Urban Canada

Urban Canada

Second Edition

Edited by

Harry H. Hiller

OXFORD
UNIVERSITY PRESS

OXFORD
UNIVERSITY PRESS

8 Sampson Mews, Suite 204, Don Mills, Ontario M3C 0H5
www.oupcanada.com

Oxford University Press is a department of the University of Oxford.
It furthers the University's objective of excellence in research, scholarship,
and education by publishing worldwide in

Oxford   New York

Auckland   Cape Town   Dar es Salaam   Hong Kong   Karachi
Kuala Lumpur   Madrid   Melbourne   Mexico City   Nairobi
New Delhi   Shanghai   Taipei   Toronto

With offices in

Argentina   Austria   Brazil   Chile   Czech Republic   France   Greece
Guatemala   Hungary   Italy   Japan   Poland   Portugal   Singapore
South Korea   Switzerland   Thailand   Turkey   Ukraine   Vietnam

Oxford is a trade mark of Oxford University Press
in the UK and in certain other countries

Published in Canada by Oxford University Press

Library and Archives Canada Cataloguing in Publication

Urban Canada / [edited by] Harry H. Hiller. -- 2nd ed.
Previous ed. published under title: Urban
Canada : sociological perspectives.

Includes bibliographical references and index.

ISBN 978-0-19-543011-0

1. Sociology, Urban—Canada—Textbooks.
2. Urbanization—Canada—Textbooks.
I. Hiller, Harry H., 1942–

HT127.U66 2009   307.760971   C2009-901458-0

2 3 4 — 13 12 11 10

Cover image: Passport Stock/Fotosearch

This book is printed on permanent (acid-free) paper ∞.

Printed and bound in Canada.

Contents

Preface and Acknowledgements

It is with pleasure that we present this new edition of *Urban Canada*. As with the first edition, our goal has been to bring together in one place a composite sketch of our knowledge of Canadian cities from a social relations perspective. We have also tried to showcase the range of expertise of urbanists across Canada who attempt to understand cities as places in which human interaction unites and divides, stimulates and antagonizes, and is structured and resisted. Cities are not just places on a map but involve people in a web of interaction that is remarkably ordered but also in process of perpetual change. In such a short book, it is impossible to cover all urban issues. For example, there is little in this book on urban planning or sustainability issues, which are critical to the future of Canadian cities. However, we are pleased to have added new chapters in this volume on inequality and social movements, housing, urban Aboriginals, and consumerism in urban life. All other chapters have been revised and updated. It is hoped that the end result is a book that enlightens those who are just entering the field but that also serves as a critical resource for those doing advanced work on specific issues.

As editor, I want to thank all contributors for their timely and significant contributions to this volume. All participants in the project have active research programs, which were often interrupted by the demands of the editorial process. Their willingness to contribute reflects their commitment to add to the literature on Canadian cities and to help us understand more clearly the dynamics of urbanization in Canada. As a group, we are grateful to all those at Oxford University Press who have helped to make this book possible: Nancy Reilly, Jennifer Charlton, and Dorothy Turnbull.

Harry H. Hiller

Contributors

Brent Berry
Department of Sociology
University of Toronto

Sonia Bookman
Department of Sociology
University of Manitoba

Jon Caulfield
Urban Studies Program
York University

Eric Fong
Department of Sociology
University of Toronto

Louis Guay
Department of Sociology
Laval University

Ron Gillis
Department of Sociology
University of Toronto

Pierre Hamel
Department of Sociology
University of Montreal

Keith Hampton
Annenberg School for Communication
Pennsylvania State University

John Hannigan
Department of Sociology
University of Toronto

Harry H. Hiller
Department of Sociology
University of Calgary

Evelyn Peters
Department of Geography
University of Saskatchewan

Bill Reimer
Department of Sociology and Anthropology
Concordia University

Gerda Wekerle
Faculty of Environmental Studies
York University

Daniyal Zuberi
Department of Sociology
University of British Columbia

Introduction: Urbanization and the City

Harry H. Hiller

The city has increasingly become the container in which most Canadians now live their lives. Calling a city a 'container' suggests that it is some kind of bounded entity. This is certainly true when we see a sign saying 'city limits', which leads us to view the city as demarcated by clear administrative boundaries. The boundary establishes the point at which a city begins. But did you ever pass such a boundary and feel that it was artificial in some way? Maybe the built-up area continued beyond the sign, or conversely, maybe there were empty spaces on both sides of the sign. The urban may no longer be so sharply differentiated from the rural, and cities may now run into one another. This suggests that to be urban might not best be represented as living in a box labelled 'Halifax' or 'Winnipeg', for example; rather, 'urban' might better be understood as a way of life or a way of perceiving life. Many people live outside of cities but either work in a city, regularly shop in a city, or watch television or receive news that focuses on the urban experience. In that sense, dramatic changes in transportation and communication mean that most people could be considered urban regardless of where they live.

Two Views of Urbanization

There are two different views of urbanization. One definition is more *demographic* in that it refers to the movement of people to cities, or the increasing size or density of cities. We often speak about a population having become more urban, meaning that more people have moved to cities or are living in them. The rural-urban shift is the best illustration of this conception of urbanization, but increasingly we are also aware that big cities keep getting bigger, not only in the number of inhabitants (**metropolitan concentration**) but also in terms of territory (**metropolitan regionalization**), which leads us to an assumption that some places are more urbanized than others. One urban sociologist, Louis Wirth (1938), took three demographic variables—size, density, and heterogeneity—and considered them the most important explanations for what makes people urban. The larger the city, the denser its population, and the wider the range of differences among people, the more urban a place was considered to be.

The second view of urbanization is more *socio-cultural* and emphasizes the pervasiveness of urban-oriented thinking, culture, and organization throughout society. In this view, it is not *where* you live that is important but *how* you live. If your life is defined more and more by ideas and organizations of urban origin, then you have become urbanized. Following this second view, even rural dwellers have become increasingly urbanized. Cities seem to serve as the primary locus of activity and new ideas that permeate all of the society. It is in cities where news emanates as represented by television stations and radio stations with strong signals. It is in cities where people congregate at the biggest structures for shopping, worship, sports, concerts, and post-secondary education. But Wirth also concluded that when you analyzed the three demographic variables identified above, it was clear that they created urbanism as a particular way of life that was somehow different because relationships lost their intimacy and became more complex and superficial. So urbanization was viewed not just as an *outcome* but as a *catalyst producing consequences*. The question that could be asked, however, is whether cities themselves are the *causes* of the changes we identify or whether cities are just the *places* where they occur.

Analyzing the City: Causes and Consequences

While urbanization might be considered a process, or even possibly a quality or lifestyle, cities are more concrete. They are places, they have names, they usually have some kind of boundaries, and they have their own mechanisms of governance. The remarkable thing is that each city is unique. Probably the thing that strikes us the most is city size. Does 'urban' mean the same thing if you live in Fredericton (a city of 51,000 and the capital of New Brunswick), Saskatoon (a city of 234,000 in Saskatchewan), or Oakville, Ontario (a city of 166,000 but part of the Toronto metropolitan area of 5.1 million)? We almost always assume that somehow size makes a difference and that bigger cities make a place more urban. Cities differ in size, form, and structure, and even their locations may make them feel very different. This suggests that cities are not just entities or objects but that they are something that is experienced. A rural-urban migrant experiences the city quite differently from a long-time resident. A homeless person experiences the city quite differently from someone who lives in an upper-class neighbourhood. Not only do people *experience* the city differently, they also *assess* the city differently. It is no wonder, then, that cities are often the focus of much debate. What one person finds exhilarating, another person experiences as anonymous and impersonal. People frequently pass judgment on city life, saying they like a particular city but don't like other cities, or they may like one section of a city but not another section of the same city. Or they might not like cities at all. These illustrations indicate that the process of urbanization almost always involves *value judgments*. For many years, especially in the industrial era, analysts of cities struggled with an anti-urban bias that pervaded much of people's thinking because cities were viewed as impersonal, chaotic, and dirty. In contrast, contemporary urbanites often express feelings of being where things are happening and feel superior to rural or small-town dwellers.

Early sociologists were intrigued by the city because they thought it represented the dawn of a new era in the way people related to one another. Ferdinand Tönnies (1855–1936), for example, described the shift as being from *Gemeinschaft* (community) to *Gesellschaft* (society) (Tönnies 1963). While these two words do not translate well from the German, they identify a change from a community where everyone knew each other intimately and had meaningful social ties to a society where people only knew each other segmentally and superficially and often competed with one another. Another analyst, Georg Simmel (1858–1918), talked about the *psychosocial* impacts of urban life in creating more competition, overstimulation from too many people, and the desire to stay aloof from others (Simmel 1950). In other words, the negative consequences of urbanization were quickly discovered, and while there might be some liberating qualities to city life, there were clearly also changes from the way life was lived in less dense or rural locations. These sociologists, along with others, are part of what we often refer to as the *German School* of urban sociology because they linked the emergence of cities with the new forces of capitalism and industrialism and sought to understand how this changed the way people related to one another.

Chicago is a good example of the way in which judgments about cities helped to foster an analysis of how cities were changing human life. It was not so much that Chicago was unique but that it represented a new kind of city that grew by attracting people from a wide diversity of backgrounds. Urban life was perceived as a kaleidoscope of people and communities as the result of immigration from abroad, migration to cities from rural areas, and the mixture of poverty (slum housing) and wealth (elite dwellings), pessimism and optimism, and industrial expansion and immigrant ghettos in which the problems of city life were all too obvious. The *Chicago School* included many sociologists, such as Robert Park (1864–1944), who saw the city as a laboratory for fieldwork (Bulmer 1984). Whereas the German

School tended to be more historical and macro in nature by assessing changes over time, the Chicago School took a more ecological approach in showing how urban behaviour was related to environment or location. In other words, a micro approach examined the different segmented spatial locations of the city, from wealthy areas to slums, from areas where juvenile delinquency or prostitution flourished, to places where gangs or hobos hung out. One of the famous illustrations of this ecological approach was the *concentric zone theory* proposed by Ernest Burgess (1886–1966), which suggested that particular types of people and behaviour could be mapped in a series of circles around the central business district (Burgess and Bogue 1967). A former student at Chicago, C.A. Dawson (1887–1964), learned much from these analyses and returned to Canada to establish at McGill University the first department of sociology in the country in 1922. Dawson led an active research program in Montreal that pursued similar objectives to those of the Chicago School: trying to understand the ecological layout of Montreal and the behaviour found within each sector (Magill 1999, 13–21; Shore 1987). Again, urban sociology was understood to be useful in that it provided a knowledge base that would help in dealing with the problems of urban complexity.

Both the German School and the Chicago School laid important groundwork for urban sociology by pointing out that city life is experienced differently by people and that the way it is organized has social consequences. If cities are becoming bigger, denser, more heterogeneous, and more complex, then it is important to understand the impact of these trends—on individuals, families, and work units. It is also important to understand that a sorting process occurs in cities that separates people with different characteristics and that instead of being chaotic, all cities possess order and structure, even if this order is not readily observable to the visitor.

The public often thinks of the city in terms of its *built environment* (i.e., the buildings, roadways, landscaping, signature structures, housing patterns, transportation patterns). In many ways, these elements of the built environment shape the nature of urban life. But humans have created the built environment. Theoretically, we call this process *externalization* because the city becomes what we make it. On the other hand, the city shapes us, and we are forced to adapt and fit in. We call this side of the process *internalization*. The relationship between these two processes of internalization and externalization is one of constant tension, which we call a *dialectic*. Understanding this dialectic is at the heart of urban sociology because we try to discern both how urban life is shaped by processes of human action and how human action is constrained by urban processes themselves.

The New Urban Sociology

Within the context of understanding more clearly how urban processes have sociological consequences, a more recent approach to understanding cities has been articulated as the *new urban sociology* (Gottdiener and Feagin 1988; Gottdiener and Hutchison 2006; Flanagan 2002). Much like the Chicago School and the German School, the new urban sociology is not a cohesive theory but a perspective clustered around a key set of ideas. Central to the new urban sociology is the idea that cities represent conflict over scarce urban space in which some groups have more power and better outcomes than others. The way cities develop, then, is the result of power relationships that have spatial outcomes. Landownership and place in the occupational production process, for example, reflect differences in power that are revealed in various forms of urban inequality, both within a city and between cities. The role cities play and the incomes of their residents are also related to global forces of power and technology so that, for example, the minimal wage of a factory worker in a city in China is intimately related to a higher standard of living for a consumer in Toronto who plays a more professional role in the global capitalist system. Thus, cities can be examined in terms of not only how power is expressed within their borders but how a particular city is related to globalizing forces. In later chapters, we will see that the decline of the industrial city in Canada and the emergence of a service-oriented post-industrial city is one reflection of this process. All of these forces shape how people live, what they do for a living, and how they relate to one another.

The German School, the Chicago School, and what is now termed the new urban sociology provide many of the interpretive perspectives in the analysis of cities that we will encounter often in this book.

Urbanization in Canada

The Extent of Urbanization

When people think of Canada, they often think of a sparsely settled country with large expanses of uninhabited territory. They may also think of small fishing settlements along the coast or perhaps the portions of land that are available for agriculture. Yet only 8 per cent of the land surface is available for agriculture, and many fishing villages have collapsed (Hiller 2006, 11). Only 19.8 per cent of the Canadian population is considered rural, and most of those people are labelled 'rural non-farm', meaning that they are not engaged in agriculture but are living in rural areas. Ironically, many of those so classified live in rural areas adjacent to urban centres. These facts all suggest that the Canadian population is much more urbanized than is often thought. In actual fact, Canadian society is very highly urbanized.

As early as 1825, Canada was one of the most urbanized countries in the world, even though settlements were not large, because the population tended to be concentrated rather than dispersed (Stone 1967, 201). By 1961, Canada was among the top 20 per cent of the world's most urbanized countries. In 1851, the level of urbanization in what is now Canada was about 15 per cent. By 1901, it was 35 per cent, increasing to 50 per cent in 1931 and 70 per cent in 1961 (Stone 1967, 202–3). By 2006, Canada was about 80 per cent urban (Table I.1).

Table I.1 demonstrates that there are considerable differences in levels of urbanization by province or region. Atlantic Canada has much lower levels of urbanization than elsewhere in Canada. For example, Prince Edward Island is 45 per cent urban, and New Brunswick is 51 per cent urban. Among the western provinces, Saskatchewan is 65 per cent urban, and Manitoba is 71 per cent urban. All other provinces from Quebec west are at least 80 per cent urban. Overall, urban populations are more likely to be better educated and have higher levels of income, which suggests that differing levels of urbanization may be related to regional economic disparities. But it also suggests that the tendency to urbanize is continuous, because it is related to improved life conditions, at least along some dimensions, which is quite contrary to the earlier idea that cities were second-rate places to live.

Defining and Measuring 'Urban'

In some ways, this discussion of levels of urbanization may be misleading, because we have not yet established a definition of 'urban'. What is 'urban' based on? size? density? culture? tall buildings? occupational types? anything that is not rural? Certainly a case could be made for each of these indicators, or perhaps a combination of them. Statistics Canada has developed a numerical/demographic measure of urbanization. And since this is the agency that reports to Canadians on our levels of urbanization, it is important to understand how it defines 'urban'. Since 1951, the minimum definition of 'urban' has been a community with 1,000 people. This is clearly an arbitrary number that must be treated with caution, because different jurisdictions/countries may use different thresholds for defining 'urban'. For example, in the United States, the minimum definition of 'urban' is 2,500. In 1981, Statistics Canada added a density requirement of at least

Table I.1   Percentage Distribution of the Canadian Population by Community Size and Province, 2006

	Urban	Over 500,000	100,000–499,999	50,000–99,999	25,000–49,999	10,000–24,999	1,000–9,999	Total rural
Canada	80.2	46.4	12.6	5.2	4.1	4.6	7.2	19.8
Newfoundland and Labrador	57.8		29.9			8.4	19.4	42.2
Prince Edward Island	45.0				28.6	10.7	5.8	55.0
Nova Scotia	55.5		31.0		3.6	10.1	10.8	44.5
New Brunswick	51.1			33.3		7.5	10.2	48.9
Quebec	80.2	53.4	4.8	4.3	4.7	3.9	7.0	19.8
Ontario	85.1	49.7	18.3	4.2	3.9	3.3	5.6	14.9
Manitoba	71.5	55.9			3.6	3.2	8.8	28.5
Saskatchewan	65.0		39.4		6.9	6.7	11.9	35.0
Alberta	82.1	56.2		6.7	3.8	6.1	9.3	17.9
British Columbia	85.4	47.5	13.9	8.5	4.2	5.2	6.0	14.6

Note: The data in this table are based on 'census divisions', which are different from 'census metropolitan areas'.

Source: Data compiled from Statistics Canada, 2006 Census, catalogue no. 97-550-XWE2006002.

400 persons per square kilometre (Vander Ploeg et al. 1999, 9). Thus, when considering reported levels of urbanization, it is important to understand what is meant by 'urban', especially since few of us would think of communities of 1,000 as truly urban.

Because 1,000 is such a minimalist definition, it is more interesting to look at the distribution of population in larger categories. While 80 per cent of the Canadian population is urban under the minimalist definition, almost half (46.4 per cent) reside in cities of more than 500,000, and a further 12.6 per cent live in cities of more than 100,000. In aggregate terms, then, almost half of the population of Canada live in cities of more than half a million, and almost three in five Canadians live in cities of more than 100,000. Cities with a population of more than 100,000 have been categorized and labelled by Statistics Canada as **census metropolitan areas (CMA)**, and three out of five Canadians live in such cities

(see Chapter 2). Between 2001 and 2006, 90 per cent of Canada's total population growth took place in CMAs. It is clear then that large cities are more and more defining Canadian life.

Cities can also be classified in smaller population categories (Figure I.1). For example, about 21 per cent of the Canadian population live in urban centres of less than 100,000. In this category, 12 per cent live in small urban centres of less than 10,000, 4.6 per cent live in small cities with populations between 10,000 and 25,000, and 9.3 per cent live in medium-sized cities of between 25,000 and 100,000. What is perhaps surprising is how few Canadians live in these medium-sized cities. Bigger cities have clearly become the dominant pattern, while the percentage of the rural population keeps eroding. There are huge differences as well from one region/province of the country to another (Table I.1). No cities in the Atlantic provinces have a population of more than half a million, and the percentage

> ### Box 1.1 *Multiple Municipalities and Census Metropolitan Areas*
>
> A census metropolitan area is not a singular entity but a complex urban form. The base definition of a CMA is that it is an area with a population of at least 100,000 including an urban core of at least 50,000 people. Note that a CMA is an area and not just one city. The Montreal CMA has nearly 100 municipalities, such as Mirabel, Longueuil, and Laval. A CMA, however, does take on the name of the central, more dominant municipality. In some cases, most of the CMA may be a single municipality. For example, 92 per cent of the Calgary CMA forms the city or municipality of Calgary, and 91 per cent of the Winnipeg CMA forms the municipality of Winnipeg. On the other hand, only 27 per cent of the Vancouver CMA consists of the municipality of Vancouver. Seventy-three per cent of the Vancouver CMA includes other municipalities, such as Surrey, Langley, and Richmond. Just over half of the Toronto and Montreal CMAs contain the municipality for which they were named, meaning that almost half of the CMAs of these two cities is made up of other municipalities. Unless some mergers take place, such as occurred in cities like Ottawa where Kanata and Rockcliffe were absorbed into the municipality, or Montreal where Pierrefonds was absorbed into the municipality of Montreal, or Toronto where the borough of East York became part of Toronto, most CMAs, and particularly the larger ones, consist of multiple municipalities.
>
> Source: Turcotte 2008

of people living in small towns and rural areas is much higher than elsewhere in Canada. Saskatchewan and Manitoba in the western interior also have a significant rural and small-town population, even though the majority of Manitoba's population is located in one city, Winnipeg. The

Figure 1.1 **Percentage Distribution of the Canadian Population by Community Size, 2006**

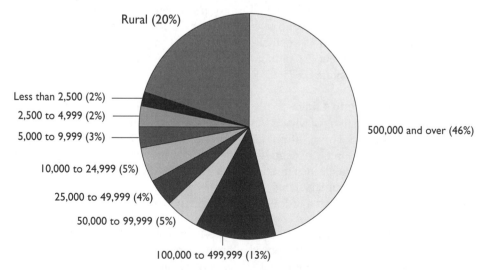

Source: Data compiled from Statistics Canada, 2006 census, catalogue no. 97-550-XWE2006002d

Note: The data in this figure is based on 'census divisions', which are different from 'census metropolitan areas'.

two central Canadian provinces (Quebec and Ontario) and the two far western provinces (Alberta and British Columbia) all have about half of their populations living in cities of more than half a million. In contrast, the populations of the territories (Yukon, Northwest Territories, and Nunavut) not only are small but have comparatively tiny main cities (Whitehorse, 18,000; Yellowknife, 18,000; and Iqualuit, 6,000).

Six metropolitan areas in Canada have populations of more than one million (playfully referred to as the 'millionaires club' by Statistics Canada). They are (in descending order) Toronto, Montreal, Vancouver, Ottawa-Gatineau, Calgary, and Edmonton, and *nearly half* of the Canadian population (45 per cent) reside within them. Toronto is by far the most populous CMA (more than 5 million) and serves as the core of an urban region called the greater Golden Horseshoe (discussed in Chapter 2). The urban region is home to 8 million people, two-thirds of the population of Ontario, and *one quarter of all Canadians*. It consists of more than 100 municipalities, including large ones such as Mississauga (670,000), Hamilton (500,000), and Brampton (430,000). The Montreal CMA consists of about 100 municipalities and 3.6 million people, which is about half of the total population of Quebec. The Vancouver CMA also contains about half of the provincial population, but it is smaller (about 2.1 million) and includes about 40 municipalities.

Political Definitions of the City

While the demographic definitions of what is 'urban' are determined by arbitrary cut-off points, the political definition of the requirements for a place to be called a city usually depends on provincial policies governing municipalities. Artibise (1981, 216–23) has shown that at least in western Canada, settlements in the past took on the designation of 'city' because their civic boosters (i.e., the commercial and land elite) viewed the attainment of city status as a tool for growth. For example, Winnipeg never did go through stages from village to town to city but became a

city in 1873 merely by incorporation by the provincial legislature. Even though Winnipeg had only 1,600 residents, city status was viewed as a means of attracting more residents and more investment. Somewhat differently, Edmonton became a town in 1892 with only 700 residents and became a city in 1904 with 8,350 residents. The point is that there was no clear minimum definition of what a city was, but it was a coveted status that presumably made land more valuable and that could be used to mobilize resources for infrastructural development. City status more accurately reflected optimism and expectations about future growth than existing reality.

Since then, as communities grow, every province makes its own decisions on whether a place should be considered a city. The impetus for becoming a city as an autonomous municipality is usually related to a desire for eligibility for grants from higher levels of government and a preference for more local control.

Suburbanization and rapid urban growth has meant that cities have spread out over larger areas that incorporate both older towns and villages and new communities that have suddenly sprouted on the fringes of a larger centre. This process, sometimes referred to as **urban spread**, means that urban places often become an amalgamation of municipalities (though one municipality may dominate) to form an **urban region**. An increasing trend is for these adjacent municipalities to join together to form a regional municipality (McAllister 2004; Rothblatt and Sancton 1998; Sancton 1994). In Canada, the Constitution Act (Section 92) puts all municipal institutions under provincial control. The provinces set out the rules by which municipalities operate, whether in terms of rules of incorporation, election procedures, taxation, or debt management (Lightbody 2006). Because municipalities are the lowest tier of government and lack both adequate financial resources for their needs and the power to control their own destinies, it is not surprising that provincial governments have viewed urban regional amalgamation as a way for cities to

Box 1.2 Municipal Reorganization: Ottawa-Gatineau

Ottawa is Canada's capital city. Yet using a single city name ignores other realities that are important to understanding this urban area.

In the first place, Ottawa itself is the result of municipal restructuring. In 2001, seven municipalities (Ottawa, Nepean, Kanata, Rockcliffe Park, Gloucester, Vanier, and Cumberland) as well as rural townships were amalgamated by the province of Ontario to form the single municipality of Ottawa.

In the second place, directly across the Ottawa River from the City of Ottawa were many municipalities in the province of Quebec that were really part of the Ottawa metropolitan region. For example, many people lived on the Quebec side but worked on the Ontario side of the Ottawa River. As the result of the rise of Quebec nationalism in the 1960s, the federal government wanted to include Quebec more directly into the national fabric. Among the measures taken was the establishment of the policy of federal bilingualism and greater employment of francophones in the federal public service. Since the city of Hull in Quebec was just across the river from the Parliament Buildings, the federal government built several government office towers there, as well as the spectacular Canadian Museum of Civilization somewhat later. These measures led to the creation of what the federal government refers to as the National Capital Region (NCR), a federal designation linking the urban areas on both sides of the border. However, unlike Washington, DC, which is a separate political jurisdiction, the NCR has no formal status as an independent entity.

On the Quebec side of the NCR, the city of Hull was the oldest city but adjacent to other municipalities such as Aylmer, Buckingham, Gatineau, and Masson-Angers. In 2002, the government of Quebec amalgamated these cities into one new municipality called Gatineau. While the former municipality of Gatineau was somewhat bigger in both population and territory than the others, renaming the entire urban region as Gatineau was also politically significant to Quebec in that it not only described an area with its well-known hills and river but also had a French name. This forced the federal government to change the name of the NCR from Ottawa-Hull to Ottawa-Gatineau.

Ottawa-Gatineau is the only CMA in Canada that crosses provincial boundaries. About one-quarter of the population of the CMA live on the Quebec side, which means that the Ontario side is considerably larger. The CMA is not identical to the National Capital Region, although it is almost as large. While Gatineau has a large bilingual population, 80 per cent of its residents have French as their mother tongue, and about two-thirds of Ottawa's residents have English as their mother tongue. Another important difference is that Ottawa has a higher proportion of residents whose mother tongue is neither English nor French than Gatineau does.

better govern and provide services (e.g., roads, policing, transit). A unicity concept was introduced to Winnipeg in 1970, and Toronto became a megacity in 1998. Thirteen municipalities had previously been consolidated into the City of Toronto, as well as the boroughs of Etobicoke, York, North York, East York, and Scarborough in 1966, but all of these units were consolidated further into the one City of Toronto in 1998 in order to support greater efficiency.

Similar urban regionalization has occurred in other locations as well, although on a smaller scale. For example, Halifax joined with its surrounding municipalities (including Dartmouth) to form the Halifax Regional Municipality. In a different context, Fort McMurray in the burgeoning oil sands region of northern Alberta joined with its surrounding municipalities to become the Wood Buffalo Regional Municipality. The trend towards a single government (rather than fragmented municipalities) is often controversial, because it removes local control (Sancton 2000). Yet the expansion of urban regions seems to respond to the need for more co-ordinated direction in the provision of services and infrastructural planning. Nevertheless, continued urban spread has meant that independent municipalities often coexist with regional municipalities, or at least as satellites of more dominant municipalities, which makes the issue of boundaries between urban jurisdictions much more complex.

The Plan of This Book

The goal of this book is to contribute to our understanding of Canadian urbanization from a social relations perspective. The authors have drawn from the global literature, and particularly the North American literature, in their analyses of different aspects of Canadian urbanization. But to what extent that work has contributed to a uniquely Canadian theory of urbanization is debatable and perhaps still in process. What is needed first is an attempt to bring together the diverse literature on the many dimensions of Canadian urbanization. Our work has also been framed by the need to understand what urbanization means to Canadians and how they experience it. We begin with a historical and global perspective and review the major theoretical traditions in the literature. Each chapter begins with an introductory s ection titled 'Getting Perspective' to prepare the reader for what is to follow. These sections were written by the editor rather than the author of the chapter (except for the first two chapters, for which editor and author are synonymous). Wherever possible and appropriate, Canadian examples and the most significant Canadian studies are cited on the topics covered. If Canadians are truly an urban people, then understanding the dynamics of Canadian urbanization is an absolute imperative, and this book seeks to contribute to that goal.

References

Artibise, Alan F.J. 1981. 'Boosterism and the development of Prairie cities, 1871–1913'. In Alan F.J. Artibise, Ed., *Town and City: Aspects of Western Canadian Urban Development*, 209–35. Regina: Canadian Plains Research Centre.

Bulmer, Martin. 1984. *The Chicago School of Sociology: Institutionalization, Diversity, and the Rise of Sociological Research*. Chicago: University of Chicago Press.

Burgess, Ernest W., and Donald S. Bogue. 1967. *Urban Sociology*. Chicago: University of Chicago Press.

Flanagan, William G. 2002. *Urban Sociology: Image and Structure*. 4th edn. Toronto: Allyn and Bacon.

Gottdiener, Mark, and Joe Feagin. 1988. 'The paradigm shift in urban sociology'. *Urban Affairs Quarterly* 24 (2): 163–87.

Gottdiener, Mark, and Ray Hutchison. 2006. *The New Urban Sociology*. 3rd edn. Toronto: McGraw-Hill.

Hiller, Harry H. 2006. *Canadian Society: A Macro Analysis*. Scarborough, ON: Pearson Prentice-Hall.

Lightbody, James. 2006. *City Politics, Canada*. Peterborough, ON: Broadview Press.

McAllister, Mary Louise. 2004. *Governing Ourselves: The Politics of Canadian Communities*. Vancouver: University of British Columbia Press.

Magill, Dennis. 1999. 'Social science paradigms'. In D. Magill and W. Michaelson, *Images of Change*, 1–38. Toronto: Canadian Scholars Press.

Rothblatt, Donald N., and Andrew Sancton. 1998. *Metropolitan Governance Revisited: American/Canadian Intergovernmental Perspectives*. Berkeley, CA: Institute of Governmental Studies Press.

Sancton, Andrew. 1994. *Governing Canada's City-Regions: Adapting Form to Function*. Montreal: Institute for Research on Public Policy.

———. 2000. *Merger Mania: The Assault on Local Government*. Montreal and Kingston: McGill-Queen's University Press.

Shore, Marlene. 1987. *The Science of Social Redemption: McGill, the Chicago School, and the Origins of Social Research in Canada*. Toronto: University of Toronto Press.

Simmel, Georg. 1950. *The Sociology of Georg Simmel*. Glencoe, IL: Free Press.

Stone, Leroy. 1967. *Urban Development in Canada*. Ottawa: Dominion Bureau of Statistics.

Tönnies, Ferdinand. 1963. *Community and Society*. New York: Harper and Row.

Turcotte, Martin. 2008. 'The city/suburb contrast: How can we measure it?' *Canadian Social Trends*, Catalogue no. 11-008. Ottawa: Statistics Canada.

Vander Ploeg, Casey G., et al. 1999. *Cities @ 2000*. Calgary: Canada West Foundation.

Wirth, Louis. 1938. 'Urbanism as a way of life'. *American Journal of Sociology* 44: 3–24.

Chapter 1 Getting Perspective

If cities, as we know them today, have reached a size and scale never seen before, how and why did this happen?

No one can see the vats of fresh water that it takes to shower or have a drink. The water just seems to appear magically from the faucet, whether you live on the 24th floor of an apartment building or work in a warehouse. Like water, many things in urban life are taken for granted. Cities seem organized in some way—public transit and freeways just seem to be there, and restaurants and food markets are always somewhere around the corner to respond to our needs. The concrete and asphalt, the bread and oranges, are somehow there and help to make our urban life much more pleasant. What we need to understand is that it has not always been that way and that because these things are readily available in our cities, urban life has taken on a character much different from what it was even 50 years ago.

Sociology is only one of many disciplines that are useful in helping us to understand cities and urban life. When many people think of cities, they think of enormous buildings, interesting architecture, and the infrastructure of complex roadways—even systems that dispose of waste. But cities are also economies, they are administratively organized, and they are distributed in space in different patterns around different topographical formations. So geography, political science, and economics, as well as other disciplines, have much to say about how cities work.

This chapter focuses on the origins, evolution, and spread of cities and uses the insights of history, archaeology, and anthropology. What makes our discussion sociological is that we apply these insights to our understanding of the nature of urban life and particularly to how city residents interact with each other to make urban life possible. In addition, the pace and nature of urbanization appear to vary considerably at different locations on the globe. Exploring these issues should help us to obtain a better perspective on urbanization in Canada.

1 Canadian Urbanization in Historical and Global Perspective

Harry H. Hiller

Learning Objectives

- To understand how and why cities have evolved.
- To understand the differences between the pre-industrial, industrial, and post-industrial city.
- To understand the causes and consequences of current trends in urbanization.
- To differentiate urbanization in the developed world from that in the developing world.
- To lay the groundwork for understanding urbanization in Canada and to put that urbanization in a global context.

Introduction

Urbanization in Canada makes little sense without a historical and global perspective. After all, cities evolved elsewhere first, and cities in other parts of the world have a more illustrious history than Canadian cities. In addition, some of these cities have played or continue to play a more dominant role on the world stage than Canadian cities. As we will see, the emergence of cities in Canada cannot be understood just by understanding urbanization within the country. Canadian urbanization has been intimately linked to urban power and urban factors elsewhere in the world.

Before we can explicitly trace the process of urbanization in Canada (Chapter 2), we need to understand how urbanization has evolved historically. Global processes such as colonialism are related to Canadian urban development, but more recent trends, such as restructuring within the global economy, have changed the way Canadian cities work. We begin, though, by sketching how cities emerged and how their roles have been transformed over time.

The City in History

In some ways, it might seem that it only makes sense to think that people have always lived in cities. Cities might not have been as large as they are today, but towns, villages, and cities must surely have always existed. However, for most of human history, people were hunters and gatherers. A nomadic form of existence was necessary, because people had to move to new sources of food and water. In that sense, settlements were only temporary, since survival required mobility, often in the face of competition from other human groups.

Much of our knowledge about early cities is based on archaeological excavations. The discovery of the remains of larger buildings and other elements of culture in a confined area has led some archaeologists to conclude that settlements were once located in these places, housing around 600 people and more. In other cases, similar communities have been excavated in surrounding areas, suggesting that there may have been a series of settlements in a general location. How large these communities were and how long they existed is open to considerable debate, but they are often referred to as the beginnings of urbanization.

Cities have existed for about 10,000 years, with the oldest city (Jericho) dating back to around 9000–8000 BC. While some of these early cities were located in the Middle East, evidence of early cities has also been found in India, China, Mesoamerica, and elsewhere (Figure 1.1). It appears that urbanization did not have one place of origin from which it spread but that human settlements occurred both as a response to the need for protection and as a reflection of power. In addition, the development of agriculture—of people growing and raising their food rather than being always on the move in search of it—allowed for a more sedentary way of life. As settlements grew in permanence and size, they developed forms of government and systems of law. The release of people from agricultural pursuits and their settlement in cities facilitated the development of writing, literature, and science. And the need for cooperation is reflected in various types of engineering to support density and compactness (especially for defence), irrigation networks for fresh water and sanitation, and significant public monuments.

The earliest known settlements of any size are usually thought to be Jericho in what is now Israel, dating to 9000 BC, and Catal Huyuk in what is now Turkey, dating to 6500 BC (Higham 1974; Hamblin 1973). A somewhat later node of cities (such as Ur, about 3000 BC) developed around the Tigris and Euphrates rivers in what is now Iraq but was formerly known as Mesopotamia. Around the same time, cities emerged in Egypt, as evidenced by the huge labour pools needed to build the large pyramids. In the Indus River Valley in what is now Pakistan, settlements known as Moenjo-Daro and Harappa existed around 2500 BC (Kenoyer 1998). Somewhat later (about 2000 BC), a series of cities that were part of the Shang dynasty in China emerged. And in the Americas, the Mayas created cities around 500 BC in what is now Mexico, as did the Incas in Peru (Unstead 1981). Most of these ancient cities

were located on river plains where the rich soil would yield good crops.

What were the characteristics of these early cities? First, they were the *centres of a civilization* in which there was some sort of *dominant authority*. Whether it was the priest-kings in Mesopotamia, the pharaohs in Egypt, or the Shang dynasty in China, a principal factor in the organization of larger and more permanent settlement was leadership, not only to organize people but also to build the structures necessary for more compact living. For example, walls were necessary for defence, and some kind of rudimentary sanitation system was required. But a dominant leader usually also represented a dynamic culture that included writing and art, various forms of architecture, and even early forms of science. Second, *none of these early settlements grew continuously*. In fact, all of them collapsed and were essentially lost until they were rediscovered by archaeologists. This helps us to see that the process of urbanization originated in fits and starts. It also means that these urban centres were not linked but were scattered throughout the world. Some of the details as to why these early cities collapsed are not known, but one reason is that the authority structures eroded, leaving people in disarray and thereby contributing to the abandonment of the city.

The Agricultural Revolution: Precursor to the Modern City

The key for the development of permanent settlements was the *domestication of plants and animals*. This is usually understood as the first stage in the **agricultural revolution** (the second stage, the mechanization of agriculture, occurred later) (Childe 1950). No longer did humans have to move with their food supply. They were now able to settle down and plant seeds to grow their own food and maintain their own livestock. Without a sense of territorial permanence, cities would not have been possible. But that is not the only important factor. When agriculturalists

Figure 1.1 Early Centres of Civilization

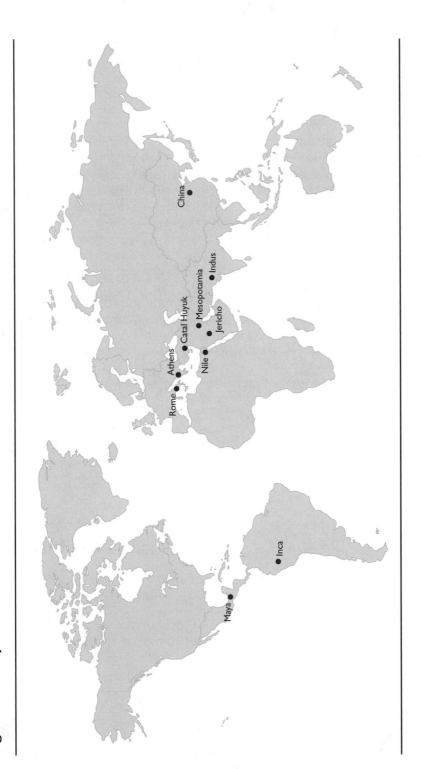

produced more than they needed to survive, it meant that some people could be released from food production. This food *surplus* could support city dwellers who would thus be free to build, think, invent, and create. Consider the modern city, with literally millions of people having no connection to agricultural pursuits and depending on the surplus production of others. These urban dwellers, like people in the earliest cities, are *released from subsistence concerns* and can create works of art, build bridges and public buildings, and focus on health care or leisure pursuits as careers. This agricultural revolution made it possible for cities to grow and develop with a much more complex division of labour.

Sociologically, the ability to produce a surplus had four consequences. The first consequence, as already noted, was the development of a much more *complex division of labour* in which people could specialize in various non-agricultural pursuits, from religion to trade to art. Second, the production of a surplus supported a more *hierarchical society* in which the leaders could extract a portion of the surplus in the form of a tax, which could then be used to control those not engaged in agriculture (Whitehouse 1977, 188). Rulers were often in a position to control the entire surplus and could then redistribute the surplus to

subjects in exchange for their loyalty. They could redirect that surplus to their favourite projects, many of which honoured them and gave their cities a distinct character. Visitors to excavated sites of early cities, such as the pyramids in Egypt and the Maya ruins in Central America, are often amazed at the complexity of urban life at that time. Third, the existence of a ruler-controlled surplus required an *administrative structure* to manage the surplus and the social controls that rewarded those who conformed to the wishes of the leaders and punished those who did not. This led to differences in the redistribution process, which accentuated *social inequalities*, the fourth consequence. Some people were allowed to live a more leisurely life, while others had a slave-type existence. Although the rewards may no longer be simply agricultural products, all cities include people in a more privileged position and others who have fewer resources. In short, the production of an agricultural surplus had important social consequences that structured the organization of urban life.

It is often thought that the fullest development of the ancient city can be seen in the cities of Greek and Roman culture from about 1000 BC to AD 300. Athens and Corinth became in some sense the cradle for democracy as the notion of

---

Box 1.1 *Catal Huyuk*

The ruins of Catal Huyuk (pronounced 'Chatal Hooyook') were discovered as a huge mound in south-central Turkey in the 1960s. It covered about 32 acres and housed at least 6,000 persons. Through various dating methods, it was determined that the city could be traced back to perhaps about 8000 BC. The mud brick buildings were built in a terraced formation, with typical entry through an opening in the roof, suggesting that ladders were in constant use. One hundred thirty-nine buildings were studied, as were 288 skeletons of men, women, and children. Tooth enamel showed evidence of disease, and the lifespan of the residents was probably about 30 years. What is amazing is the city's achievements in terms of design and planning. Archaeological excavations have unearthed wonderful examples of art, implement creation, pottery design, and perhaps most surprising, weaving that produced magnificent fabric. As with other ancient cities, it is totally unclear why the city was abandoned about 5600 BC.

Source: Hamblin 1973, 43–77.

the city-state—self-governing cities that often rivalled one another—was born (Mumford 1961). Architecturally, these cities were known for their central high point, known as the acropolis, around which the city was built. The dominant role of the agora or marketplace was also a distinctive feature. But the most significant city of that era was Rome, which probably had more than 1 million residents—much more than any city had ever had up to that time. Rome represented massive strides in urban living, with a complex road system, a water system of aqueducts, splendid public spaces like the public baths, and structures like the Forum and Colosseum.

The Rise and Fall of Cities

Perhaps one of the most notable things about cities at this point in history is that they were almost always the centre of some kind of empire. Whether it was in the Assyrian or Persian Empire, the Mayan Empire, or the Greek or Roman Empire, the city needed a vast **hinterland** to supply its needs and therefore was often the centre of trade and commerce. Cities also reflected the desire of their leaders to expand their territorial influence. Thus, settlements became the objects of attacks by would-be conquerors, and with the dawn of the city came accentuated organized warfare. One of the reasons that Rome became so influential and powerful was that it was the centre of a vast empire. The Romans contributed to an urbanization process that stretched as far away as Britain, where the city of London still contains remnants of that early Roman influence.

In almost all cases, the collapse of an empire had a devastating effect on the city that had been created as its centre—so great that it literally disintegrated and was abandoned. This was the case with the Roman Empire, and its collapse ushered in the Dark Ages, lasting until about the eleventh century. Settlements once again became small and scattered, with walls for defence as had been typical of settlements in the past. Control by

local lords who engaged in repeated acts of warfare required castle-like structures surrounded by walls and a moat. However, the later medieval period and the Renaissance, from the twelfth century through the sixteenth century, are generally known as a time of growth and rebirth as the small cities of Europe (e.g., Venice, Paris) began to blossom with new ideas as expressed in art and literature. As the population of these cities increased to 50,000–100,000, residents were forced to move beyond the walls of the city. Lack of adequate sanitation and crowded conditions made the cities less than hospitable, and about one-third of the population of Europe died as a result of plagues, such as the Black Death of the mid-fourteenth century.

Capitalism, Industrialism, and the City

Trade had always been an important urban function, and the location of a city was often related to its position on trade routes. Since one of the big issues for an urban resident was finding a means of survival, a significant development in the feudal and post-feudal period was the emergence of craft production, money exchange, and trade, which produced a new social class of urban entrepreneurs who over time became more powerful. This development is often referred to as the emergence of capitalism, which transformed social life and established what is called a *market economy* in which labour was no longer exchanged for non-monetary subsistence but could be exchanged for monetary reward. Ultimately, this set the stage for the selling of labour in factory production. But it also opened the door to social stratification no longer dependent solely on status and property but also related to income and achievement.

The **Industrial Revolution**, often dated from the invention of the steam engine in England in 1775 (but normally considered as originating much earlier, around 1700, and extending to 1850), symbolizes the dawn of a new era that had huge significance for cities. The machine now had the capacity to manufacture consumer products for which urban markets were eminently suitable, but most of all it required a different type of labourer than was typical in handcraft work. In contrast to cottage crafts based in the household, such as baking, blacksmithing, and weaving, the factory separated place of work from place of residence. It also introduced a more complex class system—an increasingly powerful entrepreneurial class on the one hand and a poorly paid class of labourers on the other, with a new middle class of merchants and administrators. Thus, both slums and middle-class suburbs emerged with the Industrial Revolution (King and Timmins 2001). Because metalwork and the manufacture of textiles were capital-intensive activities, factory owners had to minimize costs to make a profit and often exploited labour (including that of children) for maximum gain. Workers were needed, and as people flooded into the cities to take advantage of these new opportunities, there was little infrastructure to support them. The result was the image and reality of the industrial city as polluted, with poor working conditions and crowded living conditions—in short, the Dickensian city. In some ways, the city is still fighting an image of urban living that harks back to this earlier era, an image suggesting that poverty, filth, and crime are necessarily urban

problems when in fact these problems resulted from early industrial capitalism.

From an urban perspective, the factory became an important symbol of a new kind of city because it represented *space-intensive* and *labour-intensive* activity. In short, large numbers of people could find gainful employment in a relatively small space (the factory), which made larger, denser cities possible. But it also introduced for the first time the concept of unemployment, whereby labour could be released in response to changing market conditions. In spite of these problems, people rushed to the cities of England and northern Europe in record numbers. In contrast to the kind of urbanization that later occurred in Third World cities in which people were attracted to the cities because they were in essence pushed off the land, in Europe people flocked to the cities because of the new opportunities that industrial capitalism provided. England was at the heart of the Industrial Revolution, and it offers a good marker of the rapid rate of urbanization that was in many ways caused by industrialization. In 1801, London had 865,000 residents; no other English city had a population of more than 100,000, and only 14 cities had more than 20,000 inhabitants. Ninety years later, in 1891, London had more than 4 million residents, 23 cities had populations of more than 100,000, and the

Box 1.2 What Limited the Size of the Pre-industrial City?

Among the factors that limited the size of the pre-industrial city was the need for an immediate hinterland of supplies for daily survival. For example, firewood was needed for heat and cooking, and one estimate has suggested that each urban dweller in Europe used between one and 1.6 tons of firewood per year. If a horse-drawn cart could carry one ton of firewood, a community of 10,000 residents would then require between 27 and 44 cart trips per day. For cereal grain, 10 cart trips per day would have been necessary. Both of these requirements put significant strain on adjacent forests and fields. It is no surprise that cities were often built adjacent to waterways, which not only facilitated the transport of these supplies but also extended the distance and size of the hinterland.

Source: van der Woude, Hayami, and de Vries 1990, 8.

populations of 161 other cities exceeded 20,000 (Weber 1963, 46). In the two centuries from 1600 to 1800, the population of English cities (5,000 or more) increased by 600 per cent, the rural non-agricultural population grew by 249 per cent, and the rural agricultural population increased by only 9 per cent (van der Woude, Hayami, and de Vries 1990, 107). This was urbanization at a scale previously unknown.

Colonialism and the Rise of New Cities

Another factor in world urbanization was the rise of the nation-state in Europe as central governments sought to consolidate their power over their own territories. But the emergence of dominant cities such as London, Amsterdam, and Lisbon made them not only the administrative and trade centres of their own political entities but centres of imperialist expansion to new territories throughout the New World. This process, known as **colonialism**, entailed European nation-states seeking to control the new lands not only as a means of extending their influence but also to satisfy the demands of their urban marketplaces. As wealth and power grew in European cities, a consumer base existed for materials and products brought from far-flung countries. In order to export precious metals, fish, furs, spices, or tropical fruit, a port city was usually established in the new territory that would serve as the beachhead for colonial influence and trade. From 1500 to 1900, the Dutch, Spanish, Portuguese, British, and French eagerly explored the globe, and throughout the Americas, Africa, and Asia, cities were developed to serve as conduits for extraction and domination. New York, Boston, Halifax, Hong Kong, Singapore, Kingston (Jamaica), Delhi, Cape Town, Lagos, and Sydney (Australia) were just a few among many cities that grew as the result of the interests of foreign empires. As we will see in Chapter 2, urbanization in Canada cannot be understood without acknowledging the interests of European empires and their cities.

What were some of the characteristics of these colonial cities? First, they were *administrative centres* structured by representatives from the empire government, its financial institutions, and its merchants. Second, they served as an *intermediary* between the empire and the colonial hinterland and its treasures. To put it another way, these colonial cities were conduits of economic and cultural penetration into the colony. Third, a *social polarity* existed between the expatriates and the unskilled or semi-skilled indigenous peoples. Where indigenous peoples were in greater numbers (e.g., Africa) and/or had an established urban culture (e.g., India), colonial cities were divided between the foreign elite and the poorer indigenous people. Where indigenous people were fewer in number or lacked permanent settlements (e.g., North America and Australia), cities were built essentially by moving indigenous peoples out of the way. In both cases, the colonial city reflected the interests of the colonizers in architectural design, layout, and law (King 1990). What is critical to understand is that the city-forming process throughout the world was greatly spurred by the capital accumulation goals of European empires (Castells 1977).

Colonial cities often became **primate cities**, which greatly surpass the size of any other urban area in a country. They are usually located on or near the coast and serve as the major conduit for foreign influence into the country. In that sense, the values and way of life of people in a primate city are considerably different from those of the people who live in the surrounding countryside. But the primate city has extraordinary power and control over its national territory. Many primate cities started out as colonial cities, and for reasons of geography and power, their influence grew. Cities like Rio de Janeiro, Lima, Lagos, Jakarta, and Bangkok all experienced strong colonial influences but have since gone on to play a dominant role in their countries (Dogan and Kasarda 1988).

Urban Restructuring and the World Economy

The linking of merchant capitalism with industrial capitalism energized and supported global urbanization, which is under-girded by what we now call the *world economy*. Ultimately, this came to mean that the manufacture and trade of goods would no longer just be the prerogative of one section of the world but that there would now be a global economy and a global division of labour. While the world economy is structurally defined more by the modern transnational corporation than by political states, it has several defining characteristics. One is that it distinguishes between *core countries*, which have the greatest pools of capital, technological innovation, and management skills—and therefore control—and *peripheral countries*, which are poorer and whose primary assets are cheap labour and resources. For example, the United Kingdom, the United States, and Japan are considered core countries because they have investment capital and consumer demand, but they need the resources or cheap labour of peripheral countries like Nigeria, China, and Taiwan. The core countries and the peripheral countries need each other, but it is clear that the core dominates and exploits the periphery for its own interests. The second thing about the world economy is that cities serve as both the primary destination and the conduit of this international activity. Often, countries have one or two large cities that serve as the centres of finance and decision-making within the nation-state and that have intimate links with other key cities in the global community. Canadian cities will be discussed later, but the role that Canada plays on the world stage as a major supplier of resources (though certainly not cheap labour) has sometimes led to perceptions of a semi-peripheral status.

In many ways, the process of globalization, which is critical to a world economy, is a relatively new development, because the key to the prosperity of the cities in core countries since the Industrial Revolution had always been manufacturing. Textiles and garments, appliance and automobile manufacture and assembly, as well as steelmaking and other forms of production, required a broad range of blue-collar workers. The idea was that manufacturing should be as close to the big markets as possible, so companies brought all the raw materials to the job sites located in the same region that controlled all aspects of the production process. This idea of localized control is called **horizontal integration**, since all aspects of the manufacturing process are closely linked together. Around the 1970s, this process began to change as companies began to use supplier companies that competed against each other for just-in-time delivery of component parts and sometimes even for the finished product. These competitive contracts encouraged supplier companies to seek out production wherever labour was cheaper. It also meant that the main company no longer engaged in all aspects of the production process but segmentalized the process in what is called **vertical disintegration**. The end result was that much manufacturing was transferred away from core countries and their cities, resulting in their **deindustrialization**. This has meant that cities in these countries were no longer considered industrial cities but post-industrial cities, with much of the industrial process off-loaded to cities where employee benefits and pollution standards are not nearly as strict and where labour is plentiful and cheap. At the same time, cities in the core countries have become increasingly dominated by service industries, from finance to leisure and from computer technologies to health care services.

This transfer of roles in a global marketplace is referred to as *urban restructuring* and has produced what is known as the **post-industrial city**. The cities in the developed world have undergone a transformation from manufacturing-based to service-based, and growing cities in the developing world have become more industrial. Not only has this shift altered the cities in both locations, but it has also created a sense of interdependence between cities with highly paid labour and cities with poorly paid labour. Core cities are normally no longer engaged in production but focused on product design and development, research, and marketing. Workers in developing countries need jobs, and residents of core countries want cheaper consumer goods. Ironically, the standard of living of people with good jobs and high rates of pay in core countries is supported by cheap labour elsewhere.

As populations in the less developed parts of the world increasingly urbanize (Gugler 2004), the question of how they will support themselves becomes an issue. Attracting a foreign-owned industry to manufacture goods for export back to more prosperous countries is often considered as better than no employment at all, even though the wages offered by the industry are pitifully low by the standards of the developed countries. For example, the government of Mexico has encouraged the development of manufacturing facilities inside their borders so that North American (and even European) companies can take advantage of their enormous pools of urban labour in special tax-free havens known as *maquiladoras*. Many of the products we use and the clothes we wear have been manufactured offshore, sometimes under controversial conditions. The point is that core cities have lost their manufacturing industries to cities in peripheral regions, which has not only changed their cities but our cities as well. All of this reinforces the idea that we now live in a global economy.

Global Differences in Urbanization

It is important to know that there was a significant lag between urbanization in the developed world and in the developing world. The *first wave* of urbanization took place in Europe and North America and is usually identified with the period between 1750 and 1950. This was the age of industrialization, which provided consider-

able employment for urban dwellers. During that period, the urban population in that region of the world grew from about 15 million to 423 million. The *second wave* of urbanization is linked to the rapid urbanization that took place after 1950, particularly in the developing regions of the world, where urban populations grew dramatically, from less than those of the developed world (309 million) to a projected 3.9 billion by 2030. Or, to look at it over the entire course of the twentieth century, the developed regions of the world had more than twice as many urban dwellers (150 million) as the developing regions (70 million) at the beginning of the century, but by the beginning of the twenty-first century, the developing regions had more than 2.6 times as many urban dwellers (2.3 billion) as developed regions (0.9 billion) (UNPF 2008).

The year 2008 represents an important milestone in world urbanization because it marks the year in which more than half of the population was considered urban. But the differences in levels of urbanization are significant. Three-quarters of the more developed regions are urbanized, but just over 40 per cent of the less developed regions are (Table 1.1). Even within less developed regions, there is a considerable difference in levels of urbanization, with about 85 per cent of Latin America and the Caribbean but less than 40 per cent of Asia and Africa urbanized.

In sheer numbers, there are already more urban dwellers in Asia than in any other region of the world, and more people are living in cities in Asia than in North and South America, Oceania, and Europe combined (Table 1.2). By 2030, Asia will have more urban dwellers in total than the rest of the world. Note as well the low point at which Africa started in 1950 but that it is projected to become the second most urbanized region by 2030.

We can examine this shift in a different way by looking at cities of 10 million and more (Table 1.3). In 1950, New York and Tokyo were the only cities with a population of more than 10 million. By 2005, the number had increased to 20 cities.

Table 1.1 Percentage Urban Population and Urbanization Rate by Region, 1950–2030

	Urban				Urbanization Rate	
	1950	1975	2005	2030	1950–2005	2005–30
World	29.0	37.2	48.7	59.9	0.94	0.83
More developed regions	52.1	66.9	74.1	80.8	0.64	0.35
Less developed regions	18.1	26.9	42.9	56.1	1.57	1.08
Northern America	63.9	73.8	80.7	86.7	0.42	0.29
Latin America and Caribbean	42.0	61.2	77.4	84.3	1.11	0.34
Oceania	62.0	71.5	70.8	73.8	0.24	0.17
Europe	50.5	65.6	72.2	78.3	0.65	0.33
Asia	16.8	24.0	39.8	54.1	1.57	1.23
Africa	14.7	25.4	38.3	50.7	1.75	1.12

Note: Northern America includes the United States and Canada.

Source: Prepared from United Nations Population Division. 2006. *World Urbanization Prospects: The 2005 Revision*. Tables 3 and 4. New York: United Nations Population Division.

Table 1.2 Urban Population (Millions) by Region, 1950–2030

	1950	1975	2005	2030
Northern America	110	180	267	347
Latin America and Caribbean	70	197	434	609
Oceania	8	15	23	31
Europe	277	443	526	546
Asia	234	575	1553	2637
Africa	33	105	347	742

Source: Prepared from United Nations Population Division. 2006. *World Urbanization Prospects: The 2005 Revision*. Table 2. New York: United Nations Population Division.

New York had slipped to third position, Tokyo had become even larger, and 17 other cities had passed the 10-million threshold, with Sao Paulo and Mumbai threatening to surpass New York and indeed projected to do so by 2015. It is cities in the less developed regions that are swelling in population numbers, particularly cities such as Calcutta, Dhaka, Jakarta, Lagos, and Karachi. The significant difference with the developed region is that employment was not adequate for this rush of urban growth, leading to considerable poverty in these cities. The urban growth rates have been the highest in sub-Saharan Africa and Asia, but these are the places where urban slum populations have been the largest. More than half of the world's slum population can be found in Asia (581 million), and the slum growth rate is highest in sub-Saharan Africa (199 million).

Table 1.3 Population of Megacities (Cities with 10 Million Inhabitants or More), 1950, 1975, 2005, and 2015 (Millions)

	1950			1975			2005			2015	
	City	Population		City	Population		City	Population		City	Population
1	New York	12.3	1	Tokyo	26.6	1	Tokyo	35.2	1	Tokyo	35.5
2	Tokyo	11.3	2	New York	15.9	2	Mexico City	19.4	2	Mumbai (Bombay)	21.9
			3	Mexico City	10.7	3	New York	18.7	3	Mexico City	21.6
						4	Sao Paulo	18.3	4	São Paulo	20.5
						5	Mumbai (Bombay)	18.2	5	New York	19.9
						6	Delhi	15.0	6	Delhi	18.6
						7	Shanghai	14.5	7	Shanghai	17.2
						8	Calcutta	14.3	8	Calcutta	17.0
						9	Jakarta	13.2	9	Dhaka	16.8
						10	Buenos Aires	12.6	10	Jakarta	16.8
						11	Dhaka	12.4	11	Lagos	16.1
						12	Los Angeles	12.3	12	Karachi	15.2
						13	Karachi	11.6	13	Buenos Aires	13.4
						14	Rio de Janeiro	11.5	14	Cairo	13.1
						15	Osaka	11.3	15	Los Angeles	13.1
						16	Cairo	11.1	16	Manila	12.9
						17	Lagos	10.9	17	Beijing	12.9
						18	Beijing	10.7	18	Rio de Janeiro	12.8
						19	Manila	10.7	19	Istanbul	11.4
						20	Moscow	10.7	20	Osaka	11.3
									21	Istanbul	11.2
									22	Guangzhou	10.4

Note: These population numbers are urban agglomerations, which refers to populations sharing a contiguous territory. This may include cities that are administratively distinct but functionally linked (e.g., New York includes Newark in the state of New Jersey, Los Angeles includes Long Beach and Santa Ana, and Tokyo includes Kawasaki and Yokohama).

Source: Adapted from United Nations Population Division. 2006. *World Urbanization Prospects: The 2005 Revision*. Table 7. New York: United Nations Population Division.

Lack of durable housing, overcrowding, poor water and sanitation, and lack of secure tenure prompted the United Nations to specifically address this huge urban problem through its Millennium Development and Urban Sustainability Project (UN Habitat 2006).

Migration to cities at such a rate that new residents cannot be adequately integrated is called *overurbanization*. The inability to find **standard employment** (i.e., employment with regular hours and pay) results in *subsistence urbanization* in which the struggle for survival is the main objective of daily living. Innovative ways to earn money (e.g., selling things on the street) or to save money (e.g., getting things through barter or exchange) are part of what is known as the *informal economy*, which thrives in Third World cities but does not produce an adequate living or the tax supports to allow these cities to provide both services and the infrastructure necessary for a decent standard of living for urban residents.

Not all the people in cities in less developed countries are poor—especially not in primate cities. A foreign elite representing core country organizations as well as an indigenous elite are always present, although in smaller numbers, and a middle class comprising those who have standard employment and own their own homes is also likely to be found. The contrast, however, with those in abject poverty is striking. This phenomenon is often referred to as a *dual economy* in which the lifestyle and values of those in poverty contrast sharply with those of urban residents who are educated and who have financial resources. One prominent symbol of this contrast is the presence of iron gates or walls around the property of those with the financial means to reduce their vulnerability to the masses of the poor in these cities.

The New Urban Order

While the number of inhabitants, or demographic size, may be one measure of the importance of a city in the world, it is far from the most important indicator of significance. Some cities are more important than others because they are critical to the forces of market capitalism that are redefining the world beyond the borders of the nation-state (Sassen 1991).

One of the most important advances in our thinking about cities in a globalized world came from the observation that cities are not so much places as they are a *process* by which centres are connected in a globalized network (Castells 1996). From this perspective, cities should not be viewed as bounded territories but as connected, not only with their hinterlands but also with other cities. For example, the cities of Taipei and Kuala Lumpur are important not only because of their pivotal role in their own countries (Taiwan and Malaysia) but because they manufacture products for international markets, have ties with international corporations located in other cities, and utilize foreign capital and technologies that keep them in constant communication with other cities. The fact that the tallest buildings in the world are situated in these cities (Taipei 101 Tower and the Petronas Twin Towers) reflects the fact that they, and others like them in Asia, cannot simply be dismissed as Third World cities (in fact, eight of the 10 tallest buildings in the world today are in Asia). Cities like Bangkok, Singapore, or Hong Kong are important because they are part of a world system in which there are significant exchanges and complementary roles connecting them with other cities.

Nevertheless, it is true that some cities, by the nature of the roles they play, are more strategic than others. A *world city* or **global city** is a city that has a heightened position as a command and control centre in the global economy. It may play a particularly important role in finance or in the economic sector, but it often also plays a pivotal role culturally and politically. While there is some debate about which cities should be considered global, there is considerable agreement that London and New York are the most functionally comprehensive global cities, although Paris and

Box 1.3 *The World Trade Center and 9/11*

On 11 September 2001, the attack on the World Trade Center (WTC) in New York led to the death of more than 2,600 people in the two towers. Why was the WTC such a critical target?

Being a world city meant that New York was the centre of considerable decision-making and control. Not only was the city the site of the United Nations and an important American city, but it was also the centre of banking and finance with a global outreach as represented by the New York Stock Exchange and Wall Street. Publishing houses, media conglomerates, advertising agencies and insurance companies, fashion, sports, and airlines all radiate influence from New York.

The World Trade Center itself symbolized the pivotal position of this city on the world stage. About 50,000 people worked in the twin towers, which housed 430 different companies from 28 countries. Banks like the Fuji Bank, the National Bank of Taiwan, and the Asahi Bank all had offices in these buildings. The exact number of foreign nationals working there is not known, but 22 Canadians died in the attack on the WTC. Many of those who died had extensive international experience. One Canadian who died was a company vice-president and owned homes not only in New York but also in Montreal and London as the result of previous postings. While the perpetrators of the attack may have viewed the WTC as a symbol of the West or American power, it must also be noted that the twin towers housed considerable activity that demonstrated the connectivity between urban economies.

For an analysis of the impact of 9/11 on the city of New York, see Foner 2005.

Tokyo are usually also considered world cities (Taylor 2005). Depending on the indicators used, other major cities can also be ranked in descending order of importance. But instead of viewing this global process as a simple hierarchy of cities, the most important thing about these cities is that there is connectivity between them even though the world city network does have hierarchical tendencies. World cities contain institutions like banks, accounting companies, advertising companies, media conglomerates, and law firms, as well as other multinational corporations that pursue activities throughout the world. Other cities, though less functionally comprehensive, also have their niches, such as in culture (Los Angeles), religion (Rome, Mecca), banking (Zurich), and non-government agencies (Geneva), or play a strong regional role that is growing in global impact (e.g., Mumbai, Shanghai, Beijing, Hong Kong, Singapore). For this reason, world cities should be understood as leading urban centres that are enmeshed in a context of relationships with other cities elsewhere in the world. What is especially important to note is that the ranks of leading world cities are no longer restricted to the cities of the North Atlantic community of North America and Europe.

Global cities or world cities do have some unique characteristics, however (Friedmann, 1986). Because they often serve as the headquarters for major multinational enterprises, they have a significant component of highly paid and highly skilled professional workers (many of whom have been recruited internationally) that increases the demand for expensive housing and services. This has the result of pushing out the middle class who cannot afford to live in the city and who then retreat to satellite areas or move elsewhere. But it also increases the demand for low-waged labour to provide the services required by professionals and the well-to-do for which immigrants or migrants are recruited. World cities thus tend to be ethnically diverse but polarized between those in high-paying positions and those with low-paying

Box 1.4 *Urbanization in China*

It is not surprising that the country with the largest population in the world should be such an intriguing case of urbanization. With 1.3 billion people, China is less than 40 per cent urban. Yet it has more than 200 cities with populations of more than a million, and its total urban population is around 500 million (the urban population in China is more than 14 times the size of Canada's total population). The amazing thing is that this urbanization has been quite recent.

After China shook off its colonial ties in 1949 and launched the new People's Republic in Tiananmen Square, the goal was to create a self-sufficient socialist state. China then built a self-reliant, closed economy. One of the keys to this economy was the *hukou* system, which provided supplies to individual families through an arrangement of household registration. This system retarded urbanization and kept people where they were. With the advent of reforms in 1978, a socialist market economy began to develop, which drew China more directly into the global economy. One of the key ways in which this manifested itself was through the emergence of rural industries in the 1980s, essentially transforming villages into urban areas. In fact, in 1990, 90 million people were registered as working in rural industries. Through a mixture of state ownership and private ownership of industry, urbanization then occurred in situ. As industrialization strengthened and the *hukou* system weakened, urbanization occurred both in what were previously rural areas and through migration to urban areas. The result is urbanization at an enormous scale.

As China has become more integrated into the global market economy, it is not surprising that cities like Shanghai and Beijing with their gleaming office towers and high-rise apartment buildings should attract considerable attention. But a whole range of other cities in China, such as Harbin, Tianjin, Chengdu, and Guangzhou, are also impressive. However, these cities all struggle with poverty, unemployment, and inadequate housing to accommodate their burgeoning populations.

For more information on urbanization in China, see Friedmann 2005 and Logan 2008.

jobs. As the centres of these cities become more expensive, growth shifts to the towns and cities at some distance from the core, which contributes to greater *regionalization of the urban population*. For example, Mexico City and its surrounding area now contains about one-third of the national population, not only because the city is the magnet destination for Mexican people but because people relocate outside the core of the city itself while still being part of its communication and transportation structure (Aguilar 1999).

The observation that when cities grow in size and possess a strong central core but also experience deconcentration to create a growing urban region with multiple nodes has resulted in a new perspective in the analysis of cities known as the Los Angeles School (Dear 2002). Whereas the Chicago School understood cities as always having a strong central core controlling and organizing the surrounding urban population, the Los Angeles School understands metropolitan communities as consisting of a variety of urban nodes that are interconnected but are decentralized and decentred. Los Angeles is considered the epitome of this kind of development, which is also occurring elsewhere. High land prices and high labour costs in the city core result in some businesses and residents seeking cheaper suburban sites. Continued growth also demands new sites outside the core. This produces 'limitless parcelized sprawl', with all of the separate parcels linked together by advances in telecommunications and superhighways. Invariably, though, it also means that the central city itself becomes more polarized between the wealthy and the poor. More than 60 per cent of the people in Los Angeles County are immigrants, many of whom are poor. Yet other parts of the Los Angeles area, such as Hollywood, Malibu, and Bel Air, house the very rich. Some might argue that downtown Los Angeles is even less known than these satellite communities that are often thought to define the city, though mistakenly so.

Conclusion

In this chapter, we have laid the groundwork for interpreting urbanization in Canada. Among the key points that emerged was the idea that all cities require a hinterland that provides labour and resources for its needs. Obviously, the bigger the city, the more distant the hinterland, and it can surely be argued that the modern city has a hinterland that is global in nature. We will see how the hinterland for Canadian cities is both internal and international. Second, the process of urbanization was historically tied to the presence of empires, and we will see how all of Canada's major cities had their start as outposts of colonial expansion. Third, the industrialization of agriculture has played a major role in reducing rural populations and concurrently contributing to growing cities. Fourth, the global restructuring that has occurred has meant that Canadian cities are no longer based on manufacturing economies but on service economies. This also helps to explain the hierarchical order of cities—in the world and in Canada, where it has become more pronounced with the centralization of command and control functions increasingly focused on Toronto. This centralization inevitably leads to uneven metropolitan growth.

Study and Discussion Questions

1. What are the causes and consequences of the fact that more and more people are living in cities?
2. How were early cities different from modern cities? Given the way cities have evolved, how will cities of the future be different?
3. How has globalization affected the cities with which you are familiar?
4. Pick a city in North America, and explain how urban restructuring has changed that city.
5. Explain the differences between North American cities and cities in the developing world.
6. What elements of cities in less developed countries create 'culture shock' for the Canadian visitor? Explain why we react that way.
7. Are cities all the same, or are there significant differences around the world? What should be the basis for that comparison?

Suggested Reading

Gugler, Josef. 2004. *World Cities beyond the West: Globalization, Development, and Inequality*. Cambridge: Cambridge University Press. A good resource on how the process of urbanization is affecting the developing world.

Hall, Peter. 1998. *Cities in Civilization: Culture, Innovation, and Urban Order*. London: Weidenfeld and Nicolson. An interesting study of select cities (e.g., Rome, Manchester, Detroit, San Francisco, Stockholm, Los Angeles) at various points in history, focusing on distinct economic or developmental features.

Mumford, Lewis. 1961. *The City in History: Its Origins, Its Transformations, and Its Prospects*. New York: Harcourt Brace and World. A classic study of the evolution of urbanism and its consequences for human life.

Pacione, Michael, Ed. 2002. *The City: Critical Concepts in the Social Sciences*, v. 1, *The City in Global Context*. New York: Routledge. This is the first volume in a five-volume anthology of some of the best research on the complexity of cities. This volume explores the evolution of urban forms from pre-

industrial cities to post-modern urbanism.

Paddison, Ronan, Ed. 2001. *Handbook of Urban Studies*. Thousand Oaks, CA: Sage. An excellent discussion of a variety of urban issues from a global perspective.

References

Aguilar, Adrian G. 1999. 'Mexico City growth and regional dispersal'. *Habitat International* 23: 391–412.

Castells, Manuel. 1977. *The Urban Question*. London: Edward Arnold.

———. 1996. *The Rise of the Network Society*. Oxford: Blackwell.

Childe, V. Gordon. 1950. 'The urban revolution'. *Town Planning Review* 21: 3–17.

Dear, Michael J. 2002. *From Chicago to L.A.: Making Sense of Urban Theory*. Thousand Oaks, CA: Sage.

Dogan, Mattei, and John D. Kasarda, Eds. 1988. *A World of Giant Cities*. Newbury Park, CA: Sage.

Foner, Nancy, Ed. 2005. *Wounded City: The Social Impact of 9/11*. New York: Russell Sage Foundation.

Friedmann, J. 1986. 'The world city hypothesis'. *Development and Change* 17: 69–83.

———. 2005. *China's Urban Transition*. Minneapolis: University of Minnesota Press.

Gugler, Josef. 2004. *World Cities beyond the West: Globalization, Development, and Inequality*. Cambridge: Cambridge University Press.

Hamblin, Dora Jane. 1973. *The First Cities*. New York: Time-Life Books.

Higham, Charles. 1974. *The Earliest Farmers and the First Cities*. Cambridge: Cambridge University Press.

Kenoyer, Jonathon M. 1998. *Ancient Cities of the Indus Valley Civilization*. Oxford: Oxford University Press.

King, Anthony D. 1990. *Urbanism, Colonialism, and the World Economy*. New York: Routledge.

King, Steven, and Geoffrey Timmins. 2001. *Making Sense of the Industrial Revolution*. Manchester: Manchester University Press.

Logan, John R. 2008. *Urban China in Transition*. New York: Wiley-Blackwell.

Mumford, Lewis. 1961. *The City in History: Its Origins, Its Transformations, and Its Prospects*. New York: Harcourt Brace and World.

Sassen, Saskia. 1991. *The Global City: New York, London, Tokyo*. Princeton, NJ: Princeton University Press.

Taylor, Peter. 2005. 'Leading world cities: Empirical evaluations of urban nodes in multiple networks'. *Urban Studies* 42 (9): 1,593–608.

UN Habitat. 2006. *The State of the World's Cities Report 2006/2007: The Millennium Development Goals and Urban Sustainability: Thirty Years of Shaping the Habitat Agenda*. Nairobi: United Nations Human Settlements Programme.

UNPF (United Nations Population Fund). 2008. *State of the World Population 2007: Unleashing the Potential of Urban Growth*. New York: UNPF.

Unstead, R.J. *How They Lived in Cities Long Ago*. New York: Arco.

van der Woude, A.D., Akira Hayami, and Jan de Vries. 1990. *Urbanization in History: A Process of Dynamic Interactions*. Oxford: Clarendon Press.

Weber, A.F. 1963. *The Growth of Cities in the Nineteenth Century*. Ithaca, NY: Cornell University Press.

Whitehouse, Ruth. 1977. *The First Cities*. Oxford: Phaidon.

Chapter 2 Getting Perspective

How did the urban pattern in Canada develop, with some cities becoming much bigger than others—even to the point where they have become quite crowded—while other cities struggle to grow or lose population?

One hundred years ago, Canada was essentially a rural society. Since then, the country has become overwhelmingly urban, as have most other populations in the world. One of the intriguing things about this urbanization is that cities grow differentially across the country. Some villages and towns became cities, while others died. Some cities had a head start over other cities, yet they were surpassed in size and importance by relative newcomers. The cities in some regions grew to be more significant than cities in other regions. This chapter will attempt to shed light on these different patterns of urbanization.

In the previous chapter, we saw how sociology used insights from history, archaeology, and anthropology to help us understand the evolution of cities. In this chapter, we use insights from economics, geography, and political science to aid us in understanding cities not primarily as entities in themselves but as entities constructed by people with economic, political, and ideological power. Canadian cities did not just spring up from the earth like weeds but were planted by the decisions of people. Furthermore, the more rapid growth of some cities over others is also a reflection of human factors that give some places priority over others. In a real sense, people do not choose where they live but are constrained by factors that determine where they can thrive best. Someone might prefer to live in Halifax, but if the engineering job she or he wants is located in Toronto, there would appear to be little choice. But why is that engineering job located in Toronto rather than Halifax? Why can't all cities in Canada experience growth, and why does Toronto experience more of that growth than other cities? Nova Scotia might be much more compatible with the person's lifestyle and family preferences, but the metropolitan Toronto area nonetheless might become home. So what is the relationship between the pattern of cities that have developed in Canada and the political-economic decisions that have allowed some cities to grow more than others?

2 The Dynamics of Canadian Urbanization

Harry H. Hiller

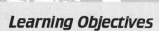

Learning Objectives

- To understand how and why urbanization has taken place in Canada.
- To interpret the shape and nature of urbanization in Canada through the political economy perspective.
- To identify both internal and external forces affecting Canadian urbanization.
- To show how concentration and centralization has resulted in uneven urbanization in Canada.

Introduction

In Chapter 1, we discovered that urbanization is a global process. But the point was not simply that cities emerged in different parts of the world at different times, or that cities elsewhere in the world have their own unique histories or economies, or even that much larger cities are found in other parts of the world. Rather, globalization means that cities are increasingly related in a world system. The key point developed in this chapter is that the different emerging patterns of urbanization, even in Canada, are not just the result of some kind of natural process but are the result of deliberate decisions and human action. This is known as the **political economy perspective** because it points out that the decisions made by people in positions of power, especially in business and politics, have a major impact on how urbanization proceeds. Government policies, political and economic power, and investment decisions have played a huge role in determining the outcomes of the process of urbanization in Canada.

Canadian urbanization, of course, is clearly related to the settlement of this country by Europeans, which proceeded in an east-to-west direction. Therefore, we would expect the first cities to have emerged along the east coast. Such a view minimizes the role of Aboriginals as the first occupants of the territory. Amerindians preceded Europeans, but in most instances they were thinly scattered across the land as hunters and gatherers. There were concentrations along the northwest coast (for example, the Salish, Haida, and Kwakwaka'wakw) and in what is now southern Ontario (the Huron and Iroquois). Among the latter group, many hunter-farmers who raised corn lived in villages with as many as 1,500 people, but they often had to move when their local resources were exhausted or as a consequence of warfare with neighbouring groups. At the site of what is now Montreal, a settlement known as Hochelaga existed around 1550 that demonstrated adaptation to farming as well as large structures known as wooden longhouses, but 100 years later it had disappeared. The Huron lived in southern Ontario between Lake Simcoe and

Georgian Bay in about two dozen villages, the largest of which may have had a population of 5,000, but they were driven from their villages, which they burned as they fled, by the Iroquois in 1649 (Dickason 2002, 50–2, 81–2).

The French and the British were interested in what we now know as Canada because of the staples (fur, fish, timber for ships) in demand in their home countries and because of colonial interest in controlling the territory. Thus, permanent European settlements in Canada were initially organized around two functions: as collection and distribution points for the staple resources and as military outposts to establish control.

Colonialism and Staples

Perhaps the most important theme in Canadian urban history is that towns, villages, and eventually cities were symbols of colonial expansion into new frontiers. Urban places were established or rose into prominence primarily because they represented the attempt to push back the frontiers of the Canadian territory. European governments and urban business interests, as well as Europeans themselves, played the major role in shaping the nature of this urbanization. A number of analysts (e.g., Innis 1933; Lithwick 1970, 69; Nader 1975, 128–200) have pointed out that Canadian development was largely triggered by the demand for staples and staple production, which included fish, fur, timber, and mineral resources and has eventually included wheat, pulp and paper, and oil and gas, all of which are products that have been or are in demand for export elsewhere. *Staples* are resource-based products that are either important for living or necessary for industry. Wherever these staples were found, as was also the case in southern Africa and Australia, for example, a process of settlement and urbanization occurred.

A common pattern we will see throughout this chapter is that settlements were sometimes formed to harvest the staple. However, in most instances, these kinds of settlements remained small or experienced considerable volatility from boom to bust. What did produce larger urban complexes was the need to administer, finance, supply, and export these commodities (Careless 1989; Davis 1971). Thus emerged a few dominant cities to service and exploit the hinterland. We call such a dominant city a **metropolis** because it is a place where manufacturing occurs and where services are provided, where capital is raised, and where decisions are made that affect the hinterland. The **hinterland** refers to those frontier places that provide staple products to sustain the metropolis and that are critical to the whole national economy. Thus, the relationship between the metropolis and hinterland is symbiotic in that they need each other, but it is also tilted in the direction of the power of the metropolis, which absorbs population as well as resources from the hinterland. There is also a hierarchical relationship between metropolitan communities in that regional metropoles may be dominated by national or international metropoles. This relationship between metropolis and hinterland helps us to distinguish conceptually between the components of the national urban system: the two surpassingly large cities in Canada (Toronto and Montreal), their relationship to smaller regional cities, and conceptions of the remaining territory as hinterland. It also helps us to understand how conflict, competition, and animosity may develop between regions and their cities.

The two earliest and most important staples were fish and fur, with lumber a secondary export. St John's, NL, has the distinction of being the first settlement in Canada, but habitation was often seasonal, and the first settlements were essentially fishing stations (Nader 1975, 155). Ships and their crews would often come to the cod-rich Grand Banks in the spring, dry their fish on the land, and in late summer take their cargo back to Europe. St John's harbour also made it important as a military outpost conveniently located as the North American land closest to Europe. While

Newfoundland had settlements that go back to the early 1500s, by the early 1800s the population of St John's was only around 8,000, even though it was an important commercial and administrative centre for the colony.

Halifax, founded in 1749, was another port city that was important both for its fish and for its strategic location for British Empire interests (Stelter and Artibise 1977, 5–14). Halifax also had an advantage in that it was not on an island, as were St John's and Louisbourg/Sydney (on Cape Breton Island), which was a French military outpost. Instead, Halifax was on the edge of the continent, which enabled it to become a transit point for the collection and distribution of goods and people between North America and Europe. As the French fur trade began to grow, the need for more inland ports became evident, and the early settlements at Quebec City (the first fur-trading settlement, established in 1608) and Montreal along the St Lawrence River became more and more important because they could handle ocean-going vessels (Nader 1975, 131). Quebec City in particular played an important role as a military post and became symbolic for control of the continent. Quebec City is where the famous battle was fought between the British and French on the Plains of Abraham in 1759 and is well known for its walled encampment, still an important marker for this historic city. In spite of conquest by the British, Quebec City became and still is an important centre for French language, culture, and politics. Montreal, on the other hand, became more important as a commercial centre under anglophone business control because it was well located on the fur trade's river canoe routes to the continental interior. Although Quebec City (7,500) was bigger than Montreal (3,500) in 1750, over time Montreal grew to become more prominent (Nader 1975, 160). Montreal was surrounded by fertile agricultural land that provided an immediate hinterland as settlement became more permanent. This was a very important new stage in Canadian urban development, for neither St

John's nor Halifax was located on land suitable for significant agricultural activity to sustain rural settlement and thereby support urban nodes. Halifax had the fertile Annapolis Valley about 100 miles away, and local farming within and on the outskirts of St John's largely sustained the St John's population until after World War II (Murray 2002), but the farmlands of the St Lawrence were much more extensive. Montreal also had the most inland port for ocean transport between Canada and Europe and therefore ultimately became the most important commercial and financial centre in the country as expansion into the interior took place. It was no accident that Montreal became an important banking centre, with the head offices of the Bank of Montreal and the Royal Bank located there.

Commercial Cities and Agricultural Hinterlands

The emergence of agriculture in what is now southern Quebec and southern Ontario in the latter part of the eighteenth century had several consequences of urban significance (Careless 1978). First, it set the stage for a more permanent population than the nomadic fur trade could support. Second, it fostered the development of towns that served as community and retail centres for the agricultural population. Third, it led to the development of regional centres of commerce and administration, which allowed towns to become larger cities and to take on a function that was different from merely serving as a military outpost or as an exchange point for sending good to and receiving them from Europe. Eventually, the increase in size of such cities was brought about by the need to furnish goods and supplies to the agricultural community through manufacturing and capital. This was particularly clear as English, Scots, and Irish people immigrated from overseas and Loyalists fled the American Revolution after 1776 to settle on the farm frontiers of Upper and Lower

Box 2.1 Urbanization by 1850

The year 1850 represents a significant point when colonialism, with its focus on overseas interests, was becoming less prominent and commercialism focused on internal markets was increasing in prominence. The largest cities were in French Canada, with Montreal at 79,700 and Quebec City at 45,500. Toronto (30,800) was slightly bigger than St John's (30,500). The two Maritime cities of Saint John, NB, and Halifax were next in size at 23,700 and 20,700. Hamilton (17,600) was just starting to experience new growth that would increase in the industrial era, and Kingston was the next largest at 11,600. Quebec City and Saint John were particularly important at this time because of their role in wooden shipbuilding.

This date also represents an important dividing point in urbanization because thereafter, railways and industrialization transformed the roles of cities by reducing dependence on water transport, opening up new hinterlands for agricultural settlement, and supporting indigenous industry and growing populations in Canadian cities. One indication of this was that between 1821 and 1871, the number of urban places with populations of more than 5,000 grew from five to 19. By 1871, Montreal had 107,000 residents, and Toronto had 56,000. After 1850, too, the importance of wooden sailing ships declined as they were replaced by iron steamships, which seemed to elevate the importance of Montreal over Quebec City.

Sources: Driedger 1991, 57; Stelter and Artibise 1977, 5–160; Nader 1975, 177; Stelter 1982, 13.

Canada. While Toronto (formerly York) was first coveted for its harbour to defend British territory from American invasion and to facilitate the fur trade, it became increasingly clear that Toronto and Montreal were the economic engines supplying the agricultural hinterland and served as the dominant connection with foreign interests and foreign markets.

As the military role of communities like Quebec City and Kingston diminished when British interests no longer felt threatened by American expansionism, the northward attempt of which ended with the War of 1812, these settlements either lost their significance (e.g., Kingston), developed new roles (e.g., lumbering at Quebec City), or were surpassed by new centres of significance (e.g., manufacturing at Hamilton). The opening of the Erie Canal in 1825 provided a new water outlet from the Great Lakes to New York, which supported added commercial options for Toronto and Montreal. In short, by 1850 British North America was no longer just a hinterland for European interests; its cities were indeed developing

their own internal hinterlands of agriculturalists and were trading with American cities.

Railways and the Industrial City

Until the 1850s, the economy of what is now Canada was shaped by water transportation. Access to rivers and oceans determined where settlements were established, and the vitality of these settlements was related to export demands and staple availability. For example, when the lumber industry replaced the fur trade, different employment opportunities developed in places like Ottawa and Quebec City, and shipbuilding using wood helped to support residents in places like Halifax and Saint John. However, the coming of the railway created a new range of options. First, the railway provided an all-seasons link between cities and settlements that did not end with freeze-up and supported more robust commercial ties. Second, the railway made it possible for new settlements not serviceable by water transport to emerge in the interior (e.g., London, ON).

Not surprisingly, the first rail lines were established from Montreal, Toronto, and Hamilton to various American cities in the 1850s, but a line (Grand Trunk) was also established between Rimouski, QC, and Sarnia, ON, covering much of the settled area of central Canada (Careless 1978). Several other smaller lines were built in Nova Scotia and New Brunswick, which enlarged the hinterland for all cities that used the rail lines as the centrepiece for their growth. Obviously, cities able to serve as transshipment nodes linking rail with water transportation would have a particular advantage in pursuing growth and expansion, but railways in general seemed to support a more diversified economy and solidified the growth of a capitalist class of entrepreneurs and promoters. Local banks such as the Bank of Montreal and the Royal Bank in Montreal, the Bank of Nova Scotia in Halifax, and the Bank of Toronto and Bank of Commerce in Toronto became major players in investments to strengthen not only regional economies but also the dominance of their respective cities in the national economy after Confederation in 1867.

While it is too simplistic to say that the railways and the banks consolidated the dominance of Montreal and Toronto, it is indeed the case that the presence of capital and a growing business class in these cities led to investment decisions, even political decisions, that seemed to make these two cities the hubs of local, regional, and national life. At the time of Confederation, Ottawa was named the national capital, a city roughly halfway between Toronto and Montreal. The Bank Act of 1871, which established a centralized national branch banking system instead of a string of local banks, clearly centralized financial power. Perhaps most significant was the fact that central Canadian business interests influenced the federal government to enact policies benefiting them that had enormous urban consequences. In particular, the National Policy of 1879 established a tariff wall around the new nation that taxed imports and that gave priority to Canadian-produced products (Nader 1975, 202–10). Thus, indigenous manufacturing could replace foreign imports, the investments of the capitalist class would be safer, and jobs in Canadian cities would be created. The benefits of this tariff accrued especially to those locations where the capitalist class made investments, and for geographical, business, and political reasons, much of the capital investment occurred in central Canada. The end result of these actions was a process known **as concentration** and **centralization**, which had differential urban effects. When the Intercolonial Railway linking Halifax to Montreal and Toronto was completed in 1876, rather than strengthening the urban economies of the Atlantic region, it led to the buying out of budding industries in the Atlantic region that could not compete with central Canadian capital (Acheson 1972). In conjunction with the decline in the building of wooden ships, which had been a major industry in the Atlantic region, promising urban growth in the region was arrested, and in many ways the region's cities became a hinterland to central Canadian cities. Thus, centralization strengthened some cities and weakened others.

A second impact of the National Policy that had urban significance was the development of the Canadian West, which was clearly identified as the new region of promise, particularly for central Canadian economic interests. The expansion of Canada 'from sea to sea' required an infusion of population into the largely unoccupied spaces to settle as agriculturalists. Thus emerged a recruitment campaign not only within Canada but also in the United States and particularly in Europe for immigrants to settle the region. The offer of land to homesteaders was used to lure new residents to the Canadian West. But key to the entire plan was the building of a national railway linking central Canada to the West. The creation of the Canadian Pacific Railway (CPR) explicitly for that purpose linked the two dominant cities in central Canada with the West, reaching all the way to Port Moody, BC, near Vancouver, in

1885. The railway was envisioned to take settlers to the western interior and also to serve as the conduit for finished goods needed by the settlers. Returning east, the railway was to carry the agricultural products the farmers produced. But from an urban perspective, the railway, in conjunction with the tariff wall, ensured that the West served as a captive market for central Canadian urban industries. Thus, employment grew dramatically in central Canada, not only to supply central Canadian consumers but to provide steel, farm implements, textiles, and various consumer goods for the markets both to the east and to the west. Thus grew an urban complex of industries, finance, and administration in central Canada that made populations elsewhere their hinterland (Spelt 1972, 198–211). This pattern, then, has a long history in Canada and contributed to the urban dominance of Montreal and Toronto and their metropolitan regions.

Urbanization in the West

The Canadian Shield serves as a formidable barrier between central Canada and western Canada. The barren rocky terrain is not suitable for agriculture, and therefore its settlement is sparse at best. The Shield stretching across central, northern, and northwestern Ontario stands in stark contrast to the agriculture and dense urban settlements of southern Ontario. West of the Shield is the Western Interior, often referred to as the Prairies, which are bounded by the Rocky Mountains on the west, leading to the Pacific coast region. Obviously, Vancouver's coastal location along with Victoria's location on Vancouver Island meant that settlement would occur there before settlement in the Western Interior. This is indeed what happened, although the growth of these two cities did not occur as rapidly as did the growth of cities on the east coast. Victoria had its origins as a British naval base and an outpost of the Hudson's Bay Company around 1850, but by 1864 it still had only about 4,000 residents.

Vancouver received its impetus with the arrival of the CPR in 1887, but what differentiated Vancouver from other western cities was that its strategic seaport facilitated international trade (especially with Asia) rather than just internal trade (Macdonald 1982). When the Panama Canal was opened in 1914, the west coast was more easily linked to European markets. Yet becoming a mainland rail terminus also linked Vancouver more closely with Canada as well. By 1891, Vancouver still had a population of only about 13,000, but its transshipment functions ensured that its role would exceed that of the provincial capital, Victoria. With its coastal international access, Vancouver has also served somewhat as a regional counterbalance to the Western Interior's orientation towards central Canada.

The opening up of the western plains through the National Policy played a huge role in the emergence of Winnipeg as the third largest city in Canada. The Hudson's Bay Company had established a fur-trading post at the junction of the Red and Assiniboine rivers in Manitoba at the eastern end of the plains. A small farming settlement, the Red River Colony, had also existed there, and waterways linked Winnipeg with St Paul, Minnesota, to the south. Manitoba had become a province in 1870, and within four years Winnipeg had a population of 3,700 (Artibise 1975, 10). By 1890, the population had reached 25,000, after which impressive growth brought the population to 136,000 by 1911, the year that Winnipeg became the third largest city in Canada. Much of this growth was due to the fact that Winnipeg had obtained a rail connection to the east in 1885 that established Winnipeg as the launching pad for western settlement. From 1890 to 1910, several hundred thousand migrants flooded into the West, mostly through Winnipeg. Some stayed in Winnipeg, creating a truly multicultural community, particularly in the North End. Two more railways came to Winnipeg (including the Canadian Northern, later a major component of the amalgamation that created Canadian National Railways in 1919), and

Box 2.2 *Winnipeg: Chicago of the North*

Just as Chicago became the vanguard city for the opening of the American West as an industrial base to supply its growth, so Winnipeg was hailed as the new metropolis that would be the dominant urban centre for the Canadian West. Indeed, from 1880 to 1910, Winnipeg was one of the fastest-growing cities in North America. And the nickname 'Bull's Eye of the Dominion' presumably reflected the importance of Winnipeg's central geographical location.

An area of the central core at Portage and Main (now known as the Exchange District and a historic site) symbolized Winnipeg's importance as the western centre for finance, investment, and distribution. Dominated by architecturally resplendent buildings made of stone, marble, and stunning terra cotta, all built in the early 1900s, the Grain Exchange, the Royal Bank Building, the Great West Life Building, the Confederation Life Building, and even a well-known vaudeville theatre known as the Pantages Theatre became symbols of prosperity and urban boom. The Exchange District contains 117 buildings that predate 1914, and many of these buildings even reflect Chicago-style architecture. Big warehouses like Ashdown's and Marshall Wells contained consumer goods for distribution throughout the West. Eaton's department store not only had an imposing retail building but also had a mail-order centre to accept orders from dispersed rural dwellers. More than 250 manufacturing firms were attracted to Winnipeg, but the railways were the largest employers, with 3,500 employees for the CPR alone.

The growth of a commercial elite and the emergence of all the trappings of their position made Winnipeg a cultural haven with sophistication. On the other hand, Winnipeg also had its share of chaos as the city became a magnet for immigrants, many of whom did not speak English, were poor, and settled in the rail-dominated North End. One of the more famous events in Canadian urban history was the Winnipeg General Strike of 1919 when workers rose up to protest their impoverished position and marginalization.

Winnipeg failed to become the industrial centre that Chicago did, partly because central Canadian dominance was too strong. Its prominence was largely due to its role as 'the Gateway to the West'. The railways from the east all passed through Winnipeg and from there to Vancouver, with the Canadian Pacific operating a southern route through Regina and Calgary and the Canadian Northern (National) running farther to the north through Saskatoon and Edmonton. Even after agricultural settlement was completed, immigrants flooded into the West after both world wars, and Winnipeg's train stations bustled with activity. Given this historical background, it is not surprising that the decline in the relative importance of Winnipeg is related to the fact that the railway is no longer a dominant mode of transportation. Winnipeg is no longer a wholesale centre, and new urban growth has occurred farther west where the regional population fulcrum is now in Alberta.

Source: Partially based on Artibise 1975.

the rail yards became a virtual beehive of activity, with space for more than 10,000 rail cars. Grain was shipped east to what is now Thunder Bay, and finished goods were shipped from central Canada to Winnipeg warehouses for storage and distribution throughout the West through large wholesalers located there. One large wholesaler—Ashdown's—had a supply train that travelled throughout the West, providing goods needed by agriculturalists. In short, the urban optimism in Winnipeg was unbelievable, and the city was hailed as the 'Chicago of the North'.

Beyond Winnipeg, the settlement of the prairie West was largely framed by the railway and the North West Mounted Police (NWMP) (Nader 1975, 245). The agencies of empire that had gone into the West with the fur trade and preceded settlement were the Hudson's Bay Company, the North West Company, and the representatives of the Catholic Church and the Anglican Church. Trading outposts and mission settlements were small, although some later served as nuclei for larger settlements, especially if they became stops along a railway. Regina had its beginnings not only as the capital of the North-West Territories but as the headquarters of the North West Mounted Police, suggesting again how military functions were important to early Canadian settlements. NWMP posts were scattered throughout the region but could easily be relocated as population nodes developed. Edmonton, for example, had been a fur-trade post, a missionary station, and a military post; eventually, it became a government centre when the province of Alberta was established in 1905. At the same time, Regina was named the capital of the new neighbouring province of Saskatchewan.

In general, though, the railways were the driving force in the establishment of new communities. Both the major stops for transcontinental service and the sites of grain elevators established as collecting points every seven to 10 miles along the complex of branch lines became the locations for towns, each with a school, one or more churches, and basic retailing. Many of these towns were small, but they were part of what has been called the prairie community system, with many independent towns and dependent villages dotting the prairie landscape (Zimmerman and Moneo 1971). Some of these locations had become major stops along the rail line either because the railway identified those places as rail centres or because of government functions or administrative/commercial functions that made them more important. For example, the decision to locate the University of Saskatchewan in Saskatoon helped to solidify that city's role as a major

centre in the northern part of the province.[1] Similarly, the decision of the CPR to make Calgary a major rail centre strengthened its commercial role in agriculture and ranching. Artibise (1982) has argued that almost always, local commercial elites—**civic boosters** who promoted economic and population growth—made the difference between the success or failure of one new community compared to that of another so that some urban centres prospered more than others.

By the end of the World War II, the settlement pattern for Canada had been well established. Two key points about these urban developments can be identified.

1. All early settlements and urban centres were established initially as the result of the interests of trade and empire—French or British entrepreneurs who found a demand for New World staple products in urban Europe. To the extent that cities were formed, they were commercial/exchange centres for the extraction of these staples. This required locating these urban centres on waterways, since shipping was the only means of transportation. Thus, all of the early cities and the largest cities of Canada were located along bodies of water. But it was not just trade interests that spurred these forays into the New World but imperial interests of control as well. Early urban centres in Canada were either fortresses of some kind or had a strong military/police presence so that representatives of the home country could administer the surrounding territory.

2. As agriculture introduced a more permanent population, more inland settlements developed. Here the role of the railway made it possible for new towns and cities to emerge in the interior. Because some cities were both railway hubs and ports for shipping lanes, they developed into more dominant cities with entrepreneurial and commercial elites. These cities were not only hinterlands of foreign markets but centres developing

their own interior hinterlands. The most successful of them also developed links to American urban centres. In general, however, up to the end of World War II, most of these cities were comparatively small, although the dominance and size of Montreal and Toronto were unrivalled.

Increasing the Scale of Urbanization: The Twentieth Century

The largest city in Canada in 1901 was Montreal, with a population of 267,000. By 1951, it had grown to 1.4 million residents. Similarly, Toronto had increased in size from 208,000 to 1.1 million over the same period. Other cities were not nearly as large, but their growth also suggested that the process of urbanization was proceeding at an enormous pace. This urban growth has continued to the extent that by 2006, Toronto had more than 5.1 million residents and Montreal had a population of more than 3.6 million. Three types of factors made this rate of urbanization and the growth of other Canadian cities possible: technological, external, and internal.

Technology

The shift from staples and water transportation to industry and rail meant that cities could become much larger in population and territory and more complex. The streetcar, for example, now made it possible for residents to live farther from the core. Industrial capitalism led to more employment options in cities with large production facilities and also meant that a waged working class became a more prominent feature of urban life. All of this began in the latter part of the nineteenth century but continued as electricity replaced steam power, making the factory an ever more dominant feature of the city landscape. The emergence of the automobile and its mass production created new options for urban spatial growth and ultimately supported the need for high-speed urban free-

ways. Structural steel made tall office towers and residential high-rises possible, thereby increasing urban density. Perhaps the most important consequence was the *suburbanization of residence* as the consequence of urban growth and eventually even the *suburbanization of industry*, which led to the growth of urban regions, not just single cities themselves. All of this was occurring at the same time that huge advances were taking place in agricultural technologies, which led to bigger farms and displaced many agricultural workers. Air travel, especially after World War II, also increased interurban exchange across greater distances, meaning that internal hinterlands could be more easily serviced from big cities and international air access would become a key indicator of a city's relationship to other global cities.

External Factors

The two world wars accelerated industrial growth as the demand for manufactured goods increased, and this growth also supported a more urban population. The aftermath of the wars brought an influx of postwar migration from war-torn Europe to Canada, increasing the urban population. The decisions made by foreign investors also framed urbanization in Canada, particularly American direct investment through the creation of Canadian subsidiaries in central Canada, as in the automobile industry. Large multinational corporations set up plants and production facilities in southern Ontario and Quebec, solidifying that region's urban growth and dominance. Somewhat later, inward investment from Hong Kong played a significant role in the urban development of Vancouver. Migration from Third World countries where opportunities were limited or from which people had to flee as refugees also played an important role in changing Canadian cities, especially Toronto, Vancouver, and Montreal.

Internal Factors

Rural-urban migration, or **rural depopulation**, became a significant cause of urban growth as family farming was slowly transformed into consolidated agribusiness. In 1941, there were a record-high 733,000 farms in Canada. This number shrank to 481,000 farms in 1961 and declined further to 229,000 farms by 2006 (Statistics Canada 2006). While the number of farms shrank to one-third of the 1941 total over this time, the size of farms almost tripled. In the postwar period, young rural women were disproportionately displaced by this shift because there was nothing for them to do, and men soon followed (Stone 1968, 203). The result has been a continual movement of people not only from rural areas and small towns but also from smaller cities to larger cities (interurban migration) that have a broader range of employment opportunities (Lithwick 1970, 83). The postwar baby boom also played a role in the demand for new housing, which often meant single detached housing for nuclear families in new suburbs, and these burgeoning suburbs pushed out the boundaries of cities. Government policies, such as those encouraging home ownership through the Canada Mortgage and Housing Corporation, and immigration policies that expanded the source countries of immigration also affected the shape and texture of cities.

We have already seen the way that the National Policy had huge urban effects in that it supported the industry and growing populations in the St Lawrence Lowlands of southern Ontario and Quebec, creating a heartland-hinterland effect. As industrialism progressed, this pattern became even more accentuated. The population of the country became more concentrated, and as a consequence political power and economic power came to be located in one urban region. Sometimes referred to as 'the main street' of Canada, the Windsor–Quebec City urban axis (see Figure 2.1) is a rectangular area stretching from Quebec City to Windsor, ON, and includes such places as Trois-Rivières, Sherbrooke, Montreal, Ottawa-Gatineau, Kingston, Peterborough, Oshawa, Toronto, Hamilton, Kitchener, St Catharines, and London (Yeates 1975). More than half of the population of Canada resides in this corridor, and seven out of 10 manufacturing jobs in

the country are located there (Yeates 1991). It is not only the core region or economic engine for internal trade but has also become the focus of international trade and is referred to as 'a North American region state' (Courchene and Telmer 1998). The problem is that this form of urban dominance creates a sense of peripheralization in the rest of the country that is difficult to change.

The continued growth of the Toronto metropolitan area and the southwestern Ontario urban region in particular accentuates this concentration. The area along the western shore of Lake Ontario from Oshawa to Niagara is known as the 'the Golden Horseshoe' because of its shape and because it is a prosperous, continuous urban agglomeration including Oshawa, Toronto, Hamilton, Oakville, Mississauga, and St Catharines (see Figure 2.1). This phenomenon is known as a *conurbation* because it involves continuous urban sprawl where there are few marks of differentiation from one city to another.

Changing Features of the Canadian Urban System

The Canadian urban system evolved into a basic structure that has been relatively stable over time in spite of its characteristic uneven urbanization. Nonetheless, forces of change continue to alter these well-established patterns. We now turn to a discussion of some of these changes.

I. A Changing Urban Hierarchy

In spite of the pattern of urban concentration and dominance that has developed in Canada, some changes both within the Windsor–Quebec City urban axis and elsewhere suggest that the urban system is dynamic rather than static. Table 2.1 shows the 10 largest cities in Canada by rank order every 10 years since 1901. Notice how many cities that were among the biggest in 1901 tended to move down the list (e.g., Quebec City, Hamilton, and Winnipeg) and even off the list (e.g., cities in the Atlantic region) by 2006. Other cities,

Figure 2.1 Census Metropolitan Areas, 2006

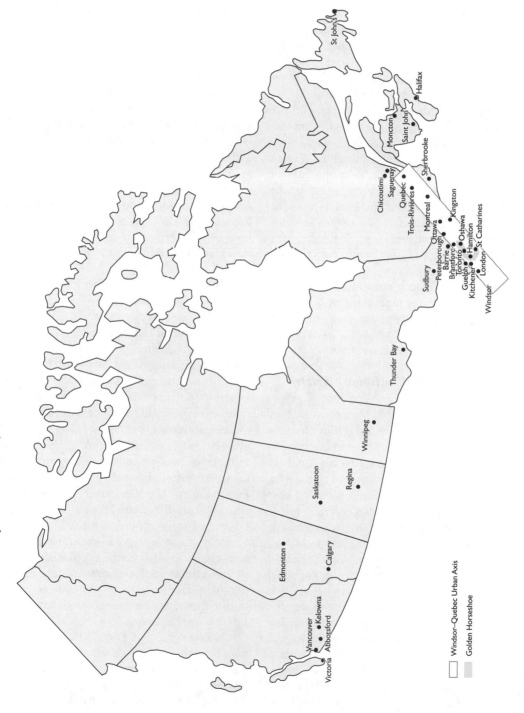

St John's

Halifax

Moncton
Saint John

Sherbrooke

Chicoutimi
Saguenay
Québec
Trois-Rivières
Montreal
Ottawa
Kingston
St Catharines
Peterborough
Barrie
Brantford
Hamilton
Toronto
Oshawa
London
Guelph
Kitchener
Windsor

Sudbury

Thunder Bay

Winnipeg

Saskatoon
Regina

Edmonton
Calgary

Vancouver
Kelowna
Abbotsford
Victoria

☐ Windsor–Quebec Urban Axis

▨ Golden Horseshoe

such as Ottawa-Gatineau, Calgary, and Edmonton, were not among the 10 largest Canadian cities 100 years ago but are now the largest among the second-tier cities behind the megacities. Six new cities (Brantford, Guelph, Barrie, Peterborough, Moncton, and Kelowna) were added to the list of census metropolitan areas (a Statistics Canada category for urban areas of at least 100,000 population) in 2006, bringing the total number of CMAs in Canada to 33. Fifteen of these CMAs are located in Ontario, including four of the six new metropolitan areas (Table 2.2). In the Atlantic region, Moncton experienced the fastest growth and has now surpassed Saint John as the largest city in New Brunswick. Some CMAs have lost population in recent years (e.g., Saguenay, Saint John) or experienced little growth (e.g., Thunder Bay, Regina). It is also noteworthy that whereas Montreal was the biggest city in Canada for more than 100 years, it was superseded by Toronto in 1981, which is now larger by more than 1.5 million persons (Table 2.1). This shift is an important aspect of Canada's urban transformation.

2. Toronto More Dominant Than Montreal

As we have already noted, Montreal's original dominance was related to its critical location for water transportation.[2] As Canada's orientation shifted from Europe to the North American continent, Toronto's importance increased (Nader 1975, 214–23). The opening of the St Lawrence Seaway in the late 1950s played a role in this shift of economic strength to the Great Lakes and American cities such as Detroit and Cleveland, but rail links (and even trucking) had become more significant than water links, which made Toronto's central position more strategic. Perhaps even more important was the fact that Ontario's urban population and Toronto's satellite cities, such as Hamilton, grew more rapidly with supporting industries than did regional cities in Quebec. In conjunction with the fact that Toronto was closer to the growing population of the West, the centre of gravity of Canada shifted westward

from Montreal. The Quiet Revolution in Quebec also played a role in the transfer of capital and influence away from Montreal. As resentment in Quebec grew over the dominance of the economy by anglophones who owned the means of production and had higher incomes, francophones demanded greater participation in the economy. When such feeling supported the rise of the independence movement, it encouraged the shift of finance (such as life insurance and money markets) and other corporate services away from Montreal to Toronto. Out-migration from Montreal occurred, less in-migration from other parts of Canada took place, and more immigrants chose Toronto over Montreal as their destination (Newbold 1996). Thus, a combination of factors has now made Toronto the dominant city in Canada.

3. Urban Growth in the Far West

There is clearly a long history of central Canadian urban dominance in Canada. However, an important trend of increasing significance is the growth of urban areas in the far West. The Vancouver metropolitan area, often referred to as the Lower Mainland of British Columbia, has grown from a population of half a million in 1951 to more than two million 50 years later. It includes municipalities such as Surrey (394,000), Burnaby (203,000), and Richmond (175,000) and a number of smaller municipalities, and a new CMA, Abbotsford, has emerged to the east in the Fraser Valley. The Vancouver CMA is still considerably smaller than Toronto and Montreal, but its coastal location has made Vancouver the Canadian gateway to Asia—a connection of new importance. It also benefits from what is known as the **climatological urbanization effect** in that urbanization in the region is fostered by its mild climate, which attracts both internal and international migrants.[3]

Vancouver is not a world city or global city like Toronto, Tokyo, or New York, but it is an interesting case of how a second-tier city-region has been changed by forces of globalization. At one time, Vancouver was largely defined by its

Table 2.1 Ten Largest Cities in Canada in Rank Order For Select Years, 1901–2006

Rank	1901	1911	1931	1941	1951	1961	1971	1981	1991	2001	2006
1	Montreal 267,730	Montreal 467,986	Montreal 818,577	Montreal 1,145,282	Montreal 1,395,400	Montreal 2,109,509	Montreal 2,743,208	Toronto 3,130,392	Toronto 3,898,830	Toronto 4,682,897	Toronto 5,113,149
2	Toronto 208,040	Toronto 376,471	Toronto 631,207	Toronto 909,928	Toronto 1,117,470	Toronto 1,824,481	Toronto 2,628,043	Montreal 2,862,286	Montreal 3,209,100	Montreal 3,426,350	Montreal 3,635,571
3	Quebec 68,840	Winnipeg 136,035	Vancouver 246,593	Vancouver 377,447	Vancouver 530,728	Vancouver 790,165	Vancouver 1,082,352	Vancouver 1,268,183	Vancouver 1,602,590	Vancouver 1,986,965	Vancouver 2,116,581
4	Hamilton 52,634	Vancouver 120,847	Winnipeg 218,785	Winnipeg 299,937	Winnipeg 354,069	Winnipeg 475,989	Ottawa-Hull 602,510	Ottawa-Hull 743,821	Ottawa-Hull 941,815	Ottawa-Hull 1,063,664	Ottawa-Gatineau 1,130,761
5	Winnipeg 42,340	Hamilton 81,969	Hamilton 155,547	Ottawa-Hull 226,290	Ottawa-Hull 281,908	Ottawa-Hull 429,750	Winnipeg 540,262	Edmonton 740,882	Edmonton 841,130	Calgary 951,395	Calgary 1,079,310
6	Halifax 40,832	Quebec 78,118	Quebec 130,594	Quebec 224,756	Quebec 274,827	Hamilton 395,189	Hamilton 498,523	Calgary 625,966	Calgary 754,035	Edmonton 937,845	Edmonton 1,034,945
7	Saint John 40,711	Halifax 46,619	Calgary 83,761	Hamilton 197,732	Hamilton 259,685	Quebec 357,568	Edmonton 495,702	Winnipeg 592,061	Winnipeg 660,450	Winnipeg 671,274	Winnipeg 694,668
8	London 37,976	London 46,300	Edmonton 79,197	Windsor 123,973	Edmonton 173,075	Edmonton 337,538	Quebec 480,502	Quebec 583,820	Quebec 645,535	Quebec 682,757	Quebec 715,515
9	St John's 29,594	Calgary 43,704	London 71,148	Halifax 98,636	Windsor 157,672	Calgary 279,062	Calgary 403,319	Hamilton 542,095	Hamilton 599,760	Hamilton 662,401	Hamilton 692,911
10	Vancouver 29,432	Saint John 42,511	Windsor 63,108	Edmonton 97,842	Calgary 139,105	Windsor 193,365	St Catharines-Niagara 303,429	St Catharines-Niagara 342,645	London 381,520	London 432,451	London 457,720

Sources: Statistics Canada 1951 Census, v. 1, tables 9 and 12; 1961 Census, catalogue no. 92541, tables 17 and 18; 1971 Census, catalogue no. 92708, v. I, bulletin 1.1-8, table 7; 1986 Census, catalogue. no. 92-104, table 2; 1996 Census; 2006 Census, Population and Dwelling Counts, Census Metropolitan Areas.

Table 2.2 Characteristics of Census Metropolitan Areas for Select Indicators, 2006

CMA	Population	% Change 1996–2006	Density per Square Km	Median Age	% Foreign-Born	% Visible Minorities
St John's	181,113	4.7	225.1	38.4	2.9	1.9
Halifax	372,858	3.8	67.8	39.0	7.4	7.5
Moncton	126,424	6.5	52.5	39.4	3.4	2.0
Saint John	122,389	−0.2	36.4	40.5	4.2	3.1
Saguenay	151,643	−2.1	86.5	43.4	1.2	0.9
Quebec City	715,515	4.2	218.4	41.7	3.7	2.3
Sherbrooke	186,952	6.3	151.8	40.2	5.6	3.8
Trois-Rivières	141,529	2.9	160.8	43.8	2.2	1.6
Montreal	3,635,571	5.3	853.6	39.3	20.6	16.5
Ottawa-Gatineau	1,130,761	5.9	197.8	38.4	18.1	16.0
Kingston	152,358	3.8	79.9	40.7	12.5	5.8
Peterborough	116,570	5.1	77.4	42.8	9.4	2.7
Oshawa	330,594	11.6	366.0	37.5	16.4	10.3
Toronto	5,113,149	9.2	866.1	37.5	45.7	42.9
Hamilton	692,911	4.6	505.1	39.9	24.4	12.3
St Catharines-Niagara	390,317	3.5	279.3	42.1	18.3	6.6
Kitchener-Waterloo	451,235	8.9	545.6	36.4	23.1	13.8
Brantford	124,607	5.5	116.1	39.6	13.0	5.5
Guelph	127,009	8.2	335.6	36.8	20.4	12.7
London	457,720	5.1	171.7	38.6	19.3	11.1
Windsor	323,342	5.0	316.1	37.7	23.3	16.0
Barrie	177,061	19.2	197.3	36.7	12.8	5.8
Sudbury	158,258	1.7	46.8	41.0	6.7	2.1
Thunder Bay	122,907	0.8	48.2	41.8	10.4	2.7
Winnipeg	694,668	2.7	131.0	38.8	17.7	15.0
Regina	194,971	1.1	57.2	37.5	7.7	6.6
Saskatoon	233,923	3.5	44.9	35.8	7.7	6.4
Calgary	1,079,310	13.4	211.3	35.7	23.6	22.2
Edmonton	1,034,945	10.4	109.9	36.4	18.5	17.1
Kelowna	162,276	9.8	55.9	43.4	14.8	5.2
Abbotsford	159,020	7.9	254.1	36.8	23.3	22.8
Vancouver	2,116,581	6.5	735.6	39.1	39.6	41.7
Victoria	330,088	5.8	474.7	43.1	19.1	10.4

Source: Adapted from Statistics Canada publication *Census Trends, 2006 Census*, Catalogue no. 92-596-XWE, http://www.12.statcan.gc.ca/english/census06/data/trends/index.cfm.

Box 2.3 Toronto: The Centre of the Canadian Universe

Is it surprising that in Canada, southern Ontario or the Toronto metropolitan region is referred to as 'the centre of the universe'? Toronto-based newspapers such as *The Globe and Mail* and *The National Post* are distributed everywhere in Canada. The CBC national news is broadcast from Toronto. Canada's only major league baseball team (the Blue Jays) and only professional basketball team (the Raptors) are based in Toronto. The financial hub of the country is the Toronto Stock Exchange. More companies have their corporate headquarters in Toronto than in any other city. Toronto has more non-stop flights to foreign cities and is serviced by more foreign airlines than any other Canadian city. Is there any demographic reason for this dominance?

More than 8 million people reside in the Greater Golden Horseshoe, which is two-thirds of the population of Ontario (Canada's province with the most people) and *one-quarter of the total population of Canada*. The city of Toronto itself houses 2.5 million people, but it is surrounded by about 100 other municipalities that make up the Toronto metropolitan area. Sixteen of these municipalities have populations of more than 100,000, such as Mississauga (670,000), Hamilton (505,000), and Brampton (435,000), but there are also other growing municipalities such as Markham, Vaughan, Kitchener, Oakville, Barrie, and St Catharines. The corridor from Hamilton through Toronto along Lake Ontario to Oshawa is the largest continuous urban corridor in Canada. In economic terms, Toronto is considered a 'big market' that can support a wide range of activities. The Toronto census metropolitan area is unrivalled in Canada as a region of power and influence and clearly reflects the processes of concentration and centralization.

resource-based hinterland of forest products and minerals, but it has now been transformed by both the markets and the people of the Asia-Pacific region.[4] Vancouver lacks significant manufacturing and a high-technology sector, it is not a capital with large numbers of public-sector employees, and it is not home to a large number of corporate head offices. Yet the city experienced remarkable growth through immigration and expansion of the service sector. One of the major reasons for this change was the fact that many of the immigrants to Vancouver were entrepreneurial and brought capital and professional skills with them. The result has been the development of the city less in the direction of the Canadian urban system or the Canadian West but with more emphasis on capital flows, trading networks, socio-cultural patterns, and travel networks throughout the Pacific region. Thus, Vancouver's transformation has involved it becoming less inward-looking in a Canadian sense and more oriented to and affected by global forces.

The other growth dynamic in the West has taken place in Alberta. Often understood as driven by oil and gas (staples in high demand), the cities of Calgary and Edmonton in particular have experienced dramatic growth during two boom cycles, 1975 to 1981 and the period since 1996. Calgary had the highest percentage growth of any major city in Canada from 1996 to 2006, and Edmonton was close behind. What is particularly interesting about the population growth of these two cities is that it was largely due to domestic migration from other parts of Canada, whereas Toronto and Vancouver grew primarily as the result of international migration. Edmonton played a crucial role during World War II and thereafter as 'the gateway to the North'. The North was important for defence purposes, and Edmonton became the staging point for that operation as well as the service point for later development, especially resource extraction. Edmonton became an important medical, educational, and supply centre for northern peoples as well. Coupled with the fact that Edmonton was also the seat of the provincial government, it was larger than Calgary until the late 1990s when Calgary overtook Edmonton in size. As the administrative centre for the oil and gas industry, Calgary has the second highest number of major corporate headquarters offices in Canada and has attracted other supporting services and capital investment that link the city to international markets. In recent years, Calgary has also become a regional transportation hub and a distribution centre for the West.

In many ways, the growth of Vancouver as Canada's primary city on the west coast is fully understandable. What has perhaps been surprising is the explosive growth of Edmonton and Calgary in the Western Interior. In 1951, Edmonton had only 173,000 residents, and Calgary had 139,000. Both cities have now passed the 1-million mark and serve as the anchors for the province of Alberta, which has experienced unusual growth since 1996. Whether this growth is part of a power shift to the West is, of course, an intriguing question. However, there is no doubt that Calgary and Edmonton are transforming urban dynamics within the country. These two cities can be called **arriviste cities** because they are upstart urban centres that are challenging the existing urban hierarchy on the basis of their newfound brash power and influence (Hiller 2007). While they are still regional cities, they have moved beyond that in important respects and have become important players in the national and international economy in an unexpected way.

4. Immigration: The Importance of Gateway Cities

Another trend of some significance is that urbanization is also closely tied to immigration. Cities that play a dominant role in receiving immigrants are known as **gateway cities**. In 2006, the foreign-born made up almost 20 per cent of the Canadian population. Immigrants were not evenly distributed throughout the country but were concentrated in the largest cities. Almost two-thirds (62.9 per cent) of all foreign-born in Canada reside in three cities: Toronto, Montreal, and Vancouver,

and about 70 per cent of all immigrants to Canada since 1996 have chosen these three cities. Among the three cities, one in particular has become the preferred destination for immigrants: Toronto received more than 40 per cent of all immigrants to Canada during that period, and its foreign-born population is now the highest among all major cities in the world at 45.7 per cent. Vancouver is second at 39.6 per cent, compared to cities such as Miami (36.5 per cent), Los Angeles (34.7 per cent), Sydney, Australia (31.7 per cent), and New York (27.9 per cent). Of further significance is that immigration has become the primary reason for the demographic growth of these cities, since fewer people are choosing to move to them from within the country and their existing population is moving farther from their centres cities or moving to other cities. It is clear, then, that immigration is changing the social landscape of Canada's largest cities in a way that places them in sharp contrast with Canada's smallest cities, which have a much smaller proportion of foreign-born (see Table 2.2).

Another indicator of the way that immigration is changing some Canadian cities in particular is the change in the place of origin of many immigrants to these cities, reflected in the growth of the visible-minority population. As recently as 1981, visible minorities made up only 4.7 per cent of the Canadian population because the primary source-countries for immigration were European. But by 2006, 16.2 per cent of the Canadian population consisted of visible minorities, particularly from Asia, who were not evenly dispersed throughout the country but were concentrated in Canada's largest cities. Toronto and Vancouver, for example, had visible-minority populations of more than 40 per cent, whereas smaller cities like Saskatoon, Moncton, and Oshawa had small populations in this category (Table 2.2).

Table 2.2 indicates as well that the largest cities have the highest densities. Furthermore, cities growing the fastest also have the lowest mean age, suggesting that migrants bring youthfulness to a city. Most cities with slower rates of growth or declining populations have older populations.

5. Urban Restructuring

Another development of considerable importance has been the emergence of what is called the post-industrial city. In Chapter 1, we saw how the restructuring of the global economy has led to deindustrialization and the rise of urban service economies. From the 1970s to the present, a huge paradigm shift has been taking place in which production of goods has shifted offshore and employment in Canadian cities has increasingly focused on service industries. Finance, management, computing, and a wide range of specialized services—for example, tourism and recreation—have replaced manufacturing as the primary form of urban employment growth, and contractual and self-employment have risen (Coffey 2000). In short, employment has become more technical and specialized, and telematics dominates the way work is performed. Most of this work occurs in the largest urban centres, again supporting the growth of large cities, and smaller cities have been unable to compete. Even cities without an industrial background that have experienced more recent growth have done

Box 2.4 Halifax: A Regional Metropole

Halifax had shown much promise and had a head start as the result of its pivotal location in the settlement of Canada. It was also a principal reception point for immigrants after both World War I and World War II. More than one million immigrants came through Pier 21 between 1928 and 1971 (switching from ship to rail), yet few stayed in the area.

Halifax fared much better when British North America was oriented almost exclusively towards Europe. As the Canadian economy became more directed towards the North American continental economy, a location on the margin became a disadvantage, and employment opportunities were not as plentiful. Nova Scotia did have an active industrial base supporting manufacturing and coal and steel production, which was scattered around Nova Scotia in places like Sydney, New Glasgow, and Amherst rather than centralized in Halifax. The fact that populations grew faster in central Canada meant that the Atlantic region did not have a large enough consumer base. Thus, regional industries were ripe for takeover and closure by central Canadian capital. Furthermore, residents of the Atlantic region often migrated westward in response to opportunities in the prairie West and urban industrial central Canada.

One significant role that Halifax has always played in the national context has been in defence because of its strategic location and deepwater port. In the American Revolutionary War, Halifax was an important naval base and attracted Loyalists from the US when it was over. In later wars, it was also an important departure point for cross-Atlantic convoys and other strategic manoeuvres, even including military operations in the Middle East. The famous Cunard Line had its beginnings in Halifax, and containerized shipping made Halifax an important transshipment point for large ocean-going vessels. Halifax had some competition from Saint John in the early years but has since become the commercial/financial centre for the entire Atlantic region.

Halifax is now 'Atlantic Canada's Toronto', or the unofficial business capital of Atlantic Canada. It is the largest CMA in the Atlantic region and the regional business centre and has the most hotels to handle large conventions. It serves as regional headquarters for many federal government and private-sector operations and acts as a growth pole for regional innovation. In recent times, Halifax joined with the cities of Dartmouth and Bedford to form the Halifax Regional Municipality.

Sources: McCann 1982; Nader 1976.

so because they have developed industries related to the knowledge or information economy. The city of Ottawa, for example, which was previously important primarily because it was the seat of the federal government, has now developed a pivotal national and international role in technology industries such as telecommunications, microelectronics, and software. Another example of the new information economy is the emergence of call centres in a variety of Canadian cities that provide employment for workers who use telecommunications equipment. Epitomizing this change in the economy are the Nova Scotian coal miners who have been retrained and are now employed as shift workers at a call centre. In general, the shift away from blue-collar work to white-collar work requiring specialized skills has meant that better-educated Canadians have moved to cities that offer these specialized career opportunities.[5] At the same time, the need for lower-paid service workers, which is often met by new immigrants, remains.

6. Single-Industry Communities: Volatile Urbanization of Small Cities

A continuing aspect of urbanization in Canada is the emergence of single-industry communities (Lucas 1971). These communities exist only because of a corporate decision to extract or process a non-agricultural product in a particular place or to provide the support for a single industrial process. The existence of such a town or city depends largely on one industry for its growth and/or survival. Some of these towns are

---

Box 2.5 *Fort McMurray: An Urban Municipality Like None Other*

Fort McMurray is the name of a city in northern Alberta, 400 kilometres northeast of Edmonton, that is not strictly speaking a city because it is joined together with nine rural communities to form the Wood Buffalo Regional Municipality for governing purposes. Fort McMurray has received global acclaim because it is the base for the extraction of oil from sand that is now acknowledged as containing the second largest oil deposit in the world. The increasing price of oil and the growing world demand for oil has attracted billions of dollars of investment into costly oil sands extraction methods, which has required the construction of elaborate refining facilities. Consequently, Fort McMurray has experienced explosive growth.

The first oil sands plant opened in Fort McMurray in 1967, and the population was around 2,000 people. Suncor and Syncrude were the major employers, and the population of the city grew into the early 1980s. In the late 1990s, expansion of oil sands plants began again, and new investment meant thousands of jobs in construction as well as operations. An increasing population also meant a growing need for a wide range of services (e.g., health, education), which also required employees. In such a resource boom, it was difficult to count the population. For example, the federal 2006 census found 51,000 people in the municipality, but the census undertaken by the municipality reported that 80,000 people resided there. One of the reasons for the difference was that the city census identified 13,000 people as a *shadow population* including those who lived in work camps, campgrounds, or had regular jobs but lived in hotels/motels because of the housing shortage. The housing shortage also meant that many residents were not reported, since people were sharing dwellings often beyond what was normally considered capacity. Including the shadow population, the population of the urban region increased 114 per cent from 1996 to 2006. Fort McMurray represents one of the most unusual resource-based urban settlements in Canadian history.

Source: Partially based on the 2006 municipal census, Wood Buffalo Regional Municipality.

quite isolated and are truly company towns, with the company even laying out the town, which often means that the town has a constricted class structure consisting of management, professionals, and workers (Stelter and Artibise 1982, 413–34). Some single-industry communities have had a short lifespan, the result of either a drop in the market for the natural resource being extracted or the exhaustion of the resource (e.g., Tumbler Ridge, BC, and Uranium City, SK), while others remain small. Still others grow and become reasonably stable. The city of Sudbury in Ontario is a good example of a community based on nickel mining that continues to survive. Other communities based on coal mines and pulp and paper mills that can employ hundreds of workers continue to thrive. The problem is that these communities have limited growth opportunities beyond what a single industry (and sometimes only one employer) can provide. The continued existence of single-industry communities reminds us of the ongoing importance of staples in the process of Canadian urbanization.

Conclusion

The goal of this chapter has been to explain the national and international dynamics within which urbanization in Canada has taken place. The political economy perspective stresses the role of economic and political power and decision-making in how cities develop and which cities grow. Of particular importance is the role that staples have played in urban development. While Canadian cities initially developed as a response to French and British interests, those external ties are now being expressed through globalization. Today, Canadian urban growth is producing metropolitan concentration in a few urban places. When the external factor of globalization is combined with internal factors in which political and economic power is also concentrated and centralized, the result is uneven urbanization, with some cities surpassingly larger and getting bigger while the development of other urban nodes has been arrested.

Notes

1. The decisions regarding the location of the provincial capital and the first major university were major issues in all new provinces. Often, the capital and the university were established in the same city, but in Saskatchewan the capital was situated in Regina and the university in Saskatoon. Saskatoon had experienced remarkable growth from 'a community of shacks to a city of almost 30,000 in 12 years' by the time this decision was made in 1906, which triggered considerable celebration in the streets (Kerr and Hanson 1982, 37–9, 78–87).

2. This discussion is based on Higgins 1986.

3. In a slightly different way, southern Ontario (especially the Niagara Peninsula) also has a milder climate than some other parts of the country, making it a pleasant place to live in. Ironically, it is in these limited places where fragile fruits can be grown that fruit farming is being replaced by the concrete city.

4. This discussion is based on Hutton 1998.

5. The growth of a more professionalized urban workforce has also supported more upscale inner-city housing. For a good account of this process, see Rose 1996.

Study and Discussion Questions

1. What is the dominant metropolis in your area? How is it related to other Canadian cities? Is it directly or indirectly related to international cities?

2. What is the urban history of the Canadian city that is most significant to you? Why is it not larger (or smaller)?

3. Why have western cities in Canada grown faster than cities in the Atlantic region even though the latter had a head start?
4. Select some technological change (e.g., the automobile, the computer), and discuss how it has changed cities and urban life.
5. Why are larger Canadian cities more attractive to people and thus growing faster than smaller ones?

6. Discuss the consequences of growing concentration and centralization in the Golden Horseshoe of Ontario.
7. Discuss the implications of the fact that immigration has changed some cities more than others in Canada.

Suggested Reading

Artibise, Alan F.J., Ed. 1981. *Town and City: Aspects of Western Canadian Urban Development*. Regina: Canadian Plains Studies Centre. A study of key factors in the development of western Canadian towns and cities.

Careless, J.M.S. 1978. *The Rise of Cities in Canada before 1914*. Ottawa: Canadian Historical Association Booklet no. 32. Ottawa: Canadian Historical Association. A concise and readable history of the early emergence of Canadian cities.

Driedger, Leo. 1991. *The Urban Factor: Sociology of Canadian Cities*. Toronto: Oxford University Press. This book deals with urbanization in Canada and is a good general reference from a sociological perspective.

Isin, Engin F. 1992. *Cities without Citizens: The Modernity of the City As a Corporation*. Montreal: Black

Rose. An interesting argument that concern for British governance and control led to Canadian cities being incorporated as subordinate entities to provinces and the federal government, leaving citizens of cities with relatively little control.

McGahan, Peter. 1995. *Urban Sociology in Canada*. 3rd edn. Toronto: Harcourt Brace. Chapter 3 of this book provides a good summary statement of the process of urbanization in Canada.

Nader, George. 1975, 1976. *Cities of Canada*, v. 1, *Theoretical, Historical, and Planning Perspectives*; vol. 2, *Profiles of Fifteen Metropolitan Centres*. Toronto: Macmillan. Volume 1 contains an excellent review of the development of urbanization in Canada. Volume 2 provides a good synopsis of the history and development of major cities.

References

Acheson, T.W. 1972. 'The National Policy and the industrialization of the Maritimes, 1880–1910'. *Acadiensis* 1 (2): 3–28.

Artibise, Alan F.J. 1975. *Winnipeg: A Social History of Urban Growth 1874–1914*. Montreal and Kingston: McGill-Queen's University Press.

———. 1982. 'In pursuit of growth: Municipal boosterism and urban development in the Canadian Prairie West, 1871–1913'. In Gilbert A. Stelter and Alan F.J. Artibise, Eds, *Shaping the Urban Landscape: Aspects of the Canadian City-Building Process*, 116–47. Ottawa: Carlton University Press.

Careless, J.M.S. 1978. *The Rise of Cities in Canada before*

1914. Canadian Historical Association Booklet no. 32. Ottawa: Canadian Historical Association.

———. 1989. *Frontier and Metropolis: Regions, Cities, and Identities in Canada before 1914*. Toronto: University of Toronto Press.

Coffey, William J. 2000. 'Canadian cities and shifting fortunes of economic development'. In Trudi Bunting and Pierre Filion, Eds, *Canadian Cities in Transition: The Twenty-First Century*, 121–50. Toronto: Oxford University Press.

Courchene, Thomas, with Colin Telmer. 1998. *From Heartland to North American Region State: The Fiscal, Social and Federal Evolution of Ontario*. Toronto:

University of Toronto, Faculty of Management.

Davis, Arthur. 1971. 'Canadian society and history as hinterland and metropolis'. In Richard J. Ossenburg, Ed., *Canadian Society: Pluralism, Change and Conflict*, 6–32. Scarborough, ON: Prentice-Hall.

Dickason, Olive. 2002. *Canada's First Nations: A History of Founding Peoples from Earliest Times*. Toronto: Oxford University Press.

Driedger, Leo. 1991. *The Urban Factor*. Toronto: Oxford University Press.

Higgins, Benjamin. 1986. *The Rise—and Fall?—of Montreal*. Moncton: Canadian Institute for Research on Regional Development.

Hiller, Harry H. 2007. 'Gateway cities and arriviste cities: Alberta's recent growth in Canadian context'. *Prairie Forum* 32 (1) :47–66.

Hutton, Thomas A. 1998. *The Transformation of Canada's Pacific Metropolis: A Study of Vancouver*. Montreal: Institute for Research on Public Policy.

Innis, H.A. 1933. *Problems of Staple Production in Canada*. Toronto: Ryerson Press.

Kerr, Don, and Stan Hanson. 1982. *Saskatoon: The First Half-Century*. Edmonton: NeWest Press.

Lithwick, N.H. 1970. *Urban Canada: Problems and Prospects*. Ottawa: Central Mortgage and Housing Corporation.

Lucas, Rex A. 1971. *Minetown, Milltown, Railtown: Life in Canadian Communities of Single Industry*. Toronto: University of Toronto Press.

McCann, L.D. 1982. 'Staples and the new industrialism in the growth of post-Confederation Halifax'. In Gilbert A. Stelter and Alan F.J. Artibise, Eds, *Shaping the Urban Landscape: Aspects of the Canadian City-Building Process*, 84–115. Ottawa: Carleton University Press.

MacDonald, Norbert. 1982. '"C.P.R. Town": The city-building process in Vancouver, 1860–1914'. In Gilbert A. Stelter and Alan F.J. Artibise, Eds, *Shaping the Urban Landscape: Aspects of the Canadian City-Building Process*, 382–412. Ottawa: Carleton University Press.

Murray, Hilda Chaulk. 2002. *Cows Don't Know It's Sunday: Agricultural Life in St. John's*. St John's: ISER Books.

Nader, George A. 1975. *Cities of Canada, v. 1, Theoretical, Historical, and Planning Perspectives*. Toronto: Macmillan.

———. 1976. *Cities of Canada, v. 2, Profiles of Fifteen Metropolitan Centres*. Toronto: Macmillan.

Newbold, K. Bruce. 1996. 'The ghettoization of Quebec: Interprovincial migration and its demographic effects'. *Canadian Studies in Population* 23 (1): 1–21.

Rose, Damaris. 1996. 'Economic restructuring and the diversification of gentrification in the 1980s: A view from a marginal metropolis'. In Jon Caulfield and Linda Peake, Eds, *City Lives and City Forms: Critical Research and Canadian Urbanism*, 131–72. Toronto: University of Toronto Press.

Spelt, Jacob. 1972. *Urban Development in South-Central Ontario*. Toronto: McClelland and Stewart.

Statistics Canada. 2006. *Census of Agriculture*. Catalogue no. 95-629-XWE. Ottawa: Statistics Canada.

Stelter, Gilbert A. 1982. 'The city-building process in Canada'. In Gilbert A. Stelter and Alan F.J. Artibise, Eds., *Shaping the Urban Landscape: Aspects of the Canadian City-Building Process*, 1–29. Ottawa: Carleton University Press.

Stelter, Gilbert A., and Alan F.J. Artibise, Eds. 1977. *The Canadian City: Essays in Urban History*. Toronto: McClelland and Stewart.

———, Eds. 1982. *Shaping the Urban Landscape: Aspects of the Canadian City-Building Process*. Ottawa: Carleton University Press.

Stone, Leroy O. 1968. *Urban Development in Canada*. Ottawa: Dominion Bureau of Statistics.

Yeates, Maurice. 1975. *Main Street: Windsor to Quebec City*. Ottawa: Macmillan.

———. 1991. 'The Windsor-Quebec corridor'. In Trudi Bunting and Pierre Filion, Eds, *Canadian Cities in Transition*, 178–208. Toronto: Oxford University Press.

Zimmerman, Carle C., and Garry W. Moneo. 1971. *The Prairie Community System*. Ottawa: Agricultural Economics Research Council of Canada.

Chapter 3 Getting Perspective

How do theories of urban life help us to interpret and analyze cities?

One way to approach theory is to perceive it as an explanation based on a series of assumptions that are only tentative because our understanding of a phenomenon is not yet complete. In the interim, however, people often argue strenuously that their theory is better than someone else's, and for that reason their explanation of a particular phenomenon is superior to others. Sometimes these kinds of theories, often presented with great complexity, are virtually considered a preferable truth. But another way to view a theory is as a particular window on the world. A theory from this point of view is a perspective or a way of seeing. It is an interpretation that follows a consistent logic and produces a valuable insight on the phenomenon in question.

If we wanted to understand your family, one way of doing so would be to look at your physical features—e.g., skin colour, height, or body shape. Another way would be to focus on your values and how you were brought up and how you relate to one another as family members. Still another way would be to focus on the amount of money you have and the occupation of the wage-earners in your household and how this has affected the choices you made. Somebody else would say that it might be more important to know in what neighbourhood you grew up and who your friends were. Which one of these approaches is best? None of them is wrong; they each provide a different perspective.

Analyzing cities can be done in a similar way. We can take a macro perspective and compare cities with each other. We can compare communities within a city with each other. We can see how power is wielded within a city and how it affects the city as a whole. We can attempt to understand how global factors affect a particular city. But we can also take a more micro perspective in which we not only compare such things as rates of criminal behaviour between cities (the more macro perspective) but can also attempt to understand what it is about life in a city that fosters criminal behaviour by talking to people who engage in criminal behaviour within that city (the more micro perspective). The micro perspective sees the city as consisting of individuals in interaction with each other. How do people present themselves to others who are essentially strangers but yet people they superficially interact with on a daily basis, such as the bus driver or the store clerk or even the neighbour? The macro perspective looks at big-picture questions about cities, and the micro perspective understands cities from the point of view of the individual urban dweller.

Macro and micro perspectives are two of the dominant themes that play into theories of cities and city life. Theories about cities, then, are different ways in which cities can be interpreted and understood. Some analysts feel that some theories or some methods of studying them are better or more useful tools—or even more powerful tools—of interpretation than others. The goal of this chapter is to help you become familiar with these interpretive models and how they further our understanding of cities.

3 Analyzing and Interpreting the City: Theory and Method

John Hannigan

Learning Objectives

- To determine what makes urban life particularly different from life in society in general.
- To present five different theoretical approaches for interpreting urban life.
- To understand the importance of the Chicago School in the development of urban sociology.
- To explore a variety of methods—from census data to interviews to participant observation—that sociologists use to study urban life.

It is often said nowadays that there is no special urban sociology. What goes on in the city, it is claimed, is merely an expression of general processes at work in a national industrial society. . . . I believe there is some truth in this view, but I also believe that there are particular processes at work in the concrete urban situation (Rex 1968, 211).

Writing 40 years ago, at a time when the basic foundations of urban sociology were being vigorously questioned, the British sociologist John Rex captured the essential dilemma that has long dogged theory and research in the field. On the one hand, the development of cities has advanced in lockstep with that of society itself, making it difficult to parse out those structures and processes that are distinctly urban. At the same time, life in the city has always seemed to possess its own unique dynamic. While recognizing that the history of urban sociology is discontinuous, possessing no cumulative tradition, Savage and Warde (1993, 2–3) nevertheless are able to identify eight 'recurrent threads and themes' around which the field revolves:

1. what it feels like to live in a modern city and whether there is any universal 'urban' experience;
2. whether, by contrast, places are distinctive and why people become attached to them;
3. how urban life is affected by the features of local social structure such as class, gender, and ethnicity;
4. how informal bonds develop and to what extent affective (emotionally charged) relationships with family, neighbours, and friends are determined externally;
5. how to explain the history of urbanization and population concentration;
6. the basic features of the spatial structures of cities and whether different spatial arrangements generate distinctive modes of social interaction;
7. the nature of and solutions to 'urban' problems such as congestion, poverty, and street violence;
8. how urban politics are conducted, what influences political participation, and what impact the state has on the daily life of its local citizens.

In their efforts to make sense of these multiple, and often divergent, themes and topics and thereby to assemble a cohesive body of theory and research, urban sociologists have encountered three deep-cutting and partially overlapping cleavages: a culturalist versus a structural orientation; a spatial versus an associational emphasis; a realist versus a constructionist interpretation.

Flanagan (2002, xvii) distinguishes between two distinct urban sociologies. The **culturalist orientation** deals with the experiential aspect of cities, addressing how urban life feels, how people react to living in an urban setting, and how the city organizes personal lives. The **structuralist orientation**, by contrast, holds that the ultimate causes of urban ways of thinking and acting are found externally in wider patterns of power and wealth in society. As we begin the twenty-first century, the processes driving urban change are said to be global in scope, rather than national or local. Consistent with Flanagan's distinction, Merrifield (2002) has identified two different and conflicting features of the contemporary urban world: the sterile, profit-dominated exchange values embedded in globalized, capitalist economies that can wreak havoc on urban life ('urbanization') and the more socially rich, locally determined use (livability) values that urban life can potentially represent for human beings ('urbanism').

A second division among urban sociologists has revolved around the importance that should be accorded physical (geographical) space in explaining patterns of behaviour. For most of its first half-century, the field was dominated by a human ecological perspective that described the processes whereby urban populations were sifted and sorted out into areas or territories according to the rules of a set of underlying economic principles. Slums, for example, were interpreted as the products of a fundamental division of labour in industrial society rather than as the result of deliberate government policies directed towards poverty and public housing. The residents of these segregated neighbourhoods were seen as being wired into their own small, localized social worlds, each with its own distinct moral code, while, at the same time, being cast adrift in a wider metropolis lacking any shared sense of belonging and identity. From the 1970s onward, urban sociologists, notably those closely identified with the social networks approach, have consistently downgraded the importance of territorial, neighbourhood-based factors. Instead, they have emphasized alternative, non-spatial forms of community, noting that the great majority of city dwellers are far from isolated from one another; rather, they are enmeshed in non-spatialized networks of family and friends (Effrat 1974, 19).

A third cleavage has revolved around the degree of realism embedded in urban phenomena. In other words, do city dwellers have any degree of agency or power to shape the physical and social space in which they reside and work, or is it rigidly predetermined by ecological or economic factors beyond their immediate control? In addition, are the details of their everyday lives dictated by the entrenched realities related to wealth, class, and power, or do people possess the capacity to inscribe meaning on their thoughts and actions? As will be discussed near the end of this chapter, urban researchers are increasingly embracing a 'social constructionist' interpretation that depicts urban life as an ongoing negotiation of cultural meaning involving different individuals, groups, and organizations, each striving to make its own interpretation hegemonic (dominant). For example, in the 'rebuilding' of the World Trade Center site in Manhattan, various conflicting visions have emerged, from those emphasizing 'patriotic tourism' to those recommending a spiritual simplicity to aggressive business strategies that detect an unparalleled opportunity to relentlessly market New York's cultural attractions and competitive advantages (Greenberg 2003, 410–12). In this view, the city is visualized as a 'text' with multiple authors possessing differing degrees of power striving to insert their own 'preferred meanings' into the text.

Table 3.1 Key Approaches to the Sociological Study of Cities

Approach	Peak Period	Key Figures	Research Methods
Human ecological	1920s and 1930s (orthodox)	Park, Burgess, and McKenzie	Urban growth modelling
	1950s and 1960s (neo-orthodox)	Shevsky, Bell, and Williams	Social area analysis; factor analysis
Urban-community studies	1950s and 1960s	Gans, Suttles, and Whyte	Participant observation; ethnography
Interactionist	1970s and 1980s	Fischer, Lofland	Network analysis; participant observation
Political economy	1980s and 1990s	Castells, Harvey, Logan, and Molotch	Grounded historical case study
Social constructionist	2000+	Beauregard, Smith	Discourse analysis

Slums, for example, do not exist independently of how we socially define them. While developers and urban planners tend to treat any working-class neighbourhood with stretches of older residential housing as 'blighted', its residents see the same area as alive and vital.

Since its emergence as a distinct subdiscipline in the 1920s and 1930s, the sociological study of the city has been punctuated by five identifiable approaches: human ecological; community studies; social interactionist; political economic; and social constructionist. As indicated in Table 3.1, their emergence has been more or less chronological, although at certain points there has been significant overlap. Several of them (human ecological, political economic) approach the status of full theoretical paradigms; others (social interactionist) more closely resemble methodological strategies equipped with some basic underlying theoretical assumptions.

In this chapter, I will outline each approach in greater detail, highlighting its contribution to the cumulative wisdom of urban sociological theory and research methods. Before doing so, however, it makes good sense to visit briefly the origins of the field as set out in the writing of Robert Park and the 'Chicago School' of urban sociology.

The Beginnings of Sociological Interpretations of Cities: The Chicago School

In 1915, University of Chicago professor Robert Park, a former journalist, published a landmark essay in the *American Journal of Sociology* entitled 'The city: Suggestions for the investigation of human behavior in the city environment' (Park 1915). By no means the first notable piece of writing to consider seriously the nature of the metropolis and urban life, 'The city' was nevertheless a pioneering attempt to outline a scientific program for understanding the essence of the industrial city both conceptually and empirically. In contrast to the prevailing tradition of abstract philosophizing and sweeping generalization, Park advocated an agenda that favoured 'sharp, researchable questions about institutions and processes that could be immediately observed and investigated' (Smith 1988, 1–2). Park's manifesto inspired a formidable outpouring of books, research monographs, articles, and doctoral theses throughout the 1920s and 1930s by a cast of students and colleagues who have subsequently become collectively known as the 'Chicago School of Urban Sociology'. Up until the rise of the political economy paradigm in the 1970s, the ideas and research methods associated with Park and his colleagues effectively dominated the sociological study of cities.

It is generally acknowledged that the Chicago School studies may be divided into two distinct categories, reflecting the two 'nested themes' (Flanagan 2002, 83) in Park's thinking describing how the spatial features of the urban environment centrally influence its organization and experience. First, Park was interested in the evolving physical form of the city—its different types of land use and the manner in which its various populations, services, and industries arrange themselves over space. This inspired an approach known as human ecology. Second, Park believed that the city was composed of a constellation of different social worlds or natural areas, each with its own distinct language, traditions, and way of life (Choldin 1985, 15). He urged his students to venture forth, much like anthropologists, and study urban culture and social organization first-hand. This nurtured a way of studying local neighbourhoods and sub-communities that has come to be called **urban ethnography**. Among the groups and activities to be investigated in this manner were gangs, homeless men (hobos), and taxi dance halls (see Box 3.1).

While differing somewhat in their interpretations, the Chicago School researchers generally shared a view of the city derived from the writings of a clutch of European social theorists from the late nineteenth and early twentieth centuries. To these early sociologists, the main story was the shift from a traditional rural way of life to a modern, industrial social order. In the former, known variously as *Gemeinschaft* (Ferdinand Tönnies) or mechanical solidarity (Émile Durkheim), social life was characterized by an emphasis on kinship, village togetherness, and a minimum of diversity in language, work roles, and culture. People obeyed the rules of social life because not to do so would be to risk being shunned by other members of the community. Starting in the nineteenth century, the populations of western

Europe and North America began to shift from the small town and rural village to the burgeoning metropolis. Life in this *Gesellschaft*, or organic solidarity type, was demonstrably different. The social cement formerly provided by church, family, work, and neighbourhood seemed to be crumbling. City dwellers put individual interest ahead of the collective good. Money became the central arbiter of all relationships. Social order was no longer maintained by normative means but by the rule of law—specifically, by a formal system of regulations, police, courts, and jails. Dependency among urban dwellers was purely functional and based on a complex division of labour. That is, rather than personally carrying out most tasks—from growing food to fixing machinery to disposing of household refuse—as farm families did, residents of cities performed specialized jobs while looking to the grocer, the plumber, and the cab driver to attend to sundry needs.

The first-generation urban sociologists were generally pessimistic about the impact of the rural-urban shift on individuals and communities. Above all, they saw this leading to a crisis of social disorganization. In *The Polish Peasant in Europe and America*, their massive study of the problems of adjustment faced by Polish immigrants to Chicago at the beginning of the twentieth century, William Thomas and Florian Znaniecki (1918–20) documented numerous cases of marital breakdown, juvenile delinquency, and even murder among newcomers to that city. Rather than attribute this to the disruptions caused by the immigration and resettlement process, they blamed the transition from rural village to big-city environment. In *The Gold Coast and the Slum*, perhaps the most extensive and powerful field study of one of Chicago's natural areas in the 1920s, Harvey Zorbaugh spotlighted the lack of community in a rooming-house area on the near–north side of Chicago, which he characterized as 'a world of political indifference, of laxity of conventional standards, of personal and social disorganization' (Zorbaugh 1929, 82). Furthermore, he concluded that there was no connecting

Box 3.1 *Doing Ethnographic Research at the Taxi-Dance Hall*

Despite their pioneering role in laying the foundations of urban sociology, the Chicago School sociologists rarely addressed methodological techniques or issues in a comprehensive manner. For example, the reports in the University of Chicago Press Sociological Series initiated by Robert Park all lack any explicit discussion of the methodologies employed (Bulmer 1983, 95). One major exception is a classic piece of ethnographic field research by Paul G. Cressey (1932) entitled *The Taxi-Dance Hall*.

In 1920s Chicago, the taxi-dance hall catered to various male clients who were considered marginal to more mainstream gendered relationships: those who suffered from physical disabilities and members of ethnic minority groups who faced racial discrimination, such as Filipinos. The hall employed female dance partners who could be engaged by purchasing a ticket for each dance.

In an unpublished paper written in 1932, Cressey provided what is possibly the first systematic account of the challenges and ethical dilemmas of doing ethnographic research. One immediate difficulty arose with regard to how to enter into the research site. Faced with the reluctance of dance-hall proprietors to talk at any length about their employees and the difficulty of doing formal interviews, Cressey and his observational team of four took on the role of the 'anonymous stranger', covertly hanging out at various taxi-dance halls across Chicago. Rather than identify themselves as sociologists, they invented fictional identities. Cressey himself used various such identities, including that of an ice-cream truck driver. This tactic occasionally backfired when he had trouble recalling what cover story he had told to whom. He also encountered difficulty in speaking the same language as other patrons; on one occasion, his chat with a flashily dressed bootlegger (illegal liquor salesman) ended abruptly when the fellow demanded to know 'Who the hell are you?'

Anticipating the future possibility of tape-recorded interviews, Cressey predicted that 'a pocket Dictaphone may at some time be available to make the recording of conversations more accurate' (1932, 118), thereby allowing the researcher to record conversations verbatim. While he did not consider the ethical and privacy-related difficulties associated with this technique, he did reflect on the fact that remaining anonymous permits the research subject to reveal her or his inner thoughts, ambitions, and fantasies, especially those of a sexual nature, to a greater extent than would be possible in a more standard interview in which the interviewer is perceived as an authority figure. Cressey worried that this anonymous relationship between observer and subject bestowed a 'non-moral' character upon the former.

These are significant issues still relevant to the conduct of ethnographic research in urban settings.

tissue strong enough to hold together the different subpopulations within the city. Any potential overarching sense of community was fractured by differences in social position (residents of the wealthy Gold Coast mansions along the shore of Lake Michigan had virtually no contact with the adjacent rooming-house area and Sicilian slum), rising rates of geographic mobility, and people's preoccupation with their work lives and careers.

In his influential article 'Urbanism as a way of life' (1938), a restatement and elaboration of German social theorist Georg Simmel's seminal essay, 'The metropolis and mental life' (1950 [1903]), Louis Wirth argued that the increasing size and population density characteristic of urban growth crucially affect the city's pattern of social organization, notably in terms of leading to a higher degree of heterogeneity (diversity) both in occupational roles and in social worlds. Echoing Simmel, Wirth asserts that this leads to a preponderance of social contacts that are impersonal, superficial, transitory, and segmental (do not go beyond the context of the encounter). Typical is the interaction between a customer and a clerk at the ticket counter of a railway station where neither is likely to know the other personally or care to do so. At the same time, the increasing heterogeneity of urban life can allow greater social mobility, making it possible for those at the lower levels of the social ladder to escape the social class associated with their birth. In addition, the more diverse and tolerant environment of the city is a boon for artists, musicians, and other creative types, who are freer to experiment both in their work and in their personal lives without being censured by those in control.

In the 1920s, several students of the Chicago School came to McGill University in Montreal. Carl Dawson, who had studied with Robert Park and was the founder of the Department of Sociology at McGill, researched the experience of ethnic groups on the Canadian Prairies. At the time, this was seen as somewhat controversial in that Dawson was perceived as supportive of a mosaic model of ethnic relations at a time when the dominant British group in Canada was pressuring the federal government to restrict immigration to groups from Britain and the countries of northern Europe (Driedger 2001, 423). Even more controversial was the work of Everett Hughes, who used ethnographic methods to study the small Quebec town of Cantonville. In his classic work *French Canada in Transition* (1963), Hughes argued that the segregation between the French and English populations of the town did not change appreciably even when Cantonville began to industrialize. This contradicted Park's assimilation model of ethnic and race relations that predicted that each newly arrived ethnic group would eventually be brought into the wider society as they established themselves economically and socially.

Five Theoretical Models

I. Human Ecology Model

As Wirth has written, numerous studies of urban land use, housing, and the incidence of poverty, disease, and crime employed 'methods which subsequently have been called ecological long before human ecology was recognized as a distinctive field of scientific activity' (1945, 179). For example, the nineteenth-century British social reformer Charles Booth published a gargantuan 17-volume work, *Survey of the Life and Labour of the People in London* (1892), that classified the urban population of that city into seven categories and mapped out, street by street, the occupations of the residents, the housing conditions in which they dwelt, and the problems of poverty they faced. It was left to Park, however, to systematize these studies and cast them within a larger theoretical framework derived from the rapidly developing scientific field of plant and animal biology. For most of his time at Chicago, Park treated human ecology as at best a loose collection of concepts (competition, invasion, succession, symbiosis) borrowed from plant and animal biology and applied to human collectivities. It was only after his retirement that he attempted to convert a loose ecological 'approach' into a 'theory' of human ecology (Smith 1988, 137).

Simply put, Park conceptualized human ecology as the breakdown of the city into separate communities bounded by transportation or other barriers within which distinct cultures developed. In the natural world, order and balance result from a continual process of competition, symbiotic interdependency, and adaptation. In similar fashion, the human ecologists argued, the city reflects the 'sub-social' competition for space and resources that you can find in settings ranging from the western prairie to a backyard pond. In human societies, the equivalent to competition and

Box 3.2 *Elephants and Watering Holes: Analyzing Spatial Residential Clustering in 15 Ontario Cities*

Adopting the metaphorical language of classic human ecology, Driedger (2003) describes metropolitan centres in Canada as 'watering holes' serving the regions that surround them. He conceptualizes class, race, and ethnicity as boundaries that enhance or detract from access to water, separating people from 'economic, political, social, and spiritual sources of sustenance' (2003, 594). In this urban ecosystem, residents of British ancestral background are the elephants who dominate politically and economically, but as the demographic, cultural, and social dynamics of the city increase, 'water fights can be expected to increase.'

Factor-analyzing more than 100 variables from the 1991 Canadian census, Driedger compares the three largest urban centres in Canada (Toronto, Vancouver, Montreal) to a dozen smaller cities in Ontario. From this, he derives four 'ecological social types'—the visible minority type (Toronto), the British/Loyalist type (Brantford, Kingston, London), the industrial blue-collar type (Hamilton, Windsor), and the northern fringe type (North Bay, Thunder Bay). With the first of these, race appears as a major factor in shaping residential segregation. Recent immigrant visible minorities from Latin America, the Caribbean, Asia, and Africa are spatially separated, especially from those who are non-immigrants of northern European background. With the second type, race is less important in predicting residential patterns, while higher social class plays a greater role. It is still possible in cities such as London and Kingston to find pockets of residents with British/Loyalist backgrounds, as was once the case in Toronto. In the third type, epitomized by Hamilton, social class seems to be a major factor, with northern European and upper-middle-class residents separating themselves from blue-collar workers. Finally, in northern fringe communities such as Thunder Bay, an important factor is First Nations people, who are separated from the British and northern European middle class, mine workers, and immigrants who arrived between 1961 and 1980.

Driedger concludes that all three factors—class, ethnicity, and race—are important in predicting where residents of Ontario urban centres live, something that can be deduced from Shevsky and Bell's social area analysis model from the 1950s.

dominance in nature is economic competition in the marketplace, as described in the classical economic theories of Adam Smith and his disciples (Abu-Lughod 1991, 222–3). Furthermore, just as the Serengeti Plain in Africa is dominated by the lion (see Box 3.2), American industrial cities were said to be dominated by industrial and commercial interests. According to the well-known 'concentric zone' model of urban growth formulated by Park and his colleague Ernest Burgess in 1923, the shape of the metropolis was directed by rapid commercial growth in the centre core. As land became scarcer and more prohibitively expensive in the central business district (CBD), more marginal uses such as warehousing and light manufacturing established themselves in the surrounding 'zone in transition', as did illegal activities such as prostitution that need to be fairly close to tourist and other clienteles in the city core. As Zorbaugh demonstrated in *The Gold Coast and the Slum*, immigrant slums and skid rows were also located there. In turn, this forced higher-rent residential land uses outward towards the periphery of the city where they were no longer in direct competition with industrial or commercial users. Three years later, Roderick McKenzie (1926, 172–81) set down four key ecological processes: specialization and the segregation of dissimilar populations and land uses; the centralization of popular and specialized services and activities; population concentration as the result of concentrated patterns of commercial and industrial growth; and **invasion and succession**—the processes whereby one segment of the urban population makes an incursion into the territory of another and eventually replaces it.

Despite its attempt to systematize the processes of urban growth, 'orthodox' human ecology, as presented in the work of Park, Burgess, McKenzie, and others associated with the Chicago School, encountered some scathing criticism. In one of the first and most frequently cited critical volleys, Alihan (1938) dismissed their emphasis on sub-social, ecological forces as wrong-headed; the dominant influences on the city, she insisted, were social and cultural. Form (1954) argued that land values were not determined by impersonal, automatic mechanisms; rather, they were linked to political processes such as zoning and urban renewal. Hatt (1946) disputed the assumption that natural areas could be immediately identified in Chicago and other industrial cities. It makes more sense, he claimed, to regard these natural areas as deliberately 'constructed' from census tract data by the urban researcher. As such, they are 'only as good as the indices from which they have been constructed and are useful only if they are appropriate to the purposes for which they were designed' (Abu-Lughod 1991, 202). In the 1970s, criticism of orthodox human ecology took on another, more stridently ideological tone. It was guilty, critics charged, of pretending to be scientifically neutral while in fact supporting a politically conservative outlook (Fainstein 1999, 251). That is, by accepting that the city was an outgrowth of inexorable natural processes such as invasion and succession rather than a product of the human exercise of wealth and power, the human ecologists inherently supported the status quo and discouraged the formation of a more change-directed politics that focused on racism, inequality, and democratic decision-making.

After the 1930s, orthodox human ecology lost much of its appeal in sociology and moved off into other disciplines, notably geography. However, in the 1950s and 1960s, it experienced a revival of sorts with the addition of more sophisticated, analytical procedures. There was also some attempt to respond to past criticisms by paying more attention to social and cultural variables. The first of these new methods to garner widespread attention was **social area analysis**, introduced by Eshref Shevsky and his colleagues Wendell Bell and Marilyn Williams (Shevsky and Williams 1949; Shevsky and Bell 1955). The researchers hypothesized that areas of the city differ from one another according to three basic population characteristics: socio-economic status, family size and status, and racial and ethnic makeup. Combining these and using census data for Los Angeles and San Francisco, they identified 18 different types of residential neighbourhoods.

Social area analysis soon gave way to more powerful computer-assisted techniques known as factorial ecology that allowed researchers to analyze a far greater number of variables than the three used by Shevsky, Bell, and Williams. For example, one study of Toronto (Murdie 1969) employed 83 primary census variables. Reviews of factorial ecology research in North America concluded that urban communities vary along six dimensions: socio-economic status, family status, ethnicity, residential mobility, population, and functional size (Lyon 1987, 46). Factorial ecology had the advantage of allowing comparative research extending beyond America; for example, analyses were published for Cairo and Calcutta. Where factorial analysis faltered was on the shoals of interpretation. Even if a cluster of variables could be identified as statistically associated with one another and differing in magnitude from one area of the city to another, it was not always clear what this really meant.

Ultimately, neither social area analysis nor factorial ecology added substantially to the theory of city growth articulated earlier by the Chicago School (Thorns 2002, 29). Nonetheless, as Savage and Warde (1993, 67) have pointed out, mapping social segregation in cities remains an important descriptive exercise that holds the promise of taking on an even greater degree of theoretical significance if its practitioners are able to better account for the 'why' as well as the 'how'.

One relatively recent expression of territorial urban segregation is Massey and Denton's (1993) book, *American Apartheid*. Here, the authors argue that racial segregation is a primary variable in explaining the economic decline and growing impoverishment of inner cities in the United States during the 1970s and 1980s. Their data indicate that blacks were effectively left behind as jobs and housing shifted to the suburbs in the second half of the twentieth century. Unlike the central and southern European immigrants who arrived in the United States prior to the 1920s, African Americans remained segregated in ghetto areas that have become permanent features of US cities. Consistent with Savage and Warde's advice, Massey and Denton not only charted these settlement patterns but also attempted to account for them by referring to such practices as 'red-lining' (see Chapter 11) by banks and other mortgage lenders that prevented African Americans from purchasing suburban homes.

2. Community Studies Model

After a relative hiatus during World War II and its immediate aftermath, urban sociology was reinvigorated in the 1950s and 1960s by a series of research studies based in residential neighbourhoods and sub-communities. These urban community studies contradicted some key assumptions about city life that had carried over from the work of the Chicago School. Whereas the development of urban theory was closely associated with the idea of the rise of a 'mass society' leading to isolation and alienation as the predominant features of city life, the community study sought to uncover evidence of close social ties and supportive relations in the city, as manifested in bonds of friendship, kinship, and neighbourliness.

While several of these classic community studies, most notably William Foote Whyte's *Street Corner Society* (1943), were published before or during the war, most appeared between 1955 and 1970 and focused on a combination of working-class, ethnic, and minority populations. Liebow's *Tally's Corner* (1967) explored the lives of African-American 'streetcorner men' in Washington, DC; Young and Wilmott's *Family and Kinship in East London* (1957) analyzed the impact of moving from a poor working-class neighbourhood in the dock area of East London to a suburban 'new town'; Suttles's *The Social Order of the Slum* (1968) focused on territorial identity in the Addams area of Chicago, a poor multi-ethnic neighbourhood undergoing invasion and succession; and Gans's *The Urban Villagers* (1962) noted the effect of urban redevelopment on a working-class, second-generation neighbourhood of Boston in the late 1950s. One of the few studies that looked at a more affluent neighbourhood was *Crestwood Heights* (Seeley, Sim, and Loosley 1956), a community located at the outer fringe of Toronto in the 1950s (see Box 3.3). As Abrahamson (1976, 156) has noted, the research subjects in these studies were inclined, to a greater or lesser extent, to create intimate village-type communities within the central city, thereby preventing them from becoming 'personally urbanized'—that is, from displaying the reserved and impersonal characteristics theoretically associated with an urban way of life.

One difficulty with these urban community studies, however, is that they tend to focus exclusively on local areas with a strong ethnic, racial, or class-based identity and dense networks of interaction—what has been termed the 'defended neighbourhood' (Suttles 1972, 21–35)—where solidarity arises from common residence. These researchers were much less inclined to select neighbourhoods containing a wide range of social types, partly because access would have been more difficult there than in the more segregated ethnic neighbourhoods and partly because they idealized the intimate, face-to-face relationships

Box 3.3 *Crestwood Heights*

Arguably the most celebrated community study ever done in Canada, *Crestwood Heights* is one of the few case studies in this genre involving an upper-middle-class area. *Crestwood Heights* has long been presented as an early empirical exploration of suburban life. In truth, it is a pseudonym for the affluent North Toronto neighbourhood of Forest Hill, which in the 1950s was on the margins of the city but not an example of the postwar suburban housing boom that produced packaged suburbs such as Don Mills.

The authors, John Seeley, Alexander Sim, and Elizabeth Loosley, worked out of a mental health agency in the local school and thus were sensitized to issues of family life, child development, and socialization. They depicted the community as an 'elite dormitory' (Seeley, Sim, and Loosley 1956, 38) where pursuit of career and social status was paramount while tradition was being devalued. Successful childrearing was a preoccupation. To this end, children were placed in the care of a host of external institutions and experts—nursery schools, summer camps, pediatricians, educational psychologists, and counsellors—so that they might emerge competent, mature, and capable of enhancing their parents' status by achieving a visible degree of success. Seeley and his fellow researchers judged this to be stress-producing, especially for the mothers of Crestwood Heights, who were said to be racked with uncertainty about the nature of their own parental role and the effectiveness of their childrearing strategies.

Although it has been a half-century since this community study was conducted, some of the authors' observations about everyday life and culture still seem terribly important. Particularly pertinent is the concept of 'rushing at experience' whereby Crestwood Heights children were enrolled in the nursery school at two years of age, were taken to the hairdresser at four, started dating at 10, and had rented tuxedos for a prom at 12. All this took place because parents were caught in 'an inflationary system where normal controls are inoperative' (Stein 1960, 216). Today, children just out of kindergarten are entered in beauty contests, and drug use among young teenagers is routine, yet the underlying process is similar. Also of contemporary interest is the chapter on home furnishing, fashion, and entertaining. The authors describe how the home was visualized as a stage on which to play out demonstrations of one's 'good taste'. Witnessing this privileging of display over utility, the authors suggested, was the first step in the formation of a marketing self-image for children in which they see themselves as a commodity.

Crestwood Heights was important for several reasons. Unlike most of the American community studies that focused on some form or another of the classic 'urban village', *Crestwood Heights* was more firmly rooted in modernity. The central social unit was the nuclear family cut loose from the traditional larger kinship group. In place of the kin group, close friends played a surrogate role (Gist and Fava 1964, 374). A host of specialized experts in the community—pediatricians, nursery school teachers, psychologists—assumed functions previously performed by the family. *Crestwood Heights* was also one of the few community studies to emphasize gender effects in addition to ethnic and social-class differences. The authors identified women as being in the vanguard of a changing value system, as opposed to their male spouses, who were more likely to represent traditional views that were already weakening in North American society (Warren 1972, 133).

of small rural villages. As a result, the research methods used in these studies 'yield their own blinders and biases' (Abu-Lughod 1991, 299). Among their other failings were that they were non-cumulative and difficult to compare systematically, made a minimal contribution to urban theory, and were concerned only with processes internal to the community (Savage and Warde 1993, 105). The value of these case studies is that the immersion of the researcher in local life meant that both the participant observer and the reader came to know a particular setting more intimately and gain a more 'authentic' feel for it (Flanagan 2002, 105).

3. Social Interactionist Model

A vastly different approach to the study of social organization in the urban environment developed in the 1970s. In common with the community studies scholars and contrary to the Chicago School, the social interactionists believed that people in the city maintained close ties with one another, as opposed to being isolated and anonymous. However, they were convinced that the basis of this contact was not the proximity supplied by the local neighbourhood per se but rather common interests in a wide variety of political, religious, and leisure pursuits. Webber (1970) labelled this 'community without propinquity'.

One influential version of this approach is Claude Fischer's **subcultural theory**. Fischer (1975; 1984) argued that Wirth was essentially correct in attributing importance to the increasing size, density, and heterogeneity that accompanied urbanization. Rather than destroying social groups, however, urbanism strengthened them by promoting the formation of diverse subcultures. In a small town, for example, there might be only one or several residents who are fans of blues music or Latin dancing, but in the big city you will likely find hundreds or thousands. As a result, those who share these interests will find one another and set up a blues society or a Latin dancing club. The urban setting contributes to this process in two ways.

First, it has the 'critical mass' of population necessary to spawn and sustain a multitude of social worlds or subcultures. Second, these subcultures are likely to be intensified by the conflict and competition of urban life.

A second version of the interactionist perspective is the dramaturgical interpretation. Rather than locating the connective tissue among urbanites in shared interests and leisure pursuits, as does Claude Fischer, this approach seeks to identify ways in which smaller units of space shape social life in the city.

In her widely praised book *A World of Strangers*, Lyn Lofland (1985) poses the question: 'Given the stranger-filled character of cities, how is it possible for people to live in them?' The answer, she says, is that city dwellers transform public space into private or semi-private space, thereby personalizing everyday experience in a setting characterized by being surrounded by a large number of persons one does not know. Lofland specifies three prime methods of privatizing public space: (1) the creation of home territories; (2) the creation of urban villages; (3) the creation of temporary mobile 'homes' by means of the travelling pack (1985, 118).

By home territory, Lofland means 'a relatively small piece of public space which is taken over and turned into a home away from home'. In recent years, upscale coffee shops such as Second Cup, Starbucks, and Timothy's have become ubiquitous examples of this, especially for the growing population of Canadians who maintain a home office. Although he prefers the traditional European coffeehouse, such places nonetheless illustrate Ray Oldenburg's (1989) concept of the 'third place', which is neither fully private nor fully public and welcomes strangers. Regular patrons of such establishments are often on a first-name basis with the staff, who know what they want to eat and drink without having to ask. Sometimes they are accorded special privileges, such as use of the telephone. It is not unusual, however, to find a certain tension between the regulars, who seek to take over public space and make it their own, and more occasional customers. For example, regular riders on urban commuter trains lay claim to the same seats each day, even though there is no formal reservation system. They are not pleased when a casual traveller attempts to claim 'their' seat.

Whereas a home territory tends to be primarily restricted to persons who either work in it or hang about in it, an urban village encompasses the entire daily life of its residents. All of its inhabitants know one another personally, their relationships are long-lasting, and there is minimal need to look beyond its boundaries for stores and services. The best known are ethnic urban villages like 'Little Italy', some of which are almost totally transplanted from the country of emigration.

Travelling in packs, Lofland says, is a strategy for avoiding the city while living in it. An example is a group of out-of-towners attending a convention who temporarily colonize spaces such as streets, parks, boardwalks, and public squares. Not infrequently, its members 'begin to act in a way that is in stark contrast to the actions of those in the same locale who are alone or with one or two others' (Lofland 1985, 139).

In a subsequent book, Lofland (1998, xi) argues that the city quite uniquely provides a kind of social psychological environment not duplicated elsewhere. This unique form of space or territory is known as the **public realm**, and it is characteristically 'a world of strangers' whose inhabitants only know one another within a limited context—for example, as transit operator and customer. In the public realm, face-to-face interaction is governed by five principles: cooperative motility (e.g., standing on the right side of an escalator so those in a hurry can pass on the left); civil inattention (e.g., avoiding the gaze of others in subway cars or in elevators); audience role prominence (e.g., a crowd gathered around a sidewalk chalk artist); restrained helpfulness (e.g., giving directions to a tourist who is lost); civility towards diversity (e.g., ignoring the teenager in the booth next to you who sports blue hair and multiple nose and lip rings).

In *The Public Realm*, Lofland takes pains to distinguish her dramaturgical approach from other competing paradigms. In particular, she explicitly rejects the notion central to both the Chicago School and the community studies researchers that primary social relationships with friends and neighbours are more 'authentic' and morally desirable than public-place attachments are. To the contrary, she insists, the secondary, person-to-person connections of 'familiar strangers' (Milgram 1977) can be both long-lasting and 'uniformly positive in emotional ambience' (Lofland 1998, 59). Witness the sorrow felt by neighbourhood parents and children when a beloved school crossing guard retires or dies. Furthermore, as noted social commentator Richard Sennett (1970; 1977) has declared, the public realm has social value because it is the only setting where diverse people can learn to act together in a civil fashion without necessarily being the same. In other words, it is a testing ground for both tolerance and cosmopolitanism.

Social interactionist research has made a valuable contribution in moving the sociological discussion of community among urbanites away from an exclusive concentration on the kind of primary ties most characteristic of 'urban villages'. Most city residents today do not live in this type of setting (although many yearn for it), and it makes sense to map their more widely dispersed repertoire of networks. At the same time, neither Fischer's subcultural theory nor Lofland's dramaturgical approach represents a very complete way of approaching urban sociology as a whole. Neither addresses issues of power, governance, inequality, and conflict in any meaningful fashion, although *The Public Realm* concludes by suggesting that the demands of tourism are increasing pressure towards the development of cities that are both artificial and segregated, thus restricting the chance that the public realm will flourish.

4. Political Economy Model

In the late 1960s and early 1970s, the field of urban sociology radically changed direction (see Chapter

11). The reigning 'social organization' paradigm, especially its human ecology version, was criticized for its failure to consider the crucial role of power, politics, and interest groups in urban affairs. The classic texts contained virtually no discussion of 'the role of political parties, mayors and city planners, of captains of industry and developers, all of which were part of Chicago in the 1920s and 1930s' (Thorns 2002, 29). In both Europe and America, a new generation of scholars was powerfully influenced by the temper of the times, which included urban riots, protests against the Vietnam War, the civil rights movement in the US, and student-led urban revolts in France, Germany, and Italy. For inspiration, principal figures in this emerging new paradigm on cities (notably Manuel Castells, David Harvey, and Henri Lefebvre) looked to Marxist analysis, which they adapted to the case of cities. These writers developed different (in some cases conflicting) but related approaches to understanding the city, but within each approach was the prevailing notion of a city that worked in the interests of (investment) capital accumulation and exploitation (Bridge and Watson 2000, 15). During the 1980s and 1990s, economic restructuring and the globalization of the economy further made the case for a new way of thinking about urbanization that conceptualized the city as something more than the outgrowth of natural processes such as invasion and succession.

While political economy assumed various theoretical and empirical shapes, its proponents did agree on some basic concepts (see Gottdiener and Feagin 1988; Gottdiener 1998; Kleniewski 2002). First, cities are depicted as more than just the products of natural processes, as human ecology had stated. Rather, they are shaped by the actions of powerful economic and political players who control key resources. The configuration of the Toronto waterfront, for example, has been irreversibly determined by property developers who for decades have exerted their muscle at city hall, securing permission to build a wall of highrise condominiums that more or less block off Lake Ontario from the downtown core.

Second, urban patterns and social life, it is claimed, are dominated by racial, ethnic, and class antagonisms. One dramatic example occurred during the 1992 Los Angles riot when more than 2,000 Korean-owned businesses were destroyed and damaged by African and Hispanic residents who resented their ownership of the majority of liquor stores and other retail outlets in ghetto areas (Walton 1993, 316).

Third, the state continues to be a significant force in urban life. Witness, for example, the high media profile attached to each political party's platform in the 2004 Canadian federal election with regard to an urban aid package that would assist municipalities in funding crucial infrastructure projects such as repairing roads, sewers, and bridges. Or consider the fact that the ongoing debate over how best to dispose of our garbage and other waste will be resolved not in the open marketplace, as human ecologists would predict, but in the political arena, where economic, environmental, and quality-of-life considerations all joust for supremacy.

Fourth, connections to the system of capitalism and its global dynamics matter a great deal. Economic restructuring, for example, has meant that manufacturing industries have pulled out of Canadian and US communities in record numbers and relocated offshore where labour costs are much lower. This has led to an unfortunate string of consequences for cities: increased unemployment, erosion of the municipal tax base, the need to undertake expensive place marketing campaigns, and an eventual shift from industrial to service jobs.

Although it makes a strong theoretical case, the political economy perspective has not always been inclined to offer up a wealth of empirical evidence in support of its claims. One approach that has been useful is statistical analysis of the distribution of investment capital in real estate across the city. Harvey's original study of Baltimore remains a model, clearly indicating how discrimination by investors and government programs leads to inner-city areas becoming rundown and abandoned. Political economy theorists have also conducted case studies that have become as memorable as the urban community studies of the 1950s and 1960s. Arguably, the best of these is Sharon Zukin's *Loft Living*, first published in 1982. Zukin traces the evolution of lofts in the SoHo district of New York from garment industry sweatshops, to places to live and work in for bohemian artists, to gentrified apartments for urban professionals. In the final stage of gentrification, artists were largely priced out of the local housing market and forced to move to a poorer habitat. This transformation was engineered by property developers who cannily marketed the lofts as offering a 'cutting-edge' lifestyle. Zukin was thus one of the first urban sociologists to show how art and culture were becoming vital components in the changing tool kit of capitalism.

While the political economy approach has certainly revolutionized the field of urban sociology, it has encountered difficulty in recent years in finding something new to say. Fifteen years ago, John Walton (1993) noted that despite its impressive accomplishments, urban political economy 'seems to be flagging of late' and its research 'has become repetitive'. He attributed this partly to the tendency of 'overconfident' practitioners to mechanically apply the same theory to each and every empirical case and partly to its 'economism' (that is, its predilection to explain each and every urban situation by referring to the nature of capitalism and class relations).

5. Social Constructionist Model

One relatively new direction in urban sociology has been to focus on the meaning attributed to places, events, and conditions by social actors within the city. The idea here is that these meanings are not self-evident but open to different (and conflicting) interpretations. Which of these interpretations triumphs depends on the degree of power possessed by various social actors.

Despite their familiarity with the symbolic interactionist approach in early American sociology, the Chicago School urban sociologists tended to adopt a 'mass society' outlook. This tendency probably derived from Robert Park's close acquaintance with European collective behaviour theory, which emphasized the notion of the 'group mind' in crowds and publics. This mindset was not really questioned until the late 1940s, when a small maverick faction within human ecology demonstrated that, economic constraints aside, urban residents deliberately choose their ideal residential environments. These socio-cultural ecologists, notably Walter Firey and Christian Jonassen, insisted that choice of location is powerfully shaped by cultural factors, especially sentiment and symbolism. In the early 1960s, Kevin Lynch (1960) discovered that people construct their own personal maps of the city, emphasizing some elements (parks, signs, stores, railway tracks) and not others. Finally, in the 1970s, University of Toronto sociologist William Michelson (1973) proposed a way of looking at residential settings called environmental-opportunity theory. It stated that people actively choose where they want to live depending on the extent to which a particular place either meshes with or constrains their preferred lifestyle. These pieces of research were largely confined to the level of environmental psychology, but they were important in that they demonstrated that urban dwellers actively construct their own versions of the city.

More recently, some urban researchers have taken this perspective considerably further and suggest that we study more than just how people attribute meaning and importance to their immediate spatial and residential environments. It is particularly important, they insist, to examine how powerful groups in the community impose their constructions on less powerful citizens. This is the theme of Kay Anderson's prize-winning book on racial discourse and the social construction of Vancouver's Chinatown (see Box 3.4). In another particularly helpful work, Michael Peter Smith (1999) argues that it is wrong to treat the 'global city'—the object of some recent cutting-edge research by urban sociologists—as something totally objective that can be found by measuring the relative absence or presence of a series of identifiable economic attributes. Rather, he maintains, the global city constitutes a 'discourse' constructed by academics, planners, and politicians and communicated through a variety of channels—conferences, the media, the classroom. Smith prefers to conceptualize contemporary global currents as constituting what he calls 'transnational urbanism'. It is neither a thing nor a continuum of events that can easily be quantified. Instead, ordinary people are viewed as creative actors who construct transnationalism out of the social networks in which they are situated. In that regard, Guarnizo, Portes, and Haller (2003) have studied networks of Latin American transnational migrants to Canada and the United States who literally lead their lives across international borders, maintaining links with family and political links in their home countries for reasons of economic, social, and emotional support.

Another illustration of the construction of urban discourses can be found in Robert Beauregard's *Voices of Decline* (2003). Beauregard contends that the idea of 'urban decline' in America is the result of more than just objective reporting. Rather, it was deliberately constructed and sold to the public, in part to justify embracing the opportunities provided by suburban growth and to avoid having to accept responsibility for inner-city poverty. This discourse 'functions ideologically to shape our attention, provide reasons for our actions, and convey a comprehensive, compelling story of the fate of the twentieth century US city' (Beauregard 2003, xi). Beauregard traces the urban decline discourse by analyzing mass-market magazines, national newspapers, government reports, and various public forums from the era. In similar fashion, Canadian sociologist Rob Shields stresses the importance of the media in discourse construction. In *Places on the Margin* (1991) he introduces the term **social spatialization** to designate how particular places are defined as good, bad, sites of danger, or sites of work. These place designations may even be mythical. Such place myths are constructed in novels, periodicals, soap operas, and advertisements.

In such cases, rather than urban meaning being an obvious and uncontested quality of the architecture or layout or physical boundaries of the area, meaning is determined socially. For example, in the mid-1990s a conflict arose over a 94-acre parcel of undeveloped land on the Downtown Eastside of Vancouver. To the Vancouver Port Authority and its private partners, 'Portside Park' was privately owned, semi-derelict land that could profitably be redeveloped as 'Seaport Centre', which would entail a cruise ship facility, a hotel, and a casino. To Downtown Eastside activists, the same parcel of land was a public space known as Crab (Create a Real Available Beach) Park with the capacity to become a large, natural green space with special meaning to First Nations people (Blomley 2004, 46). In this case, the activists eventually succeeded in defeating the seaport proposal, thereby preserving their 'construction' of a 'people's park'. In many other cases, however, the definitions associated with elite urban growth coalitions predominate, especially in the media.

Another contested social construction is that of the 'skid row'. In the early urban sociology literature, the term referred to a 'natural area' where the city's most disenfranchised residents could be found. As Huey and Kemple (2007) observe, it was 'a relatively neglected and protected space' to which individuals who had hit rock bottom, sometimes as a result of a personal tragedy, could withdraw. To a degree, the skid row carried with it a romantic image of adventure and resistance to conformity. Over time, this image changed. Today, skid rows such as San Francisco's Tenderloin district or Vancouver's Downtown Eastside have morphed into 'a civic space for the containment of moral and material dereliction'. In particular, the police implement various strategies of containment there, ranging from arrests to cautions to 'move along'. Journalists depict the skid row not so much as a magnet for the victims of hard luck as a social sore infected by drug addicts and prostitutes.

John Walton, who remarked on the dead end into which political economy had backed itself,

Box 3.4 *Constructing 'Chinatown' in Vancouver and Quebec City*

Some of the most accomplished scholarly work in the social constructionist mode has dealt with the concept of 'Chinatown'. In Canada, perhaps the best example is Kay Anderson's (1991) book *Vancouver's Chinatown*.

Anderson argues that the stereotypical Chinatown with its restaurants, pagodas, and neon lights is not something intrinsically connected to the Chinese and their immigrant experience but rather a Western 'construction' imposed on an urban district by outsiders. Around the turn of the twentieth century, Chinatown, located along Pender Street, was depicted as something exotic and vaguely dangerous, with its residents perceived as clannish and heathen, sleeping 12 to a room, conversing in a strange language, and addicted to opium and gambling. This shared characterization allowed Canadians of European ancestry to affirm their own identities as 'normal' as opposed to the 'otherness' of the Chinese newcomers.

Later, Chinatown was framed in less overheated terms but always in line with the economic exigencies and political ideologies of the day. During the 1950s, as the iron cage of 'race' was finally being dismantled by Canadian policy-makers, Chinatown was viewed as epitomizing a 'slum'. Consistent with the postwar ideology of progress, the area was to be bulldozed as part of Vancouver's urban renewal effort. Ironically, it was only spared by virtue of its constructed identity as a tourist area and ethnic neighbourhood. In the 1970s, Chinatown was singled out for special status by local authorities as part of a wider effort to encourage the imaginative reuse of existing but declining neighbourhoods in order to contribute to the quality and richness of city life. For example, it was recommended in a municipal restoration report that all new signs should reflect the traditional ethnic character of Chinatown and that the use of neon tubing for illumination purposes be emphasized.

Anderson points out that 'Chinatown was not a neutral term, referring somehow unproblematically to the physical presence of people from China in Vancouver' (1991, 30) but rather was an evaluative term that ignored how the residents of that territory might define themselves. Over time, some elements in the neighbourhood, notably local businesses, learned to manipulate this social construction for their own purposes—for example, to attract tourist dollars or frustrate urban planners. Anderson's work on Vancouver's Chinatown, Huang and Chang (2003, 81) point out, provides a good example of 'the changing discourses of place at different points in time'.

Today, little has changed, as the curious tale of Quebec City's Chinatown indicates. Never very large (at its peak in the 1940s, its population numbered less than 200), most of Quebec City's 'Chinatown' disappeared in the early 1970s, in part because of the construction of the Dufferin-Montmorency expressway. But now, city hall has joined forces with a local entrepreneur, who operates a chain of martial arts studios, in a plan to rebuild. Among the landmark features will be an ornate archway donated by the Chinese city of Xian, new shops and restaurants, two imposing bronze lions, and a park designed according to *feng shui* principles (Hamilton 2004, A1). All that is missing are local Chinese Canadians, the majority of whom have dispersed to the suburbs, retired to China, or departed for Montreal, Toronto, or Vancouver.

has himself started using the tools of social construction. In *Storied Land* (2003), Walton frames a history of Monterey, CA, as a web of competing stories from a contested past. Some of these stories won out and became history; others lost and were consigned to the archives. In general, it was the 'American' version of Monterey's past that persisted over the Native American, Spanish, and Mexican interpretations. This reflects the power differentials among the different segments of the community over the years.

Conclusion

In considering the state of theory and method in urban sociology at the beginning of the twenty-first century, Gotham (2001, 444) makes three salient observations. First, research in urban sociology is currently in a state of theoretical and methodological flux in which ideas about how to proceed vary tremendously and in somewhat opposite directions. This is not necessarily a negative development in that it may produce a creative tension in the field. At the same time, the different camps tend to operate in parallel fashion rather than engage one another. Second, urban questions do not lend themselves easily to approaches using a single method or only a particular type of data, nor do they lead to sweeping theoretical explanations of change. Third, the best kind of methodological strategy relies on multiple kinds of data—quantitative and qualitative—so as to provide both a generalized overview and a nuanced observational account. Indeed, there is no reason why the methods favoured by one approach to studying cities and urban life cannot be fruitfully applied within the framework of a competing theoretical perspective. For example, the method of urban ethnography, developed by figures in the Chicago School and refined by community studies researchers in the 1950s and 1960s, can be most useful in gauging the impact of globalization. An ethnographic approach to globalization, Gille and O'Riain (2002, 285) suggest, 'requires the understanding of locally, socially, and culturally specific ways in which people understand the place of their locality in the global scheme of things and the actions they take to shape that place'. It may be at this synapse of the local and the global that urban sociologists will finally come to grips with the dilemma posed by John Rex almost 40 years ago.

Study and Discussion Questions

1. Is there a distinct 'urban' way of thinking, relating, and behaving? If so, what are its main features?
2. In *The Gold Coast and the Slum* (1929), Harvey Zorbaugh concluded that Chicago in the 1920s lacked any resilient connective issue strong enough to hold together the different subpopulations of the city and create an overall sense of 'community'. Is this an accurate representation of Canada's larger cities in the early twenty-first century?
3. Are social network researchers correct in saying that interpersonal ties have become 'detached' from the local neighbourhood? To help answer this, map out your own personal network of family, friends, neighbours, and others with whom you maintain regular social relationships.
4. Think of a neighbourhood in your city that has been officially designated as a 'tourist zone' and/or 'historic district'. How has this identity been 'constructed' by local merchants, planners, politicians, the media, and residents?
5. Recently, an increasing chorus of voices in government and the media has been calling for a 'new deal for cities', especially with regard to affordable housing, transportation, and a sustainable urban environment. What shape do you think this urban revival should take?

Suggested Reading

Caulfield, Jon, and Linda Peake, Eds. 1996. *City Lives and City Forms: Critical Research and Canadian Urbanism.* Toronto: University of Toronto Press. Collection of articles by Canadian researchers dealing with current themes within the urban field: economic restructuring and gentrification, public versus private in the underground city, and social construction of 'Aboriginality' in relation to cities. The common thread is an orientation towards 'critical urban study'.

Çinar, Alev, and Thomas Bender, Eds. 2007. *Urban Imaginaries: Locating the Modern City.* Minneapolis: University of Minnesota Press. Cities, the authors of this book argue, exist as much in the collective imagination of their residents as they do in fixed physical spaces. This point is effectively illustrated by intriguing case studies from Brazil, Cameroun, France, India, Israel, Jordan, Lebanon, Turkey, and the United States.

Duneier, Mitchell. 2001. *Sidewalk.* New York: Farrar Straus and Giroux. Prize-winning contemporary urban ethnography of a three-block stretch of lower Sixth Avenue in New York's Greenwich Village populated by book and magazine street vendors, some of them homeless. Manages to be both sociologically insightful and emotionally moving.

Sassen, Saskia. 1991. *The Global City.* Princeton, NJ: Princeton University Press. An instant classic. Documents the increasing concentration of control and management of the international financial services industry in a handful of major cities. Note especially Sassen's linkage of these changes to the appearance of a widening economic and social polarization in New York and London.

Tajbakhsh, Kian. 2001. *The Promise of the City: Space, Identity, and Politics in Contemporary Social Thought.* Berkeley: University of California Press. Thoughtful and even-handed discussion of key theories and theorists associated with the contemporary urban scene. Note especially the rigorously argued chapters on Manuel Castells and David Harvey.

References

Abrahamson, Mark. 1976. *Urban Sociology.* Englewood Cliffs, NJ: Prentice-Hall.

Abu-Lughod, Janet L. 1991. *Changing Cities: Urban Sociology.* New York: HarperCollins.

Alihan, Mila. 1938. *Social Ecology.* New York: Columbia University Press.

Anderson, Kay J. 1991. *Vancouver's Chinatown: Racial Discourse in Canada, 1875–1980.* Montreal and Kingston: McGill-Queen's University Press.

Beauregard, Robert A. 2003. *Voices of Decline: The Postwar Fate of U.S. Cities.* 2nd edn. New York: Routledge.

Blomley, Nicholas. 2004. *Unsettling the City: Urban Land and the Politics of Property.* New York: Routledge.

Booth, Charles. 1970 [1892]. *Life and Labour of the People in London.* 17 vols. New York: AMS Press.

Bridge, Gary, and Sophie Watson. 2000. 'City imaginaries'. In Gary Bridge and Sophie Watson, Eds, *A Companion to the City.* Oxford: Blackwell.

Bulmer, Martin. 1983. 'The methodology of the taxi-dance hall: An early account of Chicago ethnography from the 1920s'. *Urban Life* 12 (1): 95–120.

Choldin, Harvey M. 1985. *Cities and Suburbs: An Introduction to Urban Sociology.* New York: McGraw-Hill.

Cressey, P.G. 1932. *The Taxi-Dance Hall: A Sociological Study of Commercialized Recreation and City Life.* Chicago: University of Chicago Press.

———. 1983. 'A comparison of the roles of the "sociological stranger" and the "anonymous stranger" in field research'. *Urban Life* 11 (4): 407–20.

Driedger, Leo. 2001. 'Changing visions in ethnic relations'. *Canadian Journal of Sociology* 26 (3): 421–51.

———. 2003. 'Changing boundaries: Sorting space, class, ethnicity and race in Ontario'. *Canadian Review of Sociology and Anthropology* 40 (5): 593–621.

Effrat, Marcia Pelly. 1974. 'Approaches to community: Conflicts and complementaries'. In Marcia Pelly Effrat, Ed., *The Community: Approaches and Applications*, 1–32. New York: Free Press.

Fainstein, Susan. 1999. 'Can we make the cities we want?' In Robert Beauregard and Sophie Body-Gendrot, Eds, *The Urban Moment: Cosmopolitan Essays on the Late 20th-Century City*, 249–72. Thousand Oaks, CA: Sage.

Fischer, Claude S. 1975. 'Toward a subcultural theory of urbanism'. *American Journal of Sociology* 80: 1,319–41.

———. 1984. *The Urban Experience*. 2nd edn. New York: Harcourt Brace Jovanovich.

Flanagan, William G. 2002. *Urban Sociology: Images and Structure*. 4th edn. Boston: Allyn and Bacon.

Form, William. 1954. 'The place of social structure in the determination of land use: Some implications for a theory of urban ecology'. *Social Forces* 32: 317–23.

Gans, Herbert J. 1962. *The Urban Villagers: Group and Class in the Life of Italian Americans*. New York: Free Press.

Gille, Zsuzsa, and Séan O'Riain. 2002. 'Global ethnography'. *Annual Review of Sociology* 28: 271–95.

Gist, Noel P., and Sylvia Fleis Fava. 1964. *Urban Society*. 5th edn. New York: Thomas Y. Crowell.

Gotham, Kevin Fox. 2001. 'Redevelopment for whom and for what purpose? A research agenda for urban redevelopment in the twenty-first century'. In Kevin Fox Gotham, Ed., *Critical Perspectives on Urban Redevelopment (Research in Urban Sociology*, v. 6), 429–52. Amsterdam: JAI.

Gottdiener, Mark. 1998. 'Urban sociology: Feagin-style'. In Joe R. Feagin, Ed., *The New Urban Paradigm: Critical Perspectives on the City*, 331–8. Lanham, MD: Rowman and Littlefield.

Gottdiener, Mark, and Joe R. Feagin. 1988. 'The paradigm shift in urban sociology'. *Urban Affairs Quarterly* 24: 163–88.

Greenberg, Miriam. 2003. 'The limits of branding: The World Trade Center, fiscal crisis and the marketing of recovery'. *International Journal of Urban and Regional Research* 27 (2): 386–416.

Guarnizo, Luis Eduardo, Alejandro Portes, and William Haller. 2003. 'Assimilation and transnationalism: Determinants of transnational political action among contemporary migrants'. *American Journal of Sociology* 108 (6): 1,211–48.

Hamilton, Graeme. 2004. 'Quebec's Chinatown like a ghost town'. *The National Post* 9 January: A1, A5.

Hatt, Paul. 1946. 'The concept of natural area'. *American Sociological Review* 11: 423–7.

Huang, Shirlena, and T.C. Chang. 2003. 'Selective disclosure: Romancing the Singapore River'. In Robbie B.H. Goh and Belinda S.A. Yeoh, Eds, *Theorizing the Southeast Asian City As Text*, 77–105. Singapore: World Scientific.

Huey, Laura, and Thomas Kemple. 2007. '"Let the streets take care of themselves": Making sociological and common sense of "skid row"'. *Urban Studies* 12: 2,305–19.

Hughes, Everett C. 1963. *French Canada in Transition: The Effects of Anglo-American Industrialization upon a French-Canadian Town*. Chicago: Phoenix Books.

Kleniewski, Nancy. 2002. *Cities, Change, and Conflict: A Political Economy of Urban Life*. 2nd edn. Belmont, CA: Wadsworth Thomson Learning.

Liebow, Elliot. 1967. *Tally's Corner*. Boston: Little, Brown.

Lofland, Lyn. 1985 [1973]. *A World of Strangers: Order and Action in Urban Public Space*. Prospect Heights, IL: Waveland Press.

———. 1998. *The Public Realm: Exploring the City's Quintessential Social Territory*. New York: Aldine De Gruyter.

Lynch, Kevin. 1960. *The Image of the City*. Cambridge: Technology Press.

Lyon, Larry. 1987. *The Community in Urban Society*. Chicago: Dorsey Press.

McKenzie, Roderick. 1926. 'The scope of urban ecology'. In Ernest W. Burgess, Ed., *The Urban Community: Selected Papers from the Proceedings of the American Sociological Society, 1925*, 167–82. Chicago: University of Chicago Press.

Massey, Douglas S., and Nancy A. Denton. 1993. *American Apartheid: Segregation and the Making of the Underclass*. Cambridge, MA: Harvard University Press.

Merrifield, Andy. 2002. *Dialectical Urbanism: Social Struggles in the Capitalist City*. New York: Monthly Review Press.

Michelson, William D. 1973. *Environmental Change*. University of Toronto Research Paper no. 60. Toronto: Centre for Urban and Community Studies.

Milgram, Stanley. 1977. *The Individual in a Social World*. Reading, MA: Addison-Wesley.

Murdie, Robert A. 1969. *Factorial Ecology of Metropolitan Toronto, 1951–1961: An Essay in the Social Geography of the City*. Chicago: Department of Geography, University of Chicago.

Oldenburg, Ray. 1989. *The Great Good Place: Cafes, Bars, Hangouts and How They Get You through the Day*. New York: Paragon House.

Park, Robert. 1915. 'The city: Suggestions for the investigation of human behavior in the city environment'. *American Journal of Sociology* 20: 577–612.

Rex, J.A. 1968. 'The sociology of a zone in transition'. In R.E. Pahl, Ed., *Readings in Urban Geography*, 211–31. Oxford and London: Pergamon Press.

Savage, Mike, and Alan Warde. 1993. *Urban Sociology, Capitalism and Modernity*. Houndmills, UK: Macmillan.

Seeley, John A., Alexander Sim, and E.W. Loosley. 1956. *Crestwood Heights*. Toronto: University of Toronto Press.

Sennett, Richard. 1970. *The Uses of Disorder: Personal Identity and City Life*. New York: Vintage.

———. 1977. *The Fall of Public Man*. New York: Alfred A. Knopf.

Shevsky, Eshref, and Wendell Bell. 1955. *Social Area Analysis: Theory, Illustrative Applications and Computational Procedures*. Stanford Series in Sociology no. 1. Stanford, CA: Stanford University Press.

Shevsky, Eshref, and Marilyn Williams. 1949. *The Social Areas of Los Angeles*. Berkeley: University of California Press.

Shields, Rob. 1991. *Places on the Margin: Alternative Geographies of Modernity*. London: Routledge.

Simmel, Georg. 1950. 'The metropolis and mental life'. In Kurt W. Wolff, Ed. and trans., *The Sociology of Georg Simmel*, 409–24. Glencoe IL: Free Press.

Smith, Dennis. 1988. *The Chicago School: A Liberal Critique of Capitalism*. New York: St Martin's Press.

Smith, Michael Peter. 1999. 'Transnationalism and the city'. In Robert Beauregard and Sophie Body-Gendrot, Eds, *The Urban Moment: Cosmopolitan Essays on the Late 20th-Century City*, 119–39. Thousand Oaks, CA: Sage.

Stein, Maurice. 1960. *The Eclipse of Community: An Interpretation of American Studies*. Princeton, NJ: Princeton University Press.

Suttles, Gerald D. 1968. *The Social Order of the Slum: Ethnicity and Territory in the Inner City*. Chicago: University of Chicago Press.

———. 1972. *The Social Construction of Communities*. Chicago: University of Chicago Press.

Thomas, W.I., and Florian Znaniecki. 1918–20. *The Polish Peasant in Europe and America*. 5 vols. Boston: Richard G. Badger.

Thorns, David C. 2002. *The Transformation of Cities: Urban Theory and Urban Life*. Houndmills, UK: Palgrave Macmillan.

Walton, John. 1993. 'Urban sociology: The contribution and limits of political economy'. *Annual Review of Sociology* 19: 301–20.

———. 2003. *Storied Land: Community and Memory in Monterey*. Berkeley: University of California Press.

Warren, Roland L. 1972. *The Community in America*. 2nd edn. New York: Rand McNally.

Webber, Melvin M. 1970. 'Order in diversity: Community without propinquity'. In Harold M. Proshansky et al., Eds, *Environmental Psychology*, 533–49. New York: Holt, Rinehart and Winston.

Whyte, William Foote. 1943. *Street Corner Society*. Chicago: University of Chicago Press.

Wirth, Louis. 1938. 'Urbanism as a way of life'. *American Journal of Sociology* 44: 3–24.

———. 1945. 'Human ecology'. *American Journal of Sociology* 50: 483–8.

Young, Michael, and Peter Willmott. 1957. *Family and Kinship in East London*. Baltimore, MD: Penguin.

Zorbaugh, Harvey Warren. 1929. *The Gold Coast and the Slum*. Chicago: University of Chicago Press.

Zukin, Sharon. 1982. *Loft Living: Culture and Capital in Urban Change*. New Brunswick, NJ: Rutgers University Press.

Chapter 4 Getting Perspective

What comparison in discussing cities has been the most powerful, the most long-standing, and yet the most perplexing contrast in the history of urban analysis?

Contrasts are all around us—night and day, black and white, rich and poor, high and low, better and worse. They represent opposites that reflect and shape our thinking. One of the most dominant contrasts in urban analysis is the comparison between rural and urban. Early urban analysts intuitively understood that urban life was significantly different from rural life, and they struggled to specify what the difference was and how it changed the way people lived. Urban residents have always seemed to compare life in cities with life in rural areas. For a while, they thought that rural life was better and cities were only to be tolerated. Later, rural areas were spoken of more negatively by city dwellers as behind the times and not progressive. More recently, rural life has experienced even more transformations so that the difference between rural and urban life has become blurred. 'Rural' used to be defined as individual farmers engaged in agriculture, but now agriculture has become corporate agribusiness. Rural areas are no longer used just for agriculture, forestry, and fishing but for tourism, lower-density living, and recreation as well. The stark contrast between rural and urban is gone, and yet we still struggle with the difference that low-density living makes in comparison to high-density living, because rural-urban comparisons still lurk in our thought. Even though proportionally fewer and fewer people who live in rural areas are engaged in primary production (agriculture, forestry, fishing, or mining), we need to understand how the rural and the urban need each other and relate to one another. Is the primary difference between rural and urban merely a matter of different densities, or is there something distinctly different about rural life as opposed to urban life?

4 Rural and Urban: Differences and Common Ground

Bill Reimer

Learning Objectives

- To understand the historical evolution of rural Canada.
- To understand the characteristics of contemporary rural Canadian society.
- To understand the relationship between rural and urban society.
- To identify common issues shared by rural and urban people.

Introduction

Rural and urban Canada are inextricably linked. Rural places provide the timber, food, minerals, and energy that serve as bases of urban growth. Rural places also process urban pollution, refresh and restore urban populations, and maintain the heritage upon which much of our Canadian identity rests. In return, urban Canada provides the markets for rural goods, much of its technology, and most of its financial capital and manufactured goods, along with a good deal of its media-based culture. To understand urban regions, therefore, one must understand their relationship to the rural context in which they exist.[1]

Canada is a highly urbanized society, so it is easy to forget that the urbanization we experience today is relatively new. When my father was born, most people in Canada lived in rural areas. Only by 1931 did urban people outnumber rural dwellers, but after World War II this difference increased rapidly (see Figure 4.1). Now, only about 22 per cent of Canadians live in rural areas. At the same time, many of the differences between urban and rural places have diminished.

Services, facilities, consumer products, and many of the same cultural artifacts can be found in small towns as well as in major urban centres. But many differences remain and will continue to affect the character of rural places. Rural places will remain less dense, with greater distances separating people and settlements. They will continue to have a narrower range of services, and they will continue to reflect the types of social relations that come with relative isolation.

It is not a simple matter to define 'rural'. Many people would do so with reference to the geographical characteristics—typically referring to population density and distance. Others challenge this approach, arguing that 'rural' (as 'urban') is a social construction and therefore should be treated as a sociological concept—with an emphasis on perception, identity, power, and symbols (Mormont 1990; Halfacre 1993; Shucksmith 1994).

Those adopting the latter perspective point to the way in which the rural/urban distinction has no compelling theoretical value, since it differentiates neither causes nor consequences. One can find many urban-like relations in rural areas, just

Figure 4.1 Rural/Urban Population Trends, 1851–2006

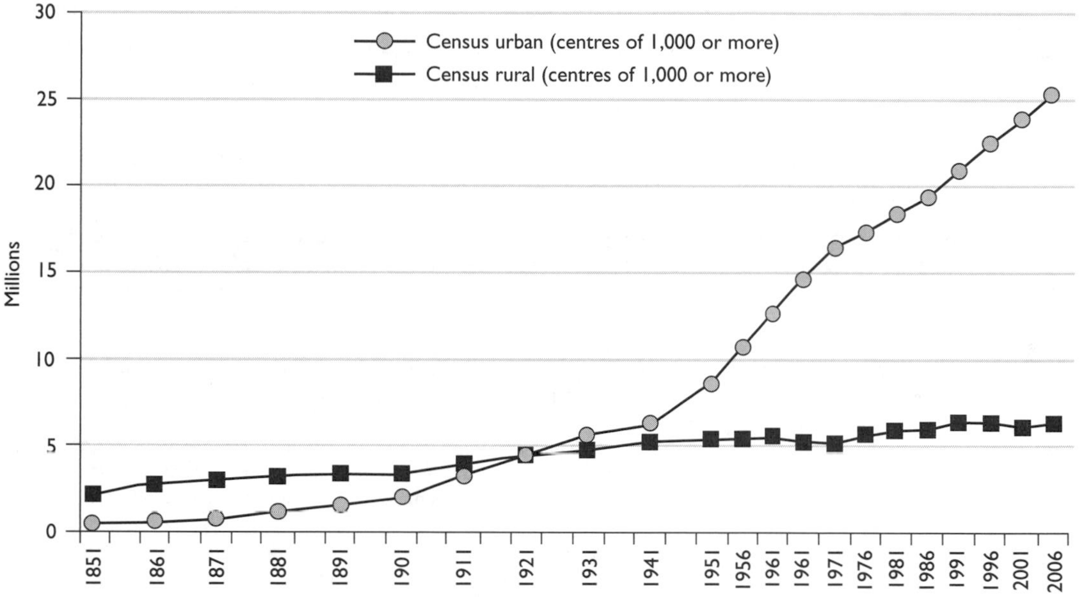

Note: Data are tabulated in the boundaries applicable at the time of the given census.

Source: From Statistics Canada publication *Structure and Change in Canada's Rural Demography: An Update to 2006 with Provincial Detail, Agriculture and Rural Working Paper Series*, Catalogue no. 21-601-MIE2008090, http://www.statcan.gc.ca/bsolc/olc-cel/olc-cel?lang-eng&catno=21-601-M2008090.

as one can find rural-like relations in urban centres (Pahl 1966; Newby 1986). Instead, they argue that 'rural' should be viewed as a social construction—important because of the way in which particular definitions provide advantages to one group over another. If, for example, rural is identified as the spaces where our raw materials are located, then communities, plants, and animals play a secondary role: as the means to extract those materials or as obstacles to efficient extraction. If, on the other hand, rural is defined in terms that emphasize heritage or amenities, then the preservation of towns and villages is likely to take precedence over clear-cut logging, industrial agriculture, and fish farms. Thus, the definition of rural becomes a struggle between interested parties wishing to champion their vision for particular outcomes and a focus for examination of the political and social processes supporting these visions.

Whatever the response, the answer usually depends on the reason one has for asking it. To students of urban regions, 'rural' may mean everywhere outside of urban centres, and whether regional centres, small towns, villages, or hamlets are included depends on the vision of urban being considered. Economists like Jane Jacobs (1984) or Laurence Solomon (2003), who focus on the ability of urban places to generate economic wealth through import substitution, tend to relegate 'rural' to undifferentiated areas outside the major urban centres. Government policy analysts with a mandate to increase wealth, provide social services, and solve problems of inequities are likely to have a much more variegated view of rural, since the requirements for services in a mid-sized town are significantly different from those in a village or an unorganized rural area (Canada 1998). Rural citizens are likely to

Table 4.1 Definitions of Rural

Definition	Main Criteria, Thresholds
Census rural area	Population living outside places of 1,000 people or more, or population living outside places with densities of 400 or more people per square kilometre.
Rural and small town (RST)	Population living outside the main commuting zone of larger urban centres (of 10,000 or more).
Census metropolitan area and census agglomeration influenced zones (MIZ) OECD rural communities	MIZ disaggregates the RST population into four subgroups based on the size of commuting flows to any larger urban centre (of 10,000 or more). Population in communities with densities of less than 150 people per square kilometre.
OECD predominantly rural regions	Population in regions where more than 50 per cent of the people live in an OECD 'rural community'.
Non-metropolitan regions	Population living outside of regions with major urban settlements of 50,000 or more people. Non-metropolitan regions are subdivided into three groups based on settlement type and a fourth based on location in the North. Non-metropolitan regions include urban settlements with populations of less than 50,000 people and regions with no urban settlements (where 'urban settlements' are defined as places with populations of 2,500 or more)
Rural postal codes	Areas serviced by rural route delivery from a post office or postal station; '0' in second position of a postal code denotes a rural postal code.

Source: Abridged from du Plessis, Beshiri, and Bollman 2001.

emphasize the culture or way of life they find in their location as the primary point of reference for distinguishing it from urban areas.

Taking a geographical point of view, du Plessis, Beshiri, and Bollman (2001) identify six different definitions of rural frequently used by analysts and policy-makers in Canada (Table 4.1). Each definition carries implications for the type of analysis being conducted (e.g., labour force, geographical settlement, administration) and also makes use of various units of analysis—from the small regions covered by a census enumerator to areas equivalent to counties. In most cases, however, they reflect an important relationship with urban areas—often being defined with respect to their proximity to such areas or the extent to which they lie in or near the labour force catchment areas of urban regions.

In the end, du Plessis et al. recommend that the definition chosen should be selected on the basis of the question being asked. Pressed to give a baseline reference, they propose that their 'rural and small town' definition be considered. By this definition, 'rural' is the population living in towns and villages outside the labour force commuting zone of larger urban centres (10,000 population or more). It places towns the size of Bonavista (NL), Souris (PEI), Inverness (NS), Sackville (NB), Baie-Saint-Paul (QC), Tweed (ON), Gimli (MB), Humbolt (SK), Banff (AB), and Hope (BC) in the category of 'rural and small town' but relegates Corner Brook (NL), Summerside (PEI), Truro (NS), Bathurst (NB), Lachute (QC), Kenora (ON), Thompson (MB), Moose Jaw (SK), Grand Prairie (AB), Dawson Creek (BC), and Whitehorse (YT) to 'urban'. A brief review of these lists should make it clear how controversial the distinction can be.

History of the Transformation (How Did We Get Here?)

The Canadian economy and society have their historical roots in the international trade of *staples*. The exploitation of fish, forests, furs, grain, dairy products, minerals, and petroleum have fundamentally shaped the history of Canada. Even our current urban centres bear the marks of this past. Our major cities are located at key points for the transfer and movement of commodities, international trade in those commodities remains a significant part of our ability to pay for urban needs and desires, and urban people play in the harbours and canals that were once the pathways for these commercial products (Innis 1995; Wallace 2002, 74).

The Short-Distance Society

At the time of Confederation, most people lived in rural areas. Travel was costly, so economic and social activities were conducted in relatively small centres located close to the natural resources on which they depended. The high birth rates in rural areas provided labour for the local industries, with any surplus population moving to growing urban centres. Many of our early manufacturing industries were born in small towns, often in response to the needs of farmers and loggers for improvements to their productivity. Miner's (1963) classic study of a small Quebec parish documents how the natural resource and manufacturing industries were intimately integrated into the social relations of small communities. Persson, Westholm, and Fuller (1997) identify this as a period when rural Canada was a 'short-distance society' (see Figure 4.2). Work, family, commercial, and recreational activities occurred within a similar (often local) geographical space because of the constraints of travel. Community systems were characterized by considerable overlap among these various spheres of life.

At a national level, the dominance of primary production was evident in the organization of our political institutions. The departments of agriculture (1867), fisheries (1868), and forestry (1899) were established to ensure conditions for high productivity—all emphasizing the commodity trade orientation of our national policies (Anderson 1985). When the settlement of the Prairies was deemed essential for Confederation, for example, the Department of Agriculture was given the mandate to organize the immigration policies and practices (Knowles 1997, 47–8). These sectoral distinctions remain with us today, although in forms that have been modified to reflect the changing conditions of Canadian society.

The Industrial Society

Persson, Westholm, and Fuller (1997) argue that this 'short-distance society' gave way to an 'industrial society' sometime during the late nineteenth and early twentieth centuries (Figure 4.2). Small rural-based processing and manufacturing activities became amalgamated in larger centres, the mobility of people and goods increased with improved transportation infrastructure and technology (primarily associated with the automobile and related vehicles), and citizens began to conduct more of their social and economic lives between places rather than within one place.

The reduction in costs for transportation and processing fit well with the organization of production that we now identify as **Fordist**. It is characterized by the use of assembly lines, the standardization of products, and the organization of industrial production in vertically integrated corporations that flourished from the mid-1940s to the early 1970s (Allen 1996a, 281; 1996b, 546). The raw materials for such production were concentrated or shipped in large quantities to central locations (most often urban areas), with significant savings in transportation and co-ordination costs over the piecemeal production of the 1800s.

All of the primary and rural-oriented industries were significantly affected by these changes.

Figure 4.2 Transformations in Rural Society

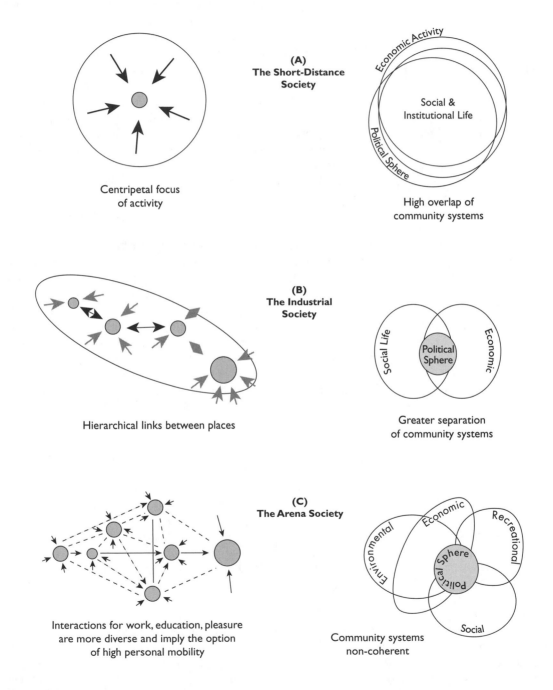

(A)
The Short-Distance Society

Centripetal focus
of activity

High overlap of
community systems

(B)
The Industrial Society

Hierarchical links between places

Greater separation
of community systems

(C)
The Arena Society

Interactions for work, education, pleasure
are more diverse and imply the option
of high personal mobility

Community systems
non-coherent

Source: Fuller (1994: 135).

Specialization in food crops, increasing farm size, larger fishing vessels, and the use of more advanced technology (machinery, fertilizers, refrigeration, and selective breeding techniques) resulted in major increases in the production of food from the 1950s to the 1980s. The use of heavy machinery in the forests, at sea, and in the mines resulted in the exploitation of forest, fishery, and mineral resources at an unprecedented scale. We were able to produce much more with many fewer people—both in the extraction and harvesting of resources and in the associated processing plants. Even during the past few years, this trend continues. For example, primary-sector **gross domestic product** (GDP) from 1981 to 2002 increased by 12 per cent, yet during the same period the number of people employed in those industries decreased by 26 per cent (CAN-SIM Tables 3790017 and 2820008).

The Canadian government was a champion of this approach, pursuing a policy advocating business-oriented farming, forestry, fishing, and mining based on scientific research and large-scale production (Canada 1969; Fairbairn 1998). This policy included major subsidies and controls over both supply and marketing of some agricultural and aquacultural products—a policy appealing to the demand for cheap food from urban Canadians and predictable markets for producers. The negative effects of this policy on family farms, rural communities, food quality, and the environment would only become apparent later (see Box 4.1).

The social structure of rural places continued to reflect primary production but in modified forms. The classic study of this transition by Hughes (1963) documents how regional centres emerged from small processing and manufacturing enterprises in Quebec, drawing in labour from more remote areas, then shedding that labour as technology took over many of the tasks. The details of this process varied considerably throughout rural areas, but the general pattern was common: increased mobility, greater levels of mechanization, and lower demand for labour

(Sinclair and Westhues 1974; Marchak 1983; Dunk 1991).

Hodge and Qadeer (1983, 115–16) identify the local social structure that emerged as '*truncated*', pointing to the way in which many of these towns lacked 'managerial functions and the social strata that dominate national or provincial decision-making processes, for example, a bureaucratic elite, corporate executives, or political leadership'. This resulted in communities that were predominantly composed of the working and lower-middle classes. It placed them at a significant disadvantage with respect to larger urban centres, especially when it came to influencing the corporate and political structures that determined so many of their opportunities.

This disadvantage was mitigated by the relatively high level of political representation of rural regions in provincial and national legislatures. Since the allocation of ridings is largely determined by population distribution, the historically high proportion of rural people and the length of time required for redistribution of these allocations meant that rural interests were a key part of political decision-making—especially when they converged with the commodity production and trade objectives of urban leaders. This was all to change, however, as advances in technology, the expansion of global trade, and the roles of governments shifted.

The Arena Society

As the advantages of Fordist production diminished through the increased use of computers, global competition, and the increasing diversification of tastes, mass production gave way to **flexible production** that was more responsive to competition and demand. A wider range of products, **just-in-time** reorganization of distribution, and a flattening of the institutional structure of management were consistent with the expansion of computer technology, almost instant communication, and more extensive and efficient transportation that developed after the 1950s (Chaykowski 1997; Wallace 2002, 117, 244).

Box 4.1 Farm Families: A Case Study of Rural-Urban Interdependence

Since the 1960s, Canadians' demand for consumer goods has increased considerably because of population growth, the desire for cheap, diverse, and safe food, and greater competition from foreign sources. This demand has been enthusiastically met by government policy, corporate reorganization, technical innovations, and marketing strategies. Urban Canadians now have access to food from around the world no matter what the season, with a minimal risk of contamination, for prices that are among the lowest in the world.

To satisfy this demand, however, a high price has been paid in terms of the social and cultural bases of rural Canada. In order to pay for the bananas and tomatoes we desired, it was necessary to produce wheat, grains, butter, and beef in large quantities. Newer, bigger machines, specialized crops, and extensive use of fossil fuels and fertilizers were required to produce the quantities necessary and meet the health regulations associated with large-scale production. At the same time, labour prices rose as urban jobs became more desirable.

Farm producers were forced to invest in the new technology, increase their landholdings, and cut labour costs in order to survive. Many farmers and their families were unable to cope with the increasing costs and lower prices so turned to off-farm work to supplement their farm incomes, sold their farms, or leased the land to others who were able to expand. This cost-price squeeze resulted in increases in family breakdown, abuse, and even suicide as farmers faced stress and failure from forces beyond their control. Farm communities suffered as well, since workers moved to urban centres, disposable incomes were reduced, and the number of farms decreased.

Agricultural production in Canada has been radically transformed in the process. Although production continues to grow, the number of farms is decreasing along with agricultural employment. Less than 2 per cent of Canadian farms make more than $1 million per year, but they are responsible for more than 35 per cent of agricultural receipts (Statistics Canada 2002, 15). In 2000, farm families received only 26.5 per cent of their income from farming activities, supplementing it with off-farm and non-farm work (Statistics Canada 2000). The narrow profit margins make farmers particularly vulnerable to natural disasters and market crises such as the droughts of 2001 and 2002 and the BSE crisis of 2003 (see Box 4.2).

Urban Canadians and policy-makers have responded to these trends in piecemeal fashion, often unaware of how their concerns for cheap food have undermined farm families and rural communities. Other nations have not all followed this pattern, however. Japan and France, for example, have recognized the interdependence of urban and rural areas and have implemented special taxes on water and food that go to support rural development. Other nations have implemented supports for farmers to offset the rising costs of farm inputs and lower prices. Citing free-market rhetoric and buoyed by an overall positive balance of trade in agricultural products, the Canadian government has minimized transfer payments to farmers—thereby supporting the trends in farm and community structure that began 50 years ago.

These economic and social changes have created conditions considerably different from those of the old industrial economy. Persson, Westholm, and Fuller (1997) identify this as the 'arena society' (see Figure 4.2), a society that is more inclusive, diverse, complex, dynamic, and confusing. Transportation and communication costs have become so low that people interact with different networks for work, education, and recreation. It means that geographically based community systems have lost most of their coherence and new social, economic, and institutional systems are more diverse and flexible (Chaykowski 1997, iii).

Coincident with these changes came increasing pressure on the Canadian state to turn over its potentially profitable activities to the private sector and to limit its restrictions on international trade (Marchak 1991). Increased spending during the post–World War II years had left the government with a sizable deficit, which was used as a justification for decreasing and reorganizing spending. During the 1980s and 1990s, this pressure resulted in a gradual reduction and reorganization of the Canadian welfare state (Britton 1996; Rice and Prince 2000) and the negotiation of free trade agreements with the United States, Mexico, and other nations in Central and South America.[2] Rural communities were hard-hit by the reorganization of government services. As the government moved to a fiscal model of delivery, there was a substantial reduction in schools, post offices, hospitals, and government offices throughout rural areas, leaving many small towns even weaker as they became less able to attract and maintain their dwindling populations (Bruce and Halseth 2001). These pressures exacerbated the ongoing migration to regional and urban centres.

The negotiations for free trade included two issues that were particularly relevant for the rural economy. The first was the separation of sectoral policy from social and environmental policy. The Canadian government argued that agriculture and forestry policies, for example, were to be considered on their own—separate from social or environmental issues that might be implicated in any tariff or trade reorganization. European nations and Japan, on the other hand, have long argued that social and environmental issues could not be separated from those of trade in commodities—a policy of entitled **multi-functionality** (Shrybman 2001). Farmers, for example, provide

scenic landscapes, manage water supplies, and contribute to national security as they produce foodstuffs. Sustainable forestry also supports carbon sequestration, biodiversity, water quality, and recreation—all important functions that are not reflected in trade debates, which focus strictly on single-sector commodities (Apedaile 2003, 1). Multi-functional advocates argue that tariffs and subsidies are some of the ways by which farmers and foresters can be compensated for providing these public services in addition to those they produce for the market. Canada and the US (among other nations) felt that such subsidies were 'trade-distorting' and gave European and Japanese farmers and industries an unfair advantage in international trade (United Nations Food and Agriculture Organization 1999).[3]

The second issue involved several programs that Canada had established to protect particular interest groups and regional development. In western Canada, for example, a long-standing arrangement with the railways involving low freight rates for shipping grain (the 'Crow rate') was ended in 1995. Changes have also been made to the federally co-ordinated provincial milk marketing boards, including the phasing out of direct subsidies for industrial milk. Provincial restrictions on quota holdings by individual producers and federal upper limits on subsidy eligibility are also being gradually reduced (OECD 1996). Similar challenges to the Canadian Wheat Board, which markets Canadian wheat internationally, reflect this pressure to reduce government involvement in agricultural trade (Kneen 1995).

The challenges remain unresolved. On the matter of trade, negotiations continue in a context of tariff imposition and trade tribunals—sometimes compounded by dramatic action over disease control or food quality concerns. For example, in 2003 the US banned all imports of beef from Canada when a cow with bovine spongiform encephalopathy (BSE) was discovered in Alberta—see Box 4.2. The safety of **genetically modified organisms** (GMOs) has also been a hotly debated topic since the beginning of this

Box 4.2 *Bovine Spongiform Encephalopathy*

Bovine spongiform encephalopathy (BSE), commonly known as 'mad cow disease', is a chronic degenerative disease affecting the central nervous system of cattle (Canadian Food Inspection Agency 2003a). Its human form (variant Creutzfeldt-Jakob disease) can be acquired by eating meat containing brain and spinal cord tissue from infected animals. In May 2003, the Canadian Food Inspection Agency announced that a single case of BSE had been discovered on an Alberta farm (Alberta Agriculture, Food, and Rural Development 2003). Between May and November, more than 30 countries imposed restrictions on beef products exported from Canada, although the United States and Mexico began to import beef products within six months of the initial detection of BSE (Canadian Food Inspection Agency 2003b). While Alberta was the hardest hit, the export ban led to massive losses of revenue and unemployment in both rural and urban places across Canada, leading some provinces to take emergency steps to provide financial relief to laid-off workers (Wilson 2003; Saskatchewan Party 2003; Alberta Agriculture, Food, and Rural Development 2003).

century. Consumer concerns for non-GMO food and GMO labelling of food has led some regions to restrict or ban the production and trade of GMO-produced foods (e.g., potatoes in PEI).

Characteristics of the New Rural Economy in Canada

The economic changes over the past 60 years have been so substantial that they have been identified with their own special designation: the New Economy. The rural economy has been a part of these changes (Bollman 2007). Five key elements are outlined below.

1. The New Rural Economy Is More Diverse and Complex

The traditional image of rural Canada as a simple mix of farmland, mining towns, mill towns, and railway towns (Lucas 1971) is more often the result of nostalgia than of reality. The remnants of resource extraction industries remain, but how they are organized no longer reflects the small-scale, simple-product focus of the past—either within rural communities or across them. Wallace (2002, 127–8) points out, for example, that 36 per cent of gross farm receipts were produced by

3.1 per cent of Canadian farms grossing income of more than $500,000 each. As discussed in Box 4.3, small agricultural producers, processors, and manufacturers have been largely replaced by huge vertically integrated corporations such as Cargill. Similarly, the small woodlots, sawmills, and bush camps of the forestry sector have been replaced by vast timber reserves, long-haul trucking of timber to large centralized pulp- or sawmills, and multinational corporations that buy and sell materials, mills, and labour with an eye to competition from Europe, the US, Asia, and Latin America (Marchak 1995). Small fishing boats are less likely to be found at the docks of picturesque harbours on our east and west coasts. Instead, sea products are caught, cleaned, and frozen at sea on large vessels or farmed in pens scattered among coves or rivers. The production of forest and mineral products has become the purview of large corporations, an industrial-style division of labour, and marketing strategies requiring speedy communication and complex knowledge.

These changes in the labour force and population have had a profound impact on the number, structure, and distribution of rural communities. Stabler, Olfert, and Fulton (1992) provide a dramatic illustration of this process in Saskatchewan, where 38.4 per cent of the rural

Box 4.3 *Cargill*: *A Corporate Food Giant*

Cargill was created in 1865 as a regional grain merchandiser in the US. Since then, its operations have expanded immensely, and it now maintains a near-monopoly in many sectors of the food system throughout the world. By 1995, Cargill had become the largest private company in the US and the eleventh largest company, public or private, in terms of sales. As of 1995, Cargill was also the largest grain trader, producer of malt barley, and processor of oilseeds—and the second largest producer of phosphate fertilizer in the world. In the US, it is the third largest beef packer, the fourth largest cattle feeder, the sixth largest turkey producer, and the third largest flour miller (Kneen 1995).

Today, Cargill Incorporated has achieved *vertical integration* throughout the food system. It is involved in the 'marketing, processing and distribution of agricultural food, financial and industrial products and services' (http://www.cargill.com). It has also achieved a substantial degree of horizontal integration in the agri-food sector around the world. In December 2003, Cargill had 98,000 employees in 61 countries.

Cargill also has a major presence in Canada. The Canadian subsidiary, Cargill Limited, was established in 1928 as a grain merchandising operation. Today it is present in the processing of eggs, malt, meat, chocolate, and oilseeds and the manufacturing of starch, sweeteners, feed, salt, and fertilizers, as well as grain handling and merchandising (Cargill 2003). In 1995, Cargill was the largest beef packer in Canada (Kneen 1995), and with the establishment of the Saskferco plant in 1992 in Saskatchewan, of which Cargill owns 51 per cent of the shares, it is now one of North America's largest producers of ammonia and granular urea (Saskferco 2003). The Saskferco plant produced 33 per cent of Canada's total granular urea fertilizer in 2001 (Saskferco 2003; Statistics Canada 2003).

Cargill's corporate strategy for the consolidation of storage and processing has had significant effects on rural and urban people alike. Larger grain storage facilities have meant a decrease in employment and in the viability of small communities. Larger processing plants have attracted workers from those small communities, further exacerbating the urbanization process on a regional level.

communities provided fewer commercial services in 1990 than in 1961. Parts of Newfoundland and Labrador, Cape Breton Island, northern New Brunswick, and the Gaspé region of Quebec show a pattern of community population decline similar to that of rural Saskatchewan.

Not all of rural Canada faces this type of challenge, however. Parts of the North, central BC, southern and western Alberta, southern Ontario, southwestern Quebec, and rural regions surrounding the larger cities in the Atlantic provinces have experienced population growth over the past 20 years. Two elements in this growth seem particularly important: proximity to urban centres and availability of natural amenities. Both of these features foreshadow new elements in rural-urban relations: the changing patterns of commuting and the growing importance of natural amenities for urban people. Coping with the tensions this generates and anticipating the opportunities it creates for rural areas are some of the pressing issues on the current agenda for many small towns.

In short, rural Canada is heterogeneous. Like its urban counterpart, it is undergoing change, with considerable diversity of conditions and results. Some of the diversity of the new rural economy is captured by the research of Hawkins and

Bollman in their analysis of the characteristics of rural **census divisions** (Hawkins and Bollman 1994). As shown in Figure 4.3, they identify seven different types of clusters to represent rural Canada. The map illustrates the following points. Agriculture is only a small part of the rural context (see 'agro-rural', largely centred in the Prairies, southern Quebec, the Annapolis Valley region of Nova Scotia, and several sections in BC). 'Resourced areas', located in northern regions of the western provinces and territories, northern Ontario, and Labrador, are the primary locations for Canadian mineral and petroleum resources. 'Rural Nirvana' areas—the regions doing relatively well in economic and social terms—are largely situated near urban centres in southern Ontario. Many of the urban regions in Canada have associated 'urban frontiers'—rural areas strongly integrated into their economic activities. Most of the 'rural enclaves' are located in the Gaspé region of Quebec, parts of New Brunswick and Nova Scotia, and much of Newfoundland. In general, we see considerable diversity among rural areas.

2. Services and Amenities Are Growing

The extraction of natural resources and trade in commodities remain important bases for the new national economy. Our overall **balance of trade** relies to a great extent on exports from the resource sectors. In 2007, for example, we largely paid for imports of machinery and consumer products with exports from forestry, energy, and agriculture (Table 4.2). In that year, these primary-sector products offset the overall trade deficit of the manufacturing sector. Growth in the service sector has shown the largest increase, however, becoming the main sector for employment growth and an increasing focus for international trade. In 1966, the service sector made up only 54.7 per cent of employment and 57.4 per cent of GDP (Wallace 2002, 113), but by 2006 these figures had increased to 78.2 per cent of employment and 69.4 per cent of national GDP (CANSIM Tables 3830010 and 3790023).

The growth in the service sector has not been sufficient to absorb the decline in primary-sector employment, however (Freshwater 2001). Unlike during the industrial period, the urban economy can no longer employ surplus rural workers. This has created major problems of unemployment in urban areas and forced governments to search for methods to increase employment opportunities in rural areas. Considerable effort has been made on the part of government agencies to diversify the types of

Table 4.2 Canadian Merchandise Trade by Commodity Group, 2007

Commodity Group	Imports ($ million)	Exports ($ million)	Surplus (Deficit) ($ million)
Agriculture and fisheries	463,051	25,496	8,874
Energy	34,370	36,569	55,078
Forestry	91,647	2,995	26,268
Industrial goods	104,421	85,132	19,289
Machinery & equipment	93,428	116,632	(23,204)
Automobile products	77,304	80,002	(2,698)
Consumer goods	18,737	54,794	(36,057)
Special & unallocated	13,880	13,385	495
Total	463,051	415,006	48,046

Source: CANSIM Table 3760006: Balance of international payments, current account, goods, annually (dollars).

Figure 4.3 A Preliminary Typology of Rural Canada

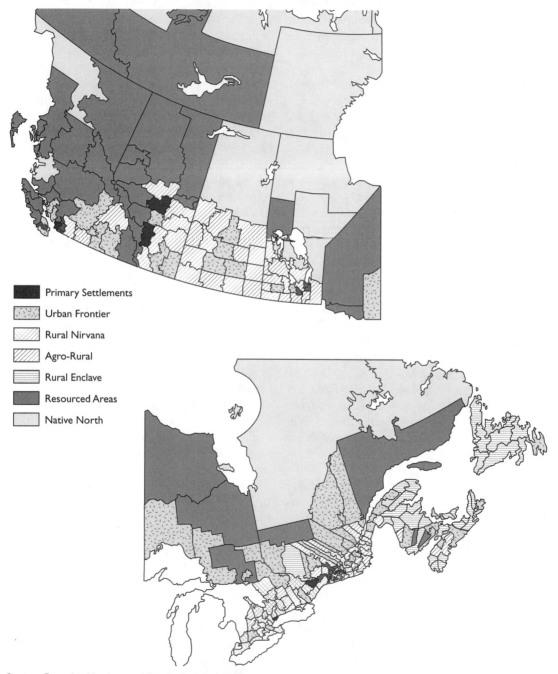

Source: From Liz Hawkins and Ray D. Bollman, 'Revisiting Rural Canada—It's not all the same', *Canadian Agriculture at a Glance* (1994): 78-80.

activities in which communities become involved, but with only moderate success. Some
remarkable examples of diversifying and innovative initiatives can be found, however, even in
regions that are economically peripheral.[4]

3. The New Rural Economy Is More Mobile

In spite of the declines in primary-sector employment, the population in rural and small-town
Canada is still growing. Since 1976, this population has consistently increased from one census
period to the next (Mendelson and Bollman 1998).
However, the growth of population in urban areas
has been greater. Along with the amalgamation
of some rural areas into their nearby urban centres, this has meant that the overall proportion
of people in rural areas has declined from about
34 per cent in 1976 to 22 per cent in 2001 (du
Plessis, Beshiri, and Bollman 2001). Most of the
population increase in rural areas (70 per cent) is
the result of *natural increase*, with the rest due to
migration (Beshiri and Bollman 2001).

Improvements in transportation and communication technology and infrastructure have
made it possible for people to move more frequently and farther. In rural Canada, this has
meant that small towns are less isolated than
they were 60 years ago, not only with respect to
having access to goods and services but also in
regard to the movement of people. One of the
biggest impacts has been on the mobility of
young people. Over the past few decades, this
movement has been largely towards urban areas,
often for education (Rothwell et al. 2002; LeBlanc
and Gauthier 2001).

Return migration occurs in a patterned fashion as well. Movement to some of the more remote towns is often linked to the employment
structure of those towns. Resource towns, whose
raison d'être is mining, oil/gas production, hydro-
electricity, or forestry, are places of destination for
seasonal or long-shift workers who move there for
part of the year before returning to urban centres
as part of a work/vacation cycle. In regions close to

urban centres, increasing numbers of people commute long distances to work on a daily, weekly, or
monthly basis. This option has become easier as
both roads and high-speed communication have
improved in their range and reliability. Since the
early 1990s, the rate of in-migration has slightly
exceeded the rate of out-migration from rural and
small-town regions, although it is highly age-
specific, with younger people (20 to 24) predominating among those moving out and older people
(25 to 65) predominating among those moving in
(Rothwell et al. 2002).

Although some have argued that the Internet
provides a new hope for rural revitalization, it is
likely to have the same mixed effects as the technological innovations before it. The establishment
of efficient postal services and telephone infrastructure, for example, undermined the monop-
oly of local retailers by making the sales catalogue
possible, but these conveniences also provided
opportunities for rural people to start their own
mail-order businesses. Paved roads had a similar
effect: it became much easier for people to shop
outside their local community, once again weakening the advantage of local retailers but at the
same time opening up new markets for the most
enterprising of them. The Internet holds the same
promise—a communication innovation that may
challenge existing economic and social relations
while opening new opportunities for business,
knowledge acquisition, and social relations.

The Canadian government has given high
priority to the establishment of high-speed communication infrastructure in most parts of the
country. The programs put in place have made
Canada one of the best-equipped countries in
the world for remote communication (Industry
Canada 2003b), but the spread of its actual use
has been rather uneven, resulting in a rural–
urban gap of experience (Sciadas 2003, 8). As
infrastructure, skills, and personal access are
improved, we are likely to see an increase in the
long-distance communication, changing local
social relations, and wider markets that are characteristic of the 'arena society'.

Box 4.4 Looking Back: The Collapse of the Atlantic Cod Fishery

In 1992, the Canadian government declared a moratorium on the cod fishery in Atlantic Canada. The primary reason was the decline (90 per cent over five years) in the stocks of cod and other groundfish (Industry Canada 2003a). This drastic change had significant social and economic repercussions throughout Atlantic Canada. The 1992 moratorium put 40,000 Atlantic Canadians out of work and cost approximately $4 billion in aid programs. Newfoundland and Labrador were particularly hard-hit because the groundfish fishery made up 80 per cent of the total provincial catch. However, in some areas this fishery was as high as 100 per cent.

During the crisis, many factors were singled out and blamed, but no single cause has yet been identified. Rather, it appears that multiple factors acted to reinforce and exacerbate the mounting crisis. They included government mismanagement in permitting overly high catches, overoptimistic scientific projections, inaccurate data on commercial fishing activities, destructive fishing practices, ecological change, and government labour policy (Wallace 2002; Industry Canada 2003a).

Attempts to reopen the cod fishery since the 1992 moratorium have largely failed, and it was completely closed down in April 2003 by the Department of Fisheries and Oceans. Although not nearly as severe in terms of impacts, this closure affected 900 fishers and cost the Atlantic region as much as $30 million in lost annual revenues (CBC News 2003).

4. External Relations Are Important in the New Rural Economy

The Canadian rural economy has always been part of the global economy. As a colony of France and Britain, it was intimately linked to the economic objectives of these European countries, and later, as trade developed with the US, the Pacific Rim, and the Americas, these international connections expanded. However, the development of high-speed communication, improvements in transportation, and the reorganization of global finance have greatly increased the exposure to global influence. While the United States has remained the largest host country for Canadian foreign direct investment (FDI), the American share of Canadian FDI declined significantly from its peak of 68.5 per cent in 1980 to 58 per cent in 1992 (Industry Canada 1994). Between 1981 and 1991, the share of other European countries (excluding the UK) in Canadian foreign direct investment increased from 5.2 to 6.9 per cent.

A significant feature of the new economy is the variety and level of competition among natu-

ral resource producers around the world. Traditionally, Canada has had an advantage merely because of its vast forests, abundant fisheries, fertile soil, and extensive mineral deposits. However, we are now facing dramatic examples of the limits to that resource abundance—from the collapse of the cod fisheries in the Atlantic region (Box 4.4) to the depletion of soil quality in the Prairies. Even our forest production is stressed. As we harvest our huge boreal forests, we have found that reforestation and forest management are increasingly important, that our resources are vulnerable to pests and climate change, and that Canada's northern location means that replenishing forest stocks takes more years than is the case in more temperate climates—thus reducing our comparative advantage (Marchak 1995).

5. The New Rural Economy Requires a Wider Range of Knowledge

The knowledge required for commodity production before World War II was relatively focused. One could learn to be a farmer, forester, or fisher

Table 4.3 Old and New Rural Economies

Old Rural Economy	New Rural Economy
Homogeneous culture	Diverse culture
Simple and repetitive	Complex
Resource commodities	Services and amenities
Low mobility	High mobility
Local relations important	External relations important
Low knowledge demands	High knowledge demands

by following the lead of one's parents—the knowledge was craft- and artisan-based. Knowledge of international or even national market conditions, currency levels, nutrient composition of feeds or fertilizers, trade policy, accounting practices, or computer operation was not essential to economic survival or even success. Under the new rural economy, such ignorance could easily place one in jeopardy. Agriculture, forestry, fishing, and mining require a considerably expanded level and range of knowledge, with all signs pointing to a continuation of this pattern. As in other parts of the economy, access to knowledge and the ability to apply it in innovative ways have become key conditions for success.

Rural Canada is in a transition period at this point (Table 4.3). Education levels are rising, although they remain behind those in more urban areas, largely because of the older age structure in rural areas. The pattern of youth out-migration found in many rural sites reflects this situation (Rothwell et al. 2002; LeBlanc and Gauthier 2001; Looker et al. 2001).

Rural-Urban Interdependence in the New Economy

Rural-urban interdependence means that what happens in rural areas will affect the welfare of urban people just as urban conditions and change will affect those in rural places. The ways in which this occurs are often indirect, but they can be seen with

respect to four broad characteristics: exchange, institutions, the environment, and identity.

Interdependence through Exchange

Rural-urban interdependence is most often represented in terms of the exchange and trade of goods, services, finances, or people. Some of this exchange is direct—as when rural-grown food is shipped to feed urban populations, urban-based financial capital is used to build rural businesses, or rural-based commuters travel to and from urban centres on a daily, weekly, or even yearly cycle. Much of it, however, is indirect, as when our natural resources are shipped to other nations in exchange for manufactured goods and consumer items. In this case, rural-urban interdependence becomes enmeshed in a complex web of crop yields, trade agreements, commodity prices, and political issues that can make it difficult to trace but no less important for the welfare of both urban and rural people.

Tariffs and subsidies under the control of other nations mean that Canadian producers have more difficulty competing in international trade. This in turn affects our ability to pay for the consumer products and variety of foods that we have come to enjoy. For the majority of Canadians, this threatens to decrease our standard of living in unacceptable ways. However, many features of that standard of living would be endangered if tariffs and subsidies were completely removed. Full exposure to international competition—which is based primarily on gaining profits for corporate owners and shareholders

Figure 4.4 Percent Commuting to the Toronto CMA, 2001

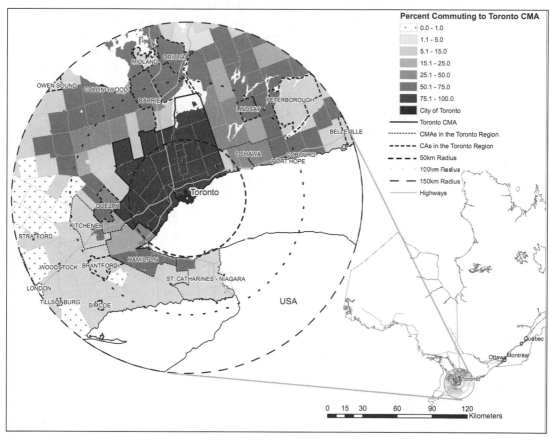

Source: http://crerl.usask.ca/infrastructure/ON_album/p 1_jpg.htm. This work was funded, in part, by an Infrastructure Canada grant.

and on the dubious assumption that science and technology in the future can rectify whatever environmental damage is done today—has resulted in the collapse of fish stocks, depletion of topsoil, and erosion of amenities through clear-cut practices in logging (Shrybman 2001). To compete with deregulated trading partners, we would be under considerable pressure to remove rather than enhance regulations that limit this type of damage.

Rural-urban interdependence is also reflected in more direct types of exchange. An analysis of daily commuting patterns around Toronto, for example, shows that a substantial number of people move back and forth between the urban core and surrounding rural areas on a daily basis. Commuting even originates as far as 150 kilometres from the centre of the city (see Figure 4.4). This is a pattern that is replicated throughout the country (see http://crerl.usask.ca/infra.php). Urban centres depend on rural labour, while rural people depend on urban employment.

Interdependence through Institutions

Rural and urban areas are also interdependent through the institutions they share. Governments and their departments, corporate organizations, and voluntary associations are all likely to include both rural and urban places in their jurisdictions, with common policies for all. This interdependence of jurisdictions can create many challenges for small places, especially with respect to policies that are effective only in an urban context yet are uncritically applied to rural regions. Examples are plentiful within the context of service provision, since this is where the distance and agglomeration challenges for rural areas are most strongly felt (Bruce and Halseth 2001). Amalgamation of services may make fiscal sense in urban centres where public transportation is extensive, but in rural areas it isolates the poor and dependent by requiring access to a car. Specialization of health professionals is also a rational approach to the increasing complexity of medical services, but it becomes unworkable in small centres where only one doctor is available (Halseth, Sullivan, and Ryser 2002). At a time when urban centres are facing their own financial pressures, it may be difficult to justify the extra spending required to overcome these challenges in rural areas.

The management of food safety and security provides another example of institutional interdependence between rural and urban places. The new economy brings new challenges to this issue as food production, processing, marketing, and retailing become more concentrated, integrated, and global. The establishment and monitoring of standards at each point in the food chain have become increasingly complex, and even minor failures in the system have had major impacts. In Canada, this is clearly illustrated by the BSE crisis (Box 4.2) and by the contamination of the water supply in Walkerton, ON, in May 2000, which killed seven people and made 2,300 others ill (CBC News 2000). Justice O'Connor's final report for the inquiry into the Walkerton tragedy concluded that Walkerton's contaminated water supply—by E. coli bacteria from runoff on a nearby farm—was the result of improper chlorination and structural problems caused by funding cutbacks in provincial and federal institutions (O'Connor 2002).

Interdependence through Shared Environments

The condition of the environment is another issue that binds rural and urban people. In many cases, it involves differing interests that cannot be easily resolved by market forces alone. Since we share the air, water, vistas, and land, it becomes impossible to separate the impacts of urban and rural activities. Urban sulphur and carbon dioxide emissions create acid rain that weakens rural vegetation. Rural fertilizers and biological wastes can leach into water supplies that endanger rural and urban citizens alike. Both urban and rural activities have altered climatic conditions that promise to have long-lasting effects on our whole way of life (see Box 4.5) (Wackernagel and Rees 1996).

We have very few social institutions that can deal adequately with these types of challenges—those where the resources and impacts are shared 'in common'. Most of our institutions are organized with the assumption that property is privately held and that the outcomes of actions can be regulated by the give and take of market transactions. Under these conditions, the environment is like **common property** and therefore in danger of being exploited for its resources or used as a dumping ground. Government regulations provide some means to limit the negative effects of these conditions, but they have been restricted in their effectiveness as a result of fiscal pressures, vested interests in private property, erosion of state autonomy, and the complex nature of environmental–social relationships (Marchak 1987).

Non-government organizations have made some contributions to highlighting and dealing with some of these challenges. Demonstrations, marches, and publicity events have brought some of the issues to public attention, and institutional innovations have provided examples of possible resolutions. Ducks Unlimited (http://www.ducks.org), for example, in its desire to preserve wetlands for waterfowl, provides compensation to landowners for removing land from cultivation. Several organizations have campaigns to purchase forest lands to preserve biodiversity.

Box 4.5 *The Ecological Footprint of Urban Places*

The ecological footprint represents the extent to which people in a particular region (e.g., city, province, country) make use of natural resources (e.g., water, land, energy). It is calculated by estimating the area of productive land required to provide resources and assimilate waste products for all the people and activities in that region (Centre for Human Settlements 2003).

According to 1999 data, the *ecological footprint* of the average Canadian was 8.8 hectares (21.8 acres, or about five and a half city blocks). This is the total amount of land required for food, housing, transport, and consumer goods and services. Energy is the largest component of this amount. The second largest component is agriculture for food supply and consumer goods. Forestry—to supply the fibre for housing and consumer goods—is the third largest component. The average ecological footprint for a world citizen is 2.3 hectares (5.6 acres), but only about 1.9 hectares (4.7 acres) of biologically productive land and sea area are available (not counting the amount required for non-human life) (Wackernagel, Monfreda, and Deumling 2002). This means that we require 1.2 earths (2.3 divided by 1.9) to sustain our current global lifestyle and 4.6 earths (8.8 divided by 1.9) if all world citizens were to share the Canadian lifestyle.

Organizations dedicated to the preservation of wildlife species, heritage buildings, or other rural amenities can serve similar purposes (e.g., the Nature Conservancy of Canada, http://www.natureconservancy.ca). In each case, they provide opportunities for rural-urban exchanges and dialogue that may be pursued to create new alliances.

Interdependence through Shared and Complementary Identities

People are also bound by the identities they share. In many cases, these identities are transitory phenomena, but they can also be fundamental attributes of both personal and collective capacity. Research on youth suicide in BC and Quebec, for example, illustrates how individual identity is intimately linked to family and place-based history, increasing the chance of suicide when this identity is undermined (Chandler et al. 2003; Dagenais 2007). At a collective level, we see how Quebecers' national and cultural identity has contributed to a unique rural policy, one that identifies rural-urban interdependence as a collective asset for growth (Quebec 2006). The power of shared identity has also been used more explicitly as a basis for rural-urban collaboration among the city of Edmonton and its surrounding villages (http://www.albertahub.com/), the Toronto Greenbelt Plan (http://www.mah.gov.on.ca/Page5275.aspx), and the promotion of direct-marketing initiatives in many of Canada's cities.

Conclusion

Rural and urban Canada are interdependent parts of the national and social whole. Their economies are interdependent, their institutions are most often the same, their cultures are intertwined, and their populations are intermixed. At the same time, there are, and will continue to be, important differences in this relationship (Wilkinson 2003; Alasia and Rothwell 2003). The particularities of location will ensure that most broad changes or policies have unique effects because of local organizations and culture. Continued urbanization will produce ghost towns, bedroom communities, playgrounds, industrial towns, manufacturing clusters, and retirement centres according to location, facilities, policy, services, population, and knowledge levels. One will always have to travel farther in rural than urban areas, just as one will continue to have access to a wider range of services in cities.

Important as the issue may be, it is difficult to anticipate the future of rural Canada in any detail. The general trends, however, seem reasonably clear. Rural Canada will continue to become more mobile, complex, global, and diverse than in the past. It will also continue to change—in ways that cannot be predicted. As a result, just as in the urban context, knowledge will become increasingly important—knowledge regarding the changes, knowledge regarding the fundamental processes of these changes, and knowledge about the opportunities emerging from them.

Notes

1. The ideas in this chapter reflect the contribution of many people in the New Rural Economy Project (NRE) of the Canadian Rural Revitalization Foundation (CRRF). I thank them for their insights and inspiration. Although I have borrowed liberally from their ideas, the particular formulation here is not an official position of the NRE or CRRF. Angela Briscoe, Becky Lipton, and Moses Tiepoh have been particularly helpful with the preparation of this material. Primary funding support for this project has been provided by the Social Sciences and Humanities Research Council of Canada.

2. In recent years, Canada has signed free trade agreements with Chile, Costa Rica, Israel, the US, and, through NAFTA, with Mexico. Canada has also signed numerous other regional and bilateral types of arrangements (Hart 2000; www.dfait-maeci.gc.ca/tna-nac/reg-en.asp).

3. Throughout these discussions, the US continues to maintain one of the highest levels of farm subsidies of any OECD country, however. In 1999, American wheat producers received 46 per cent of their income from subsidies, EU farmers received 58 per cent, and Canadian wheat producers received 11 per cent (Wallace 2002, 138). On 18 May 2002, *The Guardian* reported that the US had just passed a farm bill that would increase subsidies by $180 billion over the next 10 years, an increase of 70 per cent.

4. Two well-documented examples are found in Moncton, NB (Polèse and Shearmur 2002) and Mackenzie, BC (Halseth and Sullivan 2002).

Study and Discussion Questions

1. In what ways are urban and rural regions interdependent? In what ways are they unique? Where do their interests coincide?

2. What policy options are likely to reduce the disadvantages of rural people arising from the cost of distance or lack of density? What policies might increase those disadvantages?

3. How would our use of rural regions vary if one defined rural as:
   - the location of raw materials for industry?
   - a heritage of small towns and villages?
   - a context for biodiversity?
   - majestic vistas and peaceful scenery?
   - traditional and backward?

4. For each of the definitions in question 3, whose interests does the definition serve?

5. Calculate your ecological footprint (see Box 4.5). In what ways is it dependent on rural Canada? Cf. http://www.lead.org/leadnet/footprint/intro.htm.

6. Urban demands for cheap, diverse, and safe food have contributed to the decline in small farms and rural communities. Should this be allowed to continue? What strategies would you propose to deal with the hardships and loss of heritage it implies?

7. Should we preserve rural communities that are no longer economically viable (e.g., Murdochville, QC, Schefferville, QC, Hearne, SK, Anthracite, AB, Napier, ON, Davis Inlet, NL)? Why? How? Who should provide compensation (if anyone) when a community decides to close?

8. Lipton (1977) argues that urban centres are draining rural areas of resources, labour, and

services. As result, they function to ensure that the poor stay poor. Jacobs (1984) argues that urban centres drive the economy through agglomeration effects that enhance innovation and

economic efficiency. Are these two sides of the same coin? What options does it suggest for the future of rural communities and populations?

Suggested Reading

Bollman, R.D. 1992. *Rural and Small Town Canada*. Toronto: Thompson Educational Publishing. An excellent introduction to many of the major trends and issues affecting rural Canada, this collection of papers covers such topics as rural labour markets, business activities, well-being in rural Canada, and economic diversity.

Halseth, G., and L. Sullivan. 2002. *Building Community in an Instant Town: A Social Geography of Mackenzie and Tumbler Ridge, British Columbia*. Prince George: University of Northern British Columbia Press. The 'social-geographic' point of view provides an introduction to the major theoretical issues related to community analysis while giving the reader a good sense of local life.

Wackernagel, M., and W. Rees. 1996. *Our Ecological Footprint: Reducing Human Impact on the Earth*. Gabriola Island, BC: New Society. Discusses some of the accounting procedures used to estimate the amount of land required to sustain specific cities

and highlights the interdependence between urban places and the natural environment.

Wallace, Iain. 2002. *A Geography of the Canadian Economy*. Toronto: Oxford University Press. Although a book on the Canadian economy as a whole, its geographic focus means that rural Canada plays an important part throughout. The author examines the international context of the Canadian economy, specific economic sectors, and four regions in Canada (Atlantic, Central, Western, and Northern and Aboriginal).

Winson, A. 1992. *The Intimate Commodity: Food and the Development of the Agro-industrial Complex in Canada*. Toronto: Garamond Press. A critical analysis of the historical development and current structure of the Canadian food system, this book presents a valuable account of the organization of the food we eat, its production, trade, and the corporate structure within which it is organized.

References

Alasia, A., and N. Rothwell. 2003. 'The rural/urban divide is not changing: Income disparities persist'. *Rural and Small Town Canada Analysis Bulletin No. 4*. (4 March): 1–17.

Alberta Agriculture, Food, and Rural Development. 2003. 'Bovine spongiform encephalopathy investigation in Alberta'. Press release in association with the Canadian Food Inspection Agency and the Government of Canada. http://www.gov.ab.ca/acn/200305/14425.html.

Allen, J. 1996a. 'Fordism and modern industry'. In Stuart Hall et al., Eds, *Modernity: An Introduction to Modern Societies*, 280–306. Oxford: Blackwell.

———. 1996b. 'Post-industrialism/post-Fordism'. In

Stuart Hall et al., Eds, *Modernity: An Introduction to Modern Societies*, 533–63. Oxford: Blackwell.

Anderson, F.J. 1985. *Natural Resources in Canada: Economic Theory and Policy*. Toronto: Methuen.

Apedaile, L.P. 2003. 'The new rural economy'. Canadian Rural Revitalization Foundation. http://nre.concordia.ca.

Beshiri, R., and R. Bollman. 2001. 'Population structure and change in predominantly rural regions'. *Rural and Small Town Canada Analysis Bulletin No. 2*. Catalogue no. 21–0060-XIE.

Bollman, R.D. 2007. 'Factors driving Canada's rural economy'. *Rural and Small Town Canada Analysis Bulletin No. 83*. Catalogue no. 21-601-MIE.

Britton, J.N.H. 1996. *Canada and the Global Economy: The Geography of Structural and Technological Change*. Montreal and Kingston: McGill-Queen's University Press.

Bruce, D., and G. Halseth. 2001. *Long Run Role of Institutions in Fostering Community Economic Development: A Comparison of Leading and Lagging Rural Communities*. Montreal: Canadian Rural Revitalization Foundation. http://nre.concordia.ca.

Canada. 1969. *Canadian Agriculture in the 70s*. Ottawa: Queen's Printer.

———. 1998. *'Think Rural' and the Canadian Rural Partnership: The Government's Response to the 'Think Rural' Report of the Standing Committee on Natural Resources*. Ottawa: Agriculture and Agri-Food Canada.

Canadian Food Inspection Agency. 2003a. 'Bovine spongiform encephalopathy (BSE) in North America'. http://inspection.gc.ca/english/anima/heasan/dismala/bseeb/bseebindexe.shtml.

———. 2003b. 'Frequently asked questions about BSE and the investigation of a BSE case in western Canada'. http://www.inspection.gc.ca/english/anima/heasan/disemala/bseeb/bsefaqe.shtml.

CBC News. 2000. 'Ontario's rural heartland in shock'. http://www.cbc.ca/news/indepth/walkerton/#top.

———. 2003. 'To the last fish: The codless sea'. CBC News Online, St John's. http://stjohns.cbc.ca/features/CodFisheries.

Centre for Human Settlements. 2003. 'Our ecological footprint'. Vancouver: Centre for Human Settlements, University of British Columbia. http://www.ire.ubc.ca/ecoresearch/ecoftpr.html.

Chandler, M.J., et al. 2003. *Personal Persistence, Identity Development, and Suicide: A Study of Native and Non-Native North American Adolescents*. Monographs of the Society for Research in Child Development, serial no. 273, 68 (2).

Chaykowski, R.P. 1997. *Fostering Human Resources in the 'New Economy': Challenges to the Way Ahead*. Kingston, ON: IRC Press.

Dagenais, Daniel. 2007. *Recherches sociographiques* XLVIII (3: special issue on suicide).

Dunk, T.W. 1991. *It's a Working Man's Town: Male Working-Class Culture in Northwestern Ontario*. Montreal and Kingston: McGill-Queen's University Press.

du Plessis, V., R. Beshiri, and R.D. Bollman. 2001. 'Definition of rural'. *Rural and Small Town Analysis Bulletin No. 3*: 1–17.

Fairbairn, B. 1998. 'A preliminary history of rural development policy and programmes in Canada, 1945–1995'. Canadian Rural Revitalization Foundation. http://nre.concordia.ca.

Freshwater, D. 2001. 'Delusions of grandeur: The search for a vibrant rural America. Lexington: University of Kentucky, Department of Agricultural Economics, TVA Rural Studies Program. http://www.rural.org/publications/reports.html.

Fuller, A. 1994. 'Sustainable rural communities in the arena society'. In J. Bryden, Ed., *Toward Sustainable Rural Communities*. Guelph, ON: University School of Rural Planning and Development.

Halfacre, K.H. 1993. 'Locality and social representation: Space, discourse, and alternative definitions of rural'. *Journal of Rural Studies* 9 (1): 23–37.

Halseth, G., and L. Sullivan. 2002. *Building Community in an Instant Town: A Social Geography of Mackenzie and Tumbler Ridge, British Columbia*. Prince George: University of Northern British Columbia Press.

Halseth, G., L. Sullivan, and L. Ryser. 2002. 'Service provision as a part of resource town transition planning: A case from northern BC'. *Rural Matters*. Miramichi, NB: CRRF. http://www.mta.ca/rstp/crrfconf/halseth_slides.ppt.

Hart, M. 2000. 'The road to free trade'. In L.I. MacDonald, Ed., *Free Trade: Risks and Rewards*. Montreal and Kingston: McGill-Queen's University Press.

Hawkins, Liz, and Ray D. Bollman. 1994. 'Revisiting rural Canada—It's not all the same'. *Canadian Agriculture at a Glance*, 78–80. Ottawa: Statistics Canada.

Hodge, G., and M.A. Qadeer. 1983. *Towns and Villages in Canada: The Importance of Being Unimportant*. Toronto: Butterworths.

Hughes, E.C. 1963. *French Canada in Transition*. Chicago: University of Chicago Press.

Industry Canada. 1994. *Canadian-Based Multinationals: An Analysis of Activities and Performance*. Ottawa: Industry Canada.

———. 2003a. 'The history of the northern cod fishery'. http://collections.ic.gc.ca/cod/home1.htm.

———. 2003b. 'Rankin Inlet, Nunavut'. http://infrastructurecanada.gc.ca.

Innis, H.A. 1995. *Staples, Markets, and Cultural Change: Selected Essays of Harold A. Innis*. Montreal and Kingston: McGill-Queen's University Press.

Jacobs, Jane. 1984. *Cities and the Wealth of Nations*. New York: Vintage Books.

Kneen, B. 1995. *Invisible Giant: Cargill and Its Transnational Strategies*. Halifax: Fernwood.

Knowles, V. 1997. *Strangers at Our Gates: Canadian Immigration and Immigration Policy 1540–1997*. Toronto: Dundurn Press.

LeBlanc, P., and M. Gauthier. 2001. *La migration des jeunes de milieu rural*. Montreal: Ministère des régions, Gouvernement du Québec, INRS Urbanisation, Culture et Société.

Lipton, M. 1977. *Why Poor People Stay Poor: A Study of Urban Bias in World Development*. London: Temple Smith.

Looker, D., et al. 'Longitudinal research on youth transitions in English Canada, from the 1970's to the 1990's'. In M. Gauthier and D. Pacom, Eds, *Spotlight on Canadian Youth Research*. Quebec City: Les Éditions de L'IQRC.

Lucas, R.A. 1971. *Minetown, Milltown, Railtown: Life in Canadian Communities of Single Industry*. Toronto: University of Toronto Press.

Marchak, M.P. 1983. *Green Gold: The Forest Industry in British Columbia*. Vancouver: University of British Columbia Press.

———. 1987. *Uncommon Property*. Toronto: Methuen.

———. 1991. *The Integrated Circus: The New Right and the Restructuring of Global Markets*. Montreal and Kingston: McGill-Queen's University Press.

———. 1995. *Logging the Globe*. Montreal and Kingston: McGill-Queen's University Press.

Mendelson, R., and R.D. Bollman. 1998. *Rural and Small Town Population Is Growing in the 1990s*. Agriculture and Rural Working Paper no. 36.

Ottawa: Statistics Canada.

Miner, H. 1963. *St. Denis, a French-Canadian Parish*. Chicago: University of Chicago Press.

Mormont, M. 1990. 'Who is rural? Or, how to be rural'. In T. Marsden, P. Lowe, and S. Whatmore, Eds, *Rural Restructuring: Global Processes and Their Responses*, 21–44. London: Fulton.

Newby, H. 1986. 'Locality and rurality: The restructuring of social relations'. *Regional Studies* 20 (3): 209–15.

O'Connor, H.D.R. 2002. *Report of the Walkerton Inquiry: The Events of May 2000 and Related Issues*. Toronto: Queen's Printer for Ontario. http://www.attorneygeneral.jus.gov.on.ca/english/about/pubs/walkerton.

OECD (Organisation for Economic Co-operation and Development). 1996. *Reforming Dairy Policy*. Paris: OECD.

Pahl, R. 1966. 'The rural-urban continuum'. *Sociologia Ruralis* 6.

Persson, L.O., E. Westholm, and T. Fuller. 1997. 'Two contexts, one outcome: The importance of lifestyle choice in creating rural jobs in Canada and Sweden'. In R.D. Bollman and J.M. Bryden, Eds, *Rural Employment: An International Perspective*, 136–63, New York: CAB International.

Polèse, M., and R. Shearmur. 2002. *The Periphery in the Knowledge Economy*. Montreal: Institut national de la recherche scientifique.

Quebec. 2006. *Politique nationale de la ruralité*. Ministre des Affaires municipales et régions, Bibliothèque et archives nationales du Québec. http://www.mamr.gouv.qc.ca/publications/regions/ruralite/ruralite_politique.pdf.

Rice, J.J., and M.J. Prince. 2000. *Changing Politics of Canadian Social Policy*. Toronto: University of Toronto Press.

Rothwell, N., et al. 2002. 'Migration to and from rural and small town Canada'. *Rural and Small Town Canada Analysis Bulletin No. 3*, 1–24.

Saskatchewan Party. 2003. http://www.skaucus.com/news/2003/May-2003/052903a.htm.

Saskferco. 2003. http://saskferco.com.

Sciadas, G. 2003. 'Connectedness series: Unveiling the digital divide'. Ottawa: Statistics Canada.

http://www.statcan.ca/english/research/56F000
4MIE/56F0004MIE2002007.pfd.

Shrybman, S. 2001. *The World Trade Organization: A Citizen's Guide*. Toronto: Canadian Centre for Policy Alternatives and James Lorimer.

Shucksmith, M. 1994. 'Conceptualizing post-industrial rurality'. In J. Bryden, Ed., *Towards Sustainable Rural Communities: The Guelph Seminar Series*, 125–32. Guelph, ON: University of Guelph.

Sinclair, P., and K. Westhues. 1974. *Village in Crisis*. Toronto: Holt, Rinehart and Winston.

Solomon, L. 2003. 'Rural separatism: Western alienation is largely a misnomer. The real threat to Canadian unity, and to the Canadian economy, comes from the countryside'. *The Financial Post* 30 May: FP11.

Stabler, J.C., J.R. Olfert, and M. Fulton. 1992. *The Changing Role of Rural Communities in an Urbanizing World*. Regina: Canadian Plains Research Centre.

Statistics Canada. 2000. 'Total income of farm families'. Ottawa: Statistics Canada. http://www.statcan.ca/english/freepub/21-522-XIE/21-XIE02001.pdf.

———. 2002. 'Farming facts 2002'. Ottawa: Statistics Canada. http://www.statcan.ca/english/freepub/21-522-XIE/21-522-XIE02001.pdf.

———. 2003. 'Production and shipments of industrial chemicals and synthetic resins'. CANSIM II, vol. V39271. Ottawa: Statistics Canada. http://0-dc2.chass.utoronto.ca.mercury.concordia.ca/cgibin/cansim2/getSeries.pl?s=V39271.

United Nations Food and Agriculture Organization. 1999. 'The UN Food and Agriculture Organization warns against subsidies and protectionism in developed countries'. News release, UNFAO. http://www.fao.org/WAICENT/OIS/PRESS_NE/PRESSEN6/1999/pres99Fb76.htm.

Wackernagel, M., C. Monfreda, and D. Deumling. 2002. 'Ecological footprints of nations—2002 update'. http://www.redefiningprogress.org/publications/ef1999.pdf.

——— and W. Rees. 1996. *Our Ecological Footprint: Reducing Human Impact on the Earth*. Gabriola Island, BC: New Society.

Wallace, I. 2002. *A Geography of the Canadian Economy*. Toronto: Oxford University Press.

Wilkinson, D. 2003. *A Commentary on Statistics Canada's Rural and Small Town Analysis Bulletin (Released June 12, 2003) and Its Relevance to Northeastern Ontario and Greater Sudbury*. Sudbury, ON: Laurentian University, the NRE Project. http://nre.concordia.ca.

Wilson, Barry. 2003. 'US capitalized on BSE turmoil'. *The Western Producer* 13 November.

Chapter 5   Getting Perspective

How has urban living changed social relationships? Is there something about cities that changes the way people relate to one another?

Because human beings are eminently social, we assume that people will always seek out those with whom they have interests or values in common and that they will therefore find a sense of belonging. When people lived in villages and small towns, it was easy to see how *community* worked. Everyone knew each other on a face-to-face basis, and there were strong norms controlling behaviour. When people became more urban, such community could not always be found. In fact, to the dismay of many, people did not even know their neighbours. If you lived in a high-rise apartment building, you might never even see them, let alone know them. If you lived in a suburb, you might watch your neighbours out of the front picture window, or your children might introduce you to the neighbours because they played with the neighbours' children. But that was not the same as really knowing them. People did not necessarily send their children to the local school or attend the local church because of differences in faith. Their children did not even necessarily play on the same community sports teams because of the grading of skill levels. It was easy to see why many lamented the loss of community and saw cities as retrograde urban environments.

The important thing to learn, however, is that the nature of human relationships has changed. In the old model, community was based on *place*. People who shared a common location automatically bonded, and there were clear boundaries between communities. In contemporary society, community is more likely to be based on *interest*. That is, people do not look to people near their place of residence for meaningful social ties but rather look to interests. Religious or political values, hobbies, occupational interests, sports, and various other interests and shared characteristics lead people to move about anywhere within a city to seek out those with whom they feel most comfortable. Thus, rather than being depersonalized and atomized as individuals, urban residents seek and find their social ties in new ways. And developments in technology are leading to even more change.

This chapter will help you to understand these changing patterns of social ties, why they are occurring, and what the changes mean. We now understand that community is a much more complex set of relationships that operates at several different levels and is not restricted to relations with neighbours within a local community. None of this understanding, however, will silence the continuing debate about evaluating the changes and what they mean for urban society in the long run.

5

Social Ties and Community in Urban Places

Keith N. Hampton

Learning Objectives

- To compare and contrast different stages of sociological thought regarding the impact of the city on community.
- To critically assess how classical sociological theory interpreted the transition from rural, pre-industrial society to complex, urban industrial society.
- To understand the role of the Chicago School in early interpretations of how social relationships were transformed by urban life.
- To identify how the urban ethnographic tradition transformed sociological understanding of relationships in the city and suburbs.
- To define social capital and interpret its relationship to social network analysis.
- To critically examine the impact of new information and communication technologies on the way people maintain social contact and exchange support with members of their communities.

Introduction

As early as the late nineteenth century, sociologists began to theorize about community. Sociologists perceived, even then, that the changing nature of society was having an impact on people's social relationships. Ferdinand Tönnies (1957 [1887]) identified what he termed *Gemeinschaft* (usually translated as 'community') relations. He described as *Gemeinschaft* those social relationships that included neighbourliness and informal social control and that valued the needs of the group over the individual. *Gemeinschaft* was described as a sense of togetherness based on commonality, physical proximity, and stability. Tönnies argued that in a village or small town, *Gemeinschaft* relations predominated. Émile Durkheim (1993 [1893]) used the term 'mechanical solidarity' to define the same homogeneous, pre-industrial society. Mechanical solidarity was a solidarity that developed out of common beliefs and sentiments

within a group. It was a solidarity that brought people together based on similarity in their daily labour and the proximity of their daily lives. Even today, the concepts associated with *Gemeinschaft* and mechanical solidarity represent what many consider to be the 'ideal community'.

At the start of the twenty-first century, Canadians are faced with complex societal changes. We live in a rapidly changing, globalized, post-industrial society. New information and communication technologies are redefining how we relate to the world and to each other. It is unclear whether the concepts that described everyday life more than a century ago are still relevant in describing community today.

The late nineteenth century was also a time of change. Western society was increasingly industrial, bureaucratic, urbanized, and capitalist. Tönnies believed that social relations were increasingly less characteristic of *Gemeinschaft* and growing more characteristic of *Gesellschaft*. He described

Gesellschaft as a direct result of the transformation from a folk-type society to a modern, urban, capitalist society. Little was deemed positive about *Gesellschaft* relations; they were characterized as formal, impersonal, and individualistic in nature. Durkheim also argued that society was in transition, that as a result of an increasingly complex division of labour, mechanical solidarity was in decline, replaced by organic solidarity. Unlike mechanical solidarity, organic solidarity was not seen by Durkheim as a communal solidarity based on common values or shared understanding. Organic solidarity favoured impersonal, bureaucratic control over informal support and individualistic freedom over community control.

Sociologists, politicians, and the media often paint divergent pictures about how the changes of the twenty-first century are influencing the structure of our communities. It is clear that we are in transition; the question is, to where? Are we becoming increasingly individualistic and cut-off from those around us? Is the ideal community still one defined by physical proximity and face-to-face contact? Did we ever, or do we now want to, relate to those around us in the same way epitomized by traditional folk-like society? Do recent social changes hold the potential of reconnecting us to community?

To understand how our relations to those around us have changed in the transition from small villages to larger cities through to the rise of spaceless virtual communities, we must understand how community has changed in the 100-plus years since the writings of Durkheim and Tönnies.

Urbanization and Community

In America, Durkheim's concern about a complex division of labour and Tönnies's concern about the loss of a folk-type society were replaced early in the twentieth century by concern about the fate of community as a result of urbanization. At North America's first Department of Sociology, the sociologists who comprised the Chicago School became particularly well known for their work in a new area of study, **human ecology**: the relationship between people and their environment. Robert Park (1915) suggested that the 'modern methods of urban transportation and communication—the electric railway, the automobile, and the telephone—have silently and rapidly changed in recent years the social and industrial organization of the modern city.' The nature of these changes, according to Park, was in the substitution of 'indirect, "secondary" for direct face-to-face, "primary" relations in the association of individuals in the community'. Primary relations, or **primary groups**, were described by Charles Cooley (1909) as those intimate associations characterized by face-to-face association important in forming group norms and ideals. **Secondary relations** are better described as 'interactions' than as relationships. They are fleeting exchanges between strangers or routine instrumental interactions, such as those between customer and store clerk.

Much of the work of the Chicago School was pessimistic about the way the city affected social relationships. In 1938, Louis Wirth published *Urbanism As a Way of Life*, which would dominate sociology's perception of social relationships in the urban environment for the next 20 years. Wirth argued that city and rural life were polar opposites. The *size* of the urban environment made it impossible for all urban residents to know each other and as a result necessitated the shift from primary to secondary relationships. Urbanites interacted not as individuals but within roles (for example, as store cashier, bank teller, or cab driver). People were incapable of developing deep, personal connections. Moreover, Wirth observed that the *density* and *heterogeneity* of the urban environment led people to live in homogeneous groups—what Park (1915) referred to as 'natural areas'. Wirth argued that mixing across groups was difficult, and as a result urban residents were highly segmented. To Wirth, urbanites were characterized by a blasé

Box 5.1 *Looking Back: Misreading, Then Rereading, Nineteenth-Century Social Change*

Early social theorists may have over-idealized the locally bounded, solitary structure of earlier stages of human existence. Charles Tilly (1988) suggested that by the late eighteenth century, the European world was already mobile and well on its way to being industrialized. The scale of European villages had changed; there had been a significant decrease in the proportion of the population involved in agricultural production and a significant increase in the scale of manufacturing. While the household remained the typical production unit, networks of households would produce cheap goods, particularly textiles, for both national markets and international trade. The seasonal nature of agricultural production freed up segments of the population to travel from village to village in search of agricultural and industrial labour. A steady flow of migrants travelled between Europe and abroad. Tilly estimates that in the eighteenth century alone, 45 million Europeans migrated out of Europe, the majority to the Americas, and 10 million returned home.

The ideal dense, local, agricultural community of the nineteenth century was never observed by early social theorists like Tönnies and Durkheim. What they feared had been lost was as abstract to them as it is to us today and may never have truly existed at all.

attitude; their interpersonal relations were impersonal, superficial, and transitory. In the urban setting, 'bonds of kinship, neighbourliness, and sentiments arising out of living together for generations under a common folk tradition' were said to be 'absent or, at best, relatively weak in an aggregate' (Wirth 1938). As late as 1970, scholars such as Stanley Milgram (1970) described the 'tendency of urban dwellers to deal with one another in highly segmented, functional terms' and an 'acceptance of non-involvement, impersonality, and aloofness in urban life'. It was generally agreed that if urban residents did not have some form of psychosis, then at minimum the urban environment was itself responsible for the atrophy of community and traditional ways of life.

Studies of Urban Communities

The Chicago School treated the urban environment as a laboratory, and many of its members, including Robert Park and Ernest Burgess, were devout empiricists. In addition to setting the foundation for urban sociology, the Chicago School was instrumental in legitimizing what came to be known as the 'urban ethnographic

tradition'. The tradition of urban **ethnography** relies heavily on anthropological methods. Sociologists typically embed themselves within an urban setting and attempt to blend in and share in the experiences of the setting as would any other social participant. Well-known studies from this tradition include *Tally's Corner* (Liebow 1967), *A Place on the Corner* (Anderson 1978), and Everett Hughes's study of *French Canada in Transition* (1943). Hughes was one of the first urban sociologists to adopt the ethnographic approach, and his study of ethnic relationships in Cantonville, QC, remains one of the best known from this tradition. A member of the Department of Sociology at McGill University, Hughes observed how urbanization and the growth of new industries—run exclusively by English-speaking managers—affected the structure of local social relationships, work, church, government, and voluntary organizations in a traditional rural Quebec town. In the late 1930s, Hughes left McGill to become part of a new generation of sociologists at the Chicago School who focused on the ethnographic tradition. Ultimately, the observations of urban ethnographers would be instrumental in overturning the prevailing and relatively pessimistic view of community that had been established through the work of Wirth (1938) and the original Chicago School.

One example of the influence of the urban ethnographic tradition on the prevailing understanding of community can be found in the writings of William Foote Whyte's *Street Corner Society* (1943). In 1937, Whyte moved into an Italian-American 'slum district' in the eastern United States. 'Cornerville' was the pseudonym Whyte used to describe the neighbourhood that he would later reveal as Boston's North End. Whyte moved in with a local family, befriended local residents, and spent more than two years embedded within the community. By hanging out on the 'corner' with a group of local men and with the aid of his key informant, 'Doc', Whyte participated in the everyday life of the neighbourhood. His detailed observations revealed that contrary to the accepted notion of urban community as disorganized, role-oriented, and aloof, Cornerville had a complex social structure of supportive and enduring social relations. Neighbourhood friendships were formed early in life and remained important throughout the life course. Social relations were supportive, stable, trusting, and reciprocal. It would seem that Whyte had rediscovered community in the least likely of places, an area that most regarded as a poor, immigrant, urban slum.

Whyte was not alone in rediscovering community within urban neighbourhoods. In the late 1950s, Herbert Gans moved into a neighbourhood that bordered on Whyte's Cornerville, Boston's West End. Like Whyte, Gans was a participant observer; he and his family 'lived in the area, and used its stores, services, institutions, and other facilities as much as possible' (Gans 1962, 337). From outside appearances, the West End was very much a slum, full of old buildings with shabby exteriors. At the time, most assumed that areas like Boston's West End were terrible places to live. The choice to live in such a community was assumed to be an act of desperation,

a last alternative. In contrast, Gans discovered that *The Urban Villagers* of the West End enjoyed a rich social life, full of intense local kinship and friendship relations. While their houses were dilapidated on the outside, residents devoted considerable energy to improving and maintaining the interiors of their homes. The local Italian-American community maintained a number of local ethnic associations and close ties to the Catholic Church and enjoyed a rich public life in local bars and cafés. Living in the West End was a conscious choice, and very few had any intention of moving out of the neighbourhood and into the growing suburbs. The residents of the West End valued the dense urban environment in which their community was based. However, not everyone valued the West End or recognized the supportive environment that existed within its borders. Despite the cohesive social relations within the community, residents were not able to prevent their neighbourhood from being destroyed by the process of urban renewal. The West End was ultimately bulldozed and replaced by a series of luxury apartment buildings.

Suburbanization

While community had been rediscovered in urban neighbourhoods, a new social trend was emerging on the urban fringe: *suburbanization*, the growth of low-density, single-family residential communities on the outskirts of the central city. Mass-produced suburban housing first appeared in Canada in the late 1940s. Until that time, buildings in cities were typically placed close together or were directly attached; they were built to maximize space on a building lot and were within a relatively short distance of workplaces and most services. With the rise of the automobile and highway, it was possible to live farther from the urban core and for housing to be segregated from work and commercial areas. Expectations as to how this new urban form would affect social relations were expressed by writers, politicians, and sociologists with scepticism, if not deep pessimism.

A move to the suburbs was alleged to foster over-conformity, hyperactivity, anti-individualism, conservatism, momism, dullness and boredom, and status-seeking, as well as a host of specified psychological and social ills including alcoholism, sexual promiscuity, and mental illness (Popenoe 1977, 3).

Various concerns about social relationships in the suburbs were expressed. The mass production of homes meant that whole subdivisions were composed of nearly identical structures. The suburbs also tended to attract or exclude certain types of people based on occupation, income, religion, race, and ethnicity. The homogeneity of the environment and of those who moved to the suburbs was thought to produce conformity. Jane Jacobs (1961) felt that the densely constructed, mixed-use, diverse environments of the city offered the kind of safety and social contact that was not possible through suburban design. People who moved to the suburbs were thought to be searching for anonymity, exchanging community for privacy. Housewives were thought to be isolated and alone, cut off from traditional kinship and community ties. Some critics just found the suburban streetscape unattractive. A popular media image of the day was of a man lost, in search of his home among identical-looking suburban houses.

Ethnographic studies were important in using direct observation to identify the differences between suburban and traditional urban and rural life. One of the earliest suburban ethnographies was Seeley, Sim, and Loosley's study of the Toronto suburb of Forest Hill, *Crestwood Heights* (1956). Seeley et al. noted the important role that children played in the decision to move to the suburbs, particularly the emphasis that families who moved to the suburbs placed on their children's education. They also noted the loss of existing kinship, friendship, and institutional ties as a consequence of the suburban move, as well as the resulting importance of the automobile and new suburban institutions, such as schools,

clubs, and associations. While identifying significant differences in suburban lifestyles, the ethnographic tradition ultimately offered **empirical** observations that countered many of the early, pessimistic claims of suburban life.

Herbert Gans's (1967) study of *The Levittowners* is one of the best-known studies of suburban life. As with his study of Boston's West End, Gans moved to the New Jersey suburb of Levittown and lived there for two years. While living in Levittown, Gans participated in community activities, joined local organizations, and surveyed and interviewed local residents. Contrary to early concerns about suburbia, Gans found that the residents of Levittown were devoted to family life, were involved in intensive socializing with neighbours and between couples, and had high levels of participation in voluntary organizations. The suburbs did not cause psychological illness or other malaises. Instead, Gans found that those who moved to the suburbs came from environments that frustrated their desire for certain behaviours, such as apartment buildings that lacked sufficient neighbouring. People moved to the suburbs in the expectation that a suburban setting would support behaviours that they valued. Similarly, S.D. Clark found that people moved to Toronto's suburbs in the belief that suburban living offered possibilities that could not be achieved in the inner city (see Box 5.2). Not only was life in the suburbs not as damaging as originally predicted, but contrary to the view of human ecology, the suburban environment did not directly determine the behaviour of its residents.

William Michelson (1977) furthered Gans's observations about environmental choice with a detailed longitudinal survey of residential mobility in urban and suburban Toronto. Michelson found that people self-selected for neighbourhood and housing type based on stage in the life cycle and expectations for how different housing environments would support specific behaviours. While some degree of physical determinism might exist, people's behaviours were not directly determined by their environments. This conclusion played

Box 5.2 *The Suburban Society*

A pioneering study of the new phenomenon of suburbia was undertaken by S.D. Clark, first chair and founder of the Department of Sociology at the University of Toronto. Clark was critical of the human ecology of the Chicago School and was keenly aware that the study of suburban life was part of an ongoing debate about the changing nature of community.

> A generation ago, the student of American society, then in background truly a man of the country, could find in the big city all that was evil, depraved, and corrupt in the American way of life. . . . In the quarter century or so that has since passed, the student of American society has learned to love the city in the manner that he has long loved the country, and now it is suburbia, portrayed in terms of slavish conformity, fetish of togetherness, and craze for organization, which is set over against a romantic image of the city (Clark 1966, 4–5).

Clark studied 15 suburbs in the Toronto area. Together with his students, he conducted more than 1,200 interviews with residents and organizational leaders. The focus of Clark's work was as much on the decisions and trade-offs involved in moving to a suburb as it was on the social life that evolved in these new settings. Clark recognized that the majority of those who moved to the suburbs made the choice to do so in order to invest in behaviours that they could not support in the urban setting. For those who moved for these reasons, Clark found the suburban setting to be 'disturbingly healthy'.

One of the trade-offs that Clark focused on was the decision to leave behind neighbourhood friendship and kinship ties. Clark found that many previous neighbourhood relationships were lost as a result of the suburban move. The commute and the cost of long-distance telephone calls made the expense of regular contact too great. Still, Clark recognized that while many of these ties would be lost, suburbanites did manage to maintain social contact with ties that were spread out across the larger city. Sources for immediate aid and support were found nearby, while suburbanites kept in touch with kin and key friends from outside the area.

a significant role in reducing the dominance of the Chicago School's human ecology approach within the study of urban sociology.

Community and Social Networks

Urban ethnographic work rebutted the concerns of early urban sociologists that cities were a source of social disorganization. Still, in identifying the existence of supportive social relations, researchers failed to consider completely the concerns of early community theorists that a complex division of labour and the move to a modern urban industrial society had in some way affected community. The ethnographic focus on solitary relations in very specific localities—neighbourhoods and workplaces—ignored the existence of weaker social ties, non-clustered ties, and ties to those at a distance. In the late 1960s, urban sociologists began to address these concerns by examining social structure from a social network perspective.

Even though supportive social relations continue to exist in the neighbourhoods and workplaces of the modern urban environment, they are not of the folk-type community idealized by Tönnies. As explored by the human ecologists of the Chicago School, cities are extremely heterogeneous, residents are highly mobile, and people regularly come in contact with diverse others in a variety of social settings. The development of transportation and communication technologies, such as public transportation, the automobile, the telephone, and more recently the Internet, facilitate the formation and maintenance of social relationships at a distance. These technological changes have contributed to a decentralization of social relations. Indeed, most people have more friends outside their neighbourhood than within it.

The social network perspective explores the extent to which supportive social ties exist between individuals regardless of locality. In contrast to human ecology, which examines the relationship between people and their environment, **social network analysis** examines the relationships between social actors—people, organizations, and institutions. This perspective addresses the possibility that supportive social relations are physically dispersed, extend across multiple areas of activity, and are less dense in their structure than identified in previous models. Rather than looking at community in terms of groups—social relations clustered together based on a shared neighbourhood or workplace—community is defined as a network of social relations. In this perspective, community is no longer defined exclusively as a 'neighbourhood' but is what Melvin Webber (1963) referred to as 'community without propinquity': social affinity independent of shared place.

Subcultural Theory

In his 'subcultural theory', Claude Fischer (1975) explores why in the urban environment, social relations tend to be more physically dispersed, not neighbourhood-based. Contrary to Wirth's (1938) argument that the size, density, and heterogeneity of the modern city alienates individuals, Fischer suggests that it is precisely the urban environment's ability to attract diverse people that facilitates the formation of dispersed social ties. Individuals in the city have access to a large population, which enables them to seek out others

who have interests similar to their own, interests that they may not have been able to explore in small rural settlements and under the mechanical solidarity documented by Durkheim.

Georg Simmel, in his study of 'The metropolis and mental life' (1950 [1903]), noted that pre-modern society generally limited the size of people's social circles to kin, neighbours, and occupational guilds. The diversity of the urban environment frees the individual from what Simmel referred to as the 'the pettiness and prejudices' of rural life. In small settlements of highly interconnected others, beliefs that varied from those of the group would have been regarded as deviant and repressed in the absence of a critical mass of like-minded individuals. Thus, the size of the urban environment frees the individual to explore beliefs and interests that would not have been supported in a smaller setting.

Subcultural theory highlights the importance of social ties formed through shared interest and mutual identification rather than simply based on shared location. While subcultural theory does not exclude the idea that similar people are likely to live and participate in 'natural areas' (Park 1915), it does suggest that similarity of interest is more important in forming relations than similarity of setting.

Studying Social Networks

Social network analysis is a useful way to study community without assuming that it is confined to a local area. In studying social networks, researchers are concerned with *nodes* or *actors* and the *ties* between them. For example, in a study of community life among students, the students in a classroom could be considered network *actors* and a *tie* the presence of a relationship between any two students. While the focus of this chapter is on the social ties between people in urban communities, social networks can also be studied on a more macro level, such as those between countries or organizations.

In studying social networks, there are at least nine dimensions of network variation:

1. *Network size*, i.e., the number of actors in a network or the number of actors connected to the central actor under study.
2. *The frequency of contact* between actors.
3. *Spatial proximity* or availability of network members.
4. *Duration* of a social tie, i.e., how long one actor has known another actor.
5. The *multiplexity* of a tie, i.e., the number of different resources or types of support exchanged between actors.
6. *Density*, or the number of ties present within a network based on the total number possible.
7. *Range* or *diversity*, related to both the size and the heterogeneity of a network, which is a measure of network composition.
8. *Centrality*, a measure of actor or network control over the flow of information or resources.
9. *Tie strength*, i.e., the closeness or intimacy of a tie between actors.

Each dimension is accompanied by a theory, which attempts to explain the effect of a dimension on an outcome, and a method for observing and analyzing variation. Social network analysis is therefore both a theory and a method. An example of a social network theory is the 'Strength of weak ties' (Granovetter 1973). While we all can recognize the value of strong ties—close family members and close friends are a regular source of emotional and instrumental aid—Mark Granovetter argued that *weak ties*—social relationships that are not particularly close or intimate—play an important role in the flow of resources. Granovetter recognized that weak ties provide access to unique sources of information. In a network of strong ties, everyone is connected to everyone else, and as a result everyone has access to the same information. Weak ties can provide bridges between otherwise unconnected networks. These 'bridging ties' are a source of unique information, important in search processes, such as finding a job, and in mobilizing resources. For example,

Figure 5.1 Whole Network

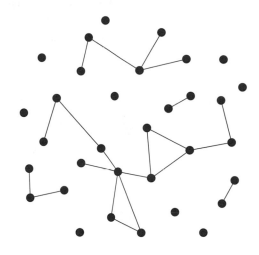

Granovetter pointed out that while Herbert Gans observed the cohesive qualities of Boston's West End, residents of the community were not able to organize collectively to prevent their neighbourhood from being destroyed by urban renewal. Granovetter argued that cohesive cliques in the community ensured that each person was tied to everyone else in his or her clique but not across cliques or to important outsiders. As a result, it was difficult for residents to share information, to mobilize resources, and to come together as a collective. Granovetter's theory of weak ties suggests that strong, cohesive social ties may be only part of what makes up a healthy, supportive community. In studying social networks, there are two ways to conceptualize a network, as a *whole network* or as a *personal community* (also called a personal or ego network). Whole networks (Figure 5.1) view community as 'aliens might view the earth's people: hovering above and observing the relationships linking all members of the population' (Wellman 1999, 18). Generally, it is possible to study whole networks only when all actors in a community can be enumerated (for example, a club, an organization, or the residents of a neighbourhood). To identify membership, boundaries must be imposed on a community, if not geographic boundaries then limits on what constitutes membership. Since whole networks have boundaries, important relationships can be missed if boundaries are mistakenly specified or key actors are excluded. This is the same problem that was experienced by those who adopted the urban ethnographic tradition—failing to consider the importance of ties outside the boundaries of a community.

Given the problems associated with examining community as a whole network, many community researchers adopt the personal community perspective. A personal community is defined from the standpoint of a focal individual, the ego. Those who study personal communities take a sample of people and compare the structure of their personal networks. Typically, a network analyst asks people a series of survey questions about those with whom they receive and give social support. Examples of studies of this nature include those of Barry Wellman (see Box 5.3) and Claude Fischer (1982).

Figure 5.2 is an example of a personal network. The ego's personal network is composed of social ties from a number of different areas: kin (immediate and extended), co-workers, neigh-bours, and other friends. The ego has a small number of strong ties and a greater number of weak ties (for simplicity, ties from the ego to each actor are not included in Figure 5.2). Kinship ties are a densely knit cluster in comparison to the ties between other personal network members. Few of the ego's social ties are crosscutting: neighbours do not know workmates, workmates do not know other friends, and friends generally do not know kin, and so on. The focus of personal networks on the provision of social support avoids the problems associated with defining community spatially.

Collective Efficacy

Despite the challenges of whole network studies, in recent years there has been a resurgence of interest in ecological, or spatial, influences and community. Social disorganization theory, first used by the Chicago School to explain the breakdown of local community as a result of urbanization, has been reformulated by Robert Sampson and his colleague into a theory of *collective efficacy* (Sampson and Groves 1989). Collective efficacy is defined as local social cohesion and the shared expectation for action (Sampson 2006). This theory has been most extensively used within the

Box 5.3 The Community Question

Barry Wellman's (1979) article 'The community question: The intimate networks of East Yorkers' examined the personal communities of residents in the Toronto borough of East York. Wellman conceptualized the debate about the impact on community of industrialization, urbanization, and a complex division of labour by developing the well-known concepts of community lost, saved, and liberated.

Wellman described the cumulative positions held by Tönnies, Durkheim, Milgram, the work of the Chicago School (e.g., Wirth 1938), and others who focused on the disintegration of community relations, as the 'Community Lost' perspective. Wellman argued that:

> Because of its assumption that strong primary ties naturally occur only in densely knit, self-contained solidarities, the argument has unduly neglected the question of whether primary ties have been structurally transformed, rather than attenuated, in industrial bureaucratic social systems (Wellman 1979, 1,204–5).

The 'Community Saved' argument runs counter to the Lost perspective. In the urban ethnographic tradition, the Saved perspective suggests that social solidarities, neighbourliness, and civic involvement continue to flourish in the urban setting. This argument recognizes that urban residents continue to have a need for social support and control. It also recognizes the importance of neighbourhoods and workplaces in the formation and maintenance of intimate, supportive, stable relationships.

The 'Community Liberated' argument accepts the underlying principles of both the Lost and Saved perspectives. Community in the modern urban environment has changed, but social support has not atrophied. Community is no longer directly associated with 'neighbourhood'; instead, supportive relations exist as a network that extends across distance and multiple sources of activity.

> The Liberated argument has developed out of the analytic juxtaposition of the Lost and Saved arguments. The Liberated argument affirms the prevalence and importance of primary ties but maintains that most ties are not now organized into densely knit, tightly bound solidarities (Wellman 1979, 1,206).

Wellman tested his hypothesis that community had been liberated in the modern urban setting with a survey of 845 adults in East York. Participants were asked to provide detailed information on the six people to whom they felt 'closest'. Consistent with the expectation that urbanites continued to have supportive social relations, 98 per cent of participants identified at least one 'close' social tie and 61 per cent listed five or more. Wellman found that people tend to maintain different social milieus, that friendship and kinship ties tended to cluster into groups with few crosscutting relationships. Wellman also found that the closest social ties were with kin (adult children, parents, and siblings) and then friends. When neighbours were identified at all, they were weaker in tie strength when compared to other ties. Few had more than one close tie with someone living within close proximity, although the majority of close ties were within Metropolitan Toronto. Contact with close ties was maintained principally through the use of the telephone, not through in-person contact. Where there were high levels of telephone contact, there were frequent in-person visits, and conversely so. Most important, East Yorkers could rely on members of their personal networks to provide them with help in emergency situations and in dealing with everyday matters.

Wellman's study of East York has become one of the most important contributions to the study of community. He demonstrated empirically that modern community consists of supportive, far-flung social networks. This realization has led to the acceptance of social network analysis as the preferred method and theory in the examination of community relations.

In the late 1970s, Wellman returned to East York to conduct in-depth personal network interviews (Wellman and Wortley 1990). The second East York study was one of the first to show the dispersed nature of community relations and that different kinds of relationships (parents, children, neighbours) provide different types of support (financial aid, companionship, emotional support). In 2004, Wellman returned for a third East York study to examine the impact of media use, specifically the Internet, on personal networks and household relations (Wellman et al. 2006).

Figure 5.2 Personal Network

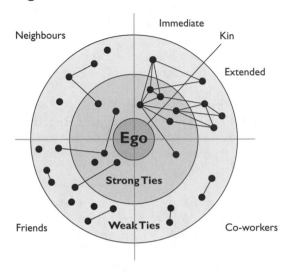

study of criminology in which the presence of collective efficacy has been associated with lower rates of crime and delinquency.

Collective efficacy recognizes that dense social networks are a measure of local social cohesion. Importantly, this perspective acknowledges that social ties vary in strength and does not argue that idealistic strong ties must dominate neighbourhood networks for social cohesion to be present. For social cohesion to enable social control, neighbours may not need to be friends. On the contrary, consistent with Wellman (1979), not only are intimate neighbour relations not the norm, but frequent neighbourly contact does not increase local surveillance, the formation of community norms, informal social controls, or community intervention in local disturbances beyond what is achieved through a minimal level of interaction (Bellair 1997). In fact, as explored by Granovetter (1973), the prevalence of dense, strongly tied, cohesive cliques may be indicative of local social structures that are focused on the exchange of resources important for daily survival but poorly organized for linkages to outside resources that are instrumental to successful collective action.

A central tenet of collective efficacy theory is that neighbourhood context matters for local network formation. Neighbourhood effects, such as the concentration of racial segregation, family disruption, and residential instability, have been found in the United States to undermine the formation of collective efficacy (Sampson 2006). Community-level instability constrains friendship choices and reduces local social cohesion. Areas with a concentration of disadvantage—neighbourhoods with high levels of poverty, unemployment, and racial segregation—are indicative of a context that has been found to predict low levels of collective efficacy and, in turn, high rates of crime and victimization. While segregation based on visible-minority status is less common and rates of violent crime are lower, similar neighbourhood effects pertaining to crime have been found in Canada as well (Oreopoulos 2003).

Social Capital and the Privatization of Community

The social network perspective has done much to demonstrate the persistence of supportive social ties; still, evidence suggests that over the past 30 years there has been a significant decline in community in terms of what has been called social capital. Social capital was first discussed in the study of community by Seeley, Sim, and Loosley (1956) in their Toronto study of *Crestwood Heights* and by Jane Jacobs in *The Death and Life of Great American Cities* (1961). However, it was not until the more recent work of Robert Putnam (2000) that social capital became a prominent concept within the study of community.

The definition of social capital remains a subject of considerable debate. Most sociologists recognize that *social capital* exists at both individual and group levels and that it is related to the ability to access resources through social networks. Putnam defines social capital along two dimensions, *bonding* and *bridging*. Bonding social capital is formed through the interaction of tightly

Table 5.1 The Decline of Social Capital

	Year	Change (%)
Number of club meetings attended per year	1975–99	−58
Number of times entertained friends at home per year	1975–99	−45
Served as an officer of a club or organization	1973–94	−42
Attended a public meeting on town or school affairs	1973–94	−35
Number of social evenings spent with someone who lives in the same neighbourhood	1974–98	−33
People who spend time in an average day on informal socializing	1965–95	−26

Source: Reprinted with the permission of Simon & Schuster, Inc., from *Bowling Alone: The Collapse and Revival of American Community* by Robert D. Putnam. Copyright © 2000 by Robert D. Putnam. All rights reserved.

knit networks. Communities high in this form of social capital tend to provide generalized social support and to be high in reciprocity, but they can also be repressive and tend to be racially, culturally, behaviourally, and ideologically homogeneous. While social capital is usually referenced in the context of its positive social benefits, the repressive, ostracizing, closed nature of bonding social capital can have negative effects for both groups and individuals. Bridging social capital, closely related to Granovetter's (1973) concept of weak ties, exists through access to diverse social ties that provide specialized social support and access to novel information and resources. Research has shown that individuals with more bridging social capital, which comes from participation in diverse social milieus, are more trusting, demonstrate greater social tolerance, cope with daily troubles and trauma more effectively, tend to be healthier, and have greater access to information and resources. Communities with high bridging social capital mobilize faster and are more successful in collective action.

In his book *Bowling Alone* (2000), Putnam provides evidence to suggest that recent generations in the United States are far less involved in both formal and informal community life than people were less than a half-century ago. People are spending less time with friends, relatives, and neighbours; they are more cynical and less trusting; and they are less likely to be involved in clubs and organizations. Table 5.1 provides a summary of some of the forms of community involvement that Putnam identifies as having declined in the last 30 years of the twentieth century.

There is still debate within the sociological community as to whether social capital has declined, or whether people are just engaging in different types of communities in new ways, and whether Putnam's observations can be generalized to Canada and the rest of the world. John Helliwell (2002) uses survey data to argue that social capital has declined in Canada. It remains higher than in the United States but is lower than what is found in Scandinavia. Helliwell also identifies important differences in social capital between Canada and the United States; in particular, American policies towards the assimilation of immigrant communities have led to lower levels of social capital than have Canadian policies of multiculturalism (Helliwell 2003).

According to Putnam (2000), there are a number of possible causes for the recent decline in social capital. They include suburbanization, globalization, changing family structures, racial and gender inequalities, the growth of the welfare state, and changing financial and temporal pressures. Putnam's evidence has led him to conclude that these factors account for very little of the social capital that has been lost. The two biggest contributors identified by Putnam, which he estimates to account for 75 per cent of lost social capital, are (1) generational change—i.e., the replacement of a heavily involved 'long civic generation' by their less-involved children and grandchildren—and (2) the growth of television.

By *generational change* Putnam is referring to the death of a generation born in the first third of the twentieth century, a generation that was far more involved in community life than generations born since. As this civic generation passes away, Putnam believes that social capital will continue to decline as more recent generations make up a greater proportion of the population. This trend is amplified, according to Putnam, by television. Putnam argues that time devoted to watching television has come at the expense of participation in other activities, primarily those that take place outside the home. Spending time in the home in front of the TV reduces exposure to other social settings and limits the formation of diverse social ties.

The trend of decreasing public participation in exchange for increasing private interactions is referred to as **privatism**. Concern over the movement of social ties from the public to the private realm originates at least as early as the Chicago School but is most prominently found in Richard Sennett's (1977) *The Fall of Public Man*, in Ray Oldenburg's (1989) discussion of 'third places', and in Lyn Lofland's (1998) *The Public Realm*. Privatism is closely tied to concerns over the implications of new technologies. As Putnam is concerned about the influence of television, Claude Fischer (1992) argues that the telephone has shifted communication out of public spaces and into the private space of the home. Similarly, an influential article by McPherson, Smith-Lovin, and Brashears (2006) identifies a significant shift over the past 20 years in the structure of people's core discussion networks. Using social network analysis, they found that the size of discussion networks has decreased by about a third, from a mean of 2.94 to 2.08, that personal networks are closer and more interconnected, and that networks contain fewer non-family members, particular those found outside of the immediate household. McPherson et al. concluded that a large social change, such as the introduction of the Internet and mobile phone, must be responsible for this dramatic change.

What are the potential long-term effects of declining social capital and increasing privatism? The decline in public activities has been met by a corresponding increase in private activities. People are increasingly likely to socialize in small groups in private homes rather than with large groups in public spaces. Divesting themselves of public participation by focusing on small-scale domestic interactions with close friends and family may mean that bridging social capital is being sacrificed for bonding social capital. People are forming closed, personal communities in exchange for diverse, broadly reaching networks of opportunity.

Community in the Network Society

The micro-technology revolution of the late twentieth century introduced a host of new technological innovations to the Western world, including the Internet, home computing, and mobile phones. Some argue that these new technologies have initiated the transition to a new form of society. Manuel Castells (1996), in his influential trilogy on the Information Age, refers to this new age as *the network society*. Within the network society, new information and communication technologies (ICTs) have facilitated a compression of space and time. It is increasingly easy to communicate in real time regardless of distance. The compression of space-time in the network society could be viewed as part of a historical trend. As the train, automobile, and telephone reduced the friction of space in the urban industrial city, the Internet further compresses time and space in the post-industrial city. It is easier for people to communicate across space, with less cost and in a shorter period of time. Castells argues that the network society is more than the next step in a historical trend; he suggests that a threshold has been reached, that a new social space has been created.

> Our societies are constructed around flows: flows of capital, flows of information, flows of technology, flows of organizational interactions, flows of images, sounds, and symbols. Flows are not just one element of social organization: they are the expression of the processes dominating our economic, political, and symbolic life . . . I propose the idea that there is a new spatial form characteristic of social practices that dominate and shape the network society: the space of flows. The space of flows is the material organization of time-sharing social practices that work through flows. By flows I understand purposeful, repetitive, programmable sequences of exchange and interaction between physically disjointed positions held by social actors (Castells 1996, 412).

According to Castells, in the network society we live in the 'space of flows' and not in the 'space of places' characteristic of earlier ages. People can communicate and share resources in real time across great distances as if they shared the same physical space. As with the transition from an agrarian to an urban industrial society, the transition to the network society has ignited a debate on the impact of societal change on community.

What's Old Is New Again: Community Lost or Saved?

Critics of the network society argue that new technologies, such as the Internet, contribute to an incomplete lifestyle that withdraws people from in-person contact and disconnects people from their communities. While new information and communication technologies originated too late to be responsible for the decline in social capital reported by Robert Putnam (2000), some argue that these new technologies exacerbate the trend towards privatism and community disengagement.

On the other side of the fence, with what should now be a familiar argument, are those who hail the community-expanding possibilities of computer-mediated communication. They contend that the Internet has created a whole new form of community, the **virtual community** (Rheingold 1993). Virtual communities refer to groups of people who use computer-mediated communication—typically the Internet—to form and maintain social relationships. Those who favour this position celebrate the transformative, space-liberating power of the Internet to connect people in supportive communities of interest. Ethnographic reports of life in virtual agoras hail the potential to rediscover—online—the densely knit, supportive communities 'lost' in the modern urban environment.

Will virtual communities fill the void left by the absence of 'traditional community'? Will people find relationships on-line that are more intense than those in the physical world? Will this redefine community, eroding the boundary between the 'real and the virtual, the animate and the inanimate' (Turkle 1997)? Will the space of flows be so immersive and fulfilling that people are lured away from 'real-life' community?

Studies of the Internet and Community

Concern for the loss of community—as a result of societal change in the forms of a complex division of labour and the transition from an agrarian to an urban industrial society and as a result of urbanization and suburbanization—was only curtailed as it was accepted that supportive community relations could be found outside of the local setting. Supportive community relations are not limited to specific places, nor are they limited to regular in-person encounters. Despite what the concept of 'virtual community' has done to highlight the potential for communities to form beyond the confines of geographic space, many who study new information and communication technologies have ignored the lessons of this earlier debate.

Barry Wellman and Milena Gulia (1999), in one of the earliest and most influential contributions to the study of the Internet and community, heavily criticize early speculation about the Internet and community as being manichean, presentist, unscholarly, and parochial. They argue that there was a tendency among scholars, politicians, and the mass media to:

- suggest that Internet use either destroys or saves community, ignoring more subtle transformative possibilities;
- treat the Internet as an isolated social phenomenon, failing to take into account how its use fits into other aspects of everyday life;
- ignore the long history of sociological debate about the transformation of community (e.g., Durkheim and Tönnies) and the methodologies of community studies (e.g., social network analysis).

As of 2007, 85 per cent of Canadians had access to the Internet, and they spent an average of 14.3 hours per week on-line (Ipsos-Reid 2007). As new ICTs have become increasingly embedded into everyday life, hype and speculation have been replaced by empirical studies of how the technologies of the network society influence the composition and maintenance of social networks. With few exceptions (e.g., Kraut et al 1998; Nie, Hillygus, and Erbring 2002), most research has converged on the finding that Internet use is associated with a high frequency of interaction with existing ties—on-line, on the telephone, and in person—as well as larger and more diverse social networks (Quan-Haase et al. 2002; Boase 2008). A 2006 study found that while the telephone remains the most common way for social ties to connect, in an average week Internet users send e-mail to a full 40 per cent of their closest and most significant social ties (Boase et al. 2006). E-mail use in particular appears to facilitate the expansion of social networks to include more weak ties (Zhao 2006; Miyata, Boase, and Wellman 2008). As new web technologies specifically geared to-wards social networking proliferate, it may become even easier to maintain personal networks. In 2007, 29 per cent of Canadians had a profile on a social networking service (Ipsos-Reid 2007) such as Facebook, and participation on these sites has been found to be associated with higher bridging social capital (Ellison, Steinfield, and Lampe 2007).

Local and Public Spaces in the Network Society

Some suggest that there may be a paradox in the space of flows (see Box 5.4). While new information and communication technologies may compress time and space, facilitating access to people and resources across distance, they may also facilitate very local interactions. A survey of 4,500 workplace Internet users in nine countries found that in France, Germany, Italy, and the US, one in every four e-mails never leaves the building in which it originates. More than 40 per cent of Internet users in Canada and the US reported that most of their e-mails travel no farther than across town (KRC Research 2003). E-mail may facilitate local interactions as much as it allows people to engage across distance. Still, the Internet is only one technology among many in the network society, and other technologies such as mobile phones may have other effects.

In some respect, wireless technologies such as mobile phones would appear to address the concerns of Putnam and others about the growth of privatism. Wireless devices increasingly bring social contact out of the home and into public spaces. Barry Wellman suggests that this may represent the rise of *networked individualism*, a shift from 'place-to-place' to 'person-to-person' interactions. Wireless communication 'shifts community ties from linking people-on-places to linking people wherever they are. Because the connection is to the person and not the place, it shifts the dynamics of connectivity from places—typically households or work-sites—to individuals' (Wellman 2001).

Mobile communication devices allow for instantaneous access to social network members;

Box 5.4 Netville

Netville was a pseudonym for a newly built middle-class neighbourhood of 109 single-family homes in suburban Toronto. It was one of the first residential communities in the world to be built with a telecommunications infrastructure that provided access to the Internet and a series of experimental information and communication technologies. The residents of Netville had free high-speed Internet service (10Mbps), a videophone, an on-line jukebox, on-line health care services, local discussion forums, and a series of on-line entertainment and educational applications. It was a model for the network society and what many envisioned to be the future in residential computer connectivity.

Netville provided an early opportunity to observe the effects of broadband Internet use on social relationships within an urban community. By studying Netville, it was possible to address the question of whether the technologies of the network society advance privatism, cutting people off from those around them, or whether they provide new opportunities for local social interaction. Combining the urban ethnographic tradition and social network analysis, in the fall of 1997, Keith Hampton moved to the neighbourhood of Netville to study the social networks of local residents. For two years, Hampton worked from home, attended local meetings, participated in on-line activities, and walked the neighbourhood of Netville, chatting and observing.

Hampton adopted a whole network perspective in the study of neighbourhood social relations. Residents were given a roster listing all other adult residents who lived in the local area. They were asked to identify those they recognized, talked to, visited, and communicated with over the telephone and by e-mail. A comparison of Internet and non-Internet users was facilitated by the presence of a demographically similar comparison group of non-wired residents.

Compared to non-Internet users, the wired residents of Netville recognized three times as many of their neighbours, talked to those neighbours twice as often, visited them 50 per cent more often, made four times as many local phone calls, and further boosted their local communication with neighbours through on-line exchanges (Hampton and Wellman 2003). When the personal networks of Netville residents were examined, the Internet was found to have facilitated few new long-distance exchanges in contact and support (Hampton and Wellman 2002). Since it focused on different types of social ties, not just the small number of 'strong' social ties in the average personal network, Internet use in Netville was found to be particularly useful in encouraging the formation of relatively weak local social ties.

As hypothesized by Mark Granovetter (1973) in his theory of 'The strength of weak ties', the presence of a large number of weak ties in Netville helped residents mobilize for collective action. As an ethnographer, Hampton had the opportunity to observe residents organizing local events—on- and off-line—and mobilizing to deal with community issues (Hampton 2003). Residents mobilized against the local housing developer to address problems they had with their newly constructed homes and against their Internet service provider when it was announced that they would be losing the free services with which they had been provided. Hampton observed that residents used their Internet connectivity to communicate and organize off-line events and their off-line meetings to plan future on-line interactions.

Why did the Internet, a technology that is supposed to facilitate distant communication, have such an impact on social ties within Netville? Hampton (2002) argues that Fischer's subcultural theory only partially accounts for why urban residents have few local social ties. A large, diverse urban population with subcultures that match every interest provides the motivation for people to form social ties outside of the local area. However, access is equally important in tie formation to the desire to find compatible social ties. Canadian neighbourhoods often lack opportunities for social contact. With local institutions such as clubs and organizations in decline (Putnam 2000) or geographically distant or absent from suburban settings, there are few opportunities for people to form local social ties. Internet services that provide forums for local communication provide an opportunity for people to meet locally based others suitable for friendship formation.

The findings of the Netville study were contrary both to utopian predictions about the space-liberating potential of the Internet and to dystopian concerns about the privatization of community. Indeed, contrary to predictions that computer-mediated communication would be most beneficial in increasing contact with distant social ties, the residents of Netville experienced the greatest increase in social contact with those who were nearby. Follow-up studies to the Netville project conducted in established suburban developments report similar findings: when residents use e-mail to communicate locally, they tend to experience an increase in the number of local weak social ties (Hampton 2007). In addition, a study comparing middle-class suburban with inner-city neighbourhoods located within a concentration of disadvantage—high levels of poverty, unemployment, and racial segregation—found that disadvantaged neighbourhoods had higher than expected collective efficacy when neighbours adopted e-mail as a means to communicate (Hampton, 2009). Hampton and Wellman have referred to the observation that the Internet can afford both global and very local interactions as *glocalization*.

aid and support are instantly accessible, anytime and any place. However, Rich Ling (2008), who has been studying mobile phone use in Norway, argues that by engaging with mobile devices in public spaces, people cut themselves off from public spaces by creating private spheres of mobile interaction. This private 'bubble' may reduce the likelihood of serendipitous public encounters and has been shown to contradict common expectations for public behaviour. Outgoing and incoming mobile phone calls divert attention away from co-present others. Moreover, the evidence suggests that mobile phones are primarily used to reinforce contact among existing social network members, particularly strong social ties. 'Those who have come into our sphere of friendship are always available' (Ling 2000).

In an increasingly mobile network society, the existing trend towards people socializing in small groups in private homes rather than with large groups in public spaces may be augmented by a new tendency to socialize remotely with small, tightly knit groups in any space, at any time. By divesting themselves of public participation, people may continue to sacrifice bridging in exchange for bonding social capital.

However, technology continues to change, and it is increasingly possible for people to connect electronically while on the go, not just using mobile phones but through mobile computing. Until recently, Internet use in North America was primarily confined to the home and workplace. However, with the advent of wireless Internet (Wi-Fi) and broadband mobile phone networks, the Internet is increasingly accessible in restaurants, coffee shops, and public spaces. Examples include the City of Toronto's municipal Wi-Fi network (spanning more than 235 city blocks), the City of Fredericton's *Fred e-Zone*, and the community wireless project *Île sans fil* in Montreal (Powell and Shade 2006).

Keith Hampton and Neeti Gupta (2008), in a study of wireless Internet use in cafés, found that while a shift in Internet use away from the home and workplace and into coffee shops is by definition a shift away from privatism, the majority of Wi-Fi users did not use their public presence for public interaction. Instead, many used the Wi-Fi café as an extension of the workplace, they actively resisted the public, and they attempted to erect barriers, physically in the form of inter-action shields and sociologically through their avoidance of gaze and verbal contact. The activi ties and interactions of Wi-Fi users in cafés were more private than public.

However, a study of wireless Internet use in seven public parks, plazas, and markets located in Toronto, New York, Philadelphia, and San Francisco found that mobile Internet users had very diverse social networks. Wireless Internet use within urban public spaces was found to afford interactions with existing acquaintances that were more diverse than those associated with mobile phone use. However, wireless Inter-net users interacted with fewer co-located others and were less involved in the public setting than most users of these spaces. Yet the activities that wireless Internet users engaged in while on-line were found to involve diverse social interactions and activities that build bridging social capital. The finding that young adults, who are, in gen-eral, less civically engaged than previous genera-tions, use wireless connectivity in urban public spaces to communicate with broad-reaching net-works and to consume and create information suggests that an infrastructure for wireless Inter-net connectivity within urban public spaces may have positive consequences for community and social capital formation (Hampton, Livio, and Sessions, in press).

Conclusion

At the end of the nineteenth century, Tönnies and Durkheim left us with a picture of traditional community life. Community, we were told, con-sisted of densely knit relationships with similar others involved in everyday, place-based inter-actions. The urban environment replaced tra-ditional, small-town life with a setting that was significantly larger, denser, and more heteroge-neous. While this new environment may have freed the individual from the repressive norms and values of smaller social settings, it was also argued that it replaced deep, personal connec-tions with formal, impersonal, secondary rela-tionships. The sociologists of the Chicago School interpreted this new environment as one that alienated the individual from those around her or him. It was not until the empirical observations of urban ethnographers that sociologists recog-nized that community endured in the city. The environment, it would seem, did not have the di-rect deterministic impact on social relations that sociologists of the Chicago School first believed. Modern social relationships are not of the densely knit, localized community recognized by Tönnies and Durkheim. In fact, community may never have been as local as Tönnies and Durkheim described. Communities consist of far-flung so-cial networks of kinship, workplace, friendship, neighbourhood, and interest group ties that to-gether form a social network. This network of relations provides aid, support, social control, and links to multiple social settings. Face-to-face contact is but one mode of social contact, in ad-dition to telephone, postal mail, e-mail, and other forms of communication that can be used in the maintenance of community relations.

Just as Tönnies and Durkheim recognized that the transition from an agrarian to a com-plex, urban industrial society would have an im-pact on community, we too recognize that our society is undergoing changes that may affect how we relate to those around us. There is some indication, in the work of Robert Putnam (2000) and others, that community may face new chal-lenges in the twenty-first century. Television and other technologies may promote a privatism that removes us from diverse networks of social ties important to community. Alternatively, technologies of the network society may provide opportunities to explore interests and connections that far exceed the diverse interactions offered by the urban environment. How the structure of our communities changes in the twenty-first century will ultimately depend on how the next generation of Canadians meets the challenges and innovations of the network society.

Study and Discussion Questions

1. Why has the concept of 'neighbourhood' been almost synonymous with the concept of 'community'? How has the emphasis on the study of locality within the study of community been problematic for understanding the structure of urban social relations?

2. The average person's social network consists of only a small number of broadly supportive 'strong' social ties. How many 'weak' social ties do you think an average person has? How might the availability of a large number of weak ties be an advantage? How might it be a hindrance?

3. Are face-to-face social relationships an essential element to community? Are they an essential element to giving and receiving social support?

4. How might the technologies of the network society increase the number of local, place-based social relationships? How might it decrease the number of local relationships?

5. Are there significant differences in the structure of American and Canadian communities? How would you conduct a study to find out? Discuss from both a spatial and a social network perspective.

6. Do you agree with Robert Putnam's assessment that television reduces social capital and leads to increased privatism? Do all types of television viewing have the same effects? What about home computers and Internet use?

Suggested Reading

Castells, Manuel. 1996. *The Rise of the Network Society*. Oxford: Blackwell. The first book in Castells's trilogy on the Information Age includes a discussion on the micro-technology revolution, the space of flows, and the rise of the new economy.

Gans, Herbert. 1967. *The Levittowners*. New York: Pantheon. An ethnographic study of life in the suburbs. It includes a detailed account of the ethnographic method.

Hughes, Everett. 1943. *French Canada in Transition*. Chicago: University of Chicago Press. An ethnographic study of the impact of urbanization and industrialization on ethnic and community relationships in small-town Quebec.

Putnam, Robert. 2000. *Bowling Alone: The Collapse and Revival of American Community*. New York: Simon and Schuster. This description of various indicators of social capital and historical trends over the twentieth century discusses why social capital is in decline, why we should care, and what can be done to reverse this trend.

Simmel, Georg. 1950 [1903]. 'The metropolis and mental life'. In *The Sociology of Georg Simmel*, 409–24. New York: Free Press. A classic essay on the transformation from rural to urban life and the impact of the urban environment on social relationships.

Wellman, Barry. 1999. *Networks in the Global Village*. Boulder, CO: Westview. An introduction to the social network perspective with a focus on studies of personal communities from around the world.

References

Anderson, Elijah. 1978. *A Place on the Corner.* Chicago: University of Chicago Press.

Bellair, P.E. 1997. 'Social interaction and community crime: Examining the importance of neighborhood networks'. *Criminology* 35 (4): 677–703.

Boase, Jeffrey. 2008. 'Personal networks and the personal communication system'. *Information, Communication and Society* 11 (4).

Boase, Jeffrey, et al. 2006. 'The strength of Internet ties'. Washington, DC: Pew Internet and American Life Project.

Castells, Manuel. 1996. *The Rise of the Network Society.* Oxford: Blackwell.

Clark, Samuel D. 1966. *The Suburban Society.* Toronto: University of Toronto Press.

Cooley, Charles. 1909. *Social Organization: A Study of the Large Mind.* New York: Scribner.

Durkheim, Émile. 1993 [1893]. *The Division of Labor in Society.* New York: Macmillan.

Ellison, N., C. Steinfield, and C. Lampe. 2007. 'The benefits of Facebook "friends"'. *Journal of Computer-Mediated Communication* 12 (4): article 1.

Fischer, Claude. 1975. 'Toward a subcultural theory of urbanism'. *American Journal of Sociology* 80: 1,319–41.

———. 1982. *To Dwell among Friends.* Berkeley: University of California Press.

———. 1992. *America Calling: A Social History of the Telephone to 1940.* Berkeley: University of California Press.

Gans, Herbert. 1962. *The Urban Villagers.* New York: Free Press.

———. 1967. *The Levittowners.* New York: Pantheon.

Granovetter, Mark. 1973. 'The strength of weak ties'. *American Journal of Sociology* 78: 1,360–80.

Hampton, Keith. 2002. 'Place-based and IT mediated "community"'. *Planning Theory and Practice* 3: 228–31.

———. 2003. 'Grieving for a lost network: Collective action in a wired suburb'. *The Information Society* 19: 417–28.

———. 2007. 'Neighborhoods in the network society: The e-Neighbors Study'. *Information, Communica-*

tion and Society 10 (5): 714–748.

Hampton, Keith. 2009. 'Internet use and the concentration of disadvantage: Glocalization and the urban underclass'. International Communication Association, Chicago, Il.

Hampton, Keith, and Neeti Gupta. 2008. 'Community and social interaction in the wireless city: Wi-Fi use in public and semi-public spaces'. *New Media and Society* 10 (5).

Hampton, Keith, Oren Livio, and Lauren Sessions. In press. 'The social life of wireless urban spaces: Internet use, social networks, and the public realm'. *Journal of Communication.*

Hampton, Keith, and Barry Wellman. 2002. 'The not so global village of Netville'. In Barry Wellman and C. Haythornthwaite, Eds, *The Internet in Everyday Life, the Internet and the Network Society,* 345–71. Oxford: Blackwell.

———. 2003. 'Neighboring in Netville: How the Internet supports community and social capital in a wired suburb'. *City and Community* 2: 277–311.

Helliwell, John. 2002. *Globalization and Well-being.* Vancouver: University of British Columbia Press.

———. 2003. 'Immigration and social capital: Issue paper'. In *2003 International Conference on the Opportunity and Challenge of Diversity: A Role for Social Capital.* Montreal: Government of Canada.

Hughes, Everett Cherrington. 1943. *French Canada in Transition.* Chicago: University of Chicago Press.

Ipsos-Reid. 2007. 'The 2007 Ipsos Canadian Inter@ctive Reid Report: Fact guide'. Toronto: Ipsos Group.

Jacobs, Jane. 1961. *The Death and Life of Great American Cities.* New York: Random House.

Kraut, Robert, et al. 1998. 'Internet paradox: A social technology that reduces social involvement and psychological well-being?' *American Psychologist* 53: 1,017–31.

KRC Research. 2003. 'Email use survey: Survey of "professional email users" in the UK, France, Germany, Italy, Spain, Denmark, Sweden, the United States and Canada'. London: Weber Shandwick.

Liebow, Elliot. 1967. *Tally's Corner*. Boston: Little, Brown.

Ling, Rich. 2000. 'Direct and mediated interaction in the maintenance of social relationships'. In A. Sloane and F. van Rijn, Eds, *Home Informatics and Telematics: Information, Technology and Society*, 61–86. Boston: Kluwer.

———. 2008. *New Tech, New Ties*. Cambridge, MA: MIT Press.

Lofland, Lyn. 1998. *The Public Realm*. New York: Aldine de Gruyter.

McPherson, M., L. Smith-Lovin, and M.E. Brashears. 2006. 'Social isolation in America'. *American Sociological Review* 71 (3): 353–75.

Michelson, William. 1977. *Environmental Choice, Human Behavior and Residential Satisfaction*. New York: Oxford University Press.

Milgram, Stanley. 1970. 'The experience of living in cities'. *Science* (March): 1,461–8.

Miyata, Kakuko, Jeffrey Boase, and Barry Wellman. 2008. 'The social effects of keitai and personal computer e-mail in Japan'. In James Katz, Ed., *Handbook of Mobile Communication Studies*. Cambridge, MA: MIT Press.

Nie, Norman, Sunshine Hillygus, and Lutz Erbring. 2002. 'Internet use, interpersonal relations and sociability: A time diary study'. In Barry Wellman and C. Haythornthwaite, Eds, *The Internet in Everyday Life, the Internet and the Network Society*, 215–43. Oxford: Blackwell.

Oldenberg, Ray. 1989. *The Great Good Places*. New York: Paragon House.

Oreopoulos, Philip. 2003. 'The long-run consequences of living in a poor neighborhood'. *The Quarterly Journal of Economics* 118 (4): 1,533–75.

Park, Robert. 1915. 'The city: Suggestions for the investigation of human behavior in the city environment'. *American Journal of Sociology* 20: 577–612.

Popenoe, David. 1977. *The Suburban Environment*. Chicago: University of Chicago Press.

Powell, Alison, and Leslie Regan Shade. 2006. 'Going Wi-Fi in Canada: Municipal and community initiatives'. *Government Information Quarterly* 23: 381–403.

Putnam, Robert. 2000. *Bowling Alone: The Collapse and Revival of American Community*. New York: Simon and Schuster.

Quan-Haase, Anabel, et al. 2002. 'Capitalizing on the Internet: Network capital, participatory capital, and sense of community'. In Barry Wellman and C. Haythornthwaite, Eds, *The Internet in Everyday Life, the Internet and the Network Society*, 291–324. Oxford: Blackwell.

Rheingold, Howard. 1993. *The Virtual Community: Homesteading on the Electronic Frontier*. Reading, MA: Addison-Wesley.

Sampson, Robert. 2006. 'Collective efficacy'. In Francis T. Cullen, John Paul Wright, and Kristie R. Blevins, Eds., *The Status of Criminology Theory*. New Brunswick, NJ: Transaction.

Sampson, Robert, and W. Byron Groves. 1989. 'Community structure and crime: Testing social disorganization theory'. *American Journal of Sociology* 94: 774–802.

Seeley, John, Alexander Sim, and Elizabeth Loosley. 1956. *Crestwood Heights*. Toronto: University of Toronto Press.

Sennett, Richard. 1977. *The Fall of Public Man*. New York: Knopf.

Simmel, Georg. 1950 [1903]. 'The metropolis and mental life'. In *The Sociology of Georg Simmel*, 409–24. New York: Free Press.

Tilly, Charles. 1988. 'Misreading, then rereading, nineteenth-century social change'. In B. Wellman and S. Berkowitz, Eds, *Social Structures: A Network Approach*, 332–58. Cambridge: Cambridge University Press.

Tönnies, Ferdinand. 1957 [1887]. *Community and Society*. C.P. Loomis, trans. East Lansing: Michigan State University Press.

Turkle, Sherry. 1997. *Life on the Screen: Identity in the Age of the Internet*. New York: Simon and Schuster.

Webber, Melvin. 1963. 'Order in diversity: Community without propinquity'. In J. Lowdon Wingo, Ed., *Cities and Space: The Future Use of Urban Land*, 23–54. Baltimore, MD. Johns Hopkins University Press.

Wellman, Barry. 1979. 'The community question'.

American Journal of Sociology 84: 1,201–31.

———. 1999. *Networks in the Global Village*. Boulder, CO: Westview.

———. 2001. 'Physical place and cyberplace: The rise of networked individualism'. In L. Keeble and B. Loader, Eds, *Community Informatics: Shaping Computer-Mediated Social Relations*. London: Routledge.

Wellman, Barry, et al. 2006. 'Connected lives'. In Patrick Purcell, Ed., *Networked Neighbourhoods*. Heidelberg: Springer.

Wellman, Barry, and Milena Gulia. 1999. 'Net-surfers don't ride alone'. In Barry Wellman, *Networks in the Global Village*, 331–366. Boulder, CO: Westview.

Wellman, Barry, and C. Haythornthwaite, Eds. 2002. *The Internet in Everyday Life, the Internet and the Network Society*. Oxford: Blackwell.

Wellman, Barry, and Scott Wortley. 1990. 'Different strokes from different folks'. *American Journal of Sociology* 96 (3): 558–88.

Whyte, William Foote. 1943. *Street Corner Society*. Chicago: University of Chicago Press.

Wirth, Louis. 1938. 'Urbanism as a way of life'. *American Journal of Sociology* 44: 3–24.

Zhao, Shanyang. 2006. 'Do Internet users have more social ties?' *Journal of Computer-Mediated Communication* 11 (3): article 8.

Chapter 6   Getting Perspective

How is inequality expressed in the form and structure of cities, and what issues does it raise?

Inequality is often most sharply visually available in cities. In urban places, an ironic thing takes place. On the one hand, because of sheer proximity, people are more likely to be aware of the existence of wealth or its absence. They see it in the places where people live, in the restaurants that they frequent because they are either too pricey or too cheap, in the mode of transportation that they choose, and in the type of work (or lack of work) that they encounter in other urban residents. It is from these observations that stereotypes are formed, statuses are developed, and stigmas are built. On the other hand, while people are easily made aware of these forms of inequality in cities, it is also in cities that a sorting-out process occurs, which reduces contact with people and places associated with different levels of inequality from their own.

Urban space is divided in ways that reflects inequalities. For example, the labelling of some areas as ghettos or slums is one way in which urban space is coded that separates certain population types (and especially the poor) and their activities and defines these places as problematic. Similarly, the presence of gates or security personnel helps to define other areas as exclusive and only for the wealthy. Middle-class persons may choose to flee the city into the suburbs as a mechanism for sanitizing their environments from people with characteristics different from theirs. Thus, ironically, even though in the city we are all brought closer together, we find ways of staying apart in a manner that reflects inequalities.

Sometimes, however, it is in central city urban spaces that inequalities encounter each other in a public way. For example, street culture makes us more aware of homelessness when we see people sleeping on sidewalks, in building corners, on heating grates, or in makeshift shelters. Aggressive panhandling might be encountered in the form of squeegee kids, or fear may be conjured up by the sight of street skinheads. Often in cities, the visibility of poverty leads people to associate poverty with older buildings, which are then demolished and replaced by gleaming new buildings, without regard for the loss of cheaper housing needed by the poor. Thus, in many ways, inequality is responsible for the way cities develop, since those with more economic resources organize themselves differently in urban space from those with less. Attempts to reduce the public expressions of inequality (e.g., loitering and panhandling bylaws), however, do not eliminate its less visible forms or even its existence altogether.

6 Urban Inequality and Urban Social Movements

Daniyal Zuberi

Learning Objectives

- To understand how inequality is experienced in Canadian cities.
- To discuss some of the causes and consequences of urban inequality.
- To critically examine the ways in which the wealthy and powerful protect and reproduce their privileges in cities.
- To study the ways in which people organize as part of urban social movements to protect their communities as well as to advance social justice or the common good.
- To discuss several examples of urban social movements in Canada and globally.

Introduction

Walking past the boutiques and upscale grocery stores of South Granville Street in Vancouver, you are surrounded by signs and symbols of privilege. The sparkling high-end luxury cars parked beside the sidewalk shimmer in the sunlight as window displays showcase the latest fashions. At the grocery store, everything is organic, free-range; even a bottle of mineral water can cost as much as $6, not including tax. This street features some of the top restaurants in Canada, where a romantic dinner for two can easily cost $300 or more. Continuing south on Granville Street, you enter Shaughnessy, one of the wealthiest neighbourhoods in Vancouver. The bucolic tree-lined streets curve elegantly; they rise gently and provide stunning vistas of downtown Vancouver and the North Shore mountains beyond. Originally designed as a suburb for the corporate executives of the resource industry, the Shaughnessy neighbourhood features elegant mansions with ornate landscaped gardens, many with four, five, or even six bedrooms and three-car garages. After years of rapid inflation in the housing market, the homes

in this area typically sell for $3 million or more. On a typical summer afternoon, Shaughnessy is extremely quiet, except for the occasional buzz of a lawnmower or leaf blower, usually operated by a hired landscaping assistant who certainly does not live in the neighbourhood.

In contrast, walking down East Hastings Street in Vancouver, only a few kilometres away, you find yourself entering one of the highest-poverty neighbourhoods in Canada: the Downtown Eastside. Once east of Cambie Street, you walk past boarded-up shops and crumbling buildings. You step over litter and broken glass, maybe even a crack pipe or a used syringe. Far from the elegant storefronts on South Granville Street, the few shops that remain include convenience stores with extensive security bars and grates on the windows and doors. Many of the other buildings are rundown **SRO (single room occupancy) hotels** that provide extremely low-cost housing featuring very small rooms, with shared kitchen and bathroom facilities, frequently infested by rats and roaches. The neighbourhood is far from quiet. To enter the building that houses Vancouver's Co-op radio, for example, you would probably have to ask a few drug addicts in the process of inhaling or shooting up to move aside so that you can ring the security intercom to be buzzed in. Men walk by with all their worldly possessions in rattling shopping carts. Others sleep listlessly on heating grates, in building alcoves, or on the sidewalk.

There are public services and institutions here, including the venerable Carnegie community centre and library and the controversial InSite supervised injection facility. If you turn left and head down towards the water, you will discover an area of abandoned warehouses and 'hungry ghosts' (Maté 2008) from which close to 100 prostitutes were lured and then brutally murdered by a serial killer. Throughout the Downtown Eastside, you can also see signs of gentrification, including the construction of a soaring condominium tower at the site of the former Woodwards department store.

Despite this gentrification initiative, the neighbourhood remains one of the poorest in Canada. Approximately 16,000 people live in the Downtown Eastside, and the average annual income is roughly $12,000. According to census data, approximately 30 per cent of the residents are of Aboriginal descent (Robertson and Culhane 2005). The HIV/AIDS infection rate is among the highest in the developed world. While it is estimated that a staggering 6,000 of the 16,000 residents regularly inject heroin, cocaine, or other drug combinations, the overwhelming majority are not drug-users or sellers. They include people living on social assistance or on disability or low pensions and the working poor (Robertson and Culhane 2005).

In both Shaughnessy and the Downtown Eastside, children make their way to school every morning, and adults venture out to earn a living or attempt to make ends meet. Yet the resources at hand for residents of these two neighbourhoods to realize their hopes and dreams differ dramatically even though they live just a few kilometres apart. This juxtaposition demonstrates the crux of urban inequality in Canadian cities: life is lived day by day at polar opposite ends of the urban metropolis. Every Canadian city features these wealthy and low-income neighbourhoods at two extremes of the socio-economic hierarchy: from Rosedale to Regent Park in Toronto, from Westmount to Pointe St-Charles in Montreal.

How is inequality experienced in Canadian cities? This chapter begins by describing some of the common measures used to examine inequality trends in Canadian cities. Then it delves into some of the current sociological research on urban inequality in Canada and internationally. It describes some research on the causes and consequences of urban inequality and how these factors manifest themselves in Canadian cities. Next, it explores some of the ways in which the wealthy and powerful organize to protect their privileges. Finally, it describes non-elite urban social movements and details some of the ways in which other people and groups, from disadvantaged workers to environmental community coalitions, organize to demand services and improve their communities.

Inequality in the City

Sociologists and urban scholars have had a long-standing interest in urban inequality. The city is increasingly becoming the spatial location where the wealthiest and poorest members of society coexist and interact. Globally, members of the elite work and live in major urban centres. Increasingly, the rural poor are relocating to cities in search of work and a better life. Today, the slums of the cities of the Global South swell with new migrants whose growing ranks currently comprise more than 1 billion people (Neuwirth 2006). These rapidly expanding slums are reshaping urban life—consider the now iconic image of a multinational CEO in Rio de Janeiro, Brazil, commuting daily by helicopter from his guarded, secure penthouse luxury apartment building to the roof of the shiny glass office tower across town, soaring over the crowded, dangerous, disease-ridden, and violence-plagued

Recently evicted from her downtown rooming house, a Vancouver woman fastens crack-cocaine pipes onto surgical tubing to prevent burning her lips while smoking. (Photo copyright © Ryan Koopmans. Reproduced by kind permission of the artist.)

favelas below. In this new urban dystopia, highly reminiscent of England's cities during the dawn of the Industrial Revolution, the wealthy and elite attempt to protect themselves and their growing assets from the burgeoning masses of urban poor (Davis 2007). Yet organizing and social activism happens on both sides of the socio-economic divide as residents of the slums also form coalitions and act politically to improve the quality of their lives and communities, fighting for basic property rights, sanitation, schools, and medical care (Neuwirth 2006).

As anyone who has recently visited an American city or watched the TV show 'The Wire' knows, the sharing of the city by the poorest and wealthiest in society is not reserved for the me-tropolises of the Global South. Walking down a major urban shopping street in a Canadian city means walking past BMWs and Gucci boutiques as well as people sleeping on the sidewalk. Indeed many of the trends in urban development—from rapid suburbanization and sprawl to the growth of gated communities—can only be understood in light of increasing levels of urban inequality. In Canada, it is in cities where millionaires live cheek-by-jowl with poor struggling single parents and the homeless. Yet very like North America in the early 1960s as described by Michael Harrington in his classic *The Other America* (1997 [1962]), the daily reality of the urban poor is both extensive and largely hidden, particularly among visible minorities.

Box 6.1 *Cuts to Social Welfare Increase Inequality in Vancouver*

In British Columbia, the freezing of social assistance benefit rates has increased the hardship and desperation of recipients in Vancouver. In addition, new eligibility rules have made it much more difficult for people in financial need to receive benefits. Based on in-depth interviews in the Vancouver region with welfare recipients, Klein and Pulkingham (2008) found that many were dependent on food banks and other charities to meet their basic needs. While approximately 77 per cent received food from a food bank, soup kitchen, or drop-in centre during the previous month, 43 per cent had done so 10 times or more. A shocking 46 per cent reported that they had often been hungry during the previous month. Of the women in the study, one-third experienced abuse by their partners, and several reported staying in these relationships for financial reasons. One-fifth reported engaging in prostitution or survival sex to make ends meet. Hardships and deprivation among the urban poor appear to be worsening in Vancouver.

Measuring Urban Inequality

What is inequality? How do sociologists measure inequality and inequality trends? Urban inequality can be measured and compared in several different ways, which often results in different understandings of the causes of and trends in urban inequality. Most scholars focus on *income inequality* as one important and easy way to measure inequality. Annual individual or household income is clearly one critical proxy to understanding well-being. Income is relatively easy to measure and compare across cities and even countries. One way to study urban inequality is to examine the differences in income between those at the top of the income distribution and those at the bottom. Sociologists and economists frequently employ standard measures like the P90/P10 ratio and the Gini Coefficient, which basically compare the level of income of the wealthiest with that of the poorest. Based on income inequality statistics alone, Toronto and Vancouver are the most unequal cities in Canada.

Many scholars also recognize, however, that these individual or household income measures are limited in terms of understanding urban poverty and inequality. They theorize that for those living in high-poverty neighbourhoods with many other poor households, the experience of being poor is different from what it is for people living in less poor neighbourhoods (Wilson 1996). Many urban scholars also compare the median household income in the wealthiest neighbourhoods to that in the lowest-income neighbourhoods. For example, Shaughnessy's median household income was $136,252 in 2001 compared to $15,647 for the Downtown Eastside community in Vancouver (Statistics Canada 2001).

Among urban sociologists, one common measure used to understand urban inequality is to examine the percentage of households living in poverty in order to assess whether a census tract should be considered as featuring *concentrated poverty*. Using this type of measure, neighbourhoods are considered high-poverty if more than 20 per cent of the households have incomes below the poverty line, while in extremely high-poverty neighbourhoods (or ghetto poverty neighbourhoods), 40 per cent of households have incomes below the poverty line (Wilson 1996). Research suggests that youth growing up in a poor household in an extremely high-poverty neighbourhood face even more serious barriers than those living in a lower-poverty neighbourhood.

Comparing the percentage of households with income below the **Low Income Cut-Off** (**LICO**) poverty line is very useful for understanding the extent of urban inequality. For example,

Box 6.2 *Understanding Urban Inequality*: The Need for a Multi-dimensional Approach

Based on ethnographic fieldwork in a gentrified Boston neighbourhood, Mario Small (2004) argues in his book *Villa Victoria* that urban inequality researchers must look beyond comparing quantitative data on census tracts to understand the process by which urban inequality is generated and reified in the city. Drawing on Pierre Bourdieu's concept of distinction and ethnographic evidence, he demonstrates how the well-off residents of a downtown Boston neighbourhood separate and isolate themselves from the urban poor living in public housing within their community. Landscaping, signage, doors, and other symbols demarcate which buildings are in the public housing complex and which belong to the wealthy living in the community. Different kinds of stores cater to different residents. Members of each group begin to stereotype the others as areas become 'no-go' zones for members of the other group. His research demonstrates that inequality operates at a micro level within neighbourhoods as well as across larger metropolitan areas.

in Vancouver, 79.8 per cent of the population lived in households surviving on incomes below the poverty line in the Downtown Eastside compared to 13.1 per cent in Shaughnessy. However, Canada has avoided the dramatic expansion of high and extremely high-poverty urban neighbourhoods that has occurred in many US cities. Fong and Shibuya found that while Canadian cities do not feature vast areas of blighted neighbourhoods, as is the case in many US cities, there were high levels of residential separation for visible minorities in selected Canadian cities (2000). While Canadian cities are experiencing greater levels of segregation, the neighbourhoods with high concentrations of visible minorities do not also feature extremely high levels of poverty (Walks and Bourne 2006). Yet there are many neighbourhoods in Canadian cities where a high proportion of families subsist on incomes below the poverty line, some of which are forced to choose between buying food or paying their rent on time (Hurtig 1999).

However, studying urban inequality only through the lens of income distribution leaves out some of the most important dimensions of inequality, especially if you are interested in understanding the social reproduction of urban inequality and the passing of privileges from the elite to their children or the disadvantages experienced by urban poor youth. Sociologists Melvin L. Oliver and Thomas M. Shapiro (2007), in their book *Black Wealth/White Wealth*, demonstrate that while the black/white income gap has somewhat declined in the US over the past several decades, much larger differences persist in terms of assets and wealth accumulated between white and African-American households (of which more than 60 per cent have no financial resources). This *wealth gap* is a legacy of the segregation and exclusion of African Americans from 'good neighbourhoods' as well as the protection of privilege by the wealthy, who pass on estates to their children. Inequalities in wealth are much greater than income inequalities. Wealth and assets—accrued through real estate, stocks, bonds, and savings—are transferred from one generation to the next. Despite some redistribution through taxation, generations of privilege and the historical legacies of exploitation live on in the transfer of resources from elite parents to their children.

Wealth inequality is an important dimension of urban inequality in Canadian cities. As real estate prices soar in major Canadian cities, it is often only with the help of large inheritances that younger Canadians, even professionals, are able to afford to purchase their first homes. What about those without high incomes or six-figure inheritances? They are simply priced out of the real estate market—one critical avenue to generating wealth and building a solid financial future. However, it is important to remember that forms of wealth vary: some assets are more liquid than others. Some households are wealthy in terms of income but struggle to make high monthly payments on their homes. Many elderly people, for example, theoretically benefit tremendously from the boom in real estate prices in Vancouver and Toronto. Yet if they are low-income seniors, they struggle to cope with higher property tax assessments.

While it is more difficult to access high-quality data on wealth inequality in urban areas, many sociologists argue that it is critical to go beyond comparing income statistics in order to begin to gain a multi-dimensional understanding of the dynamics of urban inequality, as well as of how these inequalities emerge and are reified. In other words, it is important to consider what advantages high income and wealth provide for the elite and how a lack of resources on top of a low income can result in hardship or limited opportunities.

Inequality also goes beyond income and wealth. Certain groups are disadvantaged in terms of access to the resources and opportunities in the city. For example, the visually impaired do not have the same ability to enjoy all of the city's resources and thus are in some ways socially excluded. In Canadian cities, specific groups or people are much more likely to be disadvantaged, including youth, the elderly, visible minorities, Aboriginals, transgendered people, homosexuals, and physically disabled individuals. For example, according to a City of Toronto staff report in 2006, 26 per cent of the 'outdoor' homeless in the city were Aboriginal (SSHA 2006). Although it is beyond the scope of this chapter to describe the various ways in which these groups are disadvantaged by unequal access and limited resources in Canada's cities, it is important to highlight the multiple and interacting dimensions in which inequality excludes them.

Explaining Urban Inequality Trends

Evidence suggests that high levels of inequality have deleterious consequences for a city. For example, countries with greater levels of income inequality also tend to have lower life expectancies than similar countries with more income equality (Kawachi and Kennedy 2002). Living in a high-poverty neighbourhood has been shown to be literally bad for your health. For example, Ross et al. found that among neighbourhoods in urban Canada, those with higher numbers of people with less than a high school education also had a higher average Body Mass Index (BMI), an indicator of greater levels of obesity (2007), and that across North America, higher levels of inequality are also associated with higher mortality rates (2000).

We also know that greater inequality in a city promotes *social exclusion* and reduces *equality of opportunity*. Yet inequality persists and is increasing in many Canadian cities. Why? Myles, Picot, and Pyper (2000) argue that urban inequality is worsening in many Canadian cities as a result of increasing economic segregation as well as the growth of income inequality between urban households (2000). That means that as rich people get richer compared to the rest of Canadians, they increasingly tend to live in neighbourhoods with other rich people, leaving poor people more geographically concentrated (*residential segregation*). So while the rich get richer, wealthier neighbourhoods also enjoy increasing income levels relative to poorer neighbourhoods in the same city (Heisz and McLeod 2004).

Part of the explanation for growing urban inequality includes 'macro' factors beyond the city level. For example, changes in the global economy are centrally important (Sassen 2001). The rise of neo-liberalism and cuts to social programs at the federal and provincial levels are also salient factors (Allahar and Côté 1998). Suburbanization and the flight of the middle class from city centres has also been identified as an important dynamic contributing to urban inequality (Wilson 1996).

Many of the wealthy do not need to physically leave the city to isolate themselves from the rest of the population. Although **gated communities**—communities that feature limited access by means of a gatehouse staffed by private security and surrounded by fences or other kinds of barriers—are not as extensive in Canada as in the United States, they are a growing phenomenon (Grant 2005). These communities tend to be homogenous in terms of social class and race. Their development is a visible symbol of inequality.

There are other signs of growing urban inequality in Canada. More than 25 per cent of inner-city census tracts in Canada experienced gentrification between 1981 and 2001, and while it changed the composition of who lives in inner-city Canada to include younger households with higher education and income levels, it did not increase the population of these central urban areas, instead contributing to decentralization in Canadian cities (Meligrana and Skaburskis 2005).

Saskia Sassen contends that urban inequality is likely to continue to increase globally as a result of shifts in technology and globalization (2001). In *The Global City*, she argues that advances in computer technology have facilitated a global re-ordering of production in which major cities will no longer necessarily be the sites of manufacturing—as they once were during Fordist industrialization—but rather the sites of producer services for increasingly complex and highly profitable transactions relating to the global economy. In this new economy, highly educated symbolic analysts—as described by Robert Reich in his book *The Work of Nations* (1992)—locate in major regional or international cities in order to provide the complex tax, insurance, and other corporate financial services necessary to underwrite the highly profitable needs of the new global economy. These cities provide the kind of density of social connections and expertise needed to create a competitive advantage in these new nodes of the global economy (Sassen 2001).

Based on this theory of globalization, major cities will experience greater inequality as these highly paid symbolic analysts are serviced by masses of immigrant and other poorly paid cleaners and service workers at the opposite end of the service sector hierarchy. While many in the service sector do indeed provide support and services for the elite (for example, those working in upscale hotels), many others—such as employees in the retail, food services, and health care sectors—provide services for other non-elite service workers. The consequences of these macroeconomic changes, coupled with cutbacks in government spending, negatively affected those with lower levels of education, particularly young black men in the US with less than a high school education, as manufacturing left city centres and relocated to suburban office parks, the US southwest, and overseas (Wilson 1996).

Inequalities in Urban Institutions

Some of the most important research on urban inequality has examined the deleterious consequences of inequality for the worst-off. Using a longitudinal ethnographic approach, including volunteer work in a low-income Boston area housing project, Jay MacLeod, in his *Ain't No Makin' It*, compares the experiences and fortunes of one group, the white 'Hallway Hangers', with another, the African-American 'Brothers' (2009). MacLeod examines the dynamics of these two groups over time and demonstrates how class inequality works to limit the social mobility of young men, even those with high aspirations.

In another important example, Elijah Anderson, in his classic books *Streetwise* (1990) and *Code of the Street* (1999), compares two neighbourhoods in Philadelphia. In the neighbourhood with extremely high poverty, Anderson finds that youth have to develop certain strategies and master 'codes' of behaviour, language, and stance to avoid becoming a victim of violence. You have

Box 6.3 *Hurricane Katrina*: *Urban Inequality and the Consequences of a Natural Disaster*

The horrific consequences of Hurricane Katrina for the city of New Orleans highlight the central role of urban inequality in understanding the outcomes of a natural disaster. Simply put, the wealthy of New Orleans escaped the most deleterious consequences of the hurricane. When the levees threatened to break, they piled into their cars, headed out of town to stay with friends or in a hotel, and returned to file insurance claims to repair the damage. Certainly they were inconvenienced, but almost all escaped alive with their families and loved ones and now are quickly returning to a normal life. Many of the wealthy lived in neighbourhoods where they were least at risk in the event of a hurricane.

On the other side of the wealth divide, the poor of New Orleans suffered and continue to suffer unspeakable tragedies in one of the wealthiest countries in the world. For all too many, the rupturing of the levees had the most severe negative outcome of all: more than 1,800 died as a result of the hurricane, many drowning because they did not own a car that could have easily brought them to safety. Urban residents dependent on public transportation had to wait to be shepherded into crowded evacuation facilities until water had already begun flooding the city. Of those who survived, many endured extreme discomfort and heartbreak during the evacuation and the weeks following. For example, many of these poor families were forced to abandon their beloved pets to drowning. As Naomi Klein describes in *The Shock Doctrine* (2007), while nurses gave mercy overdoses to immobile patients before abandoning them at the overwhelmed public hospitals that largely serve the poor, the wealthy—with generous private health insurance—continued to receive care and treatment in well-funded private hospitals and clinics in the city.

The consequences of inequality continue to shape the aftermath of this natural disaster. While the wealthy have been able to quickly rebuild and resume their lives, much of the damaged public housing for the poorest has been completely demolished and the residents permanently displaced, despite organizing and demonstrations by the former residents. For survivors who had little to begin with, the hurricane and rupturing of the levees cost them their homes and any opportunity to return. Political reforms that will probably disproportionately benefit the wealthy have also been rapidly implemented since the disaster. For example, the public school system has been privatized, with mass layoffs of unionized teachers in reforms that would have been unthinkable before the disaster (Klein 2007). New Orleans will never be the same city again. A natural disaster turned into the worst kind of manmade disaster for the poor of New Orleans.

to look tough and project confidence and street smarts. Unfortunately, in combination with racial stereotypes and discrimination, these very 'codes' make it even more difficult to secure living-wage employment in the formal economy, particularly for young men (Anderson 1990). The transformation away from the manufacturing economy in the US has undermined the social order of US urban ghettos. The traditional 'old head'—the senior male members of the community—have lost prestige and influence over youth as their own economic security has disappeared. Instead, an epidemic of crack cocaine swept into inner cities and created new 'role models' in the illicit economy (Anderson 1990). The decline in social organization creates new and almost insurmountable barriers for children growing up in poor neighbourhoods. Since the early 1980s, as manufacturing jobs have disappeared, there has been a rapid increase in imprisonment in the US, particularly of those convicted of non-violent drug crimes. A *carceral* state has emerged in which disproportionate percentages of African-American men have been imprisoned, often for non-violent offences (Wacquant 2007). Criminal records make it even more difficult to get jobs, furthering social exclusion. The collapse of the economy and rising levels of imprisonment have combined to make life even harder for blacks living in high-poverty urban neighbourhoods (Western 2006).

Despite having lower levels of urban poverty than the US, Canada has much higher poverty rates than many European countries. Indeed, all too many Canadians still suffer hardships from a lack of adequate resources for themselves and their families (Hurtig 1999). The economically disadvantaged in Canadian cities struggle to make ends meet. While some of the urban poor are not formally employed and rely on government programs for financial support, many low-income households have at least one formally employed person (Newman 1999). Unaffordable housing is increasingly becoming a problem for Canadian families, with growing numbers spending more than 30 per cent of their income on housing (Laird 2007). Increasing numbers of the financially worst-off Canadians live in shelters or on the street.

Evidence from the US suggests that the **working poor** can be worse off in terms of hardships than social assistance recipients. Based on their in-depth interviews with low-income families in Chicago and San Antonio, TX, Kathryn Edin and Laura Lein reported in their important book *Making Ends Meet* (1997) that working poor parents were actually worse off than similar public assistance recipients. They noted that in the survey data, low-income families tended to report greater expenditures than income. So they re-interviewed members of their sample until they could account for the source of every dollar spent by the household. They found that public assistance benefits

alone were too low for a family to make ends meet and that these payments were supplemented by a host of informal (and formal) economic arrangements, including bartering, child care, gifts, and employment. Although working in formal employment for or near the minimum wage provided more income than public assistance or welfare payments, the additional expenses of working—child care, transportation, clothing, and frequently health insurance—meant that these households experienced greater hardships in terms of being able to provide food and adequate clothing for their children. Indeed, in families not on public assistance, with a lone parent working close to full-time and earning about minimum wage, parents and children were going hungry and lacked adequate winter clothing.

Similarly in Canada, employment is increasingly no longer adequate protection against poverty, and many of the poor actually have part- or full-time jobs. The erosion of the Canadian safety net since the mid-1990s has increased the hardships of the working and non-working poor, while the incomes of the richest Canadians have been rising rapidly. Rising urban inequality is making housing unaffordable for more Canadians. Over the past several decades, **gentrification**, urban revitalization, and urban renewal schemes have reduced the amount of affordable housing available for low-income households in Canadian cities (Dear and Wolch 1993).

From a Comparative Perspective: The Mitigating Role of Public Investment

Given that Canada and the United States have undergone very similar shifts economically towards the dominance of the service sector as a result of globalization over the past 35 years, why have Canadian cities largely avoided the rapid expansion of high-poverty and extremely high-poverty neighbourhoods as observed in so many similar US cities?

Based on a comparison of national-level data from multiple sources in Canada, the United States, and Australia, sociologist Jeffrey Reitz's book *Warmth of the Welcome* (1998) demonstrates that social welfare, labour, and policy differences create the context for the differences in the way that new immigrants are incorporated into society in the three countries. Greater levels of inequality in the US means that immigrants to that country are more disadvantaged than similar immigrants to Canada, where there is a lower level of inequality.

Yet do these same national-level differences matter when we compare cities? Goldberg and Mercer (1986) describe several systemic differences between Canadian and US cities, including a greater role of government versus private interests in planning and urban development in Canadian cities. Others explicitly argue that there is much similarity between Canadian and US cities; for example, Reese and Sands (2007) argue that cities in Michigan and Ontario continued to use similar economic development policies from 1990 to 2005.

Despite some research pointing to certain similarities between Canadian and US cities, recent research demonstrates the important impact of policy differences on urban poverty and inequality. The book *Differences That Matter* carefully examines the role of differences in social welfare, labour, and other policies for explaining trends in poverty and inequality in Canada and the United States (Zuberi 2006). Based on in-depth interviews with 77 hotel employees who worked in the same jobs for the same multinational chains in Vancouver and Seattle, the findings reveal that differences in policies have an important impact on the quality of life and levels of hardship experienced by similar workers. *Differences That Matter* also argues that the greater levels of urban public infrastructure investment in community-based and universally available public recreation mitigates some of the deleterious consequences of increasing income inequality for Canadian cities compared to US cities. From equitable formulas for determining per-pupil school funding to high-quality community centres, local libraries, transit, and accessible, well-maintained parks, public investment improves the quality of life for the working poor in Vancouver as compared to that of their counterparts in Seattle (Zuberi 2006). Yet federal spending cutbacks since the mid-1990s onward in these kinds of programs have had serious consequences, increasing both hardship for the urban poor and inequality in Canada. For example, the number of homeless individuals reported during annual street counts in Canadian cities has increased dramatically over the past several years (Laird 2007).

While research highlights the importance of macro-level factors—including changes in the economy and government programs—for understanding urban inequality dynamics, many of the causes of urban inequality also occur at the local level. The ways in which groups mobilize in the city and in their communities also helps to shape the dynamics of urban inequality.

Urban Social Movements

You've worked hard and played by the rules. Attended university. Went to law school. Got married. Saved up. Had two children. Used your life savings as a down payment and took out a mortgage for a small house in the best neighbourhood in the city. A bedroom community with quaint single-family homes. The neighbourhood where your children would go to the best public schools. With nice parks. That you now love.

One morning, you get a flier in your mailbox. The city has purchased a large building on your favourite shopping street only a five-minute walk away. You had noticed that the building was for lease and had wondered what would replace the old gardening centre. A new upscale bakery? Wine boutique with the best of France? Instead, the flier tells you that the city plans to install a massive drug-treatment facility in the building. You are surprised. You start to worry. You read on.

You talk to your neighbour. Had she heard of the city's plans? She tells you about her friend on the east side whose house was broken into by addicts desperate for a fix. She also heard of another area where a treatment centre caused property values to go down as desperate owners were forced to sell and move.

You talk to your spouse about your fears. While you are all for drug treatment, you worry about the safety of your children. Will they be safe playing in the yard? Walking to school? You decide to attend the next residents' association meeting, where you find out that you are not alone in your concern. The president makes a speech: 'The community was not consulted in the city's decision.' 'It is not fair.' 'This kind of facility shouldn't be in anyone's backyard, certainly not mine.' The crowd gets roused up. 'What can we do?' someone asks. The president replies, 'We have to act now, we have to fight city hall to save our community.' The organizing begins. One committee strikes up a petition. The other prints fliers calling for a new meeting to 'Save Our Community'. Everyone is encouraged to write letters to the mayor, city councillors, and other representatives.

Someone at the meeting has a great idea. There is an all-candidates forum coming up in the election campaign for the next city council. 'Let's mobilize community members and show up to tell them how we feel about these plans for the drug-treatment centre and get them on record to prevent it from being built in our neighbourhood,' he says.

At the all-candidates forum, 300 people from the community show up. And they line up to speak. And every speaker talks about why the drug-treatment centre should not be opened. 'It should not be in any neighbourhood, but least of all in this community.' 'Why not use the space for seniors' housing and address a community need?' And so, in the face of a large elite crowd of voters, the candidates commit to working with the community to find another use for the space if they are elected. The drug treatment centre is never built in the community. Instead,

other sites, such as some in the poorest neighbourhoods (after all, that is where so many addicts live) are considered.

The city has always been a *site of collective action* where people and organizations wage campaigns to create social change. Much of the organizing for the peace movement, the women's rights movement, and the anti-poverty movement took place in the major global metropolises. These urban social movements continue today, focusing on a variety of issues and a diverse range of campaigns and tactics. Historically, social movement organizing has not always been to extend rights or to benefit the disadvantaged. The wealthy and powerful frequently mobilize to protect their privileges and their community. From NIMBYism to Business Improvement Districts (BIDS), these movements often elevate the interests of a powerful few over many. At the same time, in an increasingly global world, people and groups also organize at a local level to promote social justice, protect their communities, and create a greater good. In this dance of competing campaigns and often competing interests—in response to local and global forces—movements help shape the future of cities and society.

Reproducing Inequality: How the Wealthy and Powerful Organize to Protect Privileges

The wealthy elite in a city utilize their resources in order to advance their financial interests and protect their advantages. Harvey Molotch classically argues in an *American Journal of Sociology* article 'The city as a growth machine: Toward a political economy of place' (1976) that elites exert their influence on local governments to advance their own interests over competing interests, such as unemployed workers or other marginalized groups. With extremely high levels of urban inequality, the elite turn to an array of measures and tactics to protect their advantages. In *City of Quartz*, Mike Davis (1992) describes how these measures and tactics play out as 'class warfare at the level of the street' in Los Angeles, including the use of walled enclaves or gated communities, 'panoptic surveillance', and the militarization of the city in response to urban inequality.

In cities, the wealthy frequently form coalitions to lobby city council against perceived threats to their economic interests or community. For example, the scenario described in the previous section is based on what happened in Vancouver a few years ago. The community in this case—Dunbar—is among the wealthiest in the city. The Dunbar Residents Association mobilized 300 residents to attend a meeting of candidates for a future civic election to oppose the construction of a drug rehabilitation centre in their neighbourhood (CBC News 2005). The story received much media coverage at the time, and similar events have occurred time and again in Canadian cities throughout their histories.

The organizing of the elite to protect or advance their interests has further evolved in recent times. In the book *Sidewalk*, Mitchell Duneier (2000) describes how downtown business owners organize and fund Business Improvement Districts (BIDs) that focus on advancing their interests, which are often at odds with those of the street vendors he studied. For example, BIDs lobby for and encourage the enforcement of 'quality of life' policing initiatives to restrict street vending and busking. At one of New York's major train stations—Penn Station—these associations work with local business owners and police to 'evict' homeless people living in the station and sleeping on benches and in train cars. In Canada, business owners in downtown Vancouver along the Granville Street corridor have created a similar program, complete with paid 'ambassadors' who provide assistance to tourists and other potential customers in the downtown core. Beyond using ambassadors, these organizations work to promote the interests of business owners against others whom they see as creat-ing problems or hurting business; these others generally include those with less power, such as panhandlers, buskers, and street vendors.

While the wealthy often organize to protect their privileges, they also act politically to benefit financially. Developers lobby city council for easements on ordinances to build condo towers taller than allowed by city ordinances. Occasionally, city councils can use these exceptions to code to require developers to construct a social good, such as public waterfront walkways or social housing.

Some scholars argue that the elite also promote mega-events, such as Expo86 in Vancouver and the Olympics, in order to create highly profitable development and other business opportunities (Altshuler and Luberoff 2003; Hall 2006). Urban elites use these mega-events to create opportunities for rapid development and profit, without many of the normal checks and balances in place (Hall 2006).

Yet understanding how urban elites maintain their social position also requires studying how they utilize urban institutions in order to pass along their privileges. For example, public schools and public education are supposed to be an equalizing institution in cities, providing the same opportunity for all. Yet parents from different class backgrounds adopt different strategies to raise and educate their children. Based on in-depth qualitative research with 24 low-income and middle-class families, Annette Lareau (2003) identifies different class-related parenting strategies that have consequences for the long-term achievement of children. While middle-class parents with resources act as advocates by focusing on the concerted cultivation of their children through extra-curricular activities and their own active engagement in their children's schools, working-class and low-income parents focus on simply meeting the basic needs of their children—such as food, shelter, and safety—and expect teachers and public institutions to be responsible for their children's education. This trend disadvantages children of lower-income families,

Box 6.4 Broken Windows Theory vs Eyes on the Street

The response of the wealthy towards urban inequality tends to exacerbate the development of non-diverse communities and can challenge the vibrancy of city life. As classically argued by Jane Jacobs in *The Death and Life of Great American Cities* (1961), suburbanization and the increasing segregation of communities by class reduces the very diversity of urban street life that makes living in cities so wonderful. In her book, she promotes the power of the 'eyes on the street' as people with diverse backgrounds and resources occupy the same social space and watch out for each other, thus maintaining social order and limiting victimization of the marginalized. Greater levels of urban inequality challenge this admittedly utopian version of city street life. While Jacobs's writing was based on her experiences in Greenwich Village at the time, Mitchell Duneier, in his more recent study of African-American book vendors in Greenwich Village during the 1990s, argues that greater class and racial inequality has undermined the foundations of Jane Jacobs's vision for vibrant urban street life. In its place, a new paradigm, based on the broken windows theory, has emerged to support a new approach to policing and managing urban public space. In this new context of greater inequality, politicians, the elite, and police are encouraged to 'fix broken windows' and attack any signs of social disorder in order to discourage more serious violence (Duneier 2000). While many support the removal of graffiti and other physical signs of disorder, the application of 'fixing broken windows' policies to marginalized people seen as undesirable, such as the street homeless and vendors, threatens not only the rights of these disadvantaged people but the vibrancy of street life itself.

because the teachers generally hold middle-class expectations of parental involvement. So not only do wealthy and elite parents fundraise for special programs or facilities and thus advantage their children's schools over those located in poorer neighbourhoods, they also actively engage these urban institutions in order to pass along their own advantages to their children.

The US urban schools for the poorest—largely black and Hispanic—children feature security metal detectors at the schoolhouse doors, blast walls, crumbling infrastructure, metal chains locking plastic trash cans and even the toilet paper rolls to the wall, bars on windows, and a lack of supplies. The schools for the wealthiest in a metropolitan area—often private schools or extremely well-funded public schools in exclusive suburban enclaves—have sparkling, well-maintained buildings or campuses complete with the latest computer technology, including free access to Lexus/Nexus and Ebsco Academic

Search Premier. As detailed in the book *Savage Inequalities* by Jonathan Kozol (1992), these inequalities in educational institutions hobble inner-city poor youth at the starting gate, disadvantaging them in one of the few legitimate ways they have for achieving a larger piece of the economic pie. Educational inequities destroy equality of opportunity. Indeed, with the prevalence of the meritocratic myth in North American society, education translates systemic disadvantage into the kinds of outcomes that make people then blame themselves for their failure to advance.

In Canadian cities, with lower levels of racial segregation and sprawl as well as more equitable provincial school funding policies, inequalities among schools are less stark but still very real. The parents of children in the wealthy west side of Vancouver and in West Vancouver use their resources to raise funds for better equipment, programs, and facilities for their public schools than those of east side Vancouver public schools.

These schools then have greater resources to teach privileged students who actually require fewer resources, since their student body generally has lower levels of need.

Canadian public schools in poor urban areas face serious challenges and frequently lack the resources to address these needs. In many of these schools, libraries are only open part-time, such as three days a week. Arts and music programming is limited. Smaller problems are overlooked as resources are focused on students with serious learning or behavioural problems. Schools overwhelmed with needy children cannot sustain the program, counselling, or extra educational support required because of a lack of funds. Some even lack adequate supplies. These inequalities reproduce inequality in the city and block equality of opportunity; they set up the children of the successful to succeed and condemn the children of the urban poor to share the fate of their parents.

Urban Social Movements: How the Disadvantaged Organize to Improve Their Lives and Communities As Well As Rights and Services in the City

In cities, not only the wealthy and powerful organize to protect or advance their interests. People and organizations frequently form *coalitions* to pressure various levels of government, from city councils to local police, to *improve the quality of their lives and communities*. Sociologists have been interested in studying these movements and how they create social change. One classic example is the welfare rights movement in the United States as researched by Piven and Cloward in their seminal book *Poor People's Movements* (1978). Another classic by Manuel Castells, *The City and the Grassroots*, compares several urban struggles for community self-determination and political power (1984). Globally, several examples of

urban social movements and resistance are discussed in *Global Ethnography* by Michael Buroway et al. (2000) and in Peter Evans's *Livable Cities?* (2002). While some movements focus on radical protest to change the system, others focus more on capacity-building or work in partnership with the city and community to enact change, from constructing affordable housing to improving access for the disabled. Some emerge in response to external forces or local campaigns; others seek to bring together people from diverse backgrounds to promote common interests.

Often, urban social movements form to block perceived threats to a community or neighbourhood. These movements are not necessarily positive; witness the extensive organizing to attempt to prevent the integration of schools through busing in US cities during the late 1960s and through the 1970s. Yet many of these urban social movements have successfully preserved the character and quality of life for residents of certain neighbourhoods.

According to Hamel, Lustiger-Thaler, and Mayer (2000), understanding urban social movements requires going beyond the opposition between global elites and poor disenfranchised workers in cities. They categorize urban social movements today as including: those concerned with 'bread and butter' urban issues (traffic, sprawl); community-based organizations fighting to improve their communities; and other, broader movements to fight neo-liberal cuts to the welfare state.

In both Toronto and Vancouver, notable urban social movements blocked the construction of enormous highways that would have required the demolition of dynamic urban communities that thrive today. In Toronto, activist and urban scholar Jane Jacobs led the charge in the coalition to block the Spadina Expressway expansion that would have devastated her community (Wellman 2006). In 1971, the East Toronto Community Coalition organized a 'Stop the Spadina!' campaign and successfully lobbied to halt plans for an expressway that would

United We Can is a Vancouver charitable organization that promotes social and environmental improvement in the inner city. The program, which began in 1995 with the establishment of this bottle depot, offers recycling services to local businesses while providing employment opportunities and training to disadvantaged people living in the city's downtown. (Photo copyright © Ryan Koopmans. Reproduced by kind permission of the artist.)

have sliced through the heart of today's vibrant Chinatown community. Similarly in Vancouver, a coalition of environmental activists joined the Chinese community to prevent the demolition of the Strathcona neighbourhood by blocking the construction of a major freeway through the heart of downtown Vancouver. Today, a coalition of environmental groups in Vancouver has been less successful in their attempts to block the twinning of the Port Mann bridge and expansion of the freeway in Greater Vancouver south of the Fraser river (SPEC 2008).

Many of today's urban social movements focus on environmental and poverty issues. While these urban social movements sometimes occur at a city-wide level, at other times their cam-

paigns can be extremely local and focused on just one neighbourhood. For example, in east side Vancouver, parents and school officials have joined local community centres in efforts to prevent prostitutes and drug dealers from soliciting near school grounds. On the other hand, in some high-poverty neighbourhoods in the US, community leaders and politicians sometimes form unusual alliances with gang leaders in order to secure playground areas and other resources for community events and to mediate local conflicts (Venkatesh 2008).

Sometimes urban social movements succeed, and other times they fail. For example, a movement that attempted to prevent Vancouver from hosting the 2010 Winter Olympics failed to

Box 6.5 Tent City in Victoria

In the city of Victoria, BC, there are only 350 permanent shelter beds for a homeless population of approximately 1,500. Where do the homeless go? While many remain invisible, sleeping outside under bridges or in hidden coves, a small group of 10 homeless people set up a permanent camp in Victoria's Cridge Park (Koch 2008). Their forced eviction resulted in a court challenge and major victory for homeless rights advocates. On 14 October 2008, the BC Supreme Court declared that the municipal bylaw forbidding the construction of shelters on public spaces in Victoria was illegal and that the eviction of the homeless was a violation of their rights as protected by the Canadian Charter of Rights and Freedoms. As a result, new legislation allows homeless individuals to construct temporary shelters in Victoria parks through the night, from 9 pm to 7 am (Magi 2008).

The victory is far from complete. The mayor of Victoria opposes the court decision, for example, on the grounds of community opposition and public safety concerns (Koch 2008). Only two weeks after the court ruling, police removed daytime homeless campers and protesters from Victoria's Beacon Hill Park. As in the case of many homeless tent cities, police cited concerns about drug abuse, criminal activity, and environmental damage. Organizations such as Vancouver's Pivot Legal Society hope to challenge other urban bans on camping in public spaces. While they do not see this as a long-term solution to homeless problems, they hope that it will create pressure on municipalities to open more permanent shelter beds and begin to address some of the root causes of growing homelessness (Fong 2008).

garner enough votes at the ballot box to block the city's application. Advocates argued that the expense of hosting the Olympics took away from other critically important priorities, such as dealing with increasing rates of homelessness and child poverty and the need for increased transit infrastructure investment. On the other hand, environmental groups in Canada have successfully pressured municipalities across the country to ban the use of pesticides for cosmetic purposes.

Sociological research on urban social movements often describes the factors that contribute to their emergence and outcomes. Janet Conway describes how social movement activists and organizations in Toronto formed the Metro Network for Social Justice (MNSJ) to fight for social justice causes in the city. She documents their challenges in terms of organization and resources as well as how the coalition succeeded by responding to global shifts, including neo-liberal policies and program cutbacks. For example, the group joined forces with labour to fight cuts in social programs

implemented in Toronto by the provincial government under Mike Harris (Conway 2004).

Many urban social movements do not focus on a specific target or on blocking some initiative or policy. In many cities across Canada, capacity-building movements are innovating and changing urban life and development, from creating community gardens to bringing back streetcars, from car-sharing to the cooperative housing movement and the promotion of sustainable development. Newman et al. examine the role of social capital in a successful urban social movement that worked to create a temporary pedestrian-only zone in the Kensington market district of Toronto as part of a broader urban sustainable development initiative (2008). They found that involvement in the Streets Are for People! coalition and P.S. Kensington network both utilized and built on the social capital of participating members and organizations. In other cases, urban social movements focus on improving neighbourhoods. Anderson et al. (2005) found that community

Box 6.6 *Outsourcing of Hospital Workers and the Living Wage Movement in Vancouver and Victoria*

In 2004, as a result of BC provincial legislation, virtually all of the hospital support jobs in Vancouver and Victoria—including cleaning, maintenance, and food service work—were outsourced to major multinational companies. Thousands of workers were laid off, and those who were rehired now earned between $9 and $12 per hour as compared to approximately $18 before the outsourcing. Beyond the wage cuts, the workers in the new jobs complained of high levels of stress, inadequate training, and poor working conditions (Stinson, Pollak, and Cohen 2005). The Hospital Employees' Union (HEU) reorganized the workers and has negotiated a better collective agreement for these health care support workers, but they still earn far less than they did before. The union is working with First Call, a coalition of child care advocates and local community organizations, to raise awareness of the plight of workers who do not earn enough to make ends meet. The BC Office of the Canadian Centre for Policy Alternatives convened a living wage working group that included academics, union representatives, and anti-poverty activists to calculate a living wage for Vancouver and Victoria. The *Working for a Living Wage* report encourages employers to pay their workers a wage and/or provide benefits that will allow a two-parent family with two young children to make ends meet and be socially included. This hourly wage, $16.74 in Metro Vancouver and $16.39 in Greater Victoria, is much higher than the statutory minimum wage in BC, which has not been increased in several years (Richards et al. 2008). The process has helped to raise awareness of the struggles and hardships experienced by low-income families as well as bringing together a diverse coalition to improve the quality of life for the working poor in both cities.

development initiatives by a coalition funded by both public and private resources in the West Broadway neighbourhood of Winnipeg helped to improve older housing, although it also resulted in some gentrification.

In the United States, a growing immigrant rights movement saw millions of people march in Los Angeles (Milkman 2006). Unions have begun organizing immigrant workers—including janitors in a successful Justice for Janitors campaign (see Hamel et al. 2000) and, more recently, domestic workers. Labour movements pushing for a living wage have successfully promoted legislation in many US cities and in the UK and are now beginning to do the same in Canada as well. The UNITE HERE union's Hotel Workers Rising! campaign has targeted multinational corporations and seeks to improve the economic fortunes of low-wage workers in Canada and the United States (Zuberi 2007). Other campaigns

target the low-wage employers themselves, often singling out the biggest corporation: Wal-Mart. People have organized to prevent the construction or opening of new Wal-Mart stores in hundreds of municipalities across Canada and the United States (Sprott 2005).

These new urban social movements are based on a resurgence in 'community-based unionism' that involves coalitions between labour unions and grassroots community groups in order to mobilize people in disadvantaged communities to advance social justice causes and force concessions from elites. The movements work to build a *sense of efficacy and power* while improving the lives of citizens and neighbourhoods. In cities, the complex reality of Canadian multiculturalism is enacted every day, creating opportunities for participatory politics (Wood and Gilbert 2005). As global, national, and local forces create challenges and opportunities for city residents, new forms and coalitions of social action promise to help shape the destiny of Canadian cities.

Conclusion

There is nothing inevitable about globalization in terms of increasing urban inequality. At the same time, global trends are towards greater urban inequality, unless corresponding policy reforms and infrastructure investment serve to improve the lives of those disadvantaged by economic changes. Without a strengthened social safety net, more families will fall through the cracks and suffer hardship as urban inequality increases. Inequality research demonstrates that greater inequality is not only detrimental for the poor but for society more generally as well.

Similarly, cities featuring high levels of inequality are less pleasant to live in. They are less safe. Public infrastructure tends to be neglected as the wealthy and privileged organize to maintain their own advantages. While the elite sometimes literally physically flee to incorporated suburbs, particularly in the US where this type of sprawl has been heavily subsidized by the government, at other times they simply create gated communities within the city, using fences, gates, and security intercoms to separate themselves and their families from the masses of their fellow citizens.

Growing urban inequality not only threatens equality of opportunity but also challenges the basic principles of democracy predicated on equal rights and equal treatment. While the urban elite organize and act politically to maintain advantages and resources, people and groups also organize to protect their own communities as well as to advance social justice and the common good through urban social movements. These competing movements enliven urban life and help residents to shape the future of their cities.

Study and Discussion Questions

1. How do sociologists measure urban inequality?
2. What dimensions of urban inequality do you think are most important?
3. Describe some of the negative consequences of urban inequality.
4. How does urban inequality in Canadian cities compare to that in American cities?
5. What are some of the causes and consequences of urban inequality?
6. What kind of policies or programs would reduce urban inequality?
7. Who joins urban social movements, and why?
8. Describe some examples of how the wealthy or elite lobby to protect their privileges in a Canadian city.
9. What kinds of causes have people and organizations campaigned for in urban social movements in Canada?
10. What tactics do urban social movements use to promote their causes?

Suggested Reading

MacLeod, Jay. 2009. *Ain't No Makin' It: Aspirations and Attainment in a Low-Income Neighborhood*. 3rd edn. Boulder, CO: Westview Press. MacLeod's classic book provides rich insights into the challenges facing low-income youth in highly unequal urban America. He follows the lives of two groups of urban poor youth—one African-American and one white—as their hopes and dreams meet the barriers and reality of blocked opportunity.

Newman, Katherine S. 2000. *No Shame in My Game: The Working Poor in the Inner-City*. New York: Vintage. This award-winning book challenges the notion that all of the urban poor lack work in the formal economy. It provides a thoroughly researched portrait of the lives of fast-food workers in inner-city New York and the immense challenges they face making ends meet and getting ahead in a new urban economy dominated by low-wage service sector jobs.

Neuwirth, Robert. 2006. *Shadow Cities: A Billion Squatters, A New Urban World*. New York: Routledge. Neuwirth transports the reader into the rapidly expanding urban slums of the metropolises of the Global South. This book provides a critically important perspective for understanding urban inequality trends from a global perspective.

Robertson, Leslie, and Dara Culhane. 2005. *In Plain Sight: Reflections on Life in Downtown Eastside Vancouver*. Vancouver: Talonbooks. A collection of seven life stories of people living in Vancouver's Downtown Eastside neighbourhood, this book challenges stereotypes and provides an important perspective on the lives of the disadvantaged in a Canadian city.

Wilson, William J. 1996. *When Work Disappears: The World of the New Urban Poor*. New York: Knopf. This classic text in urban sociology provides statistical and qualitative evidence to link changes in the economy, racial discrimination, and declines in social support to the expansion and deepening of urban poverty in American cities over the past 30 years. Wilson concludes this influential work with a call for political organizing to promote common causes and policy reforms, including increasing the minimum wage, early childhood education, and public sector jobs for the unemployed.

Zuberi, Dan. 2006. *Differences That Matter: Social Policy and the Working Poor in the United States and Canada*. Ithaca, NY: Cornell University Press. This book contrasts the fortunes of room attendants and other hotel workers who work for the same hotel chains in Vancouver and Seattle. The book reveals that social policy differences in labour, health care, social welfare, and urban infrastructure development result in higher levels of hardship and lower quality of life for the Seattle employees as compared to their Vancouver counterparts. The book includes policy recommendations for improving the lives of low-income service workers in these cities and a call for urban social movement organizing.

References

Allahar, Anton L., and James E. Côté. 1998. *Richer and Poorer: The Structure of Inequality in Canada*. Toronto: Lorimer.

Altshuler, Alan, and David Luberhoff. 2003. *Megaprojects: The Changing Politics of Urban Public Investment*. Washington: Brookings Institution.

Anderson, Ayoka, et al. 2005. 'Social investment in the inner-city: Community and capital in West Broadway, Winnipeg'. *Canadian Journal of Urban Research* 14: 8–31.

Anderson, Elijah. 1990. *Streetwise: Race, Class and Change in an Urban Community*. Chicago: University of Chicago Press.

———. 1999. *The Code of the Street: Decency, Violence, and the Moral Life of the Inner-City*. New York: W.W. Norton.

Buroway, Michael, et al. 2000. *Global Ethnography: Forces, Connections, and Imaginations in a Postmodern World*. Berkeley: University of California Press.

Castells, Manuel. 1984. *The City and the Grassroots: A Cross-Cultural Theory of Urban Social Movements*. New edn. Berkeley: University of California Press.

CBC News. 2005. 'Residents oppose rehab centre in Vancouver neighbourhood'. http://www.cbc.ca/canada/british-columbia/story/2005/11/08/bc_rehab-meeting20051108.html.

Conway, Janet M. 2004. *Identity, Place, Knowledge: Social Movements*. Halifax: Fernwood.

Dear, Michael J., and Jennifer Wolch. 1993. 'Homelessness'. In Larry S. Bourne and David F. Ley, Eds, *The Changing Social Geography of Canadian*

Cities, 298–308. Montreal and Kingston: McGill-Queen's University Press.

Davis, Mike. 1992. *City of Quartz: Excavating the Future in Los Angeles*. New York: Vintage.

———. 2007. *Planet of Slums*. Reprint edn. New York: Verso.

Duneier, Mitchell. 2000. *Sidewalk*. New York: Farrer, Strauss, and Giroux.

Edin, Kathryn, and Laura Lein. 1997. *Making Ends Meet: How Single Mothers Survive Welfare and Low-Wage Work*. New York: Russell Sage Foundation.

Evans, Peter, Ed. 2002. *Livable Cities? Urban Struggles for Livelihood and Sustainability*. Berkeley: University of California Press.

Fong, Eric, and Kumiko Shibuya. 2000. 'The spatial separation of the poor in Canadian cities'. *Demography* 37 (4): 449–59.

Fong, Petti. 2008. 'Police break up Vancouver's tent city: New bylaw rushed in after court rules earlier shelter ban was unconstitutional'. *Toronto Star*. http://www.thestar.com/News/Canada/article/519783.

Goldberg, Michael A., and John Mercer. 1986. *The Myth of the North American City: Continentalism Challenged*. Vancouver: University of British Columbia Press.

Grant, Jill. 2005. 'Planned responses to gated communities in Canada'. *Housing Studies* 20: 273–85.

Hall, Michael C. 2006. 'Urban entrepreneurship, corporate interests and sports mega-events: The thin policies of competitiveness within the hard outcomes of neoliberalism'. *The Sociological Review* 54: 59–70.

Hamel, Pierre, Henri Lustiger-Thaler, and Margit Mayer. 2005. 'Urban social movements: Local thematics, global spaces'. In Jan Lin and Christopher Mele, Eds, *The Urban Sociology Reader*. New York: Routledge.

Harrington, Michael. 1997 [1962]. *The Other America: Poverty in the United States*. New York: Scribner.

Heisz, Andrew, and Logan McLeod. 2004. *Low-Income in Census Metropolitan Areas 1980–2000*. Ottawa: Statistics Canada.

Hurtig, Mel. 1999. *Pay the Rent or Feed the Kids: The Tragedy and Disgrace of Poverty in Canada*. Toronto:

McClelland and Stewart.

Jacobs, Jane. 1961. *The Death and Life of Great American Cities*. New York: Vintage.

Kawachi, Ichiro, and Bruce P. Kennedy. 2002. *The Health of Nations: Why Inequality Is Harmful to Your Health*. New York: New Press.

Klein, Naomi. 2007. *The Shock Doctrine: The Rise of Disaster Capitalism*. Toronto: Knopf Canada.

Klein, Seth, and Jane Pulkingham. 2008. 'Living on welfare in BC: Experiences of longer-term "expected to work" recipients'. Vancouver: Canadian Centre for Policy Alternatives, BC Office. http://www.policyalternatives.ca/documents/BC_Office_Pubs/bc_2008/bc_LoW_summary_web.pdf.

Koch, David G. 2008. 'Victoria allows homeless to sleep in parks'. *McGill Daily* 98 (13). http://www.mcgilldaily.com/article/5164-victoria-allows-homeless-to-sleep.

Kozol, Jonathan. 1992. *Savage Inequalities: Children in America's Schools*. New York: Harper Perennial.

Laird, Gordon. 2007. 'SHELTER—Homelessness in a growth economy: Canada's 21st century paradox'. Calgary: Sheldon Chumir Foundation for Ethics in Leadership. http://www.cbc.ca/canada/story/2007/06/26/shelter.html.

Lareau, Annette. 2003. *Unequal Childhoods: Class, Race, and Family Life*. Berkeley: University of California Press.

MacLeod, Jay. 2009. *Ain't No Makin' It: Aspirations and Attainment in a Low-Income Neighborhood*. 3rd edn. Boulder, CO: Westview Press.

Magi, Kim. 2008. 'UVic students host tent city forum'. *Martlet*. http://martlet.ca/article/5970-uvic-law-students-host-tent.

Maté, Gabor. 2008. *In the Realm of Hungry Ghosts: Close Encounters with Addiction*. Toronto: Knopf Canada.

Meligrana, John, and Andrejs Skaburskis. 2005. 'Extent, location, and profiles of continuing gentrification in Canadian metropolitan areas, 1981–2001'. *Urban Studies* 42: 1,569–92.

Milkman, Ruth. 2006. *LA Story: Immigrant Workers and the Future of the U.S. Labor Movement*. New York: Russell Sage Foundation.

Molotch, Harvey. 1976. 'The city as a growth machine: Toward a political economy of place'. *American Journal of Sociology* 82 (2): 309–32.

Myles, John, G. Picot, and W. Pyper. 2000. 'Neighbourhood inequality in Canadian cities'. No. 160. Ottawa: Statistics Canada.

Newman, Katherine S. 1999. *No Shame in My Game: The Working Poor in the Inner City*. New York: Alfred A. Knopf/Russell Sage Foundation.

Newman, Lenore, et al. 2008. 'Sustainable urban community development from the grassroots: Challenges and opportunities in a local street initiative'. *Local Environments* 13: 129–39.

Neuwirth, Robert. 2006. *Shadow Cities: A Billion Squatters, a New Urban World*. New York: Routledge.

Oliver, Melvin L., and Thomas M. Shapiro. 2007. *Black Wealth/White Wealth: A New Perspective on Racial Inequality*. New York: Routledge.

Piven, Francis Fox, and Richard Cloward. 1978. *Poor People's Movements: Why They Succeed, How They Fail*. New York: Vintage.

Reese, Laura A., and Gary Sands. 2007. 'Making the least of our differences? Trends in local economic development in Ontario and Michigan'. *Canadian Public Administration* 50: 79–99.

Reich, Robert B. 1992. *The Work of Nations: Preparing Ourselves for 21st Century Capitalism*. New York: Vintage.

Reitz, Jeffrey G. 1998. *Warmth of Welcome: The Social Causes of Economic Success for Immigrants in Different Nations and Cities*. Boulder, CO: Westview Press.

Richards, Tim, et al. *Working for a Living Wage: Making Paid Work Meet Family Needs in Vancouver and Victoria*. Vancouver: Canadian Centre for Policy Alternatives, BC Office.

Robertson, Leslie, and Dara Culhane. 2005. *In Plain Sight: Reflections on Life in Downtown Eastside Vancouver*. Vancouver: Talonbooks.

Ross, Nancy A, et al. 2000. 'Relation between income inequality and mortality in Canada and in the United States: Cross sectional assessment using census data and vital statistics. *British Medical Journal* 320 (7,239): 898–902.

———. 2007. 'Body Mass Index in urban Canada: Neighborhood and metropolitan area effects'. *American Journal of Public Health* 97: 500–8.

Sassen, Saskia. 2001. *The Global City: New York, London, and Tokyo*. 2nd edn. Princeton, NJ: Princeton University Press.

Small, Mario. 2004. *Villa Victoria: The Transformation of Social Capital in a Boston Barrio*. Chicago: University of Chicago Press.

SPEC. 2008. 'Stop Highway 1 expansion'. http://www.spec.bc.ca/project/focusarea.php?focusID=25.

Sprott, Greg. 2005. *Wal-Mart: The High Cost of Low Price*. New York: Disinformation Company.

SSHA (Shelter, Support and Housing Administration of Toronto), General Manager. 2006. 'Street needs assessment: Results and key findings'. Toronto: City of Toronto Staff Report. http://www.toronto.ca/housing/streetneeds.htm.

Statistics Canada data. 2001. Accessed at http://www.city.vancouver.bc.ca/commsvcs/Census2001/Shaughnessy03.pdf and http://www.city.vancouver.bc.ca/community_profiles/downtown_eastside/documents/DowntownEastsideDemographics.pdf.

Stinson, Jane, Nancy A. Pollak, and Marcy Cohen. 2005. *The Pains of Privatization: How Contracting out Hurts Health Care Workers, Their Families and the Health Care System*. Vancouver: Canadian Centre for Policy Alternatives, BC Office.

Venkatesh, Sudhir. 2008. *Gang Leader for a Day: A Rogue Sociologist Takes to the Streets*. New York: Penguin Press.

Wacquant, Loic. 2007. *Urban Outcasts: A Comparative Sociology of Advanced Marginality*. London: Polity Press.

Walks, R. Alan, and Larry Bourne. 2006. 'Ghettos in Canada's cities? Racial segregation, ethnic enclaves, and poverty concentration in Canada's urban areas'. *The Canadian Geographer* 50: 273–97.

Wellman, Barry. 2006. 'Jane Jacobs the Torontonian'. *City and Community* 5 (3): 217–22.

Western, Bruce. 2006. *Punishment and Inequality in America*. New York: Russell Sage Foundation.

Wilson, William J. 1996. *When Work Disappears: The World of the New Urban Poor*. New York: Alfred A. Knopf.

Wood, Patricia K., and Liette Gilbert. 2005. 'Multiculturalism in Canada: Accidental discourse, alternative vision, urban practice'. *International Journal
of Urban and Regional Research* 29: 679–91.

Zuberi, Dan. 2006. *Differences That Matter: Social Policy and the Working Poor in the United States and
Canada*. Ithaca, NY, and London: Cornell University Press.

———. 2007. 'Organizing for better working conditions and wages: The UNITE-HERE! Hotel Workers Rising campaign'. *Just Labour* 10: 60–73.

Chapter 7 *Getting Perspective*

How are Canadian cities being transformed by immigration?

If there was a time when immigrants primarily came to Canadian cities because they were stopping-off points to settlement in rural and small-town communities elsewhere in the country, that is certainly not the case today. Some immigrants had always chosen to settle in Canadian cities, even though most might have moved on, but now virtually all immigrants settle in cities, especially in the largest cities.

There are three major implications of this settlement pattern. First, cities that receive immigrants are becoming quite different from those that do not receive immigrants on such a scale. Cities that receive immigrants are growing faster and becoming much more diverse than those that receive relatively few immigrants. Thus, Canada's largest cities are developing a character considerably different from that of the rest of Canadian society. At one time, residents of rural areas and of cities had similar ethnic backgrounds, but today many new immigrants to cities come from different countries and represent quite different cultures from those of long-time residents.

The second implication of the recent swell in immigrant residents to a selective number of Canadian cities is that it raises the issue of *residential segregation*—that is, the spatial clustering of ethnic/racial groups. If people choose to live in the same area as others with a common culture, it is called *voluntary segregation*. If they are forced by lack of financial resources or discrimination to live adjacent to others of the same cultural group, it is called *involuntary segregation*. Whether the spatial clustering of a group is voluntary or involuntary is often a complex matter, but it is usually considered most problematic when an ethnic/racial group is segregated not just as an initial launching point for integration into a city but when a clustering represents a permanently depressed class producing the infamous ghetto.

The third implication of recent immigration is that it often contributes to the colour and diversity of a city through the creation of *ethnic villages*. Although the term 'ethnic ghetto' usually has a negative connotation, 'ethnic villages', on the other hand, are often viewed as quaint but robust contributions to urban life. Not only are they unique gathering places for persons of a particular group, but they are also valued by outsiders for their unique stores and restaurants. This is a very different concept of segregation, for the ethnic village may primarily be a centre for retailing and leisure consumption. Urban residents and planners often debate whether ethnic/racial clustering or segregation is a good thing and should be encouraged or whether dispersion is a better option.

7 Immigration and Race in the City

Eric Fong

Learning Objectives

- To understand that most Canadian cities have a large proportion of immigrants.
- To understand why most recent immigrants have settled in the major Canadian cities.
- To appreciate the consequence of increasing racial and ethnic diversity in major Canadian cities as a result of immigration.
- To note the economic attainments of immigrants and understand recent explanations for the patterns.
- To understand theoretical frameworks and empirical findings regarding racial and ethnic residential patterns in Canada.
- To understand the supply and demand perspectives of ethnic business development.

Introduction

If we stroll along the streets, take public transportation, and dine in restaurants in major Canadian cities, it is not unusual to hear someone next to us speaking another language. As we drive around these cities, we see vibrant ethnic communities with ethnic shops and churches, often with signs in foreign languages. If we park our cars and walk into these ethnic shops, it is not difficult to find ethnic newspapers for sale and bulletin boards full of information about activities organized by ethnic voluntary organizations, meetings of ethnic religious institutions, and promotion of ethnic products sold by ethnic businesses. Without doubt, major Canadian cities are experiencing unprecedented growth in racial and ethnic diversity, which is largely a result of immigration. Immigrants and their adaptation process have become integral components of understanding Canadian cities.

In the years from 1980 to 2006, about 5.2 million immigrants arrived in Canada (Citizenship and Immigration Canada 2003b; 2008).

The foreign-born population represented about 20 per cent of the total Canadian population in 2006. In other words, there are on average two immigrants among every 10 Canadians we meet. The immigrant representation is even higher in urban areas. About 29.5 per cent of residents in the 11 largest Canadian cities are foreign-born (Chui, Tran, and Maheux 2007; Statistics Canada 2007). Obviously, major Canadian cities disproportionately attracted immigrants.

In the following sections, we will trace the history of immigration in Canada and examine how the racial and ethic composition of cities has evolved over the years as a result of immigration. We will then discuss the settlement patterns of immigrants, the diversity of the city, and the socio-economic backgrounds of immigrants. This information provides a glimpse of the immigrant situation in cities and serves as background to the discussion of three important topics related to immigration and the city: economic attainments of immigrants, race and ethnic residential patterns, and ethnic businesses.

Figure 7.1 Number of Immigrants to Canada, 1860–2006

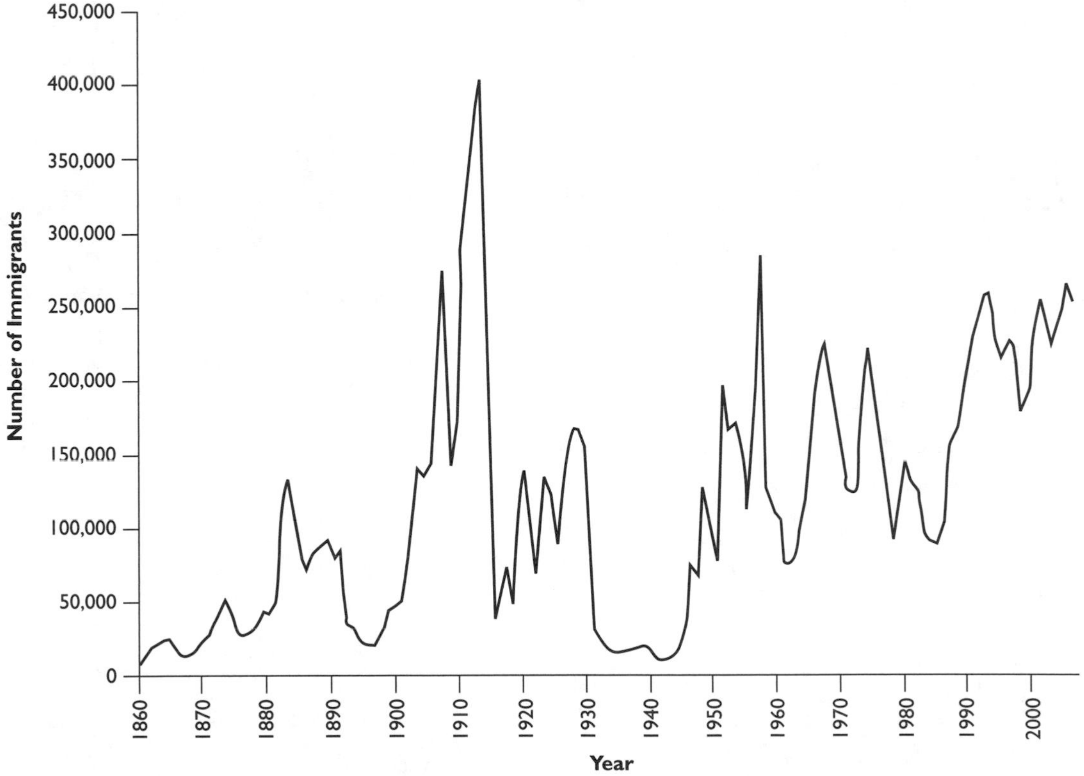

Source: Facts and Figures 2002, Immigration Overview, Immigration-Historical Perspective (1860–2002), Citizenship and Immigration Canada (http://www.cic.gc.ca/english/pub/facts2002/immigration/immigration_1.html); Facts and Figures 2006: Immigration Overview-Permanent and Temporary Residents (http://www.cic.gc.ca/english/resources/statistics/menu-fact.asp#2006)

History of Immigration

Canada is a country of immigrants. About 13 million immigrants arrived in this country in the twentieth century. A large number of them arrived in Canada at the beginning of the last century. Between 1900 and 1929, more than 1 million immigrants came to Canada each decade (Citizenship and Immigration Canada 2003a). In the 1910s alone, Canada received up to 1.9 millions immigrants (Figure 7.1). The flow of immigrants slowed down in the 1920s and 1930s. However, the number of immigrants once again increased in the 1950s. Between the 1950s and 1980s, more than 1.2 million arrived in Canada each decade. Most recently, in the 1990s, more than 2.2 million immigrants arrived, the largest number in any decade since the nineteenth century (Citizenship and Immigration Canada 2003a). During the first six years of the new millennium, about 1.4 million immigrants settled in Canada (Citizenship and Immigration Canada 2008).

Throughout the history of immigration in Canada, people from different parts of the world arrived in the country in different time periods.

Table 7.1   Major Sources of Immigrants to Canada by Periods of Immigration

	1926–45	1946–55	1955–66
British Isles	47.8	34.1	32.9
Northwestern Europe	24.4	30.2	20.7
Central and eastern Europe	19.1	15.1	7.7
Southeastern and southern Europe	4.5	15.3	29.9
Jewish	3.4	3.5	2.2
Asian and other origins	0.8	1.7	6.5
	1966–1970	**1971–1975**	**1976–1980**
British and Republic of Ireland	25.2	16.4	14.1
United States of America	11.4	14.3	9.9
Northern and western Europe	15.8	6.8	6.8
Central and eastern Europe	1.8	1.4	2.3
Southern and southeastern Europe	22.8	15.6	8.8
Israel	0.8	0.6	0.9
Australia	2.6	1.7	1.4
Asia			
South, Southeast, and East Asia	9.4	20.7	31.7
Middle East and North Africa	2.1	2.3	4.8
All others	8.1	20.2	19.3

Source: Kalbach 1987, 93.

In the early years of the last century, from the 1920s to the 1940s, most immigrants came from the British Isles and northwestern European countries. British immigrants comprised 48 per cent of those who arrived between 1926 and 1945. These immigrants were followed by northwestern Europeans, who represented 24 per cent of the immigrants in the same period (Table 7.1). Together, they represented 72 per cent of all immigrants who arrived during that period. The majority of these immigrants settled in the West, especially on the Prairies.

The number of immigrants from southern and southeastern Europe grew during the period before and after World War II. Their percentage rose from 4.5 per cent of all immigrants between 1926 and 1945 to 30 per cent between 1955 and 1966. Large numbers of them came from Italy

and Greece. At the same time, Asian immigration also increased, rising from less than 1 per cent between 1926 and 1945 to 7 per cent between 1955 and 1966 (Kalbach 1987).

While the number of new southeastern and southern European immigrants gradually declined after the mid-1960s, the number of Asian immigrants rapidly increased. The Asian population in Canada grew considerably in the 1970s and 1980s. The percentage of Asian immigrants among all immigrants rose from about 7 per cent between 1955 and 1966 to 32 per cent in the next 20 years.[1] With a continuing influx of Asian immigrants, immigration from non-European countries has dominated recent immigration trends. As a result of these waves of immigration from different regions of the world, Canada has become a multi-ethnic society.

Table 7.2 shows the regions from which immigrants came between 2000 and 2006. Immigrants from the Asia and Pacific region clearly dominate, followed by immigrants from Africa and the Middle East. Immigrants from the Asia and Pacific region comprised about 50 per cent of the immigrants who arrived in Canada each year. Immigrants from the traditional sending areas—the United States, Europe, and the United Kingdom—represent only about 20 per cent of total annual immigration (Citizenship and Immigration Canada 2003b). This pattern has been consistent for six consecutive years. To further illustrate, Table 7.3 indicates the percentage of immigrants from major sending countries from 2000 to 2006. These countries are predominantly non-European. With the increasing number of immigrants from non-European countries, Canadian cities are becoming more racially and ethnically diversified.

Where Immigrants Settle

Most immigrants at the beginning of the last century did not settle in cities. Considerable numbers resided in rural areas. As Canada experienced urbanization, immigrant settlement patterns reflected the general population distribution at the time. Their settlement pattern began to shift towards cities in the middle of the twentieth century.

However, recent immigrants have not settled evenly throughout Canadian cities. The majority have chosen to settle in large cities. They are attracted to the availability of jobs there and to the possibility of ethnic networks. A large proportion of recent immigrants have settled in the five largest Canadian cities: Toronto, Vancouver, Montreal, Ottawa-Gatineau, and Calgary. Together, these five cities held 77 per cent of those who immigrated to Canada between 2001 and 2006 (Chui, Tran, and Maheux 2007). In some cities, such as Toronto and Vancouver, because large numbers of recent immigrants have settled there, the immigrant population represents a substantial proportion of the city population. For instance, the immigrant populations of Toronto and Vancouver were 46 per cent and 40 per cent respectively in 2006 (Chui, Tran, and Maheux 20007). The percentages in these two cities are higher than they are for other major immigrant-receiving cities in other countries, such as Sydney, Australia, with 32 per cent, Los Angeles with 35 per cent, and the New York metropolitan area with 28 per cent (Chui, Tran, and Maheux 2007).

Although recent immigrants are highly concentrated in a few major cities, a cursory check suggests that most Canadian cities have large proportions of immigrants. Immigrants comprise at least 17 per cent of the population in the 10 largest Canadian cities, with the exception of Quebec City (Statistics Canada 2008). Despite the high concentration of recent immigrants in a few cities, the relatively high representation of immigrants in most cities suggests that earlier immigrants settled in a larger set of cities (Statistics Canada 2008). Nevertheless, not all cities have high proportions of immigrants. Cities in eastern Canada and in Saskatchewan have a smaller share of immigrants. For example, cities in the Maritimes and Quebec have low percentages of immigrant population—Saint John, Halifax, and Sherbrooke have only 4.2 per cent, 7.4 per cent, and 5.6 per cent, respectively (Statistics Canada 2008). The uneven distribution of recent immigrants in the major cities suggests that some cities face issues related to immigrant adaptation more than others do (Figure 7.2).

Racial and Ethnic Composition in Cities

Given that immigrants from different countries have arrived throughout the history of Canada and that each group has demonstrated a unique settlement pattern, the racial and ethnic composition varies from city to city. Table 7.4 presents the distribution of the six largest ethnic groups in

Table 7.2 Immigration by Source of Regions, 2000-2006

	2000		2001		2002		2003		2004		2005		2006	
	Number	%	Number	%	Number	%	Number	%	Number	%	Number	%	Number	%
Africa and the Middle East	40,821	18	48,097	19	46,113	20	43,678	20	49,531	19	49,275	21	51,861	21
Asia and Pacific	120,552	53	132,792	53	118,899	52	113,735	51	114,577	53	138,054	49	126,474	50
South and Central America	16,954	7	20,137	8	19,417	8	20,349	9	22,255	8	24,636	9	24,302	10
United States	5,815	3	5,902	2	5,288	2	6,013	3	7,507	2	9,262	3	10,943	4
Europe and the United Kingdom	42,888	19	43,225	17	38,841	17	37,569	17	41,902	17	40,908	18	37,946	15

Source: Facts and Figures 2002: Immigration Overview, Citizenship and Immigration Canada (http://www.cic.gc.ca/english/pub/facts2002/immigration/immigration_5.html). Reproduced with the permission of the Minister of Public Works and Government Services Canada, 2009.

Table 7.3 Major Countries Where Immigrants Came From, 2000–2006; Facts and Figures 2006: Immigration Overview—Permanent and Temporary Residents

	2000		2001		2002		2003		2004		2005		2006	
	Number	%	Number	%	Number	%	Number	%	Number	%	Number	%	Number	%
People's Republic of China	36,750	16.2	40,365	16.1	33,307	14.5	36,256	16.4	36,429	15.5	42,292	16.1	33,080	13.2
India	26,123	11.5	27,904	11.1	28,838	12.6	24,593	11.1	25,575	10.8	33,148	12.6	30,753	12.2
Pakistan	14,201	6.2	15,354	6.1	14,173	6.2	12,351	5.6	12,795	5.4	13,575	5.2	12,332	4.9
Philippines	10,119	4.5	12,928	5.2	11,011	4.8	11,989	5.4	13,303	5.6	17,525	6.7	17,717	7.0
Iran	5,617	2.5	5,746	2.3	7,889	3.4	5,651	2.6	6,063	2.6	5,502	2.1	7,073	2.8
Korea, Republic of	7,639	3.4	9,608	3.8	7,334	3.2	7,089	3.2	5,337	2.3	5,819	2.2	6,178	2.5
Romania	4,431	2.0	5,589	2.2	5,689	2.5	5,466	2.5	5,658	2.4	4,964	1.9	4,393	1.8
United States	5,828	2.6	5,911	2.4	5,294	2.3	6,013	2.7	7,507	3.2	9,262	3.5	10,943	4.4
Sri Lanka	5,849	2.6	5,520	2.2	4,968	2.2	4,448	2.0	4,135	1.8	4,690	1.8	4,490	1.8
United Kingdom	4,649	2.0	5,360	2.1	4,725	2.1	5,199	2.4	5,062	2.6	5,865	2.2	6,542	2.6
Total	121,206	53	134,285	54	123,228	54	119,055	54	122,864	52	142,642	54	133,501	53

Note: Percentage refers to the percentage to the Total Immigrant Population.

Source: Facts and Figures 2006: Immigration Overview: Permanent and Temporary Residents (http://www.cic.gc.ca/english/resources/statistics/facts2006/index.asp). Reproduced with the permission of the Minister of Public Works and Government Services Canada, 2009.

Figure 7.2 Percentage of Immigrants in 10 Largest Cities by Periods of Immigration, 2006

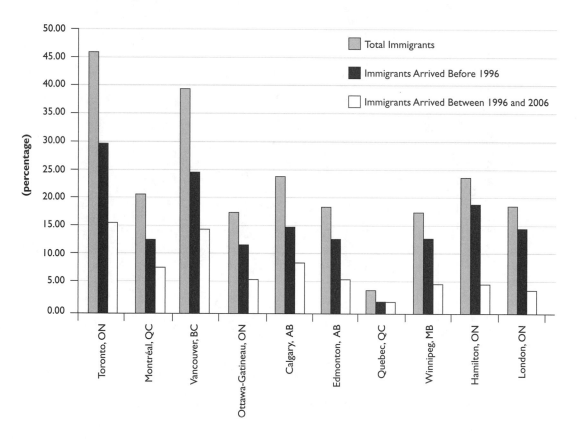

Source: Adapted from Statistics Canada publication *Immigration and citizenship, 2006 Census*, Catalogue 97-557-XIE2006001, http://www.statcan.gc.ca/bsolc/olc-cel/olc-cel?catno=97-557-XIE2006001&lang=eng.

each of the six largest cities in Canada. Given the complexity of how Canadians consider their ethnic identities, the Canadian census asked individuals to name up to four ethnic backgrounds.[2] In our discussion, we have reported the total number of those who gave only one ethnic background and those who reported more than one. This information is very important. It reflects how Canadians view their ethnic identities. Canadians are commonly identified with more than one ethnic background. This is especially true in cities where intermarriage occurs because of frequent geo-

graphic and social mobility. The large number of individuals who reported only one ethnicity suggests strong ethnic retention within these groups or possibly higher immigrant population and their children, while the large number of individuals who reported multiple ethnic backgrounds indicates high intermarriage rates in these groups.

The ethnic representations in different cities vary. If we compare all individuals who reported multiple ethnic backgrounds, we find English, French, Scottish, and Irish are always among the largest six groups in the largest six cities. In

Table 7.4 Population by Top 5 Ethnic Origins in the 6 Largest CMAs in Canada, 2006

Total Response

Toronto	%	n	Montreal	%	n	Vancouver	%	n
English	15.9	804,100	French	26.1	936,990	English	23.1	484,340
Scottish	11.1	561,050	Italian	7.3	260,350	Chinese	19.2	402,000
Chinese	10.6	537,060	Irish	6.0	216,415	Scottish	16.1	337,225
Irish	10.5	531,865	English	4.1	148,095	Irish	12.0	251,695
East Indian	9.6	484,655	Scottish	3.3	119,365	German	9.7	203,715
Italian	9.2	466,155	Haitian	2.4	85,780	East Indian	8.7	181,895
Total	66.9	3,384,885		49.2	1,766,995		88.8	1,860,960

Ottawa - Gatineau	%	n	Calgary	%	n	Edmonton	%	n
French	26.1	291,735	English	27.2	291,375	English	24.7	252,950
English	19.6	219,490	Scottish	20.8	223,000	German	19.2	196,575
Irish	19.1	213,475	German	7.1	182,940	Scottish	18.9	194,180
Scottish	15.8	176,720	Irish	16.4	175,575	Irish	16.2	165,590
German	7.1	79,835	French	10.2	109,180	Ukrainian	14.1	144,615
Italian	4.0	45,005	Ukrainian	7.1	76,240	French	12.8	131,225
Total	91.7	1,026,260		88.8	1,058,310		105.9	1,085,135

Single Response

Toronto	%	n	Montreal	%	n	Vancouver	%	n
Chinese	13.4	462,460	French	14.0	362,450	Chinese	28.0	356,845
East Indian	11.3	390,325	Italian	6.2	161,910	East Indian	12.5	159,200
Italian	8.1	312,925	Haitian	2.7	70,155	English	7.6	96,540
English	5.2	177,495	Chinese	2.6	67,990	Filipino	4.7	59,305
Filipino	4.0	136,495	Québécois	1.9	48,300	Korean	3.5	44,055
Portuguese	3.8	130,865	Greek	1.8	45,555	German	3.1	39,880
Total	45.8	1,610,565		29.2	756,360		59.4	755,825

Ottawa - Gatineau	%	n	Calgary	%	n	Edmonton	%	n
French	11.2	66,405	Chinese	11.8	61,450	Chinese	9.0	44,035
English	5.7	34,190	English	9.8	51,030	Ukrainian	8.5	41,665
Chinese	5.0	29,755	East Indian	7.7	40,405	German	8.1	39,345
Irish	3.9	23,465	German	6.3	32,675	English	8.0	38,935
Lebanese	3.0	18,045	Scottish	4.4	22,860	East Indian	5.8	28,415
Italian	2.9	17,100	Filpino	3.8	19,910	Scottish	3.5	17,140
Total	31.7	188,960		43.8	228,330		42.9	209,535

Source: Adapted from Statistics Canada publication *Ethnic Origin and Visible Minorities, 2006 Census,* Catalogue no. 97-562-XWE2006006, http://www.statcan.gc.ca/bsolc/olc-cel/olc-cel?catno=97-562-X2006006&lang=eng.

other words, a significant proportion of Canadians residing in these cities identified themselves as having part of their cultural roots from these groups. Despite this common pattern, there are considerable differences in representation of members who identified themselves as having roots from other ethnic groups. In Montreal, a large percentage of the population identifies partial French identity. In Toronto and Vancouver, which have large proportions of recent immigrants, many individuals identify visible minority groups as part of their ethnic background. In western cities such as Calgary and Edmonton, large percentages of individuals identified Ukrainian and German as part of their heritage. These patterns reflect the settlement patterns of the early immigrants and possibly a large representation of groups from intermarriage.

Those who reported only single ethnic backgrounds are most likely immigrants or children of immigrants. The representation in cities of groups based on single ethnic origins is obviously different from the representation based on multiple ethnic origins. Among the three largest cities, the largest six groups based on single ethnic origin include a number of groups that do not appear in the list based on multiple origins. This may reflect the large number of recent immigrants settled in these cities. Other major cities in Ontario show large proportions of southern and eastern Europeans, such as Italians, Poles, and Portuguese (Statistics Canada 2004). Among the major western cities, Calgary and Edmonton also attract diverse racial and ethnic groups, although Edmonton is still dominated by European ethnic groups.

In short, the demographic information tells two stories. First, individuals with partial ethnicity of the early immigrant groups such as British, French, and northern and western European, can be found in most major cities. This pattern may suggest the geographic dispersion of these groups and their high percentage of intermarriage. Second, individuals of various ethnic groups who identified themselves as having single ethnic origin—most likely immigrants and their children—are not evenly distributed. They are concentrated in a few major cities.

Immigration and Ethnic Relations in Cities

Since most recent immigrants have come from diverse countries, especially from non-European countries, and since most of them have settled in major cities, the Canadian urban landscape has become dramatically diverse in recent decades. Consequently, the study of group relationships in Canadian cities has become more complicated. Studies today have to go beyond the simple dichotomy of majority and minority. Most discussions of group relations are guided by theoretical frameworks derived from the European experiences at the beginning of the twentieth century or from the unique historical and political British-French relations. These frameworks may not be applicable to relations among today's diverse groups, a considerable proportion of whom are from non-European backgrounds.

In the following sections, we provide a glimpse of racial and ethnic relationships in Canadian cities. First, we present the socio-economic background of immigrants. Given that in 2006 less than 17 per cent of recent immigrants (i.e., those who arrived within the previous five years) were from European countries, it is important to bear in mind that information about the socio-economic background and economic achievements of immigrants largely reflects the experience of visible minority groups. In fact, the study of group relations in Canadian cities today has to take immigration and its racial components into full consideration.

Next, we explore the theoretical framework for understanding racial and ethnic residential patterns. The study of racial and ethnic residential patterns has a long history of describing group relations in cities. We highlight the limitations of previous models that were based on earlier European experiences and discuss some recent attempts to update these models.

Finally, we discuss ethnic businesses, which have attracted a lot of attention from researchers in recent decades. As most ethnic communities increase in size, ethnic businesses become an important and integral part of understanding an ethnic community.

Socio-economic Background of Immigrants

To better understand the lives of immigrants in the city, we need to consider their educational experience and workforce participation. The economic situation of immigrants is important, because almost everyone, including immigrants, has to work to pay living expenses. Since immigrants usually do not have extensive social networks, education is a critical credential for them to earn a living in their new country.

Table 7.5 shows the socio-economic backgrounds of immigrants and indicates that immigrants have higher levels of education than the Canadian-born population. Although both immigrant and Canadian-born populations include many people who have not completed high school, the percentage is lower among immigrants, especially recent immigrants. About 26 per cent of recent immigrants aged 15 or over did not have a high school graduation certificate, compared to 32 per cent of the Canadian-born population. In addition, more immigrants have completed university than have Canadian-born residents. About 21 per cent of immigrants aged 15 or over have completed university, compared to only 14 per cent of Canadian-born residents. The percentage is even higher (28 per cent) for recent immigrants.

Knowing at least one of the two official languages is important for most immigrants to Canada to become economically and socially integrated. Proficiency in one or both official languages allows them to compete in the labour market, to develop new social relations, and to extend their social networks. As would be ex-pected, a higher percentage of immigrants than of the Canadian-born population do not know either French or English. However, immigrants have a higher percentage than the Canadian-born of knowing only English. This suggests that even those who have language skills are most likely competitive in jobs that only require English but may have difficulty competing with others for jobs involving French in the workplace.

Despite a higher level of education, immigrants are not able to compete well in the labour market. These patterns are revealed by various indicators. First, immigrants aged 15 or over have a lower employment rate, at 57 per cent, while the employment rate for the Canadian-born population is 63 per cent. Second, a higher percentage of immigrants are not in the labour force, at a rate of 39 per cent compared to 32 per cent for the Canadian-born population. Third, even among those who are employed, fewer are working full-time and more are employed part-time in comparison to the Canadian-born population. About 38 per cent of the Canadian-born population work full-time, compared to 35 per cent of immigrants and only 30 per cent of recent immigrants. Finally, although a higher proportion of immigrants have completed university and research shows that educational level is related to income, immigrants still are not able to attain a higher income than the Canadian-born population. In fact, recent immigrants have a much lower average income level than people born in Canada. Because of the relatively unfavourable performance of immigrants in the labour market and because recent immigrants have largely settled in just a few major cities, the issue of accommodating immigrants in local labour markets confronts individual cities in different magnitudes.

Economic Attainments of Immigrants

In the previous section, we briefly touched on the topic of economic integration among immigrants. In this section, we will explore this topic

Table 7.5 Selected Socio-economic Background by Immigration Status, 2001

		Immigrant Status and Period of Immigration		
	Total	Canadian-born Population	Immigrant Population	Recent Immigrants[1]
Highest Level of Education				
Less than high school	31.3%	31.6%	30.4%	25.6%
High school graduation	14.1%	14.7%	12.0%	12.8%
University degree	15.4%	13.8%	20.8%	28.4%
Knowledge of Official Language				
English only	67.5%	65.1%	78.1%	75.6%
French only	13.3%	15.6%	3.5%	4.4%
English and French	17.7%	19.0%	12.0%	10.6%
Neither English nor French	1.5%	0.3%	6.4%	9.4%
Labour Force Participation				
In the labour force	66.4%	68.0%	61.4%	65.5%
Employed	61.5%	62.9%	56.9%	58.1%
Unemployed	4.9%	5.0%	4.5%	7.5%
Not in the labour force	33.6%	32.0%	38.6%	34.5%
Work Activities				
Did not work in 2000	31.2%	29.4%	37.1%	34.3%
Worked full-year full-time	37.1%	37.8%	34.9%	29.5%
Worked part-year or part-time	31.7%	32.8%	28.0%	36.2%
Average income $	29,769	29,952	29,337	21,281

1 Recent immigrants are those who immigrated between 1991 and 2001.

Sources: Statistics Canada 2003a; 2003b; 2003c; 2003d.

in more detail. In fact, the **economic integration** of immigrants in the city has drawn considerable attention from those who study immigration and cities, because economic opportunities for immigrants not only affect their integration process but also have possible economic consequences for the city economy, such as increasing the supply of labour and affecting the quality of the labour force. In addition, the fact that the majority of recent immigrants settled in urban areas suggests that the economic attainment of immigrants is an urban issue.

The dominant perspective that has guided the discussion of economic integration of immi-grants is the assimilation perspective. As mentioned earlier, this perspective is largely based on the experience of European immigrants at the beginning of the last century. The theory expects that immigrants usually start out from humble beginnings in a new country. They gradually move up the occupational and social ladders as they accumulate more working experience, learn the language, and expand their social networks as their stay in the country lengthens. Eventually, immigrants reach the same level of economic achievement as the native-born population.

Current research, however, does not seem to support this optimistic picture for recent immigrant groups. First, a persistence of lower earnings for immigrants in comparison to the Canadian-born is found even when these immigrants have been in the country for a long period of time and taking into consideration their education and language ability (Preston, Lo, and Wang 2003; Verma and Chan 2000; Christofides and Swidinsky 1994). A study by Li (1988) based on the 1981 census showed that immigrants, including those groups who had been in the country for a longer period, had lower earnings than the Canadian-born population. Christofides and Swidinsky (1994) confirmed this with more recent data. With the economy of cities having been transformed from an industrial to a knowledge-based economy—and those who work in the knowledge-based sector are highly rewarded—research controlling for other demographic and labour market factors reveals that immigrants in that sector still experience lower earnings than the Canadian-born (Ooka and Fong 2002). In addition, the results show that immigrants who are members of visible minorities experience particular disadvantages.

To explain the differences in economic achievements between immigrant and Canadian-born populations, research has pointed to several causes. First, the social networks of immigrants are usually less extensive than those of the Canadian-born. Since information about the job market is largely conveyed among friends, a less extensive social network could affect the job search results of immigrants (Waldinger 1997). The pattern is most acute among immigrants who reside in ethnic neighbourhoods with limited resources. Second, some researchers have suggested that the foreign credentials and foreign working experience of immigrants are discredited (Li 2001). This is reflected in studies showing that immigrants who hold a foreign university degree earn less than people born and trained in Canada. Finally, some researchers suggest that there is differential treatment of immigrants in the labour market in relation to job attainment and promotion (Li 1988). The effect is more obvious

in cities with large proportions of ethnic groups. Local residents may perceive that the presence of a large number of ethnic members in their cities may affect their job security.

To complicate the picture of economic attainment of immigrants, recent studies have revealed that not only are the economic attainments of immigrants lower than those of the Canadian-born but the economic attainments of *recent* immigrants are disproportionately lower than those of *earlier* immigrants when the length of time in the country is taken into consideration. Baker and Benjamin (1994) have demonstrated that the earnings of earlier immigrants are higher than those of recent immigrants, controlling for amount of time in the country. Using the 1981, 1986, 1991, and 1996 censuses, Waslander (2003) focused his study on the eight largest cities and found drastic differences in earnings and employment after the first few years of arrival between recent immigrants and earlier immigrants. Recent immigrants earned less and include a higher proportion of unemployed than earlier immigrants did when they first arrived.

Another complication in understanding the economic attainment of immigrants is the growing divergence of economic integration among immigrants (Portes and Zhou 1993). The patterns imply no single path to economic integration. Immigrants with skills and education are sought in the labour market, and their experience and expertise are well rewarded. However, immigrants with limited skills and low levels of education may have difficulty securing job opportunities. Subsequently, the economic progress of immigrants with different levels of education and skill can vary. This pattern reflects the considerable structural changes in the city economy in recent decades. Globalization creates a strong job surge in the banking, financial, and business sectors (Sassen 1991). Most of the jobs created in these sectors require considerable training and education. Individuals with such qualifications are in demand, and immigrants are no exception in this regard. At the same time, manufacturing jobs have been lost in urban Canada (Norcliffe, Goldrick, and Muszynski 1986). To lower production and operation costs, most manufacturing has moved out of Canada to developing countries that offer lower labour costs. Consequently, manufacturing jobs have been lost, and local labour markets have not been able to absorb the low-skilled workers. Immigrants with fewer skills have to compete with other workers for limited job opportunities.

Racial and Ethnic Residential Patterns

We know by now that immigration contributes to the racial and ethnic diversity in Canadian cities. To further appreciate the dynamics of growing diversity, we now turn to an exploration of the racial and ethnic residential patterns in major Canadian cities.

This topic has long been a tradition in the study of immigration and the city. Social scientists have been interested in the subject because each neighbourhood is associated with particular social and physical characteristics, such as income level or crime level. Research has pointed out that the neighbourhood social and physical environments are related to the social, psychological, and economic well-being of residents. For example, neighbourhood environments are found to be related to marital patterns (Wilson 1987), fertility patterns (Mayer 1991), mental health (Ross and Mirowsky 2001), and the job search experiences of residents (Wilson 1987). In his seminal book *The Truly Disadvantaged* (1987), Wilson has pointed out that living in a very poor neighbourhood may adversely affect the job search process, constrain job networks, and limit exposure to positive role models. If some groups disproportionately reside in neighbourhoods with less desirable environments, their full integration into society and their ability to share resources can be affected.

Racial and ethnic residential patterns have also been an important research topic, because

they are thought to reflect inter-group relations (Fong and Wilkes 2003). Sharing neighbourhoods with other groups offers more occasions for a group to interact with members from other groups, which in turn facilitates inter-group understanding and friendship (Fong and Isajiw 2000). Given that Canadian cities have become highly diversified, the topic of racial and ethnic relations is becoming more important than ever.

Early studies of residential patterns in Canada by Lieberson (1966) focused on the residential patterns of language groups. He found that individuals with a high level of French-language retention were associated with higher levels of **residential segregation**. Another study, by Balakrishnan (1976), based on the 1951 and 1961 censuses, found substantial variations in ethnic residential segregation among Canadian cities. The study indicated that cities with larger populations had higher levels of ethnic residential segregation. Therefore, cities such as Montreal, Toronto, and Vancouver had exceptionally high levels of ethnic residential segregation. However, these studies focused on European groups. Few of the early studies on Canadian residential patterns paid attention to the various other racial and ethnic groups. As Canada's racial and ethnic composition becomes more diversified as a result of immigration, the racial and ethnic residential patterns of groups in cities become more complicated (Murdie and Teixeria 2003), and the information needs to be updated.

Explaining Immigrant Settlement Patterns: Classical View

The Chicago School has provided both macro and micro perspectives on the settlement process of immigrants, based on the experiences of European immigrants at the beginning of the twentieth century. The macro perspective refers to the general settlement patterns of immigrants at the city level; the micro perspective discusses racial and ethnic composition within individual neighbourhoods.

Macro Perspective: Concentric Zone Model

Ernest Burgess (1967), in his well-known **concentric zone model** (see Figure 7.3), depicted both the temporal and spatial dimensions of the immigrant adaptation process.[3] Based on his observation of Chicago at the beginning of the twentieth century, Burgess suggested that although the settlement of immigrants seems to be unplanned, it reflects a unique pattern. He argued that when immigrants arrive in a new country with limited resources and language skills, they usually stay close to other members of their ethnic group. Residential proximity with others from one's own group facilitates information-sharing, including job assistance, among ethnic friends. Close neighbourhood proximity to ethnic members also makes it easy to draw support from the ethnic community.

Since their residents have limited financial resources, these *immigrant neighbourhoods* are usually located in the 'zone in transition', which is characterized as the 'deteriorating area' with low land values adjacent to the city business centre. As immigrants stay in the country longer, save money, and come to know the country better, they move out of the ethnic neighbourhoods in the 'zone in transition' and move into the 'zone of workingmen's homes'. These neighbourhoods are associated with better amenities but higher housing costs. Burgess also pointed out that native-born families usually settle in the outskirts of the city, which implies that children of these immigrants will follow that path.

Micro Perspective: Invasion-Succession Model

Burgess supplemented the discussion on changes in ethnic residential patterns by describing the process of ethnic composition changes in neighbourhoods—particularly those neighbourhoods in which a large proportion of population shifts from the majority group to a minority group—in his *invasion-succession model*. Instead of focusing on broad city-wide residential patterns, the model focuses at the micro or neighbourhood level. The first stage of the process is penetration,

Figure 7.3 Concentric Zone Model

Central Business Zone
Zone in Transition
Zone of Workingmen's Homes
Residential Zone
Commuters' Zone

in which a few ethnic minority families with socio-economic resources move into a neighbourhood with the established group. The invasion stage follows when large numbers of ethnic minority members move into the neighbourhood and the established group begins to move out. Eventually, the ethnic composition change will lead to a stage of consolidation when the neighbourhood has a large number of ethnic minority members. It is important to note that this discussion was mainly focused on the composition changes between blacks and whites in American neighbourhoods (Box 7.1).

Explaining Immigrant Settlement Patterns: Recent Developments

In recent years, a new perspective has emerged to broaden the understanding of immigrant settlement patterns in the city. Massey and his colleagues (Massey and Denton 1985; Massey and Mullan 1984) proposed the **spatial assimilation perspective** to update Burgess's concentric zone model. Spatial assimilation ameliorates residential segregation and is one of the key

Box 7.1 *Creating and Sustaining Community in Canadian Cities*: *The Transnational Ties of Indian Immigrants*

Newcomers from India have constituted a major immigrant group in Canada over the past two decades. Like other recent immigrant groups, they maintain strong contacts back home while gradually adapting to and integrating into Canadian society. Many of them maintain long distance connections with their home towns and villages to keep up-to-date with developments there. The attachment to the community in India is renewed each year as many of them visit their home towns and villages.

Indian immigrants also construct their identity in Canada through association with their home towns and villages. For example, immigrants from Punjab, following the same path as other immigrants from India, have retained ties with their associated villages, districts, and former colleges there. The connection is largely facilitated by fundraising in Canada for events in their home countries. Project directors and other dignitaries appeal for assistance particularly from immigrants who still maintain strong identification with their home villages and districts. One example is the Phagwara Association of Surrey, BC. The association is composed of immigrants from Phagwara and nearby villages. Many of them attended the same colleges and immigrated to Canada in the late 1960s and 1970s. They visit their home towns or villages in Punjab regularly, every one or two years. Because of their strong attachments, they have helped to raise funds for their colleges and villages. For example, commitments were made at the annual gathering on 9 December 2001 to raise funds to build more classrooms for the school and purchase a school bus in their home town. Each table of members at the annual gathering provides information about the college and a letter to outline funding needs. The event provides a good opportunity for key community leaders in Canada to strengthen their ties with each other and to their home communities and to demonstrate that they will continue to support and have an impact on their home communities despite being in another country.

Source: Based on Margaret Walton-Roberts 2003.

processes to achieving full integration among immigrants. Massey and Mullan (1984) argued that all aspects of group interaction have to occur in space, such as school, supermarket, and workplace. Therefore, spatial assimilation precedes all forms of integration.

From the spatial assimilation perspective, the sharing of neighbourhoods by racial and ethnic groups is affected by two factors: socio-economic resources and the duration of time in the country. Since housing values vary, if two groups share a similar level of socio-economic resources, it suggests that they might share the same neighbourhood. Group members tend to stay close to one another for support and for ethnic activities when they first arrive in the country. As they stay in the country for a longer period, their social networks extend and their knowledge of the country grows, and consequently they are likely to move out of these ethnic neighbourhoods. In other words, racial and ethnic residential patterns reflect economic differences and similarities among groups and their possible preference to stay together in a new country when they first arrive. The perspective suggests that racial and ethnic residential patterns reflect resource differences and duration in the country among groups. Therefore, the perspective predicts that racial and ethnic groups are more likely to share neighbourhoods when they have similar levels of socio-economic resources and when they have been in the country for a longer period.

This perspective has met a mixed response. On the one hand, research has shown that some groups, as expected, have increased their residential proximity with other groups as their stay in the country lengthens and they accumulate more resources (Fong and Wilkes 1999). On the other hand, results also have shown that some groups remain segregated even when they have been in the country for a fairly lengthy period of time and have increased their financial resources (Hou and Milan 2003). Fong and Wilkes (1999) used 1991 Canadian census data to show that the spatial assimilation perspective fits the European immigrant experience but not the experience of recent immigrant groups such as Asians and blacks. Similarly, Balakrishnan and Hou's study (1999), drawn from 1986 and 1991 Canadian census data, showed that some groups with a longer history in the country do not necessarily experience lower residential segregation. In other words, these groups still experience a higher level of residential segregation even though they arrived earlier. In a similar vein, Fong and Gulia (2000) found that groups usually move to neighbourhoods with better social and physical environments when they have greater socio-economic resources and have spent a longer time in the country. Despite the improvements, some groups are still living in neighbourhoods with better social and physical amenities than those of the neighbourhoods in which other groups with similar financial resources live. The researchers further found that when socio-economic resources are factored in, there are stable patterns of residential environments among groups. In Canada, the charter groups (British and French) and northern and western Europeans usually reside in neighbourhoods with more desirable qualities, followed by eastern and southern Europeans. Visible minorities reside in the least desirable neighbourhoods.

It seems that groups' socio-economic resources do not fully explain the residential patterns.

To address the anomalies, largely in response to the high segregation patterns of African Americans in spite of socio-economic improvement, Alba and Logan (1993; 1991) and Logan and Alba (1993) in a series of papers proposed an alternative explanation, the **place stratification perspective**, which argues that locations are usually associated with resources, prestige, and status. Those who live in desirable locations with more resources, higher prestige, and status are likely to maintain the status quo and to safeguard their neighbourhoods from any change, especially from groups with whom they prefer not to share their neighbourhoods. The inevitable outcome is that some groups are less likely to move into these neighbourhoods despite their socio-economic resources or duration in the country. This explanation focuses on the involuntary aspect of residential patterns.

Another attempt by some researchers to explain the anomalies is to consider the change in immigrant backgrounds in recent decades. Given changes in immigration policy over the past 30 years that have made education, language, and skills especially important for applicants, as well as the creation of the investment category of immigrant, recent immigrants are not necessarily disadvantaged upon arrival in Canada. On the contrary, they may bring financial resources with them. Consequently, unlike previous generations of immigrants, they often buy homes at an early stage of settlement. The unique settlement patterns of these groups can have enduring effects on ethnic neighbourhoods. In a recent study of neighbourhood patterns of four groups in Toronto, Myles and Hou (2004) revealed that the residential patterns of Chinese are quite different from the assimilation perspective. They found that Chinese who came to Canada with financial capital purchased homes near other members of their ethnicity shortly after their arrival. Their argument emphasizes the voluntary dimension of residential segregation (Box 7.2).

Box 7.2 Suburban Ethnic Malls

The emergence of large-scale Chinese ethnic malls in suburban areas is a new urban phenomenon, even though for years there have been Chinese ethnic shops and restaurants in the Chinese neighbourhoods and Chinatowns of many Canadian cities. Toronto is a prime example in terms of the number and diverse geographic distribution of Chinese ethnic malls. These malls are not very different from conventional malls and plazas. However, they have a few unique features that are not commonly found among conventional malls and plazas. Most of the ethnic Chinese malls are anchored with supermarkets, diverse restaurants, or banks, in contrast to conventional malls and plazas that are anchored by the major department stores. The stores inside the Chinese ethnic malls are usually small in size. Their opening and closing hours are largely determined by the individual store owners rather than by the mall management, as is customary in most conventional malls. Finally, the mall management has no control over the mix of stores in Chinese ethnic malls. Therefore, it is quite common to find a number of shops selling similar products located side by side.

As well as being major sources for co-ethnic products, Chinese ethnic malls also become an important location for social and cultural activities organized in the Chinese communities. On weekends and holidays, Chinese immigrants visit these malls, where they meet co-ethnic friends. This is a common activity for Chinese immigrants, especially those from Hong Kong, who are accustomed to spending their weekend time with friends and family for lunch, dinner, and shopping. The malls also become a place where major social events are organized.

Despite their importance to the Chinese community, not all of these malls are doing well. Some of them have a large number of vacant units. The Pacific Mall/Market Village complex has been considered the most successful in Toronto. The total retail space is more than 500,000 square feet. There are more than 500 stores and more than 1,500 indoor and outdoor parking spaces. Given its size, it can be recognized as a regional store. Without doubt, it is one of the largest Chinese malls in a North American city. For that reason, it has become one of the major attractions for Chinese tour groups from different North American cities and even from other continents. On 3 September 2000, York Regional Council decided to designate the mall as an official tourist area, a status shared in the Greater Toronto Area.

Source: Based on Lucia Lo 2006, 150–1

Explaining Neighbourhood Changes: Recent Development

The growing diversity of ethnic composition in the city also challenges the conventional understanding of **neighbourhood changes** based on two racial groups suggested by Burgess. The new urban landscape is no longer limited to changes involving only two groups but encompasses an array of groups. To update the understanding of neighbourhood change in multi-ethnic cities, Fong and Gulia (2000) used the 1986 and 1991 Canadian census data to explore the racial and ethnic composition changes in neighbourhoods of three major metropolitan areas—Toronto, Montreal, and Vancouver—where most immigrants reside. They discovered two pathways to neighbourhood change, with opposite consequences.

The first pattern is the path to diversity. These neighbourhoods become more racially and ethnically diverse. The change begins mostly in neighbourhoods with a majority of residents from charter groups when other Europeans first move in, followed by Asians and blacks. In a similar vein, Hou and Milan (2003) concentrated on the residential patterns of three recent immigrant groups—blacks, South Asians, and Chinese—and found that these groups have increased their representation in all neighbourhoods, especially those with a lower initial representation of their groups. It suggests that Canadian neighbourhoods have become more diversified.

The second pattern of neighbourhood change is the path to homogeneity (Fong and Gulia 2000). This pattern commonly occurs in multi-ethnic neighbourhoods. The outcome of the process usually is a reduced presence of visible minorities, especially blacks. This pattern directly questions the applicability of the invasion-succession model proposed by Burgess. The process of ethnic composition change is no longer simply that the majority group in the neighbourhood becomes replaced by the minority group.

In short, as cities of racial and ethnic diversity grow, racial and ethnic residential patterns become increasingly complex. Recent findings have challenged the classic explanations based on European immigrant experiences in the last century (Logan and Alba 1993; Fong and Wilkes 1999), and a few attempts have been made to offer alternative explanations.

Ethnic Businesses

Given that ethnic businesses make up a large proportion of businesses in most major Canadian cities and that a considerable proportion of ethnic businesses are owned by recent immigrants, the study of ethnic businesses is an essential topic regarding immigration, race, and city.

Although many studies have explored the issue of ethnic businesses, the debate on how to define ethnic businesses is far from reaching any consensus (Logan, Alba, and McNulty 1994). Most scholars agree that ethnic businesses should be defined as including only those businesses owned by members of an ethnic group (Fong

and Ooka 2002; Light et al. 1993). However, some argue that ethnic businesses should also include businesses that are not owned by ethnic group members but are managed by them and have a significant proportion of ethnic employees (Bonacich and Modell 1980). The definition, in this view, should emphasize workplace ethnic composition rather than business ownership. Other researchers emphasize the importance of language usage to define ethnic businesses, because using an ethnic language in the workplace creates a major distinction from other businesses (Reitz 1980). Despite an array of definitions of ethnic businesses, a common point is the importance of ethnic presence.

A number of suggestions have been offered to explain why ethnic businesses grow. They can be grouped into *supply-side* and *demand-side explanations* (Light and Rosenstein 1995). The first set of explanations, usually referred to as the supply-side explanation, links the participation in ethnic business to the resources and experiences held by individual ethnic group members. Groups with more members who have business experience or substantial socio-economic resources are more likely to participate in ethnic businesses. With experience in business operations and familiarity with the risks associated with running a business, such members find their background useful in managing their business (Light and Gold 2000). Running a business also requires the mastery of complex documents, interaction with customers and agencies from different backgrounds, and managing the personnel relations and finances of the business. Ethnic group members with education, language ability, and other relevant skills are definitely in a good position to meet these challenges. Finally, some argue that the likelihood of immigrants participating in ethnic businesses may be related to experiences of blocked career mobility. Immigrants may find that for various reasons, their opportunities to move into certain levels of jobs are limited. With perceived limited mobility, immigrants may find entrepreneurship attractive.

The demand-side explanation, in contrast, argues the importance of the market contexts (Light and Rosenstein 1995). One of the obvious market contexts is the size of the ethnic population. As the ethnic population increases, the demand for ethnic products and services rises. Recent research, however, suggests that it is not only the size of the ethnic group that matters but the residential concentration of the group as well (Fong and Lee 2003). A larger group with a higher level of residential concentration fosters the development of ethnic *completeness* (Breton 1964). An ethnic community with 'completeness' is characterized by extensive ethnic businesses and institutions, including religious, political, commercial, and professional institutions, to serve an array of needs of the ethnic group. In an extreme case, a fully completed ethnic community allows members to carry out all social and economic activities within the community. This proliferation of businesses and institutions results partly from the residential proximity of ethnic group members, which facilitates more social interactions that generate demand for ethnic services and products, and partly from the availability of a critical mass to support the growth of ethnic businesses.

Other market contexts have also been suggested in the literature as affecting the development of ethnic businesses (Light and Gold 2000; Fong and Lee 2003). Researchers have documented that the state of the city economy is strongly related to the development of ethnic businesses (Light and Rosenstein 1995). A weak economy may encourage ethnic members to seek an alternative path. Since ethnic businesses with their special niche provide employment advantages to ethnic members, they can attract individual members to participate. Moreover, research has also pointed out that the level of globalization of the local economy may bring in foreign investment, especially to ethnic businesses, which may stimulate the growth of ethnic businesses (Light 2001).

In sum, understanding ethnic businesses is complicated because various definitions have been used in previous studies. Nevertheless, most agree that the participation in and the operation of ethnic businesses are shaped by the supply and demand factors. Both sets of factors should be considered in order to obtain a more comprehensive picture of ethnic businesses.

Conclusion

In this chapter, we explored the topic of immigration and the city. We highlighted that most Canadian cities have a large proportion of immigrants and that most recent immigrants have settled in the major Canadian cities. Thus, the study of Canadian cities cannot be complete without understanding immigrant adaptation. The discussion also covered three major urban phenomena related to immigrants: economic attainment, racial and ethnic residential patterns, and ethnic businesses. We briefly reviewed the theoretical understanding of these topics. The review suggests the growing complexity of these phenomena, and thus the theoretical frameworks for understanding them need to be updated.

Notes

1. The 7 per cent figure included Asian and all other origins that were neither European nor British. Given that the number of those who were not Asian was very small, this percentage largely represents Asian immigrants.

2. Specifically, individuals were asked to name all ethnic or cultural origins of their ancestors. The ethnic question in 1996 and 2001 censuses allowed respondents to report up to four ethnic origins. Those who reported only one ethnic ori-

gin are considered as having single ethnic origin. Those who indicated more than one ethnic group have multiple-ethnic origins.

3. The concentric zone model suggested by Burgess consists of five zones. The 'central business zone' where commercial and major civic activities are held is located at the centre of the city. The second zone is the 'zone in transition' where factories and deteriorating housing are located.

Living conditions in this zone are not desirable. The 'zone of workingmen's homes' is the third zone. It is inhabited by those who have resources to move out of the 'zone in transition' but who prefer or need to live close to the workplace. The fourth zone is the 'residential zone' where the middle class reside in single detached dwellings. Finally, the 'commuters' zone' is the suburban area that requires a long commute to work.

Study and Discussion Questions

1. What are the implications of the high concentration of recent immigrants in a few major Canadian cities?
2. What are the implications of the divergent paths of economic integration among immigrants?
3. As immigration continues, do you expect the level of residential segregation to rise or to decline? Why?
4. Do you think residential segregation is an asset or a problem for cities?
5. Find examples of ethnic or racial segregation in the city where you live. Give concrete illustrations of how this segregation expresses itself and evaluate them.

Suggested Reading

Burgess, Ernest W. 1967. 'The growth of the city'. In Robert E. Park and Ernest W. Burgess, Eds, *The City*. Chicago: University of Chicago Press. A classic work that lays the foundation for understanding immigrant residential patterns.

Fong, Eric, and Milena Gulia. 2000. 'Neighborhood change within the Canadian ethnic mosaic, 1986–1991'. *Population Research and Policy Review* 19 (2): 155–77. A recent study that documents

the racial and ethnic changes in the neighbourhoods of major Canadian cities.

Light, Ivan, and Steven Gold. 2000. *Ethnic Economies*. New York: Academic Press. A good summary of the literature on various aspects of ethnic business.

Sassen, Saskia. 1991. *The Global City: New York, London, Tokyo*. Princeton, NJ: Princeton University Press. A classic that discusses how globalization, immigration, and the city are related.

References

Alba, Richard D., and John R. Logan. 1991. 'Variations on two themes: Racial and ethnic patterns in the attainment of suburban residence'. *Demography* 28: 431–53.

———. 1993. 'Minority proximity to whites in suburbs: An individual-level analysis of segregation'. *American Journal of Sociology* 98: 1,388–427.

Baker, Michael, and Dwayne Benjamin. 1994. 'The performance of immigrants in the Canadian

labor market'. *Journal of Labor Economics* 12 (3): 369–405.

Balakrishnan, T.R. 1976. 'Ethnic residential segregation in the metropolitan areas of Canada'. *Canadian Journal of Sociology* 1 (4): 481–98.

Balakrishnan, T.R., and Feng Hou. 1999, 'Residential patterns in cities'. In Shiva S. Halli and Leo Driedger, Eds, *Immigrant Canada: Demographic, Economic, and Social Challenges*, 116–47. Toronto:

University of Toronto Press.

Bonacich, Edna, and John Modell. 1980. *The Economic Basis of Ethic Solidarity*. Berkeley: University of California Press.

Breton, Raymond. 1964. 'Institutional completeness of ethnic communities and the personal relations of immigrants'. *American Journal of Sociology* 70: 193–205.

Burgess, Ernest W. 1967. 'The growth of the city'. In Robert E. Park and Ernest W. Burgess, Eds, *The City*. Chicago: University of Chicago Press.

Chui, Tina, Kelly Tran, and Hélène Maheux. 2007. *Immigration in Canada: A Portrait of the Foreign-Born Population, 2006 Census*. Catalogue no. 97-557-XIE. Ottawa: Statistics Canada.

Christofides, L.N., and R. Swidinsky. 1994. 'Wage determination by gender and visible minority status: Evidence from the 1989 LMAS'. *Canadian Public Policy* 20: 34–51.

Citizenship and Immigration Canada. 2003a. 'Facts and figures 2002: Immigration overview, Immigration—historical perspective (1860–2002)'. http://www.cic.gc.ca/english/pub/facts2002/immigration/immigration_1.html.

———. 2003b. 'Facts and figures 2002: Immigration overview—Immigration by source area'. http://www.cic.gc.ca/english/pub/facts2002/immigration/immigration_5.html.

———. 2008. 'Facts and figures 2006: Immigration overview: Permanent and temporary residents'. http://www.cic.gc.ca/english/resources/statistics/facts2006/index.asp.

Fong, Eric, and Milena Gulia. 2000. 'Neighborhood change within the Canadian ethnic mosaic, 1986–1991'. *Population Research and Policy Review* 19 (2): 155–77.

Fong, Eric, and Wsevolod W. Isajiw. 2000. 'Determinants of friendship choices: A perspective from minority groups'. *Sociological Forum* 15 (2): 249–71.

Fong, Eric, and Linda Lee. 2003. 'Ethnic economy within the city contexts: Economic returns of participating in ethnic economy revisited'. Unpublished paper.

Fong, Eric, and Emi Ooka 2002. 'The social conse-quences of participating in ethnic economy'. *International Migration Review* 36: 125–46.

Fong, Eric, and Rima Wilkes. 1999. 'The spatial assimilation model re-examined: An assessment by Canadian data'. *International Migration Review* 33: 594–620.

———. 2003. 'Racial and ethnic residential patterns in Canada'. *Sociological Forum* 18 (4): 577–602.

Hou, Feng, and Anne Milan. 2003. 'Neighborhood ethnic transition and its socio-economic connections'. *Canadian Journal of Sociology* 28 (3): 387–413.

Kalbach, Warren. 1987. 'Growth and distribution of Canada's ethnic populations, 1871–1981'. In Leo Driedger, Ed., *Ethnic Canada*, 93–110. Toronto: Copp Clark Pitman.

Li, Peter S. 1988. *Ethnic Inequality in a Class Society*. Toronto: Wall and Thompson.

———. 2001. 'The market worth of immigrants' educational credentials'. *Canadian Public Policy* 27 (1): 23–38.

Lieberson, Stanley. 1966. 'Bilingualism in Montreal: A demographic analysis'. *American Journal of Sociology* 71: 10–25.

Light, Ivan. 2001. 'Globalization, transnationalism, and trade'. *Asian and Pacific Migration Journal* 10: 53–80.

Light, Ivan, et al. 1993. 'Internal ethnicity in the ethnic economy'. *Ethnic and Racial Studies* 16: 581–97.

Light, Ivan, and Steven Gold. 2000. *Ethnic Economies*. New York: Academic Press.

Light, Ivan, and Carolyn Rosenstein. 1995. *Race, Ethnicity, and Entrepreneurship in Urban America*. Hawthorne, NY: Aldine de Gruyter.

Lo, Lucia. 2006. *Suburban Housing and Indoor Shopping: The Production of the Contemporary Chinese Landscape in Toronto*. In W. Li, Ed., *Suburban Asian Immigrant Communities: From Urban Enclaves to Ethnoburbs*, 134–54. Honolulu: University of Hawaii Press.

Logan, John R., and Richard D. Alba. 1993. 'Locational returns to human capital: Minority access to suburban community resources'. *Demography* 30: 243–68.

Logan, John R., Richard D. Alba, and Tom L. McNulty.

1994. 'Ethnic economies in metropolitan regions: Miami and beyond'. *Social Forces* 72: 691–724.

Massey, Douglas S., and Nancy A. Denton. 1985. 'Spatial assimilation as a socioeconomic outcome'. *American Sociological Review* 50: 94–106.

Massey, Douglas S., and Brendan P. Mullan. 1984. 'Process of Hispanic and black spatial assimilation'. *American Journal of Sociology* 89: 836–73.

Mayer, Susan E. 1991. 'How much does a high school's racial and socioeconomic mix affect graduation and teenage fertility rates?' In Christopher Jencks and Paul Peterson, Eds, *The Urban Underclass*, 321–41. Washington: Brookings Institution.

Murdie, Robert A., and Carlos Teixeira. 2003. 'Towards a comfortable neighbourhood and appropriate housing: Immigrant experiences in Toronto'. In Paul Anisef and Michael Lanphier, Eds, *The World in a City*, 132–91. Toronto: University of Toronto Press.

Myles, John, and Feng Hou. 2004. 'Changing colours: Spatial assimilation and new racial minority immigrants'. *Canadian Journal of Sociology* 29: 29–58.

Norcliffe, Glen, Michael Goldrick, and Leon Muszynski. 1986. 'Cyclical factors, technological change, capital mobility, and deindustrialization in metropolitan Toronto'. *Urban Geography* 7: 413–36.

Ooka, Emi, and Eric Fong. 2002. 'Globalization and earnings among native-born and immigrant populations of racial and ethnic groups in Canada'. *Canadian Studies in Population* 29 (1): 101–22.

Portes, Alejandro, and Min Zhou. 1993. 'The new second generation: Segmented assimilation and its variants among post-1965 immigrant youth'. *Annals of the American Academy of Political and Social Sciences* 530: 74–96.

Preston, Valerie, Lucia Lo, and Shuguang Wang. 2003. 'Immigrants' economic status in Toronto: Stories of triumph and disappointment'. In Paul Anisef and Michael Lanphier, Eds, *The World in a City*, 192–262. Toronto: University of Toronto Press.

Reitz, Jeffrey G. 1980. *The Survival of Ethnic Groups*. Toronto: McGraw-Hill Ryerson.

Ross, Catherine E., and John Mirowsky. 2001. 'Neighborhood disadvantage, disorder, and health'. *Journal of Health and Social Behavior* 42: 258–76.

Sassen, Saskia. 1991. *The Global City: New York, London, Tokyo*. Princeton, NJ: Princeton University Press.

Statistics Canada. 2003a. *Selected Cultural and Labour Force Characteristics, Immigrant Status and Place of Birth of Respondent, Age Groups, Sex and Immigrant Status and Period of Immigration for Population 15 Years and over, for Canada, Provinces, Territories and Census Metropolitan Areas, 2001 Census—20% Sample Data*. Catalogue no. 97F0009XCB01042. Ottawa: Statistics Canada.

———. 2003b. *Selected Demographic and Cultural Characteristics, Immigrant Status and Place of Birth of Respondent, Age Groups, Sex and Immigrant Status and Period of Immigration for Population, for Canada, Provinces, Territories and Census Metropolitan Areas, 2001 Census—20% Sample Data*. Catalogue no. 97F0009XCB01040. Ottawa: Statistics Canada.

———. 2003c. *Selected Educational Characteristics, Immigrant Status and Place of Birth of Respondent, Age Groups, Sex and Immigrant Status and Period of Immigration for Population 15 Years and over, for Canada, Provinces, Territories and Census Metropolitan Areas, 2001 Census—20% Sample Data*. Catalogue no. 97F0009XCB01041. Ottawa: Statistics Canada.

———. 2003d. *Selected Income Characteristics, Immigrant Status and Place of Birth of Respondent, Age Groups, Sex and Immigrant Status and Period of Immigration for Population, for Canada, Provinces, Territories and Census Metropolitan Areas, 2001 Census—20% Sample Data*. Catalogue no. 97F0009XCB01043. Ottawa: Statistics Canada.

———. 2004. 'Population by selected ethnic origins. 2001 Census, census metropolitan areas'. http://www.statcan.ca/english/Pgdb/popula.htm#ori.

———. 2007. *Portrait of the Canadian Population in 2006, 2006 Census*. Catalogue no. 97-550-XIE. Ottawa: Statistics Canada.

———. 2008. 'Population by immigrant status and period of immigration, 2006 counts, for Canada and census metropolitan areas and census agglomerations—20% sample data'. http://www.chass.utoronto.ca.myaccess.library.utoronto.ca/datalib/cc06/tbt06.htm#97-562.

Verma, Ravi B.P., and Kwok Bun Chan. 2000. 'Economic adaptation of Asian immigrants'. In Leo Driedger and Shiva S. Halli, Eds, *Race and Racism: Canada's Challenge*, 116–33. Ottawa: Carleton University Press.

Waldinger, Roger. 1997. 'Black/immigrant competition reassessed: New evidence from Los Angeles'. *Sociological Perspectives* 40: 365–86.

Walton-Roberts, Margaret. 2003. 'Transnational geographies: Indian immigration to Canada'. *Canadian Geographer* 47 (3): 247–8.

Waslander, Bert. 2003. 'The falling earnings of new immigrant men in Canada's large cities'. In Charles M. Beaches, Alan G. Green, and Jeffrey G. Reitz, Eds, *Canadian Immigration Policy for the 21st Century*, 335–72. Montreal and Kingston: John Deutsch Institute for the Study of Economic Policy and McGill-Queen's University Press.

Wilson, William Julius. 1987. *The Truly Disadvantaged*. Chicago: University of Chicago Press.

Chapter 8 Getting Perspective

Is there an expectation that groups with a distinct identity should assimilate into the dominant patterns of urban life, or is it possible for them to retain a distinct identity within the city?

Many groups in cities struggle to maintain their distinct identities. The old idea, of course, was that cities eroded group identities in order to deal with the masses of people and that assimilation was the natural outcome. Assimilation meant that a group would be forced to lose its distinctive identity through the pressures of conformity, which was a requirement for large agglomerations of people to coexist in cities.

We now realize that cities may support differentiation in some ways and assimilation in other ways. A more recent term to describe this phenomenon is *differential incorporation*. This concept is built from the observation that different groups have different outcomes in terms of their acceptance and adaptation to urban life and that all groups, because of circumstance and disadvantage, cannot be treated the same way. Instead of the assimilation that European immigration had taught us to expect, some groups struggle to retain their culture within the urban environment and yet also try to find their place in urban life. Whether a result of personal cultural commitments or of discrimination and prejudice, or both, these groups struggle to make difficult adjustments to city living.

Aboriginal peoples are among those who have found adjustment to urban life difficult and trying at times. In many ways, they are indeed a special case. They hold a unique place in Canadian history, and their relegation to rural reserves by Euro-Canadians has made it difficult for them to be prepared for urban living. Yet the Aboriginal population in Canadian cities is growing, and a legacy of confusion, breakdown, and movement back and forth between at least some reserves and cities has produced a sad condition for at least some Aboriginal people that is an embarrassment to a progressive society. Because this is a matter of particular concern in Canada, it is important that we understand the dynamics of what is occurring.

8 Aboriginal Peoples in Urban Areas

Evelyn J. Peters

Learning Objectives

- To gain familiarity with some of the socio-economic characteristics of urban Aboriginal communities.
- To understand some dimensions of urban Aboriginal diversity.
- To appreciate the importance and potential contribution of Aboriginal cultures in urban areas.
- To think critically about popular perspectives on Aboriginal urbanization and poverty.
- To evaluate the nature and significance of urban Aboriginal settlement patterns.

Introduction

In the 1940s, relatively few **Aboriginal** people lived in cities in Canada. Since then, the urban Aboriginal population has increased steadily. According to the 2006 census, 53.2 per cent of Aboriginal people lived in urban areas (Statistics Canada 2008). Aboriginal populations comprise the largest minority group in many Prairie cities, and their social and economic conditions are central to the future of these cities. While researchers and popular accounts document Aboriginal 'migration' to urban areas, it is important to emphasize that many Aboriginal people are travelling within their traditional territories and that the urban centres they migrate to are often built on traditional settlement places of different Aboriginal groups. Urban Aboriginal people are most often viewed through lenses of poverty and marginalization, but they also bring unique cultures and perspectives that can enrich urban life. Nevertheless, the ongoing effects of colonial dispossession mean that there are particular challenges for many of them. All of these factors provide a strong basis for exam-

ining the situation of Aboriginal people in urban areas of Canada.

This chapter is organized around four questions that represent common perspectives on urban Aboriginal communities. These perspectives are that Aboriginal people are abandoning reserves and rural communities and moving to cities, that Aboriginal cultures are incompatible with success in urban areas, that the urban Aboriginal population is comprised primarily of socio-economically marginalized people, and that Aboriginal people are increasingly concentrated in inner-city neighbourhoods. Using demographic data and drawing on Aboriginal peoples' own perspectives on urban life, this chapter evaluates these perspectives.

Are Aboriginal People Abandoning Reserves and Rural Areas and Moving to Cities?

Expectations that Aboriginal people would leave their reserve and rural communities and move to

Table 8.1 Urbanization Patterns for Different Groups of Aboriginal People, 1996–2006

	Total Aboriginal Identity*	Métis**	First Nations***	Inuit	Registered Indian
Total population 1996	1,101,960	204,115	529,040	40,220	488,040
Total population 2006	1,172,790	389,780	698,025	50,480	623,780
On reserve, 1996 (%)	32.8	1.5	47.4		46.0
On reserve, 2006 (%)	26.3	1.1	43.1	0.9	48.1
Rural, non-reserve, 1996 (%)	20.4	31.4	12.8		13.0
Rural, non-reserve, 2006 (%)	20.5	29.5	12.2	61.5	11.3
Urban, 1996 (%)	46.8	67.1	40.0	28.0	41.0
Urban, 2006 (%)	53.2	69.4	44.7	37.6	40.6

* Total Aboriginal identity includes persons who reported more than one Aboriginal identity group and those who reported being a Registered Indian and/or band member without reporting Aboriginal identity.

** Statistics are based on single responses to census questions about Aboriginal ancestry. Some individuals identifying as Aboriginal claimed more than one Aboriginal origin.

*** The term used in the census is North American Indian

Sources: Siggner 2003; Norris and Clatworthy 2003; Statistics Canada 2003; 2008.

urban areas have a long history in Canada. Early 'Indian' policy assumed that reserve lands would be abandoned as First Nations peoples assimilated (Tobias 1983). Urbanization was seen as a partial solution for reserve and rural poverty, and the Department of Indian Affairs organized a relocation program designed to assist First Nations to move to urban areas (Peters 2002). Census data show that since the 1950s, the proportion of the Aboriginal population found in cities increased steadily. Table 8.1 describes changes in urbanization between 1996 and 2006 for individuals who identified as Aboriginal in response to census questions. Between 1996 and 2006, the proportion of the Aboriginal population living on reserves and in rural areas declined from 53.2 per cent to 46.8 per cent, while the proportion living in urban areas increased from 46.8 per cent to 53.2 per cent.

There are differences in urbanization for different legal categories of Aboriginal peoples. Métis people are most highly urbanized, with almost 70 per cent living in urban areas. While this pro-

portion is lower than the Canadian urbanization rate, which is above 80 per cent, it is substantially higher than the rate for other Aboriginal groups. Inuit people have the lowest proportion living in cities. Urbanization for First Nations increased from 40 per cent to almost 45 per cent between 1996 and 2006. However, the proportion of Registered Indians (First Nations people registered under the Indian Act) living in cities remained relatively constant at close to 40 per cent.

However the interpretation of the data in Table 8.1 is more complex than it appears at first glance. For several census periods, a number of reserves have refused to participate in census-taking. As a result, the number and proportion of First Nations and especially Registered Indians living on reserves are underestimated. Norris and Clatworthy (2003, 54) suggested that if unenumerated reserve populations had been included in 1996, approximately 60 per cent of Registered Indians would have been found to be living on reserves. Moreover, when we look at absolute numbers rather than proportions, both reserve *and* urban Aboriginal populations increased between 1996 and 2006. In other words, reserves are not being depopulated as urban First Nations populations grow.

It is also clear that reserves and rural places of origin remain important to many Aboriginal people living in cities. Migration data are not available yet for 2006, but data from 1986 to 2001 show a substantial movement back and forth between cities and reserves and rural areas (Norris and Clatworthy 2003). While some migrants may return to reserve and rural communities because of problems with urban life, researchers found that these communities of origin remain important for individuals (Wilson 2000). Studies on migration internationally suggest that migrants maintain connections with areas both of origin and of destination through political and economic ties and movement back and forth (Portes 1999). These connections are an important part of cultural identities. Many Aboriginal people emphasize ties to the land as a continuing element of their cultural identity, and migration may be one reflection of these ties (Todd 2000/2001). Migration back to rural and reserve communities may also represent an attempt to maintain vital and purposeful community relationships.

Another process affects our interpretation of Table 8.1. The growth in the Aboriginal population in recent decades cannot be explained only by population measures such as fertility, mortality, and migration (Guimond 2003). Legislation allowing for the reinstatement of First Nations people who had lost their status through a variety of processes accounts for part of the increase. However, another component of the increase was created by individuals who did not identify as Aboriginal in previous census years now choosing to do so. Researchers have documented a similar phenomenon in the US, identifying as contributing factors US ethnic polities that embraced ethnic pride and Indian activism (Nagel 1995). Siggner (2003) suggested that changing attitudes towards Aboriginal peoples in Canada have been important in changing patterns of self-identification. US researchers suggested that urban residents were more likely to reclaim their Indian identities, and similar processes may be occurring in Canadian cities.[1] Clearly, there are more Aboriginal people living in cities in 2006 than there were in 1996, but this increase is not a simple result of migration.

Are Aboriginal Cultures Incompatible with Urban Life?

There is a long history in western thought that sees urban and Aboriginal cultures as incompatible (Berkhoffer 1979). Early writing about Aboriginal migrants to urban areas reflected ideas that Aboriginal cultures were an impediment to successful adjustment to urban society. As a result, services to Aboriginal migrants emphasised integration (Peters 2002). Ideas about the incompatibility of urban and Aboriginal cultures have not dissolved. Presenters to the Urban Roundtable of the **Royal Commission on Aboriginal Peoples** (RCAP) talked about cities as 'an environment that is usually indifferent and often hostile to Aboriginal cultures' (RCAP 1993, 2).

However, presenters to the public hearings of RCAP saw vibrant urban Aboriginal cultures as important elements of Aboriginal people's success in cities (Box 8.1). For example, Nancy Van Heest (1993, 14), working in a pre-employment program for Aboriginal women in Vancouver, told RCAP:

> Today we live in the modern world, and we find that a lot of our people who come into the urban setting are unable to live in the modern world without their traditional values. So we started a program which we call 'Urban Images for First Nations People in the Urban Setting', and what we do is we work in this modern day with modern day people and give them traditional values so that they can continue on with their life in the city.

Box 8.1 Urban Areas As 'Hubs' in Aboriginal Networks

Renya Ramirez (2007), Winnebago/Ojibwe ethnographer and professor at the University of California, Santa Cruz, provides an interesting perspective on the role of urban areas in Native American cultural networks. Ramirez references the fact that in the popular imagination, Native Americans in cities are assumed to be dysfunctional, without culture, 'forever stuck in a liminal space not still traditional and also somehow not modern' (2007, 6). In contrast, she suggests that seeing cities as 'hubs' of contemporary Native American cultures provides a concept that resonates with Native ideas of community, identity, and belonging away from tribal lands of origin and that incorporates Native perspectives on mobility. The city, she says, 'acts as a collecting center, a hub of Indian peoples' new ideas, information, culture, community, and imagination that when shared back "home" on the reservation can impact thousands of Native Americans' (2007, 2). Ramirez notes that in contrast to expectations that urban Native Americans will be assimilated into urban centres, many remain rooted in their communities of origin. When urban Native Americans move back and forth to their reservations, they take along some of these ideas to be adapted in their home communities. The idea of cities as 'hubs' acknowledges that there are continuing connections between urban areas and tribal communities of origin and that these connections contribute to the dynamic evolution of both urban and rural communities.

While Ramirez's study is based on Native Americans in the Silicon Valley, researchers in Canada have also presented cities as part of Aboriginal peoples' circulation networks (Levesque 2003). These perspectives begin to undermine expectations that migration to urban areas represents a loss of Aboriginal cultural identities and dissociation with communities of origin.

David Chartrand (1993, 565), president of the National Association of Friendship Centres, had this to say:

Aboriginal culture in the cities is threatened in much the same way as Canadian culture is threatened by American culture, and it therefore requires a similar commitment to its protection. Our culture is at the heart of our people, and without awareness of Aboriginal history, traditions, and ceremonies, we are not whole people, and our communities lose their strength. . . . Cultural education also works against the alienation that the cities hold for our people. Social activities bring us together and strengthen the relationship between people in areas where those relationships are an important safety net for people who feel left out by the mainstream.

Chartrand told RCAP that the most effective way to solve problems Aboriginal people face in the city was to catch them before they start through strengthening individual's identities and awareness of the urban Aboriginal community. Building on testimonies such as these, RCAP recommended that all levels of government initiate programs to support Aboriginal cultures in urban areas (RCAP 1996, 537). RCAP suggested support for urban Aboriginal institutions, initiatives concerning languages, and access to land and elders.

Native studies professor David Newhouse (2000) argued that the urbanization of the Aboriginal population is occurring along with the reinforcement of cultural identities. In other words, these phenomena are not mutually exclusive. At the same time, Aboriginal cultures in urban areas are not simply transplanted non-urban cultures. Instead, Newhouse noted that

Table 8.2 Cultural Characteristics of the Aboriginal Identify Population in Selected Cities, 2006

	Vancouver	Victoria	Edmonton	Calgary	Regina	Saskatoon
Total Aboriginal	40,310	10,905	52,100	26,570	17,110	21,535
% of CMA	1.9	3.4	5.1	2.5	8.9	9.3
% First Nations	60.6	64.4	44.2	42.0	56.8	54.3
% Métis	38.9	34.3	54.6	57.0	43.0	45.4
% Inuit	0.5	1.3	1.2	1.0	0.1	0.3
% With knowledge of an Aboriginal language	3.2	5.7	9.1	4.8	4.9	13.8

Aboriginal people are reformulating western institutions and practices to support Aboriginal cultures and identities so that Aboriginal people can survive as distinct people in contemporary societies.

One sign of the importance of cultural identities and practices in urban areas is the growing number and role of urban Aboriginal organizations. Friendship Centres represent the earliest formal urban Aboriginal organizations. Established as a referral service, the first centre opened in Winnipeg in April 1959. At present, there are 117 Friendship Centres in cities throughout the country. Since the 1950s, many other Aboriginal organizations have emerged to address a wide variety of issues. Some recent research in Edmonton, Winnipeg, and Saskatoon found that in addition to Friendship Centres, other organizations, primarily related to non-profit housing, have existed for many decades (Peters 2005). In larger cities, urban Aboriginal organizations are found in a wide variety of policy sectors, including economic development, child, youth, family, and senior services, educa-

tion, and justice, as well as in cultural fields (e.g., language, dance, theatre, music, and media). Organizational development occurs differently in different places. In Winnipeg, for example, the Aboriginal Centre of Winnipeg emerged in order to provide political representation for all urban Aboriginal residents in the city, while organizations in Saskatoon and Edmonton emphasize separate service provision for urban First Nations and Métis communities.

The development of urban Aboriginal institutions contributes to urban Aboriginal communities' quests for sovereignty. Hibbard and Lane (2004, 97) note that indigenous movements for sovereignty rights around the world have emphasized three interlocking matters: 'how to have some measure of political autonomy; how to maintain particular sets of social relations and more or less distinct cultural orders; and how to maintain or regain control over resources, especially land'. While resource issues are not central in most urban Aboriginal communities, RCAP suggested that the development of urban Aboriginal organizations creates meaningful levels

Table 8.2 *Continued*

	Winnipeg	Thunder Bay	Toronto	Ottawa - Gatineau	Montréal
Total Aboriginal	68,385	10,055	26,575	20,590	17,865
% of CMA	10.0	8.3	0.5	1.8	0.5
% First Nations	38.5	75.4	68.6	55.3	60.6
% Métis	61.0	24.1	30.1	41.0	36.0
% Inuit	0.5	0.5	1.3	3.7	3.4
% With knowledge of an Aboriginal language	8.7	12.2	3.1	3.9	3.9

Source: Statistics Canada. 2008. *Aboriginal Population Profile. 2006 Census.* Catalogue no. 92-594-XWE. http//www12. statcan.ca/english/census06/data/profiles/aboriginal/index.cfm?Lang=E.

of control over issues that affect urban Aboriginal residents' everyday lives (RCAP 1996, 584). Aboriginal-controlled social services generally have greater scope in delivering programs that incorporate Aboriginal principles, beliefs, and traditions; they create important employment opportunities for urban Aboriginal residents; and they result in significant economic benefits for Aboriginal communities (Hylton 1999, 85–6). The active involvement of urban Aboriginal people in defining ways to meet the needs of Aboriginal populations reflects and creates cultural vitality in urban areas.

The size of the urban Aboriginal population influences the number and diversity of urban Aboriginal organizations that a particular city can support. Table 8.2 provides information from the 2006 census for census metropolitan areas (CMAs) with Aboriginal populations of 10,000 or more. Winnipeg had the largest Aboriginal population (nearly 70,000) in 2006. The next largest urban Aboriginal populations were found in Edmonton and Vancouver, respectively. The composition of the urban Aboriginal population is also an important influence on the structure of urban Aboriginal organizations. In many Prairie cities, half or more of the urban Aboriginal population self-identifies as Métis. In many of these cities, Métis organizations have emerged to provide culturally specific services to these populations.

When Aboriginal people represent a relatively large component of the total city population, they exert an important influence on opportunities and challenges facing urban areas. Cities like Vancouver, Toronto, Ottawa-Gatineau, and Montreal may have numbers of Aboriginal people larger than or similar to those of Prairie cities, but Aboriginal people comprise a smaller proportion of the urban population. In Winnipeg, the Aboriginal population comprised one-tenth of the total population of that city. In Saskatoon, Regina, and Thunder Bay, more than 8 per cent of the total CMA population was Aboriginal. In some smaller cities, an even larger proportion of the population was Aboriginal, most notably Prince Albert with a total population of 39,800 of whom 34.1 per cent identified as

Aboriginal. In contrast, in Vancouver and in the more eastern cities, Aboriginal people comprise between less than 1 per cent and 1.9 per cent of the population. Cities like Vancouver, Toronto, and Montreal have many other minority groups living in them, and as a result Aboriginal issues receive relatively less attention. Because Aboriginal people comprise such a large component of urban populations in Prairie cities, research on Aboriginal issues has tended to concentrate in these areas.

The Urban Aboriginal community is more complex, culturally, than the statistics in Table 8.2 suggest. For example, RCAP found that in 1991 in Vancouver, the largest Aboriginal cultural group contained less than 15 per cent of the total Aboriginal population and that more than 35 other Aboriginal cultures were represented in the city. A participant in a recent study of urban Aboriginal identities in Saskatoon gave an example of the challenges faced by Aboriginal groups whose culture was in a minority in the Aboriginal population. He expressed the difficulty of being Saulteaux in a city where Cree culture was dominant.

Like if you wanna talk about being Saulteaux, what our culture is all about, the language and the value systems and also the traditions or if there's a council dance or a sweat on my reserve and I have no way to get there then I'm, you know, I'm hooped. I can't do it because it's all the way over there. So, I mean, if I wanna go to a sweat then I have to, say, call [Cree elders] which, if it's as good as it gets then okay, I'll sweat, but I'm sweating with Cree culture not Saulteaux culture and there goes the beginning of Pan Indianism where, um, as a Saulteaux Indian wanting to follow Saulteaux identity the nearest accessibility that I have, or have knowledge of, is calling Cree elders, you know. And I have a lot of respect for them and I've, you know, but at the end of the day it's me following a Cree custom not Saulteaux. So with that said, it's pretty difficult in my opinion to maintain a

cultural identity here in the city of Saskatoon (Peters, Maaka, and Laliberté 2008).

Because many urban Aboriginal people want to practise their particular cultures, Aboriginal organizations often attempt to involve elders and representatives from a variety of cultures in their programs and services. Nevertheless, urban Aboriginal people who live in cities where their culture of origin is a minority in the urban Aboriginal population find that in order to access culturally specific services, they need to visit or return to their communities of origin (Wilson and Peters 2005).

Obtaining predictable and adequate funding is also a challenge to urban Aboriginal organizations. Although the Canadian Constitution Act (1982) defined Aboriginal people as the Indian, Métis, and Inuit people and guaranteed their existing Aboriginal rights, it has been difficult for Aboriginal people living in cities to benefit from these rights. The federal government has maintained that it is responsible only for Registered Indians and that these responsibilities are limited to reserve borders (Morse 1989).[2] The federal government has regarded all other Aboriginal people as a provincial responsibility. In turn, the provinces have argued that the federal government has responsibility for all Aboriginal people. RCAP noted that the result is a 'policy vacuum'.

First, urban Aboriginal people do not receive the same level of services and benefits that First Nations people living on the reserve or Inuit living in their communities obtain from the federal government. . . . Second, urban Aboriginal people often have difficulty gaining access to appropriate programs available to other residents. . . . Third, . . . they would like access to culturally appropriate programs that would meet their needs more effectively (RCAP 1996, 538).

Although some urban programs have been established through federal, provincial, and municipal funding, these initiatives are unevenly distributed, with short-term and often limited funding (Hanselmann 2001). Annual grants place an enormous administrative burden on Aboriginal organizations and limit their ability to build successful programs over time. Dependence on government funding creates concerns about sustainability and the ability to shape aspects of programming to reflect cultural needs (Graham and Peters 2002). Nevertheless, the federal government has shown some leadership in addressing urban Aboriginal issues through the Urban Aboriginal Strategy (Box 8.2).

Vibrant Aboriginal cultures can contribute positively—not only to Aboriginal communities in cities but also to non-Aboriginal communities. Researchers have found that skilled workers are attracted to particular cities for social, not only economic, reasons. Cultural diversity has been one of the elements that has made cities attractive (Bradford 2002). Aboriginal cultures have the potential to be part of this cultural diversity, extending beyond elements such as art, dance, theatre, music, food, and media and including such contributions as new perspectives on governance, a greater depth to urban histories, and different approaches to environmental issues and educational practices.

Are Aboriginal People Marginalized in Urban Areas?

There is a literature originating around the 1940s that suggests that Aboriginal migration to cities would pose challenges for migrants but that because of their poverty, their movement into cities would also challenge the capacity of municipal governments to provide for them (Peters 2007). These concerns are echoed in contemporary research, which shows that Aboriginal people are overrepresented among the urban poor in Canadian cities and are more likely than the non-Aboriginal population to live in poor urban neighbourhoods (Heisz and McLeod 2004, 7).

A comparison of socio-economic indicators for Aboriginal and non-Aboriginal people in Canada's largest cities suggests that urban Aboriginal people are economically marginalized in comparison to non-Aboriginal people (Table 8.3). The unemployment rate among urban Aboriginal people is more than double that of the non-Aboriginal population in most cities. Aboriginal people are under-represented in managerial, supervisory, and professional occupations. On average, more than twice as many Aboriginal as non-Aboriginal individuals in private households have incomes below the poverty line. The large proportion of parents or spouses (including common-law partners) who are lone parents is much higher among urban Aboriginal people than among non-Aboriginal people, and Aboriginal people are more likely to live in dwelling units that need major repairs. Aboriginal people's difficulty in finding quality housing means that they are more likely to have to depend on kin, friends, or services to find housing and more vulnerable to becoming absolutely homeless (National Homelessness Initiative 2005). Almost twice as many non-Aboriginal as Aboriginal people earn good incomes.[3] In the cities described in Table 8.3, Aboriginal people comprise 1.6 per cent of the total population but 3.6 per cent of poor families. Aboriginal people are much less likely than non-Aboriginal people to have a university degree. Aboriginal gangs are increasingly being identified in urban areas, particularly in the Prairie provinces, and their emergence is viewed in part as evidence of poverty and marginalization in urban areas (Box 8.3).

At the same time, there are substantial variations between cities. Thunder Bay, Regina, and Saskatoon have the highest Aboriginal unemployment rates and the largest differentials between Aboriginal and non-Aboriginal populations. Ottawa-Gatineau and Toronto have the lowest unemployment rates, with 7.3 and 8.7 per cent respectively. Aboriginal people are most disadvantaged in Thunder Bay, Winnipeg, Regina, and Saskatoon. They comprise almost one-fifth of the poor population in Thunder Bay and

Box 8.2 Urban Aboriginal Strategy

The Urban Aboriginal Strategy (UAS), introduced in 1998 by the federal government, was an attempt to address the serious socio-economic needs of urban Aboriginal people. The federal interlocutor for Métis and Non-Status Indians is the lead federal minister responsible for the UAS, with eight other federal departments collaborating. The UAS began as a four-year, $50-million initiative that was introduced in the follow-up to *Gathering Strength: Canada's Aboriginal Action Plan*, the federal government's response to the report of the Royal Commission on Aboriginal Peoples. Funding was renewed in 2003, and between 2003 and 2006 more than 300 pilot projects were funded. As of 2007, the federal government had committed another $68.5 million over the next five years.

The UAS demonstrates two key policy principles guiding contemporary federal government policy for urban Aboriginal peoples—partnership and the involvement of local expertise and perspectives (Graham and Peters 2002). The UAS has attempted to involve all levels of government in decision-making and funding of projects. At present, the UAS has three main foci. One is to improve life skills by working with a variety of partners in activities such as mentorship programs, summer camps, transitional services for students and families, and leadership programs in order to achieve better educational outcomes. A second focus brings federal, provincial, and municipal partners together to improve Aboriginal representation in the labour force. A third initiative supports Aboriginal women, children, and families to reduce poverty, provide transitional support to migrants to the city, and promote healing and positive life choices (Department of Indian and Northern Affairs 2008).

The UAS has also emphasized local participation in identifying priorities and projects and in administering funding. Steering committees have been formed in each participating community, with varying composition. For example, in Prince Albert, the steering committee is comprised of six Aboriginal people (three Métis and three First Nations individuals) with three non-voting advisory members representing the city, the province, and the federal government. The Calgary steering committee includes members from Calgary's urban Aboriginal community as well as federal, provincial, municipal, private-sector, and charitable organizations.

Initially implemented in eight cities, the UAS has expanded to 12 cities with large Aboriginal populations—Vancouver, Prince George, Lethbridge, Calgary, Edmonton, Prince Albert, Regina, Saskatoon, Winnipeg, Thompson, Toronto, and Thunder Bay. Projects have been initiated across a wide spectrum of policy areas, including education, performing and visual arts, health, justice, sports and recreation, and housing, and have been directed towards people of all age groups. The UAS has enabled urban community groups to fund new initiatives in their communities and has also supported the continuation of existing programs.

Source: Department of Indian and Northern Affairs 2008

Winnipeg and slightly more than one-quarter of the poor population in Regina and Saskatoon. In other words, a perspective that sees Aboriginal people through the lenses of marginalization and poverty is not equally applicable to all cities.

RCAP (1996, 817) identified two main approaches to improving urban Aboriginal economic situations. One approach focuses on improving individual Aboriginal participation in mainstream economies through employment and

Table 8.3 Socio-economic Characteristics, Aboriginal Identity Population, Selected Cities

	Vancouver	Victoria	Edmonton	Calgary	Regina	Saskatoon	Winnipeg	Thunder Bay	Toronto	Ottawa-Gatineau	Montreal
Unemployment rates											
Aboriginal	10.7	8.8	9.8	7.3	13.8	14.6	11.3	9.3	8.7	8.8	8.7
non-Aboriginal	5.6	4.3	4.6	4.0	4.8	5.2	5.0	7.4	6.7	5.7	6.9
% Management occupations											
Aboriginal	6.9	6.7	6.2	6.9	6.6	6.6	6.0	8.0	10.1	11.5	7.9
non-Aboriginal	11.3	10.7	10.5	11.1	9.6	9.0	9.3	8.0	11.6	11.1	10.3
Median individual income ($)											
Aboriginal	18,203	18,132	19,735	24,329	17,842	16,480	18,620	16,724	24,138	25,838	20,362
non-Aboriginal	27,596	28,541	29,195	30,831	29,308	26,112	26,334	27,546	26,754	32,219	25,161
% Families in poverty*											
Aboriginal	34.3	30.4	34.7	28	51.3	50.9	46	38.5	23.2	19.9	28.3
non-Aboriginal	17.1	8.4	11.5	10.4	8.0	10.0	11.8	8.3	14.3	11.8	17.5
% of parents or spouses who are lone parents											
Aboriginal	20.7	19.3	23.5	17.5	33.4	29.7	26.9	23.1	17.7	16.5	15.7
non-Aboriginal	8.2	8.7	8.8	7.7	10.6	9.8	10.2	10.0	9.2	8.9	10.0
% Units needing repair											
Aboriginal	14.0	11.9	11.6	9.0	12.8	11.8	14.2	12.6	11.3	12.7	14.1
non-Aboriginal	6.8	5.9	5.8	4.8	7.8	6.0	8.4	7.4	6.0	6.5	7.7
% Earning good incomes*											
Aboriginal	16.8	13.4	15.1	16.5	10.5	11.3	10.3	15.2	24.3	25.5	14.4
non-Aboriginal	27.9	28.3	27.7	31.1	27.1	24.1	23.8	28.3	30.7	35.8	24.0
% with university degree or certificate											
Aboriginal	8.7	10.1	5.9	9.4	8.4	11.2	8.3	12.8	12.8	15.5	10.3
non-Aboriginal	24.6	23.6	18.3	24.7	18.4	19.4	19.0	14.8	26.7	28.7	21.0

* These data are from the 2001 census. Statistics Canada did not provide 2006 census data for Aboriginal populations in these cities.

Sources: Statistics Canada. 2003. Aboriginal Peoples of Canada. 2001 Census. Catalogue no. 97F0011XCB2001051, Catalogue no. 97F0011XCB2001053, released 19 November 2003; Catalogue no. 97F0011XCB2001047, released 10 December 2004. http://www12.statcan.ca/english/census01/products/standard/themes/ListProducts.cfm?Temporal=2001&APATH=3&THEME=45&FREE=0.

Box 8.3 *Aboriginal Gangs As a New Form of Aboriginality*

In a 2006 paper, Dr Chris Andersen, Associate Professor, School of Native Studies, University of Alberta, explored why the urban environment was such a fertile ground for the formation of Aboriginal gangs and what the implications of these gangs are for the identity of group members. The following is an excerpt from that presentation.

The definition of a 'gang' is contested, and it depends on who is defining it (e.g., police and corrections, government legislation, academics, or social service agencies). Researchers argue that one way to differentiate between an actual Aboriginal street gang and a group of 'wannabes' is whether the street name self-identification survives prison; wannabe gangs get absorbed into others once their members become incarcerated. One of the defining features of Aboriginal gangs in Canada is the extent to which prisons operate as a primary tool of recruitment, longevity, and legitimacy.

Four 'national' Aboriginal gangs exist in Canada: (a) Native Syndicate; (b) Redd Alert; (c) Indian Posse; (d) Warriors (Manitoba, Saskatchewan, and Alberta chapters). Aboriginal gangs claim certain territories within Canada's major cities, including (but not limited to) Winnipeg; Saskatoon, Regina, and Prince Albert; Edmonton and Calgary. Collectively, Aboriginal gangs make their money off prostitution, intimidation, and selling drugs for Hell's Angels and various Asian gangs, as well as any acts individual gang members carry out to support various drug and alcohol habits (such as robbery and property crimes). Aboriginal gangs borrow heavily from elements of black gangs in the US—'tagging' (using graffiti to mark territory); flashing gang signs; elaborate use of gang-specific tattoos; and elevated levels of violence, particularly in 'jumping in' and 'jumping out' ceremonies.

While Aboriginal gangs are also active in rural and reserve areas, cities are central to gang formation and longevity. Gangs constitute one form of resistance (albeit a malignant one) to largely white, middle-class attempts to 'control' urban Aboriginal populations. For example, urban Aboriginals don't make social policy, and they have little control over municipal housing policies, which affect Aboriginal location and concentration. In addition, cities are filled with people who constitute an important avenue of profit for Aboriginal gang activities. Cities also provide fertile grounds for gang recruitment. The intergenerational impacts of the residential school syndrome, which have eroded parenting skills, white, middle-class notions of 'child endangerment', which resulted in the removal of Aboriginal youth from otherwise loving families, astonishing poverty and its accompanying social pathologies have each torn the connective tissue that connects Aboriginal youths to their families. Gangs purport to fill this void.

Gang membership represents a new form of Aboriginality. Aboriginal gang members identify strongly with their gang, and for them, more established categories such as 'First Nations, Métis, Inuit' or even 'Cree, Dene, Saulteaux' must compete with gang affiliations. Many Aboriginal youth who now find themselves in gangs are products of a child welfare system that has been largely indifferent to Aboriginal cultures. Urban Aboriginal youth are living in an environment in which they endure racism—both 'in their face' and more structurally—yet have little understanding of their heritage other than as it relates to this discrimination. More specifically, Grekul and Laboucane-Benson argue that 'when young Aboriginal men choose to take on a personae generated by African-American gangs, they lose their connection to their people and their identity as a Cree, Blackfoot, Lakota, Dene, Métis, etc.' (2006, 8–9).

Box 8.4 Urban Reserves

Approximately one-quarter of all reserves in Canada are found within or near CMA boundaries. Many have developed enterprises that attempt to take advantage of urban markets. In Saskatchewan, for example, three First Nations—Whitecap Dakota First Nation, Muskeg Cree Nation, and the Lac La Ronge Indian Band—are partners in the $4-million Dakota Dunes Golf and Country Club venture 28 kilometres southeast of Saskatoon. Recently, a number of First Nations have successfully established new reserves in urban areas. Most of these reserves have been established in Saskatchewan, where bands have purchased urban lands under the Treaty Land Entitlement Process (TLE) established to resolve the shortfall in land allocated to First Nations pursuant to treaty promises. However, this form of economic development is available across Canada under the federal Additions to Reserves (ATR) policy, which governs the process through which First Nations can expand their reserve base or, in the case of landless First Nations, create a reserve.

First Nations in Saskatchewan have used urban reserves to purchase office buildings or to develop enterprises that generate an income. Businesses on these reserves are tax-exempt because of the status of reserves under the Indian Act. However, the First Nation enters into an agreement with the municipality to pay for services in lieu of taxes (Barron and Garcea 1999). First Nations and municipal governments also harmonize land-use by-laws. The Muskeg Lake Cree First Nation Urban Reserve in Saskatoon was the first urban reserve to be created through negotiations with a municipal government. Negotiations with the city of Saskatoon began in 1988 and were completed in 1993 (Western Economic Diversification Canada 2005). There are currently more than 40 businesses operating on the Muskeg Lake reserve, employing more than 300 people. The reserve has provided benefits to the city of Saskatoon by attracting Aboriginal businesses and entrepreneurs and through the fees for services it pays for previous unused and derelict land. The development of the reserve has increased the land value of surrounding businesses, increasing the city's tax base. The reserve provides the Muskeg Lake Cree First Nation with access to urban markets and services and provides an important source of income.

In addition to their financial spin-offs, urban reserves can serve as spaces where Aboriginal culture within the city can be cultivated through daily commercial and service activities if not explicit cultural events (Barron and Garcea 1999, 281). They also serve a symbolic function, symbolizing Aboriginal empowerment, the will and capacity to retain a distinct place in Canadian society, and the potential for 'harmonious coexistence' between Aboriginal and non-Aboriginal society in a shared urban community (Barron and Garcea 1999, 289–90).

training initiatives—this is the most common approach followed by governments and non-profit (including Aboriginal) organizations. A second approach is aimed at increasing economic opportunities within a distinct Aboriginal economy, such as urban reserves (Box 8.4) and community economic development. The latter has been particularly important in Winnipeg, where Aboriginal community activists, loosely affiliated under the umbrella of Winnipeg Native Family Economic Development (WNFED), have established a number of initiatives over the years, including an Aboriginal workers' co-op that operates a grocery store (Neechi Foods Co-op), a housing cooperative (Payuk Inter-Tribal Co-op), and a daycare centre (Nee Gawn Ah Kai Day Care) (Loxley and Wien 2003). These initiatives attempt to minimize economic leakages from the inner city, strengthen inner-city networks, provide long-term employment, and support local decision-making in order to strengthen community self-determination.

While attention to urban Aboriginal marginalization can highlight social inequalities and create pressure on governments to bring about change, a focus on this aspect of urban Aboriginal life alone can have some negative spin-offs. First, it can turn attention away from the historic context for urban Aboriginal poverty. It is extremely important to provide a context for the economic marginalization of urban Aboriginal communities. Silver et al.'s (2006, 11–15) interviews with 26 urban Aboriginal community leaders identified a number of factors affecting Aboriginal people's economic situation in urban areas, including the failure of both residential and non-residential schools to provide them with the skills required in urban employment, the experience of racism, often on a daily basis, and the resulting destruction of self-esteem and identity. The urbanization of Aboriginal people in Canada occurred at a time when urban economies increasingly required education and skill levels that relatively few Aboriginal people received during their educational experience. Some contemporary research suggests that education and employment conditions in many rural Aboriginal communities continue to create disadvantages for migrants to cities (Levitte 2003, 58–70).

An emphasis on marginalization also perpetuates negative stereotypes that view all urban Aboriginal people as destitute. It can deflect attention from the success that many urban Aboriginal residents experience, and it can create the perception that there is no capacity among Aboriginal people to contribute to both the Aboriginal and the non-Aboriginal community in urban areas. Siggner and Costa's (2005) study of urban Aboriginal conditions reported that between 1981 and 2001,[4] school attendance among Aboriginal youth improved and rates of post-secondary completion increased. Employment rates improved in most cities, dependence on government transfer payments decreased, and there

was a 28 per cent growth of Aboriginal income-earners making $40,000 annually (adjusted for comparison with 1981). Wotherspoon (2003, 155) noted that in urban areas, 'many public and private sector agencies in both Aboriginal and non-Aboriginal sectors have created initiatives, programs, and hiring policies to attract highly qualified Aboriginal candidates.' According to Wotherspoon (2003, 156), this replicates the way that the non-Aboriginal middle class emerged historically with 'the expansion of state functions to train and maintain a healthy population, manage the marginalized segments of the population, and administer public services'.

Increasing education levels offer a further mechanism for reaching middle-class positions. Silver et al. (2006, 18) identified three important 'paths' that community leaders follow in overcoming barriers to socio-economic mobility in the city. They include adult education, employment in Aboriginal organizations, and involvement in activities because they were parents. Focus groups with Aboriginal middle-class Toronto residents highlighted the importance of recognizing the socio-economic diversity of urban Aboriginal people. The Toronto study indicated that middle-class urban Aboriginal people did not access Aboriginal organizations because these organizations are primarily service organizations focusing on a variety of social problems. Instead, they emphasized the need for Aboriginal language and cultural programs that addressed their aspirations.

Are Aboriginal People in Cities Forming Neighbourhood Concentrations?

The settlement patterns of urban Aboriginal people have been of concern to governments, social agencies, and a variety of academic researchers ever since the number of Aboriginal people in cities began to increase in the 1950s. With increasing numbers in cities, researchers and policy-makers expected that Aboriginal people would create poverty-stricken concentrations in inner-city areas (Peters 2007). Some more recent government reports show that concerns about the possibility of concentration and its implications for Aboriginal people and for cities have not evaporated (Sgro 2002, 21).

Concern about Aboriginal concentration has roots, explicitly or implicitly, in a literature on the emergence of inner-city ghettoes in large US cities. In the US, the concept of the 'underclass' developed to describe connections between intense poverty, its concentration over very large areas, and resulting social isolation from mainstream society and values (Wilson 1987). Wilson (1987) described how the movement of employment opportunities to suburban locations drew away working- and middle-class families, leaving behind an increasingly isolated and politically powerless 'underclass'. Inner-city disinvestment and growing welfare and illicit economies in response to the lack of employment opportunities resulted in the collapse of public institutions and the development of a set of attitudes and practices of everyday life that isolated populations from the rest of urban society. Other work has explored 'neighbourhood effects' suggesting that concentration itself can create negative effects, such as the development of antagonistic cultures and isolation from the rest of urban society (Buck 2001).

One approach to the question of concentration is to assess whether Aboriginal people comprise a large proportion of certain neighbourhoods in urban areas. The 2006 census showed that except for Winnipeg, there were no **census tracts** in which Aboriginal people comprised more than half of the population. In Winnipeg in 2006, 61.7 per cent of the population of one census tract was Aboriginal. In all other census tracts, the proportion of the population that was Aboriginal was less than 50 per cent. In most of the cities examined for this study—Vancouver, Victoria, Edmonton, Calgary, Toronto, Ottawa-Gatineau, and Montreal—no census tracts existed in which Aboriginal people comprised more than one-third of the population.

The distribution of Aboriginal populations in the four other cities studied for this chapter is graphed in Figure 8.1. The graph shows that the population of the majority of census tracts in Regina, Saskatoon, Winnipeg, and Thunder Bay was also less than one-fifth Aboriginal. A small proportion of census tracts had Aboriginal populations of between 30 and 49 per cent. As mentioned earlier, one census tract in Winnipeg had a majority Aboriginal population. In contrast, black populations in inner-city areas in US cities, which generated the concept of the 'underclass', often comprised 85 per cent or more of the residents of these neighbourhoods (Jargowsky 1997).

Clearly, Aboriginal people are not dispersed evenly across all census tracts or neighbourhoods. However, neither is it the case that Aboriginal people are highly segregated in Canadian cities. Segregation indices consistently document low to low-average segregation in the urban Aboriginal population (Darden and Kamel 2002). Aboriginal people in Winnipeg and Edmonton interviewed in the context of a study on Aboriginal settlement patterns felt that the levels of concentration that existed were associated with the location of low-cost housing (Peters and Starchenko 2008). The relative poverty of urban Aboriginal people results in a lack of choice of location in the city for many. Looking at Aboriginal settlement patterns over time, Peters and Starchenko (2006) found that Aboriginal people were increasingly dispersed in urban areas rather than increasingly concentrated in a few inner-city neighbourhoods. This may be related to the emerging Aboriginal middle class. The Ontario Urban Aboriginal Task Force (Urban Aboriginal Strategy 2005) found that Aboriginal middle-class participants were dispersed throughout different middle-class neighbourhoods.

Conclusion

This chapter has used demographic information and the perspectives of urban Aboriginal residents to evaluate four common perspectives on

Figure 8.1   Aboriginal Settlement Patterns, Selected Cities, 2006

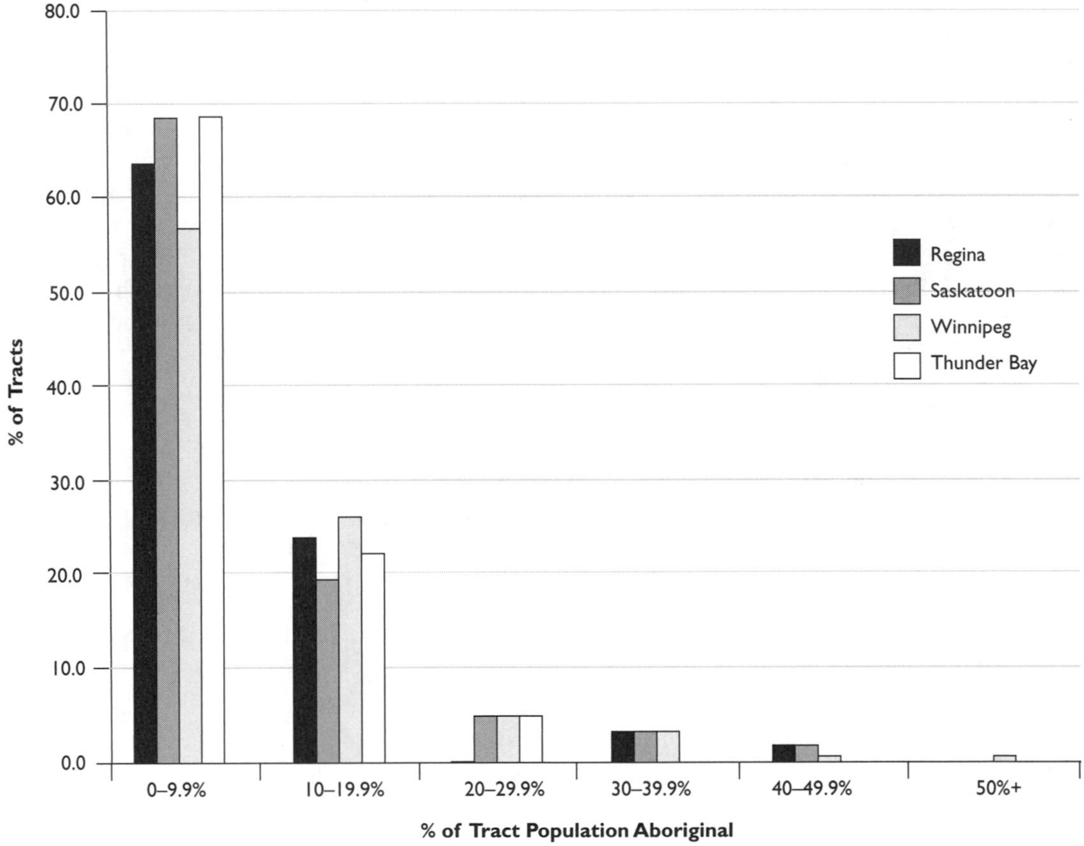

urban Aboriginal peoples. The data suggest that the perception that Aboriginal people are leaving reserves and rural communities and moving to urban areas needs to be carefully examined. Census data show that an increasing proportion of the Aboriginal population lives in cities, but there are variations by Aboriginal group, and under-enumeration, back-and-forth movement between cities and reserves, and changing patterns of self-identification complicate that picture. While the proportion of Aboriginal people living in the city has increased according to census data, rural areas and particularly reserves continue to hold importance in many Aboriginal people's lives.

Aboriginal cultures can facilitate successful adaptation to urban life for urban Aboriginal res-idents. Like other cultural groups, urban Aboriginal cultures are dynamic and creative attempts to adapt values and practices to a new environment. Urban Aboriginal cultures are reflected in, and reinforced by, a variety of urban Aboriginal organizations. While these organizations face challenges related to cultural complexity and un-stable government funding, they are an important element of contemporary urban Aboriginal communities. These cultures can also contribute to the richness of urban cultural life.

Many depictions of urban Aboriginal people view them primarily as poor and service-dependent. Clearly, poverty is a serious issue in urban Aboriginal communities, and strategies for incorporating them into the labour force or developing distinct Aboriginal economies may offer opportunities for change. However, a focus only on marginalization can hide the history of colonialism that failed to develop reserves and rural communities, education systems that did not teach them the skills necessary for economic success in contemporary economies, and racism and discrimination in urban areas. It can also hide the successes that urban Aboriginal people are experiencing in urban areas. Finally, despite continuing concerns about Aboriginal peoples' concentration in inner-city areas, their settlement patterns are quite different from those of minority groups in US inner cities. Inner-city areas continue to have Aboriginal and non-Aboriginal people living in them, and increasingly, Aboriginal people are found in all areas of cities.

Notes

1. In the United States, the commonly used term for Aboriginal people is 'American Indian'.
2. Some federally funded services are available to Registered Indians generally, no matter where they live. The most notable of these are non-insured health benefits and post-secondary educational assistance. The federal government also supports friendship centres through the Department of Canadian Heritage and the Urban Aboriginal Strategy (Box 8.2).
3. 'Good incomes' were defined as $40,000 or more in 2000. I recognize that variations in the cost of living in different cities mean that this income

level has varying purchasing power. However, this measure provides a useful comparison of Aboriginal and non-Aboriginal people in particular urban areas.
4. While the 1981 census did not ask respondents whether they identified as Aboriginal, analysis of the 1981 ethnicity question, which asked whether individuals had Aboriginal ancestry, indicated that the 1981 cohort that answered positively to the question was largely similar to that which identified as Aboriginal in the 1991 census (Kerr, Siggner, and Bourdeau 1996).

Study and Discussion Questions

1. What do you know about the Aboriginal history of the urban area in which you live? In which cultural territory is it located? Was it historically part of the territory of more than one Aboriginal group? Do you know which Aboriginal groups are represented in your urban area? How does your city acknowledge the Aboriginal histories and contemporary presence of urban Aboriginal people in your city?
2. What urban Aboriginal organizations exist in your city? Are they organized to address the needs of particular Aboriginal groups? What different areas do they represent (e.g., housing, employment, language, culture)? Can you compare the structure of urban Aboriginal organizations to organizations created for particular ethnic groups in your city?

What are the similarities and differences?
3. Are Aboriginal gangs seen as an issue in your city? What initiatives have been taken by the Aboriginal and non-Aboriginal leadership to address gang membership in your area? What are the perceptions of gangs created by the media in your city? Can you identify alternative perceptions and approaches to the issue?
4. What do you know about the history and contemporary situation of reserves and Métis communities in your area? How could these conditions contribute to the marginalization of Aboriginal people who move to the city?
5. Are you aware of racism and discrimination against Aboriginal people in your area? Do Aboriginal and municipal organizations create

initiatives to combat this racism? How are you complicit in the perpetuation of racism against urban Aboriginal people?

6. What do you know about the settlement patterns of urban Aboriginal people in your community?

Does 2006 census data show that Aboriginal people are mostly found in a few census tracts in inner-city areas, or are they present in all neighbourhoods in the city?

Suggested Reading

Barron, F. Laurie, and Joseph Garcea. 1999. *Urban Indian Reserves: Forging New Relationships in Saskatchewan*. Saskatoon: Purich. Describes the process of creating Canada's first urban reserve, provides examples of other reserve creation initiatives, and includes important legal and political information for First Nations wishing to pursue this avenue of economic development.

Lawrence, Bonita. 2004. *'Real' Indians and Others: Mixed Blood Urban Native People and Indigenous Nationhood*. Vancouver: University of British Columbia Press. An insightful depiction of the ways that federal policies that define Aboriginal identities affect 'mixed blood' urban Aboriginal people and sever them from their communities. The book also shows the resilient and innovative ways that individuals cope with these challenges to their identities.

Newhouse, David, and Evelyn Peters, Eds. 2003. *Not Strangers in These Parts: Urban Aboriginal Peoples*. Ottawa: Government of Canada (Policy Research Initiative). The papers in this volume address a wide variety of issues, ranging from issues emerg-

ing from changing patterns of self-identification in the census, to migration patterns, Aboriginal languages in urban areas, self-government, and economic development. It provides useful background material.

Royal Commission on Aboriginal Peoples. 1996. Chapter 7, 'Urban perspectives'. In *Report of the Royal Commission on Aboriginal Peoples*, v. 4, *Perspectives and Realities*, 519–621. Ottawa: Supply and Services Canada. This chapter describes a variety of issues facing Aboriginal peoples in urban areas and makes some important recommendations.

Silver, Jim, et al. 2006. *In a Voice of Their Own: Urban Aboriginal Community Development*. Winnipeg: Canadian Centre for Policy Development. This study describes the experiences of community development of 26 Aboriginal individuals identified as community leaders by the Winnipeg Aboriginal community. The participants describe the challenges they faced individually in working in an urban environment, as well as strategies for Aboriginal community development in urban areas.

References

Andersen, Chris. 2006. 'Aboriginal gangs as a new form of Aboriginality'. Canadian Indigenous Native Studies Association, Congress of the Learned Societies, Saskatoon.

Barron, F. Laurie, and Joseph Garcea. 1999. *Urban Reserves: Forging a New Relationship in Saskatchewan*. Saskatoon: Purich Publishing.

Berkhoffer, Robert F. 1979. *The White Man's Indian: Images of the American Indian from Columbus to the Present*. New York: Vintage.

Bradford, Neil. 2002. *Why Cities Matter: Policy Research*

Perspectives for Canada. CPRN Discussion Paper no. F/23. Ottawa: Canadian Policy Research Networks.

Buck, Nick. 2001. 'Identifying neighbourhood effects on social exclusion'. *Urban Studies* 38: 2,251–75

Chartrand, David. 1993. *The Electronic Series: Public Hearings*. Public hearings, Royal Commission on Aboriginal Peoples, Toronto, ON. CD-ROM. Ottawa: Minister of Supply and Services.

Darden, Joe. T., and Samuel M. Kamel. 2002. 'The spatial and socioeconomic analysis of First Nation people in Toronto CMA'. *The Canadian Journal of Native Studies* 22: 239–68.

Department of Indian and Northern Affairs. 2008. 'Urban Aboriginal Strategy: Backgrounder'. http://www.ainc-inac.gc.ca/interloc/uas/index-eng.asp.

Graham, Katherine, and Evelyn K. Peters. 2002. 'Aboriginal communities and urban sustainability'. In F.L. Seidle, Ed., *The Federal Role in Canada's Cities: Four Policy Perspectives*. Ottawa: Canadian Policy Research Networks.

Grekul, Jana, and Patti LaBoucane-Benson. 2008. 'Aboriginal gangs and their (dis)placement: Contextualizing recruitment, membership, and status'. *Canadian Journal of Criminology and Criminal Justice* 50: 1.

Guimond, Eric. 2003. 'Fuzzy definitions and population explosion: Changing identities of Aboriginal groups in Canada'. In David Newhouse and Evelyn Peters, Eds, *Not Strangers in These Parts: Aboriginal People in Cities*, 35–50. Ottawa: Policy Research Initiative.

Hanselmann, Calvin. 2002. *Uncommon Sense: Promising Practices in Urban Aboriginal Policy-Making and Programming*. Calgary: Canada West Foundation.

Heisz, Andrew, and Logan McLeod. 2004. *Low Income in Census Metropolitan Areas, 1980–2000*. Catalogue no. 75-001-XIE. Ottawa: Statistics Canada.

Hibbard, Michael, and Marcus B. Lane. 2004. 'By the seat of your pants: Indigenous action and state response'. *Planning Theory and Practice* 5 (1): 97–104.

Hylton, John H. 1999. 'The case for self-government: A social policy perspective'. In John H. Hylton, Ed., *Aboriginal Self-Government in Canada*, 78–91. Saskatoon: Purich Publishing.

Kerr, D., A.J. Siggner, and J.P. Bourdeau. 1996. *Canada's Aboriginal Population, 1981–1991*. Ottawa: Canada Mortgage and Housing Corporation.

Jargowsky, Paul A. 1997. *Poverty and Place: Ghettos, Barrios and the American City*. New York: Russell Sage Foundation.

Levesque, Carole. 2003. 'The presence of Aboriginal peoples in Quebec's cities: Multiple movements, diverse issues'. In David Newhouse and Evelyn Peters, Eds, *Not Strangers in These Parts: Aboriginal People in Cities*, 23–34. Ottawa: Policy Research Initiative.

Levitte, Yael M. 2003. *Social Capital and Aboriginal Economic Development: Opportunities and Challenges*. Unpublished PhD thesis, Geography Department, University of Toronto.

Loxley, John, and Fred Wien. 2003. 'Urban Aboriginal development'. In David Newhouse and Evelyn Peters, Eds, *Not Strangers in These Parts: Aboriginal People in Cities*, 217–42. Ottawa: Policy Research Initiative.

Morse, B. 1989. 'Government obligations, Aboriginal peoples and Section 91 (24): Aboriginal peoples'. In D.C. Hawkes, Ed., *Government Responsibility and Aboriginal Peoples: Exploring Federal and Provincial Roles*, 59–92. Ottawa: Carleton University Press.

Nagel, Joan. 1995. 'American Indian ethnic renewal: Politics and the resurgence of identity'. *American Sociological Review* 60: 947–65.

National Homelessness Initiative. 2005. 'Fact sheet on Aboriginal housing'. http://www.homelessness.gc.ca/home/infoabo_e.asp.

Newhouse, David. R. 2000. 'From the tribal to the modern: The development of modern Aboriginal societies'. In Ron F. Laliberté et al., Eds, *Expressions in Canadian Native Studies*, 395–409. Saskatoon: University of Saskatchewan Extension Press.

Norris, Mary Jane, and Stewart Clatworthy. 2003. 'Aboriginal mobility and migration within urban Canada: Outcomes, factors and implications'. In David Newhouse and Evelyn Peters, Eds, *Not Strangers in These Parts: Aboriginal People in Cities*, 51–78. Ottawa: Policy Research Initiative.

Peters, Evelyn J. 2002. '"Our city Indians": Negotiating the meaning of First Nations urbanization in Canada, 1945–1975'. *Historical Geography* 30: 75–92.

———. 2005. 'Geographies of urban Aboriginal people in Canada: Implications for urban self-government'. In Michael Murphy, Ed., *State of the Federation 2002*, 39–76. Kingston, ON: Institute of Intergovernmental Relations, Queen's University.

———. 2007. 'First Nations and Métis people and diversity in Canadian cities'. In Keith Banting, Tom

J. Courchene, and F. Leslie Seidle, Eds, *Belonging? Diversity, Recognition and Shared Citizenship in Canada*, 207–46. Ottawa: Institute for Research on Public Policy.

Peters, Evelyn J. and Oksana Starchenko. 2008. *Neighbourhood Effects and Levels of Segregation for Aboriginal People in Large Cities in Canada*. Ottawa: Canada Mortgage and Housing Corporation.

Peters, Evelyn J., Roger Maaka, and Ron Laliberté. 2008. *Urban First Nations and Métis Identities in Saskatoon*. Unpublished data.

Peters, Evelyn J., and O. Starchenko. 2006. 'Changes in Aboriginal settlement patterns in two Canadian cities: A comparison to immigrant settlement models'. *Canadian Journal of Urban Research* 14 (2): 315–37.

Portes, Alejandro. 1999 'Conclusion: Toward a new world—the origins and effects of transnational activities'. *Ethnic and Racial Studies* 22: 463–77

Ramirez, Renya. 2007. *Native Hubs: Culture, Community and Belonging in Silicon Valley and Beyond*. London: Duke University Press.

RCAP (Royal Commission on Aboriginal Peoples). 1993. *Aboriginal Peoples in Urban Centres*. Ottawa: Minister of Supply and Services.

———. 1996. Chapter 7, 'Urban perspectives'. In *Report of the Royal Commission on Aboriginal Peoples*, v. 4, *Perspectives and Realities*. Ottawa: Minister of Supply and Services.

Sgro, The Hon. Judy. 2002. *Canada's Urban Strategy: A Vision for the 21st Century*. Ottawa: Prime Minister's Caucus Task Force on Urban Issues.

Siggner, Andrew. 2003. 'The challenge of measuring the demographic and socio-economic condition of the urban Aboriginal population'. In David Newhouse and Evelyn Peters, Eds, *Not Strangers in These Parts: Urban Aboriginal Peoples*, 119–30. Ottawa: Policy Research Initiative.

Siggner, Andrew, and Rosalinda Costa. 2005. *Aboriginal Conditions in Census Metropolitan Areas, 1981–2001*. Catalogue no. 89-613-MIE, no. 008. Ottawa: Statistics Canada.

Silver, Jim, et al. 2006. *In a Voice of Their Own: Urban Aboriginal Community Development*. Winnipeg: Canadian Centre for Policy Development.

Statistics Canada. 2003. 'Aboriginal peoples of Canada'. http//www12.statcan.ca/English/census01/products/analytic/companion/abor/Canada.cfm.

———. 2008. 'Aboriginal peoples in Canada in 2006: Inuit, Métis and First Nations, 2006 census'. http://www12.statcan.ca/english/census06/analysis/aboriginal/index.cfm.

Tobias, John L. 1983. 'Protection, civilization, assimilation: An outline history of Canada's Indian policy'. In Ian A.L. Getty and Antoine S. Lussier, Eds, *As Long As the Sun Shines and Water Flows: A Reader in Canadian Native Studies*, 29–38. Vancouver: University of British Columbia Press.

Todd, Roy. 2000/2001. 'Between the land and the city: Aboriginal agency, culture, and governance in urban areas'. *The London Journal of Canadian Studies* 16: 48–66.

Urban Aboriginal Strategy. 2005. 'Urban Aboriginal Task Force progress report phase 1'. http://www1.servicecanada.gc.ca/en/on/epb/uas/reports/uatfphase1.shtml.

Van Heest, Nancy. 1993. *The Electronic Series: Public Hearings*. Public hearings, Royal Commission on Aboriginal Peoples, Toronto, ON, BC. CD-ROM. Ottawa: Minister of Supply and Services.

Western Economic Diversification Canada. 2005. 'Urban reserves in Saskatchewan'. http://www.wd.gc.ca/rpts/research/urban_reserves/default_e.asp.

Wilson, Kathi J. 2000. *The Role of Mother Earth in Shaping the Health of Anishinabek: A Geographical Exploration of Culture, Health and Place*. Unpublished PhD thesis, Department of Geography, Queen's University, Kingston, ON.

Wilson, Kathi, and Evelyn J. Peters. 2005. '"You can make a place for it." Remapping urban First Nations spaces of identity'. *Society and Space* 23: 395–413.

Wilson, W. Julius. 1987. *The Truly Disadvantaged: The Inner City, the 'Underclass' and Public Policy*. Chicago: University of Chicago Press.

Wotherspoon, Terry. 2003. 'Prospects for a new middle class among urban Aboriginal peoples'. In David Newhouse and Evelyn Peters, Eds, *Not Strangers in These Parts: Aboriginal People in Cities*, 147–66. Ottawa: Policy Research Initiative.

Chapter 9 Getting Perspective

Is there something about cities that makes life there more dangerous or risky, or have cities been given a bad rap because urban-based media always focus on the sensational?

This is a tough question, because although many people love cities—and the bigger the better—at the same time many others fear them. Urbanites love the vibrant culture, the range of opportunities, the shared energy of being in big crowds whether at sports events, symphonies, or civic gatherings, and they love sitting in a sidewalk café with a drink, watching other people. For these folks, city life is exciting, and smaller communities are boring.

On the other side, some people find the city threatening. They react negatively to line-ups, congestion, and unlike Blanche Dubois in *A Streetcar Named Desire*, they feel uncomfortable being dependent on the kindness of strangers. The idea of living in a high-rise full of strangers makes them feel vulnerable. Sirens wailing through the night disrupt sleep, as do the voices of late-night revellers out on the town. Watching the local news before bedtime is unlikely to relax any city dweller, since it will invariably report a shooting, a robbery, a serious accident, just as on the international and national news. But in the case of the metropolis, the mayhem is not distant—it is just outside. For people who are made anxious by this focus on violence, the biggest cities in particular are to be avoided—nice to visit, perhaps, but only occasionally and certainly not as places to live.

Analysts have struggled with determining why people hold these negative assessments. One possibility is that such fearful folks suffer from anxiety or some other psychological disorder. On the other hand, cities may really be dangerous, and the people who live in them, like people living on earthquake fault lines, are reckless, willing to expose themselves and their families to unnecessary risks. At the top of the list of the possible causes of such fears is that problems arise in cities because of their higher levels of population density. *Density* refers to the ratio between the size of an area and the number of people it contains, the number of rooms in a dwelling, or the number of dwellings in a building. Cities often contain more people than the space allows, making individuals feel crowded, which is in the end unhealthy. Another explanation has to do with the social mix of urban residents and the lack of meaningful ties with each other. This perspective is known as *social disorganization* because it implies that it is difficult to maintain supportive ties in large cities where many people seem strange and nearly all are strangers to each other. Another approach refers to cities as places of *stimulus overload* where people are constantly bombarded with dramatic sights, sounds, smells, and the surging movement of people and cars. Urban residents may simply learn to tune it all out by emotionally withdrawing, or 'cocooning', and becoming non-reactive, blasé—'urbane'.

This chapter examines the evidence on whether cities are indeed best characterized as havens of high culture, such as Paris and New York, or behavioural sinks of social and personal pathology, with names like Sodom and Gomorrah, or a complex combination of both.

9 Cities and Social Pathology

A.R. Gillis

Learning Objectives

- To appreciate the reality of rural life and how populations were civilized through urbanization.
- To understand the nature of the relationship between population density and social pathology.
- To know how the size of urban populations is related to specialization in goods and services.
- To grasp why Canadian and US patterns of suburbanization have been so different.
- To see where and why deviance service centres originate.
- To realize why we expect the relationship between city size and rates of homicide to be U-shaped.

Introduction

This chapter examines the relationship between urbanization and social pathology. The review of ideas and evidence pertaining to the relationship shows that students of cities have characterized it as both *positive* (the greater the urbanization of a population, the *greater* its rate of disreputable behaviour) and *negative* (the greater the urbanization of a population, the *lower* its rate of disreputable behaviour). One synthesis of these two viewpoints is that the relationship is actually *non-linear* (U-shaped), with both low and high extremes of urbanization associated with mayhem, and middle levels relatively peaceful.

The chapter begins by questioning the accuracy of the notion that cities are dangerous dens of iniquity and whether their size is positively related to social pathology. It examines the relationship between urbanization and the civilization of Western populations and concludes that at least until recently, it was rural areas that were high in mayhem, while towns and cities, with their greater degree of local and state control, were rela-

tively safe. Because of this inhibition of crime and violence in urban areas, urbanization was historically a *negative predictor* of illegal activities overall. Further, as time passed and more and more of the population lived in urban areas, rates of serious crime began falling. This decline, which started in Europe with the Renaissance and **re-urbanization**, continued for more than 500 years.

The chapter next looks at contemporary ideas and research on the relationship between population density and social pathology. We show that from time to time, people and other animals seem to prefer high density, or at least the action associated with it. This suggests that whether population density causes distress depends on other factors, such as duration of exposure, options for escape, or just a chronic desire to affiliate with others. However, most of the time, people flourish at middle levels of population density and suffer more at the extremes—prolonged exposure to either high density (**crowding**) or low density (isolation) is associated with distress. For the most part, then, the relationship between population density and pathological reactions to it is non-linear—specifically, a *U-shaped curve*.

The next section shows how in contemporary populations, the size of cities is *positively (or directly) related* to the degree of specialization of services and activities that they can develop and sustain. This includes increases in the rates of occurrence of deviant subcultures and criminal behaviours, ranging from panhandling to prostitution. When the provision of these immoral and illegal goods and services cluster in one section of the city, or in any geographic area, we call it a **deviance service centre**. These concentrations of disreputable activities often emerge in disorganized areas of the city where there are few legitimate economic opportunities and a reduced presence of state control. Together, this disorganization and the fact that people who enter into illegal contracts must depend on informal mechanisms of enforcement (usually themselves): these areas are similar to rural regions where the state's monopolization of violence is weaker and rates of serious crime are higher.

In sum, we deduce that today, rates of pathological behaviours and conditions will be most prevalent in rural regions and in particular sections of the largest cities. Rates will be lowest in mid-sized cities, where the presence of state control is more widespread and complete. To test this argument, we examine the relationship between rates of homicide and the numbers of people in each of Canada's 26 census metropolitan areas (CMAs) and the population living outside CMAs at four points in time over a 10-year period. The results are generally consistent with our argument but with one important exception: Toronto.

CMAs are localities with a population of 100,000 or more, and two out of three Canadians live in one. The Toronto area is by far the largest CMA in the country, with more than five million people. Although it usually leads the nation in the *number* of annual homicides and may be inclined to tell the whole country about them when they occur, Toronto's murder *rate* is actually relatively low, even lower than that of the country as a whole. We suggest reasons for this as well as for why Toronto, with a location and size so similar to Chicago's, lags so far behind its sister city in rates of social pathology. We also suggest that the divergence in rates of homicide between Canada and the United States is due largely to the differences between patterns of homicide in Canada's large metropolitan areas and those found in the north-central and eastern cities of the US.

The Image of the City

The relationship between urbanization and disreputable and unhealthy or pathological behaviour is probably close to invariant, at least in the minds of Canadians. Homicides and other dramatic crimes as reported on TV seem to be more likely occurrences in urban areas and more often in large cities than in small ones. Even the Bible, with its accounts of the Tower of Babel and of Sodom and Gomorrah, portrays cities as at best impossibly chaotic and at worst dens of iniquity, with size directly related to the problem. Scholars have also been suspicious of cities (White and White 1962). Social scientists are no exception (Mills 1942) and with good reason. After assessing the scientific literature on the topic, Berelson and Steiner (1964, 628) concluded that urbanization was a significant correlate of crime and that fear of crime and danger had become the most important reason for American urbanites wanting to leave cities for the suburbs. It is noteworthy, however, that for such urbanites, the ideal suburb is a settlement within 30 miles of a metropolitan area and its amenities (Fuguitt and Zuiches 1983; Fischer 1984; for Canada, cf. Clark 1966; Michelson 1976).

On the other hand, Glassner (2000) argues that in their search for drama, the media have created a 'culture of fear'. Urban violence is a case in point. Large cities produce more murders and other kinds of disreputable behaviour than do smaller ones. This should not be newsworthy in itself. There are simply more people in larger centres. To fairly calculate the likelihood of victimization, one has to divide the number of offences by the number of people inhabiting a location. For example, in 2003, Chicago had 599 homicides—about the same number of murder victims (582) as in all of Canada for 2002. It would be absurd to argue that in view of these numbers, Chicago and Canada are equally dangerous. The former has one-tenth the population of the latter. Unless one examines *rates* instead of number of cases—or, worse still, the dramatic incidents that are shown on television—urban areas will get an unfair reputation as dangerous, and big cities will look worse than smaller ones. More than a century ago, Sir Arthur Conan Doyle (1856–1930), in *Copper Beeches*, speaking through his character, Sherlock Holmes, was sceptical of the social decay of cities:

> It is my belief, Watson, founded upon my experience, that the lowest and vilest alleys of London do not present a more dreadful record of sin than does the smiling and beautiful countryside.

Conan Doyle's suspicion alerts us to the fact that pastoral scenes contain much more mayhem than people seem to believe. Part of the general misconception is based on the antagonism to cities mentioned above. However, many people venerate our rural past and traditions, arguing that only in these Eden-like settings can humans be good and true. This position, exemplified by Thoreau, and the concept of 'the noble savage' are determined far more by nostalgia and sentimentality than by fact (see Edgerton 1992) and further tempt us to distrust both cities and urban culture as corrupters of human potential. In view of this, it is ironic that the terms 'civil', 'civilize', and 'civilization' derive from *civis*, the Latin word for 'city'.

History: Urbanization and the Civilization of Europe

Except during the past five or six decades, serious crime has been in decline in the West since the waning of the Middle Ages (Johnson and Monk-konen 1996; see also Lafree 1998 on more recent periods). Since it was during this epoch that Europe became urbanized, the growth of cities is more likely over the long run to have been more a cure than a cause of human misery.

The burgeoning cities that heralded the end of the Middle Ages were more than simply large concentrations of people. They contained more diligent populations in specialized occupations or trades, which were controlled by guilds, as well as a court of law. In this respect, urban areas were not only accumulations of economic capital but repositories of other forms of capital as well.

From the standpoint of the individual, access to urban markets demanded the possession of economic capital (e.g., tools, resources), human capital (technical skills and abilities), cultural capital (shared beliefs, valued knowledge), and social capital (reliability, trustworthiness). The last form of capital included the willingness to habitually observe the laws, norms, and obligations of the city fathers (see Hirschman 1977 on the surrender and sublimation of passions to rational interests).

On a macro level, whether civility preceded or followed urbanization is unclear. On the one hand, a minimal level of order, social stability, and trust would have been required to enforce the obligations, agreements, contractual arrangements, and civil behaviour within urban populations. In view of the relationship between the expansion of state power and urban wealth, the coercive power of the former may have provided the basis for the social order of the city (Tilly and Blockmans 2000). Urban areas often maintained their own sergeant-at-arms or a constable whose task was the maintenance of order as well as political authority. Patterns of control evolved from direct coercion to more indirect, integrative control through the use of the economy (Gillis 2004), information systems (Gillis 1994a; 2004), and the courts (Gillis 1996a). Granovetter (1985) suggests that normative order is actually 'embedded' in social organization, and Coleman (1987) notes that these norms can be seen as social capital. Thus, civility may have been inherent in the emerging urban organizations. (See Berman 1983 and Braithwaite 1989 on the constraints of interdependence and the importance of public disgrace as a way of maintaining conformity and consistency.) In the end, urbanization was probably both cause and consequence of the development of a specialized economy, the formation of an organized system of social control, and an increasing degree of public safety, especially for those willing and able to abide within the walls and within the moral, legal, and political framework of the city.

Writing in nineteenth-century Strasbourg, Simmel (1970) observed that the relatively personal and spontaneous style of living in sparsely populated rural environments was less evident in cities. He suggested that urban life required adaptation to an environment that included large numbers of personal contacts and a greater demand for predictability and punctuality associated with a more complex division of labour (see also Durkheim 1964 [1893]). Feeling was divested from the majority of social relationships, which became more task-specific, superficial, and emotionally inconsequential.

> [T]he sophisticated character of metropolitan psychic life becomes understandable—as over against small town life which rests more upon deeply felt and emotional relationships. These latter are rooted in the more unconscious layers of the psyche. . . . The intellect, however, has its locus in the transparent, conscious, higher layers of the psyche; it is the most adaptable of our inner forces. . . . Thus the metropolitan type of man . . . reacts with his head instead of his heart. . . . They (metropolitan people) share a matter-of-fact attitude in dealing with men and with things (Simmel 1970, 778).

According to Simmel, then, the metropolitan mind was more oriented to thought than to feelings, and this was imposed by the urban environment, not by municipal authorities. Urbane self-control became part of the cultural capital of the city, increasing the 'trustworthiness of the social environment', which is social capital (see Coleman 1988, S103; see also MacAulay 1963 on the need for trust for the viability of contract). Thus, Simmel's determination of the origins of the urban psyche depends more on the press of people in urban environments than on selective migration from rural areas. In either case, cities were more likely to contain more sophisticated and restrained residents than were non-urban areas (see Box 9.1 for an example of a certain lack of restraint in rural nineteenth-century Ontario).

There is scant historical support for the idea of cities as a cause of pathological behaviours and conditions before the eighteenth and nineteenth centuries, when industrialization was in full flight in Great Britain and conditions of the urban working poor were dismal. It may have been at this time that the distaste for cities became entrenched in English culture. However, the negative association between urbanization and rates of serious crime continued only until the 1960s and then reversed in the US. Gary Lafree (1998) points to institutional change as the cause of this turnaround (see also Banfield 1990). However, the decline in institutional integration and control is unlikely to have been distributed evenly across or within communities.

Historians are obsessed with details, period, and place, and as a consequence are nervous about making generalizations. Social scientists, on the other hand, see generalization as part of their job (Gillis 1996b) so are inclined to disregard the limitations of both time and space and sometimes even of species. This is dramatically illustrated in the next section in which we look at the question of urbanization and pathology from a psychological standpoint.

Population Density and Social Pathology

Louis Wirth (1938) was one of the most influential among the sociologists who examined the social consequences of urbanism in America.

Box 9.1 *Looking Back at Rural Violence*: *The Massacre of the Black Donnellys*

On 4 February 1880, five members of the Donnelly clan of Lucan, ON, just north of London, were beaten and shot to death by a mob who broke into their farmhouse in the middle of the night, slaughtered the occupants, and then burned their place to the ground. No one was ever convicted of the crime. The 'Massacre of the Black Donnellys', as the case came to be known, has inspired two folksongs by Stompin' Tom Connors, several novels and plays, and countless debates over who did it and why. Although it is clear that the massacre was the end result of a rancorous feud between the Donnellys and their equally Irish Catholic neighbours, historians disagree on whether the Donnellys were the architects of their own fate at the hands of vigilantes or were the victims of organized persecution (Hendley 2004).

A local saying at the time observed, 'The farther one lives down Roman Line Road, the tougher one is. And the Donnellys live at the end of the road.' On the other side, James Reaney challenged the demonization of the Donnellys as brawling hoodlums, brutalizing and bullying the residents of Lucan. In the first play of his trilogy, *Sticks and Stones*, Reaney suggests instead that it was the Donnellys' refusal to join a secret society (the Whiteboys), which had originated in Ireland to combat the British and to which many of the Donnellys' neighbours belonged, that so enraged the community.

Whatever the cause, the unsolved murder of the Black Donnellys ('Black' in this instance refers to 'Blackfeet', an Irish Catholic epithet for families who consorted with the British), is an example of collective rural violence ending in homicide. Due in part to the popularity of Reaney's plays, the massacre of the Black Donnellys is the most famous case of its type in Canada. However, it is by no means unique. When the presence of the state is weak or intermittent, as it often is in isolated rural areas, familism, feuding, and fighting often flourish as ways of settling disputes, administering local versions of justice, and engaging in what Katz (1990) calls 'righteous slaughter' as punishments. This is why places such as rural Mexico, Sicily, and Corsica have high rates of homicide. (See James Reaney, *Sticks and Stones,* which focuses on the years from 1847, when the Donnellys arrived in Ontario from Ireland, to 1867, when the family defied the community and stayed in Lucan. *The St. Nicholas Hotel* and *Handcuffs* are the sequels.)

Consistent with the current definition of 'urban' used by Statistics Canada, Wirth defined 'urban' in terms of the density and size, as well as the 'social heterogeneity', of a location's population. Although he intended the three variables to be considered together, interacting in their effect on outcome variables, few studies have actually examined this interaction, partly because of Wirth's vague definition of social heterogeneity as diversity in lifestyle (Gillis 1983). Thus, most of the work on the impact of urbanization on urban-rural differences has concentrated on population density or city size as the cause of what Claude Fischer (1973) calls 'urban malaise'.

By far the most influential research on the impact of population density on distress and abnormal behaviour was conducted by an experimental psychologist, John B. Calhoun (1962), who first used the term **social pathology** when he concluded that when laboratory rats are exposed to high population densities, their behaviours 'sink' into social pathology (see Box 9.2). This included both excessive passivity (somnambulism or zombie-like behaviour, asexuality, apathy, careless mothering) and excessive aggressiveness (assault, sexual assault, infanticide, and cannibalism), aberrant for rats as well as for humans. Calhoun noted that all of these

Box 9.2 *Critical Thinking: Population Density or Sex Ratio?*

Calhoun began his experiment with 80 rats, 40 of each sex, occupying a huge cage with four separate sectors of equal area, each with a constant supply of food and water and connected in a line. Because of this design, a dominant male was able to take over and defend the single entrance to each of the end pens and prevent any rats from entering except for his personal harem of eight to 10 females. Thus, the end pens became relatively low-density environments, and the rest of the rat population, 38 males and about half the number of females, were confined to the central pens. This meant that the central areas were not only high in density but also had an extremely high ratio of males to females. Overlooking this, Calhoun attributed the effects he observed exclusively to density and published his results in *Scientific American*. The Planned Parenthood Association discovered the study and widely disseminated the findings to support its position that voluntary fertility limitation was preferable to social pathology.

Sex ratio as an empirically supported alternative explanation went unnoticed. This is important, especially since asexuality and hypersexuality were two of the pathologies observed in the centre areas and both seem more logically related to an imbalanced sex ratio than to high density. Further, in light of David Courtwright's observations about sex ratio, young single men, and mayhem in inner cities of modern America, this is an extremely pertinent issue to clear up before deciding that density caused the **behavioural sink** in Calhoun's experiment.

behaviours, which he considered pathological, had the effect of limiting the growth of the population. In fact, after a period of time, fertility and mortality equalized, and net growth declined to zero (which from the standpoint of the survival of community could not be considered a pathological outcome).

Although the leap from an experimental study of rats to humans in cities is a large one, it is nevertheless obvious from a scientific viewpoint that extremely high population densities *can* cause all sorts of unpleasant experiences—including death—in humans, rats, other animals, and even plants (see Gillis 1974 for a review of other animal studies). However, before becoming alarmed about the future of urban humanity, several factors should be considered.

Non-Linearity

As acknowledged earlier, population density can undoubtedly affect people adversely. However, it should also be remembered that Calhoun's rats

in the centre pens were not only forced to endure exceedingly high levels of density (for rats) as well as an imbalanced sex ratio but did so for well over a year before displaying any signs of aberrant behaviour. These extremes in density and in duration of exposure are rarely, if ever, found in natural environments, especially with humans.

Partly because of this, the relationship between density and social pathology among humans in non-experimental settings is more complex, with far more subtle consequences than most of those described by Calhoun. For one thing, among people and perhaps among rats as well, the relationship between density and negative consequences is non-linear (Galle and Gove 1978; Gillis 1979; Regoeczi 2002). Simply put, sensory deprivation may have consequences just as negative as overstimulation does, so population density can be too low as well as too high. Solitary confinement is used by humans as a punishment, and 'isolation pay' is used to compensate for having to endure low-density circumstances. This suggests that 'splendid isolation' is not always so splendid, just as the 'madding crowd' is not always exciting or enjoyable. Thus, in time, both extremely low as well as extremely high levels of population density can be aversive.

One might conclude that moderate levels of density must be ideal. Perhaps, but it is more likely that comparable to Calhoun's rats, people sometimes prefer to experience low stimulation, while on other occasions they opt for wider social involvement. Obviously, choice depends on what people want to do on a day-to-day basis, but preferences may also vary with lifestyle choices and may be associated with certain stages of the life cycle. For example, youth and the elderly seem to prefer the stimulation of high density in downtown locations, while mid-life parents and their children are more comfortable in the lower densities of smaller centres or the suburbs (see Michelson 1976).

This suggests that population density interacts with other variables with regard to its consequences. Stated differently, whether population density causes discomfort depends on what you like to do. It also depends on who you are. Some individuals, and more importantly for sociologists, some social categories of people, seem to be more resistant to the negative consequences of high density (crowding) than are others, probably because of their ethnic history and culturally transmitted techniques for coping with such effects of crowding as psychological strain (Gillis, Richard, and Hagan 1986). For example, relative to other groups, people of Anglo-Saxon origin express antipathy for cities, seem to be more susceptible to the strains of crowding, are more inclined towards individualism and 'cocooning' (Altman 1975), and tend to be relatively formal when required to engage in social interaction. At the other extreme, Mediterraneans and Asians appear to be more resistant to feeling crowded and seem to flourish in higher-density settings. In fact, cities such as Tokyo, Hong Kong, and Calcutta are further away from becoming 'behavioural sinks' than are many smaller and lower-density locations in North America. Having said this, however, it should be acknowledged that even Asians and Mediterraneans seem to have upper limits on density (Gillis, Richard, and Hagan 1986).

One of the strengths of Calhoun's work is that because of the design of his experiment, we can have greater confidence that the observed changes in his subjects were not simply the result of selective migration or the consequences of other associated variables. It is possible that the dominant males controlling access to the end pens selected female cohabitants on the basis of their resistance to pathological behaviour. However, this does not negate the fact that prolonged exposure to the conditions in the centre pens eventually affected both male and female occupants.

The Allure of High-Density Environments

People seem to be ambivalent about high density. They voluntarily subject themselves to extremely high levels of density and even line up and pay high prices for the privilege of crowding at concerts, sports events, and other forms of entertainment. This suggests that whatever the negative impact of density may be, at least for a specific period of time negative effects are more than offset by an allure associated with high density. Calhoun's rats displayed the same ambivalence. Females from low-density pens willingly ventured into the high-density and dangerous areas of the experimental setting to dine, even though there was ample food and water at 'home', and were later allowed by their mates to return to the low-density pens after a period of time 'on the wild side'. Just as people living in the suburbs choose to leave for an evening's entertainment 'on the town', the ability of these rats to expose themselves to high density may have something to do with the fact that it was voluntary and/or that they could go home to raise young, relax, and sleep in a relatively secure low-density setting.

To summarize, the implications of the Calhoun research for people are important but must be interpreted cautiously. First, his experiment showed that one of the components of urbanization—population density—may have a dramatic effect on laboratory rats in an experimental setting. Causal direction is clear. This is crucial, because among people, research shows an association between a restricted range of density and more subtle behaviours and conditions, such as psychological strain. However, among people the causal direction is unclear. Persons with high levels of psychological strain may choose or be forced by economic factors to live in high-density environments, including cities. Stated differently, easy-going, more relaxed folks may be disinclined to move to the high-density 'rat race'.

Among humans, the relationship between density and social pathology is also non-linear, with strain and distress showing up at very low and moderately high levels of density, and at least at moderate levels, density seems to interact with other variables, including ethnicity and culture, or pathology. Note that the consequences of population density are not always negative or 'pathological' or may be more than offset by some kind of benefit. Accordingly, people voluntarily expose themselves to extremely high levels for controlled periods of time without any apparent ill effects. Unexpectedly, this was also the case with Calhoun's female rats when they left the safety of their end pens to go to where the action was. Related to this, and of central importance, is the possibility that density had little to do with what went on in the central areas. Instead, it may have been the sex ratio, with its preponderance of males, which produced both the social pathologies and the allure of the high-density areas.

City Size and Deviant Subcultures

Although population density is an element of definitions of 'urban', historians and most sociologists would be quick to point out that there is far more to cities than density. Size matters. '[B]ig cities are

not just bigger versions of smaller ones, but different things' (Simmons and Simmons 1974, 32). The reason for this is organizational: specialization, co-ordination, and economies of scale.

On the positive side, large concentrations of people enable a high level of **specialization** in the supplying of goods and services. This increases productivity organizationally without anyone having to work harder, and large-scale production can take advantage of **economies of scale** (the principle behind 'cheaper by the dozen'). In comparison with their counterparts in small-scale industries, many urban workers toil in highly specialized occupational roles, some on assembly lines, some not. As a result, residents of large cities enjoy more specialized and higher-quality medical care, for example, which translates into lower rates of physical pathology and mortality. Dispersed populations in rural areas, villages, and towns cannot provide economic support for much beyond everyday goods and services. This is why the only commercial activities in small towns and local neighbourhoods usually are general stores supplying milk, bread, and daily-use staples. Small places may not have the population base to maintain a high degree of commercial specialization and infrequently purchased consumer goods, such as new cars, high-end furniture, or specialized services that relatively few people enjoy, such as opera, oyster bars, or Fauvist art exhibits. On a more crucial level, large metropolitan areas have hospital facilities and a large number of specialists instead of a few general practitioners and, hence, the expertise to treat rare diseases and the complexities of disabilities. Without an understanding of the value of large-scale specialization and economies of scale, it might appear that large cities have more goods and services than they deserve. When the Khmer Rouge and Pol Pot controlled Cambodia (Kampuchea), they sought to rectify this perceived inequality and conducted an experiment in dependency theory by eliminating the educated citizenry and de-urbanizing the population. Before it was over, the country's cities were gone, the economy was in ruins, one in eight Cambodians had died, and the mortality rate was climbing because of a shortage of physicians (Ngor and Warner 1988; Chandler 1991). The Cambodian fact indicates that there is more to specialized statuses than simply occupying the position, and although small may indeed be beautiful, it can also be pathological.

Large concentrations of people in urban areas often support unusual or deviant activities, ranging from the collection of tropical fish to sex toys and illegal goods and services. For example, if only one out of every 500 people has an interest in regularly seeking the company of a prostitute and 100 clients are required to make prostitution an economically viable career, it follows that, other things being equal, towns with populations of less than 50,000 (500 × 100) will be unlikely to support a full-time prostitute (Fischer 1984, 106). On the other hand, a large metropolitan area offers viable careers for hundreds or even thousands of prostitutes occupying highly specialized roles or niches in the sex trade. In Toronto, for example, John Hagan and Bill McCarthy (1998) identified at least three different categories of street prostitutes, apart from gradations in age and price, each with its own territory in the same section of the city. 'Tranny Town', with transvestite prostitutes, was centred near Isabella and Sherbourne, 'Boys' Town', near Grosvenor (and the provincial Legislature), was popular with male prostitutes, and female prostitutes patrolled the northern area around Church and Jarvis. As we will see later, it is not unusual for different sexual services to be located in the same general area of the city.

Once a critical mass is attained, a subculture emerges; information networks will be established that will extend the market, attracting both new clients and service providers from far and wide. Further, like everyone else, criminals are affected by the competition and the continuity of the organization and work harder in this context (Fischer 1984). However, one of the major problems facing anyone working outside the law is the issue of trust: the question of honour among thieves. Because illegal transactions are prohibited by statutes, the civil law and the force of the state cannot be used to guarantee that both sides fulfill the terms of a contract. Thus, those who operate outside the law must be prepared to take matters into their own hands to protect their own interests. This explains why vice is often associated with other, more serious offences. In terms of the chances of becoming a victim of homicide, prostitution is one of the most dangerous occupations in Canada (Statistics Canada 1996).

Social Disorganization and the City

The students of cities who began their analyses in the nineteenth and early part of the twentieth centuries came to conclusions similar to those of Calhoun and the density researchers working at a later date. According to Simmel (1970), for example, urbanites face the need to protect themselves from the overstimulation and distraction of the press of people around them. Successful urbanites do this by learning various coping mechanisms such as cocooning (withdrawing into oneself), controlling emotional response and expression, and even watching television to disengage from surroundings and buffer the impact of density (Gillis 1979). Wirth (1938) referred to this set of culturally transmitted techniques as 'urbanism' and argued that it explained why a blasé attitude and emotional withdrawal characterize the 'way of life' for city dwellers. Unlike small-town situations, one simply cannot stop and talk to everyone on the streets of a populous city; Crocodile Dundee demonstrated the incongruity of trying to do so in New York City in the film of the same name.

However, the social isolation, angst, and anomie that Wirth (1938) attributed to the size, density, and heterogeneity of cities are as widespread in rural as in urban populations (see Leighton's 1959 study of Sterling County, Nova Scotia). This probably means that, like life in the city, life in rural areas is no paradise either. The psychological stress of the assembly line and rush-hour traffic may be more than matched by the isolation, dangers, and physical and mental stresses associated with farming, fishing, and making do with limited resources in rural areas.

Wirth and other members of the Chicago School were sceptical about the social value of cities, arguing that large populations high in levels of density and social heterogeneity have difficulty sustaining 'community'. They further argued that the absence of community was manifest in both cities and specific neighbourhoods as 'social disorganization' and that this in turn impaired social control, resulting in higher rates of crime.

There are several reasons for the disorganization of community and control. One viewpoint, drawn from the arguments of Wirth, focuses on the freedom and anonymity found in cities populated by indifferent urbanites. City folks are more tolerant of differences and non-conformity (Stephan and McMullin 1982). They also draw a sharper distinction between friends and strangers and are much more likely to treat the latter with a lack of concern. This attitude shows up in the phenomenon of 'bystander apathy', which not only allows deviants to get away with their behaviours but may even *provoke* some types of urban non-conformity. Many of the city's strange sights and activities may in fact be expressions of individualism and attempts to be noticed and gain any kind of attention (Rainwater 1970). Because it is hard to make an impression on an audience of preoccupied urbanites, some attempts may go beyond the bizarre and end up damaging property and shocking or injuring passersby.

Although Thrasher (1927) and, more recently, Katz (1990) have argued that crime and delinquency can be expressive and fun, most sociologists of the Chicago School believed that its expression and proliferation were the results of the breakdown of community and social order. In 1972, a Canadian architect, Oscar Newman, produced an interesting variant of this argument. He suggested that some types of urban architecture inhibit or prevent surveillance and control in neighbourhoods as well as within apartment buildings. High walls, underground parking areas, long corridors, and hidden spaces such as stairwells prevent residents from taking responsibility for what happens there. Criminals can lurk behind walls or in stairwells and loiter in hallways where they evade notice by either police or residents. Because of these design factors, which are typically associated with high-density housing, such areas of the city have higher rates of crime than others have.

This view of the impact of the physical environment is similar to Newman's (1973) idea that the physical environment—in this case, urban architecture—prevents or permits action rather than motivating it. Law-abiding people are not driven to thoughts of mayhem by the sight of a stairwell or a dark alley. But someone with mugging or sexual assault in mind (a propensity to commit crime) may be deterred by the absence of such secluded spaces. It is when residents are either unable or unwilling to provide informal surveillance that urban spaces can become attractive crime sites. This weakening of informal control may be aggravated by the routine activity patterns of urbanites, who frequently leave their homes unoccupied, thus lowering surveillance and providing more appealing targets for thieves (Cohen and Felson 1979).

The Chicago School has been widely criticized for focusing excessively on the negative side of urban life. For example, Wirth's notion that population size, density, and social heterogeneity has a predominantly negative effect on communal, familial, and individual life in urban areas ignores the possibility that many folks enjoy the stimulation they receive from what Charles Tilly called 'the living chaos' of the city (see also Sennett 1992). Further, even those who find cities overwhelming seem to benefit from living in them. Human beings are 'voting with their feet' as they move into cities—big ones—in record numbers. Eighteen million people live in New York City. It's likely that few would opt for living in rural Iowa if given the chance. Paris is large, dense, and socially heterogeneous and attracts more tourists than any other place on Earth. Toronto is one of the most ethnically heterogeneous cities on the planet and continues to grow in size and density. The evidence is overwhelming.

Wirth and the Chicago School have also been widely criticized for overgeneralizing and for misspecifying their level of analysis. The Chicago models are clearly unsuitable for non-industrial cities (Sjoberg 1970), and their fit with Canada is at best loose (see Driedger 1991; Gillis 1994b; Kennedy 1984). In fact, it is unlikely that the models of the Chicago School are applicable to the rest of the US or even to Chicago itself. One issue involves the level of analysis. Cities appear to be heterogeneous populations when viewed in their entirety. However, at a lower level of analysis, cities can be seen as a collection of different but socially homogeneous subpopulations within each neighbourhood, which Gans (1962) called 'urban villages' in his study of Boston. Since life is lived largely at home and in the neighbourhood, the size, density, and heterogeneity of the city as a unit is largely irrelevant.

The Chicago sociologists may also have exaggerated the importance of the physical neighbourhood and proximity in their view of 'community'. Webber (1963) notes that communities can be viable 'without propinquity' as a far-flung network of friends and acquaintances (see also Young and Wilmott 1962; Wellman 1979). Thus, cities not only contain neighbourhoods with active contacts of friendship and support but include similar networks extending over great distances as well, although low-income residents find these networks more stressful than helpful (Keane 1990).

Although these critiques of the Chicago School are well-founded, the criticisms themselves are also overdrawn and overgeneralized. Many urban neighbourhoods are indeed viable communities, and many urban residents have friends who are not neighbours. However, the fact remains that physical structure and proximity do matter, especially among the poor, and other

neighbourhoods and even some cities themselves still manifest symptoms of social disorganization or collapsed 'collective efficacy'—the capacity of residents to maintain meaningful levels of social control (Sampson, Raudenbush, and Earls 1997; Sampson 1988; Sampson and Groves 1988).

One of the most important analyses of both the origin and consequences of social disorganization in American neighbourhoods can be found in Wilson's *The Truly Disadvantaged* (1987). He argues that the core areas of many US cities were depleted of jobs and financial support from property taxes as companies moved from the centre of US cities to the suburbs following the post–World War II suburbanization of urban America. The increasing scarcity of legitimate opportunities in downtown areas produced a situation similar to that described by Merton (1938) as anomie—a disjunction between goals and legitimate opportunities to achieve them. One attempt to reconcile this situation involves entrepreneurial 'innovation' in which goods and services for which there is a demand but defined by the state as illegal are provided for profit and power, if not prestige (see also Cloward and Ohlin 1966; Gillis 2004). For a disorganized neighbourhood, then, there is strong economic pressure to become a 'deviance service centre' (see Clairmont 1974).

Deviance Service Centres

'Africville' was a neighbourhood founded by African Americans who emigrated from the US several centuries ago and became squatters on the north side of Halifax (Clairmont and Magill 1974). Over the years, the community subsisted through fishing in Bedford Basin on which it bordered, through scavenging from the nearby city dump, and by picking up coal thrown by sympathetic firemen from the trains that passed through the community. By the 1960s, the fish had disappeared (a forerunner of things to come), the dump had been closed, and steam locomotives had been replaced by diesels. Thus, Africville lost its eco-

Box 9.3 Urban Gangs

People have always seemed intrigued by youth gangs. Accounts of Robin Hood, *Oliver Twist*, and *Westside Story* have both celebrated and demonized illicit organizations as part of a general trend in Western cultures that novelist Saul Bellow referred to as 'the romance of the outlaw'. In recent years, youth gangs are portrayed as more urban in location and more lethal in their actions. The Bloods, the Crips, and gangster rap feature on the evening news and in dramas about drive-by shootings, drugs, and gang wars. All of this adds to the image of life in big cities as both exciting and dangerous. However, the menace of gang violence is probably neither as common nor as widespread as the media make it seem.

Gang violence occasionally injures outsiders and innocent bystanders, and when it happens it receives extensive media attention. However, such violence is far more often payback for real or imagined transgressions on the part of members of other gangs. Whenever group membership matters more than individual culpability, the rule is 'you fight me, you fight my gang', and violence becomes collective, beginning a cycle that even the deaths of individual combatants will not break (cf Kotlowitz 2008). This code was the fuel for Sicilian vendettas, Celtic blood feuds, and the carnage produced by the two quarrelling families in Shakespeare's *Romeo and Juliet*. It also is why at the end of the play, the Duke of Verona, representing the state, curses both sides with 'a plague on both your houses'. The 'civilizing process' only began in Western populations when emerging states monopolized violence and the concept of the individual and personal responsibility displaced the importance of membership in families and local particularism (see Elias 1982 [1939]).

In this respect, modern youth gangs are akin to the Sicilian Mafia—and there are other similarities. According to Diego Gambetta (1996), the Mafia emerged as a kinship-based alternative to the state, which was too weak to enforce contracts or to keep the peace on the Mediterranean island. Further, both the Mafia and youth gangs sustain themselves economically by supplying illegal goods and services to consumers as an ongoing business. They are able to do this only because they are organizations and are able and willing to use violence to achieve their goals. By definition, illegal commercial activities are not supported by the judicial system, so buyers and sellers have no recourse if contracts are not honoured. They have to compel compliance themselves with the threat of violence, something that neither side usually wants.

Gangs may also occasionally victimize others in their neighbourhoods. As with state protection in general and Mafia support in Sicily, the money brought into the neighbourhood and the security provided by neighbourhood gangs in North America is not without cost. Neighbourhood gangs often 'tax' residents, and failure to pay the bill for services can provoke a coercive response. This practice is also known as the 'protection racket'. Further, reporting illegitimate gang activities to the police or acting as a witness in a gang member's prosecution places residents, their families, and their friends at risk of retaliation from other gang members. Thus, when neighbourhood gangs become established, they are dangerous and difficult to dislodge.

Like all social phenomena, then, juvenile gangs in disadvantaged neighbourhoods have both positive and negative sides. On the one hand, gangs provide affiliation for underprivileged juveniles while increasing income and stability within their neighbourhoods. On the other hand, although residents may be less likely to be victims of random violence from outsiders, they live in stigmatized neighbourhoods where they are subject to coercive control from the gang members who protect them.

Although the sociological literature provides empirical support for the presence of urban youth gangs, how many there are and just how much mayhem they create is less clear. The press, the public, and even the police may at times be swept away in a 'moral panic' and overestimate the danger of urban youth gangs. As well, even some juveniles may exaggerate the situation by claiming membership in nonexistent gangs or fictitious membership in extant high-profile gangs, such as the Bloods or Crips. On the other side, politically astute gang leaders occasionally deny the reality of their gangs or define themselves as 'neighbourhood activists', implying that those with contrary opinions are racist (Venkatesh 2008). (It is worth remembering that even Al Capone defined himself as a 'public servant', not a criminal, because he provided people with what they wanted.) Unlike homicide and other serious offences, then, it is more difficult to estimate the size and number of urban youth gangs across cities and provinces, never mind countries.

With this in mind, the best information suggests that youth gangs are actually widespread in US cities and also operate within Canada. The head of Toronto's homicide squad reported that in 2003, 'virtually all' (29 of 31) of the city's firearm homicides were gang-related, with a high proportion involving victims who were African Canadians (Astwood Strategy Corporation 2004). (It is noteworthy that the overrepresentation of North Americans of African origin is more likely the product of historical rather than racial factors. Monkkonen [2001] reports that blacks were not overrepresented as offenders or victims of homicide in New York City until early in the twentieth century when large numbers of African Americans migrated from the rural South to manufacturing jobs and segregated neighbourhoods in large northern cities.)

In Canada as a whole, as in the US, juveniles from economically disadvantaged neighbourhoods are overrepresented in Canadian gangs, which are more prevalent in large Canadian cities (Wortley and Tanner 2004). Unlike the situation in the US, however, Aboriginal Canadians are overrepresented in Canadian youth gangs, particularly in the West, and not always in metropolitan areas (Astwood Strategy Corporation 2004).

As with the number of neighbourhoods that are truly disadvantaged, not only is the number of juvenile gangs and their membership in the United States greater than the number in Canada, but the divergence is greater than can be explained by the difference in size of the two populations. It is possible that there is a highly developed moral panic inflating US estimates compared to those in Canada. On the other hand, perhaps because Canada has such a small proportion of truly disadvantaged neighbourhoods, youth gangs are simply much less prevalent in this country than they are in the United States (see Table 9.1).

Table 9.1 Youth Gangs in Canada and the United States

	US (2000)	Canada (2001)
Population	281,421,906	30,007,094
Percentage of jurisdictions reporting youth gang activity	40%	23.7%
Estimated number of youth gangs	24,500	434
Estimated number of gang members	772,500	7,071
Density per 1,000 population	2.75	0.24

Source: Comparison of Youth Gangs in Canada and the United States, Youth gangs in Canada: What do we know? http://www.publicsafety.gc.ca/prg/cp/bldngevd/2007-yg-1-en.asp. Reproduced with the permission of the Minister of Public Works and Government Services, 2009.

nomic independence and institutional integrity or 'completeness' (Breton 1964) and had to look outside the community for other ways to survive. It developed what Ivan Light (1977) calls an 'ethnic vice industry'. Some residents began to provide a variety of illegal goods and services to the sailors passing through the port of Halifax as well as to native Haligonians, who would go to Africville for 'bootleg booze and some fun'. This was possible because Africville was an 'off-the-beaten path and poorly policed area' (Clairmont and Magill 1974, 64). Unfortunately, as John Hagan (1994, 8) points out, although a deviance service centre may generate income, it places the community on 'the moral as well as the physical periphery of the economic system'. In other words, it is a 'deal with the Devil'. In the case of Halifax, this disreputable status helped to justify the city's efforts to break up the community and relocate the residents to several public housing projects in and around Halifax, ending the life of Africville.

Deviance service centres, as Africville became, can be as large as national states (e.g., Thailand, with its celebrated sex trade), political units within states (e.g., Nevada, with its legalized gambling, prostitution, and quick divorces), and metropolitan areas such as Atlantic City or as small as neighbourhoods ('Storyville' in old New Orleans) or even buildings (e.g., 'speakeasies' in prohibition Chicago or 'bootleggers' in Canada). Although they are sometimes the target of moral crusades, as was Africville, deviance service centres are often tolerated both by the governing elites and by the police. Until recently, in one of Canada's smaller cities, a bootlegger sponsored a Little League baseball team and held such a popular levee on New Year's Day that the police were needed to direct traffic. Patrons report that a communal informality, friendliness, open hours, and low prices made these establishments superior to licensed bars and clubs, particularly for working-class drinkers. At one point, a vote by the city council to strike a committee to deal with these 'unlicensed liquor establishments' was defeated by a ratio of 4 to 1.

Historically, one of the most famous deviance service centres was Southwark, located directly across the Thames from London. In Elizabethan London, both Shakespeare and his Globe Theatre were run out of town after the city fathers of London pronounced the popular form of adult entertainment 'Godless'. (Although Elizabethan theatre was not declared illegal, it was seen as so disreputable that women were not allowed to be actors and their roles had to be played by men.) For the additional entertainment and comfort of the largely male clientele in seventeenth-century Southwark, an abundance of drinking establishments, hotels, brothels, and prostitutes (the latter licensed by the Bishop of Winchester) accommodated patrons who were unwilling or unable to make it back to London before curfew. Winchester Cathedral was available for repentance on the part of both prostitutes, known as 'Winchester Geese', and their clients, while a constabulary, magistrates, and gaols (jails), including the original 'Clink', dealt with more disorderly revellers. Thus, like Montmartre of nineteenth-century Paris, 'Storyville' in old New Orleans, the 'Barbary Coast' in pre-earthquake San Francisco, the red-light district of modern Amsterdam, and thousands of other deviance service centres scattered over time and place, Southwark provided disreputable entertainment for Elizabethan London without challenging the integrity of the city's moral boundaries.

Once established, deviance service centres attract patrons from a wide geographic area, and this may further exacerbate crime rates in locations containing such centres, because when it occurs, it has a double impact on increasing the crime rate (see Box 9.4). Visitors who run afoul of the law are non-residents, adding to the numerator but not the denominator of offence rates (see Gibbs and Erickson 1976). For example, Gary, Indiana, population 103,000, had 68 murders in 2003, leading the US in homicide rate for cities over 100,000 for the ninth year in a row. Police report that much of the violence in Gary is committed by Chicago residents who move their homes or drug operations to the nearby Indiana city (CNN 2004).

City Size and Social Pathology

Size matters, but contrary to popular belief, bigger is not always better. This is as much the case with cities as it is with most things in life. As noted earlier, like air temperature and humidity, population density produces discomfort when it is either too low or too high. Economists report that, sooner or later 'diminishing marginal utility' determines that the addition of more goods and services, or bigger products, fails to provide the benefit they once did. Similarly, psychologists have found that under-rewarding fails to reinforce behaviour and over-rewarding is equally ineffective. In the case of cities, size brings benefits, but only up to a point. After that, additional benefits are redundant and more than offset by the costs of size: difficulties in negotiating the greater distances to cover and problems arising from the volume of traffic, noise, pollution, and even the bombardment of choices.

Just what the optimum size for cities actually is has been debated for centuries by philosophers, planners, and social scientists—estimates range from Plato's curiously precise population of 5,040 to Le Corbusier's 3 million. But the ideal size for optimizing one factor is not necessarily the best for optimizing another. For example, fear of crime is directly related to city size (Sacco 1985). On the other side, large cities are also more likely than small centres to contain a university, highly specialized medical care, a museum, a symphony, a zoo, or a professional sports franchise. Whether a supposed higher rate of crime in the larger city is real is an empirical question and is answerable. However, whether museums, zoos, and universities are worth a greater fear of criminal victimization involves a judgment of value.

The arguments outlined earlier offer ideas about what to expect. Civilization theory maintains that throughout most of recorded history, rural areas, not cities, had higher rates of serious crime because the latter developed more effective systems of control. However, civilization theorists acknowledge that urban areas seem to have become more violent in the past half-century. Some point to a reversal of the top-down culture of civility within cities as the cause. Banfield (1990) and others (e.g., Lafree 1998) point to a decline in institutional control. On the other hand, the increase in rates of serious crime that occurred after the 1960s was small relative to the overall decline since the Renaissance and seems to have reversed again. Maybe it was just a blip.

Other contemporary explanations of modern urban pathology suggest that the higher the density and the larger the populations of cities, the greater the neighbourhood disorganization, the evidence of deviant subcultures, and the likelihood of the emergence of deviance service centres. This is supported by most cross-sectional research, which shows that urbanization is directly related to rates of serious crime (Archer and Gartner 1984).

Civilization theory is generally accurate as an explanation of declining crime in the West beginning with the European Renaissance and extending to the mid-point of the last century, after which the tide of civility began to recede within cities. In fact, this decline of civility may have begun much earlier. As far back as the nineteenth century, areas that were least urbanized were highest in levels of homicide, but the next highest rates were not found at middle levels, as a linear model would predict, but in the most urbanized areas (Gillis and Regoeczi 2000). Overall, urbanization and crime were still negative correlates, but as time passed, social pathology seems to have continued to decline in rural areas. Thus, the relationship between urbanization and social pathology was actually non-linear more than a century ago.

As urbanization increased and cities grew in size, something may have occurred to stop the civilizing process within them. This could have happened on a widespread basis, across all large urban localities and throughout all regions within them. However, disorganization theory suggests that the breakdown of moral order occurred primarily within the most populous cities and within specific sectors, where institutional integration and control faded or disappeared entirely. Nevertheless, a high incidence of social pathology within these neighbourhoods would have caused moderate increases in rates calculated for the city as whole. The end result would be a **non-linear relationship** between the size of localities and rates of crime, with institutional control weakest in rural areas and small communities and in specific sections of metropolitan areas.

Thus, non-linearity may be the key to synthesizing civilization arguments and disorganization theory. It suggests that certain rural regions and small towns may lack the population or resources necessary to maintain institutions of support and control and/or, in view of our discussion, to curtail more spontaneous outbursts and higher rates of passionate violence. To make matters worse, young males, who have a greater tendency to resist control and to engage in criminal activity, are probably overrepresented in rural regions. Such occupations as farming, fishing, mining, trapping, and hunting have traditionally been the province of this age/gender category. On the urban side, modern metropolitan centres are more likely to contain deviant subcultures, **vagrants**, and deviance service centres, as well as disorganized areas, with an associated lack of institutional control. These areas, like Calhoun's central pens, also tend to have a preponderance of single males in the population both as residents and as visitors (Courtwright 1996). Further, in line with civilization theory, rural populations are more likely to engage in spontaneous crimes of passion against spouses and in vendettas against friends and neighbours. In contrast, large metropolitan centres are more likely to be the scenes of property offences and more instrumental violence between acquaintances and strangers, including robbery (violence in conjunction with commit-

ting property crimes), and violence for purposes of enforcing illegal contracts, protecting oneself or one's business, maintaining control in the neighbourhood or criminal organization, and the like (Fischer 1984). These differences are reflected even in the weapons found in either location. The deviance service centres and subcultures of large metropolitan areas and the general fear of crime provide fertile grounds for handguns. In rural areas, rifles, shotguns, and other weapons of personal destruction are often on hand as tools of rural trades.

To examine the idea that city size and serious crime are actually non-linear correlates in Canada, we looked at rates of homicide as the dependent variable. Homicide is not representative of all types of serious crime, let alone of minor crimes. However, homicide (including infanticide) is one of the offences defined as 'social pathology' by Calhoun, who first used the term. Further, unlike suicide, assault, sexual assault, and more minor offences, homicide is more likely to be accurately measured, especially across regions and cities. Because large cities often have modern, more bureaucratic police forces than smaller centres do, more crimes, including minor offences, may be more likely to be processed 'by the book'. Smaller and less bureaucratized police forces and courts are more likely to take a less formal approach and for humanitarian or particularistic reasons may not charge or convict some offenders (Wilson 1968; Cicourel 1968; Nettler 1984).

Besides the specific issue of city size and non-linearity, some patterns in homicide are pertinent to the research question. For example, since 1979 the use of firearms has consistently accounted for around one-third of all the homicides in Canada, but by 2002 the proportion had declined to 26 per cent (Statistics Canada 2002). This decrease is due entirely to a drop in the use of rifles and shotguns as murder weapons. Before 1990, handguns represented only one-third of gun-related homicides. Since then, their use has grown to represent almost two-thirds of the 149 firearm homicides in 2002, and almost three-quarters of

Box 9.4 *City Size and the Demand for Deviant Goods and Services*

When people want specific goods or services that are illegal, the official authorities face a severe enforcement problem. 'Crimes without victims' can be policed only through surveillance and strategies bordering on entrapment, because unlike the case with most offences, there is no complainant to contact authorities or to act as a witness at a trial. Prostitution is a case in point. As Claude Fischer (1984) showed, prostitution is found in Canadian cities of 50,000 or more, and rates rise very steeply with population.

How is a city to deal with this? Most urban residents will not support having the police overlook the activity and do not want 'sexual service workers' patrolling the sidewalks in front of their homes. On the other hand, police crackdowns are expensive and time-consuming and deflect resources and personnel from offences for which there are complainants. Further, in the case of victimless crimes, repression usually serves only to drive providers and offenders to different formats and locales, such as escort services, massage parlours, or business conventions held at hotels.

These polarized perspectives are tied to political and interest groups. Sexual service workers' associations such as coyote (Call Off Your Old Tired Ethics) work for outright legalization of prostitution as part of women's rights. (In fact, in Canada, soliciting, not prostitution, is the illegal aspect of the sex trade.) On the other side, traditional religious idealists call for eradication because prostitution is a form of adultery and/or fornication, proscribed in the Judeo-Christian and other religious traditions. More contemporary abolitionists, including some feminist organizations, argue that prostitution is demeaning to women, since the majority of prostitutes go into that line of business more out of desperation or naivety than by 'free' choice. Coercive circumstances and the fact that prostitution is so dangerous for women in the trade are two relevant questions for a definition of the offence as 'victimless'.

Again, political differences play a large part in defining the nature of urban life. In some ways, the idea of a deviance service centre reflects a pluralist compromise solution to the conflict. On the one hand, prostitution is informally permitted, but only within a defined area of the city. By avoiding the area, citizens and their families can choose to avoid activities they find repugnant. On the other hand, by allowing prostitution to continue in the service sector, authorities can watch, trying to control associated problems (such as sexually transmitted diseases), and offer some measure of protection to the sex workers and their clients.

Still, sex-trade workers and drug dealers in deviance service centres suffer from extraordinarily high rates of homicide, not to mention non-fatal assaults, arrests, and the lost opportunity to have a stable family life. So why do they do it? In the case of prostitutes, the answer is often money—or the things that money can buy. 'The typical prostitute earns more than the typical architect [because the short supply of sex-trade workers is greatly outstripped by the demand for their services]. . . . As for demand? Let's just say that an architect is more likely to hire a prostitute than vice versa' (Levitt and Dubner 2005, 106). In contrast, teenage crack dealers work for less than minimum wage and usually live at home with their mothers. They are driven by the hope that if they can survive and do well, they will move up in the organization and begin to earn the big bucks (see Levitt and Dubner 2005; Venkatesh 2008).

Table 9.2 Homicide Rates by Population, 1994, 1995, 2001, 2002, 2004, 2005

Population	1994	1995	2001	2002	2004	2005
500,000 +	2.20	2.22	1.83	2.03	2.04	2.08
250,000–499,999	1.47	1.12	1.06	1.25	1.06	1.83
100,000–249,999	2.23	1.69	1.35	1.48	1.92	1.93
<100,000	1.93	1.90	1.94	1.81	2.01	2.07
Canada	2.04	1.98	1.78	1.85	1.95	1.88

Sources: Statistics Canada 1996; 2003; 2006.

these weapons were unregistered (Statistics Canada 2003). This could mean that murderers have switched from using one type of weapon to another. However, it is more likely that the percentage of rural homicides has dropped because of a decline in the rural population associated with increasing urbanization and metropolitanization (see Silverman and Kennedy 1993 for a detailed discussion of homicide in Canada).

In 1994 and 1995, the distribution of homicides across localities in Canada was remarkable in several respects, some more obvious than others. Statistics Canada noted little difference between the homicide rates in metropolitan areas and in the rest of the country (Statistics Canada 1996). The same pattern was evident in 2001 and 2002 (Table 9.2).

Of greater interest is that CMAs with a half-million or more people have virtually the same rate of homicide as communities with populations under 100,000—and this includes rural areas. More noteworthy is that in all four years, CMAs with populations between 250,000 and 499,999 are lowest in homicide rates. This indicates that the form of the relationship between CMA population and homicide rate is non-linear. To test for this more rigorously, the data for individual CMAs summarized in Table 9.2 were analyzed using a maximum likelihood time series analysis to estimate and remove any first-order auto-regressive processes that might be present due to temporal associations. The linear equation shows no relationship. However, the quadratic non-linear model with CMA population is statistically significant with $p < .05$. (It is unfortunate that recent efforts by Statistics Canada to examine patterns of urban crime cannot discover this curve because they combined all cities of 100,000 or more and classified them together as 'large' urban areas.)

The pattern shows up in the same way for each of the six years as well as in the means for the period 1992–2004. Although the medium-sized CMAs lost some of their advantage in 2005, the data point to metro areas with populations between 250,000 and 499,999 as the safest communities in Canada, at least with regard to homicide (see Table 9.3).

Insofar as rates of homicide may be accurate indicators of social pathology, we find the same non-linear pattern with it and population size as we did with population density. However, although homicide can be considered symptomatic of social pathology, other types of crime, particularly mugging and vice, may not be indicators of social pathology, although they are directly related to the size of the urban population. (See Fischer 1984, 106, 104, for a comparison of the relationship between city size and rates of homicide, robbery, and prostitution in Canada for 1978. Note that the relationship between population size and homicide rates once again appears to be non-linear, as it does for the US as well.)

In our analysis, the non-linear pattern holds over 12 years and is unlikely to have been produced by random error. However, it is uncertain what produces this relationship linking the size of urban populations and rates of homicide. We discussed a logical possibility with variation in

Table 9.3 Homicides by Census Metropolitan Area[1]

	2004[r2]			2005[r3]			Average from 1992 to 2004	
	Population	Number of victims	Rate	Population	Number of victims	Rate	Number of victims	Rate
Population 500,000 or more								
Toronto	5,218,847	94	1.80	5,306,912	104	1.96	81	1.71
Montreal	3,632,340	78	2.23	3,632,340	48	1.31	70	2.02
Vancouver	2,131,960	57	2.67	2,156,509	62	2.88	53	2.63
Calgary	1,049,678	20	1.91	1,061,524	26	2.45	15	1.57
Edmonton	1,010,938	34	3.36	1,024,946	44	4.29	24	2.49
Ottawa[4]	873,316	10	1.15	876,798	11	1.25	10	1.19
Quebec City	715,335	6	0.84	720,787	5	0.69	8	1.17
Winnipeg	694,593	34	4.89	698,791	26	3.72	21	3.08
Hamilton	691,112	9	1.30	697,239	11	1.58	12	1.74
Total	**16,018,119**	**327**	**2.04**	**16,218,661**	**337**	**2.08**	**293**	**1.96**
Population 250,000 to 499,999								
Kitchener	477,885	6	1.26	485,248	7	1.44	5	1.01
London	467,918	5	1.07	471,033	14	2.97	5	1.03
St Catharines–Niagara	432,565	7	1.62	434,347	14	3.22	6	1.35
Halifax	379,248	9	2.37	380,844	10	2.63	7	1.99
Victoria	332,779	5	1.50	336,030	2	0.60	6	1.94
Windsor	331,308	4	1.21	333,163	5	1.50	6	1.97
Oshawa	326,629	6	1.84	333,617	1	0.30	2	0.81
Gatineau[5]	281,229	1	0.36	284,963	3	1.05	4	1.33
Total	**3,029,561**	**43**	**1.06**	**3,059,245**	**56**	**1.83**	**41**	**1.43**
Population 100,000 to 249,999								
Saskatoon	243,144	8	3.29	244,826	9	3.68	6	2.49
Regina	200,634	10	4.98	201,435	8	3.97	6	3.21
St John's	179,334	1	0.56	181,527	2	1.10	2	1.14
Abbotsford	161,516	7	4.33	161,516	7	4.33	5	3.03
Greater Sudbury	160,932	0	0.00	160,912	2	1.24	3	1.59
Kingston	154,168	0	0.00	154,289	5	3.24	3	1.64
Sherbrooke	147,132	0	0.00	148,225	0	0.00	2	1.14
Saguenay	147,957	2	1.35	147,071	1	0.68	1	0.75

Table 9.3 (continued)

	2004[r2]			2005[r3]			Average from 1992 to 2004	
	Population	Number of victims	Rate	Population	Number of victims	Rate	Number of victims	Rate
Trois-Rivières	144,782	1	0.69	145,567	0	0.00	1	0.75
Saint John	145,173	1	0.69	145,363	0	0.00	1	0.94
Thunder Bay	124,821	0	0.00	124,262	3	2.41	2	1.81
Total	**1,809,593**	**30**	**1.92**	**1,816,484**	**35**	**1.93**	**32**	**1.68**
CMA totals	20,857,273	400	1.68	21,094,390	427	2.02	360	1.86
Population less than 100,000	11,117,090	224	2.01	11,176,117	231	2.07	215	0.93
Canada	31,974,363	624	1.95	32,270,507	658	2.04	576	0.88

r Revised data.

1 Rates are calculated per 100,000 people.

2 A total of 13 homicides were reported and included in 2004 but occurred in previous years: two in Montréal; one in Edmonton; six in Vancouver; and 12 in localities with less than 100,000 in population.

3 A total of 21 homicides were reported and included in 2005 but occurred in previous years: two in Montréal; one in Toronto; one in Kitchener; one in Edmonton; three in Vancouver; and five in localities with less than 100,000 in population.

4 Ottawa refers to the Ontario part of the Ottawa-Gatineau census metropolitan area.

5 Gatineau refers to the Quebec part of the Ottawa-Gatineau census metropolitan area.

Source: From Statistics Canada. 2006. Catalogue no. 85-002, v. 26. no. 6, http://www.statcan.gc.ca/bsolc/olc-cel/olc-cel?lang=eng&catno=85-002-X.

institutional control and successfully predicted the non-linearity. But this does not mean that institutional control is in fact an intervening variable, explaining the link. There may be a smaller proportion of young single males in mid-sized CMAs or fewer pockets of poverty, and either of these could account for lower rates of homicide. In fact, it may be that a lower proportion of assault victims expire because specialized medical care is easily and widely accessible in mid-sized CMAs. Thus, further research is needed to determine why there is a non-linear relationship between the size of urban communities and their rates of homicide.

Finally, apart from establishing statistical significance or suggesting intervening variables, two things must be kept in mind from this analysis. First, on a world scale, rates of murder in Canada are relatively low, averaging only two homicides per 100,000 over the years between 1992 and 2004. This rate is similar to that of France, which is about average for a highly developed industrial country—considerably below the homicide rate in the United States (5.6 in 2003) and far below Mexico's. With respect to this measure of social pathology, then, on a world scale, Canada is more socially healthy than pathological. Second, by Canadian standards, our large cities are relatively safe. Between 1992 and 2004, small, sparsely populated, and ethnically homogeneous communities in Canada averaged rates of homicide comparable to those of the largest CMAs (1.96 and 1.68 per 100,000, respectively). Ironically, Toronto, one of the most ethnically diverse cities in North America and the largest CMA in the country at just under 5 million, averaged only 1.71 homicides per 100,000 annually during this period—a long way from a behavioural sink. Why Toronto is lower in rate of homicide than other, smaller Canadian metropolitan areas and comparable US cities deserves attention.

First, Toronto's homicide rate had been consistently lower than Montreal's until 2005, when the rate of the latter dropped to 1.31 (Table 9.2). This decline may represent an interlude in or the end of a turf war between the Hell's Angels and the Rock Machine. A 'war' between these two motorcycle gangs for control of the illicit drug market had been raging for more than a decade (see Lavigne 2000) and is most likely responsible for Montreal's higher rate of homicide. Second, the other large CMAs that are significantly higher in rates of homicide than Toronto are Vancouver, Edmonton, and Winnipeg, reflecting a general trend that has persisted for years. Whether because of selective migration, east-west cultural differences, or the presence of a larger number of homicide-susceptible subpopulations in the West such as Aboriginal people, rates of homicide and other crimes increase in Canada from east to west (Silverman and Kennedy 1993). In fact, future research should examine the impact of city size and the east-west factor on rates of homicide with a multi-variate analysis to get an estimate of the impact of each, independent of the other. In the meantime, the east-west pattern pales in comparison with the north-south differ-

ence in homicide rates between Canada and the US (Goldberg and Mercer 1986).

Murder in Metro Areas, Cities, and Suburbs

In 2000, the rate of homicide for all of Canada was 1.8 per 100,000 population. The overall rate for the United States was three times greater at 5.5 per 100,000. Further, an examination of seven cities, selected by Statistics Canada and matched on size, location, and type, suggests that the difference in homicide rate between the CMAs of Canada and the US is even larger (Statistics Canada 2002). As Ouimet (2002) observes, however, the estimates of the homicide rates in the Statistics Canada study are not really comparable, since the US centres in the comparison are cities, while the Canadian settlements are CMAs, which include suburbs. Thus, Chicago's rate of 21.9 homicides per 100,000 is for the city, excluding the suburbs, while Toronto's 1.76 per 100,000 is for the CMA, which includes the suburbs. Since we know that smaller and mid-sized municipalities tend to have lower homicide rates than large cities and that on the basis of demographics and economics alone, suburban localities are likely to have lower homicide rates, the Chicago homicide rate may be overstated relative to Toronto's. Nevertheless, even if all of the Toronto CMA's homicides actually took place in the core of the city and none occurred in the suburbs, the rate for the city of Toronto would still only be 3.5, far below Chicago's 21.9 homicides per 100,000. Table 9.4 includes all of the data from the Statistics Canada comparison but also presents the homicide rates for the suburbs of each US city, which when combined with the city rate enables an estimate of the rate for each US metropolitan area.

All seven comparisons display a much higher rate of homicide in US metropolitan areas than in comparable Canadian CMAs, with the narrowest gaps in the West, between Winnipeg (2.5)

Table 9.4 Homicide Rates per 100,000 in Seven Comparable Canadian CMAs and US Cities (2000), Their Suburbs (1999), and Estimates for Metropolitan Areas

Municipality	Homicide Rate per 100,000		
	CMA*	City	Suburbs
Halifax	2.2		
Norfolk	12.0	18.9	7.5
Montreal	2.0		
Philadelphia	10.3	21.9	2.5
Ottawa-Carleton	0.9		
Washington, DC	18.9	41.7	3.7
Toronto	1.7		
Chicago	10.0	21.9	2.4
Winnipeg	2.5		
Minneapolis	6.1	13.7	1.0
Calgary	1.6		
Denver	4.3	6.0	3.1
Vancouver	2.0		
Seattle	3.6	6.5	2.6
Canada	1.8		
United States	5.5		

* CMA rates for American metropolitan areas are estimates and were calculated on the basis of the national average of 40 per cent cities, 60 per cent suburbs.

Sources: Statistics Canada 2002, tabulations based on data from the FBI and US Bureau of the Census. See: http://www.downstate.edu/urbansoc_healthdata/Urban%20Center%20Website/web%20design2/pdf%20files/Table%2011.pdf.

and Minneapolis (6.1), Calgary (1.6) and Denver (4.3), and Vancouver (2.0) and Seattle (3.6). In the East, Ottawa-Carleton (0.9) and Washington, DC (18.9), Toronto (1.7) and Chicago (10.0), and Montreal (2.0) and Philadelphia (10.3) exhibit the widest gaps. Only the suburbs of Minneapolis (1.0) had a lower rate of homicide than that city's comparable Canadian CMA, Winnipeg (2.5).

Although the homicide gap between the metropolitan areas of Canada and the US is dramatic and persistent, the divergence between the homicide rates of US cities and their suburbs is no less striking. In fact, the rates of homicide in most US suburbs are almost as low as the rates for Cana-

dian CMAs. This supports the contention of Marc Ouimet, criminologist at l'Université de Montréal, that 'the major source explaining the differences between the two countries is the huge incidence of crime in large US cities' (Ouimet 1999).

Norfolk, Virginia, is anomalous inasmuch as its suburbs have a relatively high rate of homicide. This may have something to do with the fact that like Halifax, the city contains a large naval installation with a concentration of young males who spill over into service centres on the edge of the city or in the suburbs, such as Virginia Beach. As discussed earlier, suburbs or adjacent cities may have even higher rates of crime when the peripheral community has a concentration of disadvantaged people or a deviance service centre.

Although all seven of the US metro areas are higher in homicide rates than their Canadian counterparts, much variation appears across the US cities, especially in comparison with the relative consistency of their suburbs. This has important theoretical implications. Cultural differences at the national level, such as American individualism, Canada's more European cultural orientation (Lipset 1990), a greater tendency in the US to tolerate crime by 'defining deviancy down' (Moynihan 1993), and the greater restrictions placed on the ownership of firearms and generally higher levels of state control in Canada (Hagan 1991) and national differences in population composition and social structural factors (Lenton 1989) are all plausible explanations of Canadian–American differences. However, the overall differences between Canada and the US in rates of homicide seem to be due largely to extraordinarily high murder rates in certain neighbourhoods in large cities. Thus, the general explanations developed at the macro level, for the whole population, are not only inadequate but misleading when applied at lower levels in subpopulations. For example, if it is differences between the US and Canadian cultures that produce their divergence in homicide rates, US suburbs should differ as markedly from Canadian suburbs as do the cities in the two countries—but this is not the case. This disjuncture between an explanation generated by aggregated data at one level of analysis (e.g., the nation) and patterns found at lower levels of analysis (e.g., cities, suburbs) is a 'problem of aggregation/disaggregation' (Hannan 1970) or the 'ecological fallacy' (Robinson 1950).

Chicago and Toronto

To further explore the US–Canadian differences in rates of metropolitan homicide, we examined one of the pairs of metro areas in greater detail: Chicago and Toronto. Chicago was the model for the most important school of urban sociology in the 1920s and the site for Wilson's analysis of the 'truly disadvantaged' in the 1980s, as well as for both traditional and modern versions of social disorganization theory. At more than 8 million people, Chicago's metropolitan area is much larger than Toronto's, but the population of the city of Chicago itself (2,886,251) is close in size to that of the Greater Toronto Area (GTA) at 2,481,494. Thus, the Chicago metro area is more than 60 per cent suburban, 40 per cent city, while Greater Toronto's population is about half city and half suburb. The two metro areas are only a long day's drive from each other, and they were designated as 'sister cities' in 1991. Although the US homicide rate is about three times greater than Canada's, Chicago's is six times greater than Toronto's.

Much of the divergence in rates of homicide between the two cities may derive from differences in the ethnic and racial composition and concentration. Hispanic and especially black populations tend to be higher in rates of both homicidal victimization and offending than are whites (Miethe and Regoeczi 2004), and Chicago has a large (26 per cent) Hispanic population and an even larger (36.4 per cent) and more concentrated African-American population. The latter surrounds the central commercial district, or 'Loop', and extends southward and westward, virtually splitting the city into north and south sides. Further, the postwar flight of people and positions to the suburbs left the South Side of Chicago almost entirely segregated, black, and without social amenities—as Wilson observed, 'truly disadvantaged' with respect to economic opportunities, a tax base, and social amenities. Again, the combination of a visible underclass heavily concentrated in a sector of the city with few opportunities for legitimate employment is conducive to the emergence of illegitimate occupations as a survival strategy (Merton 1938). As noted, these illegal contracts cannot be enforced within the judicial system, and neither the suppliers nor the consumers of deviant services can easily be protected by the state, since they require seclusion from the police to complete transactions. In line with this, the homicide rates in certain neighbourhoods on the South Side are extremely high and often are related to the lucrative but dangerous trafficking in illicit goods and services. (Historically African-American homicide rates were not extraordinary. Historian Eric Monkonnen [2001] found that African Americans were not overrepresented in homicide in New York City until early in the twentieth century.)

African Canadians represent not only a much smaller proportion of the Toronto population (just under 10 per cent) but also differ in ethnicity, having immigrated principally from Africa and the Caribbean, which diverge considerably in cultural patterns from those of black Americans, who have a more complex history and have developed more of a 'culture of opposition' (Kasinitz et al. 2008). Further, many in Toronto's African-Canadian population are recent immigrants, who have been selected on the basis of qualifications that guarantee certain minimum levels of human and social capital, as well as the absence of a criminal record.

Although Toronto is known for its ethnic neighbourhoods, the residential segregation of Toronto's black population is extremely low by US standards and even lower than among other visible minorities in the city. '"Black neighborhoods" are few in number and widely dispersed. More importantly, most blacks do not live in "black neighborhoods"' (Myles and Hou 2004, 52; see also Balakrishnan and Hou 1999). This is in sharp contrast to the US, where the segregation of African Americans in inner-city neighbourhoods was encouraged by welfare policies that favoured concentrations of recipients downtown rather than dispersing them throughout the city, especially in white neighbourhoods.

The Robert Taylor Homes is one of the Chicago Housing Authority's largest projects on the South Side. Like the better-known Pruitt-Igoe

project in St Louis (because it was eventually blown up), the Robert Taylor was based on the Swiss architect Le Corbusier's modernist design. It concentrated the occupants of massive-scale housing projects into a few large high-rises with open walkways, the remaining open space to serve as parkland, or a 'river of trees', complete with playgrounds. This award-winning concept made far more sense in Europe's moderate climate than in the Windy City with its lengthy and severe winters. Worse, instead of middle-class Europeans, the Robert Taylor was to contain almost 30,000 people, the vast majority of whom were African-American single mothers, with 90 per cent of them on welfare. Residents were housed in 4,400 apartments in 28 buildings, located on 7 per cent of the land. The project was placed in the middle of an already crowded black ghetto, and almost from the outset the law-enforcement officials regarded the Robert Taylor as 'too dangerous to patrol'. This housing project is also scheduled for destruction (see Venkatesh 2008).

Although on a smaller scale, the idea of concentrating public housing in a few neighbourhoods of cities was also policy in Canada until 1972. Then, as Jane Jacobs wrote (2004, 109):

> owing to the good fortune of a clever, courageous, and popular mayor, David Crombie; a housing commissioner, Michael Dennis, who was a genius at cutting red tape; creative architects; and strong citizen support, Toronto managed to win independence from the province for planning and design of assisted housing. . . . It also extricated itself from the federal government's red tape. . . . The city used its new responsibilities to build on very small, scattered sites. Architecturally the buildings varied, depending on existing surroundings. . . . Dreary vacant lots were knit back into lively city fabric.

Following this, Canadian cities have managed to avoid both abandoned inner-city neighbourhoods and the concentration of disadvantaged families in large projects in poor areas of the inner city (Ouimet 1999).

To summarize, the exodus of economic, social, and human capital that has occurred with selective migration from US cities, such as Chicago, to their suburbs has produced a duality in rates of homicide that is unmatched in Canada. This has not occurred in Toronto, where lower-income neighbourhoods are smaller, more dispersed, and even more prevalent in the suburbs than in core areas. In fact, recent research suggests that Canada's largest city is becoming 'Manhattanized', with an increasing exodus of low-income households to the suburban fringe, an increasing presence of the wealthy in downtown areas, and a fading of the middle class from the city scene (*Globe and Mail* 2007).

As in Chicago, race matters in the Greater Toronto Area. African Canadians are underrepresented in home ownership, and blacks pay more for housing in the suburbs than other minorities do (Fong 1996). Further, there is at least one neighbourhood in Scarborough and another in North Toronto where poverty and African Canadians are overrepresented (Fong and Shibuya 2000), and they may have higher rates of homicide. However, in Canada such areas are not as large, concentrated, central, racially homogeneous, or visible as they are in the inner cities of urban America. In *American Apartheid*, Massey and Denton (1993) argue that US cities where such 'hyper-segregation' has occurred have produced an underclass with a high propensity for crime. Criminologists Ruth Peterson and Lauren Krivo (1993) concur, reporting that isolation resulting from black-white segregation is an even better predictor than poverty or income inequality of differences in rates of homicide between cities in the US. Moreover, consistent with the argument regarding informal social control within deviance service centres, these researchers found that the impact of segregation on homicide patterns is that murders involve acquaintances or strangers rather than other types of homicide, such as domestic violence. In view of this, it is reasonable to explain differences in homicide rates between the US and Canada on the same basis.

Selective Suburbanization and the Development of Deviance Service Centres

Apart from racial segregation within cities, dissimilarities in the extent and generation of the suburbanization process itself may also have exacerbated differences in segregation and rates of homicide between US and Canadian cities. For one thing, the US is more suburbanized than Canada. This is due in part to American political decisions that have encouraged out-migration to the suburbs and Canadian efforts to maintain urban populations. For example, federal funding of highways has resulted in a proliferation of roads connecting US cities to their suburbs. Since the national government is responsible for maintaining these freeways, many are in poor condition in cash-strapped states. Nevertheless, this network of highways provides more convenient access between city and suburb in the US than any parallels in Canada, and this, in a nation more heavily committed to transportation by automobile than to public transit, has encouraged suburbanization in the US. Further, unlike the situation in Canada, residents of the US are able to deduct their mortgage interest payments from their taxable income. This tax rebate provides a much greater financial incentive for US residents to become homeowners, drawing them to the place where new homes are located—the suburbs (see Gillis 1994b).

On the Canadian side, as noted earlier, suburbanization has increased enormously over the past half-century, but it has not depleted the populations of the cities as it did in the United States. This has been due in part to municipal government control. Some Canadian cities deliberately constrained the complete takeover of central areas by commercial enterprises with which residential homeowners and renters cannot compete, especially during periods of economic growth. Again, Toronto mayor David Crombie reversed prevailing wisdom on the need to separate residential and commercial areas (see Jacobs 2004) and *required* that a minimal proportion of central-city neighbourhoods be developed as residential. This prevented most central business areas of the city from becoming entirely commercial—and deserted—after business hours. Further, as a result of this bylaw, when businesses failed or relocated during the inevitable economic slumps, abandonment of central areas of the city was minimized. It had an enormous impact on the quality of communal life in inner-city neighbourhoods (see Jacobs 1961; she left the US to live in Toronto) as well as on informal surveillance and the control of crime (Newman 1973). To varying degrees, this has been the case in many Canadian cities, where some deserted commercial establishments can be seen in cities but not on the same scale as in the US. Thus, unlike most American cities, the centres of Canadian cities are still among the most desirable places to live, gentrifying and attracting residents who turn former business establishments into fashionable residences and loft apartments, sustaining the neighbourhood with their presence, their shopping, and their municipal taxes. In this respect, Canadian cities are more like their European counterparts.

The depletion of the population of inner cities, combined with the growth of the suburban population, has resulted in the majority (more than 60 per cent) of the population of US metropolitan areas living in small towns and suburbs, which offer amenities and safety for the raising of families. It is likely that these suburbanites feel that they have achieved the American dream, owning a home in an area that offers a happy balance between city and countryside and a place to raise children in relative affluence and safety. However, fear of crime is one of the principal 'push factors' for leaving the city. The film *Escape from New York* presents an extreme version of this position. Meanwhile, wealthy and viable 'edge cities' (Garreau 1992) have grown around suburban shopping centres, while gated communities with their own private security services are burgeoning as another response to suburban fear of criminal victimization. (SUVs, with their widespread popularity among metropolitan populations, who rarely see, let alone drive, any off-road surfaces, may function in the psychology of their owners as gated communities on wheels.) Thus, the reputation of cities as dangerous and crime-ridden has become a major push factor for out-migration, further supporting 'Gresham's Law' that 'the bad drive out the good'.

Those left behind in the city have to cope with a worsening situation as the proportion of residents with economic and personal difficulties increases. The arrival of economically viable residents invests the suburbs with relatively high human capital and a correspondingly low probability of criminal behaviours. To the extent that this is the case, suburbanization in itself would lower the crime rate of the suburbs while increasing it in the city. However, urban crime rates may be much greater than one would expect on this purely statistical basis. For one thing, the higher rate of crime in the core area could accelerate push factors, especially for the most fearful and law-abiding, accelerating out-migration, while at the same time making the location more attractive for those who prosper or otherwise benefit from lawlessness. For example, both users and purveyors of illicit drugs must eventually complete their transactions in relative safety from arrest. Thus, in this instance, Gresham's Law functions optimistically: the bad not only drive out the good but attract more bad. Further, as the reputation of the neighbourhood spreads and some critical mass or tipping point is reached (Lieberson 1981), prejudice on the outside stigmatizes all residents, including those who abhor the violence and the degeneration of their neighbourhood (Loury 2002; Anderson 1990).

Apart from the obvious normative and methodological flaws in such stereotyping, prejudice against inner-city neighbourhoods can have important political and economic consequences, especially when the voting majority of a metropolitan population resides in the suburbs. If legislators focus on representing their own constituents, the allocation of services is unlikely to flow to inner-city areas where the need is greatest. Further, inner-city areas are stigmatized as undeserving or, worse, depraved. When this happens, the best that core areas can reasonably hope for is benign neglect and further deterioration, and the worst is the fate of Africville.

Generally speaking, the less heavily suburbanized Canadian metro areas are not as susceptible to suburban dominance at the polls as their US counterparts. However, there are other potentially serious problems in Canada. Rural, suburban, and urban populations often have completely different voting preferences, which can have dire consequences for cities. For example, when the suburban areas around Toronto switched their political allegiance from the political centre to the rural-based Progressive Conservatives, the result was a provincial government that withdrew support from many of the social programs of Toronto, which serve low-income immigrants and in-migrants from all over Canada, including rural Ontario (Dale 1999).

Although this may seem like an isolated occurrence, it reflects the political processes that have produced Wilson's truly disadvantaged in US cities and threaten to do the same in Canada. Both the US and Canadian electoral systems are heavily biased against CMAs. This bias has occurred in part because although voting constituencies were originally defined as geographic units with roughly comparable populations, migration from rural to urban areas has simultaneously depleted the populations of the countryside while increasing the populations of the cities. Add to this the fact that the vast majority of immigrants to Canada now settle in the largest cities, and it is easy to see how the principle of 'representation by population' has, over time, been seriously undermined. In Canada, although the provinces are represented in the House of Commons roughly on the basis of population, two-thirds of the population live in CMAs, with one-third of all Canadians living in just three: Toronto, Montreal, and Vancouver. Yet all three are grossly under-represented in the House of Commons in Ottawa, and they are just as under-represented within their own provincial legislatures. This situation has important political consequences. In Quebec, for example, the electoral domination of sparsely populated regions such as Lac Saint-Jean and other Parti Québécois strongholds has been at the expense of anti-PQ preferences in Montreal. It is partly because of this that although the independentist party has won a majority of the seats in Quebec's National Assembly in a number of elections, it has been unable to win a majority on a referendum favouring independence. There are similar problems in Ontario, where the Conservatives under Mike Harris were elected in the 1990s and imposed an educational curriculum that makes far more sense in unilingual rural regions than in the multicultural schools of the Toronto metropolitan area. As in Quebec, most attention has focused on the substantive issues instead of the deeper problem in the underlying political structure, which in both instances has enabled a rural minority to have disproportionate power and to dictate policy to the metro areas.

Although circumstances are similar in the US and in other countries, the situation is to say the least a peculiar version of democracy. The Canadian government has stated an intention to provide necessary financial support directly to cities and to re-establish a ministry of urban affairs to keep watch over their welfare. The funding would bypass the provincial governments, which tend to allocate funds on the basis of numbers of MPs or MLAs rather than on the basis of population or the need to sustain heavily used and gradually deteriorating infrastructures of the inner cities. Particularly galling to residential taxpayers is the fact that both provincial and federal governments receive the bulk of their income and sales tax revenue from metropolitan populations. Further, the 'fiscal responsibility' so often trumpeted by political leaders is belied by the fact that large numbers of disadvantaged people come to the city from outside and consume rather than provide resources and a multitude of commuters take advantage of the city and its facilities through the day and return to their home communities at night, taking their school and property tax dollars as well as their votes with them.

Whether the federal or provincial governments will ever actually follow through with aid to the cities is uncertain. But unless something is done to stop the decline in urban infrastructure brought on by years of overuse and underfunding, Canada's cities will increasingly resemble their crumbling counterparts in the US (for an elaboration, see Jacobs 2004). Ironically, the current economic crisis may be the stimulus that forces governments to address this problem through Depression-era work programs designed to reduce unemployment. If these programs focus on repairing and improving the urban infrastructure, the cities of both countries will be revitalized.

Conclusion

From the standpoint of criminologists, the US pattern of suburbanization accounts for a great deal of the difference between the United States and Canada in rates of homicide, but they would be quick to point out that homicide is not always a good indicator of general crime, let alone something as vague as 'social pathology' (Ouimet 1999). Others, such as Mayor Marion Barry of Washington, DC, would agree, emphasizing that 'Outside of the killings, Washington has one of the lowest crime rates in the country.' Although this statement seems bizarre, Mayor Barry was right. Cities with high rates of some types of crime, such as prostitution, car theft, and robbery (all of which are directly related to population size), do not necessarily rank particularly high for others.

From the viewpoint of a student of cities, however, this is too refined a point. Homicide is probably the crime that concerns people the most, especially when evaluating the habitability of nations, cities, and neighbourhoods. More important, however, is not that Canada is relatively safe but that large Canadian cities are *so* safe, with lower rates of homicide than even US suburbs. From this standpoint, Canadians are indeed fortunate. In spite of heavy suburbanization and an electoral system biased against them, the residents of Canadian CMAs have avoided creating depopulated inner-city areas and a residual, isolated, visible, and disadvantaged underclass.

In 1999, Marc Ouimet observed that most of the variance in the difference in crime rates between Canada and the US can be accounted for by huge amounts of crime in the latter's large metropolitan regions. This chapter supports this explanation with more recent data and points to differences in patterns and consequences of suburbanization as the cause. In the US, highly selective suburbanization has not only depleted inner-city neighbourhoods of taxpayers, resources, and responsible citizens to act as models and agents of informal control. It has isolated and impoverished a subpopulation of already disadvantaged people in inner-city ghettos. By distilling the inner-city population down to only those who cannot leave, large US cities have concentrated on a massive scale people without human, social, or economic capital in inner-city locations. This occurred more actively in the past within large public housing projects, such as the Robert Taylor housing project in Chicago and Pruitt-Igoe in St Louis. Crime became so rampant in the latter setting that residents were relocated to smaller, more dispersed projects and the high-rises of Pruitt-Igoe were demolished (Newman 1973). Accordingly, Chicago has recently begun downsizing and dispersing the residents of some of its larger projects in an effort to reduce rates of crime on the South Side.

On one level, the differences between Canada and the US in rates of inner-city homicide directly account for more of the difference in national murder rates than do cultural differences. On another level, however, the differences in the structures of Canadian and American cities reflect the fact that the US is far more laissez-faire, both socially and economically, and less of a welfare state than Canada (Adams 2004; Grabb and Curtis 2005). Canadian governments exercise relatively greater control, and this has had an impact on the urban landscape. For example, the destruction of Africville in Nova Scotia and the dispersion of residents regardless of their preferences involved much more than racism or the oppression of a powerless subpopulation. It also reflected a paternalistic tendency on the part of Canadian governments to override individual freedom and disregard popular preferences in favour of top-down government control in the maintenance of general welfare. Similarly, the Toronto City Council's decision to prevent businesses from entirely subsuming neighbourhoods in core areas of the city involved serious government intervention with market forces, presumably for the general good. These sorts of government actions are at odds with the American value of free enterprise and much more in line with the social democratic policies of European governments. In the end, then, the structures of US and Canadian cities reflect broad differences in political cultures. These distinctions are reflected in the mottos of the two countries. 'Life, liberty, and the pursuit of happiness' declares the American ideal of individual freedom. The Canadian constitutional mandate of 'peace, order, and good government' places the collective good over the freedom of the individual.

Finally, Canadians' image of their own cities seems affected more by deeply held cultural stereotypes and by a sensationalist media than by the actual likelihood of citizens being victimized. As in the US, fear of crime is directly associated with city size (Sacco 1985). However, the facts are that Canadian cities embody civility by North American standards, and the largest CMAs in the country are no more dangerous than small towns and rural areas. The safest cities, at least with respect to homicide, are mid-sized to large in population. Further, even in the most dangerous localities in the US, cities are aggregates of census tracts and neighbourhoods, and many if not most of them are relatively safe. If in Canada a few urban neighbourhoods and some isolated rural regions are out of the political, economic, and socio-cultural loops, US cities contain proportionally far more of these areas than their Canadian counterparts do. When these localities become deviance service centres, they provide employment for the down-and-out and disreputable recreation for the wider population. Between the influx of the consumers of these products, issues of territoriality, and problems of enforcing illegal contracts, signs of illegal activity become more evident, and rates of social pathology increase. As with Calhoun's rats, then, a walk on the wild side can be risky for humans too, especially when taken in the US.

Study and Discussion Questions

1. Why do so many people believe that Canadian cities are dangerous?
2. How did the re-urbanization of Europe in the Renaissance reduce rates of serious crime?
3. Who were the 'Whiteboys' and the 'Black Donnellys'?
4. Why is it difficult to conclude from Calhoun's experiment that high-density living situations are pathological for humans?
5. Why are large cities more likely than smaller settlements to contain deviance service centres?
6. Why are deviance service centres more likely

than other urban areas to have higher rates of violence and homicide?
7. Why do rural areas and large urban centres in Canada have higher rates of homicide than mid-sized cities?
8. Why do central and eastern cities in the northern US have such high rates of homicide?
9. Compare and contrast the black populations in Toronto and Chicago.
10. How may suburbanization have increased social pathology in the US but not in Canada?

Suggested Reading

Clairmont, Donald C., and Dennis W. Magill. 1974. *Africville: The Life and Death of a Canadian Black Community*. Toronto: McClelland and Stewart. A Canadian classic, *Africville* gives a detailed account of the destruction of Africville, a 'deviance service centre', and the mixture of motivations behind this 'urban renewal'.

Fischer, Claude S. 1984. *The Urban Experience*. 2nd edn. New York: Harcourt Brace Jovanovich. A classic text in urban sociology. Fischer elaborates on his idea concerning the necessary size of urban populations for the emergence and growth of specialized goods and services, including deviant subcultures.

Hagan, John, and Bill McCarthy. 1998. *Mean Streets: Youth Crime and Homelessness*. Cambridge: Cambridge University Press. This award-winning field research presents the personal accounts of homeless Toronto youth, including abuse at home, the nature of life on the street, and their assessments of efforts to provide assistance.

Monkkonen, Eric. 2001. *Murder in New York City*. Berkeley: University of California Press. Monkkonen traces the ups and downs of the Big Apple over two centuries and the relationship between these ups and downs and changes in rates of homicide, exploding one theory after another, and compares American patterns to those of Canada and Europe, arguing that US politicians should emphasize crime prevention.

Ouimet, Marc. 1999. 'A comparative analysis of crime in the United States and Canada'. *Revue canadienne de sociologie et d'anthropologie* 36 (3): 289–408. A detailed review of the literature on Canada-US differences in rates of crime, pointing to city size and region as important predictors. This study is foundational to mine on non-linearity and the application of Wilson (1987) to explain the differences in homicide rates between the two countries.

Venkatesh, Sudhir. 2008. *Gang Leader for a Day: A Rogue Sociologist Takes to the Streets*. New York: Penguin. This ethnography of a crack cocaine–dealing gang in a Chicago project gives a vivid portrayal of life in one of the South Side's largest public housing projects. By hanging out with the gang, Venkatesh was able to give a dispassionate description not only of organized crime, life, drugs, and violence in the project but also of how families and the community itself depend on the gang for peace, order, and good government. Old-time sociology at its best.

Wilson, William Julius. 1987. *The Truly Disadvantaged: The Inner City, the Underclass, and Public Policy*. Chicago: University of Chicago Press. Wilson's profoundly important thesis is that the flight of jobs and employed people to the suburbs left a black, impoverished underclass without the tax dollars to supply schools, public safety, or other amenities.

References

Adams, Michael. 2004. *Fire and Ice: The United States, Canada, and the Myth of Converging Values*. Toronto: Penguin.

Altman, Irwin. 1975. *The Environment and Social Behavior*. Monterey, CA: Brooks/Cole.

Anderson, Elijah. 1990. *Streetwise: Race, Class, and Change in an Urban Community*. Chicago: University of Chicago Press.

Archer, Dane, and Rosemary Gartner. 1984. *Violence and Crime in Cross-National Perspective*. New Haven, CT: Yale University Press.

Astwood Strategy Corporation. 2004. *Canadian Police Survey on Youth Gangs*. Ottawa: Public Safety and Emergency Preparedness Canada.

Balakrishnan, T.R., and Feng Hou. 1999. 'Residential patterns in cities'. In Shiva S. Halli and Leo Driedger, Eds, *Immigrant Canada: Demographic, Economic and Social Challenges*, 116–47. Toronto: University of Toronto Press.

Banfield, Edward. 1990. *The Unheavenly City Revisited*.

Prospect Heights, IL: Waveland.

Berelson, Bernard, and Gary A. Steiner. 1964. *Human Behavior: An Inventory of Scientific Findings*. New York: Harcourt, Brace and World.

Berman, Harold J. 1983. *Law and Revolution*. Cambridge, MA: Harvard University Press.

Braithwaite, John. 1989. *Crime, Shame, and Reintegration*. Cambridge: Cambridge University Press.

Breton, Raymond. 1964. 'Institutional completeness of ethnic communities'. *American Journal of Sociology* 70: 103–205.

Calhoun, John B. 1962. 'Population density and social pathology'. *Scientific American* 206: 139–48.

Chandler, David. 1991. *The Land and the People of Cambodia*. Toronto: HarperCollins Canada.

Cicourel, Aaron. 1968. *The Social Organization of Juvenile Justice*. New York: John Wiley.

Clairmont, Donald H. 1974. 'The development of a deviance service centre'. In Jack Haas and Bill Shaffir, Eds, *Decency and Deviance*, 30–42. Toronto: McClelland and Stewart.

Clairmont, Donald H., and Dennis William Magill. 1974. *Africville: The Life and Death of a Canadian Black Community*. Toronto: McClelland and Stewart.

Clark, S.D. 1966. *The Suburban Society*. Toronto: University of Toronto Press.

Cloward, Richard A., and Lloyd E. Ohlin. 1966. *Delinquency and Opportunity: A Theory of Delinquent Gangs*. Glencoe, IL: Free Press.

CNN. 2004. Website, 3 January; posted 4:37 pm EST.

Cohen, Lawrence E., and Marcus Felson. 1979. 'Social change and crime rate trends: A routine activity approach'. *American Sociological Review* 44: 588–608.

Coleman, James S. 1987. 'Norms as social capital'. In Gerard Radnitzky and Peter Bernholz, Eds, *Economic Imperialism*, 133–55. New York: Paragon.

———. 1988. 'Social capital in the creation of human capital'. *American Journal of Sociology* 94 (supplement): S95–S120.

Courtwright, David T. 1996. *Violent Land: Single Men and Social Disorder from the Frontier to the Inner City*. Cambridge, MA: Harvard University Press.

Dale, Stephen. 1999. *Lost in the Suburbs: A Political Travelogue*. Toronto: Stoddart.

Driedger, Leo. 1991. *The Urban Factor: Sociology of Canadian Cities*. Toronto: Oxford University Press.

Durkheim, Émile. 1964 [1893]. *The Division of Labor in Society*. New York: Free Press.

Edgerton, Robert B. 1992. *Sick Societies: Challenging the Myth of Primitive Harmony*. New York: Free Press.

Elias, Norbert. 1982 [1939]. *The Civilizing Process: Power and Civility*. New York: Pantheon.

Fischer, Claude S. 1973. 'Urban malaise'. *Social Forces* 52: 221–35.

———. 1984. *The Urban Experience*. 2nd edn. New York: Harcourt Brace Jovanovich.

Fong, Eric. 1996. 'A comparative perspective on racial residential segregation: American and Canadian experiences'. *Sociological Quarterly* 37 (2): 199–226.

Fong, Eric, and Kumiko Shibuya. 2000. 'Spatial separation of the poor in Canadian cities'. *Demography* 37 (4): 449–59.

Fuguit, Glenn V., and James J. Zuiches. 1983. 'Residential preferences and population distribution'. In Mark Baldassare, Ed., *Cities and Urban Living*, 168–80. New York: Columbia University Press.

Galle, Omer R., and Walter R. Gove. 1978. 'Overcrowding, isolation, and human behavior: Exploring the extremes in population distribution'. In Karl E. Taeuber et al., Eds, *Social Demography*, 95–132. New York: Academic Press.

Gambetta, Diego. 1996. *The Sicilian Mafia: The Business of Private Protection*. Cambridge, MA: Harvard University Press.

Gans, Herbert J. 1962. *The Urban Villagers*. Glencoe, IL: Free Press.

Garreau, Joel. 1992. *Edge City: Life on the New Frontier*. New York: Doubleday.

Gibbs, Jack P., and Maynard L. Erickson. 1976. 'Crime rates of American cities in an ecological context'. *American Journal of Sociology* 82 (3): 605–20.

Gillis, A.R. 1974. 'Population density and social pathology: The case of building type, social allowance and juvenile delinquency'. *Social Forces* 53 (2): 306–14.

———. 1979. 'Household density and human crowding: Unravelling a non-linear relationship'. *Journal of Population* 2: 104–17.

———. 1983. 'Strangers next door: An analysis of density, diversity and scale in public housing projects'. *Canadian Journal of Sociology* 8 (1): 1–20.

———. 1994a. 'Literacy and the civilization of violence in 19th-century France'. *Sociological Forum* 9 (3): 371–401.

———. 1994b. 'Urbanization and urbanism'. In Robert Hagedorn, Ed., *Sociology*, 5th edn. Toronto: Holt, Rinehart and Winston.

———. 1996a. 'Urbanization, crime, and historical context'. In J. Hagan, A.R. Gillis, and David Brownfield, *Criminological Controversies*. Boulder, CO: Westview Press.

———. 1996b. 'So long as they both shall live: Marital dissolution and the decline of domestic homicide in France, 1852–1908'. *American Journal of Sociology* 101 (5): 1,273–305.

———. 2004. 'Institutional dynamics and dangerous classes: Reading, writing, and arrest in 19th-century France'. *Social Forces* 82 (4): 1,303–31.

Gillis, A.R., and Wendy C. Regoeczi. 2000. 'Urbanization and homicide: Unraveling a non-linear relationship across time and space in 19th-century France'. Paper presented at the annual meeting of the American Society of Criminology, San Francisco, November.

Gillis, A.R., Madeline A. Richard, and John Hagan. 1986. 'Ethnic susceptibility to crowding: An empirical analysis'. *Environment and Behavior* 18 (6): 683–706.

Glassner, Barry. 2000. *The Culture of Fear: Why Americans Are Afraid of the Wrong Things*. New York: Basic Books.

Globe and Mail. 2007. 'Toronto divided: A tale of three cities'. December 10.

Goldberg, Michael A., and John Mercer. 1986. *The Myth of the North American City: Continentalism Challenged*. Vancouver: University of British Columbia Press.

Grabb, Edward, and James Curtis. 2005. *Regions Apart: The Four Societies of Canada and the United States*. Toronto: Oxford University Press.

Granovetter, Mark. 1985. 'Economic action, social

structure, and embeddedness'. *American Journal of Sociology* 91: 481–510.

Hagan, John. 1991. *The Disreputable Pleasures*. 3rd edn. Toronto: McGraw-Hill.

———. 1994. *Crime and Disrepute*. Thousand Oaks, CA: Pine Forge Press.

Hagan, John, and Bill McCarthy. 1998. *Mean Streets: Youth Crime and Homelessness*. Cambridge: Cambridge University Press.

Hannan, Michael T. 1970. *Aggregation and Disaggregation in Sociology*. Lexington, MA: Lexington Books.

Hendley, Nate. 2004. *The Black Donnellys: The Outrageous Tale of Canada's Deadliest Feud*. Toronto: Altitude Publishing.

Hirschman, Albert. 1977. *The Passions and the Interests: Political Arguments for Capitalism before Its Triumph*. Princeton, NJ: Princeton University Press.

Jacobs, Jane. 1961. *The Death and Life of Great American Cities*. New York: Vintage.

———. 2004. *Dark Age Ahead*. New York: Random House.

Johnson, Eric A., and Eric H. Monkkonen, Eds. 1996. *The Civilization of Crime: Violence in Town and Country since the Middle Ages*. Urbana: University of Illinois Press.

Kasinitz, Philip P., et al. 2008. *Inheriting the City: The Children of Immigrants Come of Age*. Cambridge, MA: Harvard University Press.

Katz, Jack. 1990. *The Seductions of Crime*. New York: Basic Books.

Keane, Carl Ross. 1990. 'Loose coupling in tight places: Gender and psychological strain among public housing residents'. PhD thesis, University of Toronto.

Kennedy, Leslie. 1984. *The Urban Kaleidoscope: Canadian Perspectives*. Toronto: McGraw-Hill.

Kotlowitz, Alex. 2008. 'Blocking the transmission of violence'. *New York Times Magazine* 4 May.

Lafree, Gary. 1998. *Losing Legitimacy: Street Crime and the Decline of Institutions in America, 1946–1996*. Boulder, CO: Westview Press.

Lavigne, Yves. 2000. *Hell's Angels at War*. Toronto: HarperCollins.

Leighton, Alexander. 1959. *My Name Is Legion*. New York: Basic Books.

Lenton, Rhonda. 1989. 'Homicide in Canada and the USA: A critique of the Hagan thesis'. *Canadian Journal of Sociology* 14 (2): 163–78.

Levitt, Steven D., and Stephen J. Dubner. 2005. *Freakonomics: A Rogue Economist Explores the Hidden Side of Everything*. New York: William Morrow.

Lieberson, Stanley. 1981. *Piece of the Pie: Black and White Immigrants since 1880*. Berkeley: University of California Press.

Light, Ivan. 1977. 'Numbers gambling among blacks: A financial institution'. *American Sociological Review* 42: 892–904.

Lipset, Seymour Martin. 1990. *Continental Divide: The Values and Institutions of the United States and Canada*. New York: Routledge.

Loury, Glenn C. 2002. *The Anatomy of Racial Inequality*. Cambridge, MA: Harvard University Press.

MacAulay, Stewart. 1963. 'Non-contractual relations in business: A preliminary study'. *American Sociological Review* 28: 55–67.

Massey, Douglas, and Nancy A. Denton. 1993. *American Apartheid*. Cambridge, MA: Harvard University Press.

Merton, Robert. 1938. 'Social structure and anomie'. *American Sociological Review* 3: 672–82.

Michelson, William. 1976. *Man and His Urban Environment*. 2nd edn. Reading, MA: Addison-Wesley.

Miethe, Terrence D., and Wendy C. Regoeczi. 2004. *Rethinking Homicide: Exploring the Structure and Process Underlying Deadly Situations*. Cambridge: Cambridge University Press.

Mills, C. Wright. 1942. 'The professional ideology of social pathologists'. *American Journal of Sociology* 49: 165–80.

Monkkonen, Eric. 2001. *Murder in New York City*. Berkeley: University of California Press.

Moynihan, Daniel Patrick. 1993. 'Defining deviancy down: How we've become accustomed to alarming levels of crime and destructive behavior'. *The American Scholar* (winter).

Myles, John, and Feng Hou. 2004. 'Changing colours: Spatial assimilation and new racial minority immigrants'. *Canadian Journal of Sociology* 29 (1): 29–58.

Nettler, Gwynn. 1984. *Explaining Crime*. New York: McGraw-Hill.

Newman, Oscar. 1973. *Defensible Space: Crime Prevention through Urban Design*. New York: Macmillan.

Ngor, Haing, and Roger Warner. 1988. *A Cambodian Odyssey*. New York: Scribner.

Ouimet, Marc. 1999. 'A comparative analysis of crime in the United States and Canada'. *Revue canadienne de sociologie et d'anthropologie* 36 (3): 289–408.

———. 2002. 'Explaining the American and Canadian crime drop in the 1990's'. *Revue canadienne de criminologie* 44 (1): 33–50.

Peterson, Ruth, and Lauren Krivo. 1993. 'Racial segregation and black urban homicide'. *Social Forces* 71 (4): 1,001–17.

Rainwater, Lee. 1970. *Behind Ghetto Walls: Black Families in a Federal Slum*. Chicago: Aldine.

Regoeczi, Wendy C. 2002. 'The impact of density: The importance of nonlinearity and selection on flight and fight responses'. *Social Forces* 81 (2): 505–29.

Robinson, W.S. 1950. 'Ecological correlations and the behavior of individuals'. *American Sociological Review* 15: 351–7.

Sacco, Vincent F. 1985. 'City size and perceptions of violence'. *Canadian Journal of Sociology* 10: 277–94.

Sampson, Robert J. 1988. 'Local friendship ties and community attachment in mass society: A multilevel systemic model'. *American Sociological Review* 53 (5): 766–79.

Sampson, Robert J., and W. Byron Groves. 1988. 'Community structure and crime: Testing social disorganization theory'. *American Journal of Sociology* 94: 774–802.

Sampson, Robert J., Stephen Raudenbush, and Felton Earls. 1997. 'Neighborhoods and violent crime: A multilevel study of collective efficacy'. *Science* 277: 918–24.

Sennett, Richard. 1992. *The Uses of Disorder*. New York: Norton.

Silverman, Robert, and Leslie Kennedy. 1993. *Deadly Deeds: Murder in Canada*. Toronto: Nelson.

Simmel, G. 1970. 'The metropolis and mental life'. In Robert Guttman and David Popenoe, Eds, *Neighborhood, City, and Metropolis*, 777–88. New York: Random House.

Simmons, James, and Robert Simmons. 1974. *Urban Canada*. 2nd edn. Toronto: Copp Clark.

Sjoberg, Gideon. 1970. 'The preindustrial city'. In Robert Guttman and David Popenoe, Eds, *Neighborhood, City, and Metropolis*, 168–76. New York: Random House.

Statistics Canada. 1996. *The Daily*. 30 July.

———. 2002. http://www.npb_cnlc.gc.ca/reports/pdf/pls_2002/08_e.htm.

———. 2003. *The Daily*, 3 October.

———. 2007. 'Homicide in Canada, 2005. *Juristat* 26 (6).

Stephan, G.E., and D.R. McMullin. 1982. 'Tolerance of sexual non-conformity: City size as a situational and early learning determinant'. *American Sociological Review* 47: 411–15.

Thrasher, Frederick. 1927. *The Gang*. Chicago: University of Chicago Press.

Tilly, Charles, and Wim P. Blockmans, Eds. 2000. *Cities and the Rise of States in Europe, A.D. 1000 to 1800*. Boulder, CO: Westview Press.

Venkatesh, Sudhir. 2008. *Gang Leader for a Day: A Rogue Sociologist Takes to the Streets*. New York: Penguin.

Webber, Melvin M. 1963. 'Order in diversity: Community without propinquity'. In L. Wingo, Jr, Ed., *Cities and Space: The Future Use of Urban Land*. Baltimore, MD: Johns Hopkins University Press.

Wellman, Barry. 1979. 'The community question'. *American Journal of Sociology* 84: 1,201–31.

White, Morton, and Lucinda White. 1962. *The Intellectual versus the City*. Cambridge, MA: Harvard University Press.

Wilson, James Q. 1968. 'The police and the delinquent in two cities'. In Stanton Wheeler, Ed., *Controlling Delinquents*. New York: John Wiley.

Wilson, William J. 1987. *The Truly Disadvantaged: The Inner City, the Underclass, and Public Policy*. Chicago: University of Chicago Press.

Wirth, Louis. 1938. 'Urbanism as a way of life'. *American Journal of Sociology* 44: 3–24.

Wortley, Scot, and Julian Tanner. 2004. 'Social groups or criminal organizations? The extent and nature of youth gang activity in Toronto'. In Bruce Kidd and James Phillips, Eds, *From Enforcement and Prevention to Civic Engagement: Research on Community Safety*, 59–80. Toronto: Centre of Criminology, University of Toronto.

Young, Michael, and Peter Wilmott. 1962. *Family and Kinship in East London*. London: Penguin.

Chapter 10 Getting Perspective

Do women live in the city differently from men?

The relationship between women and cities is intimately tied to women's changing roles. The industrial city meant the separation of place of residence and place of work for the first time. Women were first employed in low-paying industrial jobs, especially when labour was in short supply, as was the case in wartime. Later, in the expanded suburban city of the postwar period, women were primarily engaged in unpaid domestic labour in the home. Men's roles came to be defined as occurring in public space, whereas women's roles took place in private places. The more recent shift to greater participation in the labour force by women has brought about an awareness that cities are gendered places. Housing in distant suburbs presented problems for women active in the labour force who still had the greater burden of domestic work, caregiving, and nurturing within the family. As suburbs have become places in which to live and work, a more diverse range of households confronts a built form that cannot address the needs of a multiplicity of cultures, lifestyles, and stages of the life cycle.

Women's interest in the city began with the industrial city, with its substandard housing, pollution, and poverty. Activist women played a huge role in helping to transform the city into a more livable place. One such woman in the city of Chicago was Jane Addams, the first woman to win a Nobel Peace Prize. She not only worked hard to help women secure the vote but sought to improve the lives of people in slums through better housing, child labour laws, domestic violence laws, and child care facilities. She even played a role as a non-academic in the establishment of the first Department of Sociology—at the University of Chicago, where urban sociology was born. Women played similar roles in Canada, such as that of the 'Famous Five' women from Alberta who are commemorated by a bronze monument on the Olympic Plaza in downtown Calgary and a massive sculpture on Parliament Hill in Ottawa. These five women played a critical role in the constitutional recognition of women as persons in 1929 and fought for the improvement of conditions of life in cities for all, but particularly for women.

10 Gender and the Neo-liberal City: Urban Restructuring, Social Exclusion, and Democratic Participation

Gerda R. Wekerle

Learning Objectives

- To understand the ways in which neo-liberal urban restructuring contributes to social exclusion.
- To analyze four aspects of social exclusion and their impacts on urban women's lives.
- To appreciate how women's urban activism offers an alternate vision of the just city.

Introduction

Feminist urbanists like Doreen Massey (1997) have argued that we must rethink the relationship between spatiality, power, and justice. They challenge us to view globalized cities as contested terrains where narratives of economic competition and urban growth mask growing inequalities and social exclusion. Women have been at the centre of these struggles in globalizing cities, challenging social exclusion exacerbated by growing economic polarization, residential segregation, shifts in mobility, reductions in municipal services, and declining participation in local governance. Feminist urban scholars have emphasized that the differences among women need attention. They analyze how gender differences in the experience and use of urban space is mediated by class, race, and sexuality. Urban research has also delved into the details of women's urban experiences—their housing options, the diversity of women's lives in cities and suburbs, and how they move around the city. These in-depth studies frequently challenge our stereotypes of specific women in particular places and demonstrate

that many women engage in active place-making strategies rather than remaining socially and spatially isolated. Even when the stories are framed as survival strategies in the global city, the accounts often highlight how women become active agents in forging their own lives and the futures of their children. This is evident in the community food security movements spearheaded by women and in women's struggles to control and build their own housing to maintain a secure place in the global city. Women have claimed the right to the city in challenging public agencies to provide access to transportation and safety in public spaces. They articulate a vision of a just city that contrasts with the image of the global competitive city.

Issues of social polarization, spatial inequality, and the deterioration of everyday life for urban dwellers receive scant attention in the prevailing discourses of the neo-liberal city. Sociologist Joe Feagin (1998, 18–19) argues that we need to move class, race, and gender domination to the centre of our analyses of urban restructuring, change, and development in order to understand how urban transformations, which create opportunities and prosperity for some, result in increasing marginalization for others. A key theme in the literature on Canadian cities is the ways in which large Canadian cities, especially Vancouver, Toronto, and Montreal, have been reshaped as competitive entrepreneurial cities (Kipfer and Keil 2002). Cities around the world are in competition with one another to attract and serve knowledge workers in the new economy and professional and managerial classes through entertainment districts and the arts, loft and luxury condominium developments in downtown cores, and high-tech industrial parks on the exurban fringe. Larry Bourne (2000, 39) argues that 'Part of the challenge posed by economic restructuring and social change is our ability to respond to the needs of those left behind in the competition for living space and a larger slice of the urban economic pie.' In contrast to the image of the city as a generator of wealth and continuing economic growth, social researchers, policy-makers, and community activists highlight the ways in which neo-liberal restructuring contributes to social exclusion. They ask: Who is left behind in the current economic and socio-spatial restructuring of cities? And how might they be included?

Social Inclusion and Exclusion in the City

The concepts of social inclusion and exclusion were initially developed in Europe and the UK as a way to talk about poverty and inequality as both a state and a process (Hills, LeGrand, and Piachaud 2002). The term **social exclusion** refers to the syndrome of poverty and multiple deprivations, including lack of employment, low income, poor housing and health, and limited access to facilities and services that structure inequalities among urban residents. This chapter focuses on four ways in which gender and social exclusion intersect in Canadian cities. First, social exclusion is related most obviously to poverty. Income affects access to housing, including tenure, location, and the quality of life attached to living in specific types of housing and locations. Second, residential segregation structures social exclusion or inclusion. Who lives where in cities structures the availability, quality, and access to services, including education and child care, immigrant settlement services, and public transit, all of which affect social inclusion. The segregation of land uses associated with suburban low-density developments based on homeownership and the lack of alternative housing options particularly affects women's lives in cities. Third, social exclusion is increasingly linked to mobility, with the continuing spread of cities through low-density suburban and exurban development and the almost exclusive reliance on private automobiles. Travel behaviour in cities is deeply gendered, with consequences for daily life and livelihood. Finally, social inclusion also addresses participation in governance and having a political voice in cities, including the question of whose vision of the city is listened to, valued, and implemented and who has rights to the city.

Economic Polarization, Housing, and Gender

Women in Canada continue to be more vulnerable to poverty than men are. Women make up the majority in all groups that experience poverty: Aboriginal people, people with disabilities, people of colour, recent immigrants, seniors, and youth. In 2005 across Canada, women's earnings were on average 64 per cent of men's earnings—$26,800 per year compared to men's average earnings of $41,900 per year (Statistics Canada 2007a). The median income of lone-mother households was $38,347, compared to lone-father household median income of $54,431 in 2005 (Statistics Canada 2006b). In 2006, 11.6 per cent of all Canadian women between the ages of 18 and 64 were poor (as measured by low-income cut-offs), contrasted with 10.9 per cent of males in the same age group (Statistics Canada 2008). Women with disabilities, recent immigrants, and members of visible minorities have a higher incidence of persistent poverty than women as a whole. The net worth of family units—i.e., assets, including pension plans, that households can draw on to purchase housing and transportation or to pay for education—varies substantially by gender: in 2005, the median net worth of all Canadian male family units was $184,964; the median net worth of female units was $105,470. The differences among those under 35 is stark: males had a median net worth of $28,203; females had a median net worth of $9,900 (Statistics Canada 2006b). These differences in wealth between men and women and among different groups of women differentially affect available housing options and associated locational advantages and disadvantages. They affect how much income is left over after basic shelter and subsistence costs. They affect mobility and access to employment opportunities, and ability to make use of urban amenities, including recreation, that are increasingly available on a user-pay basis.

Within Canadian cities, levels of income polarization and poverty have increased, affecting where people live and work and their overall quality of life. During the 1990s, conditions worsened for those on fixed or low incomes, including refugees and some immigrants, unattached individuals, single-parent families, and elderly women living alone (Bourne 2000; Bourne and Rose 2001). In Toronto, which has experienced high growth and high housing costs, a study (United Way of Greater Toronto 2004) showed an increase of 69 per cent in the number of poor families between 1981 and 2001 compared to just a 15 per cent increase in the number of families overall. In addition, poverty is spatialized. There has been a dramatic increase in the number of higher-poverty neighbourhoods in Toronto, from 30 in 1981 to 120 in 2001, with pockets of poverty concentrated in the inner suburbs built during the postwar period. The suburban poor live in areas with declining housing stock, an aging retail sector, limited services, and inadequate public transit. Immigrant families accounted for

two-thirds of the total family population living in higher-poverty neighbourhoods.

The high cost of housing in Canada's largest cities and women's relative poverty mean that women as a group have more circumscribed housing options. Access to affordable housing affects life chances, security, and access to services. Women in Canadian cities have been particularly hard hit by the retreat in the mid-1990s by federal and provincial governments from state-funded social housing programs, the scarcity of rental housing, and reliance on the private market to meet the housing needs of most Canadians. As Walks (2006, 423) points out, 'Increasing income inequality at the household level and greater competition in the housing market translate into greater polarization between those who own their homes and those who rent. Since the mid-1970s, homeowners have become richer, while tenants have become poorer.'

Public policy decisions to virtually eliminate the construction of rental social housing and to allow for the construction of condominium housing and conversion of rental units to condominiums resulted in a decline in rental housing as a proportion of the total housing stock. Consequently, the supply of rental housing, particularly affordable housing and a choice of locations, declined at a time when urban populations continued to grow and income inequalities were exacerbated in Canada's largest urban areas (Walks 2006). Housing affordability has become a suburban problem; there are now more households spending more than 30 per cent of their income on shelter living in suburban portions of Canadian cities than in inner cities (Walks 2006). Community agencies have begun to identify problems of homelessness and people living in unregulated basement apartments in suburbs.

The Canadian housing system favours homeownership. *Neo-liberal restructuring* has put the emphasis on housing produced by the market rather than by government and on housing as a commodity and a means of capital accumulation. More than two-thirds of Canadian households (68.4 per cent) owned their dwelling in 2006 (Statistics Canada 2006a). Homeownership bestows many benefits: security of tenure and relatively good quality of housing, a range of locations, and a way to save for retirement (Wekerle 1997). But not all urban residents are in the homeownership pool. In the past, lone-mother households and women living alone had the lowest homeownership rates. This has changed somewhat. In 2006, for the first time, more than half (52.5 per cent) of lone-parent households headed by women owned their own home, still well below the two-thirds of lone fathers who owned a home. However, the number of lone mothers who spent more than 30 per cent on shelter increased between 2001 and 2006 (Statistics Canada 2006a). This may reflect their lower incomes and increasing pressures to own housing rather than renting. Women who lived alone had a higher homeownership rate (48.7 per cent) than their male counterparts, although about half of these women are over 65 and were probably widowed—i.e., they inherited the family home (Statistics Canada 2006a).

Across Canada, condominium ownership now accounts for 10.9 per cent of all homeownership. The proportion of owner households living in condominiums has risen to 31 per cent in Vancouver, 18.6 per cent in Toronto, and 13.3 per cent in Montreal (Statistics Canada 2006a). Condominiums have been particularly attractive to female one-person households and have offered a new avenue for women into homeownership. As Kern's (2007) research on young women condominium owners in Toronto demonstrates, condominiums provide a way to access the social and economic advantages of homeownership from which young single women have been excluded in the past. But the pressure to own in a shrinking rental market also means that young women with a low asset base and a relatively lower employment income may be more financially vulnerable in economic downturns.

A sizable number of women rent rather than own. Among women renters who lived alone, 56.6 per cent spent more than 30 per cent of their income on shelter costs (Statistics Canada 2006a). In Winnipeg and Toronto, anti-poverty campaigns, 'Pay the Rent or Feed the Kids', have highlighted the untenable choices and extreme hardships faced by low-income households struggling for survival. These households are further disadvantaged by limited locational options. Besides providing shelter, housing is also a locational good. Because housing is located in a specific place, it mediates access to employment opportunities and a range of other social goods, including the quality of local schools, recreation and green space, neighbourhood security, air quality, and access to grocery shopping and food, public transit, and health care. A report on Canadian women and their housing (CMHC 1997) notes that 'Location is important for reaching access to community services. Some social housing projects are situated in "second choice" locations such as redeveloped industrial lands or remote suburbs. Areas with pollution, exposure to lead or mercury, poor air quality, or few green spaces negatively affect health.'

Urban Diversity and Residential Segregation

Canada's cities are becoming ethnically and racially more diverse as a result of immigration targets of about 200,000 immigrants per year. By the 1990s, almost 80 per cent of immigrants came from Asia, Africa, the Caribbean, and Latin America, a shift referred to as 'the ethnocultural transformation of the larger cities through immigration' (Bourne and Rose 2001, 113). Among the immigrants arriving between 2001 and 2006, seven out of 10 people settled in Toronto, Vancouver, and Montreal. The largest number (40 per cent) moved to Toronto, many of them settling in suburban areas (Statistics Canada 2007b).

The residential concentration of immigrant communities and how it may relate to social exclusion is of concern to policy-makers. Studies have examined whether immigrants voluntarily choose to live within their own communities and the role that poverty plays in these choices (Preston and Wong 2002). Recent immigrants with lower incomes and young families have been attracted to lower-cost suburban locations. At the same time, older, more affluent immigrants, often postwar immigrants from Europe, continue to move into ethnic enclaves in the suburbs. The material conditions and experiences of daily life are very different, although both are considered suburban environments.

Suburbia and Social Exclusion

A dominant trend affecting the socio-spatial form of Canadian cities is the accelerating and continued growth outwards and decentralization of people, services, and jobs to the suburbs (Burleton 2002, 8). Much of this development continues to be at relatively low densities because of demands for more living space in single-family housing, parking lots for automobiles in larger retail centres for big-box stores, and the dispersion of employment throughout the region and in suburban high-tech, campus-style sites (Bourne 2000). The existing urban fabric, with separation of residential uses from employment and retail uses, has increased reliance on private automobiles for commuting to work and to meet the requirements of everyday life, since dispersed suburban development often does not provide the density of people needed to run public transit.

Yet today's suburbs are also more diverse than they have ever been, with dual-worker households, aging populations, single parents, non-family households, multi-generational families, and ethnic enclaves. Many new immigrants move directly to the suburbs, where jobs and housing are more readily available (Bourne 2000). The proportion of immigrants has reached 25 to 40 per cent and is growing in suburban municipalities such as Markham, Vaughan, and Mississauga in the Toronto CMA and Richmond and Surrey in

Greater Vancouver (Bourne and Rose 2001). This 'suburbanization of diversity' (Bourne and Rose 2001) raises concerns about whether conventionally planned suburbs can meet more diverse needs for housing, community services, and access to public space.

The increasing diversity of suburban communities is reflected in the ways that immigrant communities in Canadian cities, particularly in Toronto and Vancouver, actively construct and reshape suburbs, from the building of mosques and related schools and community centres to demands for housing designs that accommodate multi-generational families. The influx of immigrant households with varying cultural traditions as to the role of women provides opportunities to further investigate the processes of place-making and construction of gender relations. The emergence of suburban ethnic enclaves that offer ethnocultural services, religious institutions, and shopping has been framed in the media as potentially isolating ethnic communities from the mainstream of Canadian life. Others suggest that this is a positive development, heralding a process of restructuring suburban spatial patterns to make suburbs into a place to call home.

In an era of fiscal cutbacks, services to assist the settlement process were reduced in Canadian cities. Immigrants were forced to rely on the assistance of friends and family to access employment, housing, and other services (Hoernig and Walton-Roberts 2006). Immigrant women often create communities of mutual aid in Canadian cities. Through in-depth studies of immigrant women's neighbourhood networks in Montreal, Ray and Rose (2000) found that gender plays an important role in how social networks are constructed and how these networks intersect with the material conditions of real urban neighbourhoods.

Suburbanization is a long-standing socio-spatial pattern that increases the distance between affluent and poor urban residents. Critics of suburban sprawl tend to focus on the problems of gridlock, pollution, global warming, and the loss of farmland (e.g., Calthorpe and Fulton

2001). Yet there are also social costs, both for the people who live in suburban and exurban communities and for people who are excluded from obtaining housing or employment in the fast-growing suburbs. Over the past three decades, the out-migration of large-scale office, commercial, and service functions has tapped into a pool of well-educated middle-class women living in the suburbs (Frank 2008; Wekerle and Rutherford 1989). Yet this has also increased social and spatial polarization because low-income women living in city centres and older suburbs have found it more difficult to travel to these locations largely accessible only by private automobile. In some US cities, church leaders and politicians have explicitly linked suburban sprawl to racial segregation. They claim that low-density suburban development contributes to the social exclusion of the poor, immigrants, and visible minorities and serves to maintain the privilege of primarily middle-class, white residents (Dreier, Mollenkopf, and Swanstrom 2001; Orfield 1997). To combat the economic and racial segregation of racialized minorities in the core and older suburban areas of cities, some cities require *regional fair share affordable housing*—that is, suburban communities are required by state governments to construct some affordable housing. While activists in Canadian cities have also organized campaigns against sprawl, the focus has tended to be on environmental preservation rather than on issues of social exclusion and access to employment, services, and affordable housing (Wekerle and Abbruzzese, 2009).

Feminist Critiques of Housing and Suburbs

Since the 1970s, feminist urbanists have argued that housing, particularly in the suburbs, assumes a traditional nuclear family and does not reflect the diversity of household and family types or the increasing ethnic and cultural diversity of cities (Wekerle, Peterson, and Mor-

ley 1980; Keller 1981). Over three decades of research, this literature has linked urban processes, industrial restructuring, and household relationships (McDowell 1993a). A major contribution was in the studies of the *gendered division of labour*, particularly the relationships between home and work and 'the significance of women's unpaid labour in maintaining urban functions' (McDowell 1993a, 166). Feminist research on urban environments argued that a particular urban form—the suburban single-family house, built at low densities, with limited public services and reliance on the automobile—was developed on *gendered principles*. Suburban forms assumed a family type, the nuclear family, and a mother at home to care for the needs of that family. Inequalities arise because of the assumption that the tasks of reproduction—i.e., the household work and care of children—are primarily the responsibility of women (McDowell 1993a). Researchers questioned the compatibility of separating land uses into spheres of work and family life, especially as more women entered the labour force (Hayden 1981; Michelson 1985; 1988). They argued that women had dual roles, as workers in the labour market and as persons responsible for the caring work in the home, and that the built form of the city should take this into account. As families became more diverse, many women living in suburbs did not meet the conventional models of femininity, including women living in families that were single-parent, woman-led, dual-earner, single-person, retired, or intergenerational and women from other cultures where conceptions of femininity were quite different from those in the West.

Feminist urban research has documented the ways in which gender, race/ethnicity, and class intersect to constrain and shape the lives of women who are working-class, lesbian, disabled, or members of racial and ethnic minority communities (Gilroy and Woods 1994; Garber and Turner 1995; Ainley 1998; Miranne and Young 2000). Specifically, this research outlines how gender is socially constituted in particular places. For example,

Robyn Dowling's (1998) comparison of mothers in two Vancouver suburbs starts from the position that the many different household and family forms found in today's suburbs reflect a diversity of gender relations. Suburban women's lives are differentiated not only by paid work outside the home but also by differences in mothering practices, family, and religious networks.

Women and Housing

Architect Dolores Hayden provoked debate when she published an article, 'What would the non-sexist city be like?' She challenged architects and activists 'to develop a new paradigm of the home, the neighbourhood, and the city; to begin to describe the physical, social and economic design of a human settlement that would support, rather than restrict, the activities of employed women and their families' (Hayden 1981, 168). Hayden (1981; 2002) critiqued the typical urban form, which spatially separated places of residence and places of employment, offering existing examples of alternatives that would accommodate a wider diversity of households. They included communal and co-housing projects that offered collective spaces for dining, work at home, and child care. Hayden reported on ways that accessory apartments for the elderly, young singles, or tenants have been incorporated into suburban housing design. Many of these examples illustrate how to intensify land uses in suburban neighbourhoods and break down the spatial separations between home and work and the isolation between individual households and their neighbours.

Canadian women have tried to address women's limited housing options and their exclusion from the building and development industry. In the early 1980s, groups of women in cities across Canada responded to the housing affordability crisis by developing housing with women (Wekerle 1988a, 1988b; Wekerle and Novac 1989; Wekerle and Muirhead 1991; Wekerle 1993). They obtained funding from social housing programs of the federal and provincial governments to build non-profit housing cooperatives and non-profit rental housing, which would be designed by women for women and managed by the women who lived there. In cities across Canada, including Victoria, Vancouver, Calgary, Regina, Hamilton, Toronto, Montreal, Quebec City, Halifax, and St John's, women's groups were successful in building more than 100 projects, ranging in size from six to more than 100 units, for and with older women, Aboriginal women, visible-minority women, lesbians, single parents, abused women and their children, and teen mothers. This housing was built on reserves, in a converted 300-year-old convent in the centre of Quebec City, in a new suburban cul-de-sac in Peterborough, ON, as a courtyard building on a brownfield site in Toronto, and as low-rise, in-fill projects in Vancouver, Halifax, and Toronto (Figures 10.1 and 10.2). The housing that women built, while constrained by affordable housing guidelines, incorporated features that women asked for: on-site child care centres, laundry rooms that overlook playgrounds, housing for battered women, accessible units, the use of non-toxic building materials, and spaces for community-building. Because the non-profit housing was run by residents themselves, it also provided opportunities for skill-building and active participation in decision-making.

Feminist visions of the good city have suffered as Canadian women were forced to turn their energies towards defending and fighting cutbacks in social housing and essential urban services. One woman housing activist in Toronto recently commented that in an era when no new affordable housing was being built, women stopped advocating specifically for housing design that addressed gender inequities (Dale 2004, 5). With changes in government at the provincial, federal, and municipal levels, women's housing advocates have regrouped. The YWCA of Toronto recently opened a newly built 69-unit housing project for women-led households with a 62-space child care centre.

Constance Hamilton Housing Cooperative, Toronto, designed by architect Joan Simon, includes 32 apartments and a six-person transition house for women escaping violence. It is located in a new inner-city community of non-profit housing cooperatives and social and seniors housing and is close to transit and shopping.

While Canadian women used government programs to build specific housing projects to meet a diversity of needs, women in northern European cities defined their project as one of creating a more 'woman-friendly city'. 'Woman-friendly' was a flexible term that aimed to take into account the activities of women's daily lives and included designs by women architects and planners (Frankfurt), the hiring of gender planners in a city's planning department to review policies and plans from the standpoint of women (Hamburg, Berlin), and kitchen-table conversations that encouraged working-class women in neighbourhoods throughout Barcelona to develop their own plans for the city. Some concrete expressions were achieved in Goteborg, Sweden, where women planners and architects drew on women's experiences of everyday life to design a new neighbourhood based on gender planning principles that integrated employment, family life, and services. In Vienna, the city developed what it labelled a 'woman-friendly suburb' (OECD 1995). Through a housing competition, the City of Vienna's Women's Office awarded a contract to women planners and architects to develop plans and to have a new suburban community for 2,000 residents built (now fully occupied). The community plan takes into account the demands of women's everyday lives and the needs of women and diverse family types. This new suburban development of multi-family housing incorporates child care on-site and a police station with staff trained to assist victims of violence.

A Gendered Urban Sustainability?

Many of the feminist proposals for a **non-sexist city** have re-emerged under the new guise of urban sustainability. Suburban development forms have come under fire from proponents of urban sustainability and new urbanism (Roseland 1998; Duany, Plater-Zyberk, and Speck 2000; Wheeler 2004). They argue that continuing to build conventional suburbs is ecologically unsustainable. Advocates of urban sustainability propose to redesign the city and develop sustainable communities with more compact suburban development and mixed use that incorporates a range of housing and employment opportunities, the replacement of the automobile by transit, bicycles, or walking, and a reduction in the ecological footprint of each household. New suburban developments are changing in response to the high costs of energy and the costs of infrastructure such as roads, sewers, and water mains. In the Toronto region, for example, suburban cities such as Mississauga and Markham are developing mixed-use suburban downtown centres where residents can live and work. Transit-oriented housing developments are being planned as new regional public transit is developed. Developers in the region are starting to build assisted-living units for seniors in suburban locations and condominium apartment towers that would appeal to both young singles and empty-nesters. Mainstream developers are starting to offer suburban houses that are built to a very high standard of energy conservation.

In the decades since Hayden (1981) wrote her initial article on what a non-sexist city would look like, the intensification of suburbs, work at home, community gardens, and even car-sharing have been implemented in at least some communities, particularly under the ban-

Alma Blackwell's, Vancouver, a women's housing cooperative in an established neighbourhood. A group of community women developed the concept, obtained funding, and had the multi-unit structure built.

ner of sustainable communities. However, the gender and class analysis that underpinned Hayden's call for a non-sexist city is absent. This is significant in that recent proposals for smart growth that include transit-oriented developments, more pedestrian-friendly suburbs, and mixed-use suburban city centres (Calthorpe and Fulton 2001; Duany, Plater-Zyberk, and Speck 2000) emphasize design solutions and green technologies for energy conservation. But proponents neglect to point out that these are uniformly market solutions targeted to higher-income homeowners. Smart growth initiatives do not specifically address the diversity of incomes, stages of the life cycle, family types, and ethnocultural backgrounds that characterize the present-day Canadian suburb.

The sustainable suburb discussions tend to ignore issues of social equity or gender relations. In assessing proposals for sustainability from a feminist urbanist perspective, MacGregor (2002; 2006) argues that there is no discussion on who will do the extra work required to live more sustainably. Since women are still largely responsible for household labour, they will likely bear the costs of engaging in more sustainable practices such as household recycling, hanging clothes on a clothesline, composting, and using transit rather than cars. Schemes for transit-oriented housing or new urbanism developments are designed for the most affluent consumers and not for women with lower incomes, single parents, older women, or intergenerational immigrant families. Current proposals for sustainable communities diverge substantially from the vision of a non-sexist and sustainable city (Eichler 1995) in their disregard for the gendered division of labour, the gendered experience of urban space, and 'the particularities of gender, race, or class experience' (MacGregor 2002, 82).

Women in the City

Recent feminist research has challenged the simplistic delineation of space into suburbs or inner city dominated by family or non-family households (Ray and Rose 2000). In an early article (Wekerle 1984), I argued that 'woman's place is in the city' on the grounds that core areas with a public infrastructure that includes child care, shops, and transit most readily met the needs of women, particularly low-income single mothers. Yet these households are being squeezed out of central locations in Canada's largest cities. Participation of women in the labour force, particularly women working in the service economy and in professions, has increased the demand

for housing in central residential locations and has squeezed out women-led households that relied on the access to transit and social services offered by inner-city locations. (Rose 1989; Bondi 1994). The affluence of small professional households has created a market for inner-city housing, which now includes gentrified housing in older neighbourhoods, loft conversions of industrial buildings, and luxury condominiums. Leslie Kern (2007) documents how new condominium developments in Toronto offer young, single professional women not only access to all the benefits of homeownership but also the many advantages of city life, including proximity to work and recreation, access to transit and public space, anonymity, and safety. She argues that condominium marketing, which urges women to financially benefit from homeownership and take advantage of the city, is based on gendered notions of women as consumers rather than urban citizens. This raises questions about the extent to which the expressions of women's housing preferences through gentrification 'reinforce, reduce, modify, or leave unaltered existing gender divisions within the home, or in any way encapsulate new conceptions of masculinity and femininity'(Bondi 1994, 196).

Feminist urban research has focused on diverse women's experiences in urban places. It drew on concepts of the construction of women's situated and embodied local knowledge (Haraway 1991; Smith 1987; Allen and Howard 2002). Much of this research focused on how constructions of class, ethnicity/race, and sexuality mediated gender differences in the experience and use of urban space (Ray and Rose 2000). The literature addressed the differences among women, their experiences in specific urban places, and 'the salience of place in the construction of multiple female identities' (McDowell 1993b, 310). In contrast to meta-narratives of the city, these studies often take the form of detailed ethnographic accounts, case studies, or analyses of texts in which women themselves speak of their daily lives in the city.

Community studies give us insights into the particularities of women's homelessness. According to one estimate, about 30 per cent of the homeless in Canada are women (Klodawsky 2006). However, this is not a firm number, since women's homelessness is often hidden. They are less visible on the street or in shelters and more likely to rely on informal and ad hoc arrangements. While poverty, racism, and sexism are associated with homelessness, the fragility of women's shelter security is tied to shifts in welfare regimes, changing labour markets, cutbacks to funding for social housing and related services, and family violence. Homeless women in Toronto are 10 times more likely to be sexually assaulted and twice as likely to have a mental illness as homeless men (Kandor and Mason 2007). Bridgman's (2002) ethnographic study of a Toronto shelter for homeless women and Benoit, Carroll, and Chaudhry's (2003) examination of the impact of existing health clinics on homeless Aboriginal women living in Vancouver's Downtown Eastside provide insights into the daily life of homeless women living in large cities. As Evelyn Peters (1998) notes, instead of framing the city and First Nations cultures as spatially separate, urban Aboriginal women created spaces of healing where 'learning traditional values was a prerequisite for being able to live in the city'. She concludes that 'First Nations women's "place" in the city is related to both gender and Aboriginal heritage' (Peters 1998, 668).

Feminist urban researchers have also focused on how gender and sexuality intersect and the ways in which sexual orientation is inscribed within the spaces of everyday life (Valentine 1993; Peake 1993; Ray and Rose 2000). The emergence of gay and lesbian communities in inner-city neighbourhoods and their significance in maintaining social networks and political mobilization were the focus of research in Vancouver and Montreal (Ingram, Bouthilette, and Retter 1997; Ray and Rose 2000). Ali Grant's (1998) study in Hamilton, ON, focused on the spaces in which lesbian identities and activism are constructed, including lesbian women's leadership in the women's shelter movement. Podmore's (2001) interviews with lesbians living in a Montreal neighbourhood revealed that boulevard St-Laurent facilitates patterns of social interaction, place-making, and expressions of desire. She argues that 'the heterogeneity of this border zone renders this public space more accessible for lesbians' (Podmore 2001, 339).

Within the neo-liberal, competitive global city oriented to attracting investment and infrastructure that serves elite populations, women's claims have been marginalized and often reduced to struggles for basic survival (Naples 1998). Urban women have often played a significant role as activists or leaders within community organizations or their neighbourhoods in organizing around issues of daily life, including health care, housing, environmental conditions, and immigration (Wekerle and Peake 1996; Rabrenovic 1995).

While there are many such examples of women's neighbourhood-based organizing in Canadian cities, women's activism around food security has come to the fore in many cities, linking diverse women in local campaigns and in transnational movements. Women's leadership has taken a traditional women's issue, food preparation and nutrition, and made it into a tool for political mobilization (Field 1999; Moffett and Morgan 1999; Wekerle 2004a; 2005b). In the food security movements that have developed in cities across Canada, women provide the leadership in a range of initiatives that have moved beyond emergency food provision and that offer urban residents alternative approaches to meeting their food needs. For example, in Toronto, FoodShare, a community food security advocacy organization, was inspired by the experience of community kitchens organized by mothers' clubs in Lima, Peru, and São Paulo, Brazil, and farmers' markets that linked small farmers and consumers. This led to the creation in Toronto of community gardens, community kitchens, and a Good Food Box program that delivers fresh vegetables to low-income households. In reflecting on Toronto's community food security grassroots coalition, Moffett and Morgan (1999, 234) point out that it links 'the many community services that deal with women, food, and shelter in the fight for social change'.

Mobility and Social Exclusion

The role of mobility in spatially structuring racial, class, and gendered inequalities in cities is seldom discussed in the literature on global cities. Yet the power to move—and to move more than others—has taken on huge social significance in globalized cities, as Doreen Massey (1997, 112) points out. The combination of cutbacks in public services and suburban sprawl has shifted the costs of accessing jobs and essential services from the state to each individual household. The almost total reliance on suburban, low-density homeownership to meet shelter needs and the continued separation of home and work create problems of mobility, particularly for people with low incomes, women, immigrants, the elderly, and teenagers without access to adequate public transit or a private automobile (Denmark 1998; Ong 2002). Urban residents who are mobility disadvantaged have more limited life chances with less access to housing, jobs, child care, and public services.

How gender differences in mobility structure access to opportunity has been the focus of considerable urban research (Hanson and Pratt 1995; Rutherford and Wekerle 1988; Wekerle and Rutherford 1989). Much of this literature has examined the intersections of gender, race, and class in structuring social exclusion in spatially and racially segregated cities. After the introduction of work-for-welfare programs—workfare—in the mid-1990s, researchers documented the links between transit, employment, and welfare dependence. They found that welfare recipients with no access to cars were often kept out of jobs in the suburbs, where many service jobs are located (Ong 2002). People dependent on public transit to travel from city centre to suburb or across suburbs often spent substantial time in their journeys to work. Poor women, especially those with children, are penalized and forced to pay with their time because of limited choice of housing locations, spatial constraints on their job search, and transit dependence.

Research on travel behaviour has found that men and women have different mobility patterns because of differences in their incomes, jobs, family responsibilities, and power within the family. Men and women have differential access to various modes of transportation: men are more likely to have a driver's licence and to drive to work; more women take public transportation for lack of other options (Rutherford and Wekerle 1988). In 2001 across Canada, 13 per cent of the employed female labour force that travelled to work used public transit, while male riders represented 8 per cent of employed men who travelled to work. This differential held even among the age 20 to 24 group, where only 13.6 per cent of male workers took transit, contrasted with 19.8 per cent of female workers (Statistics Canada 2001). The 2006 census shows that in the Toronto census area, 37.3 per cent of people who drove to work were women and 62.7 per cent were men. In contrast, among people using transit to get to work, 59.5 per cent were women and 40.5 per cent were men (Statistics Canada 2007c). In the Region of Peel, a suburban area that has limited public transit, among those driving to work, 41.8 per cent were women, and 58 per cent were men. But women are even more predominant as transit users: 60.9 per cent were women and only 39.1 per cent were men (Statistics Canada 2007d). How do we account for this difference in transit usage between male and female suburban residents? Do women work in places more accessible to public transit, even in the suburbs? Do these women live in households where there is no money left over for a second car? Or are women more ecologically conscious than men?

The preponderance of women using public transportation to get to work has equity implications. Men's work trips tend to be between home and work; women tend to make multiple trips, including shopping and child care drop-offs, as part of their journey to and from work (Blumen 1994). This takes more time and may cost more money when bus routes do not readily connect these various locations. Linking transit routes to key services rather than just employment nodes is important to women users.

Studies have also found that women may restrict their employment to places that are closer to home in order to accommodate domestic work responsibilities and/or because lower-wage service jobs pay similar wages whether close to home or far away (Wekerle and Rutherford 1989; Hanson and Pratt 1995). Limited employment location options may affect income or advancement. When there is only one car, the male head of the household, or even a son, will use the family car;

women more often use transit. Explanations for these spatial patterns have focused on women's lower incomes, greater part-time employment, and less power in accessing scarce household resources such as the car. However, women's commuting patterns are also influenced by class: urban professionals with higher incomes may choose to live closer to work, but they also have access to an automobile; women clerical workers who live in lower-cost housing on the urban periphery may have longer journeys to work with limited access to an automobile. Box 10.1 describes some of the efforts made by women's groups to improve public transit with women in mind.

With the spatial restructuring of employment in the global city, the mobility patterns of men and women may be converging. For example, in 1991 the majority of public transit riders in Toronto were

Box 10.1 *Mobility in the Global City: Transit Equity Movements*

In some cities, urban social movements have highlighted how transportation planning is a fundamentally political process that redistributes resources among groups and communities. For the most part, women's groups have not focused on issues of mobility and access or the ways in which transportation decision-making excludes the urban residents who are most dependent on public transportation in all aspects of their daily lives. There are a few exceptions. In Whitehorse, Yukon, in the early 1980s, there was no transit service. A women's group established the Women's Minibus Society to reduce women's isolation in the home. A small van did a circular route throughout the town, picking up women and dropping them off for shopping and services. This women's minibus eventually became the basis for the public transit system of Whitehorse. In the UK in the 1990s, women-only van services in several cities offered predominantly South Asian women rides to local shopping and service centres. Women's cars on public transit have been instituted in Cairo, Tokyo, Mumbai, and Rio de Janeiro (Sussman 2006). In response to women's complaints of harassment on public transit in Mexico City, in 2008 the city began to offer a women-only bus service—the Pink Bus—to protect women from the groping and sexual harassment that is so prevalent on the public transit system (Ellingwood 2008). Women's organizations claim that such initiatives deal only with symptoms and not the inadequate transportation system and systemic gender inequalities.

Canadian women have been pioneers in calling for public transit that addresses women's needs. In the late 1980s and into the 1990s, community-based women's groups in Toronto mobilized politically to gain more equitable access to public transit and to address women's concerns about safety on the public transport system (Wekerle 2005a; 1999). Women Plan Toronto, a women's advocacy group, and the Metro Action Committee to Prevent Violence against Women and Children (METRAC) organized three large public meetings to focus on women's transit needs. Women shared their experiences of being dependent on public transportation, including the physical barriers encountered when taking children in strollers on buses and up and down long subway stairs and the problems of older women who could not walk the distance to bus stops or climb onto vehicles. They complained of bus services that ran infrequently during off-hours or on the weekend. They recounted the fear of crime that women experienced in waiting for and using public transit. Many women connected fear of crime and violence against women to the design and management of the public transport system.

Women's groups framed women's transit needs in terms of women's rights to move freely through the city. While not responding to the overall concerns about equitable access, the Toronto Transit Commission (TTC) made a commitment to work in partnership with women's community organizations to address women's safety concerns. Together with women's groups, the TTC conducted a study of women's safety in subway stations and on some bus routes (Toronto Transit Commission, METRAC, and Metropolitan Toronto Police 1989). Changes included better training of staff to deal with cases of harassment and sexual assault; hiring more women as front-line workers; physical design changes to improve safety, including lighting and signage; establishing designated waiting areas with emergency call buttons on subway platforms; and a demand-stop program that allowed women to request a stop anywhere along a bus route after 9 pm rather than disembark at designated stops. The TTC also set up a Women's Security Advisory group to provide advice on the design of a new subway line.

In the mid-1990s, the election of a neo-liberal provincial government and fiscal cutbacks at the TTC resulted in the withdrawal of commitment to working with women's groups. The TTC was under pressure to operate more as a business in a competitive marketplace than as a public service. In this environment, consultation and participatory processes were seen as 'frills' and catering to special interests. Women's community groups were no longer seen as partners who would assist in providing better services to citizens. However, the design and security changes and Request Stop Program remained in place.

This is in contrast to the situation in the UK, where the Mobility Unit of the Department of the Environment, Transport, and the Regions has produced a Public Transport Gender Audit and requires transport providers to demonstrate how they are meeting the transit needs of women (Hamilton and Jenkins 2000). In Canadian cities, not only women but transit consumers in general have not tended to organize to make their power as consumers felt in the design of public transit. Yet citizen engagement in transit policy making and implementation has become even more important as Canadian cities embark on major transit infrastructure upgrading and expansion as an economic stimulus in response to national and financial crises.

In Los Angeles, the Bus Riders' Union, led by visible-minority women, describes itself as a transit equity movement focused on the social and environmental justice dimensions of transportation provision and decision-making processes (Mann 1997; Grengs 2002). Low-income workers have organized public protests and legal challenges against a transit authority that has allocated substantial new funding to light rail transit, which serves the predominantly white and affluent suburbs, instead of improving bus service to predominantly working-class neighbourhoods. They have been successful in focusing public attention on cutbacks to an essential public service and the racialized and gender impacts of public transit cutbacks.

women—59 per cent of bus passengers and 57 per cent of subway passengers (Joint Program in Transportation 1991). The growth of new employment opportunities in low-density suburban areas has created greater pressures on all workers, including women, to use automobiles for the trip to work. Between 1986 and 1996, the percentage of Toronto women working full-time who had a driver's licence increased from 72 per cent to 78 per cent, compared to 93 per cent throughout the period for all males working full-time (Joint Program in Transportation 1998). Not only does this increase in car use contribute further to suburban gridlock, but the need to own and operate a car as a condition of employment will mean that women have less money available for other essential needs.

Concerns over global warming, carbon emissions, and the cost of gasoline increase pressures to reduce car trips. Since women have lower incomes than men, they are less able to absorb the higher costs. Smart growth advocates would like to see much more transit, cycling, and walking in cities and suburbs. There are ambitious proposals to increase public transit in Canada's major cities. None of these proposals incorporate a gender analysis of travel patterns but assume that all riders are alike. Studies show that women's concerns about safety on transit and while waiting for buses is a constraint on transit use, especially in isolated suburban areas and at night (Taylor et al. 2006). Women's dual responsibility for both household and paid labour, coupled with less time and lower incomes, means that they need flexible and affordable transportation options. Unless transit proposals take into account the circumstances that account for men and women's differing travel patterns, new schemes may not succeed or may even contribute to existing inequities.

Social Exclusion, Fear, and the Rights to the Street

A recurrent theme in feminist urban research is women's right to the public spaces of the city

and the ways in which violence against women and women's fear of crime contribute to social exclusion. A substantial theoretical and empirical literature addresses issues of social identity and fear in the city, as well as policies and programs to address fear and make cities safer (Pain 2001). The early studies emphasized the importance of gender, age, and subordinate social and economic status in the experience of fear of crime. More recent research has focused on the complexity and shifting nature of social identities that relate to fear of crime (Pain 2001). Critical studies have begun to examine the social and political construction of fear of crime and its focus on certain groups (women and older people) and disregard of others, including boys, men, and people of colour.

Rachel Pain (2001, 902) outlines how fear of crime can 'create and reinforce exclusion from social life and from particular urban spaces'. For example, people who are already socially or economically disadvantaged are most affected by fear of crime. It can affect their mobility, employment opportunities, and use of urban facilities. While women often express fear of particular public spaces in the city, feminist geographers have pointed out that attention to public violence may be misplaced, since sexual violence most often occurs in the privacy of the home (Valentine 1989).

Feminist policy interventions to make urban space or the city safer for women have tended to focus on design interventions in public transport, city centres, urban parks, streets, and housing projects (Whitzman 1992; Wekerle and Whitzman 1995; Andrew 1995; 2000). These projects, which emerged as safer community or safer city projects, were often initiated by women's community groups in Toronto, Montreal, Vancouver, Calgary, Quebec City, and Halifax in the early 1990s. They focused planners' and architects' attention on urban spaces and fear of crime from the standpoint of women. Various accounts (Wekerle 1999; Andrew 2000; Whitzman 2002) critically examine how women's local knowledge was used to create a safety audit guide, which women's groups used to evaluate specific urban spaces. In some instances, this tool empowered women's groups, while in other cases it was used to depoliticize and appropriate women's framing of urban crime. Pain (2001) argues that the focus on design change tended to ignore the wider social origins of fear of crime. It may also have inadvertently contributed to neo-liberal arguments for law and order and the surveillance and privatization of public space. Further, the exclusive focus on women, albeit women identified as young, old, lesbian, and visible-minority, may have underplayed the fear of crime and negotiation of urban space on the part of young males, in particular, and the way in which racial stereotypes of crime are gendered and sexualized. As Pain (2001, 910) concludes, 'When gender, age, and race are viewed as social relations which are based upon unequal distributions of power, they begin to explain who is most affected by fear, and where.'

Gender and Democratic Governance

One of the primary roles of municipal government is to provide the means by which urban citizens can express their collective objectives and influence decisions (Tindal and Tindal 2009). Yet **neo-liberal governance** strategies prioritize cutbacks in social welfare, downsizing and privatizing public space and services, and the treatment of citizens as customers. Increasingly, decision-making in Canadian cities reflects an interdependence and intersection of the private, public, and voluntary sectors. Governments establish or work closely with advisory bodies, such as city summits of appointed civic, business, and municipal politicians, who jointly develop a long-range vision for the city. Corporate actors are often favoured and designated as 'community' representatives. Unions, non-profit organizations, neighbourhood groups, and social

movements are increasingly excluded from these partnerships. There are concerns that growth coalitions (Molotch 1993)—the networks of development interests, financiers, business elites, and politicians that organize to support the economic growth of urban areas—have undue influence in Canadian cities. There are pressures to limit participation by reducing the numbers of elected officials and eliminating the resources devoted to citizen advisory committees. These changes raise questions about gender equity in the delivery of services and women's access to democratic participation.

Women's groups in Canadian cities have challenged what they view as the systematic exclusion of women's interests and political participation in the neo-liberal and entrepreneurial city. Throughout the 1980s and 1990s, local governments in Canada specifically addressed women's needs across a range of service areas, including public health, child care, women's shelters, and initiatives to counter violence against women. In some cities, status of women committees within city government represented women's service needs in decision-making, policy, and programs. Despite the limited mandate and relatively small successes of these committees, they often managed to increase the visibility of gender equality issues on the institutional agendas of municipal governments (Wekerle 2004b). However, the restructuring and refocusing of municipal governments towards acting like a business and treating citizens as customers resulted in funding cutbacks and the elimination or marginalization of women's committees in many municipalities (Bashevkin 2006). This raised concerns about women's access to municipal services and to participation in municipal decision-making.

Several current initiatives seek to increase women's participation in municipal government (Purdon 2004). The Regional Municipality of Ottawa-Carleton established a Working Group on Women's Access to Municipal Services in Ottawa to evaluate and propose improvements to women's access to services and employment (Working Group on Women's Access 2001; Andrew et al. 2004). A follow-up project, entitled City for All Women Initiatives, is a partnership between community women's groups and municipal staff and politicians to ensure equal access to decision-making. In Toronto, an action research project involving agencies working with people of low income from various ethnocultural groups identified women's needs and access to services and laid out an action plan involving municipal government and its agencies (Khosla 2003). This resulted in virtually no change. In 2008, only 31 per cent of the city of Toronto's councillors were women. The city has begun a project to identify young women in the community who will be mentored by women councillors to encourage more women to consider running for municipal office. This was in response to the Federation of Canadian Municipalities' (FCM) cross-Canada participatory action project, Increasing Women's Participation in Municipal Consultation Processes, to enhance women's participation in municipal consultation processes and policies (Purdon 2004). In 2006 across Canada, women constituted only 21.4 per cent of municipal councillors. The FCM has launched local educational workshops and has challenged municipal governments to attempt to increase this proportion to 30 per cent by 2026.

Such initiatives assume that women's democratic participation in municipal government will be increased by electing more women to municipal councils rather than by developing women-friendly municipal policies. This presupposes that women have interests best represented by other women, despite the broad diversity of women's interests that vary across intersecting class, race, and sexual identities. While women may bring a different viewpoint to policy-making, there are no guarantees that they will forward feminist or women-friendly agendas (Wekerle 2004b; Boles 2001). Increasing the number of women councillors does not address the wider issue of urban citizenship, which entails full membership in a community that is multi-layered and located in multiple spheres.

Conclusion

Neo-liberal city paradigms have focused on the economic restructuring of cities. Yet there has also been a significant socio-spatial re-sorting as revitalized core areas attracted more affluent and professional homeowners and new immigrants moved directly to suburbs, which are now the living and work places of a wide diversity of households. Climate change poses a significant challenge to these patterns in Canadian cities. In response to the call for more sustainable cities, urban areas are required to reduce car dependence and increase transit use, intensify and redesign suburbs for mixed uses and greater energy conservation, and maintain and enhance the vitality of city centres. Yet proposals to create more sustainable cities still emphasize the economic and competitive advantages of such changes. They fail to take into account how space and place intersect with race, class, and gender in structuring inequalities and social exclusion in cities. Women's energies and initiatives to re-envision a non-sexist and sustainable city are needed if sustainable city proposals are to succeed.

Despite decades of urban activism and substantial research on gender and cities, many gaps remain. The feminist urban literature has been limited in examining the relationships between spatiality, power, and justice and the institutional processes that contribute to gendered inequalities (Kern and Wekerle 2008). Feminist researchers tend not to examine the networks of power created by the global economic and political elites of cities. There are no gender analyses of growth-machine politics in Canadian cities or of the predominantly male-dominated development industries that reshape the countryside as suburban developments. (See Fincher 2006 for an analysis of developers' masculinist visions of housing and city form in Australia). Although there have been many small-scale studies of how built form is gendered and patriarchal, the starting point has tended to be the household and neighbourhood. Feminist urban scholars have not addressed how the intersections of gender, race, and class also underlie the dynamics of downtown redevelopment schemes, waterfront revitalization, or condominium loft developments. The owners, developers, and decision-makers engaged in these large-scale projects are primarily men operating from a masculinist experience and view of how cities work and should operate. As yet there is no feminist urban political economy that links global economic restructuring, urban growth, and change to gender equity and gender justice in Canadian cities. To forge a vision of a sustainable and just city, we must integrate visions of the non-sexist and sustainable city.

Study and Discussion Questions

1. The discourse of the global city focuses on economic competitiveness, growth, and less government intervention. What groups of women are excluded from this vision of the city?
2. The suburbanization of diversity describes the move of immigrants to the suburbs. How might suburban design and planning accommodate the needs of a wider range of women from different ethnocultural backgrounds? How do suburbs need to change to accommodate the needs of single parents, low-income women, or young single women?
3. If women's employment choice and ability to combine work and family responsibilities are related to mobility, should we encourage more women to get driver's licences? How would you design a transit system to respond to women's responsibilities in the workplace and in the household? What about women's expressed concerns about transit and urban security?
4. If you live in a large city, look at the newspaper and billboards for ads about condominium developments or loft developments in the centre of the city. How are women portrayed in this advertising? What image of the city do they convey? What kind of lifestyle is described? Who is displaced by these new projects? Where will they live?
5. How are women's needs identified and addressed by municipal government? How would you encourage women's participation in democratic governance at the municipal level? Are women's needs best addressed by electing more women to municipal councils, or are there other ways that women's voices can be heard and acted upon?
6. Plans for sustainable cities incorporate many of the proposals for changes in urban form that feminist architects and planners have espoused. But they fail to address systemic gender inequalities in labour markets and in household labour that affect how women navigate urban space. How could we bring together visions of the non-sexist and sustainable city to forge a vision of a sustainable and just city?

Suggested Reading

Bashevkin, Sylvia. 2006. *Tales of Two Cities: Women and Municipal Restructuring in London and Toronto*. Vancouver: University of British Columbia Press. Analyzing municipal restructuring in London, UK, and Toronto, Canada, women's initiatives within local government structures, and outcomes.

DeSena, Judith N. 2008. *Gender in an Urban World*. Bingley, UK: Emerald Group/JAI Press. A collection of feminist urban sociology articles on the public realm, gentrification, suburbia, the creative city, and condominium ownership in cities around the world.

Federation of Canadian Municipalities (FCM), International Centre for Municipal Development. 1997. 'A city tailored to women'. Ottawa: FCM. http://www.icmd-cidm.ca. Describes how municipal governments in Canada ensure the participation of women.

Gender, Place and Culture: A Journal of Feminist Geography. Provides a forum in human geography and related disciplines on feminist, anti-racist, and critical geographies of place, space, nature, and the environment; feminist geographies of differences and marginality.

'In Mexico: A bus of women's own'. 2008. *New York Times* 11 February. http://www.nytimes.com/2008/02/11/world/americas/11mexico.html.

Little, Jo. 1994. *Gender, Planning and the Policy Process.* Oxford: Pergamon. A feminist interpretation of contemporary urban planning in England and Wales.

McDowell, Linda. 1999. *Gender, Identity and Place:* *Understanding Feminist Geographies.* Minneapolis: University of Minnesota Press. An analysis of the gendering of specific spaces and places ranging from the workplace to the nation-state.

Wilson, Elizabeth. 1991. *The Sphinx in the City: Urban Life, the Control of Disorder and Women.* Berkeley: University of California Press. A critique of anti-urbanism through a feminist analysis of urban culture and the freedom of the city.

Women and Environments International. 2004. 62–3 (spring/summer). Special issue: 'Cities for women'. Articles focus on housing, urban design and architecture, planning and safety, transportation, sustainability, and governance.

References

Ainley, Rosa, Ed. 1998. *New Frontiers of Spaces, Bodies and Gender.* London: Routledge.

Allen, Carolyn, and Judith A. Howard, Eds. 2002. *Provoking Feminisms.* Chicago: University of Chicago Press.

Andrew, Caroline. 1995. 'Getting women's issues on the municipal agenda: Violence against women'. In Judith A. Garber and Robyne S. Turner, Eds, *Gender in Urban Research*, 99–118. Thousand Oaks, CA: Sage.

———. 2000. 'Resisting boundaries? Using safety audits for women'. In Kristine B. Miranne and Alma H. Young, Eds, *Gendering the City*, 157–68. Lanham, MD: Rowman and Littlefield.

Andrew, Caroline, et al. 2004. 'Accessing City Hall: The Working Group on Women's Access to Municipal Services in Ottawa'. *Women and Environments International* 62–3 (spring/summer): 49–50.

Bashevkin, Sylvia. 2006. *Tales of Two Cities: Women and Municipal Restructuring in London and Toronto.* Vancouver: University of British Columbia Press.

Benoit, Cecilia, Dena Carroll, and Munaza Chaudhry. 2003. 'In search of a healing place: Aboriginal women in Vancouver's Downtown Eastside'. *Social Science and Medicine* 56: 821–33.

Blumen, Orna. 1994. 'Gender differences in the jour-ney to work'. *Urban Geography* 15 (3): 233–45.

Boles, Janet. 2001. 'Local elected women and policy-making: Movement delegates or feminist trustees?' In Susan J. Carroll, Ed., *The Impact of Women in Public Office.* Bloomington: Indiana University Press.

Bondi, Liz. 1994. 'Gentrification, work and gender identity'. In Audrey Kobayashi, Ed., *Women, Work and Place*, 182–200. Montreal and Kingston: McGill-Queen's University Press.

Bourne, L.S. 2000. 'Urban Canada in transition to the twenty-first century: Trends, issues and visions'. In Trudi Bunting and Pierre Filion, Eds, *Canadian Cities in Transition: The Twenty-First Century*, 26–51. Toronto: Oxford University Press.

Bourne, L.S., and D. Rose. 2001. 'The changing face of Canada: The uneven geographies of population and social change'. *The Canadian Geographer* 45 (1): 105–19.

Bridgman, Rae. 2002. 'Housing chronically homeless women: "Inside" a safe haven'. *Housing Policy Debate* 13: 51–81.

Burleton, D. 2002. 'A choice between investing in Canada's cities or disinvesting in Canada's future'. TD Economics Special Report. Toronto: TD Financial Group.

Calthorpe, Peter, and William Fulton. 2001. *The Regional City: Planning for the End of Sprawl.* Washington: Island Press.

CMHC (Canada Mortgage and Housing Corporation). 1997. *Canadian Women and Their Housing: 1997*. Socio-economic Series no. 72. Ottawa: CMHC.

Dale, Amanda. 2004. 'No place like home: Women's housing advocacy rebirth in Toronto'. *Women and Environments International* 62–3 (spring/summer): 15.

Denmark, David. 1998. 'The outsiders: Planning and transport disadvantage'. *Journal of Planning Education and Research* 17 (3): 231–45.

Dowling, R. 1998. 'Suburban stories, gendered lives: Think through difference'. In Ruth Fincher and Jane M. Jacobs, Eds, *Cities of Difference*, 69–88. New York: Guilford Press.

Dreier, P., J. Mollenkopf, and T. Swanstrom. 2001. *Place Matters: Metropolitics for the Twenty-First Century*. Lawrence: University of Kansas Press.

Duany, A., E. Plater-Zyberk, and J. Speck. 2000. *Suburban Nation: The Rise of Sprawl and the Decline of the American Dream*. New York: North Point Press.

Eichler, Margrit, Ed. 1995. *Change of Plans: Towards a Non-sexist Sustainable City*. Toronto: Garamond.

Ellingwood, Ken. 2008. 'Mexico City's women-only buses offer relief'. *Los Angeles Times* 12 March.

Feagin, Joe R. 1998. *The New Urban Paradigm: Critical Perspectives on the City*. Lanham, MD: Rowman and Littlefield.

Field, Debbie. 1999. 'Putting food first: Women's role in creating a grassroots system outside the marketplace'. In Deborah Barndt, Ed., *Women Working the NAFTA Food Chain: Women, Food and Globalization*. Toronto: Second Story Press.

Fincher, Ruth. 2006. 'Space, gender and institutions in processes creating difference'. *Gender, Place and Culture* 14 (1): 5–27.

Frank, Susanne. 2008. 'Gender trouble in paradise: Suburbia reconsidered'. In Judith N. DeSena, Ed., *Gender in an Urban World*, 127–48. Bingley, UK: Emerald/JAI Publishing.

Garber, Judith A., and Robyne S. Turner, Eds. 1995. *Gender in Urban Research*. Thousand Oaks, CA: Sage.

Gilroy, Rose, and Roberta Woods, Eds. 1994. *Housing and Women*. London: Routledge.

Grant, Ali. 1998. 'UnWomanly acts: Struggling over sites of resistance'. In Rosa Ainley, Ed., *New Frontiers of Spaces, Bodies and Gender*, 50–64. London: Routledge.

Grengs, Joe. 2002. 'Community-based planning as a source of political change: The transit equity movement of Los Angeles' Bus Riders Union'. *Journal of the American Planning Association* 68 (2): 165–78.

Hamilton, Kerry, and Linda Jenkins. 2000. 'A gender audit for public transport: A new policy tool in the tackling of social exclusion'. *Urban Studies* 37 (10): 1,793–800.

Hanson, Susan, and Geraldine Pratt. 1995. *Gender, Work and Space*. New York: Routledge.

Haraway, Donna. 1991. *Simians, Cyborgs and Women: The Reinvention of Nature*. London: Free Association Books.

Hayden, Dolores. 1981. 'What would a non-sexist city be like? Speculations on housing, urban design and human work'. In Catherine Stimpson et al., Eds, *Women and the American City*, 167–84. Chicago: University of Chicago Press.

———. 2002. *Redesigning the American Dream: Gender, Housing, and Family Life*. New York: W.W. Norton.

Hills, J., J. LeGrand, and D. Piachaud, Eds. 2002. *Understanding Social Exclusion*. Toronto: Oxford University Press.

Hoernig, Heidi, and Margaret Walton-Roberts. 2006. 'Immigration and urban change: National, regional, and local perspectives'. In T. Bunting and P. Filion, Eds, *Canadian Cities in Transition*, 408–18. Toronto: Oxford University Press.

Ingram, G.B., A. Bouthilette, and Y. Retter. 1997. *Queers in Space: Communities, Public Places, Sites of Resistance*. Seattle: Bay Press.

Joint Program in Transportation. 1991. *Transportation Tomorrow Survey*. Toronto: University of Toronto.

———. 1998. *1986–1996 Travel Trends in the GTA and Hamilton-Wentworth*. Toronto: University of Toronto.

Kandor, Erika, and Kate Mason. 2007. *The Street Health Report 2007*. Toronto: Street Health.

Keller, Suzanne, Ed. 1981. *Building for Women*. Lexington, MA: D.C. Heath and Company.

Kern, Leslie. 2007. 'Reshaping the boundaries of public and private life: Gender, condominium development, and the neoliberalization of urban living'. *Urban Geography* 28 (7): 657–81.

Kern, Leslie, and Gerda R. Wekerle. 2008. Gendered spaces of redevelopment: Gendered politics of city building'. In Judith N. DeSena, Ed., *Gender in an Urban World*, 233–62. Bingley, UK: Emerald Publishing/JAI Publishing.

Khosla, Punam. 2003. *If Low Income Women of Colour Counted in Toronto*. Toronto: Community Social Planning Council of Toronto.

Kipfer, Stefan, and Roger Keil. 2002. 'Toronto Inc.? Planning the competitive city in the new Toronto'. *Antipode* 34 (2): 227–64.

Klodawsky, Fran. 2006. 'Landscapes on the margins: Gender and homelessness in Canada'. *Gender, Place and Culture* 13 (4): 365–81.

McDowell, Linda. 1993a. 'Space, place and gender relations: Part I. Feminist empiricism and the geography of social relations'. *Progress in Human Geography* 17 (2): 157–79.

———. 1993b. 'Space, place and gender relations: Part II. Identity, difference, feminist geometries and geographies'. *Progress in Human Geography* 17 (3): 305–18.

MacGregor, Sherilyn. 2002. 'Bright new vision or same old story? Looking for gender justice in the eco-city'. In Caroline Andrew, Katherine Graham, and Susan Phillips, Eds., *Urban Affairs: Back on the Policy Agenda*, 71–92. Montreal and Kingston: McGill Queen's University Press.

———. 2006. *Beyond Mothering Earth: Ecological Citizenship and the Politics of Care*. Vancouver: University of British Columbia Press.

Mann, Eric. 1997. 'Confronting transit racism in Los Angeles'. In R.D. Bullard and G.S. Johnson, Eds, *Just Transportation*. Gabriola Island, BC: New Society.

Massey, Doreen. 1997. 'Space/power, identity/difference: Tensions in the city'. In Andy Merrifield and Erik Swyngedouw, Eds, *The Urbanization of Injustice*, 100–17. New York:

New York University Press.

Michelson, William. 1985. *From Sun to Sun: Daily Obligations and Community Structure in the Lives of Employed Women and their Families*. Totowa, NJ: Rowan and Allen.

———. 1988. 'Divergent convergence: The daily routines of employed spouses as a public affairs agenda'. In Caroline Andrew and Beth Moore Milroy, Eds, *Life Spaces: Gender, Household, Employment*, 81–101. Vancouver: University of British Columbia Press.

Miranne, Kristine B., and Alma H. Young, Eds. 2000. *Gendering the City*. Lanham, MD: Rowman and Littlefield.

Moffett, Deborah, and Mary Lou Morgan. 1999. 'Women as organizers: Building confidence and community through food'. In Deborah Barndt, Ed., *Women Working the NAFTA Food Chain: Women, Food and Globalization*, 221–36. Toronto: Second Story Press.

Molotch, Harvey L. 1993. 'The political economy of growth machines'. *Journal of Urban Affairs* 15: 29–53.

Naples, Nancy A. 1998. 'Women's community activism: Exploring the dynamics of politicization and diversity'. In Nancy A. Naples, Ed., *Community Activism and Feminist Politics*, 327–49. London: Routledge.

OECD (Organisation for Economic Co-operation and Development). 1995. *Women in the City: Housing, Services and the Urban Environment*. Paris: OECD.

Ong, Paul. 2002. 'Transit, employment and women on welfare'. *Urban Geography* 23 (4): 344–64.

Orfield, Myron. 1997. *Metropolitics: A Regional Agenda for Community and Stability*. Washington: Brookings Institution Press.

Pain, Rachel. 2001. 'Gender, race, age and fear in the city'. *Urban Studies* 38 (5–6): 899–913.

Peake, Linda. 1993. 'Race and sexuality: Challenging patriarchal structuring of urban social space'. *Environment and Planning D: Society and Space* 11: 415–32.

Peters, Evelyn. 1998. 'Subversive spaces: First Nations women and the city'. *Environment and Planning D: Society and Space* 16: 665–85.

Podmore, Julie A. 2001. 'Lesbians in the crowd: Gender, sexuality and visibility along Montreal's boul. St-Laurent'. *Gender, Place and Culture* 8 (4): 333–55.

Preston, V., and M. Wong. 2002. 'Immigration and Canadian cities: Building inclusion'. In Caroline Andrew, Katherine Graham, and Susan Phillips, Eds., *Urban Affairs: Back on the Policy Agenda*, 24–44. Montreal and Kingston: McGill-Queen's University Press.

Purdon, Colleen. 2004. 'Strengthening women's voices in municipal processes'. *Women and Environments International* 62–3 (spring/summer): 51–2.

Rabrenovic, G. 1995. 'Women and collective action in urban neighborhoods'. In Judith A. Garber and Robyne S. Turner, Eds, *Gender in Urban Research*, 77–96. Thousand Oaks, CA: Sage.

Ray, Brian, and Damaris Rose. 2000. 'Cities of the everyday: Socio-spatial perspectives on gender, difference, and diversity'. In Trudi Bunting and Pierre Filion, Eds, *Canadian Cities in Transition: The Twenty-First Century*, 2nd edn, 502–24. Toronto: Oxford University Press.

Rose, Damaris. 1989. 'A feminist perspective of employment restructuring and gentrification: The case of Montreal'. In J. Wolch and M. Dear, Eds, *The Power of Geography: How Territory Shapes Social Life*, 118–38. Boston: Allen Unwin.

Roseland, Mark. 1998. *Toward Sustainable Communities: Resources for Citizens and Their Governments*. Philadelphia: New Society Publishers.

Rutherford, Brent, and Gerda R. Wekerle. 1988. 'Captive rider, captive labor: Spatial constraints and women's employment'. *Urban Geography* 9 (2): 116–37.

Smith, Dorothy. 1987. *The Everyday World As Problematic: Feminist Sociology*. Boston: Northeastern University Press.

Statistics Canada. 2001. *2001 Census, Where Canadian Work and How They Got There*. Ottawa: Statistics Canada.

———. 2006a. *Changing Patterns in Canadian Homeownership and Shelter Costs, 2006 Census*. Catalogue no. 97-554. Ottawa: Statistics Canada.

———. 2006b. *Net Worth of Family Units, by Selected Family Characteristics*. Survey of Financial Security, 7 December. Ottawa: Statistics Canada.

———. 2007a. *Average Earnings by Sex and Work Pattern*. CANSIM, 5 January. Ottawa: Statistics Canada.

———. 2007b. *Immigration in Canada: A Portrait of the Foreign-Born Population, 2006 Census: Immigrants in Metropolitan Areas*. 10 December. Ottawa: Statistics Canada.

———. 2007c. *2006 Community Profiles, Toronto, Ontario, 2006 Census*. Catalogue no. 92-591-XWE. 13 March. Ottawa: Statistics Canada.

———. 2007d. *2006 Community Profiles, Peel, Ontario, 2006 Census*. Catalogue no. 92-591-XWE. 13 March. Ottawa: Statistics Canada.

———. 2008. *Persons in Low Income after Tax, by Prevalence in Percent*. CANSIM, 5 May. Ottawa: Statistics Canada.

Sussman, Anna Louie. 2006. 'In Rio rush hour, women relax in single-sex trains'. *Women's eNews* 23 May. www.womensenews.org.

Taylor, B., et al. 2006. *Designing and Operating Safe and Secure Transit Systems: Assessing Current Practices in the US and Abroad*. San Jose, CA: Mineta Transportation Institute.

Tindal, Richard C., and Susan Nobes Tindal. 2009. *Local Government in Canada*. 7th edn. Toronto: Nelson.

Toronto Transit Commission, METRAC, and Metropolitan Toronto Police. 1989. *Moving Forward: Making Transit Safer for Women*. Toronto: TTC.

United Way of Greater Toronto. 2004. *Poverty by Postal Code*. Toronto: United Way.

Valentine, Gill. 1989. 'The geography of women's fear'. *Area* 21: 385–90.

———. 1993. '(Hetero)sexing space: Lesbian perceptions and experiences of everyday spaces'. *Environment and Planning D: Society and Space* 11: 395–413.

Walks, R. Alan. 2006. 'Homelessness, housing affordability, and the new poverty'. In T. Bunting and P. Filion, Eds, *Canadian Cities in Transition*, 419–37. Toronto: Oxford University Press.

Wekerle, Gerda R. 1984. 'A woman's place is in the city'. *Antipode* 6 (3): 11–20.

———. 1988a. *Women's Housing Projects in Eight Canadian Cities*. Ottawa: Canada Mortgage and Housing Corporation.

———. 1988b. 'Canadian women's housing cooperatives: Case studies in physical and social innovations'. In C. Andrew and B. Moore-Milroy, Eds, *Life Spaces: Gender, Household, Employment*, 102–40. Vancouver: University of British Columbia Press.

———. 1993. 'Responding to diversity: Housing developed by and for women'. *Canadian Journal of Urban Research* 2 (2): 95–113.

———. 1997. 'The shift to the market: Gender and housing disadvantage'. In Patricia Evans and Gerda R. Wekerle, Eds, *Women and the Canadian Welfare State*, 170–94. Toronto: University of Toronto Press.

———. 1999. 'Gender planning as insurgent citizenship: Stories from Toronto'. *Plurimondi* 1 (2): 105–26.

———. 2004a. 'Food justice movements: Policy, planning and networks'. *Journal of Planning Education and Research* 23 (4): 378–86.

———. 2004b. 'Framing feminist claims for urban citizenship'. In Lynn Staeheli, Miriam Kofman, and Linda Peake, Eds, *Mapping Gender, Making Politics: Feminist Perspectives on Political Geography*, 245–60. London: Routledge.

———. 2005a. 'Gender planning in public transit: Political process, changing discourse and practice'. In Susan Fainstein and Lisa Servon, Eds, *Gender Planning*, 275–95. New Brunswick, NJ: Rutgers University Press.

———. 2005b. 'Domesticating the neoliberal city: Invisible genders and the politics of place'. In Wendy Harcourt and Arturo Escobar, Eds, *Women and the Politics of Place*, 86–99. Bloomfield CT: Kumarian Press.

Wekerle, Gerda R., and Teresa V. Abbruzzese. 2009. 'Producing regionalism: Regional movements, ecosystems and equity in a fast and slow growth region'. *Geojournal*.

Wekerle, Gerda R., and Barbara Muirhead. 1991. *Canadian Women's Housing Projects*. Ottawa: Canada Mortgage and Housing Corporation.

Wekerle, Gerda R., and Sylvia Novac. 1989. 'Developing two women's housing cooperatives'. In K. Franck and S. Ahrentzen, Eds, *New Households, New Housing*, 223–40. New York: Van Nostrand Reinhold.

Wekerle, Gerda R., and Linda Peake. 1996. 'New social movements and women's urban activism'. In J. Caulfield and L. Peake, Eds, *City Lives and City Forms: Critical Research and Canadian Urbanism*, 263–82. Toronto: University of Toronto Press.

Wekerle, Gerda R., Rebecca Peterson, and David Morley, Eds. 1980. *New Space for Women*. Boulder, CO: Westview Press.

Wekerle, Gerda R., and Brent Rutherford. 1989. 'The mobility of capital and the immobility of female labour: Responses to economic restructuring'. In J. Wolch and M. Dear, Eds, *The Power of Geography: How Geography Shapes Social Life*, 139–71. London: Unwin and Hyman.

Wekerle, Gerda R., and Carolyn Whitzman. 1995. *Safe Cities: Guidelines for Planning, Design and Management*. New York: John Wiley.

Wheeler, Stephen M. 2004. *Planning for Sustainability: Creating Livable, Equitable, and Ecological Communities*. New York: Routledge.

Whitzman, Carolyn. 1992. 'Taking back planning: Promoting women's safety in public places: The Toronto experience'. *Journal of Architectural and Planning Research* 9: 169–79.

———. 2002. 'The voice of women in Canadian local government'. In Caroline Andrew, Katherine Graham, and Susan Phillips, Eds, *Urban Affairs: Back on the Policy Agenda*, 93–118. Montreal and Kingston: McGill-Queen's University Press.

Working Group on Women's Access to Municipal Services in Ottawa. 2001. *Making the New City of Ottawa Work for Women*. Ottawa: Federation of Canadian Municipalities.

Chapter 11 *Getting Perspective*

What forces are at work in restructuring cities in the Western world?

This chapter gives us some sense of where cities have come from, but it also raises questions about where cities are going in the future. Industrialization meant that cities were employment magnets as factories needed workers. It was no wonder that the migration of people, their adjustment problems, and the growth of suburbs as an escape from the factory environment became central issues in urban sociology. However, the restructuring of cities away from manufacturing led to deindustrialization that produced a growing service sector. It became increasingly clear that urban land was scarce and that uses changed over time. Thus, a new emphasis in urban sociology turned to how decisions about land use were made, who made these decisions, and what the impact of such transformations might be.

It became increasingly obvious that the key issue in cities was the fact that land became viewed as a *commodity*. Land could be bought and sold or even rented, but there was a clash between the *exchange value* (the economic value) of land and the *use value* (the value of land from the perspective of its users, the inhabitants) of land. Fundamental conflicts occurred—both ideologically and on the ground—between those who viewed urban space primarily as an investment and those who viewed it in terms of its meaning and value for everyday living. Decisions about how land was used reflected the interests of those making the decisions. Instead of investment in manufacturing for profits, the new emphasis became how *property entrepreneurs* made investments in land development to obtain profits. Elite coalitions of real estate developers, business owners, and government officials work together as 'growth machines' to restructure the city for more growth. The effect has been that urban growth has transformed the meaning of property.

The removal of manufacturing industries at first made the office building the new symbol of the urban economy. Increasingly, however, a new purpose has developed in central cities, with a focus on the *symbolic economy* of shopping malls, museums, art galleries and concert halls, athletic venues, bars, and themed restaurants, all of which are various forms of entertainment. These places create in people a desire to spend money in what is called 'leisure consumption'. It begins with people looking for exciting ways to spend their leisure time but ends up having them become consumers supporting a huge leisure industry on private property (e.g., malls) rather than mingling in public parks.

11 The New Urban Political Economy

John Hannigan

Learning Objectives

- To understand what the new urban political economy paradigm is and why it arose.
- To identify the contributions of the major theorists of political economy.
- To learn how cities have shifted to entrepreneurial governance as a strategy of interurban competition and economic development.

Introduction

In the late 1960s, a revolution occurred in the field of urban sociology (Walton 1993, 301) in which the human ecology paradigm (a paradigm is a set of related concepts, research questions, and theories that assist in making sense of the world) that had been dominant since the 1920s was superseded by a 'political economy' paradigm that continues to prevail three decades later. This new viewpoint emphasized investment shifts by banks, insurance companies, and international corporations that shaped cities by transferring the ownership and uses of land from one social class to another (Zukin 1996, 43). Furthermore, the political economy approach focused on how conflicts between different elements of the urban population, notably social classes and racial and ethnic populations, determined the physical and social character of the metropolis (Macionis and Parillo 1998, 198). To a certain extent, this reflected a more general shift during this era within sociological theory from a 'functionalist' to a 'conflict' perspective. However, it was more directly a product of the changing demographic, economic,

and political character of European and North American cities, as well as the rapid urbanization of Africa, Asia, and Latin America. Labelled by Zukin (1980) 'the new urban sociology', the political economy paradigm lost much of its creative vitality in the 1990s, only to bounce back over the past few years—partly as a result of its success in explaining changes related to urban marketing and the growth of a 'symbolic economy' organized around tourism, sports, entertainment, and the arts rather than manufacturing.

Factors Contributing to the Emergence of Urban Political Economy

From Order to Crisis

When urban sociology first achieved scholarly prominence and coherence as an area of inquiry in the 1920s and 1930s, it was in the context of massive migration and immigration to American cities, most notably Chicago. The sheer volume of this population growth, reinforced by the fact that many of the newcomers to the city came from small towns, villages, and rural settings, meant that a perceived crisis of adjustment loomed large. In both policy and academic terms, the mission of the early pioneers of urban sociology was to systematically discover the structure and dynamics of the modern city in order to ensure the maintenance of social order. Indeed, it appeared that the traditional bases of social integration and solidarity—the family, the neighbourhood, and the church—were all simultaneously breaking down, leading to widespread marital breakdown, juvenile delinquency, and other indicators of social disorder. By carefully charting the physical form of the city and demonstrating how it influenced urban organization and experience, academic researchers, planners, and social workers believed that they might better understand and cope with the problems and potential solutions associated with the perceived breakdown of the moral order.

Forty years later, however, the challenge facing urban researchers and practitioners had fundamentally changed. Rather than finding ways to assist legions of migrants and immigrants better adjust to life in the metropolis, the first task now revolved around interpreting and mitigating the 'urban crisis' that had captured the attention of politicians, policy analysts, and media reporters. In the United States, this meant explaining the growing incidence of civil disorders arising out of racial segregation and conflict, inequality, and poverty. Urban unrest reached its zenith in the late 1960s when riots erupted in Detroit, Los Angeles, Newark, NJ, and dozens of other American cities. In western European cities, students and working-class protesters took to the barricades to demonstrate against arbitrary treatment by government bureaucrats and other elites. It soon became quite evident that the existing social organization paradigm was not up to the task of explaining these sharp and pervasive contemporary conflicts. As Manuel Castells, an early and vitriolic European critic of the status quo in the field, later declared, 'when everything was contested, debated, fought over, and negotiated between social groups with conflicting interests

and alternative projects, the very notion of integration in a shared culture appeared utterly obsolete' (Castells 2002, 391–2).

Policy Changes

Immediately after World War II, suburban communities proliferated in Canada and the United States at a rate never before witnessed. Several alternative explanations have been advanced for this move to the suburbs. In one version, the dominant factor was the sudden spike in demand for housing following the cessation of wartime hostilities. From the start of the Depression in 1929 through the end of World War II, very few new homes had been erected. When the veterans were decommissioned and returned home in 1945, they faced a major housing shortage. Many were forced to live in crowded quarters in the central city with parents and other relatives, leading to considerable intergenerational tension. This was exacerbated by the postwar 'baby boom' in which couples who had been separated for much of the war finally decided to start a family. Sensing a potentially explosive political issue, governments in both countries introduced a new model of real estate development. The small local builders who had previously predominated gave way to large corporate developers who mass-produced new housing tracts on the edge of the city. In Canada, the template for this development was set in the relatively affluent Toronto suburb of Don Mills, while in the United States the most famous model was Levittown, a lower-middle-class development of which versions were built in New York, New Jersey, and Pennsylvania. Governments encouraged this suburban housing boom by making a variety of loans and tax incentives available to developers and low-interest mortgages requiring small or no down payments to purchasers. This change in the urban form was directly related to financial and government policies.

Race, Class, and Lifestyle Issues

Another explanation for suburban growth during this era downplays economic factors in favour of sociological considerations. Here it is suggested that those who purchased new homes in the suburbs were actively seeking a distinct lifestyle characterized by a child-centred orientation, the pursuit of status congruent with the culture of large companies such as IBM and General Motors, and intense social involvement with one's neighbours. In the United States, there was another twist: moving to the suburbs was a means of 'escaping' the waves of southern blacks and Hispanics who were flooding into the cities of the northeast in the 1950s and 1960s in record numbers. By contrast, in Canada where the racial and ethnic makeup was more homogeneous, this **escape from the city thesis** was much less of a factor (Clark 1966).

Deliberate or not, the shift of large numbers of white, middle-class Americans to the suburbs led to increasing racial polarization. Chicago, the central focus of the first generation of urban sociological studies, provides a good example. In the 1920s and 1930s, most of the non-white population was concentrated in the South Side 'Black Belt', which cut across several of the concentric zones or circles that were said to characterize the growth pattern of the city. By 1950, some minority settlement had spread to the West Side, but only 14 per cent in that area were 'nonwhite'. Yet by the early 1960s, a major transformation had occurred with 'a massive transfer of the white population out of Chicago and into the outer rings of suburban Cook County and, increasingly, into the so-called collar counties that stretched beyond Cook County' (Abu-Lughod 1999, 230–1). Soon, in a pattern that became typical of most large American cities, both middle- and working-class residents of these distant suburban rings 'mostly avoided the shopping and recreational areas of either the south or the north downtowns, preferring the massive outlying malls that the ring highways made more easily accessible' (Abu-Lughod 1999, 236). With whites rapidly retreating to zones beyond the city limits, commercial strips that previously served adjoining black and white neighbourhoods collapsed; an oversupply of available housing led to collapsing real estate values; cases of arson escalated, and riots ensued.

Urban Renewal

This period also saw the zenith of urban renewal in North American cities. From 1944 to 1964, most municipalities in Canada were targeted for a form of property redevelopment known as urban renewal. The rationale for it was that the older areas of Canadian cities had become 'rundown' and 'blighted'. Since the private real estate market had been sluggish in responding to the challenge, aggressive public investment was needed to take up the slack (Smith and Moore 1993, 358). This was facilitated by the decision of the federal government to introduce amendments to the National Housing Act in 1949 and 1956 that encouraged 'slum clearance' both by providing for joint federal-provincial participation in public housing projects and by funding urban renewal studies jointly with municipalities (the federal government paid 75 per cent of the cost through the Canada Mortgage and Housing Corporation).

While the initial intention here was altruistic—tear down the slums and replace them with decent low-income housing—urban renewal programs soon morphed into something quite different. With municipalities reaping higher taxes from commercial and industrial buildings than from new residential areas, renewal funds were increasingly deployed to 'clear' inner cities for large-scale projects such as office complexes and shopping centres. Since the official definition of blight was vague, municipalities could legally designate any residential block with older housing as 'blighted'. As a consequence, lower-income groups from inner-city neighbourhoods in Canada were forced to find comparable housing, if they could, in less accessible areas, notably on the outskirts of the city where public housing had generally been placed. In one extreme case, the Halifax community of 'Africville' was totally obliterated and its residents dispersed to public housing across the city (see Box 11.1).

Box 11.1 *Africville*

Perhaps the most extreme case of urban renewal in Canada during the 1960s was that of Africville, which in fact was on the margins of the metropolis. This primarily black community on the periphery of Halifax was totally destroyed between 1964 and 1969. At the time of relocation, Africville was essentially a small, stable community with a social life centred on the Seaview African United Baptist Church. Some residents claimed roots that extended as far back as 1848 when the first settlers came. Its negative reputation in the Halifax area derived in part from a minority of 'marginals/transients' who lacked local kinship ties or housing claims in the community and were prone to engage in various deviant behaviours (Clairmont and Magill 1999, 531).

Although its final destruction began in the mid-1960s, the community had long faced the threat of expropriation. As far back as 1947, Halifax City Council formally approved the designation of Africville as industrial land. A report to Halifax City Council in mid-1954 recommended the shifting of Africville residents to city-owned property to the southwest, noting that the area that Africville occupied, with its ocean frontage, nearby railway line, and location midway between downtown and the provincial highway, made it ideal for industrial purposes. Having been defined as a slum, the area was continually neglected by city authorities. It never, for example, obtained water and sewage services. There were no paved roads. In the mid-1950s, an open city dump was moved to the Africville area. Some residents found that they could not obtain insurance because 'they lived in an undesirable area' (Clairmont and Magill 1999, 128). Nevertheless, most residents felt that this was home and did not wish to move.

When the moment came to leave, the relocation was handled without any element of sensitivity: residents who could not afford to move on their own had their household possessions pitched into the back of a city garbage truck and taken to public housing elsewhere in Halifax. Compensation for the 400 residents amounted to less than $500 each, insufficient funds to allow any meaningful relocation. In 1970, bulldozers were sent in the middle of the night to level the remaining houses, stores, and businesses. In the end, the plans for industrial expansion never materialized, and the site became a park.

The case of Africville dramatically demonstrates how urban land use revolves around contestation among different social actors. As we have seen, city officials believed that the land was not suitable for residences but ideal for industrial development. The human rights community in Halifax 'saw the abolition of Africville as a positive government action to bring employment, education, and desegregation to a black slum' (Ward 2002). Residents and their supporters tended to view the city's action as an outright land grab in which residents were denied any meaningful voice. Furthermore, this instance of urban renewal illustrates how governmental and policy decisions affected an entire community that had been labelled in a particular way.

None of these trends—suburban growth, racial polarization, and urban renewal—were easily explained using traditional approaches such as human ecology. The existing paradigm assumed an urban economy that operated efficiently according to natural principles and without requiring any significant interference from outside forces.

However, as we have seen, suburban growth in the 1950s and 1960s was lubricated by a battery of government subsidies and incentives, many of which were extremely advantageous to the development industry. In Canada, for example, one tax concession, the capital cost allowance (CCA), permitted developers to show huge paper losses on their income properties business on their corporate tax returns, even though their audited financial statements showed that they earned substantial profits on these income properties (Lorimer 1978, 65). Furthermore, the social organization paradigm had not anticipated urban racial segregation on the scale that it appeared in the United States after World War II. It was assumed that just as European ethnic groups—the Irish, the Italians, the Poles—eventually moved to better areas of the city as they became more settled (and assimilated), so too would blacks and Hispanics. However, rather than lessening over time, racial segregation in American cities was in fact intensifying, and minority group members were finding themselves confined to racially segregated ghettos (Kleniewski 2002, 39). Until the 1970s, few found their way into suburban subdivisions. Some suburban developments, including the original Levittown, had racially restrictive protective covenants that blocked home sales to selected minorities. Banks and other financial institutions would refuse to give mortgages and/or mortgage insurance (see Box 11.2). Municipal governments maintained a number of exclusionary zoning practices—controls on the number of units on a piece of land, minimum lot and housing sizes, housing codes, prohibition of trailers—that were intended to exclude low-income populations in general and blacks in particular (Palen 1995, 123). Even after 1968 when the US government passed fair housing legislation and middle-class minorities—mostly African Americans—moved into suburbs in increasing number, few ended up in mixed neighbourhoods, settling instead in black suburbs (Macionis and Parillo 1998, 227–8).

Third World Urbanization

Political economy emerged as a more suitable way of approaching the structures and processes of Third World urbanization, an area in which the previous social organization paradigm had generated relatively little comparative work (Walton 1993, 310). Rather than developing in the same way as the cities of western Europe and North America, cities in Asia, Africa, and Latin America display unique features. Most are characterized by over-urbanization whereby the rate of urban population growth far outstrips the pace of industrialization. This has resulted in widespread unemployment, especially among the millions of rural migrants who flock to cities imagining that the streets are paved with gold. Many end up in the informal economy, bartering goods and services, scavenging in dumps for recyclable materials, and living in shantytowns without basic urban services such as sewage and water. The classic human ecology approach was unable to explain this, since it assumed that newcomers to the city would eventually prosper and inevitably move up the social ladder. Seeking guidance, some urban political economists turned to *world system theory*. This analytic approach introduced by Immanuel Wallerstein (1976) distinguished between different categories of nations. Core nations such as the United States, Britain, and France performed the functions of capital investment, economic management, and innovation, while peripheral nations exported agricultural products and raw materials such as minerals, as well as supplying cheap factory labour. Foreign investment from the core countries centrally influenced urbanization in the Third World both by relegating it to a lesser role in the global division of labour and by accelerating urban growth, pushing rural peasants off their land by imposing large-scale, capital-intensive, and export-oriented agriculture (Kleniewski 2002, 165). In addition, these global arrangements provided cheap labour for world markets while often bringing low wages and appalling working conditions to workers in Third World cities (Drakakis-Smith, 2000, 123).

Three Key Theories

Manuel Castells: The Crisis of Consumption

It is generally acknowledged that a major turning point in the shift in urban sociology from a hu-

Box 11.2 Redlining

Redlining occurs when lending institutions such as banks and insurance companies decline to make a loan on property in a specific area of the city or only do so on less than favourable terms, which leads to the continued depreciation of the property. The term arises from the story of a bank in Boston that evidently drew a red line around an area of the city where it declined to lend mortgage money (Short 1996). It is often most closely associated with racial exclusion in poorer, inner-city districts in US cities during the 1950s and 1960s, although it also used to be a characteristic practice regarding suburban property in Canada, where it was 'if anything more common' (Harris and Forrester 2003, 2,663).

Two developments in the financing of home ownership in the US led to the expansion of racially exclusionary practices and housing patterns: the long-term mortgage and federal insurance for mortgage loans (Squires 1992, 3). In the case of the former, both private appraisers and those working for the Home Owners Loan Corporation (HOLC), a federal agency created in 1933, deliberately undervalued dense, mixed, or aging neighbourhoods, most of which contained large minority populations. In the HOLC rating system, a neighbourhood coded 'red' was judged to have the lowest value. Another agency, the Federal Housing Administration (FHA), more or less required racial segregation in its insurance underwriting practices, ensuring that most of the guaranteed mortgages went to white suburbanites. The FHA justified this by claiming that it was risky to extend home financing to African-American and Hispanic home-seekers because 'a change in social or racial occupancy generally contributes to instability and a decline in values' (US Federal Housing Administration 1938, paragraph 937).

Using land registry and property assessment data from between 1935 and 1954, Harris and Forrester (2003) demonstrate that the institutional lenders (banks, insurance companies) who replaced private individuals as sources of home financing in Canada after World War II discriminated sharply in favour of the more expensive suburban Hamilton, ON, neighbourhoods of the West End—the Mountain and Bartonville—and against portions of the poorer East End that were unserviced or close to lakefront industry. They conclude that 'there is every reason to believe that Hamilton's experience was typical of other Canadian urban areas' (2003, 2,683).

The process of redlining is an especially evident example of the utility of the political economy paradigm over the human ecology approach. Two influential authors of ecological growth models in the 1920s and 1930s, the sociologist Ernest Burgess (1928) and his geography colleague at the University of Chicago, Homer Hoyt (1933), exercised significant impact on housing policy by arguing that the invasion of white ethnic neighbourhoods by blacks and Mexicans had the effect of depreciating land values, a finding that was used to justify discriminatory practices such as redlining (Squires 1992, 4–5). Redlining demonstrates that financial institutions actively influence housing opportunities and housing constraints in the city by the amount they lend, to whom they lend, and where they lend (Short 1996).

man ecological to a political economy paradigm was the 1977 publication of the English translation of Manuel Castells's *The Urban Question*. Castells, a Spaniard who did his doctoral studies in Paris, was part of a trend in French sociology in the 1960s and 1970s that saw the application of neo-Marxist theory to urban issues. Castells stood out from other contributors because he deliberately aimed his critique at a wider, international audience well beyond the confines of the introverted debates that raged within French intellectual circles of the time.

In *The Urban Question*, Castells argued that the urban problems facing Western societies in the 1960s and 1970s were very different from those that existed in Chicago in the 1920s. Rather than ballooning social disorganization (delinquency, divorce, crime, suicide, family breakdown) among recent migrants and immigrants, the major point of concern was the extent of inequality and injustice spawned by late modern capitalism. As an escalating number of inner-city riots in Britain and America and street protests in France and Italy indicated, serious cracks were beginning to appear in the social fabric of the metropolis, precipitating a sense of 'crisis'.

In his attempt to reconstruct urban sociology, Castells turned to Marxist theory but gave it a novel twist. The exploitation and alienation of the factory, he claimed, had now spilled over and been reproduced beyond the workplace. In particular, it characterized the sphere of collective consumption, that is, various services collectively provided by the state—mass housing, transport, health facilities, and so forth. The city was of major importance here because it was at the municipal level that collective consumption operated on an everyday basis.

At about the same time that Castells was delivering his critique, some leading British sociologists, notably Ray Pahl and John Rex, were formulating an 'institutional' approach to urban issues that focused on housing stratification. With housing in short supply in postwar Britain, some low-income residents, notably South Asian and Caribbean immigrants, were being systematically denied a place to live. This class struggle over housing was said to be the dominant process of the city as a social unit. Rex and his colleagues proposed a *managerialist thesis* whereby the key to understanding unequal access to housing was located in the gatekeeper actions of individual managers and supervisors in public housing agencies. The managerialist thesis was criticized on the grounds that it lacked any theoretical explanation as to why housing was in short supply and why certain groups predominated among the gatekeepers who excluded minority group members. By contrast, Castells's ideas on collective consumption seemed to provide this missing theoretical foundation.

Cities, Castells claimed, were increasingly losing their central place as the locus of production units and becoming instead the site of consumption activities: housing, health care, social services, education, transportation. These activities are vital for the efficient operation of modern capitalism but are inherently unprofitable, so the state must pick up the bill (Elliott 1980, 155). This situation contrasts with that of the past when company housing was often provided at minimal cost to workers. By providing essential services, however, the state places itself in a contradictory situation in which the interests of the corporate sector and those of working-class consumers directly clash. Rent controls, for example, benefit the latter but not the former. Furthermore, the contradictory position of the state eventually results in a fiscal crisis. As the cost of collective services rises, governments find themselves locked on the horns of a dilemma. If they keep spending, they risk losing their credit rating or going bankrupt. If they raise taxes, popular unrest may be generated. If they cut back on spending, their 'clients' may rise up in anger. The conflicts arising from the contradictions associated with collective consumption inevitably give rise to a host of urban social movements. While much of Castells's early theorizing tended to be rather abstract, he did contribute a collection of empirical case studies on such topics as urban renewal, squatting, public transport, and ecological conflicts. Perhaps the best known of the latter is his research on *Monopolville* (Castells and Godard 1974) in which he demonstrated how postwar development in the French port city of Dunkirk was centrally shaped by large corporations who turned to the state and its planners to provide the necessary infrastructure.

In 1979, Castells moved to the University of California at Berkeley. At Berkeley, he shifted away from Marxist analysis to a less economics-based and more cultural approach. Soon after arriving, he began a major study of the local urban movements that were active in the San Francisco Bay area in the late 1970s and early 1980s. Castells concluded that the social mobilizations that occurred in American cities tend to revolve around one key goal—that is, they have a single objective that is unrelated to broader issues. For example, poor people will mobilize to obtain greater welfare benefits without challenging the general employment policy or the taxation system. He identified three main 'structural issues' underlying these urban mobilizations: the preservation and improvement of residential neighbourhoods; poverty; and social and cultural discrimination. He reported this research in *The City and the Grassroots* (1983), a winner of the C. Wright Mills Book Prize from the American Sociological Association.

In the 1990s, Castells once again shifted gears, undertaking a trilogy that focused on high technology, global 'flows', and the 'network society'. In particular, he stressed that the network society is organized around the opposition between the global and the local. The former, he claimed, predominates in technology, the economy, and the media. By contrast, day-to-day work, private life, cultural identity, and political participation are all essentially local (Castells 2002, 396). While some have praised this more recent work as magisterial, others have criticized Castells for abandoning his youthful idealism and commitment to class struggle and the triumph of social movements (Fainstein 1999, 260).

In a sense, things have come full circle. Castells now claims that the issue of social integration has come again to the forefront of urban sociology. However, rather than the quest for the assimilation of urban subcommunities that was characteristic of Chicago School theory, today the challenge is said to be the sharing of the city by those possessing distinctly different cultures and identities, most notably 'haves', who are plugged into the world of e-commerce and the Internet, and 'have-nots', who are excluded from this dimension.

David Harvey: The Crisis of Accumulation

In North America, Castells's ideas were initially less influential than those of David Harvey, a British geographer working at Johns Hopkins University in Baltimore. Harvey's primary contribution is that he drew our attention to the role of real estate investment in the way cities develop.

Whereas Castells treated the urban crisis of the 1960s and 1970s as a 'crisis of consumption', Harvey viewed it as a **crisis of accumulation** (Zukin 1980, 585). In America, the 'crisis' was triggered by the decision of investors to abandon the inner city, thus calling up a battery of problems: eroding income, physical deterioration of housing, rising crime rates. In using the phrase 'crisis of accumulation', Harvey meant to convey that real estate investors characteristically tend to over-invest in a particular area because it appears to be profitable. Soon, the market is flooded, and a decline in profit or 'productive investment' occurs. When this happens, investors collectively shift their sights (and their money) to another location, leaving the original site facing economic difficulties. In the 1950s and 1960s, investors took their money out of the inner city and ploughed it into land development and house construction in the suburbs. In Canada, it has been estimated that banks and insurance companies mobilized a total of $75 billion between 1948 and 1978 to finance the development of real estate, mainly urban real estate—about $3,000 for every person in the country (Lorimer 1978, 258). This resulted in a steady decline in older areas of the central city. When suburban growth slowed in the 1980s, investors revisited inner cities, which by then were exhibiting sharply declining land values after decades of neglect. This time around, capital was invested in gentrifying neighbourhoods that middle-class newcomers were moving into, displacing blue-collar residents.

Looking to the writing of Marx and Engels, as channelled by Henri Lefebvre (1984), Harvey distinguished between three types of investment capital, each of which follows its own 'circuit'. Whereas the first or *primary circuit* flows into manufacturing, the *second circuit* of capital tends to flow into investment in land and the third or *tertiary circuit* into scientific knowledge that is produced and used to make capitalism work better. Within the corridors of Marxist political economy, there has long been a sharp debate over the extent to which these three circuits operate independently from one another as opposed to one siphoning off profits from the other. Indeed, Harvey seems to have wavered somewhat on this. In the Canadian case, the banks and financial institutions have historically tended to follow a dual strategy in which they support domestic businesses in the fields of commerce, finance, and real estate, while leaving foreign investors to finance ventures in resource development (mining, oil, forestry) and manufacturing. In the 1970s, this led some critics to call for far less money to be directed into the urban land development industry, thereby freeing up a substantial supply of Canadian investment capital for alternative uses, notably investment in new manufacturing industries (Lorimer 1978, 260–3). Today, with many manufacturing jobs having migrated offshore to Asia and Latin America, this alternative is somewhat less compelling.

Since the goal is to maximize return, where and how real estate investment is made is influenced by various factors, including the potential for profit and how stable and secure the investment will be. The problem is that what is optimal for real estate investors may turn out to be much less so for the welfare of the city and its residents. For example, banks and other lenders have a long history of declining to lend to the inner-city poor, who must therefore buy their houses, if indeed they can afford to do so, using cash and private loans or through government programs (Macionis and Parillo 1998, 200). This leads to the creation of poor inner-city neighbourhoods with low rates of home ownership and, conversely, a preponderance of slum landlords. Much of Harvey's theoretical scheme was inspired by empirical inquiries that he conducted into housing and real estate development in Baltimore in the 1970s. In that city, investment capital was most likely to be directed to middle-income areas in the northeast and southwest instead of poorer black areas that had become progressively run-down and abandoned.

Another theme closely associated with David Harvey is social justice and the right to the city. In his 1973 book *Social Justice and the City*, Harvey defines social justice as 'a just distribution justly arrived at' (1973, 98). In this highly prescriptive scheme, Harvey proposes that the right to shared resources such as good education and affordable transportation must necessarily trump individual rights. To use the example of a high-profile issue in the current Canadian political scene, it is only fair and just to use a portion of provincial gas taxes to subsidize the cost of mass transit, since the less affluent sector of society is most dependent on buses and subway travel.

Molotch and Logan: Elite Coalitions and the Urban Growth Machine

A third highly influential approach that has shaped the political economy paradigm is the 'urban growth machine' concept of Harvey Molotch and John Logan. They were centrally concerned with the agents, processes, and consequences of city building, something given short shrift by neo-Marxist writers who were preoccupied with transplanting ideas about exploitation and class conflict from the workplace to the metropolis. Molotch and Logan focus specifically on the structure of political power in the urban community rather than dwelling on the mode of production (capitalism).

The concept of the **urban growth machine** was first proposed by Molotch (1976) in his seminal journal article, 'The city as a growth machine: Toward a political economy of place' and elaborated in a book, *Urban Fortunes: The Politi-*

cal Economy of Place, co-authored with Logan a decade later (Logan and Molotch 1987). Molotch and Logan depict the city as a machine controlled by business, political, and professional elites. Members of this machine or pro-growth coalition include corporate property owners, real estate brokers, bankers, developers, public utilities (gas, water, and electric companies), local media editors, producers, news readers and reporters, sports team owners and officials, and college and university administrators. In contrast to earlier sociological attempts to depict the nature of community power and decision-making, these elites do not ordinarily congregate behind closed doors in private clubs or on exclusive golf courses, nor are they necessarily just capitalists. However, they share a common assumption: that the best interests of the city and its residents are optimally served by pursuing continuous economic growth and development. Economic growth is an ideology shared by a wide range of elites who work together to support economic development strategies, which is why it is called a machine.

To accomplish this, they advocate using the full arsenal of weapons available to politicians and planners to attract tourism, jobs, and external investment. These weapons include everything from mounting promotional campaigns (perhaps the most famous is the 'I Love New York' campaign) and offering tax incentives and holidays to prospective investors to enhancing and promoting the image of the city by attracting professional sports teams and 'hallmark events' such as the Olympics and Grand Prix auto races (see Box 11.3). Molotch and Logan argue that growth is rarely the panacea it is said to be by growth machine proponents. Among the negatives are environmental degradation, higher rents, more crime, greater traffic congestion, and an infrastructure (roads, sewers, landfills, parks, recreation centres) unable to handle an increased population (Macionis and Parillo 1998, 204). Furthermore, urban growth does not automatically convert into new jobs and prosperity for everyone. Any suggestion that

this growth has 'trickle-down' benefits for every urban resident 'is either blatant self-promotion or naive utopianism' (Langer 1984, 112). On the contrary, urban growth strategies generally result in a net transfer of wealth from the less wealthy to urban elites. Two decades after the urban growth machine thesis was first proposed, John Logan reported that the collected wisdom from a long series of empirical studies using the thesis seemed to be that there was a very limited increase in new investment and no demonstrable increase in new jobs in cities that competed vigorously for new growth (Logan, Bridges, and Crowder 1999).

The critical dimension in Molotch and Logan's model stands in stark contrast to most previous writing on cities, refracted as it was through an uncritical lens. What critique there was, Molotch (1999, 247) observes, came mostly from an aesthetic distaste for such things as the tackiness and uniformity of suburbia. The growth machine model, on the other hand, cut to the ideological core of city power and politics.

The Entrepreneurial City

Starting in the early 1970s and intensifying during the following two decades, a fiscal crisis had an impact on cities across Europe and North America. After decades of prosperity, the industrial economy was now rapidly faltering. Profits became increasingly squeezed; production was not increasing fast enough to cover promised wages and benefits to labour; and international competition was on the rise. At the heart of the crisis was the escalating process of deindustrialization—the rise of new industrial forms that were reconstituting the mass production system along significantly different lines, notably those emphasizing greater flexibility and a global scope. Manufacturing jobs that had formerly been situated in Cleveland, Montreal, or Manchester migrated to China, Mexico, or India, where wages were demonstrably lower and unions weaker or non-existent.

Box 11.3 *Racing for 'World-Class' Status*

In the stampede to generate a 'world-class' image, Canada's largest cities embraced motorsport events. Each summer, Molson Indy car races were held in Toronto and Vancouver, while the Montreal Grand Prix was a regular stop on the Formula One (F1) racing circuit. Civic boosters in each city aspired to be the 'Monaco of North America', replicating the glitz, glamour, and publicity associated with the annual Monaco Grand Prix with its resident royal family, palaces and mansions, posh hotels and casinos, yacht-filled Mediterranean harbour, and globetrotting celebrities (Lowes 2002, 14). Montreal came closest with the arrival during race week of the 'F1 clique', a colourful cast of 'Euro-trash', New York's jet set, heirs and heiresses with numbered bank accounts at Crédit Suisse, and minor aristocrats who travel from Grand Prix to Grand Prix (Gollner 2002, SP1). Indeed, having cars racing at break-neck speed through blocked city streets is itself a strange means of urban marketing and one that is clearly disruptive to normal urban life.

The alleged economic spinoffs from motorsport events are twofold. First, there are the direct revenues from taxes, tourism, and temporary jobs. It was estimated that the Montreal Grand Prix generated $75 million per year (Gollner 2002, SP1), while the Molson Indy Vancouver contributed $22 million to the local economy (Lowes 2002, 67). No less significant is the 'showcase effect' (Hiller 1989) whereby media coverage of the city generates positive publicity for months and years afterwards, especially with prospective tourists. In Australia, for example, marketing research indicated that the Adelaide Grand Prix was quite successful in altering Adelaide's image as a boring, quiet 'city of churches', an image that had formerly served to inhibit consideration of Adelaide as a travel destination for many would-be visitors (Van der Lee and Williams 1986). Furthermore, economic development planners claim that corporations are more likely to locate in cities with a 'buzz'. However, there has been substantial debate over the actual magnitude of these economic effects. In one reported case, an assessment of the 1996 Qantas Australian Formula Grand Prix, a consulting group retained by the Save the Albert Park Group concluded that claims that the 1996 Grand Prix provided a gross economic benefit of A$95.6 million were significantly overstated (Hall 2001, 170).

Not everything has gone smoothly for motorsport events in recent years. In the wake of new Canadian government regulations that prohibit sponsorship of sporting and cultural events by tobacco companies, the Montreal Grand Prix, formerly sponsored by Rothmans, was briefly removed from the F1 circuit in 2004, only to be reinstated when the governments involved agreed to pony up additional financial subsidies, allowing expansion to an 18-race schedule. More recently, Championship Auto Racing Teams (CART), the US public company that ran events in Montreal, Toronto, and Vancouver, declared bankruptcy, briefly putting events in those three cities in jeopardy before a bankruptcy judge ruled in favour of a new ownership group whose bid would keep the Canadian races alive. Then, in February 2008, Champ Car (the successor to CART) merged with the rival Indy Racing League, resulting in the cancellation of the Grand Prix of Toronto (formerly the Molson Indy race). In October 2008, the Formula One race in Montreal was cancelled and its slot in the calendar taken by Turkey. The race-car industry provides an excellent illustration of how cities use high-profile events to market themselves as a tool of economic development but with questionable marginal benefits to urban residents. Other, similar events include international sporting competitions in track or figure skating and even large conventions.

In response, economies shifted from a 'Fordist' system typified by mass production, standardized products, and large, vertically integrated companies to a flexible system—sometimes called **flexism**—characterized by small-batch manufacturing runs, high-tech production, and decentralized organization. On the factory floor, the traditional assembly line gave way to robots, computers, and 'just-in-time' delivery systems that eliminated the need for inventory storage. Manufacturers attempted to reduce risk by 'outsourcing' and subcontracting to companies that were not part of their own organizations, thus reducing the amount of vertical integration. Magna International is a good example of a Canadian company that has prospered mightily by taking over the subassembly of major components for the large auto manufacturers. Soja (2000) claims that this represents nothing less than a 're-industrialization, the rise of new industrial forms that reconstitute Fordism along significantly different lines'. While all of this made some manufacturing plants more efficient and competitive and consequently saved them from closing, many were simply shifted elsewhere, more often than not 'offshore'. Entire urban regions became economically depressed; the heavy industrial zone stretching throughout the American northeast and midwest, for example, became known as the 'Rust Belt'.

The response of cities caught in a seeming downward spiral of deindustrialization and decline was to embrace a new form of doing business that has become known as **entrepreneurial governance**. Basically, it involves a shift in the role of local government from providing services such as garbage collection and welfare to becoming promoters, pitching the opportunities and attractions of the community to everyone from tourists to sports team owners. Of course, this type of promotional activity by city governors is not entirely new. For example, the popular British motion picture, *The Full Monty*, opens with a 1950s newsreel that shamelessly hypes Sheffield, a steel production centre in the north of England, as a 'City on the Move'. The events in the movie occur four decades later when Sheffield is experiencing deindustrialization through the collapse of its steel production, forcing the workers onto welfare. Similarly, there is a long history of local communities offering subsidies to attract auto plants and other potential employers. However, in the entrepreneurial city, planners and politicians not only engage in marketing and self-promotion, they are preoccupied by these activities. Furthermore, rather than do it alone, local governments seek out partnerships with real estate developers, media and entertainment companies, sports teams, and other partners in the private sector. Having witnessed this in Baltimore in the 1980s, Harvey (1989, 7) observed that the new entrepreneurialism has as its centrepiece the notion of *public-private partnership* in which local government joins forces with private interests to undertake major projects or mega-events in the hope of reviving the flagging economic fortunes of the city.

All of this culminates in a city that looks dramatically different from its industrial predecessor. On the ropes in the 1970s, the city centre has been reborn as a glitzy showpiece for consumption-related activities revolving around tourism, professional sports, culture, and entertainment. These features include themed restaurants and bars, megaplex cinemas, casinos, various types of virtual arcades, rides and theatres, sports stadiums and arenas, retail-entertainment emporiums celebrating iconic brands such as Nike, Prada, Sony, and Disney, cultural districts, and high-concept museums designed by signature architects (see Box 11.4). In some cases, these new urban 'landscapes of consumption' may take the form of waterside leisure areas with aquariums, IMAX theatres, luxury hotels, and even urban theme parks. Whereas the industrial city operated primarily during the day, these new 'fantasy cities' (Hannigan 1998) flourish at night as well, with upmarket style and café bars and nightclubs playing a key part in the new entertainment infrastructure (Chatterton and Hollands 2003).

Box 11.4 *Rogers Centre*

While Canada does not thus far register a 'fantasy city' on the scale of Las Vegas or Orlando, Toronto's downtown core has begun to resemble one in places, especially in the areas around the Eaton Centre and just west of Union Station. The two major landmarks in the latter district are the CN Tower and the Rogers Centre.

Opened in 1989 at a cost of nearly $600 million, the Rogers Centre (originally named SkyDome, the winning entry in a public contest) is representative of an era in which American commercial culture expanded into Canada in the context of the spectacular growth of televised professional sports. By the mid-1990s, its financial success was inexorably tied to the activities of corporations and the sustained satisfaction of the elite groups it served; for example, 40 per cent of its revenues came from club seat holders and corporate box holders (Kidd 1995, 189).

A trip to a Toronto Blue Jays baseball game at Rogers Centre is a safari into the heart of consumerism and popular culture in the early twenty-first century. The stadium is flanked by a bevy of themed restaurants (Baton Rouge, Wayne Gretzky's) and contains within a Hard Rock Café and a hotel. Between innings there is a continuous stream of contests, with the winners rewarded with national brand-name pizza, subs, ice cream bars, and even free delivery from an office supply chain of stores. The centre of action often shifts from the playing field to the 33-foot-high Daktronics ProStar video screen and other electronic signage that displays player statistics, out-of-town scores, fan antics, and advertising spots. Celebrities (and near-celebrities) are in constant attendance; for example, the ceremonial first pitch on opening day 2004 was hurled by Canadian actor Eugene Levy (*American Pie*), and 'American Idol' reject William Hung sang a characteristically off-key version of 'Take Me out to the Ballgame' during the seventh-inning stretch in a game in June. It's fair to say that you don't have to be a baseball fan to go there, but you do need to be a follower of pop culture.

For the most part, urban researchers, especially those working within a political economy paradigm, have viewed these developments with some alarm (Hannigan 2003, 354). Rather than build on the solid foundation of local place distinctiveness, and identity, these new urban growth machines often prefer to imitate success stories such as Las Vegas or Orlando, importing branded projects that evoke images taken from popular motion pictures or theme park rides. In the cultural sector, commentators now cite the **Bilbao effect**. This refers to the imagined economic boost that will ensue for cities that build their own version of the Guggenheim Bilbao, a branch of the Guggenheim Museum in New York that was opened in the aging Spanish port city of Bilbao in 1997. Designed by Canadian-born star architect ('staritect') Frank Gehry, the Guggenheim Bilbao attained celebrity status in architectural and design magazines and became an instant tourist attraction. While there are conflicting opinions on the extent of its long-term contribution to urban revitalization in Bilbao, the museum has been perceived among city politicians and planners around the world as the kind of magic elixir that promises to revive the fortunes of communities hobbled by deindustrialization and other recent economic body blows. The Royal Ontario Museum in Toronto, for example, joined the fray by commissioning a major renovation and addition featuring a dramatic and controversial pyramidal glass structure conceived by Daniel Liebeskind, who achieved superstar status when he won a competition to design the replacement for the World Trade Center in New York City. Critics point out that the market can quickly become saturated with such large projects and their subsequent failure totally drains public coffers (Molotch, Freudenburg, and Paulsen 2000, 818). It is also important to note that spectacular architecture alone is unlikely to turn the fortunes of a city around. Even in Bilbao, the remarkable turnaround was not just the result of one strong piece of architecture but rather the culmination of a decade of collaborative strategic planning by local and regional officials that included e-commerce, banking, trade fairs, and waterfront revitalization (Lorinc 2006, 315).

Fantasy cities are also considered problematic by their critics on the grounds that they are becoming increasingly undemocratic (Hannigan 2003, 355). As urban politics moves from 'government' to 'governing', key decisions are made less by elected representatives and more by public/private institutions that finance and manage the facilities of tourism and entertainment (Judd and Simpson 2003, 1,057) and are not directly accountable to the public. Community input here is minimal. Referendums on major capital projects have become increasingly rare. Consistent with the principles of the political economy paradigm, exchange values consistently trump use values, meaning that the financial possibilities of a project overshadow its possible social and environmental effects. Furthermore, municipalities have shown themselves to be more than willing to set up special, privately controlled administrative bodies such as BIDs (Business Improvement Districts) and give them responsibilities such as street cleanup, garbage removal, and private policing that were formerly carried out by public agencies and departments. Some BID boards even have the power to impose property taxes. While praised by some for making city spaces cleaner and safer, BIDs lack public accountability. Essentially 'malls without walls', business improve-

ment districts represent explicit attempts to win the confidence of corporate clients, gentrifiers, middle-class shoppers, and tourists by purging disreputable elements such as homeless people and vagrants and moving them to poorer areas that cannot develop their own improvement projects or to outlying areas on the urban periphery (Graham and Marvin 2001, 262).

Too often, the entrepreneurial city passes over and excludes significant segments of the local population. It is not unusual to find some of the most deprived areas of inner-city decay, characterized by chronic dependency, poverty, and unrest, in close juxtaposition to the glitter of fantasy city–type developments (Hall and Hubbard 1998, 1). This phenomenon can be seen with uncommon clarity regarding recent events related to Hurricane Katrina in New Orleans (see Box 11.5). Urban revitalization projects of this type are frequently justified on the grounds that they will create employment for those who are disadvantaged and put consumer dollars in the pockets of local merchants and restaurant owners. However, research has generally concluded that the notion that a rising economic tide must necessarily lift all ships is fundamentally faulty. In what is perhaps the most extensive longitudinal research study of its type, Levine (1987) found that the ripples from Harborplace, a festival marketplace opened along Baltimore's Inner Harbor in the 1970s, failed to reach the city's poor, predominantly black neighbourhoods, which remained in desperate condition over the decade 1970 to 1980. These areas constituted an 'underclass city of desolate neighbourhoods marked by social exclusion, high rates of crime and drug abuse, deepening ghetto poverty, and dilapidated or abandoned housing where much of the city's predominantly black population lived' (Levine 2000, 124). If anyone gained, Levine concluded, it was out-of-town tourists, suburbanites who captured most of the well-paid professional and managerial jobs, and middle-class residents of three gentrifying neighbourhoods adjacent to Inner Harbor.

Box 11.5 *Hurricane Katrina and the Dual City*

The chasm between the entrepreneurial city and the underclass city was laid bare on 29 August 2005 when Hurricane Katrina slammed into the Mississippi Delta, with a death toll of more than 1,400, making it the deadliest natural disaster in the United States in more than 75 years.

Well before the storm, New Orleans had evolved into a dual city: the iconic French Quarter with its distinctive antebellum architecture, famed jazz establishments along Bourbon Street, and Mardi Gras excesses, and the adjacent black district, scarred by poverty, high unemployment, rising crime, and racial segregation. Efforts to preserve and brand the former as a 'Disneyfied' tourist zone were ongoing, while attempts to extend it to the latter were consistently stymied. For example, Tremé, a mostly African-American neighbourhood across Rampart Street where a good many jazz musicians lived, was marginalized, losing its majestic oak trees and vibrant boulevards to an interstate expressway (Souther 2007).

As Peter Dreier (2006, 539) has quipped, 'Katrina was not an equal opportunity disaster.' Whereas the more upscale neighbourhoods on higher ground (French Quarter, Garden District) sustained only modest damage, the poorer areas were almost totally inundated by water from Lake Pontchartrain when the levees failed. The most severe flood damage was in the Ninth Ward, which was more than 98 per cent black with poverty rates of some 36 per cent of the total population in 2000 (Baade, Baumann, and Matheson 2007, 2,073). Furthermore, most higher-income residents were able to flee the disaster, while the poor, with no means of transport, were stranded and vulnerable.

In the aftermath of Katrina, efforts to reconstruct housing, schools, nursing homes, hospitals, health clinics, and child care centres in poor, racially segregated areas quickly stalled (Dreier 2006, 540). By contrast, plans to strengthen and enhance the New Orleans brand as the birthplace of jazz intensified. A central strategy here has been to convince prospective visitors that the French Quarter and other approved tourist spaces were 'hermetically sealed enclaves that are safe and crime free' and 'clearly demarcated, disconnected, and segregated from flooded neighbourhoods' (Gotham 2007, 836). Indeed, these flooded neighbourhoods were relegated to the indignity of 'disaster tourism' as city tour buses wound their way past the Ninth Ward and rock and roll legend Fats Domino's house. Once again, the local growth machine is aggressively pursuing a 'Disneyfied' brand of tourism: 'the very economic development strategy that magnified the social disaster of Katrina' (Souther 2007).

Conclusion: The Cultural/ Symbolic Emphasis of Political Economy

As is the case with the wider discipline, there is an increasing emphasis in urban sociology on culture and the symbolic economy. An important focus here is on how various social groups in the city are differentially taken into account in the design and use of buildings and public spaces such as parks, malls, and plazas. Another key focus has been the conscious and deliberate manipulation of the arts in the selling of places (Philo and Kearns 1993, 3). Indeed, the strategy of using culture to market cities has become an absolute must for politicians and planners. In his best-selling book *The Rise of the Creative Class*, Richard Florida (2002) contends that there is a strong and direct correlation between a city's success in economic development and the size and vibrancy of its cultural scene (see Box 11.6).

Box 11.6 *The Bohemian Factor*

Much of the literature on the entrepreneurial city has described and evaluated the role played by major construction and renovation projects and by mega-events in enhancing competitiveness. Typically, Ley (1996, 29) observes that the pursuit of the "'convivial city" (a place of festivity, livability, and fun, which includes specialty retailing, heritage areas, street festivals, ethnic restaurants, and art and cultural events) has become a municipal objective reflected in arts, leisure and tourism initiatives, and public expenditures for sports stadia, convention centres, policies for the arts, and tourist attractions.' Arts policy is one example among others of this broader trend towards urban entrepreneurialism.

Richard Florida argues that the driving force behind urban prosperity is the ability to attract members of what he calls 'the creative class'. This class is composed of knowledge workers who 'possess the creative competence required by technology and design enterprises' (Lloyd 2002, 519), which is another way of saying that they are computer engineers, website designers, and other Silicon Valley types who are crucial to the success of the microchip industry. Florida believes that members of this class are not very likely to patronize theme-park urban entertainment centres or arts complexes but rather are 'drawn to more organic and indigenous street level culture' (Florida 2002, 182), notably jazz clubs, bistros, small galleries, and areas with street musicians. Cities that have a booming local arts scene will thus be more successful in attracting high-tech businesses.

To scope out a formula for success, Florida developed a 'Bohemian Index'. Bohemians here are cultural workers such as writers, dancers, actors, and singers. Using US census data from 1990, Florida discovered a robust correlation between the presence of artists in an urban region and the concentration of high-technology enterprises. Cities that rank highest on the Bohemian Index (San Francisco, Boston, Austin, TX) not only have the most creative workers, but they also rank high on measures designed to measure social tolerance and diversity. Most notably, cities with large gay communities are more likely to include a lot of artists. In similar fashion, a high ranking on the 'Mosaic Index' (percentage foreign-born residents) is correlated with the presence of both a strong Bohemian population and considerable high-tech employment. Working with Florida, Canadian economic geographer Meric Gertler has applied the Bohemian Index to the Ontario scene, with more or less similar results. The authors conclude that Ontario cities, with their social diversity and artistic creativity, have the kind of 'creative capital' needed for economic growth and competitiveness in today's world (www.competeprosper.ca/research/index.php).

As might be expected, both urban and arts planners have shown tremendous interest in the Bohemian Index. The former have seen in Florida's work a magic bullet for enhancing urban competitiveness, while the latter recognize that it gives them a strong argument for increased government funding. Academic commentators, however, have been somewhat dubious. Some critics have focused on the circular logic engulfing Florida's identification of a 'creative class' (Marcuse 2003, 41). Nothing in Florida's data, it is pointed out, proves that high-tech companies strategically choose to locate in communities rating high on the Bohemian Index. Furthermore, increased spending on the arts does not necessarily produce more artists. For example, Montreal's budget for culture and heritage is almost double that of Toronto's, but Toronto has more 'Bohemians' (9.05 per 1,000 population) than does Montreal (8.20) (Bozikovic 2003). Most recently, in a major formal test of Florida's hypotheses about metropolitan competitiveness, economic growth, and urban planning, a research group in the Department of City and Regional Planning at the University of North Carolina found that attracting the creative class is no more effective in producing positive economic outcomes than traditional strategies such as investing in quality education, upgrading the skills of the workforce, creating new businesses, or expanding existing industries. While allowing that Florida's arguments could lend support to many worthwhile activities designed to enhance the livability of urban neighbourhoods, the authors fear that 'policies based on a narrow interpretation of Florida's creative class concept may not live up to some policymakers' positive expectations and may actually do harm by misallocating scarce public resources' (Donegan et al. 2008, 181).

Some of the most important pioneering work on the role of culture in post-industrial cities has been conducted by Sharon Zukin, who first wrote on the subject in *Loft Living* (1982). This is a case study of the SoHo district in New York City, which was transformed from an area of garment industry sweatshops to a place where artists lived and worked in lofts that they themselves had converted from factory space. Art galleries and chic boutiques followed. Soon, the neighbourhood was being highlighted in the Manhattan media. This caught the eye of property developers, who commandeered the conversion of factories into lofts and sold them to well-to-do urban professionals seeking a 'cool' lifestyle. Alas, the artists and other creative types were soon priced out of the local housing market. Zukin's case study was one of the first to recognize the powerful appeal of aesthetics and culture in constructing desirable neighbourhoods for middle-class gentrifiers.

More recently, Zukin and others have focused on economic development strategies that use symbolic and cultural institutions to create the appearance of a global city. A vibrant symbolic economy, Zukin (1996, 45) observes, attracts investment capital from banks, property developers, and large property owners. Analyses such as this emphasize how cultural representations have now become an integral part of the economic structure of the city (Tajbakhsh 2001, 21). Evans (2003, 436–7) refers to the process of

'hard-branding' the contemporary city whereby museums, art galleries, and other cathedrals of culture now aggressively market their architecture, history, and collections as a branded urban consumption experience.

In all of this, however, there lies a fundamental paradox. Urban planners, architects, city managers, and property developers want to exploit the creative edge, excitement, and diversity of creative subcultures for economic development purposes, but they wish to do so entirely on their own terms. What they want to avoid at all costs are art, culture, and consumption practices that tourists and other urban visitors might find challenging and upsetting. Consider, for example, the following example.

In her case study of the revitalization of Portland, Maine, Lees (2003) documents the tensions that arose when local youths who hung out in that city's erstwhile Arts District were perceived by downtown business interests as being 'too deviant'. Among their alleged transgressions were loitering, noise-making, reckless skateboarding, panhandling, graffiti, petty theft, mock sex acts, public drunkenness, and drug abuse. Those who hung out in a small public square in front of Green Mountain Coffee were criticized for skateboarding on the metal railings and concrete barriers outside the shop and for refusing to move on when asked. The teenagers denied that their activities in the downtown posed any significant threat to public

Box 11.7 Circus City

TOHU (the name comes from a Hebrew word describing the chaos before the creation of the world) is a 'circus arts community' located on the Saint Michel Environmental Complex, a 192-hectare former limestone quarry and municipal garbage dump in one of Montreal's poorest East End neighbourhoods. In the late 1990s, Cirque du Soleil, the one-time street performers collective that now has 14 shows playing simultaneously around the world, joined forces with the national Circus School and En Piste, the Canadian circus arts network, in a bold initiative designed to creative a world-class training, production, and performance facility for the circus arts. As the project proceeded, it evolved into a combination of entertainment destination, urban park, and community help program. TOHU's general manager describes it as 'the encounter between a burgeoning arts community looking for a home, a damaged site in the process of being restored, and a poor neighbourhood unsure what to do with its rich potential (Brunelle 2008). At the centre of its 'human' component is a job readiness initiative that combines work experience with personal coaching. Furthermore, TOHU attempts to involve its neighbours in a wide array of live performances, exhibits, community celebrations, and educational events. It is too early to know whether Circus City represents a successful template that can be usefully adapted to other urban settings or whether Montreal's brand of culture-led regeneration is significantly flawed (Broudehoux 2006).

safety and accused the police and the business owners of harassing them. In such cases, Lees (2003, 614) notes, 'it is paradoxical that urban renaissance promotes cultural diversity at the same time as promoting forms of conspicuous consumption and social control that limit diversity.'

The transition to the cultural economy illustrates that we have come a long way from cities that function primarily as industrial centres. But it also illustrates that shifts in land use and economic development mean that cities are constantly changing, reflecting major impacts on local residents. Ideally, the next generation of culture-led regeneration projects can function as economic incubators at the same time that they are environmentally and socially sustainable. One notable attempt to achieve this is TOHU, the circus arts city in Montreal (see Box 11.7). However, innovative projects of this nature remain all too rare.

Study and Discussion Questions

1. In the 1920s and 1930s, urban sociologists saw their central task as maintaining social order by assisting migrants and immigrants to better adjust to life in the metropolis. Forty years later, this focus had shifted to explaining and remedying 'urban crisis' rooted in escalating conflict, poverty, and inequality. What should be the major focus of urban sociology today? Is the political economy paradigm up to the task of dealing with this challenge?

2. Molotch and Logan have depicted cities as 'urban growth machines' controlled by broad coalitions of local decision-makers united by a belief that the city is best served by pursuing a policy of continual economic growth and development. Does the city in which you currently reside and/ or attend classes follow this urban growth machine model? If so, discuss some recent commercial development projects that have resulted.

3. Many cities pursue high-profile events as a means of marketing to encourage economic growth. Do you think this works? What events has your city pursued? Does it really matter that Toronto's Summer Olympics bid was unsuccessful and Vancouver's bid for the Winter Olympics was successful?

4. Urban researchers working in a political economy paradigm have increasingly focused on how cities are 'branded' in the same manner as consumer products such as soft drinks and running shoes. Imagine that you are a consultant who has been given the assignment of branding Vancouver, Calgary, Winnipeg, and Halifax. What kind of brand identity might you formulate for each of these four Canadian cities?

5. How are Canadian urban economy and culture influenced by the wider forces of globalization? Should these influences be embraced or resisted?

Suggested Reading

Davis, Mike. 1990. *City of Quartz: Excavating the City in Los Angeles*. London: Verso. Alarming, controversial, but powerful indictment of Los Angeles in the 1990s. Davis's bleak vision of the urban future is a cautionary tale for Canadian cities aiming for 'world-class' status.

Evans, Peter, Ed. 2002. *Livable Cities? Urban Struggles for Livelihood and Sustainability*. Berkeley: University of California Press. An exciting and essential book that examines how local populations in the developing world struggle against growth machines to achieve a balance between sustainability and livability. Case studies are from Thailand, Korea, Vietnam, Hungary, Brazil, and Mexico.

Hannigan, John. 1998. *Fantasy City: Pleasure and Profit in the Postmodern Metropolis*. London and New York: Routledge. An eminently readable analysis of the post-industrial city as an entertainment hub. Hannigan asks whether the middle-class search for 'risk-free' entertainment will end up destroying inner-city communities or creating new groupings of shared identities and experiences.

Judd, Dennis R., and Susan S. Fainstein, Eds. 1999. *The Tourist City*. New Haven, CT: Yale University Press. Timely and informative case histories of urban tourism, its pivotal role in economic development, and its impact on cities. Tourist sites discussed include Las Vegas, Prague, Jerusalem, Southeast Asia, and Times Square in New York City.

Lloyd, Richard. 2006. *Neo-Bohemia: Art and Commerce in the Postindustrial City*. New York and London: Routledge. A fascinating and insightful ethnographic account of Wicker Park, a declining industrial neighbourhood on Chicago's North Side, which has become a celebrated centre of hip urban culture. With considerable verve, Lloyd demonstrates the role played by edgy cultural areas in the global economy.

Zukin, Sharon. 1995. *The Cultures of Cities*. Oxford: Blackwell. Influential and readable treatment of the rise of a new 'symbolic economy' based on tourism, the media, and entertainment. Includes chapters on Disney World, New York City restaurants, and art museums.

References

Abu-Lughod, Janet L. 1999. *New York, Chicago, Los Angeles: America's Global Cities*. Minneapolis: University of Minnesota Press.

Baade, Robert, Robert Baumann, and Victor Matheson. 2007. 'Estimating the economic impact of natural and social disasters, with an application to Hurricane Katrina'. *Urban Studies* 44 (11): 2,061–76.

Bozikovic, Alex. 2003. 'Planting urban seeds: Artscape hopes to boost our bohemian factor'. *Eye Weekly* 13 November: 11, 16.

Broudehoux, Anne-Marie. 2006. 'Circus City: Debunking culture-led regeneration in Montreal'. *Traditional Dwellings and Settlements Review* 18 (1).

Brunelle, Charles-Mathieu. 2008. 'Unusual sources for successful cultural incubators'. Keynote address to 'Creative Construct': International Symposium on Building for Culture and Creativity, Ottawa, 1 May.

Burgess, Ernest W. 1928. 'Residential segregation in American cities'. *Annals of the American Academy of Political and Social Science* 140: 105–15.

Castells, Manuel. 1977. *The Urban Question: A Marxist Approach*. Cambridge, MA: MIT Press.

———. 1983. *The City and the Grassroots: A Cross-Cultural Theory of Urban Social Movements*. Berkeley: University of California Press.

———. 2002. 'Urban sociology in the twenty-first century'. In Ida Susser, Ed., *The Castells Reader on Cities and Social Theory*, 390–406. Oxford: Blackwell.

Castells, Manuel, and Francis Godard. 1974. *Monopolville: l'entreprise, l'état, l'urbain*. The Hague: Mouton.

Chatterton, Paul, and Robert Hollands. 2003. *Urban Nightscapes: Youth Cultures, Pleasure Spaces and Corporate Power*. London and New York: Routledge.

Clairmont, Donald H., and Dennis William Magill. 1999. *Africville: The Life and Death of a Canadian Black Community*. 3rd edn. Toronto: Canadian Scholars Press.

Clark, S.D. 1966. *The Suburban Society*. Toronto: University of Toronto Press.

Donegan, Mary, et al. 2008. 'Which indicators explain metropolitan economic performance best?' *Journal of the American Planning Association* 74 (2): 180–95.

Drakakis-Smith, David. 2000. *Third World Cities*. 2nd rev. edn. London and New York: Routledge.

Dreier, Peter. 2006. 'Katrina and power in America'. *Urban Affairs Review* 41 (4): 528–49.

Elliott, Brian. 1980. 'Castells and the new urban sociology'. *British Journal of Sociology* 31 (1): 151–8.

Evans, Graeme. 2003. 'Hard-branding the cultural city'. *International Journal of Urban and Regional Research* 27 (2): 417–40.

Fainstein, Susan. 1999. 'Can we make the cities we want?' In Robert Beauregard and Sophie Body-Gendrot, Eds, *The Urban Moment: Cosmopolitan Essays on the Late 20th-century City*, 249–72. Thousand Oaks, CA: Sage.

Florida, Richard. 2002. *The Rise of the Creative Class and How It's Transforming Work, Leisure, Community and Everyday Life*. New York: Basic Books.

Gollner, Adam. 2002. 'Life in the fast lane'. *National Post* 22 June: SP1, SP3.

Gotham, Kevin Fox. 2007. '(Re)branding the Big Easy: Tourism rebuilding in post-Katrina New Orleans'. *Urban Affairs Review* 42 (6): 823–50.

Graham, Stephen, and Simon Marvin. 2001. *Splintering Urbanism: Networked Infrastructures, Technological Mobilities and the Urban Condition*. London and New York: Routledge.

Hall, C. Michael. 2001. 'Imaging tourism and sports event fever: The Sydney Olympics and the need for a social charter for mega-events'. In Chris Gratton and Ian P. Henry, Eds, *Sport in the City: The Role of Sport in Economic and Social Regeneration*, 166–83. London and New York: Routledge.

Hall, Tim, and Phil Hubbard. 1998. 'The entrepreneurial city and the new urban politics'. In Tim Hall and Phil Hubbard, Eds, *The Entrepreneurial City: Geographies of Politics, Regime and Representation*. Chichester, UK: John Wiley and Sons.

Hannigan, John. 1998. *Fantasy City: Pleasure and Profit in the Postmodern Metropolis*. London and New York: Routledge.

———. 2003. 'Symposium on branding, the entertainment economy and urban place building: Introduction'. *International Journal of Urban and Regional Research* 27 (2): 352–60.

Harris, Richard, and Doris Forrester. 2003. 'The suburban origins of redlining: A Canadian case study, 1935–54'. *Urban Studies* 40 (13): 2,661–86.

Harvey, David. 1973. *Social Justice and the City*. Baltimore, MD: Johns Hopkins University Press.

———. 1989. 'From managerialism to entrepreneurialism: The transformation of governance in late capitalism'. *Geografiska Annaler* 71: 3–17.

Hiller, Harry. 1989. 'Impact and image: The convergence of urban factors in preparing for the 1988 Calgary Winter Olympics'. In G.J. Syme et al., Eds, *The Planning and Evaluation of Hallmark Events*, 119–31. Brookfield, VT, and Aldershot, UK: Avebury.

Hoyt, Homer. 1933. *One Hundred Years of Land Values in Chicago*. Chicago: University of Chicago Press.

Judd, Dennis R., and Dick Simpson. 2003. 'Reconstructing the local state: The role of external constituencies in building urban tourism'. *American Behavioral Scientist* 46 (8): 1,056–69.

Kidd, Bruce. 1995. 'Toronto's SkyDome: The world's greatest entertainment centre'. In John Bale and Olof Moen, Eds, *The Stadium and the City*, 175–96. Keele, Staffordshire, UK: Keele University Press.

Kleniewski, Nancy. 2002. *Cities, Change, and Conflict: A Political Economy of Urban Life*. 2nd edn. Belmont, CA: Wadsworth Thomson Learning.

Langer, Peter. 1984. 'Sociology—four images of organized diversity: Bazaar, jungle, organism and machine'. In Lloyd Rodwin and Robert M. Hollister, Eds, *Cities of the Mind: Images and Themes of the City in the Social Sciences*, 97–117. New York and London: Plenum Press.

Lees, Loretta. 2003. 'The ambivalence of diversity and the politics of urban renaissance: The case of growth in downtown Portland, Maine'. *International Journal of Urban and Regional Research* 27 (3): 613–34.

Lefebvre, Henri. 1984. *The Production of Space*. Oxford: Blackwell.

Levine, Marc V. 1987. 'Downtown development as an urban growth strategy: A critical appraisal of the Baltimore renaissance'. *Journal of Urban Affairs* 9 (2): 103–23.

———. 2000. 'A third-world city in the first world: Social exclusion, racial inequality, and sustainable development in Baltimore, Maryland'. In Mario Polèse and Richard Stren, Eds, *The Social Sustainability of Cities: Diversity and the Management of Change*, 123–56. Toronto: University of Toronto Press.

Ley, David. 1996. 'The new middle class in Canadian central cities'. In Jon Caulfield and Linda Peake, Eds, *City Lives and City Forms: Critical Research and Canadian Urbanism*, 15–32. Toronto: University of Toronto Press.

Lloyd, Richard. 2002. 'Neo-Bohemia: Art and neighborhood redevelopment in Chicago'. *Journal of Urban Affairs* 24 (5): 517–32.

Logan, John R., Rachel Bridges, and Kyle Crowder. 1999. 'The character and consequences of growth regimes: An assessment of twenty years of research'. In Andrew E.G. Jonas and David Wilson, Eds, *The Urban Growth Machine: Critical Perspectives Twenty Years Later*, 73–93. Albany: State University of New York Press.

Logan, John R., and Harvey L. Molotch. 1987. *Urban Fortunes: The Political Economy of Place*. Berkeley: University of California Press.

Lorimer, James. 1978. *The Developers*. Toronto: James Lorimer and Company.

Lorinc, John. 2006. *The New City: How the Crisis in Canada's Urban Centres is Reshaping the Nation*. Toronto: Penguin Canada.

Lowes, Mark Douglas. 2002. *Indy Dreams and Urban Nightmares: Speed Merchants, Spectacle and the Struggle over Public Space in the World-Class City*. Toronto: University of Toronto Press.

Macionis, John J., and Vincent N. Parillo. 1998. *Cities and Urban Life*. Upper Saddle River, NJ: Prentice-Hall.

Marcuse, Peter. 2003. Review of Richard Florida, *The Rise of the Creative Class*. Urban Land 62: 40–1.

Molotch, Harvey. 1976. 'The city as growth machine: Towards a political economy of place'. *American Journal of Sociology* 82: 309–32.

———. 1999. 'Growth machine links up, down and across'. In Andrew E.G. Jonas and David Wilson, Eds, *The Urban Growth Machine: Critical Perspectives Two Decades Later*, 247–66. Albany: State University of New York Press.

Molotch, Harvey, William Freudenburg, and Krista E. Paulsen. 2000. 'History repeats itself, but how? City character, urban tradition and the accomplishment of place'. *American Sociological Review* 65 (6): 791–823.

Palen, J. John. 1995. *The Suburbs*. New York: McGraw-Hill.

Philo, Chris, and Gerry Kearns. 1993. 'Culture, history, capital: A critical introduction to the selling of places'. In Gerry Kearns and Chris Philo, Eds, *Selling Places: The City As Capital, Past and Present*, 1–32. Oxford: Pergamon Press.

Short, John Rennie. 1996. *The Urban Order: An Intro-*

duction to *Cities, Culture and Power*. Oxford: Blackwell.

Smith, P.J., and P.W. Moore. 1993. 'Cities as a social responsibility: Planning and urban form'. In Larry Bourne and David F. Ley, Eds, *The Changing Geography of Canadian Cities*, 343–66. Montreal and Kingston: McGill-Queen's University Press.

Soja, Edward W. 2000. *Postmetropolis: Critical Studies of Cities and Regions*. Oxford: Blackwell.

Souther, J. Mark. 2007. 'The Disneyfication of New Orleans: The French Quarter as façade in a divided city'. *The Journal of American History* 94 (3). http://www.historycooperative.org/journals/jah/94.3/souther.html.

Squires, Gregory D. 1992. 'Community reinvestment: An emerging social movement'. In Gregory D. Squires, Ed., *From Redlining to Reinvestment: Community Responses to Urban Disinvestment*, 1–37. Philadelphia: Temple University Press.

Tajbakhsh, Kian. 2001. *The Promise of the City: Space, Identity, and Politics in Contemporary Social Thought*. Berkeley: University of California Press.

US Federal Housing Administration. 1938. *Underwriting Manual*. Washington: US Government Printing Office.

Van der Lee, P., and J. Williams. 1986. 'The Grand Prix and tourism'. In J.P.A. Burns, J.H. Hatch, and T.J. Mules, Eds, *The Adelaide Grand Prix*, 39–57. Adelaide: Centre for South Australian Economic Studies.

Wallerstein, Immanuel. 1976. *The Modern World System*. New York: Academic Press.

Walton, John. 1993. 'Urban sociology: The contribution and limits of political economy'. *Annual Review of Sociology* 19: 301–20.

Ward, Linda. 2002. 'Africville—the last town'. CBC News Online, 8 July.

Zukin, Sharon. 1980. 'A decade of the new urban sociology'. *Theory and Society* 9: 575–601.

———. 1982. *Loft Living: Culture and Capital in Urban Change*. New Brunswick, NJ: Rutgers University Press.

———. 1996. 'Space and symbols in an age of decline'. In Anthony D. King, Ed., *Re-presenting the City: Ethnicity, Capital and Culture in the 21st Century Metropolis*, 43–59. New York: New York University Press.

Chapter 12 Getting Perspective

How is consumer behaviour shaping cities and urban life?

In the preceding chapters, we learned how Canadian cities have shifted from an industrial economy to a service economy and the implications this trend has for leisure consumption. This chapter follows this train of thought by focusing explicitly on consumer behaviour and its impact on urban space.

When you drive into a new city for the first time, you are probably struck by the fact that all of the major transportation arteries are lined with familiar signage. In most cases, these signs are for franchise food or drink outlets or other stores and services that are found in every other city. Furthermore, if you identify one such franchise, it is a good bet that there are other similar franchises nearby. Sometimes such clusterings are found at the intersection of two or more major roadways. Sometimes they occur near a major shopping centre. Shopping centres themselves are often central attractions for visitors as well as for local residents. In all of these cases, it is clear that consumer behaviour is a central feature of urban life.

Analyzing consumer behaviour in cities is important for a number of reasons. First, as has already been suggested, consumer outlets serve as important *landmarks* in cities. This is because they are visually available to all and are public in the sense that they invite anyone to patronize their establishment (in contrast to the private space of residences). Second, consumer outlets *structure urban space*. Mega-malls or big-box retailers, for example, have a defining presence, but so do neighbourhood convenience stores because they are strategically located. Third, consumer outlets are *places of social interaction*. Shopping is social as much as it is buying. Coffee shops are people places. Fourth, consumer outlets play a huge role in *urban place marketing*. Cities are marketed to visitors in terms of the consumer options available, and specific locations are marketed to city residents themselves in terms of consumer opportunities. It is no surprise then that retailing and food services are major factors in urban planning and design.

The importance of consumer behaviour in urban life has drawn new attention to the significance of the *public realm*—i.e., places in cities where people are co-present with others whom they may not know at all or whom they may know only partially or segmentally or only in a fleeting manner. While the public realm involves more than consumer behaviour, it is true that consumer activity is almost always part of the public realm. Healthy and robust cities require a vital and active public realm, but how will it be shaped, and who will shape it?

12 Consumer Culture, City Space, and Urban Life

Sonia Bookman

Learning Objectives

- To gain a preliminary understanding of consumer culture.
- To learn what is meant by 'brandscaping' and how it has become a prominent feature of city consumptionscapes and urban life.
- To understand how the shopping mall operates as a social space and its problematic perception and use as a public space.
- To understand the development and definition of cultural quarters and urban villages, as well as the ways in which they structure urban space and social life.
- To appreciate how the contours of city space and urban life are profoundly shaped in and through consumer culture.

Introduction

Consumer culture is intricately intertwined with contemporary city life. In Canadian cities, we encounter and engage in a range of forms and spaces of consumption as we go about our everyday urban lives, including stopping at Tim Hortons on the way to work in Halifax, shopping with friends at Yorkdale Mall in Toronto, or watching the Calgary Stampeders at McMahon Stadium. We seek out experiences of cultural consumption in the cities we visit as tourists, whether this involves shopping on Vancouver's Robson Street lined with flagship retail brands and café culture, attending the jazz festival in Montreal and taking in the vibrant nightlife it offers, or visiting The Forks heritage complex in Winnipeg. Cities have become increasingly known for their *consumptionscapes*—the various sites and spaces of consumption and the range of consumerist activities they offer. Indeed, many urban analysts argue that the contemporary city is increasingly oriented towards and defined through consumption: 'cit-

ies are no longer seen as *landscapes of production*, but as *landscapes of consumption*' (Zukin 1998, 825; Jayne 2006). The rise of consumption to prominence has significant implications for city life, shaping urban space and culture through the proliferation and pursuit of urban lifestyles, the rise of shopping as a significant leisure and tourist activity, and the establishment of new spaces of cultural consumption. In this chapter, we will explore some aspects of the complex relationship between consumption, city space, and urban life, beginning with a consideration of contemporary consumer culture and the city.

Consumer Culture and the City

Consumer culture is described by leading analyst Celia Lury (1996, 1) as a specific form of material culture that emerged in the latter half of the twentieth century and is particularly characteristic of advanced industrial societies. Consumer culture is characterized by an emphasis on the design, production, and making use of goods as cultural objects—as signs or images that convey cultural meanings. It is marked by an increased **aestheticization** of consumer goods—in other words, an intensification of cultural meaning-making in relation to goods and services. In processes of aestheticization, goods and services are imbued with aesthetic and symbolic attributes and values that they do not have inherently—for example, qualities such as 'hip' or 'authentic'. This is achieved in part through the use of visual imagery in the advertising, packaging, and display of goods and services, the application of design to enhance the appearance and material configuration of goods, as well as the presentation and 'staging' of goods and services in specific contexts. For example, think of how Nike shoes are associated with a range of cultural meanings such as empowerment, success, 'coolness', and athleticism through the extensive use of multi-media advertising campaigns promoting the 'Just Do It' slogan, the design and prominent appearance of the 'swoosh' logo on the shoes, and the ways in which they are displayed on the bodies of sponsored sports stars and teams. Through aestheticization, goods and services ranging from soft drinks and clothing to restaurants and tourist destinations become cultural products. The value of such products lies primarily in their symbolic significance and cultural meaning relative to their utilitarian value or practical functionality (Scott 2000, 3). Thus, for example, while a Gucci handbag serves a utilitarian function as a carrier of personal objects, its symbolic value as a carrier of cultural meanings, ranging from fashionability and elegance to success and high class, is of greater importance to the consumer.

Central to processes of aestheticization are the *cultural industries*, defined as those institutions that are 'most directly involved in the production of social meaning' and whose activities entail the primary aim of communicating to an audience (Hesmondhalgh 2002, 11). They include industries such as advertising, marketing, and magazine publishing, all of which are key aestheticizing agents concerned with the shaping of cultural products and their meanings through practices of design, display, packaging, and promotion. Related to the rise of consumer culture, the cultural industries have undergone significant expansion in recent decades, forming an important aspect of the new urban cultural economy (Scott 2000).

In consumer culture, cultural products and their symbolic meanings (which are by no means fixed, since they are subject to processes of interpretation and appropriation) have become important resources in processes of identity-making and expression. They are used to construct, make sense of, and fashion our selves, as well as to mark our attachments to particular social groups (consciously or not). Consider how the consumption of Apple products allows consumers to stylize themselves as creative, youthful, intelligent, and hip, not unlike the image of the 'Mac guy' in Apple advertisements. Or think about how purchasing 'natural' skincare products from The Body Shop enables consumers to fashion themselves as environmentally concerned. Alternatively, reflect on the way that Tim Hortons, located in cities (and towns) across Canada and associated with prominent aspects of Canadian culture such as hockey or multiculturalism, enables the expression of Canadian identities. In all of these scenarios, the cultural product not only is used to express individual identities but also serves as a social marker that indicates group belonging, whether it be to the 'cool' creative Mac-user crowd, a grouping of urban environmentalists, or a national community. Indeed, the consumption of certain cultural goods, services, and experiences increasingly mediates our connection to various social groups based on constructions of social class, 'ethnicity', age, and so on, and marks our membership in a growing range of lifestyle groupings formed on the basis of shared style, taste, interests, or practices (Lury 1996). At the same time, cultural products are used to make distinctions between our selves and other social groupings, operating as markers that divide one group from another. In this sense, cultural consumption is tied up with processes of social stratification, division, and exclusion. In particular, it is important to note that not everyone in society can participate equally in consumer culture; individuals are constrained by the amount of economic and cultural capital they have to engage in cultural and conspicuous consumption.

Consumer culture is deeply implicated in the shape and form of urban life, affecting both city space and urban social relations. Key urban cultural theorist Sharon Zukin (1998, 825) observes how cultural consumption and attention to urban lifestyles has contributed to significant changes in the cityscape, resulting in the proliferation of new 'highly visible' spaces of consumption such as art galleries, espresso bars, and specialty markets. It has engendered new, innovative retail strategies incorporating entertainment such as themed restaurants, mega-malls, and branded retail shops. Furthermore, it underpins the aestheticization of public space as entrepreneurial cities turn to culture and cultural consumption as a strategy of urban regeneration and re-imaging, with the aim of attracting tourists, residents, and capital. This has resulted in the development of urban entertainment zones, heritage tourist sites, spectacular stadiums, and cultural quarters. These new material and symbolic spaces of consumption shape the ways in which urbanites interact with and relate to one another, mediating particular forms of urban sociability. Spaces of cultural consumption increasingly define and demarcate social identities and groupings based on the combination of symbols, consumption practices, and cultural experiences that are assembled in a particular space, and the way in which they are used by different groups. As we will see in this chapter, they constitute spaces of belonging for some and exclusion for others. In this sense, they are part and parcel of ongoing processes of spatial and social segmentation that occur in the city; of division and distinction between various urban social groupings. In what follows, we will focus on the emergence of three popular and pivotal new spaces of consumption—the brand, the shopping mall, and the cultural quarter—outlining some of the social implications of such spaces and processes of cultural consumption in the city.

The Brand

Within contemporary consumer culture, the brand has emerged as an increasingly important market cultural form. Although brands have been around since the mid-nineteenth century, it is only recently, from the 1980s, that they have become central elements of consumer society (Arvidsson 2006). As Naomi Klein notes in her influential book on brands entitled *No Logo* (1999, 3), the rise of brands occurred when management theorists decided 'that successful corporations must primarily produce brands, as opposed to products'. Brands such as The Gap, HMV, Vespa, Boston Pizza, and Chapters are now everywhere; we encounter them on buses, bodies, and busy shopping streets. We almost take them for granted as part of our everyday urban experience. But what exactly is the brand? And how has the brand shaped our city spaces and social lives in particular ways? Brands are complex media objects that enable the communication of qualitative information (values such as 'coolness', styles such as 'modern', or qualities such as 'gourmet') through the co-ordination of advertising and marketing strategies, product design, packaging, and presentation, as well as potential consumer activity, with the aim of establishing a particular brand image or experience among consumers (Lury 2004; 2000). Brands evoke cultural meanings for a whole range of goods and services (from jeans to paint in the case of Ralph Lauren) and provide a cultural framework or context for their use: 'With a particular brand I can act, feel, and be in a particular way. With a Macintosh computer I can become a particular kind of person and form particular kinds of relations to others' (Arvidsson 2006, 8). In this sense, brands have become important cultural resources and tools that facilitate the expression and construction of identities, social relations, and lifestyles (Arvidsson 2006)

Brands are becoming increasingly spatialized through recent marketing strategies designed to enhance and develop the brand, termed **brandscaping** (Lury 2004). Brandscaping involves the organization of space by the brand, including the co-ordination of elements such as location, architecture, interior design, and atmosphere to invoke a complete aesthetic experience, engaging the senses and emotions of consumers. It is about creating a space in which consumers can interact with and experience the brand as a kind of event or performance (Lury 2004; see also Moor 2003). Examples of brandscaping include the development of entertainment retail stores such as Niketowns, where consumers participate in a sporting 'event' of sorts, encountering a world of glamorous Nike-wearing sports stars whose images fill the shop, simulated athletic games, and televised Nike commercials (Lury 1996). Combining retail and leisure in this way, brands have become destinations in and of themselves, attractive to tourists and everyday shoppers alike. Themed restaurants and cafés also reflect the strategy of brandscaping. For example, the Rainforest Café envelops consumers in a total jungle environment, complete with wild animals, exotic vegetation, and desserts named Volcano, providing a simulated safari experience. Theming provides a framework for the organization of space in a particular way to establish a unifying image, idea, or experience associated with the brand (Lukas 2007, 1).

The spatialization of brands has amplified their visibility in the city, where they increasingly dominate consumptionscapes as 'new landmarks on the urban scene', in some ways replacing the older grand department stores (Zukin 1998, 834). Branded stores are often located in prominent shopping streets and placed in 'urban entertainment destinations' in order to establish a particular image for both the brand and the urban area in which it is situated (Zukin 2004). In this sense, branded shops have been incorporated into consumption-oriented urban regeneration and revitalization strategies, either forming part of a 'standardized backdrop' for tourism, leisure, and shopping activities in downtown entertainment zones, indicating an 'up-and-coming' fashion district, or defining a particular urban village (Zukin 2004).

As mentioned earlier, these new spaces of consumption not only structure urban space but have important implications for city life, shaping urban identities and the way we experience and orientate our selves in the city. In our everyday lives, we use, relate to, and identify with particular brands and the images, lifestyles, or experiences they convey. Spatialized through strategies of brandscaping, brands serve as way-finding 'techno-aesthetic' markers that orientate our sense of self spatially in the city as our identities are mapped out through the branded spaces we inhabit and consume (Lury 1999). When we visit cities as tourists or move to new cities as workers or as students studying abroad, the global brands we are familiar with and relate to, such as Starbucks, Benetton, or McDonalds, serve to orientate our selves, grounding us as we navigate through unfamiliar urban terrain. Reproduced on a global scale, such brands are understood by some theorists as constituting 'generic spaces': branded spaces that are the same everywhere and anywhere, where one American Apparel store is interchangeable with another or one Hard Rock Café with another (Lash 2002). However, other analysts note how such spaces are used by local consumers, who inhabit them in particular ways, and as such are better understood as embodied 'generic spaces' (Yakhlef 2004). In this sense, branded spaces reflect a complex interplay between the brand and local consumers and cultures. For example, while McDonalds signifies cheap fast food in many Canadian cities, McDonalds in major Chinese cities is related to as middle-class and modern: it is a space where middle-class families go to distinguish themselves and a 'a place where young people who want to associate themselves with the symbols of emerging capitalism like to congregate and spend time' (Sturken and Cartwright 2001, 324).

Indeed, brand-based spaces of consumption are social spaces where consumers interact with the brand and with each other, where brands form the source of shared experiences and mediate certain kinds of social relation (Arvidsson 2006). For example, Starbucks cafés, with their maga-zine racks stuffed full of half-read newspapers, plush sofas, slate fireplaces, and modern artwork on the walls, resemble a bourgeois living room. A 'home-away-from-home', these branded spaces form a comfortable and familiar meeting place and 'hangout' for middle-class urbanites who co-create a shared **third place** experience with the brand (see Box 12.1 and Figure 12.1). Apple

Box 12.1 *Starbucks: A Third Place*'

The *third place*, according to Ray Oldenburg (1989), is an informal gathering place outside of home and work that serves as a neutral meeting ground for guests who engage in various interactions: exchanging glances, greetings, and especially conversation. Examples include the local pub, the hair salon, the community centre, or the coffeehouse. It is an inclusive and ac-cessible place, operating as a public space marked by playfulness, community, and camaraderie. Starbucks' branded café space is designed to invoke a third place experience. This is achieved through the creation of warm, relaxing interiors with space for chairs, couches, and fireplaces wherever possible, the establishment of a comfortable atmosphere with non-invasive jazzy music playing in the background, and the framing of 'community' through the provision of items such as newspapers and community boards and the staging of cultural events such as poetry readings, as well as the staff conveying friendliness (through 'small talk'), hospitality (providing a welcoming atmosphere), and recognition (by remembering names or favourite drinks).

In interviews with Starbucks consumers in Toronto and Vancouver, it was found that con-sumers interact with and encounter Starbucks as a social urban space. An important aspect of the branded café is the way in which it forms a space where consumers can go alone to read, work, observe, surf the Internet, or think in the presence of others. The brand provides a so-cial experience, which consumers can blend in with and feel part of. Starbucks is also a space where consumers get together with friends, conduct business with colleagues, and meet blind dates on neutral territory. Indeed, for many Starbucks consumers, the branded café resembles a third place, described by some as a 'home-away-from-home' or like being in their living room, only in public. As one consumer observed, 'they've made an environment where it is really comfortable to stay and actually spend time socializing—your social life is here.'

Nonetheless, while Oldenburg's third places are supposed to be inclusive public spaces of sociability, the third place experience generated in relation to Starbucks is less so. First of all, branded space is private space, and participation usually entails the purchase of a product, which serves to exclude those who cannot afford the 'entry fee'. Second, Starbucks is per-ceived by consumers as a middle-class or yuppie space of sociability and style. This image is based on the aesthetic information Starbucks conveys through the use of 'upscale' finishes and fabrics, hand-blown glass lights, modern artwork, and other aspects of café design. It is also premised on Starbucks' provision of 'authentic' gourmet coffee rather than basic, standard-ized coffee, prepared by knowledgeable 'baristas' rather than employees, representing a cof-fee connoisseurship intended to appeal to 'sophisticated' and discerning consumers. As such, the brand frames a particular kind of middle-class third place experience, which facilitates the gathering of those (especially, though not exclusively, middle classes) who feel comfortable and 'at home' in such a space, and enables the expression of and aspiration to middle-class lifestyles premised on shared tastes, practices, and experiences.

In this sense, branded spaces of consumption mediate belonging to and distinction from particular social groupings and lifestyles through the specific kinds of social experience they frame and enable. This was particularly evident in interviews with consumers who consistently distinguished between Starbucks, which was associated with middle-class and yuppie lifestyles on the one hand, and Tim Hortons, which consumers perceived as working-class or an 'every person's' kind of space on the other. Of course, these spaces can also be used to express multiple identities and belonging. For example, some consumers indicated that while they usually go to Starbucks or Second Cup (also considered an urban middle-class space of sociability), they frequent Tim Hortons as well. As one consumer explained, 'Um, I come from Hamilton, Hamilton has a very strong Tim Hortons culture . . . when I go to a Second Cup, it's an entirely different feel . . . it's about when I want to consider myself city-like and more urban. I like the Tim Hortons if I'm in a different mood, if I want to feel like a Hamiltonian, and kind of working-class, or Canadian.' Where do you get your coffee?

Outdoor patios and their use by consumers contribute to the brand's third place image and experience (Sonia Bookman).

Source: Bookman, 2005.

Stores, featuring a 'Genius Bar' offering technical advice and stations such as 'The Studio' where consumers can consult a 'Creative' on the use of Apple products for web design, film-editing, or other purposes, is inhabited by cultural industry Mac-users and facilitates the gathering of those who aspire to a hip urban 'bohemian' lifestyle. Mountain Equipment Co-op stores, with environmentally friendly architectural design including extensive bicycle parking, compost toilets, and green roofs, offer consumers an assortment of 'green' products and outdoor gear, suggesting a connection to and concern for 'nature'. As such, these environmentally themed spaces enable the expression of shared interests and ethics, creating common experiences among urban individuals who pursue environmentalist lifestyles.

These new branded spaces of consumption serve as significant symbolic and cultural nodes that are used in the construction and expression of identities and belonging to various social groupings in the city. In particular, they mediate and enable the development of shared experiences, ethics, interests, or tastes, which are central to the formation of myriad urban lifestyle groupings, ranging from bohemians and skateboarders to yuppies and hipsters (Shields 1992). While these spaces express membership and facilitate a sense of belonging to such groups, the brand also forms a boundary and marker of distinction between groups, contributing to social divisions on the basis of lifestyle. Indeed, Zukin (1998, 826) raises the question of whether urban populations are 'now divided by lifestyle rather than by race, ethnicity, and social class', especially considering the proliferation of urban lifestyles and the growth of cultural spaces of consumption that cater to them in the city. The extent to which lifestyle is distinct from such social groupings as class, gender, or age is debatable, however, since many lifestyles are in fact intertwined with aspects such as social class (for example, the class-based lifestyle grouping yuppies, which consists of young urban professionals with significant amounts of disposable income to spend on conspicuous consumption). Of

particular concern here is the way by which the spatialization of cultural consumption, as in the case of the branded retail store or restaurant, may be contributing to new modes of social and spatial micro-segmentation in the city, with certain social groups inhabiting particular branded terrain—in other words, how urban space is being divided up into niches occupied by distinct social groups.

The Shopping Mall

While much consumption is still routine and ordinary, oriented towards the satisfaction of everyday needs, new patterns of consumption have risen to the fore in contemporary consumer culture. Consumption has become an important leisure and tourist pursuit (after television, shopping is the second most popular leisure activity in the United States), accompanied by an increase in consumption of sports and various leisure practices (Lury 1996, 29). Cultural consumption and lifestyle shopping have become exemplary modes of consumption in consumer culture, reflecting the increasing centrality of cultural goods in the construction and expression our selves. Consumption is also politicized with the introduction of 'green' consumer guides and the establishment of 'fair trade' consumer practices (Lury 1996, 29). The expansion of new forms of shopping and consumption has paralleled an increase in shopping sites and spaces designed to facilitate such new patterns of consumerist activity, including the now ubiquitous shopping mall (Lury 1996, 29).

The origins of the shopping mall can be linked to the bourgeois shopping arcades (see Benjamin 1999) as well as to the establishment of the multi-level department store, both of which used new materials such as steel, plate glass, and electric lighting to display an ever-expanding range of newly available consumer goods for primarily wealthy, women shoppers (Shields 1992). Rooted in these significant landmarks of nineteenth and early twentieth-century commercial culture, the shopping mall is nonetheless a relatively recent development, emerging in the latter half of the twentieth century in conjunction with processes of suburbanization and the expansion of auto-mobility (see Chapter 5). Predominantly located in the suburbs, the shopping mall comprises a range of shops, boutiques, and, increasingly, chain-stores or branded retail environments, assembled on one or more levels, and is usually anchored by a department store (often a suburban branch of an original downtown store) at one end, with a food court at the other. Attracting both suburban and urban shoppers with its convenient clustering of stores and comfortable, climate-controlled atmosphere, the suburban shopping mall has drained resources and investment from downtown commercial areas and shopping streets while replicating them in enclosed, safe environments (Zukin 1998). Shopping streets are recreated in the mall through the use of landscaping with potted trees and flowerbeds, the design and implementation of wide walkways simulating urban boulevards, and the installation of street furniture, including benches or lamp posts, as well as the provision of everyday amenities from post offices to shoe repair shops.

As many writers have observed, the shopping mall is a social space where groups gather and individuals go to engage in a range of shopping and leisure activities (Shields 1992; Zukin 1998). Seniors meet in the early mornings before the mall opens to engage in the exercise of walking together, teenagers use the mall as an informal 'hangout', and friends meet to browse the shops, check out the styles others are wearing, and spend time together. Individuals exchange glances, gazes, and words with other shoppers and clerks while simultaneously developing tastes and constructing lifestyles through practices of interacting with, purchasing, and appropriating cultural goods. In this sense, the shopping mall is not only appreciated for its functional attractions but is especially valued as 'a site of communication and interaction' (Shields 1992, 5). It is a space in which people meet and where 'face-to-

face communication if not community is a practice for a huge number of people in the televisual age' (Shields 1992, 5). Thus, the shopping mall has become a public space of sociability and urban community for many, functioning as a new kind of public square. It brings together a diversity of people from all classes, ethnicities, and ages contributing to the widespread perception of the mall as public space.

Regardless of this perception, however, the mall is a private-public space. It is privately owned, operated, and controlled. The mall is closely surveilled by a private army of security guards and a host of closed-circuit television cameras, which track participants and their actions, ensuring conformity and 'good behaviour' on the part of shoppers and retailers alike (Shields 1991, 5). Some groups are monitored more closely than others (such as young, male, minority-group members), and security guards have the power to question and exclude individuals deemed a 'threat' to the safe, orderly, sanitized environment of the mall (Zukin 1998; 2004). In addition, while the suburban shopping mall appears open to all (especially since no purchase is required for participation and in any case, purchases can be kept to a minimum), access is partly limited by location and transportation options. Often situated at the intersection of major suburban 'feeder' roads or highway routes and encircled by a sea of asphalt parking lots, the shopping mall caters to private transport. It is more efficiently and easily reached by those who own or have use of a car and live in the suburbs than by those who rely on public transport and reside farther away (in the inner city, for example). In this sense, the mall is seen by many writers as linked to broader processes of privatization underpinning suburbanization and other recent forms of urban development. As one analyst indicates, 'the shift of space from the public domain of the open square and public street to the private space of the mall marks a significant shift towards greater privatization within the urban environment' (Thorns 2002, 138).

More recently, the suburban mall has been subject to competition from super-sized discount stores (such as Wal-Mart), as well as emerging suburban power centres (see Box 12.2). Partly in response to such competition and partly reflecting the intensification of consumer culture, both older and especially newer shopping malls have pursued cultural strategies of redevelopment and refurbishment, incorporating various entertainment elements. This has involved adding entertainment complexes such as Silver City multiplex movie theatres, reworking interiors to include themed shopping 'districts', and extending and reinvigorating food courts with features such as 'chalet-style' fireplaces and elaborate entertainment platforms—complete with large-screen televisions—designed to stage and project fashion shows and other cultural events such as live reality television make-overs. Intended to attract a wide diversity of consumers and, increasingly, tourists, some of the larger, most 'spectacular' shopping malls such as the Mall of America or the West Edmonton Mall (see Box 12.3) have become regional and national tourist destinations, offering complete travel packages with passes to the various cultural 'attractions' they offer, such as themed parks, aquariums, mini-golf, and speedways. Such 'spectacular' malls offer consumers a 'fantasy landscape', consisting of juxtaposed architectural styles,

Box 12.2 Power Centres

The power centre is a 'planned agglomeration of big-box retail outlets that may or may not be accompanied by conventionally sized commercial units' (Lorch 2004, 1). It is a sprawling outdoor assemblage of stores such as Rona, the Real Canadian Superstore, and Urban Barn. Based on an open-air design, stores are clustered into multiple structures separated by giant parking lots and divided by roads, resembling a 'campus-like environment' (Lorch 2004, 17). For example, a power centre might consist of two free-standing anchors (stores that occupy more than 75,000 square feet) such as Home Depot or Sobey's grocery store and several retail 'island' strips containing a number of stores, as well as a cluster of stand-alone box stores such as Chapters, Old Navy, and so on, all bound by common parking areas and intersected by various roadways. Such power centres are located in new greenfields developments at the edge of the city or in prosperous suburban areas near existing shopping malls at the intersections of major city routes.

In Canada, power centres have proliferated since the 1990s, led by key developer First Pro Shopping Centres, which operates and is currently developing more than 90 such sites in cities across the country (there are 22 power centres in Winnipeg alone) (Lorch 2004). These new spaces of consumption have significant implications for shopping and sociability. Often situated far from bus and train lines, such outdoor shopping centres rely extensively on private transport, not only to travel to the centre but also to shop there, since clustered stores are often sprawled out across roadways and over great distances with few pedestrian pathways, requiring shoppers to drive from one set of stores to another rather than walk to them. This contributes to an exclusive, privatized shopping experience, which is further enhanced by the lack of common spaces such as the mall food court where people can 'hang out', watch, meet, or simply be with others (Lorch 2004). Thus, as a space of consumption, the power centre is difficult to access for various social groups (those who rely on public transport) and offers few possibilities for public engagement other than within the walls of its big-box stores.

Source: Lorch 2004.

The Forks heritage tourist site is located at the intersection of the Red and Assiniboine rivers in the city of Winnipeg. The development and renewal of the site has revolved around the restoration and use of a set of historic buildings associated with the railway and promotion of the site as a 'meeting place' premised on its extensive history as a meeting ground for Aboriginal groups, early European colonists and settlers, and immigrants and goods arriving by train from across the country (Forks North Portage Corporation 2009). The buildings are currently host to a festive marketplace, featuring the work and produce of local artisans, as well as numerous restaurants, cafés, shops, and boutiques. The Forks also features a river walkway, gardens, and public art, as well as a park space and Scotiabank-sponsored stage where numerous public events are held. Bringing city dwellers together to celebrate major holidays such as New Year's Eve and Canada Day, The Forks serves as a key 'public square' in the city. However it is also a highly regulated and monitored space, owned and managed by an organization—The Forks North Portage Partnership—that mobilizes investment from government, institutions, and the private sector to continue redeveloping the area (Forks North Portage Corporation 2009) (Sonia Bookman).

times, activities, events, and images, to generate an entertaining shopping experience (Jayne 2006). Cultural strategies of redevelopment are not limited to suburban and 'spectacular' shopping malls but have also been applied to downtown malls and shopping areas in recent efforts to revitalize inner-city areas by bringing both people and activity back to the city centre (Thorns 2002). Centred on the production and promotion of cultural consumption, such efforts have resulted in the emergence of remodelled inner-city malls and the development of festival marketplaces encompassing shops, restaurants, markets, and entertainment. They are often linked to the development of city waterfront areas, such as Toronto's Harbourfront, or the promotion of heritage and other tourist zones, such as The Forks in Winnipeg (see Figure 12.2).

Cultural Quarters, Urban Villages

In their edited book *City of Quarters* (2004, 1), urban analysts David Bell and Mark Jayne note the near-ubiquitous presence of *urban villages or quarters* in the contemporary city. They describe them as 'distinct social and spatial areas' that have been designated and developed to convey a specific cultural image and identity and to offer a definitive urban experience. Urban villages and **cultural quarters** are organized around the principle of

Box 12.3 West Edmonton Mall: A 'Spectacular' Shopping Centre

Described on its promotional website as 'North America's largest entertainment and shopping centre and Alberta's number one tourist attraction', West Edmonton Mall features:

- over 800 stores and shops
- at least 100 restaurants and eateries
- 5.3 million square feet
- three themed shopping streets, including 'Europa Boulevard' with Parisian cafés and nineteenth-century European-style architecture, New Orleans 'Bourbon Street' with statues of jazz musicians and prostitutes, and 'Chinatown' featuring a traditional market and festive dragon
- a 'fantasyland hotel'
- the 'world's largest indoor amusement park', complete with a triple-loop roller coaster
- a five-acre Caribbean-themed water park
- an 'NHL-sized ice arena'
- sea lion and pirate shows
- several mini-golf courses
- a Las Vegas–style casino
- a recreation area with bowling, billiards, and arcade-style games
- a 'Wild West Shooting Centre'
- bungee jumping, rock climbing, and other physical activities
- an ongoing schedule of events, such as an NBA basketball 3on3 tournament, an international salsa dance competition, fundraising for global relief work, programs for seniors, teen dance parties, and more.

Source: West Edmonton Mall. 1995–2005

consumption, promoting various kinds of cultural goods and services including food, fashion, entertainment, and housing, intended to appeal to tourists, visitors, and especially the new professional, service, and middle-class city dwellers (Bell and Jayne 2004). The development of these new spaces of consumption is a relatively recent phenomenon, taken up and promoted by entrepreneurial cities (see Chapter 11) as a way of rejuvenating floundering urban areas and, perhaps even more important, constructing an image of the city as creative, diverse, and vibrant, making it desirable to domestic and international tourists, residents, and cultural workers, as well as business and mobile investment.

A range of cultural quarters and urban villages are now commonplace, including enhanced historical districts such as Gastown in Vancouver and the Distillery District in Toronto (see Chapter 15), which are aestheticized with an emphasis on the conservation and display of distinctive historical architecture, combined with unique shops, walking tours, and various events promoting heritage culture. Other urban villages are premised on the packaging and promotion of gay districts, such as Manchester's Gay Village (Binnie and Skeggs 2004). Endorsed as a zone of openness and tolerance and featuring a vibrant nightlife centred around hip clubs, gay and lesbian bars, and stylish restaurants, the village offers various kinds of sexualized cultural consumption opportunities. In addition, an array of ethnic neighbourhoods are mapped out and marketed as cultural quarters, such as the Brick

Lane area of London, branded 'Banglatown' and based on the promotion of Bengali food, culture, and entertainment as a consumer experience for tourists (Brown 2006). Another example would be the 'Golden Village' located in Richmond, BC. An area of Asian-Canadian settlement, this village is touted by Tourism British Columbia as an 'Asian attraction' where tourists can encounter a concentration of Asian-themed shopping malls, restaurants, and events, as well as significant Asian architectural sites (Tourism British Columbia 2008). In summertime, the 'Golden Village' hosts the well-publicized, Asian-themed 'Richmond Night Market' that attracts thousands of visitors each weekend.

Here it is important to point out that there is a difference between urban villages that grow out of and cater to the needs of various local communities on the one hand, and the planned packaging, branding, and promotion of these spaces by institutional alliances on the other. Urban villages and cultural quarters are constructed and produced through a process of aestheticization involving the *material and symbolic framing of space*, managed by some combination or alliance of local entrepreneurs and businesses, urban planners and local authorities, private-public partnerships such as business improvement districts (see Chapter 11), and the media (Binnie et al. 2006). This process involves the co-ordination of physical interventions in the landscape (signage, shops, street furniture), the visual staging or presentation of space (the display of architectural features, the use of colour to demarcate an area, and the beautification and cleaning of streetscapes), as well as the way in which the area is described, defined, and narrated, especially in promotional materials such as tourist brochures or city guides. The aim is to generate a coherent image or 'signature' for the designated space. According to Bell and Jayne (2004, 252), cultural quarters and urban villages, 'like museum displays, make most sense when seen as "staged" or packaged—and in that respect, they seek to speak to visitors, to provide

a narrative of place'. While such narratives make these spaces palatable for consumers, they can also serve to stereotype and 'fix' identities and cultures, which are commodified and marketed as a curiosity to tourists and consumers. Bell and Jayne indicate that this is particularly evident in the framing of 'ethnic quarters' in which 'ethnic difference is packaged for the consumption of "non-ethnic" visitors', raising concerns about voyeurism, appropriation, and cultural fossilization (2004, 252).

Nonetheless, it is important to note that the process of quartering, of producing a distinctive, coherent image and tidy 'narrative' of a particular area, is not necessarily straightforward but is complex and conflictual. Local residents and groups do not necessarily share the vision and image that is promoted by planners, and therefore it is subject to various forms of contestation. For example, the [murmer] project, carried out in various cities, including Toronto, attempts to insert the voices and experiences of local individuals into such spaces by recording their oral histories and memories of the place and making them available by telephone. Small signs are posted at each 'memory site', and the recordings provide alternative or resistant stories to balance or counter the institutionally developed narratives provided to visitors (Richards-Bentley 2008).

An exemplary kind of cultural quarter that has emerged in many different cities in slightly varied forms is the *cosmopolitan cultural quarter*. From SoHo, New York, to Manchester City Centre, to the Exchange District in Winnipeg (see Box 12.4 and Figure 12.3), cosmopolitan quarters are found in gentrified inner-city districts where they have been developed in conjunction with consumption-oriented strategies for revitalizing and regenerating urban city centres (Binnie et al. 2006). In its popular usage, cosmopolitanism 'expresses a modern style of urbanity characterized by cultural liveliness and a certain sophistication' (Haylett 2006, 187). It involves an awareness of and openness to cultural diversity and is closely related to 'urbane-ness', as in 'someone who is cultivated, refined, and at ease in the world' (Latham 2006, 95). It is this 'style of urbanity' that is packaged and produced in cosmopolitan quarters, configured through the assembling of 'sophisticated' consumer practices such as browsing designer shops, the provision of opportunities to demonstrate one's 'worldliness' through cultural connoisseurship in a range of wine bars, specialized delis, or 'exotic' ethnic restaurants, and the staging of local and international media and cultural events such as jazz, film, and fringe festivals. Cosmopolitan quarters also offer places of residence such as urban lofts, which are aesthetically designed to reflect the tastes of the new middle and gentrifying classes perceived to be seeking (and able to afford) the kind of urban 'cosmopolitan lifestyle' articulated in and through these distinctive urban spaces (Binnie et al. 2006; Young, Diep, and Drabble 2006). Indeed, participation in cosmopolitan spaces of consumption and the construction of a cosmopolitan lifestyle requires a certain level of cultural and economic capital: 'being worldly, being able to navigate between and within different cultures, requires confidence, skill, and money' (Binnie et al. 2006, 8).

Similar to brands and shopping malls, urban villages and cultural quarters are bound up with particular forms of urban sociability, as well as social divisions and exclusions. For example, metropolitan cosmopolitan quarters allow individuals to both distinguish themselves as cosmopolitan and mark their connection to other cosmopolites based on shared consumption practices such as hanging out in European-style latté-bars, the consumption and use of paraphernalia such as global fashions and gourmet food magazines, as well as property style and display. The shared practices and forms of cultural consumption that make up a particular cosmopolitan lifestyle enable mutual recognition among cosmopolites who inhabit, navigate, and feel at ease in such cosmopolitan quarters (Binnie et al. 2006). At the same time, however, these spaces are exclusionary of social groups that cannot engage with the particular forms of cosmopolitan consumption they offer because of economic constraints, as well as those who do not 'fit' the cosmopolitan image that is framed, packaged, and promoted by local authorities, businesses, and other organizations. Indeed, the 'planning of such spaces to support "cosmopolitan" consumption practices can [also,] intentionally or unintentionally, act to homogenize them and exclude difference' (Binnie et al. 2006, 25). This involves the exclusion of certain individuals and groups through subtle measures, including the implementation of surveillance and patrol programs that monitor and regulate the designated space in order to 'clean it up' and make it 'safe' for retailers and middle-class consumers (Binnie et al. 2006). Furthermore, shops, restaurants, and property all tend to become more expensive as they are oriented towards middle-class cosmopolitan consumers, thus pushing out poorer groups from the area.

Bell and Jayne (2004) suggest that the practice of quartering the city—the planned development of urban villages and cultural quarters—involves a process of social and spatial segmentation in which different urban spaces are allocated to specific social groupings: 'a place for everyone and everyone in their place' (253, italics removed). Thus, there are spaces and groups of people labelled as cosmopolitan and those that are deemed non-cosmopolitan (Binnie et al. 2006). Cosmopolitan spaces of consumption are associated with a particular segment of the middle classes for whom cosmopolitan lifestyles serve as a form of distinction from other classes. Indeed, cosmopolitan identities, lifestyles, and spaces are constructed *against* what are perceived as non-cosmopolitan identities, lifestyles and spaces, such as the supposedly culturally homogenous, mainstream middle-class suburbs, as well as various working-class spaces marked by an absence of chic lofts, latté-bars, and other kinds of consumption considered essential to an urban cosmopolitan lifestyle (Young, Diep, and Drabble 2006). In addition, the designation of certain spaces and urban villages as 'ethnic' or 'gay' based on constructs of ethnic and sexualized 'difference' involves what Bell and Jayne (2004, 253) refer to as the 'corralling of difference into distinct zones'. This entails the fragmenting and 'fixing' of particular social groups, identities, and cultures in place. Bell and Jayne note that such parcelling of different social groups into distinct areas is tied up with the production of 'tourist geographies' within the city whereby visitors can encounter a unique cultural experience at each 'site' or space of cultural consumption (2004, 253). Furthermore, quartering involves a division between these themed cultural zones of consumption characterized by a concentration of consumerist activity on the one hand and 'marginal, non-quartered zones': the borders, edges, and spaces *between* quarters that are occupied by marginalized groups on the other (Bell and Jayne 2004, 253). Thus, for example, gentrified cosmopolitan quarters may be juxtaposed with ghettos in the inner city, comprising spaces of renewal next to zones of decay. This produces an uneven and divided cityscape made up of 'peaks and troughs', contributing to social and spatial inequalities (Bell and Jayne 2004, 253).

Box 12.4 The Exchange District

In recent years, Winnipeg's historic Exchange District (see Chapter 2) has undergone a process of regeneration and redevelopment, following a standard pattern of consumption-led gentrification. Old warehouse buildings and lofts rented out to local artists as inexpensive studio space have been refurbished by property developers into fashionable condominiums for urban professionals. The main streets are increasingly lined with hip boutiques, cafés, art galleries, and trendy restaurants offering a range of culinary experiences from sushi bars to fine French cuisine, as well as a range of theatres, making the Exchange Winnipeg's theatre district. Plans are underway to redevelop the Old Market Square, a central park-like space and stage where public events and festivals such as the Winnipeg Fringe Festival are held. A cultural hub in the city, the Exchange District contains a concentration of the city's cultural industries, ranging from architectural firms and advertising agencies to film companies and software developers. In addition, a whole host of arts organizations are housed in a landmark warehouse building, Artspace, which was established in the 1980s as a non-profit cultural space facility.

The redevelopment of the Exchange District is guided in part by the Exchange District BIZ, set up as one of the city's Business Improvement Zones in 1989. A key aim of this public-private initiative is to promote the area to consumers, residents, tourists, and businesses by creating an attractive image of the Exchange District through symbolic framing and material interventions. To this end, a number of initiatives have been established. The Clean Team engages in street beautification by planting flowers as well as removing graffiti and litter in an attempt to create a clean, sanitized, standardized aesthetic appearance. A weekly farmer's market and various cultural events are organized to create a lively cultural atmosphere. The Foot Patrol program attempts to make the area appear safe by addressing '"quality of life" issues such as panhandling, litter, and graffiti' through the employment of private, uniformed patrols who 'act as "eyes and ears" for the Winnipeg Police Service' (Exchange District BIZ 2008). Furthermore, BIZ marketing initiatives promote the district through a website, tourism brochures, and other communications efforts.

In the fall of 2007, the Exchange District BIZ, along with a number of local businesses, sponsored an innovative campaign and branding exercise created by an Exchange District advertising and branding company, Vantage Studios. The award-winning multi-media campaign encompassed a series of advertisements for an event labelled 'Sex and the District' (Vantage Studios Inc. 2006). The 'New York-style' event featured a fashion show, various forms of entertainment, shopping opportunities, and culinary specialties intended to bring people, especially young women, to the inner-city area. The campaign and event were designed to establish awareness of the Exchange District while 'creating an image and lifestyle' that could be associated with the area (Vantage Studios Inc. 2008). Invoking New York's urban vibe, cultural liveliness, and sophistication in fashion and food through reference to the popular television series 'Sex and the City', the image mobilized was a cosmopolitan one (Vantage Studios Inc. 2006). Described as 'one of North America's most colourful and cosmopolitan neighbourhoods' by the Exchange District BIZ, the consumption-oriented redevelopment and re-imaging of the Exchange District, co-ordinated and managed by an alliance of private-public organizations, local businesses, organizations, and advertising agencies, can be seen as illustrative of the packaging, branding, and promotion of cosmopolitan cultural quarters, as discussed in this chapter (Exchange District BIZ 2008). Through this process, the Exchange District is being transformed into a safe, sanitized space of cultural consumption designed to appeal to the middle classes who can pursue the particular vision of a cosmopolitan lifestyle it offers.

The regeneration and re-imaging of Winnipeg's historic Exchange District as a cosmopolitan cultural quarter is marked by the introduction of café culture, upscale urban clothing shops, and boutique hotels, as pictured here (Sonia Bookman).

Sources: Exchange District BIZ 2008; Vantage Studios Inc. 2008.

Conclusion

The contours of city life are profoundly shaped in and through consumption. Various analysts suggest that the very cultural and economic vitality of cities now depends on the ability of cities to provide a wide array of consumption spaces, from entertainment districts and distinct cultural zones to mega-malls and themed parks: 'In general, the most successful cities contain the most culturally and socially diverse and innovative spaces of consumption' (Jayne 2006, 83). Such spaces contribute to the establishment of a 'vibrant atmosphere' in the city and are harnessed in the creation of an image of the city as creative, diverse, and successful (Jayne 2006, 82; Hall and Hubbard 1998).

Reflecting the influence of consumer culture, many new spaces of cultural consumption have emerged as significant components of the city's consumptionscape. These new spaces do not necessarily supplant 'ordinary', inconspicuous everyday consumption spaces such as charity shops, local farmer's markets, corner stores, and community shopping streets. However, they are increasingly prevalent in the city (Jayne 2006). Therefore, it is important to consider these spaces in terms of their configuration, how they structure urban space in particular ways, and their implications for urban life. This chapter focused on three of these new spaces of consumption— the brand, the shopping mall, and the cultural quarter—delineating some of the ways in which they implicate and shape forms of urban sociability. In particular, it was suggested that they comprise significant social spaces where identities are formed and social groupings are defined. They are spaces of belonging for some and exclusion for others. In some cases, such as the shopping mall, they bring together a wide range of disparate social groups, and in other cases they contribute to social and spatial divisions in the city. Because they are intensely implicated in our everyday lives, urban social relations, and experiences of city space, it is vital that we continue to observe, analyze, and critique the many new forms of consumption that mark our cityscapes.

Study and Discussion Questions

1. Think of an example of a cultural quarter or urban village in your city. What image or identity does it convey? How is it framed symbolically and materially in order to present this image?
2. Do you agree with Thorns's (2002, 138) observation that public space is being shifted 'from the public domain of the open square and public street to the private space of the mall'? Why or why not? What are some of the social implications of this shift? What other private, commercialized spaces besides the mall serve as semi-public squares in the city?
3. Think about your own identity. How is it constructed through the kinds of cultural objects you consume? Would someone be able to get a sense of who you are by finding out which branded spaces you occupy or interact with in the city?
4. Think about and make a list of some of the potential negative social consequences of the 'quartering' of the city.
5. Do you think that 'brandscaping' is contributing to new forms of social and spatial segmentation whereby space is being divided into distinct niches occupied by certain social and lifestyles groupings? Why or why not?

Suggested Reading

Bell, David, and Mark Jayne, Eds. 2004. *City of Quarters: Urban Villages in the Contemporary City.* Burlington and Aldershot: Ashgate. An insightful look at the development of cultural quarters and urban villages in the context of entrepreneurial governance. Includes several case studies of diverse cultural quarters and the social implications of their establishment. Discusses more inclusive alternatives to 'quartering' the city.

Binnie, Jon, et al., Eds. 2006. *Cosmopolitan Urbanism*. London and New York: Routledge. Considers different ways in which cosmopolitanism is interpreted, constructed, and consumed in grounded urban contexts. Three sections critically examine what cosmopolitan urbanism implies, how cosmopolitanism becomes associated with particular spaces and lifestyles in the city, and the ways in which it is planned and produced through cultural policies.

Jayne, M. 2006. *Cities and Consumption*. London and New York: Routledge. A comprehensive examination of the relationship between consumption and the city, including the development of the modern and post-modern city and the particular practices, spaces, and forms of consumption associated with each of them. Looks at everyday, ordinary consumption as well as spectacular forms of consumption in the city. Considers the relationship between consumption, identity, and urban cultures. Also provides a critical account of recent consumption-led processes of urban regeneration.

Lury, Celia. 1996. *Consumer Culture*. Cambridge: Polity Press. An essential, eminently readable introduction to the topic of consumer culture. Clearly defines consumer culture and evaluates different explanations of its emergence. Includes engaging chapters outlining how cultural consumption relates to constructions of class, gender, and 'race', as well as the establishment of youth subcultures. Discusses the significance of consumer culture for expressing self-identity and group membership.

Zukin, Sharon. 2004. *Point of Purchase: How Shopping Changed American Culture*. London and New York: Routledge. A lively, entertaining analysis of shopping and its impact on urban society. Covers a range of aspects related to shopping, including its history, the emergence of department stores, the democratizing effect of discount stores, the link between consumer guides and lifestylization, brands, Internet shopping, and some thoughts on what shopping should and could be like.

References

Arvidsson, Adam. 2006. *Brands: Meaning and Value in Media Culture*. London and New York: Routledge.

Bell, David, and Mark Jayne. 2004. 'Conceptualizing the city of quarters' and 'Afterward: Thinking in quarters'. In David Bell and Mark Jayne, Eds, *City of Quarters: Urban Villages in the Contemporary City*, 1–14, 249–56. Burlington and Aldershot: Ashgate.

Benjamin, W. 1999. *The Arcades Project*. H. Eiland and K. McLaughlin, trans. Cambridge, MA: Harvard University Press.

Binnie, Jon, et al. 2006. 'Introduction: Grounding cosmopolitan urbanism: Approaches, practices and policies'. In Jon Binnie et al., Eds, *Cosmopolitan Urbanism*, 1–34. London and New York: Routledge.

Binnie, Jon, and Beverly Skeggs. 2004. 'Cosmopolitan knowledge and the production and consumption of sexualized space: Manchester's gay village'. *The Sociological Review* 52: 39–61.

Bookman, Sonia. 2005. 'Framing consumption, configuring production, generating culture: An enquiry into the branding processes of Starbucks and Second Cup'. Unpublished doctoral dissertation. Manchester: Department of Sociology, University of Manchester.

Brown, Gavin. 2006. 'Cosmopolitan camouflage: (Post-)gay space in Spitalfields, East London'. In Jon Binnie et al., Eds, *Cosmopolitan Urbanism*, 130–45. London and New York: Routledge.

Exchange District BIZ. 2008. www.exchangedistrict. org.

Forks North Portage Corporation. 2009. www.the forks.com.

Hall, Tim, and Phil Hubbard. 1998. 'The entrepreneurial city and the new urban politics'. In Tim Hall and Phil Hubbard, Eds, *The Entrepreneurial*

City: Geographies of Politics, Regime and Representation, 1–23. Chichester, UK: John Wiley and Sons.

Haylett, Chris. 2006. 'Working-class subjects in the cosmopolitan city'. In Jon Binnie, et al., Eds, *Cosmopolitan Urbanism*, 187–203. London and New York: Routledge.

Hesmondhalgh, David. 2002. *The Cultural Industries*. London: Sage.

Jayne, Mark. 2006. *Cities and Consumption*. London and New York: Routledge.

Klein, Naomi. 1999. *No Logo*. Toronto: Knopf Canada.

Lash, Scott. 2002. *Critique of Information*. London: Sage.

Latham, Alan. 2006. 'Sociality and the cosmopolitan imagination: National, cosmopolitan and local imaginaries in Auckland, New Zealand'. In Jon Binnie et al., Eds, *Cosmopolitan Urbanism*, 89–111. London and New York: Routledge.

Lorch, Brian J. 2004. 'Big boxes, power centres and the evolving retail landscape of Winnipeg: A geographical perspective'. Research and Working Paper #43. Winnipeg: Institute of Urban Studies, University of Winnipeg.

Lukas, Scott. 2007. 'The themed space: Locating culture, nation, and self'. In Scott Lukas, Ed., *The Themed Space: Locating Culture, Nation, and Self*. Lanham, MD: Lexington Books.

Lury, Celia. 1996. *Consumer Culture*. Cambridge: Polity Press.

———. 1999. 'Marking time with Nike: The illusion of the durable'. *Public Culture* 11 (3): 499–526.

———. 2000. 'The united colors of diversity'. In Sarah Franklin, Celia Lury, and Jackie Stacey, Eds, *Global Nature, Global Culture*, 147–9. London: Sage.

———. 2004. *Brands: The Logos of the Global Economy*. London and New York: Routledge.

Moor, Elizabeth. 2003. 'Branded spaces: The scope of "new marketing"'. *Journal of Consumer Culture* 3: 39–60.

Oldenburg, Ray. 1989. *The Great Good Place*. New York: Marlowe.

Richards-Bentley, Christopher. 2008. 'A guide to navigation during perilous times: Queer individuals' construction and preservation of their histories, identities and activisms'. Unpublished paper presented at the Canadian Sociology and Anthropology Association annual meeting, University of British Columbia, Vancouver.

Scott, Allen J. 2000. *The Cultural Economy of Cities*. London: Sage.

Shields, Rob. 1992. 'Spaces for the subject of consumption'. In Rob Shields, Ed., *Lifestyle Shopping*, 1–17. London and New York: Routledge.

Sturken, Marita, and Lisa Cartwright. 2001. *Practices of Looking: An Introduction to Visual Culture*. Oxford and New York: Oxford University Press.

Thorns, David C. 2002. *The Transformation of Cities: Urban Theory and Urban Life*. New York: Palgrave Macmillan.

Tourism British Columbia. 2008. 'Richmond things to do'. www.hellobc.com/en-CA/SightsActivitiesEvents/Richmond.htm.

Vantage Studios Inc. 2006. 'The campaign'. www.vantagestudios.ca/sexandthedistrict/thecampaign.php.

West Edmonton Mall. 1995–2005. www.westedmontonmall.com.

Yakhlef, Ali. 2004. 'Global brands as embodied "generic spaces"'. *Space and Culture* 7: 237–48.

Young, Craig, Martina Diep, and Stephanie Drabble. 2006. 'Living with difference? The "cosmopolitan city" and urban reimaging in Manchester, UK'. *Urban Studies* 43 (10): 1,687–714.

Zukin, Sharon. 1995. *The Cultures of Cities*. Oxford: Blackwell.

———. 1998. 'Urban lifestyles: Diversity and standardisation in spaces of consumption'. *Urban Studies* 35 (5–6): 825–39.

———. 2004. *Point of Purchase: How Shopping Changed American Culture*. London and New York: Routledge.

Chapter 13 *Getting Perspective*

In what ways is housing more than simply shelter, and how are issues related to housing a reflection of the social structure of the city?

All cities have an informal sorting process whereby residents gravitate to those places that reflect their class position. Perhaps the best symbol of this sorting process is where you live. The housing you have and where it is located reflects the inequalities that exist in a city. For example, every city has its elite neighbourhoods, but it also has its slums. People also tend to classify or stereotype other areas as working-class or middle-class. No one has to draw a map, but people who live in a city grade each area of the city using their own informal criteria. These evaluations may be partially related to the amenities of the area, but they are particularly related to the cost of housing. Thus, housing and location combine to give us a pretty good indication that a sorting process is at work.

A house, then, is an important symbol. At one level, it is simply a structure providing shelter. But at another level, it is one's own space that provides a sense of security in which accessibility is controlled and privacy is ensured. When this occurs, a house becomes 'my' home. Thus, the provision of shelter might be a minimum requirement for urban living, but it is not nearly as desirable as having a home that is private and secure. A home in that sense is a 'cocoon' in which people can remove themselves from urban society, if only in a partial or temporary sense. But housing is also a reflection of social status. How one decorates one's home demonstrates tastes that reflect social position. Where one chooses to live also reflects social status so that the type of home chosen reflects who you are and communicates status and style.

One of the major issues in our society is whether people should rent or own their own dwelling. Through government policies that attempt to reduce down payments or guarantee mortgages through the Canada Mortgage and Housing Corporation, there has been a bias towards homeownership. But some people prefer rental housing, while others cannot afford regular mortgage payments or do not qualify for mortgages, and these people are vulnerable to shifting rental markets and housing supply. The poor obviously are the most clearly affected by these issues, and cities have struggled with the appropriate way of providing housing for such persons. Should this housing be government-owned? Should such housing be located as *clusters* in several places that are easily identified (and stigmatized) as low-cost housing? Or should the poor be given money to subsidize their rent anywhere they can find housing, therefore dispersing low-income people throughout the city? Should special housing be provided for those with special needs, and should they be concentrated in one area or dispersed?

Another important issue related to many of these concerns is the role of single-family housing in relation to various forms of multiple-family housing, from duplexes and villas to walk-up apartments and high-rise residential towers. Which form of housing is preferable, and for whom? How this question is resolved will critically affect the shape of Canadian cities for the future. These are all issues that cities must deal with in particular when attempting to meet the needs of the most disadvantaged. The sociology of housing is a primary indicator of urban inequality, and the issues raised in regard to housing reflect important debates about how cities should deal with the wide range of human need within them today.

13 The Sociology of Housing

Brent Berry

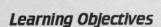

Learning Objectives

- To outline the relevance of housing for human privacy, identity, and community.
- To identify the different types of housing and tenure arrangements.
- To describe inequalities in the quality and distribution of housing.
- To examine the benefits and problems of high-rise living.
- To review housing policy and support programs.
- To describe the homeless, their shelter options, and how organizations respond to them in the city.

Introduction

Housing constitutes much more than physical shelter. People seeking housing are also seeking privacy, security, a healthy environment, neighbourly social relations, status, community facilities and services, access to jobs, investment, and control over the environment. Urban Canada has experienced fundamental change in housing over the past 100 years, including dramatic increases in suburbanization, new types of housing and tenure arrangements, high-rise living, gentrification, and urban renewal. Although the quality of housing has improved for many urban Canadians, fewer free and affordable shelter options and more hostile political responses to homelessness have exacerbated the troubles for the homeless.

Housing Differentiates Private from Public

The spaces where we live are significant to us at a deep level. Our house is where we can break from social conventions and partake in intimate social relations. More than just shelter from the elements, home shields its inhabitants from public distractions, allowing for a sense of privacy. A uniquely personal world can be created with this privacy, shaping and reflecting the identity of its inhabitants (Fitzpatrick and LaGory 2000, 51–5). The critical need to maintain a sense of privacy and control through housing is what makes homelessness the most severe form of disadvantage in modern urban societies.

The level of privacy at home has varied considerably over time. For example, in the early twentieth century, many city dwellers were densely packed into poorly constructed multistorey dwellings, sharing common facilities, suffering thin walls, and residing close to public sidewalks. Since the end of World War II, important changes in society led to large-scale construction of low-density suburban housing. The decentralization of employment opportunities from traditional downtowns has made it possible to live and work farther from city centres. Cars and extensive road networks have made it easier to work at significant distances from home, expanding the range of potential jobs for

Box 13.1 *Interior Dwellers, More Than Ever*

The Industrial Revolution brought the growing significance of artificially constructed environments. Today, our homes' interior spaces more profoundly than ever shape how we experience the world both socially and physically. This **interiorization** runs counter to the view that 'nature is a basic human need' (Gallagher 1993, 20). Interior dwelling time has risen. For example, American adults spend just an hour outdoors each day on average, spending the rest in vehicles and buildings (Robinson and Godbey 1997). This is a significant shift from two generations ago when more time was spent in public outdoor spaces doing routine activities. What are the long-term consequences of this interiorization on the human species, given that we evolved in the natural world? How can housing and other built environments be modified to rekindle our relationship with nature and public space?

a given individual. Easily available home mortgages have also spurred demand for suburban housing construction.

Suburbanization has had important consequences for experienced and expected privacy at home. In fact, the common suburban tract house is designed to emphasize privacy. Interior spaces are separated by their functional role, and exterior spaces include private outdoor areas at the back of the home that serve a role distinct from the more public front yard. Privacy is further emphasized through the diversion of local through-traffic by means of buffer zones (e.g., cul-de-sac streets). Inside the modern suburban home, technology such as personal televisions, telephones, and computers has fostered even greater privacy and public space avoidance. They make it less necessary to leave the home to satisfy a basic desire for communication or entertainment. Paradoxically, they also increase the separation between individuals sharing a home.

These changes in privacy and spatial separation in contemporary living may foster self-consciousness and personal liberty, but they also create disconnection from healthy social relations and civic engagement (Fitzpatrick and LaGory 2000). Cooley (1922) believed that immersion in a rich social environment was required to generate a sense of self. Despite the fundamental spatial needs of human beings, the fragmentation of spaces in contemporary neigh-

bourhoods and houses may exceed its usefulness to modern culture. If individual households collectively lose sight of the whole, common values such as tolerance of others may be threatened. Some now suggest that individualism has been nurtured in increasingly segmented urban society at the expense of inter-group tolerance and public civility (Fischer 1982). Others counter that new forms of community, such as those developed through Internet social networking, are supplementing and in some cases replacing existing forms of community (Castells 1996; Hampton and Wellman 2003).

Although suburban homes often provide significant privacy, housing in many older and some newly constructed areas of the city suffer from a lack of privacy. Research suggests that children living in homes with little privacy spend more of their leisure time away from these environments and the supervision they impose (Gove, Hughes, and Galle 1979). This is important, because environments without adequate adult supervision generally contain greater risk and fewer sources of protection in case of trouble.

Types of Housing and Tenure Arrangements

Housing type and **housing tenure arrangement** are two important ways to describe housing.

Table 13.1 Distribution of Households and Net Worth by Tenure and Asset Profile, Canada, 1999

Tenure and asset type	As % of all households	Share of total net worth (%)
Owners	**64**	**91**
No substantial retirement or investment assets*	28	16
with substantial retirement and investment assets	35	75
Renters	**36**	**9**
No substantial retirement or investment assets*	30	3
with substantial retirement and investment assets	6	6

Note: An asset is considered substantial if it has a minimum value of $50,000.

Source: Adapted from Statistics Canada. 1999. *The Assets and Debts of Canadians: An Overview of the Survey of Financial Security* Catalogue no. 13-595-XIE. Ottawa: Statistics Canada.

Cities contain a variety of housing types, including single **detached houses**, semi-detached houses (sharing a common wall), row houses or townhouses (joined on both sides), and multiple-family buildings. Areas with high levels of **residential density**, such as neighbourhoods along mass transit links, are more likely to contain large multi-family apartment buildings and condominiums.

The most common tenure arrangements are ownership and rental (alternative tenure arrangements are discussed below). As depicted in Table 13.1, about two-thirds of Canadian households are *homeowners* (64 per cent). The most common form of ownership is **freehold**, whereby both the land and the structure are owned. Another involves residents of a structure (e.g., a condominium) owning and co-managing the land and common areas.

Owning a home confers several social advantages. Historically, buying a home has been a good investment because it has allowed individuals and families to build equity while also providing a place in which to live. Equity accumulated through appreciation and mortgage payments has allowed families to move up to better homes and neighbourhoods as they experienced mobility. As the largest single source

of wealth, home equity can also ease financial concerns later in life as retirees cope with lower incomes. As Table 13.1 suggests, compared to renters, homeowners have a disproportionate share of total net worth and retirement assets in Canadian society. Besides economic benefit, homeownership is a visible indicator of social status. And it allows the private pursuit of activities and the independence to make personal choices about style and furnishings. In short, ownership is a widely sought after source of economic advantage, pride, and identification.

Homeownership also brings responsibilities, such as regular maintenance and extra costs associated with taxes, utilities, and unanticipated repairs (Baum and Hassan 1999). Although housing values have increased in the long term, the prices of homes do sometimes rise beyond their intrinsic value in what is called a 'bubble market' whereby price declines can put owners 'upside' down—holding a mortgage that is larger than the market value of their home. These 'market corrections' are infrequent, but they can have a jarring impact on many homeowners and their communities, as recently seen in the dramatic rise in real estate foreclosures and municipal budget shortfalls in the United States in 2007 and 2008.

Box 13.2 *Alternative Tenure Arrangements*

In recent years, the proportion of Canadians who own their own home has increased, but the affordability has declined. Partly in response to affordability pressures, alternative tenure arrangements have emerged, including **co-housing**, cooperatives, life lease projects, and shared equity arrangements (see Scherlowski and Mancer 2000). They are less common than traditional ownership and rental scenarios but have the potential to increase the range of affordable housing options to meet changes in Canadian society and consumer preferences.

Co-housing: Co-housing or collaborative housing communities provide private self-contained dwellings along with a full range of shared facilities such as group dining areas, kitchens, meeting rooms, lounges, libraries, recreation facilities, workshops, and daycare. Those attracted to this kind of housing cite a desire for intentional community, the benefits of pooling resources, sharing the burden of activities like meal preparation and facility maintenance, supervision of children, and commonality of viewpoints. Residents of co-housing communities report a high level of satisfaction, partly because they have self-selected this form of community. Gaining approval for such communities has in many cases been difficult because of zoning restrictions.

Cooperatives: Co-op residents share ownership in the cooperative that owns the land and buildings. The two basic types of housing co-ops are government-assisted co-ops in which low-income members qualify for subsidization, and equity co-ops in which members finance the co-op without government assistance.

Life lease projects: Residents of life lease housing are aged 55+ and contribute a lump sum prepayment and modest monthly fees to live in a building for the rest of their lives. Life lease housing projects are usually supported by community-based non-profit organizations. Manitoba and Saskatchewan developed the first Canadian life lease projects in the late 1980s through government joint life lease/rent supplement projects. The number of these projects has grown and is expected to continue to grow with the aging of the baby-boomers.

Shared equity arrangements: Shared equity arrangements are designed to make home-ownership easier and more accessible for those with low incomes. This approach provides workable solutions to inner-city housing problems in cities where there is low-cost inner-city housing stock in need of repair. A purchaser contributes part of the down payment on a house, and a local non-profit organization contributes the remainder. Buyers who maintain regular payments and involvement in the program build equity in their homes. Any subsequent property appreciation is shared if the property is sold.

Renters have a disproportionately smaller share of overall net worth in Canadian society (although they tend to be younger). A *renter* lacks control over what can be done with his or her housing, limiting opportunities for self-expression through housing. This can contribute to a feeling of **residential alienation** (Marcuse 1975, 183), which is 'the condition of estrangement between a person and his/her dwelling'. Such estrangement is reflected in renters spending less time at home than owners do, less likely to rate their time at home as enjoyable, and less likely to view their dwelling as a positive reflection of who they are. Ideally, rental housing should provide both decent shelter and opportunities to express individuality.

Renters move more frequently than owners do, limiting the social and economic connectedness they make with their communities. However, the ability of renters to move on fairly short

Table 13.2 Population and Dwelling Growth in Canadian Cities, 1901–1911

	Population		Dwellings		No. per Dwelling	
	1901	1911	1901	1911	1901	1911
Vancouver	27,010	100,401	5,964	21,509	4.5	4.8
Calgary	4,398	43,704	1,684	11,350	2.6	3.9
Winnipeg	42,340	136,035	7,496	19,915	5.6	6.8
Toronto	208,040	376,538	39,104	60,595	5.3	6.2
Montreal	267,730	470,480	36,503	35,677	7.6	13.3

Source: Dominion Census, as reported in Bryce Stewart. 1974 [1913]. 'The housing of our immigrant workers'. In Paul Rutherford, ed., *Saving the Canadian City: The First Phase, 1880–1920*, 152. Toronto: Univesity of Toronto Press.

notice can be a benefit. Homeowners must pay substantial transaction costs and take time to sell their homes.

Housing and Inequality

Visible minorities, recent immigrants, and the poor are more likely to live in housing that is crowded, in disrepair, and in locations that are less safe and less central to labour markets. These groups are also more likely to face discrimination in securing and keeping housing (Novac et al. 2002). Although immigrants on average are more disadvantaged than the native-born population, it is important to note that a sizable subset of recent immigrants to Canada is relatively affluent. For example, immigration from Hong Kong has contributed to large increases in the price of housing in Vancouver.

Crowding

Some of the first efforts in the early twentieth century to address housing inequality in urban Canada focused on **crowding**. Sociologist Bryce Stewart (1974 [1913]) documented the changing housing conditions of immigrant workers between 1900 and 1910, describing the poor housing conditions in several rapidly growing Canadian cities. Most of the large urban centres in Canada experienced big population increases

over a short period of time, with many new immigrants seeking work in the booming factories. Table 13.2 illustrates the extent of this pressure, showing that dwellings failed to keep pace with the rapid population growth. The number of inhabitants per dwelling increased everywhere, alarmingly so in Montreal. Social science research during this early period collectively helped to forge new standards for housing and city planning. One early influential policy was New York City's tenement law that required all new buildings to provide sufficient amounts of natural light and fresh air.

Housing Challenges for a Growing Population

Spurred by the continued growth of cities and underdeveloped housing construction and finance industries, the federal government passed the National Housing Act (NHA) in 1938 to promote both the construction of new and the improvement of existing homes. The **Canada Mortgage and Housing Corporation** (CMHC, a Crown corporation) was set up in 1945 to administer the NHA and quickly address housing shortages facing postwar families (Fallis 1994, 358). CMHC has since had a key role in addressing housing inequalities by offering home improvement loans, creating a federal-provincial public housing program, offering mortgage insurance, and developing planning guidelines for coping with growth. As a consequence of these policy changes, as well as suburbanization and post-war affluence, the rate of homeownership has increased, and crowding has decreased.

Despite these long-term improvements, many Canadians, especially new immigrants, remain susceptible to housing problems. One measure that CMHC tracks is **core housing need**. A household is considered to be in core housing need if it has no choice but to live in housing that does not meet standards of affordability, condition, and size. Adequate dwellings are those that do not require major repairs, have enough bedrooms for the family according to National Occupancy Standards, and cost less than 30 per cent of before-tax household income. Table 13.3 shows that recent immigrants are more likely than non-immigrants to experience core housing need. Although this need among immigrants declines over time to equal that of non-immigrants, rising prices for homeownership and the declining stock of affordable renting housing has increased the incidence of core housing need for everyone, not just immigrants (Bruce and Carter 2003; CMHC 2006).

Neighbourhoods with high incidence of core housing need tend to have higher *population density* (measured as inhabitants per square kilometre). Table 13.4 (top panel) shows that recent immigrants are more likely to settle in high-density than in low-density neighbourhoods. Many poorer immigrant families end up living in apartments in older high-rise buildings or in basement apartments not well suited for them.

However, the relationship between density and quality of housing is not a simple inverse one. Living in a dense residential environment does not necessarily imply crowded or unappealing housing conditions. In fact, higher-density urban neighbourhoods with well-designed housing and rich amenities within walking distance are a magnet for what Richard Florida calls the **creative class** (2005). Table 13.4 (middle panel) illustrates that persons aged 25 and older with a university degree are more likely to choose high-density neighbourhoods than the population at large (the

comparison group in the bottom panel). This is true even though newer housing (constructed between 1991 and 2001) tends to be located in lower-density neighbourhoods (Table 13.5).

Housing Segregation

Residential segregation is the tendency for groups (e.g., social classes or ethnic groups) to live in different neighbourhoods to a greater extent than would be expected by chance alone. Segregation is a powerful form of inequality because it determines the social, physical, and service environments that influence important life outcomes. For example, the quality of schools and recreational amenities varies significantly by neighbourhood. Richer neighbourhoods have better schools and public spaces. Poorer neighbourhoods have greater pollution and crime. Alarmingly, the rates of residential segregation by income, race, and ethnicity have been increasing in urban Canada. Even worse, there is an increasing concentration of the poor in the inner suburbs, communities challenged both by aging infrastructure and by inadequate access to jobs downtown and in the outer suburbs. Despite these trends, residential segregation in Canada remains significantly lower than in major American cities.

Residential segregation has been examined along numerous lines—income, race, ethnicity, age, family structure, sexual orientation, lifestyle preferences—but the bulk of research has focused on economic, racial, and ethnic forms of segregation. Segregation can arise from both *voluntary* and *involuntary* factors. For example, new immigrants often voluntarily choose to live in an **ethnic enclave** because it provides the benefits of shared language, social networks, job opportunities, and cultural familiarity during a difficult adjustment period. This kind of *self-segregation* can protect the mental health of new immigrants by allowing them to assimilate gradually.

On the other hand, practices like exclusionary zoning and housing discrimination by landlords are important involuntary causes of segregation (Novac et al. 2002). To truly understand

Table 13.3 Households and Core Housing Need, Canada, 1996–2001

		Total			Owner			Renter		
		Number of Households	Number of Households in Core Housing Need	% in Core Housing Need	Number of Households	Number of Households in Core Housing Need	% in Core Housing Need	Number of Households	Number of Households in Core Housing Need	% in Core Housing Need
All households	1996	10,027,800	1,567,200	15.6	6,494,000	446,200	6.9	3,533,800	1,121,000	31.7
	2001	10,805,600	1,485,300	13.7	7,229,700	473,800	6.6	3,576,000	1,011,500	28.3
Non-immigrants	1996	7,892,700	1,132,900	14.4	5,111,000	311,800	6.1	2,781,700	821,100	29.5
	2001	8,439,400	1,045,700	12.4	5,656,700	319,400	5.6	2,782,800	726,300	26.1
Immigrants	1996	2,096,100	418,600	20	1,376,200	133,300	9.7	719,900	285,300	39.6
	2001	2,319,900	425,600	18.3	1,563,200	153,000	9.8	756,600	272,600	36
Pre-1976*	1996	1,306,600	182,900	14	999,200	79,000	7.9	307,400	103,900	33.8
	2001	1,222,400	162,200	13.3	969,800	78,000	8	252,600	84,200	33.3
Recent immigrants**	1996	232,400	99,500	42.8	70,500	18,200	25.8	161,900	81,300	50.2
	2001	225,100	81,100	36	72,400	15,300	21.2	152,700	65,800	43.1

*Note that for 2001, the primary maintainer would have been in Canada for 25 years, compared to 20 years for 1996 data.
** Recent immigrant households represent those households whose primary maintainer immigrated to Canada in the five years prior to the Census. For 2001, the primary maintainer arrived between 1996 and 2000. For 1996, the primary maintainer arrived between 1991 and 1995.
Source: CMHC. 2001 [revised 2005]. *Households in Core Housing Need, Canada, Provinces, Territories and Metropolitan Areas, 1991–2001*.

Table 13.4 Recent Immigrants and Educated Young Adults Prefer to Live in High- vs. Low-Density Neighbourhoods

	All CMAs	Toronto	Montreal	Vancouver	Ottawa	Calgary	Edmonton	Quebec City	Winnipeg	Medium CMAs	Small CMAs
Per cent of Recent Immigrants (1991 to 2001) in											
High-density neighbourhoods	15	28	10	19	14	13	8	2	8	9	3
Medium-density neighbourhoods	10	18	5	19	7	6	6	1	5	6	2
Low-density neighbourhoods	6	11	2	12	2	7	4	1	3	3	1
Per cent of persons aged 25 Years and older with a university degree in											
High-density neighbourhoods	24	30	21	28	31	32	24	21	21	21	16
Medium-density neighbourhoods	21	25	21	21	30	24	16	19	19	18	18
Low-density neighbourhoods	20	24	18	23	28	24	18	19	18	17	15
Per cent of entire population in											
High-density neighbourhoods	23	23	47	25	22	6	12	30	10	10	13
Medium-density neighbourhoods	29	31	19	38	37	27	30	24	26	32	30
Low-density neighbourhoods	48	47	34	37	40	67	58	46	64	59	58

In low-density neighbourhoods, 66.6% or more of the housing stock is composed of single-family dwellings, semi-detached dwellings, or mobile homes. In medium-density neighbourhoods, the percentage is between 33.3% and 66.6%. In high-density neighbourhoods, these types of dwellings comprise less than 33.3% of the housing stock.

Source: Statistics Canada. 2001 Census. Table adapted from M. Turcotte, 2008. 'The city/suburb contrast: How to measure it?' *Canadian Social Trends* 85. Catalogue no. 11-008-XWE. Ottawa: Statistics Canada.

Table 13.5 Percentage of Recent Housing Construction (1991–2001) by Neighbourhood Density in Urban Canada

	All CMAs	Toronto	Montreal	Vancouver	Ottawa	Calgary
High-density neighbourhoods	17	17	26	33	13	3
Medium-density neighbourhoods	24	19	19	39	39	10
Low-density neighbourhoods	59	64	55	28	48	87

residential patterns, we must examine the complex set of causes that operate simultaneously—group preferences for similarity, the unequal availability of affordable housing, exclusionary zoning, poverty, family background, cultural resources, social networks, and discrimination. I will expand on the role of group preferences and zoning.

Group Preferences

Homophilly, or the desire to be with those who are similar to us, is a consistent finding in studies of residential preferences. When choosing housing, individuals more often prefer potential neighbours who share a common racial or ethnic background or recent immigrant perspective. Many have an aversion to living close to other groups of different ethnic background because of prejudicial attitudes about that group. For example, research on housing choice has found that whites are much less willing than blacks to live in a neighbourhood that is 50/50 black and white. The **contact hypothesis** suggests that breaking the vice of segregation requires routine group contact on an equal footing, providing the crucible for exposing and eliminating prejudices.

Individuals tend to prefer neighbours whose status is the same as or higher than their own (e.g., income level or occupational prestige). Groups also often vary in their preferences for housing type, such as new housing of a particular design (e.g., modern versus Victorian architecture), proximity to valued social institutions (e.g., church), and accessibility to work. Immigrants have, for example, been more willing to live in high-rise buildings than native-born Canadians, contributing to segregation by housing type.

Zoning and Affordable Housing

Compared to the suburbs, high-density urban neighbourhoods contain a greater mix of both substandard but affordable housing and housing that higher-income groups find appealing. This mix is rarely found in suburban neighbourhoods. Affordable housing is most likely to be built in higher-density neighbourhoods or to become affordable after once-chic apartment buildings fall into disrepair (e.g., Toronto's St Jamestown neighbourhood, once a single-professional enclave, is now an ethnic-receiving area). This in large part has to do with the zoning regulations that shape urban and suburban housing. Urban areas are more likely to practise **inclusionary zoning**, which is a set of planning ordinances that require a given share of new construction to be affordable for people with low to moderate incomes. Essentially, urban municipalities place a deed restriction on 10 to 30 per cent of new housing units in order to make ownership affordable for lower-income households. Suburban governments are in a different position because they are newly populated, often have a large amount of undeveloped land, and are generally more economically homogenous than the cities they surround. **Exclusionary zoning** aims to exclude affordable housing from a

Table 13.5 Continued

	All CMAs	Edmonton	Quebec City	Winnipeg	Medium CMAs	Small CMAs
High-density neighbourhoods	17	7	25	5	9	12
Medium-density neighbourhoods	24	16	21	10	24	27
Low-density neighbourhoods	59	77	54	85	68	62

Source: Statistics Canada 2001 Census. Table adapted from M. Turcotte, 2008. 'The city/suburb contrast: How to measure it?' *Canadian Social Trends* 85. Catalogue no. 11-008-XWE. Ottawa: Statistics Canada.

municipality through the zoning code. Many suburban municipalities have enacted exclusionary zoning and ordinances to preserve the 'character' of their community. One common exclusionary practice is to stipulate that housing lots must be of a certain minimum size and houses must be set back a minimum distance from the street (CMHC 2005; Gottdiener 1994, 222). In many cases, such ordinances make affordable housing economically unfeasible because it is cost-prohibitive to build modestly priced houses on large (expensive) lots. Consequently, many suburban communities have been able to cater to wealthier citizens through zoning and ordinances, shutting out low-income families. Whether such exclusion of low-income families was explicitly intended or not, by denying such households access to suburban communities, exclusionary zoning helps to maintain concentrated poverty in existing poor urban areas. Furthermore, developers of master-planned suburban neighbourhoods often build entire subdivisions of similar houses that are sold for similar prices, artificially narrowing the income range of a given community. What are the consequences of such exclusion and homogeneity in suburban housing?

Exclusionary zoning reinforces inequalities in local services. Wide variation in social services remains despite efforts to preserve minimum levels across neighbourhoods. Most families moving into a suburban community will be told where the best schools are located, and most will subsequently try to purchase a home in that district. Of course, areas with better schools will be among the most expensive. In this way, economic segregation perpetuates intergenerational inequalities through local services, an unfortunate consequence that emanates in part from suburban housing development.

High-Rise Living

A growing proportion of urban Canadians in all income brackets live in *high-rise buildings*. For example, in North America, Toronto is second only to New York City in the number of high-rises. Vancouver, a city with nowhere to build but up, has many residential towers in its downtown. The quality of high-rise housing varies immensely. Some high-rises are 1950s- and 1960s-era apartment buildings that house a sizable proportion of the city's low-income and new immigrant residents. Rather than being centralized, clusters of such high-rise apartment buildings dot a wide swath of cities like Toronto. The other predominant type of high-rise is the newer owner-occupied condominiums with units ranging in price from $100,000 to $10 million. These buildings tend to be close to major cultural institutions, natural landmarks, downtown employment, and mass transit corridors.

Research reveals both problems and benefits of high-rise living, suggesting that there is considerable variation. The experience of high-rise living may vary significantly by type of building (condo versus public housing), ethnicity, gender,

Box 13.3 How Much House Is Enough?

In the postwar period, Canadians raised their housing standards significantly. Newer homes were built with more floor area per person and more and higher-quality appliances (Foley 1980). House prices rose accordingly, from about two times the annual income in 1950 to nearly four times the annual income in 2000. Some charge that the homebuilding and real estate industries contribute to price increases by convincing home shoppers that they need these higher standards.

Would families opt for 'basic' housing at reduced cost? Michelson advocated for more modest but comfortable single-family homes: 'It is not the ornate features of the house that serve as the major attraction to the respondents surveyed, but rather some of its most basic characteristics—control of the premises, relative economic security, self-containment, and private open space. These are found in basic houses as well as in deluxe houses' (Michelson 1977, 367).

Despite these protests and some small movements to 'simple living' and small houses, house sizes and standards have continued to increase beyond what can be explained by need, indicating that housing is part of the social stratification system of consumer societies. Individuals strive to acquire housing not just with shelter in mind but in the same way that they seek identity, recognition, and status. Recognizing the connectedness of housing to so many other things, sociologists of housing increasingly view housing as key part of systems of power and stratification. Furthermore, the role of housing in social stratification is not just a North American problem but an issue facing all contemporary societies.

household composition, and details of the high-rise design. High-rise living is also more accepted in some societies such as Singapore and Hong Kong, where it is dominant.

A substantial amount of research in the 1960s and 1970s argued against high-rise housing. The focus was largely on the experiences of low-income residents in public housing projects. A key in the anti-high-rise advocacy was concern over the suitability of high-rises for families with young children. Access to ground-level outdoor space is often limited and crowded. Children on balconies must be closely supervised. Following the recommendations of urban sociologists, the British government ceased building residential public housing buildings over six storeys high in the 1960s. Researchers demonstrated that medium-density social housing could allow more than half of all households direct access to personal outdoor ground-level space. These planning guidelines were replicated in other countries, slowing the construction of high-rise apartments for public housing for families with children. The massive shift away from high-rise public housing for families with children shows us that social research can effectively influence housing policy.

Other research has examined the social and mental health consequences of high-rise living for adults. A significant number of adults reported feelings of impersonalization and loneliness as a result of high-rise living. Helleman and Wassenberg (2004, 15) argue that 'high-rise offers too many, similar, and not attractive dwellings for non-existent average people in the wrong places.'

Gillis (1977) found gender and ethnic differences in responses to high-rise living. For single-parent women, a higher-floor residence was associated with greater psychological strain. High-rise living detaches some individuals not only from the ground but also from the socially embedded lifestyle found in a horizontally built community. There was a strong push to abandon high-rise public housing stemming from the research on children and adults (Foley 1980).

As Abel (2003) points out, more recent high-rises tend to be privately developed, located in prime downtown locations (versus public housing projects), and taller. As high-rise public housing for families has declined, owner-occupied high-rise condominiums have grown popular. Surprisingly little research has studied the effects of high-rise living on occupants who chose to live there. Some cities that abandoned high-rise residential constructions have returned to it with a surge in private owner-occupied high-rise construction (e.g., London).

High-rise living is valued for spectacular views, the sensation of height, privacy and quietness, and, increasingly, prestige and status. Highrises also allow for the efficient use of energy (e.g., heating), infrastructure (e.g., roads, sewers), and linkages to mass transit. High-rise residents can more easily travel because they do not have a yard and other property issues to worry about. High-rise living aspirations are epitomized by the cosmopolitan lifestyle depicted in television shows like 'Frasier'. Costello (2005, 54) argues that central-city high-rise living has become a lifestyle of the global era in which convenience and sophistication merge.

Despite the allure of new high-rises, few purchasers are families with children. Most owners are single professionals, childless couples, or 'empty nester' couples downsizing from a conventional house. Indeed, few condominiums have units large enough for families with multiple children. The dearth of families in the condo-dense part of cities is a concern, given that communities with a full range of family forms are more stable. City councillors in Toronto have sought to expand inclusive zoning to ensure that new condominiums have units that are affordable and sizable enough for families.

Some cities have been so successful at building high-rise condominiums downtown that there is a shortage of space for office-building development. For example, the number of residential towers dwarfs office towers in Vancouver, creating a problematic mismatch in the supply of workers and jobs. A growing number of downtown condominium residents in big cities like Vancouver, Montreal, and Toronto are 'reverse commuting' from their downtown condos to suburban office parks.

Housing Projects and Assistance Programs

Public housing and other housing assistance programs in Canada have evolved with experience, funding changes, and changes in the disadvantaged populations themselves. The postwar period saw a number of *master-planned public housing projects* optimistically aimed at helping the urban poor. During this period, sociologist Robert Merton observed, 'Contemporary housing provides an unparalleled near-experimental setting for the study of "what might be" rather than the continued observation of "what is" and "what has been" in human relations within the local community' (Merton 1951, 185–6). Neighbourhoods consisting almost entirely of modernist high-rise towers for the poor were advocated as an efficient solution by planners and architects. Subsequent experience and research have shown that the large, monolithic high-rise housing projects did not function as intended, failing to improve the well-being of their residents. They were not practically designed for the human scale, were poorly oriented to the street, and were often located in isolated places away from attractive jobs, safe activity spaces, diverse shopping outlets, and effective public transit. Rather than being a sanctuary, the well-intended green spaces surrounding many buildings became dangerous hotspots for crime and drug dealing that were difficult for police to patrol.

Both in the US and Canada, high-rise public housing projects from this earlier period are gradually being replaced by lower-density housing that is built into mixed-income communities (Chisholm 2003). Public housing units that are indistinguishable from the private-owner-occupied housing does not stigmatize low-income residents

> **Box 13.4 *The House Keys to Successful Aging***
>
> The symbols, markers, and memories associated with our homes are of great personal significance beyond the material value of the objects themselves. Especially as we age, places and our memories of them become ever more interwoven with our sense of self. The loss of independence for an elderly person can take a great personal toll, in part because a move away from home is ultimately a loss of self. Late-life moves to an institutional facility is associated with a twofold increase in mortality (Aneshensel et al. 2000). However, some evidence suggests that relocating important personal belongings from home with the person (e.g., photos, furniture, paintings) can reduce the negative consequences of the move. When we are old, nurturing the home in our memories is more important than actual home.

by isolating them in communities that are underserved by merchants and public transit. Toronto's Regent Park, one of Canada's oldest public housing communities, is currently being rebuilt to include both **rent-geared-to-income** and owner-occupied housing. The new community will also subdivide the 'superblock', with roads and sidewalks crisscrossing the neighbourhood, providing a streetscape and access for residents, delivery vehicles, and police. These improvements in community design, however, come with a net reduction in the number of public housing units at a time when the demand for housing assistance has grown. There has been a general reduction in federal and provincial outlays for new public housing.

Publicly funded projects alone cannot house everyone in need, especially given that few new projects have been built recently. The availability of affordable units in the private rental market is critical. However, as with public housing, affordable housing construction for the private market has not kept pace with need. Low private-apartment vacancy rates and the high cost of ownership, especially in recent years, have restricted the housing options available to low-income groups.

Budget constraints, high housing prices, and low vacancy rates have shifted Canadian public housing policy towards the development of alternative approaches to affordable housing, such as non-profit and cooperative complexes (Carter 1997; Homegrown Solutions 1999; Kraus, Eberle, and Pomerleau 1994). For example, some pri-

vately initiated alternative tenure arrangements offer innovative ways to provide affordable housing for various groups (see Box 13.1). The few new public housing projects avoid the ghettoized nature of the postwar era public housing but also offer fewer rent-geared-to-income units than conventional projects. Recent efforts at all levels of government favour **public-private partnerships** in ensuring affordable housing (Fallis 1990; Pomeroy et al. 1998). For example, a municipal government will often negotiate with a condominium developer for rent-geared-to-income units in exchange for height allowances. And new models of housing that target specific disadvantaged populations have been successfully implemented in several cities (e.g., **supportive housing** for the elderly and mentally ill and **harm-reduction housing** for the under-housed with drug dependency issues). Finally, several large Canadian cities have permitted homeowners to rent out a portion of their house as a 'second suite', a flexible and market-responsive form of housing that can take some stress off public housing providers and provide additional income for homeowners.

The characteristics of the population in need of housing assistance has also changed. It increasingly consists of elderly persons with relatively low incomes, single parents who have difficulty juggling work and child care, visible minorities discriminated against in employment and housing, new immigrants whose education credentials are not accepted, and the mentally ill (Henry 1995).

Demand for public housing has shifted from the poor in need of temporarily housing assistance to the poor in need of long-term assistance because of unemployment, single-parent difficulties, insufficient old age income, and mental illness.

The cumulative deficit in affordable housing construction described above has increased the number of Canadians unable to afford the available market-rate accommodations. The private rental accommodations available are often overpriced, undersized, and poorly maintained. For example, $1,000 per month in Toronto will often pay for no more than a basement apartment with low ceilings and poor heat in the winter. Given the long lists for public housing slots, this kind of substandard housing is often the only affordable alternative.

Homelessness

Homelessness deprives people of the spaces that are essential for human needs. More than a severe form of poverty and a lack of shelter, homelessness exposes individuals to constant and overwhelming hassles and stress. The United Nations distinguishes between 'absolute' and 'relative' forms of homelessness. *Absolute homelessness* describes people who lack physical shelter and therefore must sleep outdoors, in abandoned buildings, or in other places not intended for human habitation. *Relative homelessness* is the condition of having physical shelter but one that does not meet basic standards of health and safety, such as protection from the elements, access to sanitation, clean water, personal safety, and affordability (Jencks 1994).

The actual number of homeless is unknown. Estimates vary by city, season, and method of estimation. Information most commonly used to gauge the number of homeless comes from shelter use. If we simply use shelter capacity as a good indicator of the homeless population, then about 10,000 people sleep in shelters on a given night in the 10 largest Canadian metropolitan areas, or about six per 10,000 population. Shelter counts understate

the homeless population because many homeless refuse to stay in shelters even on cold nights.

A complex set of causes contributes to homelessness. Homelessness is typically preceded by or associated with multiple life crises. Common reasons for homelessness include problems with personal relations (e.g., divorce, separation, domestic violence, or difficulties in getting along with other household members), financial difficulty, and substance abuse (Fitzpatrick and LaGory 2000, 139). Frequently, the causes of homelessness for an individual extend far back into his or her past. Negative events in childhood such as unhappiness, physical or sexual abuse, and unusual housing arrangements are associated with homelessness later in life (Piliavin, Sosin, and Westerfelt 1993).

Most researchers agree that homelessness has increased in Canada over the past two decades. There are a number of reasons for this trend. Perhaps most important, the homeless are greater in number because urban redevelopment and gentrification has diminished the stock of abandoned and underused buildings and reduced the availability of low-end rental housing. Neighbourhood redevelopment has converted many **marginal spaces**, or neglected urban areas where the homeless often prefer to live, into **prime spaces**, or more desirable and frequently used spaces where anti-homeless sentiment and enforcement of panhandling and loitering laws are often stricter. The loss of affordable housing has not only contributed to larger homeless populations but have also made the homeless more visible to urban dwellers because the homeless are increasingly found sharing 'prime' public spaces with other residents of the city. While marginal spaces and existing affordable housing have been lost, newer replacement housing has not been built. Cities have been unable and sometimes unwilling to provide housing for larger homeless populations with additional temporary shelter beds. More desirable permanent or semi-permanent housing for the homeless and those at greatest risk of homelessness has also not materialized. Public housing, and other forms of housing geared to the homeless, such as harm-reduction housing, has not benefited from consistent support at all levels of government in Canada.

Besides changes in affordable housing, changes in families, the quality of jobs, and treatment for people with substance abuse and mental health problems have exacerbated problems of homelessness. Families today are more geographically dispersed and smaller in size, diminishing their ability to offer a relative a place to live. Declines in manufacturing and other low-skilled jobs that once paid wages high enough for a self-sufficient standard of living have forced more people into poverty and closer to the precipice of homelessness. The treatment options for people with substance abuse problems and the availability of professional care and housing for people living with mental illness have also not kept pace with recommendations of researchers and professional bodies that treat these social problems.

Responses to Homelessness

Of the organizational and political responses to homelessness, only some deal directly with resolving inadequacies in housing. In their study of the homeless, Snow and Anderson (1993, 85) discern five patterns of responses describing the various organizations intervening in the lives and routines of the homeless. First, **accommodative responses** are provided by 'caretaker agencies and individuals who not only give patient care, but other kinds of aid that they think will benefit the client. The responses offer aid as an end in itself, rather than as a means to a more important end.' Accommoda-tive responses provide for basic subsistence needs, especially food and temporary shelter. They do little to help keep the homeless off the streets.

Second, **restorative responses** aid the homeless from a treatment-oriented rather than sustenance perspective. Examples include mental and regular hospitals, drug detox facilities, and some missions. These responses are geared towards attending to actual physical, psychological, or spiritual problems that are impeding a homeless person's functioning. Long-term housing fits into this category of restorative responses. Third, some organizations have **exploitative responses** because they cater to the homeless from a market-oriented perspective with little authentic concern for their well-being. For example, there are documented examples of the homeless being exploited as unpaid sources of labour and blood plasma. Some merchants extend credit to the homeless at usurious rates of interest, and others charge exorbitant fees for basic services. Fourth, the political climate in many neighbourhoods and municipalities has led to **exclusionist/expulsionist responses** to the homeless. For example, allegations that proposed homeless shelters will diminish property values and increase crime frequently succeed in the cancellation of projects, contributing to inequalities both in where the homeless live and in the capacity of communities to deal with homelessness. The homeless are routinely displaced out of fear and scorn, alleged to have chosen their way of life and deserving of being contained within a limited ecological area. Recent advocacy efforts by the homeless and their supporters have effectively countered exclusionist and expulsionist response by invoking Canada's Charter of Rights and Freedoms.

Study and Discussion Questions

1. What type of housing is most common in the neighbourhood you live in? To what extent is there a mix of the different types of housing discussed in this chapter?

2. The chapter described how housing can provide much needed privacy but can also lead to social isolation. As a society with such a diversity of people and housing, how can we best meet the

needs for privacy yet promote social integration and shared understanding? Do you think that social networking technology such as Facebook can help mediate this balance between privacy and isolation?

3. A small but growing number of Canadians have sought to create 'intentional communities' through co-housing. Describe the advantages and disadvantages of this housing arrangement. Do you think that this kind of housing would be equally attractive to people at different points of life?

4. How might exclusionary zoning exacerbate inequalities in society? Can you think of any examples? Why has it historically been more difficult to enact inclusionary than exclusionary zoning?

5. Some research suggests that over the long term, purchasing a home can both be a good investment and improve the social and psychological well-being of its owner. Do you agree or disagree with this assertion?

6. High-rise living has often been viewed as ill-suited for raising children. However, some cities have created high-density urban neighbourhoods that are viewed as desirable for raising children. What are some of the features of these family-friendly high-density urban neighbourhoods that overcome the problems of high-rises?

7. Most housing policy programs are aimed at helping to provide housing for disadvantaged populations. However, during recessions, homeowners of many income levels have trouble affording their homes. Discuss the reasons for this. What policies with regard to housing would minimize this negative potential?

Suggested Reading

CMHC (Canada Mortgage and Housing Corporation). 2008 Canadian Housing Observer. Ottawa: CMHC. A comprehensive description of housing and homeownership trends in Canada.

Dipasquale, Denise, and Edward L. Glaeser. 1999. 'Incentives and social capital: Are homeowners better citizens?' Journal of Urban Economics 45: 354–84. Investigates the social integration and civic involvement of homeowners compared to renters, addressing the often assumed hypothesis that homeowners are more involved in their communities.

Finnimore, Brian. 1989. Houses from the Factory, System Building and the Welfare State. London: Rivers Oram Press. Chronicles the industrialization and systematization of home and apartment building construction and how this trend is both a reflection of and influence on the welfare state.

Harris, Richard. 1996. Unplanned Suburbs: Toronto's American Tragedy 1900 to 1950. Baltimore, MD: Johns Hopkins University Press. An historical account of Toronto's suburban development, arguing that poor planning has had a durable effect on suburban-urban tensions, effectiveness of mass transit, and efficient resource utilization.

Joint Center for Housing Studies. 2008. The State of the Nation's Housing 2008. Cambridge, MA: Joint Center for Housing Studies, Harvard University. www.jchs.harvard.edu. An extensive review of facts and figures on American homeownership, renting, and the quality of housing stock.

Kertzer, David. 1991. 'Household history and sociological theory'. Annual Review of Sociology 17: 155–79. A fascinating historical account of how household size and composition have changed, influencing the demand for different forms of housing.

Marsh, Alex, et al. 2000. 'Housing deprivation and health: A longitudinal analysis'. Housing Studies 15 (3). An empirical investigation of how insufficient housing can have a negative influence on health.

Miron, John R., Ed. 1993. House, Home, and Community: Progress in Housing Canadians, 1945–1986. Montreal: McGill-Queen's University Press. A comprehensive review of Canadian housing policy in the postwar generation.

Popenoe, D. 1985. Private Pleasure, Public Plight: American Metropolitan Community Life in Comparative Perspective. New Brunswick, NJ: Transaction Press. An influential thesis about major shifts in society from widespread investment in public space and public institutions to their neglect. Also reviews the increasing individual time-use in private environments.

UN-Habitat. 2005. 'Financing urban shelter: Global report on human settlements 2005'. www.unhabitat. org. A review of the challenges and opportunities for addressing the housing needs around the world.

Wallis, Allan D. 1991. *Wheel Estate: The Rise and Decline of Mobile Homes*. Baltimore, MD: Johns Hopkins University Press. The fascinating story of manufactured housing, chronicling its creation in response to demand for low-cost housing and continued discrimination faced in the housing regulatory environment.

References

Abel, C. 2003. *Sky High: Vertical Architecture*. London: Royal Academy of Arts.

Aneshensel, Carol, et al. 2000. 'The transition from home to nursing home: Mortality among people with dementia'. *Journal of Gerontology: Social Sciences* 55B (3): S152–62.

Baum, S., and R. Hassan. 1999. 'Home owners, home renovation and residential mobility'. *Journal of Sociology* 35 (1): 23–41.

Bruce, D., and T. Carter. 2003 'Socio-economic trends affecting consumers and housing markets'. Ottawa: Canada Mortgage and Housing Corporation.

Carter, T. 1997 'Current practices for procuring affordable housing: The Canadian context'. In Fannie Mae Foundation, *Housing Policy Debate* 8 (3): 593–632.

Castells, Manual. 1996. *The Rise of the Network Society*. Oxford: Blackwell.

Chisholm, Sharon. 2003. 'Affordable housing in Canada's urban communities: A literature review'. CMHC research report. Ottawa: Canada Mortgage and Housing Corporation.

CMHC (Canada Mortgage and Housing Corporation). 2005. 'The impact of zoning and building restrictions on housing affordability'. Research highlights. Socio-economic Series 05-012, no. 63918. Ottawa: CMHC.

———. 2006. 'Household income, net worth and housing affordability in Canada'. Research highlights. Socio-economic Series 06-003, no. 65006. Ottawa: CMHC.

Cooley, Charles H. 1922. *Human Nature and the Social Order*. New York: Scribner's.

Costello, L. 2005. 'From prisons to penthouses: The changing images of high-rise living in Melbourne'. *Housing Studies* 20 (1): 49–60.

Fallis, George. 1994. 'The federal government and the metropolitan housing problem'. In Frances Frisken, Ed., *The Changing Canadian Metropolis: A Public Policy Perspective*, 357–89. Berkeley: Institute of Governmental Studies Press, University of California.

Fischer, Claude. 1982. *To Dwell among Friends*. Berkeley: University of California Press.

Fitzpatrick, Kevin, and Mark LaGory. 2000. *Unhealthy Places*. New York: Routledge.

Florida, Richard. 2005. *Cities and the Creative Class*. New York: Routledge.

Foley, D. 1980. 'The sociology of housing'. *Annual Review of Sociology* 6: 457–78.

Gallagher, Winifred. 1993. *The Power of Place: How Our Surroundings Shape Our Thoughts, Emotions, and Reactions*. New York: HarperCollins.

Gillis, A.R. 1977. 'High rise housing and psychological strain'. *Journal of Health and Social Behavior*. 18: 418–31.

Gottdiener, Mark. 1994. *The New Urban Sociology*. New York: McGraw-Hill.

Gove, W.R., M. Hughes, and O.R. Galle. 1979. 'Overcrowding in the home: An empirical investigation of its possible pathological consequences'. *American Sociological Review* 44: 59–80.

Hampton, Keith, and Barry Wellman. 2003. 'Neighboring in Netville: How the Internet supports community and social capital in a wired suburb'. *City and Community* 2: 277–311.

Helleman, G., and F. Wassenberg. 2004. 'The renewal

of what was tomorrow's idealistic city: Amsterdam's Bijlmermeer high-rise'. *Cities* 21 (1): 3–17.

Henry, F. 1995. *The Colour of Democracy: Racism in Canadian Society*. Toronto: Harcourt Brace Canada.

Homegrown Solutions. 1999. 'Infill development in low density non-profit and co-operative housing projects'. Ottawa: Sound Advice Consulting Co-operative.

Jencks, Christopher. 1994. *The Homeless*. Cambridge, MA: Harvard University Press.

Kraus, Deborah, Margaret Eberle, and Joffre Pomerleau. 1994. 'Affordable housing solutions: Fifteen successful projects'. CMHC Research Report no. 62013. Ottawa: CMHC.

Marcuse, P. 1975. 'Residential alienation, home ownership and the limits of shelter policy'. *Journal of Sociology and Social Welfare* 3: 181–203.

Merton, R.K. 1951. 'The social psychology of housing'. In W. Dennis et al., Eds, *Current Trends in Social Psychology*, 163–217. Pittsburgh: University of Pittsburgh Press.

Michelson, W. 1977. *Environmental Choice, Human Behavior, and Residential Satisfaction*. New York: Oxford University Press.

Novac, S., et al. 2002. *Housing Discrimination in Canada: What Do We Know about It?* CUCS Research Bulletin no. 11 (summary of CMHC report). Toronto: Centre for Urban and Community Studies, University of Toronto.

Piliavin, Irving, Michael Sosin, and A. Westerfelt. 1993. 'The duration of homeless careers: An exploratory study'. *Social Service Review* 67: 576–98.

Pomeroy, Steve, et al. 1998. 'The role of public-private partnerships in producing affordable housing: Assessment of the U.S. experience and lessons for Canada'. CMHC Housing Affordability and Finance Series, no. 61592. Ottawa: CMHC.

Robinson, John P., and Geoffrey Godbey. 1997. *Time for Life: The Surprising Ways Americans Use Their Time*. College Park, PA: Pennsylvania State University Press.

Scherlowski, David, and Kathleen Mancer. 2000. 'Alternate tenure arrangements'. CMHC Research Report no. 62284. Ottawa: CMHC.

Snow, David A., and Leon Anderson. 1993. *Down on Their Luck: A Study of Homeless Street People*. Berkeley: University of California Press.

Stewart, Bryce. 1974 [1913]. 'The housing of our immigrant workers'. In Paul Rutherford, Ed., *Saving the Canadian City: The First Phase, 1880–1920*. Toronto: University of Toronto Press.

Chapter 14 Getting Perspective

How can we explain Montreal's changing role in the Canadian urban hierarchy, and how is urbanization changing the province of Quebec?

Montreal has been and is an important city in Canada; for many years, it was the country's largest city. Montreal's significance was related to its location linking Europe and the Atlantic region with the West, its position in the heartland of the country, and its role as a meeting point between English and French cultures. Most significantly, it was the centre of shipping, finance, and industry.

The Quiet Revolution beginning in 1960 introduced some important changes. The rural way of life that had distinguished the rest of Quebec from Montreal collapsed, and rapid rural-urban migration took place not only to Montreal but to smaller Quebec centres such as Quebec City and Saguenay. Consonant with this change was the desire that francophone Quebecers play a more pivotal role in Quebec life, especially in areas requiring a more educated workforce where anglophones had previously played the dominant role. This served as the background to the rise of Quebec nationalism, with French language and culture achieving a higher profile and francophones gaining more opportunities in Quebec economic life in particular.

The end result of this transformation was that Montreal began to play a very different role in Canadian society. Whereas it was once a city in which two languages were common but English was the language of business, French was now the dominant language in daily life as well as in business. Not only did few anglophones now move to Quebec cities (and particularly to Montreal, where they had often migrated), but anglophones began leaving Montreal. The city did attract immigrants, but they were largely French-speaking immigrants from places like Morocco, Haiti, Cambodia, and Vietnam. Other urban centres in Quebec were unique, however, in that they attracted few immigrants and became overwhelmingly French-speaking as the result of interprovincial migration.

Montreal has a sterling international reputation because of its thriving urban culture and retains a unique international identity. Yet the city is struggling to find its place in the new international economy in which deindustrialization has removed many of the old pillars of economic strength. Montreal is still highly significant in the Canadian context because it is the second largest city in the country, and it holds that position with considerable advantage over the next largest city, Vancouver. It does demonstrate, though, how a city's place in the urban hierarchy may change as a result of cultural as well as economic factors.

14 Urban Change and Policy Responses in Quebec

Louis Guay and Pierre Hamel

Learning Objectives

- To learn about urbanization trends in Quebec.
- To understand recent changing economic, political, and cultural conditions in Quebec's urban system.
- To appreciate how social actors have adapted to these changes through particular planning decisions.
- To identify new challenges to the urban and territorial system in Quebec.

The city, as one finds it in history, is the point of maximum concentration for power and culture of a community. It is the place where the diffused rays of many separate beams of life fall into focus, with gains in both social effectiveness and significance. The city is the form and symbol of an integrated social relationship: it is the seat of the temple, the market, the hall of justice, the academy of learning. The goods of civilization are multiple and manifold; transformed into viable signs, symbols, patterns of conduct, systems of order (Mumford 1961).

Introduction

Paradoxically, while urbanization was a critical aspect of the modernization of Quebec, the study of the process was neglected by researchers. More attention has been paid to linguistic conflicts, cultural identity controversies, and challenges raised by multiculturalism than to political, economic, and cultural choices made by local, provincial, or federal authorities regarding the way Quebec's cities and the country-side have been planned. It is as if these problems were of secondary concern. Most researchers would tend to agree that the market is the main force in shaping space and territories.

This does not mean that some important studies have not been carried out, including works by historians (Linteau, Durocher, and Robert 1989; Dickinson and Young 1995), geographers (Courville 2000), and architects (Marsan 1994). Socio-political analyses were completed as well in reference to particular issues like housing (Rose 1996), immigration (McNicoll 1993), linguistic issues, and economic development (Levine 1990). In many ways, these studies contributed to a socio-political analysis of urbanization in Quebec. However, they have not been reinterpreted and synthesized to highlight the role of space and urbanization in the modernization of Quebec from a multi-disciplinary perspective.

We do not intend to try to overcome such a shortcoming. Nevertheless, at the outset we would like to take this flaw seriously by bringing to the fore the fact that space in modern Quebec has been not only a reflection of class conflicts and social relations but also a central component of broad social and economic changes. In that respect, recent metropolitan and regional issues cannot be dealt with without taking into account space or the specificity of spatiality in the current situation, inviting us consequently to consider the historical roots of urbanization and the collective choices, planned or unplanned, from which an urban system or order has emerged.

Theoretically, sociology has approached the city in many different ways.

Three broad schools of thought have dominated urban sociology (see Hannigan in this book: chapters 3 and 11). The Chicago School of Sociology was the first to provide a comprehensive understanding of urban areas (Park, Burgess, and McKenzie 1925). Two kinds of factors were at work in producing the form and content of city life: the ecological factors that shape the urban form and the social and cultural factors that distribute people in relatively homogeneous urban sub-areas, or in 'natural areas', to use Park's term. The Chicago School's researchers emphasized this duality, for which they were criticized. Their ecological model led them to value the city centre. The Chicago School was also keen on understanding the city as such, which led one of its members to talk of 'urbanism as a way of life' (Wirth 1938).

Distancing itself from the Chicago school, the second school was more concerned with political and economic forces in the structuring of urban spaces. The city structure was seen as the result of struggles for key positions and locations, defined as resources of consumption or objects of capitalist production. The school couched their analysis in class terms and emphasized the class conflicts in the production of (urban) space, to use Henri Lefebvre's expression. In the 1980s, this political economy perspective gave way to two competing paradigms, post-Fordism and post-modernism. While the post-Fordist researchers tried to situate the crisis of regulation that urban capitalism was facing within an historical perspective, postmodern analysis was mainly concerned with highlighting the cultural diversity emerging in large metropolitan areas in a global context.

While some (Dear 2002) contrast the Chicago School's mode of analysis with the 'Los Angeles School' of urban analysis, the leading representative of the new political economy approach, one must be wary of trying to fit into fixed models the variety of perspectives on city form and its internal dynamics, which must now be defined as urban regions. There is no longer an overarching model but very many different modes of understanding what is happening in urban areas. We propose to call this constellation of modes of analysis the *collective construction of urban space*, where actors and institutions are confronted with very many changes and, in order to respond, develop through cooperation and conflict a common understanding of the situations and select actions and policies in a socially negotiated process. This negotiated process may in some cases be limited to the urban elites or in other cases be less closed and more open to broad public participation (Savitch and Kantor 2002; Stone 2006).

This chapter is divided into four parts. First, we give an overview of Quebec urbanization up to the 1970s in order to highlight the main transformations of the urban system during the first and second waves of industrialization. Second, we focus on what has been going on since the 1970s as Quebec's society and many of its towns and cities have had to deal with deindustrialization and economic restructuring. Other important changes, such as ethnocultural composition and the new urban centrality, will also be discussed. Third, we consider how governments—local, provincial, and federal—respond to conditions that change urban and regional life. We will concentrate, however, on Montreal and Quebec City, obviously the two main urban areas of the province. Fourth, we end with a discussion of new challenges to Quebec's territorial system (Figure 14.1), particularly to its large cities, where a majority of the people live. These challenges are numerous and involve sustainable development as well as new forms of governance and public participation in decision-making.

The Evolution of Urbanization in Quebec

Urbanization under European Influence

The history of city-building in Quebec can be traced back to the beginning of the French colony. Under the French Regime, the settlement was limited to the lower St Lawrence River. Only after the British Conquest in 1760 did its territory expand.

At the end of the French Regime, the population was established along the St Lawrence, concentrated in three main centres, Quebec City, Trois-Rivières, and Montreal. At the outset, these cities were not spaces for production. Their chief functions were defined around trade, religious missions, and territorial control. And their destiny was shaped by European metropolitan centres.

The fur trade, which was the main economic activity along with the fishery, did not require a large European workforce until about 1650, which is one of the principal reasons that the population increased slowly. In the middle of the seventeenth century, the population was estimated at around 1,200 people. Mainly rural, this population settled on both banks of the St Lawrence River before moving upwards along such tributaries as the Richelieu and the Chaudière. In 1760, the largest city, Quebec City, had a population of 8,000 inhabitants. Montreal was half that size, and Trois-Rivières, with less than 800 inhabitants during the French Regime, remained a small administrative town. Added to these three main cities were a few villages responsible for servicing the rural population in their vicinity, but no real urban system existed (Dickinson and Young 1995).

After the British took over the French colony, the demographic characteristics of the population remained much the same, with the lack of immigration from France made up for by a high birth rate. During the pre-industrial period, Canada as a colony was seen mainly by the European metropoles—first Paris and then London—as a provider of natural resources. At the same time, it was a market for manufactured products coming from France and Great Britain.

Urbanization and Industrialization

At the beginning of the nineteenth century, Quebec's economy was still dominated by agricultural and craft production but not for much longer. Up to 1880, the entire society had been in transition towards industrialization as factories progressively replaced workshops. In 1816, craft-based activities were at the heart of the economy, but by 1890 their role appeared to be negligible. These changes were tremendous and had great impacts. The rise of an industrial economy was accompanied by substantial social transformations in both public and private spheres. For instance, between 1851 and 1881, the value of manufactured goods increased from $600,000 to $104 million (Dickinson and Young 1995, 163). The formation of large businesses in the transport sector provided employment to thousands of workers, especially in Montreal, which became the transport hub of Canada. Consumer goods became available to a growing portion of the urban and rural populations.

The second half of the nineteenth century was also marked by the shift from a population predominantly rural to a population predominantly urban. From the crucial year 1915 (Linteau, Durocher, and Robert 1989, 469) the urban population not only outgrew the rural population but has increased steadily up to the present (Table 14.1). It is interesting to note that the province of Quebec urbanized earlier than Ontario or the rest of Canada and by the 1931 census was fully urban—that is, more than half the population lived in a city, whether small or large—at least in a statistical sense. However, Ontario's urbanization advanced more quickly, beginning in 1971, and today Ontario is slightly more urban than Quebec. There was also a small decline in Quebec's urban population during the period 1971 to 2001, a trend that has been observed in other countries, although concluding that there

Table 14.1 Evolution of urbanization in Quebec, Ontario, and Canada as a whole

Year	Quebec % urban	Ontario % urban	Canada % urban
1851	15	14	13
1901	40	43	37
1931	63	53	54
1951	67	71	62
1971	81	82	76
1991	78	82	77
2001	80	85	80

Source: Statistics Canada. 'Recensements du Canada. Population urbaine et rurale, par province et territoire'. www40.statcan.ca/l02/cst01/demo62a_f.htm.

has been a counter-urbanization movement in Quebec is not warranted (Berry 1976; Champion 1989).

The development of the industrial city in the late nineteenth century—and particularly its expansion during the first decades of the twentieth century—modified the urban system. Montreal became the largest city in Canada, with a population of 467,986 in 1911 (Linteau 1992, 160). Almost 33 per cent of the city's workforce was employed in the manufacturing sector. As early as 1881, Montreal and its suburbs were producing 52 per cent of the goods manufactured in Quebec (Dickinson and Young 1995, 175). Simultaneously, the expansion of a service sector transformed urban space with the creation of financial and retail districts. The proximity among different urban functions that prevailed in the pre-industrial city was gradually weakened in favour of an urban organization divided into specialized zones. Moreover, residential areas were developed according to social-class cleavages. Workers lived near factories in small tenements, while the middle and upper classes resided uptown and in suburban communities. The development of large urban areas shaped by social and institutional fragmentation increased throughout the twentieth century. This was particularly the case in Montreal and Quebec City.

However, Montreal's situation differed, in large part owing to its linguistic divisions.

Many smaller cities like Shawinigan, Saint-Hyacinthe, Saint-Jean-sur-Richelieu, Drummondville, Trois-Rivières, and Sherbrooke went through similar transforming processes. Because of the proximity of water power, these cities were key centres of manufacturing, particularly in the textile industry.

Until the end of the nineteenth century, Quebec City remained an important trading and manufacturing centre. With the rise of Montreal as Canada's main financial and industrial metropolis (see Box 14.1), the province's capital lost its diversified economic base. After it was named the capital of the new province of Quebec in 1867, Quebec City became an administrative and political centre.

The relationships between the central city and its suburbs have defined the modern metropolis and its particular spatial organization. In North American cities—including Montreal—central cities have grown through amalgamating suburban communities, a trend that began in the 1870s. Most of these suburban towns faced serious financial difficulties because of their expansionist policies. They could not carry the financial burden linked to urban growth, which required infrastructure-building, forcing many local au-

Box 14.1 Montreal's Main Urbanization Phases

Before 1825
Native settlements
Colonial settlements along the St Lawrence River
Development of three main cities: Quebec City, Trois-Rivières, and Montreal

Between 1825 and 1867
Organization of trade and craftsmanship
Development of transport infrastructures
Implementation of urban services

Between 1867 and 1930
Emergence of industrial activities
Spreading out of economic activities at the metropolitan level
Heyday of Montreal as Canada's metropolis

Between 1930 and the 1950s
Diversification of industrial activities
Expansion of workforce proletarianization
Planning of urban neighbourhoods for workers and their families

Between the 1950s and the 1970s
Demographic growth and urbanization of rural land
Construction of highway network
Construction of first shopping malls
Montreal, the provincial metropolis

The 1970s onward
Deindustrialization
Decline of inner-city neighbourhoods
Definition of policies to counter middle-class exodus towards the periphery

thorities to agree to annexation to the central city. For example, between 1883 and 1918, 23 former cities became part of Montreal (Linteau 1992, 194). However, not all suburban towns agreed to be incorporated within the larger city. Some of them, like Outremont, Westmount, Mount Royal, Verdun, LaSalle, and Lachine—close 'suburbs' of Montreal—chose to remain independent.

During the second half of the nineteenth century, industrialization accelerated the process of urbanization. Between 1870 and 1901, the urban population increased much more rapidly than ever before. Moreover, by expanding the use of modern tools of communication and transportation, such as the railway, telephone, and telegraph, industrialization also contributed to the consolidation of small cities. Consequently, the urban system, which had been structured around one main metropolis, a provincial capital, and a series of small cities dispersed in the plain of

Montreal and in the Eastern Townships, became stronger than before but remained incomplete. However, the urbanization of the peripheral regions—Mauricie, Saguenay–Lac-Saint-Jean, and at the end of the period Abitibi—occurred soon afterward. Between 1897 and 1929 (Linteau, Durocher, and Robert 1989, 470), regional centres like Rimouski and Chicoutimi arose and contributed to the formation of Quebec's present urban system.

Urbanization and the Quiet Revolution

The structure of the Quebec urban system was in place by 1930. However, this does not mean that it ceased to evolve, for change has continued to take place. What occurred after World War II can be described as the reinforcement of a system that had already been entrenched in the social, cultural, and economic reality of Quebec's territory during the first decades of the twentieth century.

It is certainly true that economic, urban, and regional development has not been the same—in terms of growth and dynamism—all over Quebec's territory. Some regions and some municipalities have been more prosperous than others. Nevertheless, at the beginning of the 1960s, because of the institutional reforms initiated by the 'Quiet Revolution', winds of modernization blew over Quebec, and regional equity became a dominant framework for concerns.

The consequences of this structural transformation were numerous. Although it is impossible to review all the initiatives taken by the government of Quebec at that time to improve the quality of public services and public governance, at least two aspects should be underlined. First, one of the main objectives of the Quiet Revolution was to enhance the life conditions and administrative capabilities of regions to make them more competitive on a Canadian and continental scale. It was therefore necessary to improve public infrastructures and public utilities. Consequently, the government launched several programs to finance the building or renovation

of transport infrastructure such as motorways, harbours, and airports. Other investments went into the creation of industrial parks. In fact, public investments were made in different sectors, especially in education and the health care system in which Quebec's relative backwardness in comparison to some other Canadian provinces, especially Ontario, was well documented.

The second aspect has to do with urban and regional planning. The municipal system in place and the tools available to planners to cope with spatial and economic change appeared outdated. The planners convinced the decision-makers to initiate a vast reform of the municipal system and to create planning institutions that would give local authorities resources and legitimacy to intervene on the local and regional scenes. To this end, the Conseil d'orientation économique du Québec was reactivated, leading to the creation of the Office de planification et de développement du Québec a few years later. Subsequently the Quebec government decided to create administrative regions—10 were established in 1968, and 13 now cover southern Quebec (Figure 14.1)—giving these regions a political recognition they did not have before. Such an institutional innovation introduced a new dynamic with the provincial system, between the representatives of these regions and the government, between the regions themselves, and between the regions and Montreal as the metropolis of Quebec.

At the beginning of the 1970s, the federal government sponsored a study of the Montreal region. The report (Higgins, Martin, and Raynauld 1970) recommended an interventionist economic development strategy. The primary argument was that to reinforce the regional development of the whole territory of Quebec, it was imperative to reinforce Montreal's economy. This thesis stemmed from two observations. First, Montreal was the only development pole in Quebec. A development pole is a large urban area comprising a diversity of economic activities, particularly tertiary dynamic activities like engineering, accounting, and marketing services

Figure 14.1 Quebec's Census Metropolitan Areas (CMAs) and Administrative Regions, 1996

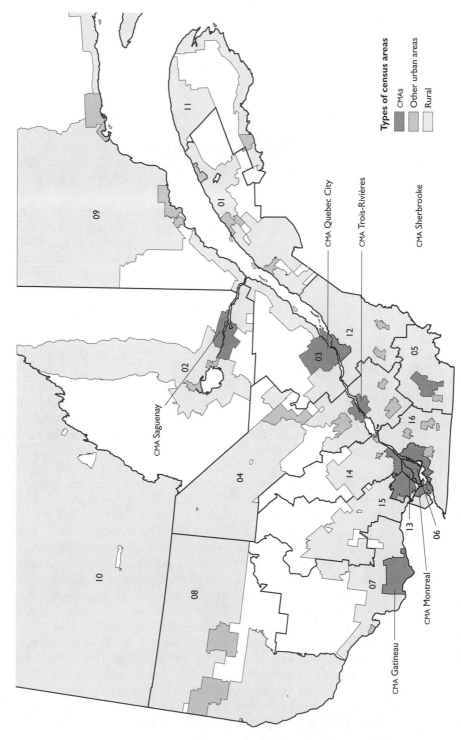

Types of census areas
- CMAs
- Other urban areas
- Rural

CMA Quebec City

CMA Trois-Rivières

CMA Sherbrooke

CMA Saguenay

CMA Gatineau

CMA Montreal

Source: Mapped by Martin Vachon.

for businesses, universities, research centres, and international firms. Second, as a development pole, the dynamism of Montreal was not strong enough to enable it to compete internationally, not to mention with a growing Toronto. Consequently, it was necessary to focus on the industrial and economic infrastructure of Montreal, not only to spark the economy of Montreal but also to improve the situation in all of Quebec through trickle-down effects. In other words, investing in the Montreal region meant that every region of Quebec would benefit.

Such a perspective was in complete opposition to the one developed by the leaders of the Quiet Revolution, who were more interested in reducing regional disparities than in understanding the changing relationships between regions and the unique characteristics and role of the Montreal region within Quebec society. From then on, a major conflict between Montreal and the regions in modern Quebec would surface at both the administrative and the political level.

Recent Factors in Quebec's Urban Transformation

Deindustrialization and Urban Restructuring

At about the same time that Quebec was modernizing and building a strong provincial state, further economic transformations were occurring. There is no better place to observe this than in Montreal. Lamonde and Martineau (1992) have studied the deindustrialization of Montreal's economy during the 1970s, which speeded up a decade later (Coffey and Polèse 1993; 2000). This economic transformation is not unique to Quebec's largest city, for many North American cities, as Lamonde and Martineau showed, have gone through the same process of structural economic change. At work were forces of *creative destruction*, to use Schumpeter's celebrated expression for describing how technological innovations can drastically change industrial systems. Schumpet-

er's conception captures two different processes: creative destruction is brought about on the one hand by a higher level of economic competition as a result of enlarging markets and opportunities and on the other hand by the industrial impacts of technological innovation. This second process may be more accurately named *destructive creation*, for destruction followed the creation and application of new ideas, whereas in the former process, competition may rely on very few, if any, new technological ideas. Montreal's phase of deindustrialization was characterized by intense international competition and opening of new markets but at the same time by an opening of domestic markets to foreign and Third World agricultural and manufactured products. As old industries closed, a new type of economy emerged. Montreal's economy suffered during the 1980s, and it took more than a decade to rebound (Tellier 1997; Manzagol 1998; Martin 1998; Germain and Rose 2000, ch. 5; Collin 2003).

The wave of **deindustrialization** was felt all along the urban hierarchy. Middle-sized towns like Sherbrooke, Trois-Rivières, Shawinigan, and many others, which had industrialized during the twentieth century based on natural resources, energy, and light or heavy industries, experienced similar difficulties. Trois-Rivières, for instance, which because of its pulp and paper production had relatively high wage levels, lost a great many of its high-paying jobs owing to the restructuring of its pulp and paper industry and to the closing of its textile and clothing plants. It thus appears that despite a relatively late industrial modernization, the same factors that forced many industrial cities to change were at work in Quebec's larger towns and cities. There has been, starting around 1960, a diffusion process of economic development over a larger and larger geographic zone.

Polèse and Roy (1999) have shown how the Montreal region lost, relatively speaking, to other regions, mainly to the Quebec City region and middle Quebec (encompassing secondary urban nodes such as Sherbrooke, Drummondville, and Trois-Rivières) in terms of economic activities and employment between 1960 and 1980. This meant that these regions grew more rapidly in economic activity than Montreal did. Despite this, all old industrial towns and cities were hit by international competition and the need to modernize their industrial technologies or radically change their economic basis. Of the industries that survived this modernization process, some, like the pulp and paper industry with help from the government, grew stronger, but others just disappeared from the industrial and urban landscape.

The consequence of this process was that cities were often left with vacant urban land and derelict neighbourhoods. This truly was a process of creating urban destruction. Municipalities had to respond to such a change. It was no longer enough to respond to accelerated urbanization; they also had to plan for revitalization of important parts of urban areas.

Suburbanization

A second change in large urban areas marked the period 1970–90. After World War II, Quebec's urbanization continued. Montreal was a city of just over a million people in 1951 and grew, as an urban region, to more than 3 million by the turn of the century. Quebec City, which had been a provincial town, became a respectable city in demographic terms during the same period. Its urbanized region is now close to 700,000 inhabitants (Table 14.1). However, if large towns increased in size, it was not by a process of densification. Like so many North American cities, suburbanization characterized this spatial and demographic change. But after *suburbanization* came *ex-urbanization*, or *counter-urbanization*, both of which describe how population grew rapidly at the periphery of large cities in smaller centres (Berry 1976; Champion 1989; Bourne 2001). People tended to move not only within close range of old urban cores but farther from these cores, though not so far away that they could not enjoy the economic and cultural benefits of a large city. Old central cities were struck by the successive changes. They lost in population, absolutely

as well as relatively, and they had to counter the trend, building on a change in attitude towards urban centrality (Germain and Rose 2000).

Suburbanization occurred first as a matter of sheer change in population size. The Montreal metropolitan area more than tripled in population size between 1951 and 1991, and the additional 2 million people had to find space in which to live. Old structures die slowly: the urban fabric could not be transformed at such a demographic pace. Second, people still valued space-consuming individual houses surrounded by small gardens, as Divay and Gaudreault have shown (1984). Third, government transport and housing policies helped to bring about this urban extension, or sprawl. These policies all favoured the private car and the construction of motorways, even close to large town centres. Quebec City, for example, is surrounded by a large motorway system that links it to the rest of the province, resulting in 21.4 kilometres of expressways per 100,000 inhabitants, compared to 8.8 kilometres per 100,000 in Montreal, and 7 kilometres per 100,000 in Toronto (Vandersmissen and Villeneuve 2001, 216, 240 n. 1). The urban renewal projects of the 1960s provided for penetration of large expressways into the city centre to get people in and out rapidly. Fortunately, these projects were never fully developed, and some expressways had to be completely redesigned in the 1990s, transformed into urban boulevards, although not all such projects have been carried to completion. Fourth, the cost of urban land for business as well as for houses was much lower in the periphery than in the central city. Moreover, derelict neighbourhoods and vacated or degraded urban land contribute nothing to the image of a business and have no appeal for prospective residents. Fifth, the telecommunications revolution helped businesses to move outward and resettle some of their activities. But again, except for a few cases, business at distance was, and still is, not the preferred choice of many employers (Polèse and Shearmur 2002). They prefer close contacts and proximity to a large urban area. This means that the area around Montreal has become more and more urbanized, expanding northward up to Saint-Jérôme and Mirabel and southward to Chambly. Eastward and westward, the spatial expansion is clearly visible. Small and medium-sized towns are gradually coming into the orbit of metropolitan Montreal. Quebec City is experiencing a similar process, although on a smaller scale. Finally, there seems to be a strong preference among the population for a suburban or even ex-urban environment. In comparing data for the late 1970s with the findings of a recent poll, Fortin and Bédard (2003) show that Montrealers value more low-density and suburban environments to high-density and central city environments. This finding indicates how difficult it would be for planners and urban administrations to reverse a long-term trend and change deep-seated preferences. It may even shatter urban professionals' dream of planning for compact cities (Canada 1996; Paehlke 1993; Alexander 2000; Sénécal and Hamel 2001).

Ethnocultural Change

The final consideration is the ethnocultural composition of Quebec's population, although this is a factor primarily in Montreal. Montreal has always been a port of entry, or gateway, and a choice of residence for waves of immigrants. In the twentieth century, eastern and southern Europeans came to settle in its central neighbourhoods. Their economic and social integration, mobility, and residential choice followed those of their particular economic group: Jewish Montrealers (who formed a large part of eastern European immigration) and Italian and Greek Montrealers moved out of central neighbourhoods to locate in middle-class and suburban areas, although members of each ethnocultural community (defined by a common language, religion, or geographic origin) tended to remain close to one another, forming suburban cultural areas (Guay 1978; Drouilly 1996; Renaud, Mayer, and Lebeau 1996). Starting in the 1970s, countries from which Canada recruited im-

migrants changed sharply (Ley 1999; Ley and Hiebert 2001). Montreal became host to people from Latin American countries and from Asia and Africa (see Box 14.2). New immigrants tend to concentrate in the central city, with pockets of residential choice in the suburbs (Renaud, Mayer, and Lebeau 1996; Germain 2002; Charbonneau and Germain 2002). Public services, including municipal services, had to adapt to this changing social and cultural composition. Although Montreal (20.6 per cent in 2006) holds in proportion today far fewer immigrant residents than Toronto (45.7 per cent) or Vancouver (39.6 per cent), a little less than Calgary (23.6 per cent), and a little more than Edmonton (18.5 per cent) and Ottawa-Gatineau (18.1 per cent), it is still an important centre of immigration in Canada and has, for most of its recent past, been by far the principal centre in Quebec with between 85 and 90 per cent of the province's foreign-born residents (Germain 1997, 247). The immigrant population of other Quebec CMAs is very small (Quebec City, 3.7 per cent; Sherbrooke, 5.6 per cent; Trois-Rivières, 2.2 per cent), which puts Montreal in a different ethnocultural category than the rest of the province (Table 14.2). Larger cities with their stronger and more diversified economies may explain this contrasting phenomenon. Also, with immigration there may be a path-dependent social process: a city that has been opened to immigrants in the past is more likely to open its door to further immigration, because previous immigrants may help new immigrants to adapt to new conditions and the host society, while maintaining their own identity, by providing them with jobs, social, religious, and linguistic services, and a community that may ease the transition process.

Consequences of These Changes

These changes are not without consequences to central city life and decision-making. Despite a relatively strong process of gentrification in Montreal and Quebec City, and to a lesser extent in middle-sized towns, Quebec's main central cit-

Box 14.2 *Ethnocultural Change in Montreal*

Montreal has always been a city of socio-cultural diversity. On a background of anglophone and francophone differentiations move patches of ethnocultural colours. Before the waves of immigration starting in the second part of the nineteenth century and accelerating in the twentieth century, Montreal had some cultural diversity: small groups of Amerindians and blacks cohabited with French settlers (Germain and Rose 2000, 216). After the Conquest, Montreal's population gradually became of British Isles origin. The strong Irish immigration of the 1815–50 period, which took place when industrialization began to take hold in Montreal and its economy, accelerated this process. Immigration over the past 100 years has changed Montreal's ethnocultural composition regularly. Up to the beginning of the twentieth century, Montreal's socio-cultural diversity was primarily linguistic, and its inhabitants were either of British or French origin. The first wave of non-British and non-French immigration came from eastern Europe, made up of people fleeing poverty or political and religious persecution, although there were small communities of Italian and Chinese immigrants before the twentieth century.

After World War II, Montreal, like some other Canadian cities, was host to succeeding waves of immigration. Southern Europeans—mostly Italians and Greeks—came first. They were followed by people from Central and South America in the 1970s and by immigrants from Asia and Africa in the 1980s and 1990s. In the 1970s, a significant community of Jewish Moroccans chose Montreal as their place of residence. Since they spoke French, they could continue to live in their own language in Montreal. A Haitian community and a small Southeast Asian group of Vietnamese and Cambodians came in the 1970s and 1980s, again because of the French language. Although there is a small community of Jamaicans in Montreal, most Jamaicans chose to immigrate to the Toronto area. In the past many, if not all, immigrants chose the English system of education for their children, but the adoption of 'Bill 101' in 1977 made it mandatory, with some exceptions, for immigrants' children to attend French primary and secondary schools.

Immigrants do not select their neighbourhoods at random. The Chicago School sociologists had observed that immigrants tend to concentrate in a small number of urban areas. This has long been the case in Montreal. Successive waves of immigrants settled along St Laurent Boulevard, the physical and symbolic line dividing French- and English-speaking Montrealers. This area was the most heterogeneous part of the city. As immigrants moved up on the socio-economic scale, they, or their children, moved out of this 'port of entry' zone. For instance, eastern European Jews moved west, deep into the anglophone neighbourhoods of Montreal, whereas most residents of Italian origin moved east into the French-speaking part (Drouilly 1996, 120–1, 124–5). Finally, although they concentrated in the central parts of the city, new immigrants tended to choose a greater variety of neighbourhoods. As Charbonneau and Germain (2002) have observed, suburbs of immigrants are now found on the south shore of the St Lawrence River and in the city of Laval.

Over the past few years, immigration has raised new concerns as it seems more and more difficult for Quebec society to retain the newcomers. This problem is mainly related to the difficulty immigrants face in integrating into the job market. Recent (arriving between 1996 and 2001) and most recent (arriving between 2001 and 2006) immigrants experience an unemployment rate two to four times higher than that of Quebeckers born in Canada. For those who immigrated less than five years ago, the unemployment rate is 17 per cent. For the North Africans

(Maghrébins), it is even higher—up to 27 per cent (Statistics Canada 2006). That is why the Quebec government decided in April 2008 to take action to help immigrants find a way of integrating into the job market. Over the next three years, $68 million is to be invested—through specific measures—in facilitating social integration of immigrants, beginning with employment.

The stakes are very high. Between now and 2010–11, Quebec will have to fill 700,000 jobs, and a large proportion of these jobs will necessarily have to be occupied by immigrants living within the Montreal city-region.

ies have continued to lose population or at least have not recovered from past losses (Germain and Rose 2000). Many of the changes mean that central city municipalities (the political and administrative cities of Montreal and Quebec, in particular) face significant financial problems. The middle classes have fled to the suburbs and ex-urbs, and apart from a very small group of rich people, the central city is occupied mainly by less well-off city dwellers. Although the central city administration may extract high taxes on their land values from commercial, institutional, and services activities, there is a limit to what they can contribute to municipal budgets. The central city remains much poorer, and with aging infrastructure, than surrounding areas (Renaud, Mayer, and Lebeau 1996; Drouilly 1996). Also, immigrants tend to settle in central neighbourhoods where they can find affordable housing and perhaps the cultural associations that may help them to find a job and integrate into the wider society. They clearly contribute to the city's physical renewal, although their incomes tend to be lower than those of the groups who have resided in the city for a longer period of time. Moreover, this relatively poorer population also has to deal with older urban infrastructure and higher costs of maintenance. This situation helps to explain the wave of municipal **amalgamations**, or 'fusions', that the provincial government decided to impose on Quebec's largest urban areas in 2000 (Collin 2002), a process that has also been occurring elsewhere in Canada (Sancton 2000).

Urban Consolidation and Policy Choices

No city of substance exists without planned intervention by some public authority. The life and economy of a city need to be co-ordinated differently from the way they are in small towns, villages, and rural settlements. Ancient urban history shows how urban life co-emerged with political authority, or the state (Weber 1958; Mumford 1961). Urban states had to have some form of policy. This policy may have included regulating public festivities and economic exchanges or protecting against crime or foes. It could also include developing plans for public or state buildings. The central area of the city might have been the main interest of urban governments, but they could not totally ignore the other areas, particularly when it came to the main lines of communication, to moving people and goods, armies, functionaries, and ruling classes in and out of town. So city life engenders an urban policy.

Administrative and Political Reform

There is, of course, no unique central city policy determined by a provincial government or even designed by each municipality. Although municipalities are the 'creation' of provincial governments, they are not a provincial government administrative unit. People elect their representatives, who can levy taxes and charge fees for urban services. Second, there is a strong, legitimate autonomy among municipal mayors and city councillors. It took almost 40 years of debate and negotiation to arrive at the creation of large, integrated, and merged municipal governments (the merged cities of regional towns, such as Trois-Rivières, Sherbrooke, and Saguenay, and the two megacities of Montreal and Quebec). Even though many newly merged suburban municipalities do not accept this state of affairs, hoping that future referendums will turn the clock back, large urban entities seem to work satisfactorily. However, one does not need a well thought out and long-term plan or policy to intervene in order to deal with urban problems. Between 1979 and 2001, Quebec's municipalities regrouped in new administrative and political structures called *urban communities* (for Montreal, Quebec, and Hull-Gatineau) or MRCS (*municipalités régionales de comté*) for all the other municipalities—there were more than 1,600 municipalities at the beginning of this reform—and these amalgamated municipalities had strong obligations to plan the development of their own territories (Baccigalupo 1990). The Loi d'aménagement et d'urbanisme (the first comprehensive and effective local planning Act in Quebec, also called Loi 125) gives powers to municipal authorities to adopt a broad policy of urban land use and planning. The legislation provides them with traditional, but now compulsory, planning tools (*Schéma d'aménagement* at the regional level and *Plan d'urbanisme* at the local level), which are not always used effectively (Guay 2002). Some use this planning tool to comply with provincial regulations, others to do much more forward-looking planning for their own municipalities. In a fine and replicated study of regional planning, Fortin and Parent (1983; 1985) have distinguished two types of regional authorities: participatory and technocratic; the choice of words may be debatable, but the two contrasting expressions are meaningful. The former have developed a strong sense of local 'empowerment' and have experimented with public participation practices, whereas the latter tend to stick to the rules and do what the law asks them to do.

Obviously, depending on their financial resources and their political determination, municipalities have a large part to play in development and land-use planning. They have reacted differently to the changes that confronted them in the 1970s and 1980s. However, some trends and similarities in the decisions and policies are clearly discernible.

Planning Decisions

Heavily hit by economic restructuring, large urban areas had to embark on the new **knowledge economy**. Montreal, Quebec City, and large (in demographic and spatial terms) suburbs of Montreal, like Laval, invested (often using provincial grant programs) in the new service- and knowledge-based economy (Doloreux 1999). The *Cité du Multimédia* (an economic area specializing in the new economy of information technology and its applications) and the *Quartier international* (an area and agencies for promoting the internationalization of Montreal's economy) came into existence in old neighbourhoods of Montreal, downtown and close to the Lachine Canal, that had been deeply downgraded by industrial closures and loss of economic activity (Choko 2002; Poitras 2002). In Quebec City, the Saint-Roch area had lost population, commercial activity, prestige, and the interest of local developers (Mercier 2002; 2003). City hall had developed many plans to revitalize this area of the *Basse-ville* (below the promontory on which the historical, tourist, and administrative functions of Quebec are located), which has had a troubling and controversial history (Hulbert 1994). Grand plans for injecting new life into the area had been conceived by a municipal party (Parti civique) and its planners. But local citizens and citizens' committees were opposed to what they perceived as a *politique de grandeur*. They had an alternative. Since Saint-Roch had previously been a thriving working-class and residential neighbourhood and a strong commercial area for the whole city as well as for local residents, they wanted it to more or less regain its 'past glory'. Instead of high-rise buildings catering to tourism, administrative functions, and better-off people, they proposed lower-density, cooperative, and social housing and, in general, that Saint-Roch should remain a neighbourhood inhabited by local people. A new municipal party (le Rassemblement populaire) took over in 1989 and brushed aside the grand plans. However, it took the new administration many years to bring about the 'renaissance' of Saint-Roch (see Box 14.3). Timely municipal investments (such as an urban park), good cooperation with Quebec City's institutional decision-makers (like the Université du Québec and its subdivisions), and close contacts with the provincial government to convince them that what had been provided to Montreal could also be done for Quebec (investing in the new technologies of information and communications) resulted in a remarkable urban revitalization job. It was accompanied by some planning decisions that helped to change the negative image of the whole area and conferred on it a new modern image, which now attracts young people, families, and professionals. However, there was also some 'social creative destruction', which poses an ethical problem for planners: the area had gradually been occupied, physically and symbolically, by low-income people, the homeless, and people on social benefits who have been displaced as a result of planning decisions favouring new businesses and new, younger, and better-off residents. This new urban dynamic in central Quebec City (namely, *La Cité arrondissement*) has been called an 'urban renaissance' (Villeneuve and Trudelle 2008).

Cities' capacity and power to bring about economic restructuring are limited. Municipal administrations cannot decree when new information and communication technology firms will emerge and where they will locate. They can only help them to choose desirable locations by offering them fiscal incentives and a physical environment that will attract and retain the best employees. But—perhaps more in Quebec City than in Montreal—municipal initiatives place pressure on firms' and institutional decisions.

In Montreal, economic actors are much more diversified, so location decisions are highly disseminated. Although a wealth of reports on Montreal's economic decline have appeared (Higgins 1986; Sénécal 1997; Hamel and Poitras 2004) and the economic elite remains deeply concerned about the city's future, its final demise has not been written. Although the city took a beating in the 1980s as a result of the recession, anglophone emigration, and an old industrial structure still too concentrated in clothing, textiles, and light industries, it has recently rejuvenated, and housing prices and construction are on the rise, a good indication of its new attractiveness to investment and to people. New economic sectors—aeronautics and aerospace, telecommunications equipment, pharmaceuticals and biotechnology, microelectronics—have prospered, and the region can now offer high-tech and high-paid jobs (Germain and Rose 2000, 133–44). It can build its long-term strength on four universities, private research and development facilities, a better-educated labour force, and closer links between public and private actors, although on some crucial economic indicators (average income per capita, high-tech professional services, and patents per person) Montreal still lags behind other North American cities, such as Boston and Seattle but also Ottawa and Calgary (Polèse and Shearmur 2004, 11–13, 19).

Urban authorities and municipal administrations can influence economic decision-making through investments in urban infrastructures. A city with a good communication systems, an airport, good and not too expensive public transport, clean parks and streets, and a low rate of crime can play on these characteristics to attract investments and people (Rondinelli 2001)—even more so when large cities compete not only in the national arena but increasingly in the world arena as well. World-city theorists (Friedmann, Hall, Sassen, and Castells, for instance) have all emphasized the new global context: a few cities are truly global cities, but many more will have to take the global context into account when planning their development. Montreal aspires

Box 14.3 *Revitalization of an Urban Neighbourhood*: *The Case of Saint-Roch in Quebec City*

Saint-Roch is located in what Quebec City residents called la Basse-ville, in opposition, geographically as well as socially, to la Haute-ville. La Basse-ville has traditionally been a working-class and industrial area. By contrast, la Haute-ville is middle-class, particularly outside the walls. The administrative functions of the provincial government are largely concentrated in la Haute-ville, although some decentralization was achieved by the provincial government in the 1970s and 1980s. La Haute-ville is also the prime tourist destination, chiefly because of Old Quebec.

Saint-Roch has experienced a fluctuating history (Morisset 2001). The main industrial centre of the region for a long period (from 1880 up to World War II), it declined rapidly in the second part of the twentieth century. The decline was economic, demographic, and physical. People who remained in the neighbourhood were captive: less well-off, they were unable to move to the suburbs.

Urban planning in Saint-Roch since 1969 can be divided into two stages (Mercier 2002). The first (1969–89) was governed by old urban renewal policies: a strong intervention by local authorities, an effort to attract private developers and residents, grand plans for high-rise buildings, the demolition of old housing and commercial and industrial stock. This planning policy was highly controversial. Urban social movements emerged to confront city hall and the planners. The second stage (from 1990 to the present) started with a change of municipal government in 1989. The new administration put a stop to previous grand plans, established close links with urban movements, and became involved in participatory planning, setting up consultation processes on urban change and projects. Many projects were on a small scale. The municipality helped local residents to change their environment and improve the quality of urban life. The residents worked independently on improving their own environment, such as establishing the community garden l'îlot fleuri (Mercier 1999). But the planners felt that they needed larger developments if the area were to be revitalized, so they pursued a policy of attracting public institutions and the new economy. Meanwhile, they had their own ideas and projects for the area. The Saint-Roch mall, which had been an subject of controversy (derided as an example of 1960s planning) in the architecture and planning professions, was radically transformed; an urban park was designed; streets and alleys were improved; private owners renovated their own properties; and new institutional buildings were constructed, with some care given to architecture and urban integration—all in order to change the area's negative image.

Owing to a large extent to municipal interventions and policies, Saint-Roch is in the process of gentrification, which is already well advanced. The urban landscape has changed dramatically. No longer is the area almost deserted and negatively perceived by non-residents: it has a thriving business (high-tech) sector and a growing residential area. Some residents who occupied the neighbourhood during most of its decline can no longer afford to live in Saint-Roch, and if the gentrification process continues, they will eventually leave it entirely.

to lead the battle of the global economy for all of Quebec, even though some regions may not need to ship goods and services internationally (Polèse and Shearmur 2002).

Central city policies also have concentrated on more urban design projects. A highly degraded built or 'natural' environment does not project an image of economic strength and social vitality.

These policies are designed to erase urban blight and modernize the central city's features. City administrations first had to 'fill the gaps' left by old industrial and housing structures. For some time, parts of the central city of Montreal have been vacant and used for car parks. Old buildings had to be replaced by new ones, and a quiet, though difficult, policy of revitalization as practised in Quebec City can bear long-term fruit. Some old buildings are worth preserving. An urban heritage policy, again benefiting from provincial money and programs, has been a declared objective of urban renewal in many Quebec cities, not only major ones like Montreal and Quebec City but also smaller towns. Heritage buildings, houses, industrial plants, and commercial shops are restored and given new functions, such as sites for regional history or art museums.

However, cities have learned that to attract younger and more educated people to live in central neighbourhoods, they have to offer them something that the suburbs cannot: a city life—and an art life in particular. This called for an urban cultural policy. For example, Quebec City, often in partnership with private investors, has invested a great deal in making its town centre a place where artists will locate and establish their studios. Combined with new cultural buildings (the municipal library in Quebec City and the Grande bibliothèque in Montreal, for instance), this policy reaffirmed central city rights on culture and cultural activities (Laperrière and Latouche 2002).

Urban design for new as well as old structures has also been an important practice in urban planning and revitalization (Piché 1991). After World War II, much urban planning was functional, oriented by economic development, obsessed with the rapid transportation of people and goods and with city accommodation to cars, with little consideration for protecting the urban heritage and historical landmarks, not to mention old neighbourhoods and their people. Urban design was rediscovered in the 1980s as a tool in planning and came to guide some urban interventions. Recently

in Quebec City, two urban expressways were redesigned as urban boulevards. Cities became more concerned with urban squares, the design and creation of small parks, and programs to embellish streets and shops in secondary commercial areas. Urban landscapes are gradually changing for the better, and planning and architecture schools now integrate greater concern for urban design criteria into planning practices.

Cities' Needs and Resources

The past two decades have not been easy for municipal finances. Municipalities and the provincial government negotiated a 'new deal' for sharing power, responsibilities, and resources. The so-called Ryan Reform (1992) has tried to establish a new contract between municipalities and the provincial government. Responsibilities were devolved to the municipalities in exchange for greater financial resources. However, this reform was not always well received and perceived by local authorities. They saw in the fiscal reform a downloading of responsibilities to the local level in order to ease the fiscal problems of higher-level governments. When the federal government, followed by some and eventually by all provincial governments, decided to eliminate the deficit and reduce its debt, many people felt that the 'buck' was being passed down. Municipalities were hard hit by the need to limit public spending. They had their own problems and sensed that the door was shut to their concerns. However, even though public spending was reduced over the past 10 years or so, large cities benefited from provincial and federal programs. A long period of central-city decline was followed by a recent period of growth. But large cities had to control their own finances more closely. Partnerships with private and local non-governmental organizations (NGOs) were struck, in part for job creation and in part for the provision of social and community services to people in need (Fontan et al. 2003). Recently, large cities have signed contracts with the provincial government, predominantly regarding investment in central cities and mainly for large infrastructure. The Liberal government has decided to accelerate the investment and infrastructure program because of the current economic situation. This strategy of contracting with higher tiers of government can open new ground for improving the relationships between local governments and the federal and provincial governments. Large cities are desperately in need of major infrastructure repair and change—a recent report by the Bureau des audiences publiques sur l'environnement (BAPE), which examined water problems in the province in preparation for a new provincial water policy, found that up to 20 per cent of clean water provided to city dwellers in some municipalities is lost through leaks in the water system (BAPE 2000). One can understand, then, why a group of large-city mayors has begun to press the federal government for immediate action and for expenditures in large urban areas. A federal prime ministerial task force has explored this avenue (Task Force 2002; Wolfe 2003), although there may be strong opposition from provincial governments, who are fiercely protective of their own prerogatives.

Challenges Ahead

Urbanization is a multi-faceted process of change. Large urban areas have always been engines of economic change, but they were also engines of social change. Paul Bairoch (1995, ch. 20), in his monumental history of cities and the economy, emphasized the capacity of cities and of large cities in particular for technological innovation. Based on the best data he could gather, he linked city size and urban life to technological innovation, although this relationship is weakening with the diffusion of the urban way of life. Why are cities the breeding ground for innovation? In essence, according to Bairoch, they diffuse new ideas more quickly, and through their own cultural, scientific, and educational activities and facilities, their population is more open to innovation. Peter Hall (1998), in *Cities in Civilization*,

shows how cities have contributed to the progress of ideas and their application to arts, government, industry, and ways of life. Canada's population continues to urbanize; the urban way of life has certainly diffused across vast spaces, but only up to a point. A recent study of moral traditionalism (a complex index of attitudes and values) by Turcotte (2001) shows that the cores of large urban regions are more tolerant of pluralistic and socially liberal values, while suburbs and urban peripheries are more like small towns and rural regions in this respect. This gives some support to the thesis that large urban areas are not only different from other inhabited areas but also harbour different urban cultures, not just one (Fischer 1984).

The population geography of Quebec is still in the process of *metropolitan concentration* in which the western part of the province is taking the lion's share of what Tellier (2003) calls 'topodynamics': the process of long-term and inevitable spatial change whereby population concentration and economic activities tend to move westward, creating poles or nodes of intense economic and social development. Some of the fastest-growing urban areas (CMAs and CAs [census areas]) are located around Montreal or in the southeast region of Montreal and in western Quebec. The fastest-growing CMAs (2001–2006) are Montreal (5.3 per cent), Gatineau (6.8 per cent), and Sherbrooke (6.8 per cent), which are expanding faster than the Quebec population as a whole (4.3 per cent) (Table 14.2). Except for Saint-Georges (some 130 kilometres south of Quebec City), the fastest-growing CAs are located fairly close to the main metropolitan area (Table 14.4). On the other hand, some resource-dependent regional towns are declining rapidly or are stagnating (Alma, Val-d'Or, Rouyn-Noranda). Jobs and economic opportunities are the main factors explaining this westward and metropolitan concentration of population in Quebec, despite (in some cases) relatively high local median family incomes, such as in Val-d'Or and Rouyn-Noranda, two traditional mining and forestry

Table 14.2 Quebec's Census Metropolitan Areas (CMAs)

CMA	Population 2006	% change 2001–2006	% Immigrants (2006)	Median family income (2005) ($)
Montreal	3,635,571	5.3	20.6	58,600
Quebec	715,515	4.2	3.7	65,299
Gatineau	242,124	6.8	8.7	68,500
Sherbrooke	186,952	6.3	5.6	56,403
Saguenay	151,643	-2.1	1.8	58,542
Trois-Rivieres	141,529	2.9	2.2	55,461

Source: Adapted from Statistics Canada. 'Profils des communautés, 2006. Régions métropolitaines de recensement'. www12.statcan.ca/english/english/census06/data/profiles/community.

towns. But there are other reasons as well. In a comprehensive study of why young people leave their regions for large urban areas, Gauthier and her colleagues attribute this regional exodus to social, personal, and educational factors, even though the young remain attached to their region of origin (Gauthier 2003). Education is a strong force in territorial mobility: to further their education at university or technical and professional colleges, the young have to leave the area where their family and relatives live. All this creates a tension between large cities and regions in Quebec's political economy, which goes a long way towards explaining the frequent changes in regional policies and structures and the need for a rural policy (*politique de la ruralité*) (Dugas 2003; Jean 2003; Vachon 2003).

Table 14.3 Quebec's Metropolitan Concentration, 2006

Population of Quebec	7,546,131
Population of CMAs	5,073,334
Population of non-CMAs	2,472,797
CMAs/total population	67.2 %
Montreal CMA/total population	48.2 %
Montreal CMA/all CMAs	71.7%

Source: Adapted from Statistics Canada. 'Profils des communautés, 2006. Régions métropolitaines de recensement'. www12.statcan.ca/english/english/census06/data/profiles/community.

Contrasting spatial, economic, and demographic evolution is only one of the challenges cities and regions face in the coming years. Others pertain to changes in urban life, governing structure, planning, and the environment. Several of these important challenges are outlined below.

1. In 2002, a number of newly merged large cities were established. The integration has been highly contested, and the election campaign leading to the choice of mayors and councillors was largely fought, in Montreal and Quebec City in particular, over the problem of *défusion* (de-merging) and whether a new provincial government would allow the merged municipalities, if they wished, to return to their previous autonomous status (Belley 2003; Sancton 2004). Ahead lurks a difficult period of uncertainty and mutual adjustment. Despite the wish of some still-opposed 'municipalities', the former municipal structure is gone. Several factors militate against its being reinstated. First, Quebec contains, comparatively speaking, a large number of municipalities, most of them small—i.e., of less than 10,000 inhabitants. Second, the provincial government has allowed referendums on de-merging, but the conditions for winning were stricter than expected. Montreal's West Island decided to de-merge, but only one city in the Quebec

Table 14.4 Regional Cities (Census Areas: Top Tier)

Census Areas	Population	% change 2001–2006	Median family income 2005 ($)
St-Jean-sur-Richelieu	87,492	9.9	60,668
Drummondville	78,108	7.3	53,518
Granby	68,352	8.4	57,755
Saint-Hyacynthe	55,823	2.9	56,683
Shawinigan	51,904	-0.3	48,747
Victoriaville	48,893	4.2	54,203
Sorel-Tracy	48,295	1.0	56,598
Rimouski	46,807	1.7	58,613
Joliette	43,595	9.8	53,005
Rouyn-Noranda	39,924	0.8	58,357
Salaberry-Valleyfield	39,672	1.7	55,952
Alma	32,603	-1.0	57,907
Saint-Georges	31,364	5.4	57,368
Val-d'Or	31,123	-1.0	60,371

Source: Adapted from Statistics Canada. 'Profils des communautés, 2006. Régions métropolitaines de recensement'. www12.statcan.ca/english/english/census06/data/profiles/community.

City region voted in favour of returning to its previous structure. Third, many mayors and municipal councillors are deeply involved in having their merged municipality work 'for the good of all residents'. Finally, urban politics in this new context and in the context of the greater importance and role devolved to large urban areas may become a more interesting and promising ground for governance, democracy, and fiscal equity (for the Metropolitan Community of Montreal, see Le Blanc 2006, 140–47). Cities like Quebec and Montreal, as well as the MRCs, have had some experience in public consultation and participation in urban affairs (Simard 2001; Hamel 1999). Whether more autonomous and newly merged cities would promote innovative forms of urban governance remains to be seen.

2. City governments, in view of their cities' changing social (notably an aging popula-

tion) and ethnocultural composition, will have to devise policies to solve new problems of integration and citizenship. The police, the school system, and social services will continue to provide for a more diversified urban population. Montreal is and will remain the experimental ground for innovative policies on social cohesion and citizen integration in Quebec's polity.

3. One consequence of metropolitan concentration will be the gradual loss of power and influence of depopulated rural and resource-dependent regions in the northern and eastern parts of the province. The urban-rural political equilibrium is bound to change. Top-tier census areas, or regional towns (between 30,000 and 100,000 inhabitants), have been experiencing contrasting demographic and economic change for three decades, with a long-term trend towards decline or stagnation for less cen-

trally located small urban areas (Carrier and Gingras 2004; Proulx 2006). Regional elites and agricultural interests will most probably lose influence over policies and the governance system. Regions and rural areas have been hoping for new resources (money, investments, infrastructure) under the recent provincial rural policy, but the policy seems to be well below their expectations. Since a majority of people live in metropolitan areas, and since these areas will need major investments in the near future, provincial as well as national resources will increasingly flow to these population centres.

4. The new knowledge economy is thriving mostly in large urban areas. It feeds on the constantly changing stock of knowledge produced by universities and research centres—institutions highly urban in the past and still greatly concentrated in large urban areas—and on close contacts and personal communication. This will most certainly reinforce large-city regions. Peripheral regions and regional towns, unless all analysts are mistaken, will not be able, at least in the near future, to compete and provide resources for building a strong knowledge economy.

5. Planning large urban regions has always been a great challenge (Hamel 2001). A strong reason for merging municipalities in Montreal and Quebec City in particular was the possibility of integrating economic policy and regional infrastructure planning. For the Montreal and Quebec metropolitan regions, 'metropolitan communities' (*Communautés métropolitaines*) were created in the wake of the recent municipal reform. They are responsible for land-use planning (*aménagement du territoire*), economic development, the public transit system, refuse collecting and disposal, arts and cultural development, and the managing of large-scale and regional facilities and infrastructure (Belley 2002, 53). These regional communities will become, one hopes, less providers of services and more planning and strategic institutions, in contrast to previous 'urban communities'.

6. Challenges in urban planning at almost all levels are real and complex. The idea of compact cities has gained some ground and devotees. Urban infrastructure is in need of major repairs or replacement. Mayors of Canadian large-city regions are hoping that the federal government will become supportive (*Globe and Mail* 2001). The past 20 years have been characterized by an urban policy concentrated on the central city; suburbs may no longer be left to 'soft' and passive planning based chiefly on applying regulations. If urban and suburban dwellers start to complain about physical conditions or, worse, start to move to ex-urbs or satellite towns—and even if they wish to remain where they live—their urban habitat will have to be cared for intensively. Planners are struggling with new ideas and new conditions: mixing urban functions is on their agenda, whereas postwar planning practices almost totally banned mixing them. Jane Jacobs has created an opening in the modernist planning armour. It may be that the entire urban habitat needs to be rethought and new models of urban living invented.

7. The biggest challenge is undoubtedly the sustainable development of large cities (WCED 1997). The Federation of Canadian Municipalities is well aware of the importance of the concept of sustainability in planning and managing (Maclaren 1992). Because they are engines of growth, cities consume a great deal of resources, and their 'ecological footprint' is deep and wide (Wackernagel and Rees 1999). Sustainable development is about economic efficiency, ecological integrity, and social equity. Since, according to Bourne and Rose (2001, 115), 80 per cent of Canadian population growth in the near future will be concentrated in the five regions surrounding highly urbanized cores (Toronto, Montreal, Vancouver, the Edmonton-Calgary corridor,

Ottawa-Gatineau), sustainable planning will be imperative. Recycling materials, reducing energy and space consumption, protecting biodiversity not only in uninhabited or poorly inhabited lands but also in towns and cities (McNeely 1995; Bulkeley 2006), reducing greenhouse gas emissions originating in cities—these are immense challenges for the industrial system as well as for the governance system, particularly in very large cities. In the industrial production system, there is an 'industrial ecology' in the making in which firms are beginning to take sustainability seriously, starting to apply scientific and technological methods to this end, and innovating to reduce the impact of the industrial system on the environment. However, as yet no comparable 'urban ecology planning system' is in action, despite some efforts and plans, particularly in the public transit system, towards 'greening' in Quebec's large urban areas (Guay 2005; Brown 2006).

Conclusion

This analysis has shown that Quebec's cities have been experiencing important change, which was partly responded to. Policies and planning decisions were paramount in facing deep transformations, whether economic, cultural, or spatial. New policies and planning decisions were brought about by interactions between actors and institutions. Although we could not document policy decisions and planning processes in greater detail, it is clear that since the 1960s, public participation has been practised in various degree, albeit far from perfectly. We have called this interactive and complex process the *collective construction of urban space*. This does not mean that all actors and institutions agree on the decisions taken, but it does means that the participation of many of them, depending on the problem at hand, is required. The economic transformation of Montreal and Quebec City would not have been possible without the active role of the provincial and federal governments. But it would not have been possible without public participation and some elites' cooperation either. Declining regional cities create significant difficulties, either for decision-makers, local authorities, or the people themselves. Many of these difficulties stem from resource exploitation. Forest-dependent communities face dire times, but the MRCs are not well equipped to respond to such challenges. Higher tiers of government must act, as indicated in the new Green Paper on the province's forest future (Gouvernement du Québec 2008). But the deep-seated trend remains urban concentration and the higher than average growth of the already large Montreal region. Finally, cities will eventually encounter the challenge of sustainable development. Lukewarm and half-measure policies will most probably not be good enough, and a deep reflection on the direction of urban development and land-use and infrastructure planning (*aménagement*) is necessary.

Study and Discussion Questions

1. What were the main characteristics of the Quebec territory during the industrial era?
2. To what extent is the structure of the Quebec urban system put in place at the beginning of the twentieth century still the same today?
3. Within large urban areas, two major changes occurred during the period 1970 to 1990 related to deindustrialization and suburbanization. What were the consequences of those changes on central-city life?
4. What have been the main challenges for planners since the 1980s in comparison to the ones they had to face after World War II?
5. How can sustainable development help cities to face urban problems of the twenty-first century?

Suggested Reading

Courville, Serge. 2000. *Le Québec. Genèses et mutations du territoire. Synthèse de géographie historique.* Sainte-Foy and Paris: Les Presses de l'Université Laval and L'Harmattan. A comprehensive account of the transformation of Quebec and its territorial evolution and of the processes of urbanization and industrialization.

Courville, Serge, and Robert Garon, Eds. 2001. *Atlas historique du Québec. Québec ville et capitale.* Sainte-Foy: Les Presses de l'Université Laval. A factual and comprehensive account of the social, economic, and cultural evolution of Quebec City, with an emphasis on its spatial and physical characteristics.

Fortin, Andrée, Carole Després, and Geneviève Vachon, Eds. 2002. *La banlieue revisitée.* Quebec City: Édi-

tions Nota Bene. The first comprehensive study of the suburbs of Quebec City that grew up after World War II and have now evolved into older areas in need of appropriate planning initiatives.

Germain, Annick, and Damaris Rose. 2000. *Montreal: The Quest for a Metropolis.* Toronto: John Wiley. A thoughtful analysis of the rise and relative decline of Montreal, its recent economic recovery, its changing social and ethnocultural composition, and the impacts of a new urban centrality.

Hulbert, François. 1994. *La comédie urbaine de Quebec. Essai de géopolitique urbaine et régionale.* 2nd edn. Montreal: Méridien. A highly critical analysis of the recent evolution of Quebec City and its suburbs, focusing on the weaknesses of urban regional planning and decision-making.

References

Alexander, D. 2000. 'The best so far: Vancouver's remarkable approach to the Southeast False Creek redevelopment is a big step towards sustainable redevelopment planning for urban sites'. *Alternatives* 26: 10–14.

Baccigalupo, A. 1990. *Système politique et administratif des municipalités québécoises. Une perspective comparative.* Montreal: Éditions Agence d'Arc.

Bairoch, P. 1995. *De Jericho à Mexico. Villes et économie dans l'histoire.* 2nd edn. Paris: Arcades-Gallimard.

BAPE. 2000. *L'eau, ressource à protéger, à partager et à mettre en valeur.* Quebec City: Bureau des audiences publiques sur l'environnement. www.bape. gouv.qc.ca/sections/rapports/publications/eau.

Belley, J.-G. 2002. 'Des communautés urbaines aux communautés métropolitaines: quelles innovations institutionnelles?' *Organisations et Territoires* 11 (3): 51–7.

———. 2003. 'L'élection municipale de 2001 à Québec: l'"interventionnisme municipal" de la ville-centre contre le "populisme fiscal" des banlieues'. *Recherches sociographiques* 44: 217–38.

Berry, B.J.L., Ed. 1976. *Urbanization and Counterurbanization.* Beverly Hills, CA: Sage.

Bourne, L. 2001. 'Urban Canada in transition to the twenty-first century: Trends, issues, and visions'. In T. Bunting and P. Filion, Eds, *Canadian Cities in Transition*, 2nd edn. Toronto: Oxford University Press.

Bourne, L., and D. Rose. 2001. 'The changing face of Canada: The uneven geographies of population and social change'. *The Canadian Geographer/Le Géographe canadien* 45: 105–19.

Brown, D.F. 2006. 'Back to basics: The influence of sustainable development on urban planning with special reference to Montreal'. *Canadian Journal of Urban Research* 15: 99–117.

Bulkeley, H. 2006. 'Urban sustainability: Learning from best practices?' *Environment and Planning A* 38: 1,029–44.

Canada. 1996. 'Le Canada urbain'. In *L'état de l'environnement au Canada* 12: 1–47. Ottawa: Ministère des travaux publics et des Services gouvernementaux.

Carrier, M., and P. Gingras. 2004. 'Les villes moyennes. Analyse démographique et économique, 1971–2001'. *Recherches sociographiques* 45: 569–92.

Champion, A. 1989. *Counterurbanization*. London: Edward Arnold.

Charbonneau, J., and A. Germain. 2002. 'Les banlieues de l'immigration'. *Recherches sociographiques* 43: 311–28.

Choko, M. 2002. 'Le Quartier International de Montréal et sa périphérie. Enjeux stratégiques'. In G. Sénécal, J. Malézieux, and C. Mazagol, Eds, *Grands projets urbains et requalification*, 25–34. Montreal and Paris: Les Presses de l'Université du Québec and Publications de la Sorbonne.

Coffey, W., and M. Polèse. 1993. 'Le déclin de l'empire Montréalais: regard sur l'économie d'une métropole en mutation'. *Recherches sociographiques* 34: 417–37.

———. 2000. *La restructuration de l'économie Montréalaise. Comparaisons avec d'autres métropoles nord-américaines*. Montreal: INRS-Urbanisation.

Collin, J.-P. 2003. 'Introduction: Montréal, tableaux d'une métropole moyenne'. *Canadian Journal of Urban Research/Revue canadienne de recherche urbaine* 12: 8–15.

———. 2002. 'La réforme de l'organisation du secteur municipal au Québec: la fin ou le début d'un cycle?' *Organisations et Territoires* 11 (3): 5–13.

Courville, S. 2000. *Le Québec. Genèses et mutations du territoire. Synthèse de géographie historique*. Sainte-Foy and Paris: Les Presses de l'Université Laval and L'Harmattan.

Dear, M.J. 2002. 'Los Angeles and the Chicago School: Invitation to a debate'. *City and Community* 1: 5–38.

Dickinson, J.A., and B. Young. 1995. *Brève histoire socio-économique du Québec*. Sillery: Septentrion.

Divay, G., and M. Gaudreault. 1984. *La formation des nouveaux espaces résidentiels. Le système de production de l'habitat urbain dans les années soixante-dix au Québec*. Quebec City: Les Presses de l'Université du Québec.

Doloreux, D. 1999. 'Technopoles et trajectoires stratégiques: le cas de la ville de Laval (Québec)'. *Cahiers de géographie du Québec* 43: 211–35.

Drouilly, P. 1996. *L'espace social de Montréal, 1951–1991*. Montreal: Septentrion.

Dugas, C. 2003. 'Le monde rural québécois et la Politique nationale de la ruralité'. *Organisations et Territoires* 12 (2): 41–7.

Fischer, C.S. 1984. *The Urban Experience*. San Diego and Toronto: Harcourt, Brace, Jovanovich.

Fontan, J.-M., et al. 2003. 'The institutionalization of Montreal's CDECs: From grass roots organizations to state apparatus?' *Canadian Journal of Urban Research/Revue canadienne de recherche urbaine* 12: 58–76.

Fortin, A., and M. Bédard. 2003. 'Citadins et banlieusards. Représentations, pratiques et identités'. *Canadian Journal of Urban Research/Revue canadienne de recherche urbaine* 12: 125–42.

Fortin, G., and L. Parent. 1983. *Les MRC et leur capacité d'extension*. Études et documents no. 39. Montreal: INRS-Urbanisation.

———. 1985. *Les MRC en devenir perpétuel*. Montreal: INRS-Urbanisation.

Gauthier, M., Ed. 2003. 'La migration des jeunes'. *Recherches sociographiques* 44: 19–139.

Germain, A. 1997. 'L'étranger et la ville'. *Canadian Journal of Regional Science/Revue canadienne des sciences régionales* 20: 237–54.

———. 2002. 'La culture urbaine au pluriel? Métropole et ethnicité'. In D. Lemieux, Ed., *Traité de la culture*, 121–34. Sainte-Foy: Les Presses de l'Université Laval/éd. de l'IQRC.

Germain, A., and D. Rose. 2000. *Montreal: The Quest for a Metropolis*. Toronto: John Wiley.

Globe and Mail. 2001. 'Cities want bigger slice of national funding pie'. 21 May: A3.

Gouvernement du Québec. 2008. *La forêt pour construire le Québec de demain*. Quebec City: Ministère des ressources naturelles et de la faune.

Guay, L. 1978. 'Les dimensions de l'espace social urbain: Montréal: 1951, 1961, 1971'. *Recherches sociographiques* 19: 307–48.

———. 2002. 'La longue et tortueuse évolution de l'aménagement du territoire'. In R. Côté, Ed., *Quebec 2002*, 51–61. Montreal: Fides.

———. 2005. 'Les options de l'aménagement du territoire à la lumière des enjeux environnementaux'. *Organisations et Territoires* 14: 25–37.

Hall, P. 1998. *Cities and Civilization*. New York: Pantheon.

Hamel, P. 1999. 'La consultation publique et les limites de la participation des citoyens aux affaires urbaines'. *Recherches sociographiques* 40: 435–66.

———. 2001. 'Les enjeux métropolitains: les nouveaux défis'. *International Journal of Canadian Studies/Revue internationale d'études canadiennes* 24: 105–27.

Hamel, P., and C. Poitras. 2004. 'Déclin et relance économique d'une agglomeration métropolitaine. Le discours et les representations des elites économiques à Montréal'. *Recherches sociographiques* 45: 457–92.

Higgins, B. 1986. *The Rise and Fall of Montreal: A Case Study of Urban Growth, Regional Economic Expansion and National Development*. Moncton: Canadian Institute for Research on Regional Development.

Higgins, B., F. Martin, and A. Raynauld. 1970. *Les orientations du développement économique régional dans la Province de Québec*. Ottawa: Ministère de l'Expansion économique régionale.

Hulbert, F. 1994. *La comédie urbaine de Québec. Essai de géopolitique urbaine et régionale*. Montreal: Méridien.

Jean, B. 2003. 'Réussir le développement des communautés rurales: dix conditions gagnantes'. *Organisations et Territoires* 12 (2): 19–30.

Lamonde, P., and Y. Martineau. 1992. *Désindustrialisation et restructuration économique. Montreal et les autres grandes métropoles nord-américaines*. Montreal: INRS-Urbanisation.

Laperrière, H., and S. Latouche. 2002. 'La Grande Bibliothèque du Québec et la requalification du Quartier latin. Une méthode, deux réalités, trois visions'. In G. Sénécal, J. Malézieux, and C. Mazagol, Eds, *Grands projets urbains et requalification*, 127–42. Montreal and Paris: Les Presses de l'Université du Québec and Publications de la Sorbonne.

Le Blanc, M.-F. 2006. *Des communautés plus ou moins civiques. La capital social et la gouvernance métropolitaine au Canada et aux États-Unis*. Quebec City: Les Presses de l'Université Laval.

Levine, M.W. 1990. *The Reconquest of Montreal: Language, Policy and Social Change in a Bilingual City*. Philadelphia: Temple University Press.

Ley, D. 1999. 'Myths and meanings of immigration and the metropolis'. *The Canadian Geographer/Le Géographe canadien* 43: 2–19.

Ley, D., and D. Hiebert. 2001. 'Immigration policy as population policy'. *The Canadian Geographer/Le Géographe canadien* 45: 120–5.

Linteau, P.-A. 1992. *Histoire de Montréal depuis la Confédération*. Montreal: Boréal.

Linteau, P.-A., R. Durocher, and J.-C. Robert. 1989. *Histoire du Québec contemporain*, tome 1. Montreal: Boréal.

Maclaren, V.W. 1992. *Pour un développement urbain durable au Canada: la mise en œuvre du concept*. Rapport de recherche préparé pour le compte du Comité intergouvernemental de recherches urbaines et régionales. Toronto.

McNeely, J.A. 1995. *Cities, Nature, and Protected Areas: A General Introduction*. Gland, Switzerland: World Conservation Union.

McNicoll, C. 1993. *Montréal. Une société multiculturelle*. Paris: Bélin.

Manzagol, C. 1998. 'La restructuration de l'industrie'. In C. Manzagol and C.R. Bryant, Eds, *Montreal 2001. Visages et défis d'une métropole*, 119–33. Montreal: Les Presses de l'Université de Montréal.

Marsan, J.-C. 1994. *Montréal en évolution: historique du développement de l'architecture et de l'environnement urbain montréalais*. 3rd edn. Laval: Éditions Méridien.

Martin, F. 1998. 'Montréal: les forces économiques en jeu, vingt ans plus tard'. *L'Actualité économique* 74: 129–53.

Mercier, G. 1999. *L'usage urbain de la nature: conflit et ralliement au quartier Saint-Roch à Québec*. Quebec City: Université Laval, Département de géographie/CÉLAT.

———. 2002. 'Essai de schématisation des modèles urbains de la revitalisation du quartier Saint-Roch à Québec'. In G. Sénécal, J. Malézieux, and C. Mazagol, Eds, *Grands projets urbains et requali-*

fication, 101–15. Montreal and Paris: Presses de l'Université du Québec and Publications de la Sorbonne.

———. 2003. 'The rhetoric of contemporary urbanism: A deconstructive analysis of central city neighbourhood redevelopment'. *Canadian Journal of Urban Research/Revue canadienne de recherche urbaine* 12: 71–98.

Morisset, L.K. 2001. *La mémoire du paysage. Histoire de la forme urbaine d'un centre-ville: Saint-Roch, Québec.* Sainte-Foy: Les Presses de l'Université Laval.

Mumford, L. 1961. *The City in History.* Harmondsworth, UK: Penguin.

Paehlke, R. 1993. 'Villes compactes, villes écologiques'. In SCHL, Ed., *Vision de la vie dans une ville écologique du 21e siècle*, 31–58. Ottawa: SCHL.

Park, R.E., E.W. Burgess, and R.G. McKenzie. 1925. *The City: Suggestions for Investigations of Human Behavior in the Urban Environment.* Chicago: University of Chicago Press.

Piché, D. 1991. 'Le design urbain: le cas de Québec. Une manière de placer l'humain et la culture au cœur de l'aménagement?' In A. Germain, Ed., *L'aménagement urbain*, 129–77. Quebec City: Institut québécois de la recherche sur la culture.

Poitras, C. 2002. 'La Cité du Multimédia à Montréal. Fabriquer l'image d'un nouveau quartier'. In G. Sénécal, J. Malézieux, and C. Mazagol, Eds, *Grands projets urbains et requalification*, 143–55. Montreal and Paris: Les Presses de l'Université du Québec and Publications de la Sorbonne.

Polèse, M., and M. Roy. 1999. 'La dynamique spatiale des activités économiques au Québec. Analyse pour la période 1971–1991 fondée sur un découpage centre-périphérie'. *Cahiers de géographie du Québec* 43: 43–71.

Polèse, M., and R. Shearmur. 2002. *La périphérie face à l'économie du savoir. La dynamique spatiale de l'économie canadienne et l'avenir des régions non-métropolitaines du Québec et des provinces de l'Atlantique.* Montreal: INRS-Urbanisation, Culture et Société et l'Institut canadien de recherche sur le développement régional. www.inrs-usc.uquebec.ca/F/inc/regions du S.

———. 2004. *Le positionnement de Montréal par rapport à 11 autres agglomérations: entre perceptions et statistiques.* Montreal: INRS-Urbanisation, Culture et Société.

Proulx, M.-U. 2006. 'La mouvance contemporaine des territoires: la logique spatiale de l'économie au Québec'. *Recherches sociographiques* 47: 475–502.

Renaud, J., M. Mayer, and R. Lebeau. 1996. *Espace urbain, espace social. Portrait de la population des villes du Québec.* Montreal: Éditions Saint-Martin.

Rondinelli, D.A. 2001. 'Making metropolitan areas competitive and sustainable in the new economy'. *Journal of Urban Technology* 8: 1–21.

Rose, D. 1996. 'Economic restructuring and the diversification of gentrification in the 1980s: A view from a marginal metropolis'. In J. Caulfield and J. Peake, Eds, *City Lives and City Forms: Critical Research and Canadian Urbanism.* Toronto: University of Toronto Press.

Sancton, A. 2000. *La frénésie des fusions. Une attaque à la démocratie locale.* Montreal and Kingston: McGill-Queen's University Press (also published in English: *The Merger Mania: The Assault on Local Government*, McGill-Queen's University Press, 2000).

———. 2004. 'Les villes anglophones du Quebec. Does it matter that they disappeared?' *Recherches sociographiques* 44.

Savitch H.V., and P. Kantor. 2002. *Cities in the International Market Place.* Princeton, NJ: Princeton University Press.

Sénécal, G. 1997. 'Les récits du déclin et de la relance de Montréal face aux défis de l'aménagement urbain'. *Cahiers de géographie du Québec* 41: 381–91.

Sénécal, G., and P.J. Hamel. 2001. 'Ville compact et qualité de vie: discussion autour de l'approche canadienne des indicateurs de durabilité'. *The Canadian Geographer/Le Géographe canadien* 45: 306–18.

Simard, M. 2001. 'L'urbanisme communautaire à Québec: utopie ou réalité?' *Organisations et Territoires* 10 (2): 81–9.

Statistics Canada. 2003. 'Le Canada en statistiques.

Proportion de personnes nées à l'étranger, régions métropolitaines de recensement'. www.statcan/francais/Pgdb/demo46b_f.htm.

———. 2006. 'Situation des immigrants sur le marché du travail, province et régions'. www.statcan.ca/francais/freepub/71-606-XIF/2007001/findings/prov-fr.htm.

Stone, C.N. 2006. 'Power, reform and urban regime analysis'. *City and Community* 5: 23–38.

Task Force (Prime Minister's Caucus Task Force on Urban Issues). 2002. *Canada's Urban Strategy: A Vision for the 21st Century*. Ottawa.

Tellier, Luc-Normand, Ed. 1997. *Les défis et les options de la relance de Montréal*. Sainte-Foy: Les Presses de l'Université du Québec.

———. 2003. 'La grande région de Montréal dans le monde: perspectives topodynamiques pour 2060'. *Organisations et Territoires* 12 (2): 57–8.

Turcotte, M. 2001. 'L'opposition rural/urbain a-t-elle fait son temps? Le cas du moralisme traditionnel'. *Canadian Journal of Sociology/Cahiers canadiens de sociologie* 26: 1–29.

Vachon, B. 2003. 'Ruralité en péril: redéfinir les consensus et argumentaires en faveur de l'occupation dynamique des territoires fragiles'. *Organisations et Territoires* 12 (2): 31–9.

Vandersmissen, M.-H., and P. Villeneuve. 2001. 'L'évolution de la mobilité des femmes à Québec entre 1977 et 1996'. *Cahiers de géographie du Québec* 45: 211–43.

Villeneuve, P., and C. Trudelle. 2008. 'Retour au centre à Québec: la renaissance de la Cité est-elle durable?' *Recherches sociographiques* 49: 25–45.

Wackernagel, M., and W. Rees. 1999. *Notre empreinte écologique*. Montreal: Éditions Écosociété.

WCED (World Commission on Environment and Development). 1997. *Our Common Future*. Oxford: Oxford University Press.

Weber, M. 1958. *The City*. New York: Free Press.

Wirth, L. 1938. 'Urbanism as a way of life'. *American Journal of Sociology* 44: 3–24.

Wolfe, J.M. 2003. 'A national urban policy for Canada: Prospects and challenges'. *Canadian Journal of Urban Research/Revue canadienne de recherche urbaine* 12: 1–21.

Chapter 15 Getting Perspective

Is Toronto a good example of how contemporary cities are evolving, or is it a special case reflecting its unique position in the Canadian urban hierarchy?

As we have already learned, Toronto has now become the largest, most dominant, and influential city in Canada. Not only is it the place where most Canadian companies have their headquarters or at least a major office, but it is the place where most international companies also locate. Whereas Toronto was once second to Montreal in size and significance, it is now the undisputed economic centre of Canada, which of course enhances other elements of strength such as in the arts and technology. It also contributes to the stunning growth of the urban region, which includes more distant cities like Hamilton, Kitchener, and London.

For this reason, it is particularly interesting to understand how this city has evolved over time. The shift from the pre-industrial period to the industrial period demonstrates how factories structured the city and in particular how elites and the working class sorted themselves out in urban space. But Toronto's role became more important because it was an administrative centre, a position it has retained to this day. Consequently, the well-being of many highly paid people in the city contrasted sharply with that of the working class, which included many immigrants. This is typical of global cities, where costs rise quickly because of demand and the ability of at least some to pay high prices. The better-off also seek to renovate old structures in the inner city that were significant in the industrial era because of their access to the central core, its jobs, and its leisure activities. This process of *gentrification* finds wealthier residents moving into older lower-class neighbourhoods, renovating buildings, and displacing the residents who had lived in these neighbourhoods.

Post-industrial Toronto displays all of the hallmarks of the new urban economy in which city cores are organized around corporate leisure or leisure consumption. The Eaton Centre, the Rogers Centre, the Air Canada Centre, the CN Tower, and waterfront luxury hotels and condominiums represent a transformation of space once dedicated to shipping and warehousing, factories, and residences.

The evolution of Toronto over the past 150 years raises the issue of what kind of city we want and how we can achieve it. We have learned that urban development does not happen by itself and that certain critical decisions make a city what it is. If big corporations are playing an increasingly important role in the shape of Canadian cities, citizens themselves also need to play a role through the *urban planning* process. The question of what cities should be like is a thorny one, yet planning is not just a matter of the physical objectives of land use or the economic objectives of marketability; rather, the social objectives of human needs for living must be considered. This chapter demonstrates how cities are constantly changing and how the outcomes of these changes give us pause for reflection about what forces drive the direction and velocity of this change in our search for more livable cities.

15 Toronto: The Form of the City

Jon Caulfield

Learning Objectives

- To understand that shifts in a city's economy over time have major effects on its built form.
- To understand that corporatization is a key force shaping urban space today.
- To understand that the fabric of the city is an ongoing work in progress.
- To understand that urban forms reflect modernist and post-modern approaches to city-building.
- To understand that urban places have a dialogical quality.

Introduction

In broad terms, Canadian cities may be described as comprised of two zones. An inner zone consists of older areas of the urban region whose **morphology** was in place by the 1950s and, in Canada's older cities, often includes districts and buildings that date to the mid-1800s or earlier. While this zone is in constant transition, it remains marked, as it has been historically, by high densities of people and activities clustered in a closely-grained mix of residential, commercial, and other kinds of **land uses**. Surrounding this inner part of the city is an outer zone developed in recent decades where densities of people and activities are usually lower and land uses are more segregated and organized around the automobile. While this sorting of Canada's urban fabric into two kinds of places simplifies a more complex reality,[1] it also identifies a key feature of current-day metropolitan space by making a distinction between traditional and recently built urban spheres.

This chapter focuses on the former zone, the older realm of urban space, and explores key features of its fabric. It does so in the con-text of Canada's largest city at the centre of its most extensive urban region, Toronto, with two thoughts in mind. First, Toronto's place in the Canadian urban system makes it worth study as a case in itself. Second, Toronto is not a solitary case. The processes of change it has experienced and the forces shaping these processes are evident in Canadian cities more widely, and readers may draw on a study of Toronto to help make sense of urban patterns elsewhere.

The chapter takes as a starting point three sites in inner Toronto that are useful places for exploring facets of Canada's modern urban landscape: an abandoned factory complex restored to life in a new way, the surroundings of a downtown church, and a 1950s-era public housing project.

The Distillery

A couple of kilometres east of Toronto's downtown is a rusted sign above the main door of a five-storey grey limestone building: 'Gooderham & Worts Limited/Distillers of Fine Whiskies Since 1832'. Built in 1860, it is the core structure

Figure 15.1 'View looking w. from near foot of Trinity Street', chromolithograph, 188–?, based on Thomas Young, General View of the City of Toronto, 1835

The Gooderham and Worts windmill was one of Toronto's earliest industrial structures. Built in 1832, it was used to process grain into flour. Until it was torn down in 1859, it was the dominant landmark on Toronto's waterfront and an orientation point for lake vessels (*Metropolitan Toronto Reference Library*).

of what was once Canada's largest liquor manufacturer. By the time of Confederation, the company employed 160 workers, who produced 2.5 million gallons of whisky yearly. Now on a summer afternoon, jazz echoes along the building's wall from a trio at the far end of a cobblestone courtyard. Across the courtyard people enjoy cappuccinos at tables outside a café. A nearby building—the distillery has more than 20—has been renovated as studios and offices for more than 50 artists and arts groups. Other buildings house art galleries, craft studios, an oyster bar, deluxe boutiques, a microbrewery, a chocolatier, stylish restaurants, and in two smartly renovated whisky-aging sheds, a drama school and theatre.

The café is in a small building where pumps once drew water into the distillery from Lake

Ontario. The lake used to be nearer. An 1836 lithograph of Toronto's shoreline shows the first structure on the distillery's site, a windmill put up in 1832 by two British immigrants, and places it close to the water (see Figure 15.1). By the time of another painting five decades later, a lot had changed. The distillery's main buildings were in place—smoke pours from their stacks—and the water's edge had been pushed back for wharves and dockside warehouses (see Figure 15.2). Later, it was pushed back still farther. Today, the distillery is separated from the harbour by railway tracks, a six-lane elevated expressway, and a stretch of forgotten industrial land.

The distillery is a useful starting point for this chapter because it clearly illustrates essential elements of Toronto's fabric across the key

Figure 15.2 Arthur Henry Hider, 'Gooderham and Worts, Ltd., Toronto, 1896'

By the 1890s, the distillery was among Toronto's largest industrial complexes, and the process of landfilling along the city's shoreline for rail lines and port facilities had begun. The lakeside warehouses in the picture's foreground are gone, but the rest of the distillery remains intact. 'To walk inside these precincts,' an observer of Toronto's architecture wrote two decades ago, 'is to leave the twentieth century behind' (McHugh 1989, 38) (*Metropolitan Toronto Reference Library*).

periods of its urban economy—pre-industrial, industrial, post-industrial[2]—a framework that is among the most useful tools for making sense of Canadian cities over time (see Table 15.1). 'Each stage has a distinctive function [and] morphology with its corresponding social landscape,' wrote historian Gilbert Stelter, and each 'represents a particular set of power relationships between people, groups, and a place, and between places and larger society' (1986, 7).

The Pre-industrial Phase

Canada's pre-industrial urban phase had two distinct parts. The first was a mercantile period, when important settlements were **entrepots** or had some other role in the trade of staple goods like fur, fish, and lumber. Toronto originated in the 1700s as a French military base whose function was helping to protect France's interest in the fur business. It was soon replaced by a British

fort. Places like this were small but still urban— colonial outposts governed by imperial officials at the frontier of European metropolitan society.

Mercantile outposts often became administrative towns—Toronto, for example, became the capital of Upper Canada—and emerged as centres of colonization during the second part of the pre-industrial phase, the commercial period. From 1831 to 1861, Toronto's population increased tenfold to more than 40,000 as rapid settlement also occurred in the surrounding agricultural region. The town was now a service centre where government was based, wholesale and retail goods were bought and sold, and key institutions like the bank, post office, and hospital were located. James Worts and William Gooderham arrived early in this period to found one of the town's first industries, a mill to process grain into flour sold retail and wholesale in the local market. The firm soon added a small distillery.

Table 15.1 Phases of Canadian Urbanism

	Urban Function	Power over Place
Pre-industrial phase		
• **Mercantile period**	Entrepots, administrative or military outposts	Officials of the imperial state and its colonial agencies
• **Commercial period**	Regional trade and services amid colonial settlement	A growing colonial elite of entrepreneurs and professionals
Industrial Phase		
• **Early period**	Small-scale industry mainly for local and regional markets	As in the commercial period, local business and professional elites
• **Later period**	Large manufacturing and extractive industries	Company owners and business elites of the industrial economy
Post-industrial phase	Business, financial, professional, and personal services	Multinational corporations and elites of the service economy

Toronto's sense of its identity at the time and a focal point of its landscape were captured in an 1845 painting of its main thoroughfare, John Gillespie's *View of King Street*, whose motifs were prosperity and civic pride. In the picture, diverse citizens stroll on a wide, well-appointed streetscape past tidy shops and the town's city hall, with the spire of a new Anglican cathedral in the background. Imperial administrators who managed the town in the mercantile period were now supplanted by a rising class of immigrant entrepreneurs and professionals. They shaped urban development through a municipal government established in 1834 and organizations like a board of trade founded in 1845 'to express the views of [the] business community [and] protect the interests of its members' (Dendy 1993, 28).

The Industrial Phase

Colonial Toronto had many small craft industries like the Worts-Gooderham mill, but manufacturing did not emerge as a key sector of its economy until the 1870s and 1880s when Confederation and the protective tariffs of the National Policy propelled industrial development in urban Canada. About 9,000 Toronto employees were classed

as 'industrial' in 1871, a number that had tripled by 1891, as did the town's population to more than 180,000.[3] Continued industrial growth in eastern cities was generated by completion of the Canadian Pacific Railway, which enabled settlement of the West—opening markets, for example, for agricultural machinery manufactured by Toronto's Massey-Harris company, which employed 2,000 workers by the turn of the century in massive factories only a few blocks away from the sites of the early French and British forts.

The industrial phase also had two distinct parts, illustrated by a simple statistic. Toronto's 26,000 factory workers in 1891 were employed in about 2,400 firms. By 1911, the number of workers had risen to more than 65,000, while the number of firms fell to 1,100. These figures reveal a basic shift in the scale and organization of the factory economy. Smaller workplaces of the early industrial period, including many family-owned shops and those of self-employed artisans, were replaced by increasingly larger factories as the full-blown form of the industrial city emerged. Buildings like the distillery's grey limestone hulk beside the plant's massive smokestacks became common in the later industrial period, especially on the lakeshore, soon landfilled half a kilometre south to make more room for factories, warehouses, and rail and harbour facilities. In some places, the land uses of the commercial period, including residential areas, were eliminated for industrial development. North of the distillery, for example, a neighbourhood where William Gooderham once lived was replaced by rail yards and factories (Goad 1884; 1923, Plate 28).

Stelter's observation that each urban period had a distinct spatial and social morphology is illustrated by the emerging dominance of large factories in the city's fabric and also by residential patterns. Toronto had earlier followed the typical course of pre-industrial cities in which privileged households lived in comfortable homes near the centre of town. Now, amid the increasing turmoil of the factory economy with its pollution and noise and with the inner-city presence of immigrant factory workers arriving in ever-rising numbers, affluent families began to leave downtown for new suburbs at the outskirts with names like Parkdale, Rosedale, and Riverdale. This patrician shift away from the centre has been described by one historian as 'unthinkable in the premodern city', but it now became the rule (Fishman 1987, 7).

It was not only in the inner city that the new working class settled but also in industrial suburbs. As factory sites near downtown became scarce, manufacturers increasingly chose outlying locations on major rail lines—for example, large plants built in 1917 by the Goodyear rubber company west of town and the Kodak camera company to the northwest (Harris 1996, 60). Workers lived in new nearby neighbourhoods, often composed of owner-built homes and rigidly segregated from the suburban havens of the middle class (Harris 1996, 200–32; 2004, 58–62).

'[P]erhaps the most characteristic feature of the social landscape of industrial towns and cities was the way in which society increasingly sorted itself,' wrote Stelter (1982, 28), and class was the most important mechanism of this sorting. While sorting also occurred in the pre-industrial city, with status generally declining farther from the centre, there was also considerable social mixing, with lower-class households often living side-by-side with the well-to-do (Fishman 1987, 6–8). But social relations of the factory era were marked by growing antagonism between workers and privileged, tension that became evident in often-violent conflicts that arose between blue-collar workers and white-collar management. This deepening fissure was clearly imprinted on the industrial city's residential fabric.

As the emergence of large factories illustrates, power over place in the industrial city was increasingly held by the elite of the manufacturing economy. As Stelter also notes, power over place included 'relationships between . . . places and larger society'. For example, the Massey-Harris farm machine company originated in Brantford, Ontario, but by the turn of the century had moved to Toronto after absorbing several scattered smaller firms in the same business (Careless 1984, 112). Another example is Guelph, Ontario, a thriving manufacturing centre in the early industrial period that later lost many firms, which either relocated to larger cities like Toronto or were taken over by companies there (Johnson 1982). Meanwhile, Toronto-based capital built mining industries and company towns at northern locations like Sudbury, a type of city sometimes termed a specialized centre because of its reliance in the wider urban economic network on the market for a single extracted or manufactured commodity.[4]

Hence the industrial period bred a number of new urban forms—large factories and manufacturing zones, vast rail yards, inner-city working-class districts, middle-class and industrial suburbs, one-industry towns—and it also bred another. Toronto's growing economic weight was rooted in the activities of relentlessly larger business firms that required suitable headquarters, which they found in the new form of the office skyscraper imported from Chicago and New York. By 1914, the city had five of these buildings, ranging in size from 10 to 20 storeys, not high by today's standards but Brobdingnagian at the time, spatial symbols of their occupants' wealth and power. The four largest are depicted in Robert Gagen's 1914 painting, *Temples of Commerce*, rising in a smoke-choked sky behind the city's industrial waterfront. Only one of the many church steeples that had dominated the skyline of the pre-industrial city is visible in the picture.

In 1921, an observer wrote of a 'vast gulf between [Toronto]'s present and its immediate but somehow almost mysterious past' (Fairley 1921, 276), a gulf reflecting the sudden shift from pre-industrial to industrial urbanism.

The Post-industrial Phase

While industry became a key sector of its economy, Toronto was never primarily an industrial city. Consistent with its pre-industrial role as southern Ontario's administrative and service centre, the number of factory workers never outnumbered employees in fields like management, finance and commerce, wholesale and retail trade, and business, government, and personal services. Even in manufacturing's peak decades, the 1910s and again in the 1940s, it accounted for only 35 per cent of the city's employment.

As its ascendancy over Ontario's manufacturing and extractive industries grew, Toronto increasingly fit J.M.S. Careless's definition of a metropolis: 'a dominant large city whose commanding status essentially expresses the commercial, transport, industrial, and financial functions of control or influence which it exerts over extensive and productive hinterland territories' (1989, 61). In the 1930s, the city passed two symbolic statistical benchmarks when the value of its stock market transactions and of cheques processed in its financial institutions surpassed the numbers for Montreal (Nader 1975, 218–19). It was emerging not only as Ontario's metropolis but as Canada's, in part a function of its role as the main headquarters for US investment in Canada, replacing British capital based in Montreal as the major source of foreign investment.

It is hard to recognize the onset of a historical epoch until afterwards. Industrialists of the 1890s,

for example, certainly did not foresee the extent to which their activities would almost wholly remake Toronto's landscape, and looking back today at the 1950s, it is apparent that those years marked a shift from one urban era to another. During that decade, the number of industrial jobs in the inner zone of Toronto dropped by 25 per cent and it continued to fall at rates of 29 and 28 per cent in the 1960s and 1970s (CATF 1974, 267; Muszynski 1985, 14). The latter figure was reported in a study whose title included a cumbersome new word, deindustrialization, meant to connote the decline of manufacturing in city economies. Toronto's industrial era had waned.

Manufacturing does continue to remain an important part of the economy of Toronto's wider urban region, accounting for about one-sixth of its workforce and one-fourth of its economic output in the 1990s (Gertler 2000, 5, 7, 23). Many factory jobs that left Toronto did not go far, only to new sites at its outskirts or elsewhere in southern Ontario as the emergence of truck transport freed industry from locations along railway lines.[5] But more dominant patterns have been the movement of manufacturing away from Canada in three directions: to highly competitive industrial nations like Japan and China, to developing countries with cheap labour markets and weak environmental regulations, and to the US as an effect of free trade accords. These patterns illustrate an important aspect of deindustrialization in Canadian cities, its close connection with economic **globalization**.

Industry's steady decline in Toronto is one dimension of the post-industrial period of its economy as other kinds of work have become increasingly important. An account of the region's employment structure from 1981 to 1996 notes 'a pronounced shift towards occupations such as managerial/administrative, the natural, applied, and social sciences, arts, culture and recreation, and sales and service' alongside diminishing factory and clerical jobs, tendencies most evident in the older inner zone of the city (Gertler 2000, 6). A 2001 planning document identified the inner zone's largest job 'clusters' as business and professional services, financial services, tourism, and information technology (CT 2001, 46).

The structure of the post-industrial economy tends in two directions towards what are sometimes termed the 'knowledge economy' and the 'McDonald's economy'. Work in prestigious realms like corporate head office management, high-end financial services, new media entrepreneurialism, and the culture industry aristocracy contrasts sharply with 'low-wage, often part-time non-unionized jobs in restaurants, hotels, cleaning, security, data-processing, and entertainment . . . sectors that serve the needs of the dominant global city classes' (Kipfer 1999, 14). The pattern of who does the latter work illustrates another feature of post-industrial globalization. Concentrated in this lower economic stratum is the half of Toronto's population born outside Canada, often immigrants from Third World countries. The heightening **bifurcation** of the job market has helped to produce 'a growing gap in income and wealth and greater polarization among Toronto's neighbourhoods' (Hulchanski 2007, 2). A 2007 report concludes that 'the number of vulnerable workers in precarious forms of employment' is a key factor in the city's becoming what a *Toronto Star* headline called 'Canada's poverty capital' (UWGT 2007; Monsebraaten and Daly 2007).

One effect of the city's new economy has been a reversal of the forces that generated middle-class movement to the suburbs of the industrial city. As factories disappeared from downtown, the working-class presence in inner-city neighbourhoods, often within walking distance of steady and well-paid industrial jobs, was destabilized and steadily diminished. Meanwhile, a growing cadre of the new post-industrial elite are inclined towards the lifeworld and lifestyle of districts in and near downtown where social diversity, a palpable presence of urban heritage and history, and the close proximity of job opportunities and urban amenities afford an everyday life they find desirable. Their movement to once-working-class neighbourhoods now frag-

mented by deindustrialization—areas that often originated as patrician districts but were then abandoned by the middle class of the industrial period—has been termed gentrification (Caulfield 1994; Ley 1996a; 1996b; Hamnett 2000).

Gentrifiers and others with a taste for urbane leisure—tourists or suburbanites out for a day on the town—are the target market for the diversions of the Distillery District. Out of the whisky business since the 1950s when its parent firm moved these operations to a Windsor plant closer to its US markets, the company continued to make rum and industrial alcohols until 1990, after which its buildings stood empty for more than a decade (White and Otto 2001; Caulfield 2005). Their restoration now, amid the lifeworld of post-industrial urbanism, is a striking example of **adaptive reuse**. One of the finest surviving examples of Victorian factory construction in North America—'to walk inside these precincts . . . is to leave the twentieth century behind,' wrote an observer of Toronto's architecture (McHugh 1989, 38)—the distillery has been reconceived as a venue where the post-industrial middle class takes its pleasures amid art galleries, boutiques, and oyster bars (see Box 15.1).

Two large hunks of anonymous machinery placed in its cobblestone courtyard as a kind of aesthetic object, their function forgotten, are a measure of how thoroughly the meaning of the distillery has been remade. It is hard to imagine what workers from the plant's industrial heyday might think if they saw the place today on the far side of another 'vast gulf between [Toronto]'s present and its immediate but somehow almost mysterious past' (Fairley 1921, 276).

Holy Trinity Church

The surroundings of the Church of the Holy Trinity illustrate as vividly as the distillery Toronto's passage across its pre-industrial, industrial, and post-industrial phases (Caulfield 2001). Holy Trinity was one of six Toronto churches built

Box 15.1 *The Distillery District*: *Two Journalists' Views*

John Lorinc and Christopher Hume provided accounts of the distillery in November 2003, soon after it opened.

This buzzing fusion of history, culture, and commerce is Toronto's next Queen Street West. Since it opened earlier this year, the refurbished Gooderham and Worts complex, together with the cluster of warehouses around it, has exerted an astonishing gravitational force on the world of arts and culture. Soulpepper [Theatre Company] is the latest arrival, with philanthropist David Young kicking in $3 million to fund the city's first major alternative theatre space since Harbourfront's Du Maurier Theatre. Coming off its first bustling summer, the Distillery District will utterly transform the adjacent . . . area, then spill under the Gardiner [Expressway] into the Portlands and Queens Quay East (where the land values are already skyrocketing, according to municipal assessment rolls), establishing an arty post-industrial mecca.

— John Lorinc. *Toronto Life*. November 2003: 70.

Since it opened last May, the former Gooderham and Worts property . . . has become Toronto's new cultural hot spot. . . . [R]eclamation of the old industrial site is moving faster than anyone expected. 'It couldn't be going any better,' says John Berman, a partner in Cityscape Developments.

. . . [T]he idea of renovating the distillery seemed implausible. Conventional wisdom had it that the start-up costs would be prohibitive and the time required too long. Few investors, it was thought, would be willing to wait so long for a return on their investment. . . . But what the Cityscape partners realized was that by plugging into Toronto's artistic community they could bring life to the place. . . .

Andrew Ellbogen of Sound Designs is showing off an $85,000 home movie system so good it would be like having your own IMAX in the basement. 'Moving here was probably the best business decision we ever made,' Ellbogen enthuses. 'It's been fantastic. Just the setting has been fantastic. The response has been phenomenal.'. . .

Ann Seymour, an art teacher . . . in Mississauga, likes to bring her classes to the Distillery. Last week, she was there with a large group of Grade 10 students, all busy taking photographs. 'It's like coming from a desert to a feast,' Seymour says. 'There's so much here. I think it's wonderful. The Distillery provides Toronto with an old and historical section, a soul.'

— Christopher Hume. *Toronto Star*.
16 November 2003: B5

(Reprinted with permission—Torstar Syndication Services)

in the 1840s amid the rapid colonial settlement of the commercial period. Placed on the north outskirts of town as a church for a low-income district located there, by the 1870s it was in the middle of the city surrounded by houses. A few decades later, the houses were gone, replaced by six- to twelve-storey factories and mail-order buildings put up by the Eaton's department store company to consolidate many small operations it had scattered around town and the work of several small suppliers it absorbed (see Figures 15.3 and 15.4). With some 5,000 employees at their peak, these buildings were among the city's largest workplaces until the 1960s when Eaton—increasingly securing its merchandise in the global market[6] and now directing its energy towards

Figure 15.3 The Surroundings of the Holy Trinity Church, 1884

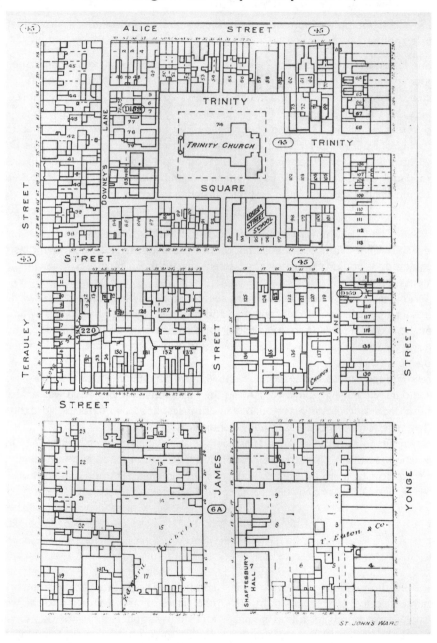

In 1884, the fabric of the pre-industrial city was still in place on the blocks around Holy Trinity Church. Apart from commercial uses along Yonge Street, the neighbourhood was mostly residential, and in photographs from the period the church dominates its surroundings, the largest building in the area. Take note of Eaton's small department store on Yonge Street south of the church (Goad 1884, Plate 9).

Figure 15.4 The Surroundings of Holy Trinity Church, 1923

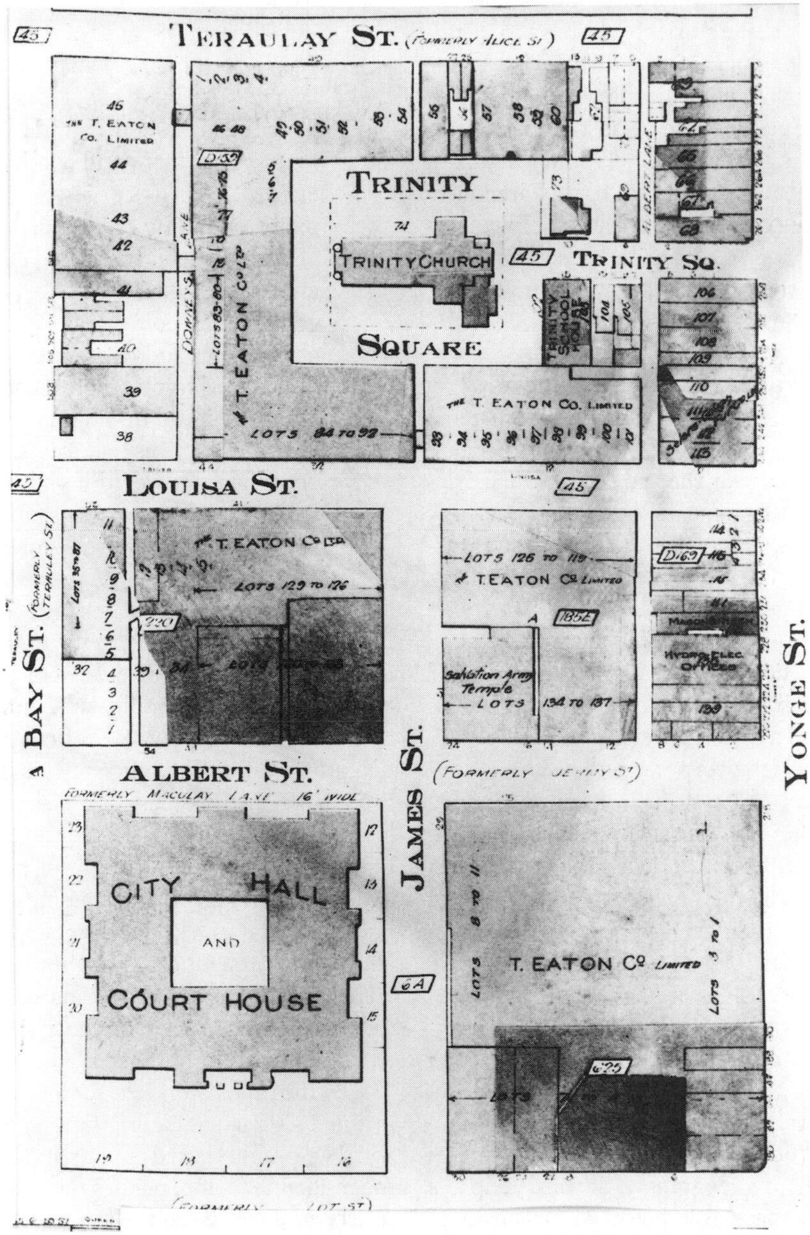

By 1923, Holy Trinity Church was surrounded on three sides by the high walls of massive factories, warehouses, and mail-order buildings put up by the Eaton department store company. A Toronto historian described the church in this new setting as 'like Truth at the bottom of a well' (Middleton 1923, 695). Two other recent arrivals in the neighbourhood were City Hall, completed in 1899, and Eaton's new, much larger store (Goad 1923, Plate 9).

stores in new suburban malls—began to curtail its manufacturing and mail-order operations.

To this point, the stories of church and distillery are much the same: a pre-industrial landscape was replaced by a major manufacturing complex that then became obsolete in post-industrial Toronto. Now the tales diverge. Unlike the distillery's buildings, no Eaton factories or warehouses remain, and their fate and the nature of what replaced them, Eaton Centre, illustrate two more of this chapter's themes, the corporatization of the city and the transience of urban fabrics.

The Corporate Urban Landscape

Today, downtown **superblock** projects are taken for granted in Canadian cities. But when Eaton first framed a plan for the site of its old factories in the mid-1960s, the idea was visionary, clearly imagining the shape of still-nascent post-industrial urbanism. It had three components: a large shopping mall (a new suburban form to be transplanted downtown) that would shift urban retail activity from the city's streets into a controlled interior environment, four commercial/residential towers, and a hotel/convention centre. Eaton's plan anticipated the corporatized city.

A key facet of the shifts from one economic phase to another is identified in Stelter's observation that the different periods embody distinct sets of power relations 'between people, groups, and a place, and between places and larger society'. In the era of post-industrial urbanism, power over place is increasingly concentrated in the hands of global corporations and their managers—for example, multinational firms based in Hong Kong that dominate redevelopment of Toronto's central waterfront and downtown rail yards. The ethos of corporate city-building is tersely defined by geographer Edward Relph: a view of urban space as 'a potential *commodity* to be exploited, managed, or manipulated in whatever ways will ensure . . . profitability' (1987, 188). Relph identifies five forms commonly used by modern development firms to commodify city space, to which we may add two more:

- office towers that not only function as workplaces but are also meant to connote power, wealth, and prestige (termed by Relph 'towers of conspicuous administration')[7];
- large tracts of suburban houses;
- luxury apartment and condominium towers;
- major shopping malls whose tenants are almost all chain stores and corporate franchises[8];
- commercial boulevards lined mostly by chain stores and corporate franchises;
- hotel/convention centre complexes that are home away from home for roving corporate executives and tourists;
- corporate leisure edifices, including professional sport venues, cineplex/amusement centres, and mega–musical theatres.

Two of these forms, housing tracts and commercial boulevards, are specific to the outer zone of the city. The other five ways of packaging urban space as a commodity are found across the metropolitan area but are often most opulent downtown—modern office towers like Toronto's Brookfield Place (formerly BCE Place) whose heroic lobby recalls a Gothic cathedral; condominium buildings that offer 'a culture of personal space and refined living . . . the epitome of urban life'[9]; luxury hotels with a dazzling array of business and tourist amenities; sport and entertainment arenas (often with corporate names) like Toronto's Rogers and Air Canada centres; multilevel interior shopping complexes like Eaton Centre.

By the time Eaton Centre was eventually built in the 1970s, after Eaton's formed a partnership with a Toronto-based multinational developer, the residential component of the project had been jettisoned. But the mall, office towers, and a hotel now encircle Holy Trinity in place of the vanished factories (see Figure 15.5). The vicinity of Eaton Centre has also been increasingly corporatized, with condominium towers, a multiplex cinema, a growing number of corporate franchises (The Gap,

Figure 15.5 Holy Trinity Church after construction of Eaton Centre

Holy Trinity was built in 1847 in a field at the north outskirts of town, meant to serve as a parish church for a working-class district located there. As seen in Figures 15.3 and 15.4, it was later surrounded by houses, then by Eaton's loft factory buildings. Today, it is surrounded by the corporate fabric of Eaton Centre. This picture was taken when Eaton Centre still had an Eaton's store before the company went out of business in 1999 (*Jon Caulfield*).

Starbucks, H&M, Hardrock Café, Guess) and some downtown versions of big-box stores. Meanwhile, the visual field of the surrounding streets is saturated with high-tech media promoting corporate product—'a noisy barrage of video screens, LED signs, oversized billboards. . . . Everywhere you look you're exhorted to buy, spend, acquire, and desire' (Hume 2008). Today, Holy Trinity Church is in the midst of a fabric of *corporate urbanism*.

The Transience of City Fabrics

The cycle of upheaval in the church's surroundings also illustrates the impermanence of urban fabric. City-dwellers are accustomed to persistent change in the outer urban zone, a process begun in Toronto 60 years ago when in only two decades, 1951 to 1971, the suburbs of North York, Scarborough, and Etobicoke collectively grew from around 200,000 residents to more than a million. Pastures, woodlots, and ravines were transformed as housing tracts, high-rise clusters, shopping malls, and expressways. This pace of change continues today with relentless development of corporate suburbs at the ever-spreading metropolitan edge.

Older parts of Canadian cities, though, may seem at first glance solid and enduring, particularly

> ## Box 15.2 'New-Build Gentrification'
>
> Condominium construction and gentrification, which are remaking urban Canada's residential geography, are both clearly parts of a single process. With each, a basic element of industrial urbanism undergoes sweeping change—gentrification in older working-class neighbourhoods and condominium development on industrial **brownfield sites** once occupied by factories, warehouses, and rail yards. Together, they compose what is sometimes described as an *embourgeoisment* of the inner zone of the city as it is resettled by middle- and upper-income households. A recent debate has centred on whether, because they are so closely entwined, the two processes should be subsumed under the same name by identifying condominium zones as *new-build gentrification*. On the one hand, condominium development 'involves middle-class resettlement of the central city, the production of a gentrified landscape, and lower-income displacement in the adjacent residential communities', but on the other, 'different groups of people are involved, different kinds of landscapes are . . . produced, and different sociospatial dynamics are operating' (Davidson and Lees 2005, 1,169). To some extent, it is a semantic debate. Whatever words are used, the essential issue is that gentrification and condominium construction are analytically distinct parts of a coherent larger process.

among younger city-dwellers who have less experience of urban change. Stability does characterize some parts of the older fabric. Toronto has buildings that have been in use for more than a century. Holy Trinity's ministry, for example, has continued unbroken 155 years. Or old buildings may be kept for historical or cultural reasons. Eaton's first superblock plan imagined demolition of Toronto's Old City Hall, a proposal undone by a citizens' group that argued the building was vital to the city's architectural heritage. Older neighbourhoods, too—usually privileged districts like Toronto's Rosedale—may experience decades of quiet stability. But processes of change are more often the rule. When cities are viewed across time, the transience of their fabrics is evident. They are constant works in progress, in continual flux.

This occurs at variable scales and speeds. Eaton Centre and Toronto's St Jamestown neighbourhood—16 high-rise apartment towers built in the 1960s on nine square blocks northeast of downtown—are examples of **cataclysmic change** involving abrupt demolition and rebuilding of a whole area. Or cataclysmic reshaping of

urban space may occur across several sites. Today, scores of condominium projects are recently built, under construction, or planned within a few kilometres of Toronto's downtown, mostly large projects at scattered locations that formerly had non-residential—usually industrial—functions (see Box 15.2). The once-sprawling rail yard beside the city's downtown—now the site of the Rogers Centre, the CN Tower, and a growing forest of condominium towers—illustrates an even more dramatic kind of change. It was built on manufactured space half a kilometre deep, four kilometres wide, created by landfilling Lake Ontario in the early 1900s for industrial, rail, and port facilities.[10]

Patterns of home renovation in older neighbourhoods illustrate processes of more **gradual change**. While gentrification, for example, sometimes occurs rapidly, it is more often piecemeal, as was a style of remodelling among Toronto's southern European immigrants in recent decades, sometimes named *mediterraneanization* (see Box 15.3). Mediterraneanization was usually done house by scattered house over many years until homes with this appearance became com-

Box 15.3 *The Social Nature of Urban Forms: Gentrification and Mediterraneanization*

Mediterraneanization and gentrification are distinct approaches to the exterior renovation of old city houses that offer a good example of the social nature of urban forms. Two key variables in these processes are social class and the cultural heritage of ethnicity. Working-class Italian, Portuguese, and Greek immigrants who renovated inner Toronto homes often installed new red brick or decorative stone facades, replaced old wooden porches with concrete verandas that featured brick arches and iron railings, and used aluminum windows, trim, and fascia in place of the original wood. In gentrified renovation, the original brick and woodwork of the facades are carefully restored or replaced, and old wood-frame windows are refurbished (and are especially valued if they are stained glass). Verandas, though, are often removed, reflecting middle-class disinclination from the active social life at the front of homes often evident in working-class districts. *Mediterraneanization* and *gentrification* illustrate that the same kind of gradual neighbourhood change—renovating house exteriors—may take quite different paths based on the social and cultural tendencies of the groups involved.

mon in an area. Old commercial areas experience a similar kind of gradual change as a store here, a store there, are renovated for existing businesses or remodelled for new ones. While change at this scale is incremental, its eventual outcome is city fabric slowly refashioned in basic ways.

The overall pace of urban change is not constant. The dramatic periods of spatial restructuring that accompanied the onsets of industrial and post-industrial urbanism happened fitfully. The 1920s, for example, was a time of concentrated city-building in Toronto that ended abruptly with the Great Depression of the 1930s when very little development occurred. Similarly, during the economic doldrums of the 1990s, downtown office construction slowed to a standstill. A project then underway was terminated with only an underground parking garage and a few storeys of elevator stack completed. Known as 'The Stump', it stayed this way for 15 years until development of the site recommenced in 2007. (The slump of the 1990s also led to the residential conversion of a modernist office building in the heart of downtown.) In contrast, in the decade 1964 to 1974, massive bank towers of 56, 57, and 72 storeys appeared on three of the four corners at King and Bay streets in the core of Toronto's financial district (with a 68-storey tower built on the fourth corner in the 1980s). Someone familiar with this intersection before the skyscrapers appeared, or familiar with the locales of St James-town or Eaton Centre before their construction, would not recognize these places afterwards, so thorough was the erasure of their earlier fabric.

A useful way to conceptualize urban change imagines shifts of urban form or urban function (built elements of city fabric and how they are used) that animate shifts of urban meaning (how city-dwellers understand and experience urban forms and functions). For example, a key goal of the managers of the Distillery District is to maintain Victorian industrial form amid total rescripting of its function. An interior factory space of rough masonry, timeworn brick, and old timbers is now a gallery showing major works of avant-garde art, change that wholly alters how users understand and experience the space—its meaning. Millions of dollars have been committed to modernizing the distillery's invisible infrastructure—its electrical, plumbing, and heating systems—with millions more spent to preserve the buildings' nineteenth-century appearance.

Viewed from down the block, their form appears much as it was when whisky was made here.

Holy Trinity Church and Old City Hall, in contrast, are the only stable elements of a fabric otherwise entirely remade. Eaton Centre's commercial space, office towers, and hotel revise the urban form, function, and meaning of the district everywhere but on Yonge Street, where the function remains retail-commercial. But a user's experience of interior corporatized space is very different from the experience of a traditional city street, and so the meaning of Yonge Street is recast.

The space of the inner zone of the city is like a kaleidoscope turning at variable speeds—impermanent and constantly in motion, sometimes slowly, sometimes at a rapid pace.

Regent Park

Regent Park, Canada's largest **public housing** project, is home to about 7,500 residents who live in 2,000 high- and low-rise apartment and townhouse units built in the 1950s on 14 square blocks east of downtown. Regent Park had three roots:

* the view of many citizens and social agencies that the life chances of low-income city-dwellers would be substantially improved if they had better housing;
* the belief of **growth-booster** business groups and civic officials that the city's 'slums' were a significant impediment to downtown development investment;
* the vision of an architectural movement named **modernism**, a main theme of this part of the chapter.

Regent Park reflects modernist design ideas in many ways. First, it was what is sometimes called clean-sweep *urban renewal* because it erased an entire neighbourhood; only a couple of churches and a school were left standing.

Second, like Eaton Centre it is a *superblock*; all but one of the streets that formerly crisscrossed the area were removed. Third, except for a few institutional buildings, Regent Park has only one function, residential; retail and other commercial uses that were part of the earlier fabric were eliminated. Fourth, the project's design is implacably utilitarian, with little architectural flourish or decoration, reflecting modernism's aesthetic code of functional efficiency (see Figure 15.6).

Regent Park is widely regarded as an idea that has not worked. Many early residents have good memories of their time there (see Box 15.4), and people who make their homes in Regent Park today often react angrily—with good reason—to stereotypes of the neighbourhood as a troubled ghetto. But it remains flawed planning, in part because its residents are almost solely low-income. Median annual household income is less than $24,000, and 70 per cent of households live below the poverty line.[11] The implications of this **demography** are amplified by Regent Park's isolation, cut off from the city by the absence of both through streets and mixed uses that might draw in outsiders. Meanwhile, the lack of variety in the kinds and ages of the buildings excludes the possibility of evolution in how the neighbourhood is used and who uses it. Trapped in time, Regent Park can never be anything other than what it is.

The Vision and Perversion of Modernism

The influence of modernist urbanism is a force deeply embedded in the fabric of Canadian cities. Common features of urban landscapes today—superblocks, segregation of land uses, high-rise residential buildings, office towers rising from concrete plazas, expressways linking zones of specialized use—originated with modernism.

The modernist movement arose in Europe during the early twentieth century in response to the devastating effects of industrialism on the physical and social fabrics of cities. Modernists believed that the fate of industrial urbanism was anarchy—that the intense crowding of people and of ever-larger factories and skyscrapers onto the template of the pre-industrial city could not

Figure 15.6 In a Courtyard at Regent Park

Modernist principles of functionality and segregated use are in evidence in Regent Park, a neighbourhood east of downtown where 14 city blocks were erased in the 1950s for the construction of public housing. Toronto's civic government now plans to replace Regent Park with a dense and socially diverse neighbourhood of mixed uses. The buildings and courtyard pictured here have already been demolished (*Jon Caulfield*).

Box 15.4 *Regent Park Remembered*

I was a child of a working-poor family that moved into one of the brand-new low rises of Regent Park in the early 1950s. . . . [H]eat and hot water were novelties, but excitement was soon replaced by the awesome reality of being warm, with hot water to wash in, of having a refrigerator that ran on electricity, instead of an ice box. . . . [I]n those first decades, Regent Park lived up to its promises . . . a neighbourhood where everyone knew each other, where everyone was house proud, where neighbours were there to help, where deliverymen brought bread and milk to the door.

I grew up in Regent Park and left only when it was time to go to university. My family, including cousins and aunts and uncles, also moved on to better things, like home ownership and good jobs. And when we get together, our memories of the neighbourhood are warm and positive. . . . For several decades, Regent Park provided what it was intended to provide: a safe, secure place for families to live, meeting the basics of human needs, like heat, water, shelter, plumbing, all of which were missing from the firetraps that were there before. But most of all, it gave security, self-esteem, pride, and hope.

— Brian McAteer, letter to the editor, *Toronto Star*, 21 March 2003: A31.

be sustained. The solution they imagined was total rebuilding of the city according to a new science of urban design.

Among their main concerns were conditions of everyday life experienced by working-class city-dwellers—the masses of industrial urbanism pressed into dense, squalid slums (Relph 1987, 106–12). Decades before, an observer of a working-class district in an early industrial city in Britain described:

wretched, damp, filthy cottages [amid] streets . . . in the most miserable and filthy condition, laid out without the slightest reference to ventilation, with reference solely to the profit secured by the contractor. . . . [N]o cleanliness, no convenience . . . no comfortable family life is possible (Engels 1987 [1845], 100).[12]

A central element of modernism's agenda was to replace this kind of slum with healthy and efficient housing oriented to **use value** rather than to the money that might be made—**exchange value**—and in so doing promote a more equitable city.

Regent Park is not what modernists had in mind. One of the movement's passionate advocates wrote in the 1930s that '[n]othing positive can be accomplished by clearing slums and simply erecting new buildings on the same sites' (Giedion 1967, 822)—exactly what Toronto did in Regent Park. Rather, modernism imagined urban planning in the context of an ambitious program of progressive social development that envisioned the city and its parts as a coherent human fabric. Regent Park, though, was built with little thought for its surroundings (so, for example, its residents have been perennially without adequate nearby essential services and shopping facilities for their families). While the project's design observes modernism's codes of functionality and efficiency, it is inconsistent with its humanitarian values. Meant as interim housing for low-income tenants, it seems to have been deliberately made 'bland and spartan . . . forestall[ing] any glimmer of aesthetic or social pleasure' (McHugh 1989: 147).

Another case of modernism abused is St Jamestown. Here, a Victorian neighbourhood was almost wholly removed for high-rise towers where

15,000 people now live. St Jamestown differs from Regent Park in that most of its buildings are not public housing (a few are) but were built for profit by private-sector corporations. A trendy middle-class neighbourhood for a few years after it was built, it soon began to deteriorate. Today it is in rough condition, and its tenants are mostly a polyglot mix of Third World immigrants, members of the post-industrial global working class. (One reason for St Jamestown's deterioration is that it accommodates a much larger population than it was meant to house because families now live in units designed for smaller non-family households.)

St Jamestown is sometimes unfairly cited as an example of the ills of modernist design—unfair because the project's modernism is only skin-deep. Modernists imagined their high-rises in parks where residents found ample green space just outside the front door, but St Jamestown's towers are set in scraps of ill-kept lawn. Modernists believed that good housing was a social right and that building housing as a commodity oriented to exchange value undermined sound planning objectives. This certainly seems to be what happened in St Jamestown. It is a parody of modernism.

Downtown office-tower development has also often abused modernist ideas. Modernists imagined large and well-designed plazas at the bases of their skyscrapers that would be contemporary versions of the public squares of classical and medieval cities—centres of civic life where city-dwellers gathered for commerce and for cultural and political expression. But most new downtown office towers in Canadian cities are built up to the sidewalk, with little provision for public space apart from occasional zones of wind-swept concrete and interior corporate malls. So while modernism has had profound effects on Canadian cities and their everyday life, it has often been a perverted modernism of design forms stripped from the contexts of a progressive social vision and comprehensive urban planning.

Evidence of what modernist city space might look like as its framers envisioned it is found in the Toronto neighbourhood of St Lawrence. Built in the late 1970s at the initiative of the city's municipal government, St Lawrence is another example of clean-sweep demolition for new housing. But in this case, the area erased was not a neighbourhood but a downtown zone of worn-out industrial and warehousing uses. St Lawrence's six- to 10-storey apartment buildings are set along a boulevard beside a well-kept park, with low-rise apartments and townhouses on side streets behind them. The area may seem akin to places like Regent Park and St Jamestown, but the resemblance is superficial. The neighbourhood is home to about 12,000 residents, many of whom live in tenant-managed **non-profit housing cooperatives** occupied by middle- and lower-income households whose rents are geared to their incomes. It has an active community life and long waiting lists of people seeking to move into one of the co-ops. Its success has helped stimulate private-sector condominium development on adjacent streets. While St Lawrence varies in some ways from modernist thinking—for example, it is knit into the city's street system—it also suggests that modernism's vision of good urban space oriented to use value is achievable (Hulchanski 1990).

The Anti-modernist Movement

In 2006, the City of Toronto began to demolish Regent Park. The plan for the neighbourhood that will replace it derives from a widespread movement against ways that ideas of modernist urbanism were being applied. Many city-dwellers and city planners were strongly critical of the indiscriminate razing of neighbourhoods for the kinds of cataclysmic projects that development corporations and government agencies were building; they did not believe that traditional urban space should be tossed in the dustbin.

One theme of the critics was that older built forms are essential parts of the history and heritage of urban places, important to the identities of cities and their citizens. This idea is reflected in *Lost Toronto*, a book about scores of demolished buildings from Toronto's 'rich treasure' of architecture, many of which were removed for redevelopment schemes. Its author argues that the 'architecture [of the past] adds an important dimension to our understanding' of a city and its people (Dendy 1993, xiii)—architecture that in many cases may now be seen only in photographs. This kind of sentiment was at the root of the opposition to Eaton's proposal to bulldoze Old City Hall. Other buildings saved from demolition for heritage preservation include Toronto's neoclassical railway terminal and a nearby locomotive roundhouse (that now houses a microbrewery), many nineteenth-century civic and institutional buildings, and dozens of old houses—structures said to embody key facets of the city's social and architectural history.

A second argument against removing older parts of city fabrics is that doing so dissolves the time-tested logic of urban space as it evolved over centuries. A key figure here is Jane Jacobs, whose *Death and Life of Great American Cities* argued that traditional urban places have qualities that allow them to serve as 'effective economic pools of use' and to regenerate over time through processes of gradual change (Jacobs 1961, 143–238):

- mixed **primary uses**, including a good measure of residential use, that draw different people into an area on different schedules for different reasons;
- a high concentration of people and closely-grained activities;
- older lower-cost buildings that act as economic incubators for commercial uses that require low rents and for innovative entrepreneurial activities;
- a crisscrossing grid of streets that draws people into and through an area along a complexity of routes.

Jacobs challenged the idea that a high-density jumble of people and activities is a recipe for urban anarchy. While older urban districts—like old Chinatowns—may look chaotic at first glance, she wrote, this surface appearance conceals a complex and durable economic logic that has its roots in urban history. Jacobs scorned clean-sweep destruction of traditional urban places. 'This is not the rebuilding of cities. This is the sacking of cities. . . . [T]he entire concoction is irrelevant to the workings of cities' (1961, 4, 25).

Jacobs's influence on city planning was considerable, illustrated, for example, by a plan written in the 1970s for the Southeast Spadina neighbourhood, the site of Toronto's own Chinatown, whose residents defeated a proposal to demolish the area for high-density commercial, institutional, and residential development. The new plan sustained the neighbourhood's old fabric and described its mix of uses, concentration of activities, and old buildings as key ingredients of a district that worked perfectly well for a diverse range of residents and businesses (CTPB 1972). Across town, people living in the Trefann Court neighbourhood resisted a 1960s proposal that their homes be razed for an extension of Regent Park. Here too the revised plan reflected Jacobs's thinking, retaining the area's closely grained uses, raising its density, and keeping its street system (Caulfield 1994, 70–1).

Post-modern City Form

Redevelopment of Regent Park will take more than a decade as the area is rebuilt piece by piece (to avoid wholly dislocating its current residents). Public- and private-sector investment will produce a residential fabric of condominiums, rental apartments, and townhouses with a social mix mirroring St Lawrence—half the units rent-geared-to-income, the remainder market-based for more affluent households. Again, the plan echoes Jacobs:

- residential density will nearly double (with no net loss of low-income units);
- a mix of uses will include street-level retail businesses throughout the district as well as offices, studios, and other kinds of non-residential space;

Box 15.5 *Post-modern Form in Suburbs*

The post-modern genre of producing new buildings that imitate traditional urban forms is common today, not only in the older realm of the city but also in newer suburbs—for example, commercial malls designed to look like rows of colonial Canadian homes (in styles that would not usually be found together, recalling Jean Baudrillard's definition of *simulation*: a copy of an original that never existed [1983]). Some new residential subdivisions feature houses that imitate the Victorian and Georgian domestic architecture of small-town and rural Ontario. Billboards at two of these projects advertised 'Heritage Inspired Homes' and 'The Traditional Village Community', an appeal to an apparent nostalgia for simpler bygone times.

Elsewhere are subdivisions derived from a mode of urban design named new urbanism that imagines suburban neighbourhoods built to resemble older parts of the city with higher densities than most suburbs, houses placed close to the sidewalk, and corner stores and other mixed uses just down the street (and cars sequestered in garages along back laneways). Similar thinking on a grander scale is reflected in the preliminary design of a new 'downtown' in the Toronto suburb of Vaughan that models the project on traditional urban centres and makes reference to streetscape features found in Barcelona, Paris, Savannah, Washington, and inner Toronto (CV 1997).

Post-modern urbanism is also evident in suburban communities where local movements arise to protect historic town centres and old rural forms threatened by the sprawl of surrounding development. Movements to preserve old town centres have both popular and official roots, on the one hand driven by sentiments of long-time community members against the erasure of local history, on the other hand supported by civic administrators who recognize the value of heritage as a draw for investment and 'desirable' new residents.

• streets removed for the 1950s superblock will be replaced, linking the neighbourhood back into the city's street grid.

Urban development in this vein—new development that replicates old city forms—is common today, one of *three key genres* of what is sometimes named **post-modern urbanism**. Replicated in Regent Park is a whole neighbourhood, built on the template of traditional city fabric. New buildings also often draw on past styles—for example, the lobby of Brookfield Place (formerly BCE Place), which echoes a Gothic cathedral, or the galleria design of Eaton Centre that recalls the architecture of nineteenth-century European shopping arcades. Post-modern form is sometimes crafted to illude, as with recent Toronto condominiums that resemble converted industrial structures or old apartment buildings. New houses made to look like nineteenth-century Victorian homes are common in the city's neighbourhoods (see Box 15.5).

A second genre of post-modern urbanism maintains old city forms with their original functions. This includes old residential neighbourhoods secured from redevelopment and buildings like Toronto's old rail station, still used as a train terminal. Other examples are nineteenth-century office buildings renovated as high-end professional and business space, commercial districts like Toronto's Kensington Market and Chinatown zoned to remain what they are, and old theatres grandly refurbished as venues for tourist-attraction productions.

A third genre of post-modern urbanism is adaptive reuse of old forms of which Toronto's most vivid current example is the distillery.

Box 15.6 *Adaptive Reuse: An Urban Tradition*

While *adaptive reuse* is common in cities today, it is not a new phenomenon but an urban tradition. This is illustrated by four examples from Toronto's Spadina District, west of downtown, that became home to Jewish immigrants in the early 1900s.

A retail district here, Kensington Market, is a part of an originally middle-class residential neighbourhood that became a commercial zone when Jewish-immigrant merchants decided to park their wagons in front of their homes and draw customers to them instead of plying the streets of the city with their wares. The wagons were eventually enclosed by extensions built onto the fronts of houses, and the market was born. The Jews are now mostly gone, but the market remains, its stores run by immigrants from the four corners of the globe.

Nearby is a large nineteenth-century home that was adapted as a synagogue after its middle-class residents sold it and decamped to the suburbs of the industrial city. Pews from a demolished Christian church were cut to fit into the house's front rooms, and stone tablets announcing the building's new identity in Yiddish script were installed by the front door. Today the building is a house again, but the tablets remain as a reminder of its past.

A few blocks away, a Christian church that fell into disuse as Jews increasingly settled the neighbourhood was sold in 1909 to a Jewish garment firm that adapted it as a small factory, and it continues to house garment-trade businesses today. While its ecclesiastical architecture is no longer apparent when the building is seen from the front, it is clearly evident when viewed from the rear.

Two other nearby churches were adapted as synagogues, a reuse that required modifying their architecture by removing the pointed steeples that clearly marked them as Christian buildings and putting rounded domes in their place. (One was later adapted as a community centre.)

Elsewhere on the waterfront, an old warehouse has been restored as posh retail, office, performance, and condominium space, and a former hydro facility beside it now houses a theatre and avant-garde art gallery. Old garment and mattress factories are remade as condominiums, the stables of the city's nineteenth-century streetcar company are now a children's theatre, and an 1899 coal-gas plant is a police station. Old downtown churches are reused as a dance theatre, academic offices, condominiums, a boutique mall, and a community centre, and old downtown houses are adapted as pubs, coffee shops, offices, and in one case, a boutique hotel (see Box 15.6).

A powerful economic motive underlies corporate and municipal support for post-modern urbanism in the context of the post-industrial city. In an era when capital and labour are highly mobile, cities competing for business and investment must offer distinction as places in which to live.

In the industrial era, white- and blue-collar workers migrated to a fixed site of capital, the factory city. But this pattern is now reversed, especially among workers in the most sought-after jobs as investment often follows high-end post-industrial labour to the most prestigious metropolitan centres. A provincial report on the future of Ontario cities advises:

> To be successful in this emerging creative age, regions must develop, attract, and retain talented and creative people who generate innovations, develop technology-intensive industries, and power economic growth. Such talented people . . . tend to concentrate within particular city regions (Gertler et al. 2002, ii).

Box 15.7 Bilbaoism

It is not only 'authentic' urban forms alive with history and heritage that cities on the make seek to encourage but also what is sometimes termed starchitecture—buildings by pre-eminent architects that will earn global attention. The model for this is Bilbao, a city in Spain whose 1997 Guggenheim museum has become an envied tourist destination (see Chapter 11). But it is not primarily tourists who are the intended audience for starchitecture but Florida's 'creative class', the human capital who will be drawn to cities with a flair for adventurous and prestigious architecture and whose presence will help breed post-industrial prosperity. Toronto culture and tourism officials advertise several new buildings in this vein, including the Royal Ontario Museum's Crystal, the renovated Art Gallery of Ontario (by Toronto native Frank Gehry, who also designed the Bilbao Guggenheim), the Four Seasons Centre for the Performing Arts, which houses the Canadian Opera Company and National Ballet, and the Ontario College of Art's Sharp Centre for Design (buildings viewable at http://www.tobuilt.ca). Urban-growth policies of the industrial era focused on infrastructural systems and municipal services to attract manufacturers. Today, culture, the arts, and architecture are the currency of growth-boosterism.

A co-author of the report, Richard Florida, has coined the term *creative class* to denote the kind of post-industrial workforce cities hope to lure (2002/4; 2005; see Chapter 11, Box 11.6). A more recent report identifies 'lessons' from Toronto that may be useful for cities framing plans 'to enhance the growth and development of [their] creative industries' (Gertler, Tesolin, and Weinstock 2006, 3, 51–2).

Critical ingredients in efforts to nurture a high quality of cosmopolitan life are the calibre of a city's built forms and the sense of urban place and culture of everyday life they afford, a context in which the craft of place-making assumes a key role in civic policy. Because an essential element of place in today's urban climate is an 'authentic' aura of heritage and history, post-modern planning and design are critical to a city's fortunes. This sense of place works together with the local culture and leisure industries to draw the human capital that will in turn attract investment (Zukin 1995; see Box 15.7).

The Dialogical Roots of Urban Form

Regent Park also illustrates another facet of urban forms, their dialogical quality.[13] The word *dialogical* may seem remote but provides a good metaphor to connote the complex roots from which urban forms often arise. In contrast with monologue, in which one voice speaks, dialogue involves at least two voices, perhaps many. In Regent Park, we hear a range of voices—of social agencies and citizens concerned about providing good-quality housing for low-income families, of growth-minded civic officials hoping to promote development investment, of modernist architects who decades earlier had sought to address the crisis of industrial urbanism. Modernism was also among the roots of St Jamestown, paradoxically joined with the impulse of property capital towards securing maximum profit from urban space, a curious dialogue of bold utopianism and opportunistic corporatization (see Figure 15.7).

At least *three* kinds of dialogue are common in urban forms. One involves intersections of different moments of a city's history, exemplified by the fit of Holy Trinity Church with its current surroundings. In the distillery, we hear the voice of Victorian industrial architecture adapted to the lifeworld of post-industrial urbanism. The Gladstone Hotel, once a railway inn serving factory-era business travellers to plants

Figure 15.7 Apartment Towers in St Jamestown

St Jamestown, a neighbourhood of 16 apartment towers built in the 1960s, is now home mostly to a polyglot mix of Third World immigrants, members of the post-industrial working class. It is an urban fabric where seemingly incompatible voices are joined together—those of modernism, whose utopian visionaries decades ago sought to imagine good housing for low-income industrial workers, and of corporate property capital seeking to secure the highest profit from a tract of urban space (*Jon Caulfield*).

like Massey-Harris, is now a hive of avant-garde cultural activity where 'creative' workers lodge in rooms designed by artists.

A second kind of dialogue arises from an interaction of more local and more global voices, illustrated, for example, by a proliferation of venues like the Distillery District on waterfronts. The near-universal post-industrial appearance of 'revitalized' waterfronts (or riverfronts) is not co-incidence but reflects a more general pattern as shorelines cease to be industrial resources and factory zones and become viewed as lucrative environmental and lifestyle amenities. But the spe-

cific ways that waterfronts are redeveloped also reflect the practices of a given city's entrepreneurs and civic officials who produce particular local expressions of the more general tendency (Desfor, Goldrick, and Merrens 1988, 110). Cityscape, for example, the company that repackaged the distillery, framed a business plan that ran contrary to accepted wisdom in the heritage industry—for example, it imagined casting working artists as a primary centrepiece of the distillery, not just a side attraction—and was termed 'economically dubious' by another heritage developer (Lewington 2002, 73).[14] It was a distinct and unorthodox

> ### Box 15.8 The Dialogical Subdivision
> The suburban subdivision of single-family homes is a good example of the dialogical nature of urban space.
>
> - The suburb derives from ideas about how to build housing at the city's outskirts that arose in late eighteenth-century Britain amid the Industrial Revolution.
> - Various principles of subdivision design, like putting homes on crescents and cul-de-sacs and grouping blocks of houses around schools, arise from an early twentieth-century planning idea, the 'neighbourhood unit'.
> - The single-family home of separate rooms with special purposes (living, dining, bed) is domestic architecture based in ideas about home and family intimacy that arose in seventeenth-century Holland (Rybczynski 1986, 15–75).
> - The ranch and split-level design of many suburban houses derives from the ideas of twentieth-century American architect Frank Lloyd Wright.
> - Placing homes on trim lawns with carefully tended gardens arises from an eighteenth-century British aesthetic movement, the 'picturesque' school.
> - Subdivisions also reflect the ambitions of local civic governments to promote the growth of their towns and of development corporations to find profitable investments.
>
> The modern suburban subdivision is a highly dialogical form in which an entire chorus of voices is audible.

approach, made in Toronto, to a process occurring in cities more globally. Cityscape also had to work within the specific local context of the city's planning and heritage preservation regulations. This kind of dialogue is also illustrated in a theatre district on King Street west of downtown. Theatre districts of this kind, where blockbuster contemporary shows are produced, are often found in post-industrial cities. But the district's location at this specific site was the work of an entrepreneur named Honest Ed Mirvish, who in 1963 when post-industrial urbanism was barely in its infancy bought the Royal Alex Theatre to save it from demolition and kept it as a theatre. The global and the local come together on King Street.

A third way that urban forms are dialogical involves collisions and conjunctions of differing political or economic interests. One voice heard in Eaton Centre, for example, is that of Toronto's civic government, which sought to promote imaginative architecture in the project, prevent demolition of Old City Hall and Holy Trinity Church, and develop a public square beside the church. Another voice was that of Eaton's, seeking the full exchange value its superblock might produce, reflected in the comment of an Eaton official about the idea of a public square on land that might have been much more profitably used: '[W]e cannot support it from any realistic commercial point of view' (CHTA 1970). But the company was later forced to recant this position because it could not complete its shopping mall plan without cutting a deal with Holy Trinity. The public square beside the church today reflects a dialogue of conflicting interests.

Grasping their dialogical quality is essential to making sense of urban forms (see Box 15.8).

Conclusion

This chapter uses urban forms in Toronto's inner metropolitan zone to explore key features of Canadian cities today. In particular, it stresses ways that a city's economy may shape its fabric, the role of corporations in producing urban space, the constant remaking of the city's landscape, the influence of the modernist and post-modern movements on the city, and the dialogical nature of urban forms. While the chapter's focus is Toronto, none of its themes are unique to that city. The challenge for readers elsewhere is to use the ideas raised as tools to explore their own urban realms, and towards this objective, the following project is suggested, 'Exploring City Places Photographically'.

Project: Exploring City Places Photographically

A good way to explore city places is with a camera. Taking photographs requires active, critical observation of urban forms in the process of deciding what pictures to make. There are many possible themes for photographs in the urban field. A few are suggested here[15] that may be pursued in a series of photographic exercises.

- an area's (or building's) location within the city and its fit with adjacent areas (or buildings);
- urban forms and their arrangement—for example, buildings (big or small, old or new, high- or low-density, in good or shabby condition?) and their architecture (and also the spaces between buildings);
- urban functions and their arrangement—for example, land uses that are observable and their mix and fit;
- evidence of urban meaning—of how people understand and experience a place (which may differ among different people);
- people and activities—for example, who is found in a place (the same kind of people or different kinds? and who is not found there?) and what they are doing, with attention both to an area's residents and to non-residents who may come there for different reasons on different schedules;
- evidence of the past—of the history that a place has experienced;
- signs of change with an eye for evidence of the pace of change and for discontinuities that may be occurring in the course of change;
- patterns and anomalies (what is typical or harmonious and what is untypical or discordant?);
- a juxtaposition of opposites, focusing on the side-by-sideness of disparate things;
- evidence of the encounter or dialogue of the global with the local, the corporate with the traditional, the modernist with the postmodern;
- the 'last-of' phenomenon, focusing on something that may be or may be about to become the last of its kind.

Notes

1. Today, the suburban sphere is sometimes imagined as two zones, an inner area built in the 1950s and 1960s, a lot of which is now home to working-class immigrant households, sometimes termed 'the in-between city' (Hulchanski 2007; Sieverts 2003), and beyond this, newer areas that are home mostly to middle-class and more affluent households.

2. This section draws on the work of Stelter (1982; 1986) and Simmons and Simmons (1974, 45–65).

3. This account draws statistical data from Careless (1984, 200–3) and Lemon (1985, 194–9).

4. An example of the latter is Oshawa, an automobile town for many decades.

5. An example is the meat processing industry,

which has mostly moved to Ontario sites away from Toronto. Its abandoned railside stockyards within the city are now the site of big-box stores and townhouse development.

6. Shoes illustrate the transition from phase to phase. They were produced in small shops by self-employed artisans in the pre-industrial and early industrial city, but their manufacture then shifted for many decades to large domestic factories like the Eaton buildings. Today they are mostly imported from developing countries.

7. The massive office towers of the post industrial city recall a definition of 'spectacle' framed by French social theorist Guy Debord: 'capital to such a degree of accumulation that it becomes an image' (1983, 34); see note 8.

8. Modern mega-malls recall a second definition Debord gave 'spectacle': 'the moment when the commodity has attained the total occupation of social life' (1983, 42).

9. *Condo Life* June 2003: 17; *Toronto Star* 25 January 2003: P7.

10. Also filled for portside industry were two square kilometres of marsh at the mouth of the Don River. More recently, Toronto has used rubble from demolished structures and earth from development excavations to push a four-kilometre peninsula into Lake Ontario east of downtown, the Leslie Street Spit.

11. These figures are from 2001 census tract data; 2006 income data were not available at the time

of writing. The figures overestimate income and underestimate the incidence of low-income because the Regent Park tracts also include some more advantaged households on adjacent streets.

12. Engels's tone in this passage was echoed in Toronto in 1934 by an early advocate of urban renewal plans that would 'enable workers to establish homes in proper houses and convince the worker's child that there are . . . lovelier flowers than those on the lithographed calendar that hangs on the cracked and crumbling and soiled wall of a murky room into which the sun's rays have never penetrated' (Fraser 1972, 52).

13. The term 'dialogical' is drawn from Russian theorist Mikhail Bakhtin (see, for example, Bakhtin 1984).

14. Earlier plans for the distillery had cast working artists in a subordinate role and had also proposed removal or reconstruction of several buildings to generate greater revenue (Caulfield 2005, 142–4). Cityscape's plan is to keep all the buildings, a less profitable short-run strategy. Its plan also includes three condominium towers on vacant corners of the site—formerly used as parking lots—that will provide a revenue stream and substantially increase the nearby residential population. Residents began moving into the first of these buildings in June 2008.

15. The author thanks Jon Rieger for sharing some of these items.

Suggested Reading and Viewing

This list identifies five books that provide information about specific Toronto buildings and districts and their roots and history. They are essential sources for studying urban forms in Toronto past and present.

Bureau of Architecture and Urbanism. 1987. *Toronto Modern: Architecture 1945–1965*. Toronto: Bureau of Architecture and Urbanism. *Toronto Modern* offers a general introduction to modernist architecture in Canadian cities and looks closely at 10 modernist buildings in Toronto that its authors

judge noteworthy.

Byrtus, Nancy, Mark Fram, and Michael McClelland, Eds. 2000. *East/West: A Guide to Where People Live in Downtown Toronto*. Toronto: Coach House Books. *East/West* views scores of buildings and neighbourhoods in inner Toronto through the eyes of architects, civic officials, urban researchers, local residents, and other observers.

Dendy, William. 1993. *Lost Toronto: Images of the City's Past*. Toronto: McClelland and Stewart. The author catalogues buildings of all kinds from Toronto's past that have been demolished, often for redevelopment. Richly illustrated and based in meticulous research, *Lost Toronto* provides an intimate account of traditional urban forms in Canadian cities and their social roots.

McHugh, Patricia. 1989. *Toronto Architecture: A City Guide*. Toronto: McClelland and Stewart. Organized as a series of 22 walks through districts and neighbourhoods in and around the city's downtown, *Toronto Architecture* provides accounts of the design and history of various kinds of structures, including houses, office blocks, factories, government buildings, banks, churches, and many others.

Sewell, John. 2003. *Doors Open Toronto: Illuminating the City's Great Spaces*. Toronto: Knopf Canada. Cited for excellence by the Ontario Association of Architects, *Doors Open Toronto* is a companion piece to an annual May weekend when scores of Toronto buildings usually closed to the public are opened for viewing.

These films, both available on DVD, touch on themes raised in the chapter and are highly recommended.

Last Call at the Gladstone Hotel. 2007. Toronto: Last Call Productions. 56 minutes. *Last Call* tells the story of a Toronto hotel that originated in the 1880s as lodging for travelling businessmen, later provided cheap digs for low-income tenants, and recently has become a hive of avant-garde cultural activity.

A Way Out. 2001. Toronto: Syncopated Productions. 54 minutes. *A Way Out* tells the stories of three people who grew up in Regent Park and found their way out of the culture of poverty and of a boy who lived there when the film was made and hoped to make his way out.

References

Bakhtin, M. 1984. *Problems of Dostoevsky's Poetics*. Minneapolis: University of Minnesota Press.

Baudrillard, J. 1983. *Simulations*. New York: Semiotext(e).

Careless, J.M.S. 1984. *Toronto to 1918: An Illustrated History*. Toronto: Lorimer/National Museums of Canada.

———. 1989. *Frontier and Metropolis: Regions, Cities and Identities in Canada before 1914*. Toronto: University of Toronto Press.

CATF (Core Area Task Force). 1974. *Core Area Task Force Technical Appendix*. Toronto: City of Toronto Planning Board.

Caulfield, J. 1994. *City Form and Everyday Life: Toronto's Gentrification and Critical Social Practice*. Toronto: University of Toronto Press.

———. 2001. 'Political economy pictured: Holy Trinity Church and the Eaton Company'. *Sociological Imagination* 38 (1/2): 29–64.

———. 2005. 'The Distillery District'. *Urban Planning Overseas 2005*. English version, 85–97. www.arts. yorku.ca/sosc/urbanst/publications.html.

CHTA (Church of the Holy Trinity Archives). 1970. Correspondence of M. Sphon to H. Casson, 6 February.

CT (City of Toronto). 2001. *Toronto at the Crossroads: Shaping Our Future*. Toronto: City Planning Division, Urban Development Services.

CTPB (City of Toronto Planning Board). 1972. *Towards a Part II Plan for Southeast Spadina: Tentative Planning Proposals*. Toronto: City of Toronto.

CV (City of Vaughan). 1997. *Vaughan Corporate Centre: Urban Design Guidelines Report*. Vaughan: City of Vaughan.

Davidson, M., and L. Lees. 2005. 'New-build "gentrification" and London's riverside renaissance'. *Environment and Planning A* 37: 1,165–90.

Debord, G. 1983. *Society of the Spectacle*. Detroit: Black and Red.

Dendy, W. 1993. *Lost Toronto: Images of the City's Past*. Toronto: McClelland and Stewart.

Desfor, G., M. Goldrick, and R. Merrens. 1988. 'Redevelopment on the North American waterfrontier'. In B. Hoyle et al., Eds., *Revitalising the*

Waterfront: International Dimensions of Dockland Redevelopment, 92–113. London: Belhaven.

Engels, F. 1987 [1845]. *The Condition of the Working Class in England*. London: Penguin.

Fairley, B. 1921. 'Some Canadian painters: Lawren Harris'. *Canadian Forum* June: 275–8.

Fishman, R. 1987. *Bourgeois Utopias: The Rise and Fall of Suburbia*. New York: Basic Books.

Florida, R. 2002/2004. *The Rise of the Creative Class: How It's Transforming Work, Leisure, Community and Everyday Life*. New York: Basic Books.

———. 2005. *Cities and the Creative Class*. New York: Routledge.

Fraser, G. 1972. *Fighting Back: Urban Renewal in Trefann Court*. Toronto: Hakkert.

Gertler, M. 2000. 'A region in transition: The changing structure of Toronto's regional economy'. Toronto: Department of Geography, University of Toronto.

Gertler, M., et al. 2002. *Competing on Creativity: Placing Ontario's Cities in North American Context*. Toronto: Ontario Ministry of Enterprise, Opportunity and Innovation.

Gertler, M., Lori Tesolin, and Sarah Weinstock. 2006. *Strategies for Creative Cities Project: Toronto Case Study*. Toronto: Munk Centre for International Studies, University of Toronto.

Giedion, S. 1967. *Space, Time, and Architecture: The Growth of a New Tradition*. Cambridge, MA: Harvard University Press.

Goad, C. 1884. *Atlas of the City of Toronto and Suburbs*. Toronto: Charles Goad.

———. 1923. *Atlas of the City of Toronto and Suburbs: Third Edition*. Toronto: Goad's Atlas and Plan Company.

Hamnett, C. 2000. 'Gentrification, postindustrialism, and industrial and occupational restructuring in global cities'. In Gary Bridge and Sophie Watson, Eds., *A Companion to the City*, 331–41. Oxford: Blackwell.

Harris, R. 1996. *Unplanned Suburbs: Toronto's American Tragedy, 1900 to 1950*. Baltimore, MD: Johns Hopkins University Press.

———. 2004. *Creeping Conformity: How Canada Became Suburban, 1900–1960*. Toronto: University of Toronto Press.

Hulchanski, D. 1990. *Planning New Urban Neighbourhoods: Lessons from Toronto's St. Lawrence Neighbourhood*. Vancouver: University of British Columbia School of Community and Regional Planning.

———. 2007. *The Three Cities within Toronto: Income Polarization among Toronto's Neighbourhoods, 1970–2000*. Toronto: Centre for Urban and Community Studies.

Hume, C. 2008. 'Iconic Dundas Square a major city asset'. *Toronto Star* 4 February: A12.

Jacobs, J. 1961. *The Death and Life of Great American Cities*. New York: Vintage Books.

Johnson, L. 1982. 'Identity and political economy in urban growth: Guelph'. In G. Stelter and A. Artibise, Eds, *Shaping the Urban Landscape: Aspects of the Canadian City-Building Process*, 30–64. Ottawa: Carleton University Press.

Kipfer, S. 1999. 'Whose city is it?' *City Scope Magazine* winter 1999/2000: 13–17.

Lemon, J. 1985. *Toronto since 1918: An Illustrated History*. Toronto: Lorimer/National Museums of Canada.

Lewington, J. 2002. 'Industrial strength'. *Report on Business Magazine* September: 72–3, 75.

Ley, D. 1996a. 'The new middle class in Canadian central cities'. In J. Caulfield and L. Peake, Eds, *City Lives and City Forms: Critical Research and Canadian Urbanism*, 15–32. Toronto: University of Toronto Press.

———. 1996b. *The New Middle Class and the Remaking of the Central City*. Oxford: Oxford University Press.

McHugh, P. 1989. *Toronto Architecture: A City Guide*. Toronto: McClelland and Stewart.

Middleton, J. 1923. *The Municipality of Toronto: A History*. Toronto: Dominion Publishing Company.

Monsebraaten, L., and R. Daly. 2007. 'Canada's poverty capital'. *Toronto Star* 26 November: A1.

Muszynski, L. 1985. *The Deindustrialization of Metropolitan Toronto: A Study of Plant Closures, Layoffs and Unemployment*. Toronto: Social Planning Council of Metropolitan Toronto.

Nader, G. 1975. *Cities of Canada, Volume 1: Theoretical, Historical and Planning Perspectives*. Toronto:

Macmillan.

Relph, E. 1987. *The Modern Urban Landscape*. Baltimore, MD: Johns Hopkins University Press.

Rybczynski, W. 1986. *Home: A Short History of an Idea*. New York: Viking Penguin.

Sieverts, T. 2003. *Cities without Cities: An Interpretation of the Zwischenstadt*. London: Spon Press.

Simmons, J., and R. Simmons. 1974. *Urban Canada*. 2nd edn. Toronto: Copp Clark.

Stelter, G. 1982. 'The city-building process in Canada'. In G. Stelter and A. Artibise, Eds., *Shaping the Urban Landscape: Aspects of the Canadian City-Building Process*, 1–29. Ottawa: Carleton University Press.

———. 1986. 'Power and place in urban history'. In G. Stelter and A. Artibise, Eds., *Power and Place: Canadian Urban Development in the North American Context*, 1–11. Vancouver: University of British Columbia Press.

UWGT (United Way of Greater Toronto). 2007. 'Losing ground: The persistent growth of family poverty in Canada's largest city'. Toronto: United Way of Greater Toronto.

White, J., and S. Otto. 2001. *The History of Gooderham and Worts*. Toronto: The Distillery District.

Zukin, S. 1995. *The Cultures of Cities*. Oxford: Blackwell.

Glossary

Aboriginal   The indigenous population of Canada, including First Nations (Indian), Métis, and Inuit peoples. First Nations people include both individuals who are registered under the Indian Act (Registered Indians) and individuals who identify as First Nations people but who do not have the rights, benefits, or status associated with registration. It is important to note that these are legal definitions that do not reflect the range of diverse nations within the population, and in many cases they do not correspond to how Aboriginal people refer to themselves.

accommodative responses to the homeless   Provide for basic subsistence needs, especially food and temporary shelter, but not longer-term housing and other assistance.

adaptive reuse   Adapting a structure for a use different from that for which it was originally built.

aestheticization   Also referred to as stylization in the context of consumer culture, involves the process of imbuing goods, services, places, and spaces with cultural meaning. In other words, the production, design, making, and use of goods as if they were signs, images, or art.

agricultural revolution   Advances in food production that created a food surplus and was marked by the shift from a nomadic hunting and gathering lifestyle to more permanent settlement that occurred around 6000 BC in its earliest form but yielded massive strides in production with mechanization after 1800.

amalgamation   A political and administrative process whereby two or more municipalities are merged into one entity. The process is as old as municipalities themselves. Recent Quebec provincial legislation forced municipalities to merge, and new, larger municipalities were created in 2002. The decision concerned urban areas throughout the province but became a divisive

political issue chiefly in the Montreal and Quebec City regions. In 2004, referendums to 'de-merge' were organized. Most of the former municipalities of the western part of Montreal decided in favour of 'de-merging', but only two out of 13 in the Quebec City region chose to do so.

arriviste cities   Cities experiencing new growth that challenges their position in the national urban hierarchy.

balance of trade   The surplus of exports over imports for a region or country.

behavioural sink   The growth of unusual behaviours (social pathologies) under conditions of high density in Calhoun's experiment with rats.

BIDS   An acronym for Business Improvement Districts, which vary in size and scope but are generally organized by central city business owners to advance agendas that they perceive as improving the business environment. These organizations generally go beyond lobbying to actually employing off-duty police or other personnel to provide privatized services, enforce municipal codes to 'clean up the streets', and so on and can act as quasi-governmental organizations.

bifurcation   A division of a population into two parts.

Bilbao effect   The imagined economic revitalization and iconic status that will ensue for cities that build their own local versions of the Guggenheim Bilbao, an art museum in a Spanish port city designed by superstar architect Frank Gehry.

brandscaping   The spatialization of a brand, involving the organization and co-ordination of space through combinations of location, architecture, interior design, and atmospheric elements to create a particular experience that is associated with the brand.

brownfield sites   Sites for development formerly occupied by polluting industrial uses (in contrast to greenfield sites at the urban outskirts).

Canada Mortgage and Housing Corporation (CMHC) The national housing agency of the federal government that insures residential mortgage loans, provides subsidies under federal housing programs, administers co-op operating agreements funded under federal programs, and conducts and publishes housing research.

cataclysmic change A term drawn from Jane Jacobs's *Death and Life of Great American Cities* that identifies major shifts in urban fabrics propelled by large investments from outside an area (in contrast to gradual change).

census division A group of neighbouring municipalities joined together for the purposes of regional planning and managing common services (such as police or ambulance services). These groupings are established under laws in effect in certain provinces and territories of Canada. For example, a census division might correspond to a county, a regional municipality, or a regional district. In other provinces and territories where laws do not provide for such areas, Statistics Canada defines equivalent areas for statistical reporting purposes in cooperation with these provinces and territories (Statistics Canada. 2003. 'Census dictionary'. Ottawa: Statistics Canada. http://www.statcan.ca/english/census2001/dict/geo008.htm).

census metropolitan area (CMA) An area with at least 100,000 people, with an urban core of at least 50,000.

census tracts Small, relatively stable geographic areas that usually have a population of 2,500 to 8,000. They are located in census metropolitan areas and in census agglomerations with an urban core population of 50,000 or more in the previous census.

civic boosters (boosterism) Urban elites with vested interests who support any efforts or campaigns that stimulate the growth of their city.

climatological urbanization effect The tendency for people to choose locations with the most favourable climate, which results in increasing levels of urbanization in these locations.

co-housing A collaborative housing tenure arrangement whereby residents maintain a private dwelling while also sharing facilities like group kitchens, dining facilities, lounges, libraries, workshops, gyms, and green space.

colonialism The role played by powerful nation-states in establishing new cities in less developed areas.

common property Property that is used by many people or organizations—no one has sole rights of ownership. Examples include the air, many of our water resources, fish in international waters, and general knowledge.

concentration (centralization) The increasing tendency for populations and economic activity in a country to be located in a few urban regions.

concentric zone model Describes the relationship between city residential patterns and the immigrant adaptation process.

consumer culture A particular kind of material culture (the way people produce, interact with, and make use of things) that has emerged in the latter half of the twentieth century and that is best defined by a process of stylization, or aestheticization.

contact hypothesis The greater the equal-status contact between individuals from opposing groups (defined by language, culture, skin colour, nationality, and so on), the greater will be the undermining of stereotypes that are the basis for prejudice and discrimination. The contact hypothesis suggests that breaking the vice of segregation requires routine group contact on an equal footing, providing the crucible for exposing and eliminating prejudices.

core housing need Occurs when an inadequate supply of housing results in a household living in housing that is in disrepair, too small relative to its family size, and costs more than 30 per cent of total income.

creative class The term social scientist Richard Florida has used to describe the group of educated adults who work in high-status, culturally connected, growth-oriented industries like the arts, media, technology, and biomedical fields. Florida hypothesizes that these groups will flock to housing options in vibrant high-density urban neighbourhoods.

crisis of accumulation   What occurs when real estate financiers over-invest in a particular urban sector, flooding the market and depressing profits. When this occurs, investors collectively shift to another location, leaving the original to decline.

crowding   A condition in which the number of residents in a household relative to its size exceeds both absolute standards for healthy human habitation and relative standards based on the culture and society.

cultural quarter   A specific urban area that has been intentionally planned, packaged, and promoted to create a distinct cultural identity or image. It is organized around the principle of consumption and is intended to provide a distinctive cultural experience for visitors.

culturalist orientation   Theoretical perspective that conceptualizes the city as giving rise to a distinguishable and characteristically urban way of thinking, relating, and behaving.

deindustrialization   The shift from cities that formerly had a strong economic base in mechanized production to an economy based more on service industries.

demography   The study of statistical features of a population, including such characteristics as income, gender, age, household type, ethnicity, and 'race'.

detached house   A common type of house that does not share any structural walls with another dwelling. The land required for this housing type is greater than for any other housing type.

deviance service centre   An area specializing in providing illegal goods and services, adjacent to another area that openly regards them as disreputable.

economic integration   Refers to economic performance of immigrants as compared to native-born residents.

economies of scale   The idea that the production of large numbers of goods can be accomplished more efficiently (at a lower per-unit cost) than with smaller production.

empirical   Relying on or providing evidence based on observations or experiments.

entrepot   Site of transshipment in the trade of a commodity.

entrepreneurial governance   Shift by cities during the 1970s and 1980s from providing welfare and collective services to policies designed to foster and encourage local growth and economic revitalization.

escape from the city thesis   An explanation for American suburban growth in the 1950s and 1960s proposing that the middle class fled the central city in order to avoid contact with minority group migrants who were flooding into the cities of the northeast in record numbers.

ethnic enclave   A small neighbourhood or community of members of the same ethnicity that socializes and cooperates economically to aid in the adjustment to a new society.

ethnography   The study of people in their natural settings; a qualitative methodology, sometimes also called 'participant observation'.

exchange value   A measure of the profitability of an object as a commodity (in contrast to use value).

exclusionary zoning   Aims to exclude affordable housing from a municipality through the zoning code.

exclusionist/expulsionist responses to the homeless   The use of fear, overzealous enforcement of existing laws, and allegations about the homeless increasing crime and diminishing property values to exclude and expel them from some areas of the city.

exploitative responses to the homeless   Responses that take a market-oriented perspective in order to profit from the labour and resources of the homeless with little or no authentic concern for their welfare.

flexible production   A form of industrial production that has emerged with the widespread use and diffusion of computers. Rather than produce many identical copies of the same product, industries are reorganized to manufacture a variety of goods or similar goods with minor variation in an efficient and flexible manner. This is often associated with a reorganization of the labour force to include multi-skilled workers and a larger proportion of temporary (contract) employees.

flexism   Industrial system characterized by small-batch manufacturing runs, high-tech production, just-in-time product delivery, and decentralized corporate organization.

Fordist production   A type of mass industrial production characterized by mechanized production of standardized goods by a large workforce in which each person has a narrow range of skills. It was championed by Henry Ford in the automobile industry and is typically associated with strong labour unions able to ensure good wages and a state that regulates the national economy.

freehold ownership   The most common form of ownership in Canada whereby residents own both the housing structure and the land it occupies.

gated communities   Communities created to allow the wealthy in highly unequal cities to increase their security by limiting access to their neighbourhoods and homes. They often feature gatehouses staffed by private security and are surrounded by fences or other kinds of barriers to limit access. These communities tend to be homogenous in terms of social class and race. They stand as a visible symbol of inequality and are becoming more common globally as urban inequality worsens.

gateway cities   Cities that serve a unique role as access points to a country, often becoming major destinations in themselves.

genetically modified organisms   Organisms with genes added from another species through the techniques of genetic engineering. This is only one type of genetic modification. In a more scientific use, genetic modification would include modification through naturally occurring or induced mutation (often through radiation). Using this more general definition, for example, all commercial strains of wheat, including organic wheat, have been (randomly and massively) genetically modified by radiation mutagenesis.

gentrification   The process of urban neighbourhood change in which a group of wealthy residents and the institutions that serve them—from high-end specialty shops to grocery stores—move into a low-income neighbourhood, thus driving up housing prices and rents and frequently displacing former residents.

global (world) city   A city that is a command and control centre in the world economy.

globalization   A term denoting the decline of regional and national economic networks in the context of worldwide patterns of trade in goods and services.

gradual change   Slower processes of change in urban fabrics propelled by small amounts of local investment (in contrast to cataclysmic change).

gross domestic product   A measure of the total of a country or region's economic production. It is typically calculated by taking the total value of all goods and services produced in a year, then subtracting the net income gained from investments in other countries or regions.

growth-booster   Describes civic officials and local business groups whose primary interest is a city's private-sector economic growth (and who have little attention for other kinds of municipal issues).

harm-reduction housing   A form of housing that provides shelter and a range of on-site services aimed at minimizing and reducing the harm wrought by drug dependency.

hinterland   Locations beyond cities that produce the food and supplies necessary for urban living.

homophilly   As the number of shared characteristics between two individuals increases, their mutual preference for interaction with and proximity to one another also increases. Homophilly as seen in housing choice helps to explain residential segregation by race and ethnicity.

horizontal integration   When most aspects of manufacturing production occur in the same general location and adjacent to the primary market for that product.

housing tenure arrangement   The relationship persons have to the housing that they reside in. The most basic tenure arrangements are ownership and renting, although alternative tenure arrangements have arisen to address concerns about housing affordability and community.

human ecology The study of the relationship between people and their environment.

inclusionary zoning A set of planning ordinances that require a given share of new construction to be affordable for people with low to moderate income.

Industrial Revolution The birth of mechanized production in factories, often linked to the invention of the steam engine, which provided employment for growing urban populations beginning in Britain and then in Europe and North America in the late 1700s and the first half of the nineteenth century.

interiorization The process over time whereby people have come to spend significantly more time indoors disconnected from the natural world.

invasion-succession Human ecological processes whereby one segment of the urban population makes an incursion into the territory of another, eventually replacing it.

just-in-time An organization of product distribution that uses high-speed communication and transportation to respond in a short time frame to consumer demand. Rather than stock many warehouses with standard products, distributors ship their products in a more piecemeal fashion in response to specific consumer requests.

knowledge economy All economy is based on knowledge, but the term characterizes a recent trend in industrialized countries to replace manual occupations with intellectual occupations. More broadly, the expression means that advanced economies are driven by technological, organizational, and social innovations, which are mainly based on scientific and technical knowledge.

land use A term used in urban planning to describe the functions of city space; the main urban land uses are residential, retail-commercial, office-commercial, industrial and warehousing, leisure and entertainment, public and private institutions, parks and open space, and transportation.

Low Income Cut-Off (LICO) Income levels calculated by Statistics Canada. Persons and families living below these income levels are considered to be living in 'straitened circumstances'. There are

35 different LICOs, varying according to family size and size of community. The LICOs are more popularly known as Canada's poverty lines.

marginal spaces Areas in the city that are viewed as undesirable by society at large. These areas are not seen as attractive to property investors, businesses, and most residents and are often not maintained or patrolled by police as regularly as other areas. With gentrification and urban redevelopment, marginal spaces have become less numerous.

metropolis-hinterland An interactive but unequal relationship between locations of high population density, decision-making, and control and locations of staple exploitation and low density.

metropolitan concentration The process that leads some cities to grow faster than others by experiencing greater population intensification.

metropolitan regionalization See **urban spread**.

modernism An approach to city-building that viewed the social effects of industrial urbanism as malignant and saw the solution as complete reconstruction of the city according to a new science of city-building.

morphology A word drawn from biology in which it refers to the structure of an organism; it is used in urban studies to denote the spatial structure and organization of a city or part of a city.

MRCs (municipalités regionales de comté) and urban communities Supra-municipal governments in Quebec, created by provincial legislation in 1979. They are responsible for regional services and interests, such as land-use planning, and can vary greatly in size and population. The MRC is headed by a *préfet*, who is chosen from and by the participating mayors. Three urban communities were created in 1969 (in Montreal, Quebec City, and the Hull region), uniting the urban cores of these areas. Before the recent amalgamation process, they were responsible for regional services, such as regional planning and the environment.

multi-functionality The trade policy position taken by various nations (e.g., many European nations) who argue that several primary-sector activities serve many functions (e.g., farmers produce foodstuffs and a scenic landscape at the same time). It is often used to justify compensating primary producers for their production of public goods (i.e., goods to which everyone has free access) as well as the goods they produce for the market.

neighbourhood changes   Racial and ethnic composition changes in neighbourhoods.

neo-liberal governance   The replacement of local government structures and procedures with a more fragmented system, including appointed special-purpose bodies, privatization of public services, and the introduction of a consumer model for the delivery of municipal services.

NIMBY   An acronym for 'not in my backyard', a term used to describe the tendency of people living in a neighbourhood to organize to prevent the location of what is perceived as a non-desired social good—such as homeless shelters, landfills, train tracks, social housing—in or near their community.

non-linear relationship   A statistically significant association in which the best-fitting line of least squares is quadratic, cubic, or some other departure from linearity.

non-profit housing cooperatives   Mixed-income, tenant-managed housing developed by private-sector non-profit corporations, often with government support, to provide market-cost units for middle-class tenants and lower-rent units for low-income tenants.

non-sexist city   A paradigm of home, neighbourhood, and city that describes the physical, social, and economic design of human settlements that would support rather than restrict the activities of employed women and their families.

place stratification perspective   Suggests that groups are stratified according to locations in the city.

political economy perspective   The interpretive framework that understands urbanization not as the result of natural processes but as the result of actions and decisions by those who have economic or political power.

post-industrial city   See **deindustrialization**.

post-modern urbanism   An approach to city-building rooted in a widespread reaction against ways that ideas of modernist urbanism were being applied. It encourages the conservation, reuse, and replication of traditional urban forms.

primary groups   Intimate associations characterized by face-to-face contact.

primary uses   Land uses that bring people into a part of town, in contrast to secondary uses that serve people who are already there.

primate cities   Cities that are surpassingly larger than other cities in a country and that are conduits to cities in more powerful regions.

prime spaces   Desirable and frequently used areas of the city that are considered valuable property for investors and of significant tax value to the city. Anti-homeless sentiment and enforcement of panhandling and loitering laws are often stricter in prime spaces.

privatism   Withdrawing from the public world into more private spaces.

public housing   Low-income housing developed and managed by a government agency.

public-private partnerships in housing   An alternative form of housing development whereby government, corporate underwriting, and real estate developers share the risk in developing housing structures that include both for-profit and low-income housing units.

public realm   A term used by Lyn Lofland to describe urban space or territory. It is characterized by a 'world of strangers' whose inhabitants only know one another in a limited context—for example, as bus driver and customer.

redlining   When lending institutions such as banks and insurance companies decline to make loans in a specific area of the city or only do so on less than favourable terms, which leads to the properties in the area continuing to depreciate.

rent-geared-to-income housing   Apartments with rents that are set at a rate low enough that low-income residents will not spend more than 30 to 40 per cent of their monthly income on housing.

residential alienation   The estrangement between a person and his/her dwelling, exemplified by renters spending less time at home than owners do, less likely to rate their time at home as enjoyable, and less likely to view their dwelling as a positive reflection of who they are.

residential density A standard measure of the number of inhabitants per unit of area (e.g., population per square kilometre) that is commonly used to compare neighbourhoods and guide planning decisions.

residential segregation The tendency for groups (e.g., social classes or ethnic groups) to live in different neighbourhoods to a greater extent than would be expected by chance alone. There are both voluntary and involuntary forms of residential segregation.

restorative responses to the homeless Responses that attend to actual physical, psychological, or spiritual problems that are impeding a homeless person's functioning, such as their lack of secure long-term housing or harm-reduction housing services.

re-urbanization An increasing proportion of a population inhabiting a settlement defined as urban within a region that previously had been experiencing a decline.

Royal Commission on Aboriginal Peoples Established on 23 April 1991 in part as a response to the Oka crisis, a land dispute between the Mohawk nation and the town of Oka, QC, which began on 11 July 1990 and lasted until 26 September 1990. The mandate of the commission was to 'examine the economic, social, and cultural situation of the Aboriginal peoples of the country'. In addition to numerous other studies, the commission published its final report in 1996, comprising 4,000 pages in more than five volumes. While relatively few of the commission's recommendations were translated into policy, it continues to set the standard for the understanding of a wide variety of issues facing Aboriginal people in Canada today.

rural depopulation Rural-urban migration that leads to a thinning of rural population.

secondary relations Fleeting interactions between strangers or routine instrumental interactions.

social area analysis Analytical approach developed by Eshref Shevsky and colleagues in the 1950s that hypothesizes that areas of the city differ from one another according to three basic population characteristics: socio-economic status, family status, and ethnicity.

social exclusion The syndrome of poverty and multiple deprivations that structure inequalities among urban residents, including locational advantages and disadvantages associated with housing and mobility, access to public service, and participation in local governance.

social network analysis The study of social structure based on an analysis of the relationships between actors—people, organizations, and institutions.

social pathology A catch-all term used by John B. Calhoun for the behaviours in the high-density pens of his experiment on rats. The behaviours included infanticide, aggression and sexual assault, asexuality, careless mothering, and apparent depression.

social spatialization Concept introduced by Rob Shields in the 1990s in his discussion of place myths to designate how particular places are centrally defined by popular culture and the media.

spatial assimilation perspective Describes the changes in patterns of immigrants sharing neighbourhoods with other groups over time.

specialization (and size) The idea that a large number of individuals in interrelated specialized roles will be more efficient organizationally and produce a greater number and higher quality of goods and services than will relatively few individuals in more generalized roles.

SRO (single room occupancy) hotels Hotels that provide extremely low-cost and low-quality housing, often to the homeless. They generally provide very small rooms and shared kitchen and bathroom facilities. They are frequently rundown, dirty, insect-infested, and even violent. Yet they offer one of the few alternatives to sleeping out on the street for the worst-off among the urban poor.

standard employment Employment providing regular and consistent income and benefits.

structuralist orientation Theoretical perspective that views urban places as manifestations of wider configurations of power and wealth that should be treated as the ultimate causes of patterns of thought, behaviour, and organization associated with urban dwellers.

subcultural theory A social interactionist–style approach to the city introduced by Claude Fischer in the 1970s that credited urbanism for strengthening social groups by promoting the formation of diverse subcultures.

superblock An urban development project that consumes several city blocks and erases the old configuration of streets.

supportive housing A form of housing that provides permanent shelter and a range of on-site and proximate services aimed at helping the mentally ill live an independent life. This form of housing may be located in a purpose-designed building or scattered-site apartments.

third place A place outside of work and home where people meet to interact in public. It is an informal, inclusive, accessible place characterized by camaraderie, friendly conversation, and community.

urban ethnography A method of studying urban culture and organization first-hand through participant observation and non-participant observation.

urban growth machine A concept proposed by Molotch and Logan that depicts urban decision-making as dominated by a public-private coalition of elites who believe that the best interests of

their city and its residents are served by pursuing continuous economic growth and development.

urban region The cluster of municipalities surrounding a dominant municipality for which a region is named.

urban spread (metropolitan regionalization) The pushing outward of cities to take in older towns, villages, new suburban developments, and other municipalities on its fringe, thereby forming a continuous urban mass.

use value Refers to the usefulness of an object apart from its market value (in contrast to **exchange value**).

vagrants Persons who manage to survive without a fixed address or any visible means of employment apart from panhandling (begging). Also known as 'the homeless' and 'street people'.

vertical disintegration When different aspects of manufacturing production occur in diverse locations and often at considerable distance from the primary markets for the product.

virtual community An electronic community on the Internet, such as a multi-user domain, a graphical world (e.g., Sims Online), e-mail lists, or chat groups.

working poor People who work in the formal economy, often full-time, who do not earn enough income to lift their families above the poverty line. Working poor parents, in particular, often struggle to make ends meet as a result of the high costs of child care and other expenses.

Index